S0-AZJ-549

PRINTED IN GREAT BRITAIN

EVERYMAN'S LIBRARY
EDITED BY ERNEST RHYS

REFERENCE

A DICTIONARY OF ENGLISH
AND AMERICAN AUTHORS
BY JOHN W. COUSIN

THIS IS NO. 449 OF *EVERYMAN'S LIBRARY*. THE PUBLISHERS WILL BE PLEASED TO SEND FREELY TO ALL APPLICANTS A LIST OF THE PUBLISHED AND PROJECTED VOLUMES ARRANGED UNDER THE FOLLOWING SECTIONS:

TRAVEL ❦ SCIENCE ❦ FICTION
THEOLOGY & PHILOSOPHY
HISTORY ❦ CLASSICAL
FOR YOUNG PEOPLE
ESSAYS ❦ ORATORY
POETRY & DRAMA
BIOGRAPHY
REFERENCE
ROMANCE

THE ORDINARY EDITION IS BOUND IN CLOTH WITH GILT DESIGN AND COLOURED TOP. THERE IS ALSO A LIBRARY EDITION IN REINFORCED CLOTH

J. M. DENT & SONS LTD.
ALDINE HOUSE, BEDFORD STREET, LONDON, W.C.2
E. P. DUTTON & CO. INC.
286–302 FOURTH AVENUE, NEW YORK

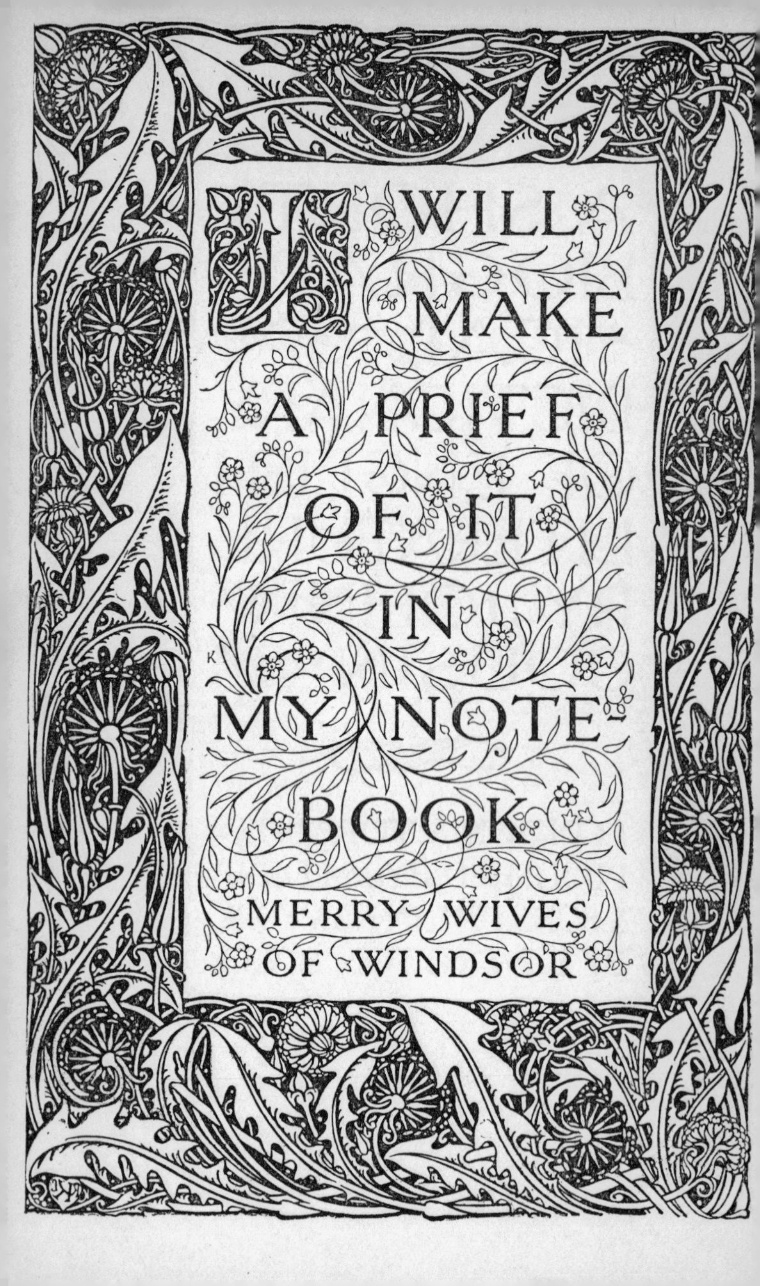
I WILL
MAKE
A PRIEF
OF IT
IN
MY NOTE-
BOOK
MERRY WIVES
OF WINDSOR

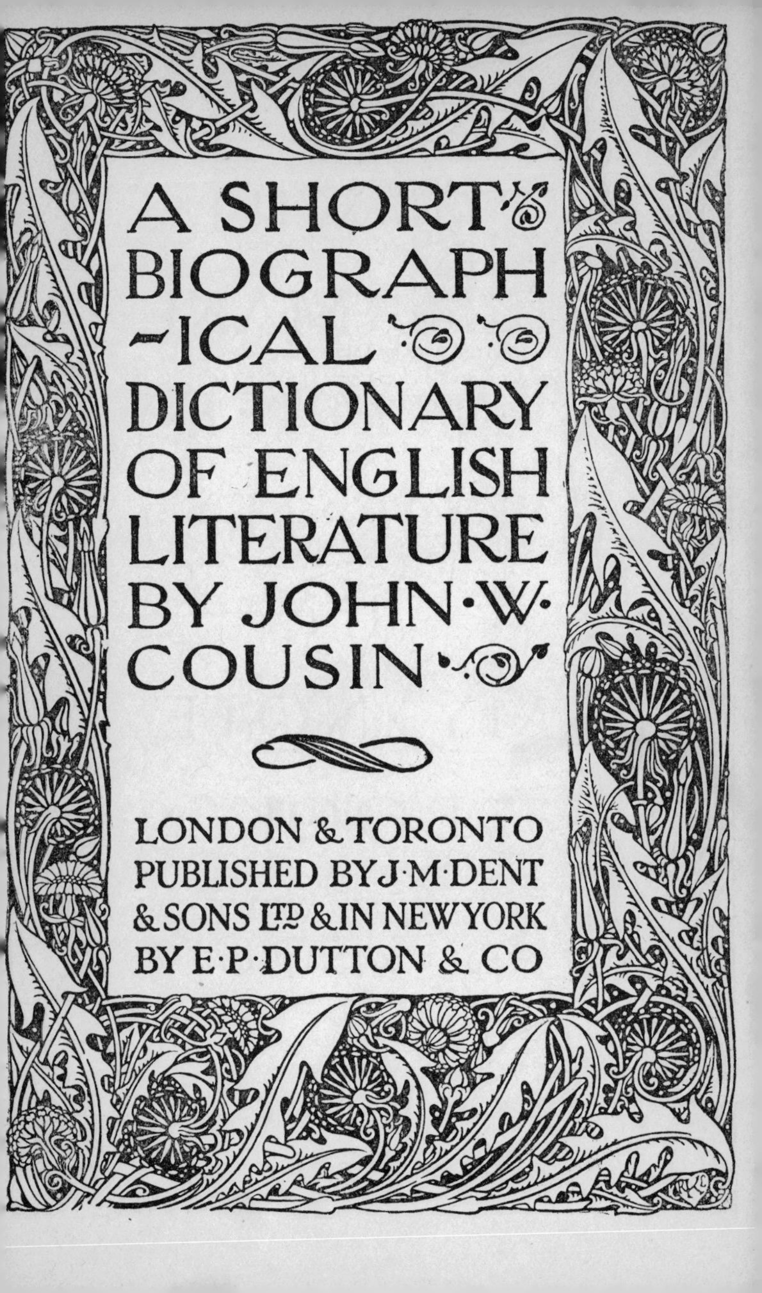

A SHORT BIOGRAPHICAL DICTIONARY OF ENGLISH LITERATURE

BY JOHN · W · COUSIN

LONDON & TORONTO
PUBLISHED BY J · M · DENT & SONS LTD & IN NEW YORK
BY E · P · DUTTON & CO

All rights reserved
Printed in Great Britain
by The Temple Press Letchworth
for
J. M. Dent & Sons Ltd.
Aldine House Bedford St. London
Toronto . Vancouver
Melbourne . Wellington
First Published in this Edition 1910
Reprinted 1910, 1912, 1916, 1921
Revised with new Appendix, 1925
Reprinted with new Addenda and Appendix, 1929, 1933

PREFACE

THE primary aim of this book is to give as much information about English authors, including under this designation American and Colonial writers, as the prescribed limits will admit of. At the same time an attempt has been made, where materials exist for it, to enhance the interest by introducing such details as tend to illustrate the characters and circumstances of the respective writers and the manner in which they passed through the world; and in the case of the more important, to give some indication of the relative place which they hold and the leading features of their work.

Including the Appendix of Later Writers, the work contains upwards of 1600 names; but large as this number is, the number of those who have contributed something of interest and value to the vast store of English Literature is larger still: and any attempt to make a book of this kind absolutely exhaustive would be futile.

The word "Literature" is here used in a very wide sense, and this gives rise to considerable difficulty in drawing the line of exclusion. There are very many writers whose claim to admission may reasonably be considered as good as that of some who have been included; but even had it been possible to discover all these, their inclusion would have swelled the work beyond its limits. A line had to be drawn somewhere, and the writer has used his best judgment in making that line as consistent as possible. It may probably, however, be safely claimed that every department of the subject of any importance is well represented.

Wherever practicable (and this includes all but a very few articles), various authorities have been collated, and pains have been taken to secure accuracy; but where so large a collection of facts and dates is involved, it would be too sanguine to expect that success has invariably been attained.

J. W. C.

The following list gives some of the best known works of Biography:—

Allibone, Critical Dictionary of English Literature and English and American Authors, 1859-71, Supplement, by J. F. Kirke, 1891; W. Hazlitt, Collections and Notes of Early English Literature, 1876-93; R. Chambers, Cyclopædia of English Literature, 1876, 1901; Halkett and Laign, Dictionary of Anonymous and Pseudonymous Literature, 1882-88; Dictionary of National Biography, ed. by Leslie Stephen and Sidney Lee, 1885, etc., re-issue, 1908, etc.; Appleton's Cyclopædia of American Biography, ed. by J. Grant Wilson and John Fiske, 1887, etc.; J. Thomas, Universal Dictionary of Biography and Mythology, 1887-89; Men and Women of the Time, 15th edit., ed. by Victor G. Plarr, 1889.

LIST OF CONTRACTIONS USED THROUGHOUT THE WORK

b.	born	Edin.	Edinburgh
c.	*circa*	*fl.*	flourished
Camb.	Cambridge	Glas.	Glasgow
Coll.	College	*m.*	married
coll.	collected	Oxf.	Oxford
cr.	created	pres.	president
d.	died	*pub.*	published
dau.	daughter	Prof.	Professor
ed.	educated	sec.	secretray
ed.	edition editor edited	*s.* Univ.	son University

NOTE TO THE 1933 EDITION

THE chief feature of this edition is that in place of the old inadequate Addenda and Appendix a completely new Appendix has been prepared, giving notices of over two hundred English and American contemporary writers. A number of important corrections have also been made in the text: several articles have been overhauled, and the omission of such names as Francis Thompson, Emily Dickinson, Gerard Manley Hopkins, has been made good.

DICTIONARY
OF
ENGLISH LITERATURE

ABBOTT, JACOB (1803-1879).—Educationalist and miscellaneous author, *b.* at Hallowell, Maine, *ed.* at Bowdoin Coll. and Andover, entered the ministry of the Congregational Church, but was best known as an educationist and writer of religious and other books, mainly for the young. Among them are *Beechnut Tales* and *The Rollo Books*, both of which still have a very wide circulation.

ABBOTT, JOHN STEVENS CABOT (1805-1877).—Historian, etc., *b.* Brunswick, Maine, and *ed.* at Bowdoin Coll. He studied theology and became a minister of the Congregational Church at various places in Massachusetts and Connecticut. Owing to the success of a little work, *The Mother at Home*, he devoted himself, from 1844 onwards, to literature, and especially to historical writing. Among his principal works, which were very popular, are: *History of Napoleon Bonaparte* (1852-55), *History of the Civil War in America* (1863-66), and *History of Frederick the Great* (1871).

À BECKETT, GILBERT ABBOTT (1811-1856).—Comic writer, *b.* in London, the *s.* of a lawyer, and belonged to a family claiming descent from Thomas à Becket. Destined for the legal profession, he was called to the Bar. In addition to contributions to various periodicals and newspapers, including *Punch*, *The Illustrated London News*, *The Times*, and *Morning Herald*, he produced over fifty plays, many of which attained great popularity, and he also helped to dramatise some of Dickens' works. He is perhaps best known as the author of *Comic History of England*, *Comic History of Rome*, *Comic Blackstone*, etc. He was also distinguished in his profession, acted as a commissioner on various important matters, and was appointed a metropolitan police magistrate.

ABERCROMBIE, JOHN (1780-1844).—Physician and writer on mental science, *s.* of a minister, was *b.* at Aberdeen, and *ed.* at the Grammar School and Marischal College there. He studied medicine at Edinburgh, in which city he practised as a physician. He made valuable contributions to the literature of his profession, and *pub.* two works, *Enquiry Concerning the Intellectual Powers* (1830) and *The Philosophy of the Moral Feelings* (1833), which, though popular at the time of their publication, have long been superseded. For his services as a physician and philanthropist he received many marks of distinction, including the Rectorship of Marischal College.

ABERCROMBIE, PATRICK (1656-1716).—Antiquary and historian, was physician to James II. in 1685; he was a Jacobite and opposed the Union in various pamphlets. His chief work was *Martial Achievements of the Scots Nation* (1711-16).

ACTON, JOHN EMERICH EDWARD DALBERG-ACTON, 1ST LORD (1834-1902).—Historian, *s.* of Sir Richard A., and grandson of Sir John A., who was Prime Minister of Naples, was *b.* at Naples. He belonged to an ancient Roman Catholic family, and was *ed.* first at Oscott near Birmingham under Dr. (afterwards Card.) Wiseman. Thence he went to Edinburgh, where he studied privately, and afterwards to Munich, where he resided in the house of Dr. Dollinger, the great scholar and subsequent leader of the Old Catholic party, by whom he was profoundly influenced. While at Edinburgh he endeavoured to procure admission to Cambridge, but without success, his religion being at that time a bar. He early devoted himself to the study of history, and is said to have been on terms of intimacy with every contemporary historian of distinction, with the exception of Guizot. He sat in the House of Commons 1859-65, but made no great mark, and in 1869 was raised to the peerage as Lord Acton of Aldenham. For a time he edited *The Rambler*, a Roman Catholic periodical, which afterwards became the *Home and Foreign Review*, and which, under his care, became one of the most learned publications of the day. The liberal character of A.'s views, however, led to its stoppage in deference to the authorities of the Church. He, however, maintained a lifelong opposition to the Ultramontane party in the Church, and in 1874 controverted their position in four letters to *The Times* which were described as the most crushing argument against them which ever appeared in so condensed a form. A.'s contributions to literature were few, and, in comparison with his extraordinary learning, comparatively unimportant. He wrote upon *Cardinal Wolsey* (1877) and *German Schools of History* (1886). He was extremely modest, and the loftiness of his ideals of accuracy and completeness of treatment led him to shrink from tasks which men of far slighter equipment might have carried out with success. His learning and his position as a universally acknowledged master in his subject were recognised by his appointment in 1895 as Professor of Modern History at Cambridge. Perhaps his most valuable services to historical literature were his laying down the lines of the great *Cambridge Modern History*, and his collection of a library of 60,000 vols., which after his death was purchased by an American millionaire and presented to Lord Morley of Blackburn, who placed it in the University of Cambridge.

ADAMNAN, ST. (625?-704).—Historian, *b.* in Donegal, became Abbot of Iona in 679. Like other Irish churchmen he was a statesman as well as an ecclesiastic, and appears to have been sent on various political missions. In the great controversy on the subject of the holding of Easter, he sided with Rome against the Irish Church. He left the earliest account we have of the state of Palestine in the early ages of the Church; but of even more value is his *Vita Sancti Columbæ*, giving a minute account of the condition and discipline of the church of Iona. He *d.* 704.

ADAMS, FRANCIS, W.L. (1862-1893).—Novelist, was *b.* at Malta, and *ed.* at schools at Shrewsbury and in Paris. In 1882 he went to Australia, and was on the staff of *The Sydney Bulletin.* In 1884 he *publ.* his autobiographical novel, *Leicester*, and in 1888, *Songs of the Army of the Night*, which created a sensation in Sydney. His remaining important work is *Tiberius* (1894), a striking drama in which a new view of the character of the Emperor is presented. He *d.* by his own hand at Alexandria in a fit of depression caused by hopeless illness.

ADDISON, JOSEPH (1672-1719).—Poet, essayist, and statesman, was the *s.* of Lancelot Addison, Dean of Lichfield. *B.* near Amesbury, Wilts., A. went to the Charterhouse, where he made the acquaintance of Steele (*q.v.*), and then at the age of fifteen to Oxford, where he had a distinguished career, being specially noted for his Latin verse. Intended at first for the Church, various circumstances combined to lead him towards literature and politics. His first attempts in English verse took the form of complimentary addresses, and were so successful as to obtain for him the friendship and interest of Dryden, and of Lord Somers, by whose means he received, in 1699, a pension of £300 to enable him to travel on the continent with a view to diplomatic employment. He visited Italy, whence he addressed his *Epistle* to his friend Halifax. Hearing of the death of William III., an event which lost him his pension, he returned to England in the end of 1703. For a short time his circumstances were somewhat straitened, but the battle of Blenheim in 1704 gave him a fresh opportunity of distinguishing himself. The government wished the event commemorated by a poem; A. was commissioned to write this, and produced *The Campaign*, which gave such satisfaction that he was forthwith appointed a Commissioner of Appeals. His next literary venture was an account of his travels in Italy, which was followed by the opera of *Rosamund.* In 1705, the Whigs having obtained the ascendency, A. was made Under-Secretary of State and accompanied Halifax on a mission to Hanover, and in 1708 was appointed Chief Secretary for Ireland and Keeper of the Records of that country. It was at this period that A. found his true vocation, and laid the foundations of his real fame. In 1709 Steele began to bring out the *Tatler*, to which A. became almost immediately a contributor: thereafter he (with Steele) started the *Spectator*, the first number of which appeared on March 1, 1711. This paper, which at first appeared daily, was kept up (with a break of about a year and a half when the *Guardian* took its place) until Dec. 20, 1714. In 1713 the drama of *Cato* appeared, and was received with acclamation by both Whigs and Tories, and was followed by the comedy of the *Drummer.* His last undertaking was *The Freeholder*, a party paper (1715-16). The later events in the life of A., viz., his marriage in 1716 to the Dowager Countess of Warwick, to whose son he had been tutor, and his promotion to be Secretary of State did not contribute to his happiness. His wife appears to have been arrogant and imperious; his step-son the Earl was a rake and unfriendly to him; while in his public capacity his invincible shyness made him of little use in Parliament. He resigned his office in 1718, and, after a period of ill-health, *d.* at Holland House, June 17, 1719, in his 48th year. Besides the works above mentioned, he wrote a *Dialogue on Medals*, and left unfinished a work on the Evidences of Christianity. The character of A., if somewhat cool and unimpassioned, was pure, magnanimous, and kind. The charm of his manners and conversation made him one of the most popular and admired men of his day; and while he laid his friends under obligations for substantial favours, he showed the greatest forbearance towards his few enemies. His style in his essays is remarkable for its ease, clearness, and grace, and for an inimitable and sunny humour which never soils and never hurts. The motive power of these writings has been called "an enthusiasm for conduct." Their effect was to raise the whole standard of manners and expression both in life and in literature. The only flaw in his character was a tendency to convivial excess, which must be judged in view of the laxer manners of his time. When allowance has been made for this, he remains one of the most admirable characters and writers in English literature.

SUMMARY.—*B.* Amesbury, *ed.* Charterhouse and Oxford; received travelling pension, 1699; *Campaign* (1704) leads to political office; goes to Ireland, 1708; assists Steele in *Tatler*, 1709; *Spectator* started, 1711; marries Lady Warwick, 1716; Secretary of State, 1716-18; *d.* 1719.

Lives in *Biographica Britannica*, *Dict. of Nat. Biog.*, *Johnson's Lives of Poets*, and by Lucy Aikin, Macaulay's *Essay*, Drake's *Essays Illustrative of Tatler, Guardian, and Spectator*; Pope's and Swift's Correspondence, etc.

The best edition of the books is that in *Bohn's British Classics* (6 vols., 1856); others are Tickell's (4 vols., 1721); *Baskerville* edit. (4 vols., 1761); Hurd's (6 vols., 1811); Greene's (1856); Dent's *Spectator* (1907).

ADOLPHUS, JOHN (1768-1845).—Historian, studied law and was called to the Bar in 1807. He wrote *Biographical Memoirs of the French Revolution* (1799) and *History of England from 1760-1783* (1802), and other historical and biographical works.

ÆLFRED (849-901).—King of the West Saxons, and writer and translator, *s.* of Ethelwulf, *b.* at Wantage. Besides being the deliverer of his country from the ravages of the Danes, and the restorer of order and civil government, Æ. has earned the title of the father of English prose writing. The earlier part of his life was filled with war and action, most of the details regarding which are more or less legendary. But no sooner had he become King of Wessex, in 871, than he began to prepare for the work of re-introducing learning into his country. Gathering round him the few scholars whom the Danes had left, and sending for others from abroad, he endeavoured to form a literary class. His chief helper in his great enterprise was Asser of St. David's, who taught him Latin, and became his biographer in a "life" which remains the best original authority for the period. Though not a literary artist, Æ. had the best qualities of the scholar, including an insatiable love alike for the acquisition and the communication of knowledge. He translated several of the best books then existing, not, however, in a slavish fashion, but editing and adding from his own stores. In all his work his main desire was the good of his people. Among the books he translated or edited were (1) *The Handbook*, a collection of extracts on religious subjects; (2) *The Cura Pastoralis*, or Herdsman's book of Gregory the Great, with a preface by himself which is the first English prose; (3) *Bede's Ecclesiastical History of the English*; (4) *The English Chronicle*, which, already brought up to 855, he continued up to the date of writing; it is probably by his own hand; (5) Orosius's *History of the World*, which he adapted for English readers with many historical and geographical additions; (6) the *De Consolatione Philosophiæ* of Boethius; and (7) a translation of some of the Psalms. He also made a collection of the best laws of his predecessors, Ethelbert, Ine, and Offa. It has been said "although King Alfred lived a thousand years ago, a thousand years hence, if there be England then, his memory will yet be precious to his country."

ÆLFRIC (955-*c.* 1022).—Called Grammaticus (10th century), sometimes confounded with two other persons of the same name, Æ. of Canterbury and Æ. of York, was a monk at Winchester, and afterwards Abbot of Cerne and Eynsham successively. He has left works which shed an important light on the doctrine and practice of the early Church in England, including two books of homilies (990-94), a *Grammar, Glossary, Passiones Sanctorum* (Sufferings of the Saints), translations of parts of the Bible with omissions and interpolations, *Canones Ælfrici*, and other theological treatises. His writings had an influence on the formation of English prose. He filled in his age somewhat the same position that Bede did in his, that of a compiler and populariser of existing knowledge.

AGUILAR, GRACE (1816-1847).—Novelist and writer on Jewish history and religion, was *b.* at Hackney of Jewish parents of Spanish descent. She was delicate from childhood, and early showed great interest in history, especially Jewish. The death of her *f.* threw her on her own resources. After a few dramas and poems she *pub.* in America in 1842 *Spirit of Judaism*, and in 1845 *The Jewish Faith* and *The Women of Israel*. She is, however, best known by her novels, of which the chief are *Home Influence* (1847) and *A Mother's Recompense* (1850). Her health gave way in 1847, and she *d.* in that year at Frankfort.

AIKIN, JOHN (1747-1822).—Miscellaneous writer, *s.* of Dr. John A., Unitarian divine, *b.* at Kibworth, studied medicine at Edinburgh and London, and received degree of M.D. at Leyden. He began practice at Yarmouth but, one of his pamphlets having given offence, he removed to London, where he obtained some success in his profession, devoting all his leisure to literature, to which his contributions were incessant. These consisted of pamphlets, translations, and miscellaneous works, some in conjunction with his sister, Mrs. Barbauld. Among his chief works are *England Delineated, General Biography* in 10 vols., and lives of Selden and Ussher.

AIKIN, LUCY (1781-1864).—Historical and miscellaneous writer, *dau.* of above and niece of Mrs. Barbauld (*q.v.*). After *pub.* a poem, *Epistles on Women*, and a novel, *Lorimer*, she began the historical works on which her reputation chiefly rests, viz., *Memoirs of the Courts of Elizabeth, James I., and Charles I.* (1818-33) and a *Life of Addison.* She also wrote lives of her father and of Mrs. Barbauld. She was remarkable for her conversational powers, and was also an admirable letter-writer. Like the rest of her family she was a Unitarian.

AINGER, ALFRED (1837-1904).—Biographer and critic, *s.* of an architect in London, *grad.* at Cambridge, entered the Church, and, after holding various minor preferments, became Master of the Temple. He wrote memoirs of Hood and Crabbe, but is best known for his biography of Lamb and his edition of his works in 6 vols. (1883-88).

AINSWORTH, WILLIAM HARRISON (1805-1882).—Novelist, *s.* of a solicitor, was *b.* in Manchester. He was destined for the legal profession, which, however, had no attraction for him; and going to London to complete his studies made the acquaintance of Mr. John Ebers, publisher, and at that time manager of the Opera House, by whom he was introduced to literary and dramatic circles, and whose *dau.* he afterwards married. For a short time he tried the publishing business, but soon gave it up and devoted himself to journalism and literature. His first successful novel was *Rookwood*, *pub.* in 1834, of which Dick Turpin is the leading character, and thenceforward he continued to pour forth till 1881 a stream of novels, to the number of 39, of which the best known are *The Tower of London* (1840), *Old St. Paul's* (1841), *Lancashire Witches*, and *The Constable of the Tower.* The titles of some of his other novels are *Crichton* (1837), *Jack Sheppard* (1839), *Guy Fawkes*, *The Star Chamber*, *The Flitch of Bacon*, *The Miser's Daughter* (1842), and *Windsor Castle* (1843). A. depends for his effects on striking situations and powerful descriptions: he has little humour or power of delineating character.

AIRD, THOMAS (1802-1876).—Poet, *b.* at Bowden, Roxburghshire, went to Edinburgh, where he became the friend of Professor Wilson, Carlyle, and other men of letters. He contributed to *Blackwood's Magazine*, and was editor of the *Dumfries Herald* (1835-63). His chief poem is *The Captive of Fez* (1830); and in prose he wrote *Religious Characteristics*, and *The Old Bachelor in the Old Scottish Village* (1848), all of which were received with favour. Carlyle said that in his poetry he found everywhere "a healthy breath as of mountain breezes."

AKENSIDE, MARK (1721-1770).—Poet, *s.* of a butcher at Newcastle-upon-Tyne, gave early indications of talent, and was sent to the University of Edinburgh with the view of becoming a dissenting minister. While there, however, he changed his mind and studied for the medical profession. Thereafter he went to Leyden, where he took his degree of M.D. in 1744. While there he wrote his principal poem, *The Pleasures of the Imagination*, which was well received, and was subsequently translated into more than one foreign language. After trying Northampton, he settled as a physician in London; but was for long largely dependent for his livelihood on a Mr. Dyson. His talents brought him a good deal of consideration in society, but the solemn and pompous manner which he affected laid him open to some ridicule, and he is said to have been satirised by Smollett (*q.v.*) in his *Peregrine Pickle*. He endeavoured to reconstruct his poem, but the result was a failure. His collected poems were *pub.* 1772. His works, however, are now little read. Mr. Gosse has described him as "a sort of frozen Keats."

ALCOTT, LOUISA M. (1832-1888).—Writer of juvenile and other tales, *dau.* of Amos Bronson Alcott, an educational and social theorist, lecturer, and author, was *b.* in Pennsylvania. During the American civil war she served as a nurse, and afterwards attained celebrity as a writer of books for young people, of which the best is *Little Women* (1868). Others are *Little Men* and *Jo's Boys*. She also wrote novels, including *Moods* and *Work*.

ALCUIN OR EALHWINE (735-804).—Theologian and general writer, was *b.* and *ed.* at York. He wrote in prose and verse, his subjects embracing educational, theological, and historical matters. Returning from Rome, to which he had been sent to procure the *pallium* for a friend, he met Charlemagne at Parma, and made upon him so favourable an impression that he was asked to enter his service as preceptor in the sciences to himself and his family. His numerous treatises, which include metrical annals, hagiographical and philosophical works, are not distinguished by originality or profundity, but he is the best representative of the culture and mental activity of his age, upon which, as the minister of education of the great emperor, he had a widely-spread influence.

ALDRICH, THOMAS BAILEY (1836-1906).—Poet and novelist, *b.* at Portsmouth, N. H., was for some time in a bank, and then engaged in journalism. His first book was *The Bells, a Collection of Chimes* (1855), and other poetical works are *The Ballad of Babie Bell, Cloth of Gold, Flower and Thorn*, etc. In prose he wrote *Daisy's Necklace, The Course of True Love, Marjorie Daw, Prudence Palfrey*, etc.

ALESIUS, ALEXANDER (1500-1565).—Theologian and controversialist. His unlatinised name was Aless or Alane, and he was *b.* at Edinburgh and *ed.* at St. Andrews, where he became a canon. Originally a strong and able defender of the Romish doctrines, he was chosen to argue with Patrick Hamilton, the proto-martyr of the Reformation in Scotland, with the object of inducing him to recant. The result, however, was that he was himself much shaken in his allegiance to the Church, and the change was greatly accelerated by the martyrdom of H. His subsequent protest against the immorality of the clergy led to his imprisonment, and ultimately, in 1532, to his flying for his life to Germany, where he became associated with Luther and Melancthon, and definitely joined the reforming party. Coming to England in 1535, he was well received by Cranmer and other reformers. While in England he studied medicine, and practised as a physician in London. On the fall of T. Cromwell in 1540 he again retired to Germany, where, at Leipzig, he obtained a professorship. During the reign of Edward VI. he re-visited England and was employed by Cranmer in connection with the 1st

Liturgy of Edward VI. Returning to Leipsic he passed the remainder of his days in peace and honour, and was twice elected Rector of the University. His writings were both exegetical and controversial, but chiefly the latter. They include *Expositio Libri Psalmorum Davidis* (1550). His controversial works refer to such subjects as the translation of the Bible into the vernacular, against Servetus, etc.

ALEXANDER, MRS. CECIL F. (HUMPHREYS) (1818-1895).—*dau.* of Maj. H., *b.* in Co. Waterford, *m.* the Rev. W. Alexander, afterwards Bishop of Derry and Archbishop of Armagh. Her *Hymns for Little Children* had reached its 69th edition before the close of the century. Some of her hymns, *e.g.* "There is a Green Hill" and "The Roseate Hues of Early Dawn," are known wherever English is spoken. Her husband has also written several books of poetry, of which the most important is *St. Augustine's Holiday and other Poems.*

ALFORD, HENRY (1810-1871).—Theologian, scholar, poet, and miscellaneous writer, *s.* of a clergyman, was *b.* in London. After passing through various private schools, he proceeded to Cambridge, where he had a distinguished career, and after entering the Church and filling various preferments in the country, became minister of Quebec Chapel, London, whence he was promoted to be Dean of Canterbury. His great work was his *Greek Testament* in 4 vols., of which the first was *pub.* in 1849 and the last in 1861. In this work he largely followed the German critics, maintaining, however, a moderate liberal position; and it was for long the standard work on the subject in this country. A. was one of the most versatile men, and prolific authors, of his day, his works consisting of nearly 50 vols., including poetry (*School of the Heart* and *Abbot of Munchelnaye*, and a translation of the *Odyssey*), criticism, sermons, etc. In addition to the works above mentioned he wrote *Chapters on the Greek Poets* (1841), the *Queen's English* (1863), and many well-known hymns, and he was the first editor of the *Contemporary Review.* He was also an accomplished artist and musician. His industry was incessant and induced a premature breakdown in health, which terminated in his death in 1871. He was the friend of most of his eminent contemporaries, and was much beloved for his amiable character.

ALISON, ARCHIBALD (1757-1839).—Didactic and philosophical writer, was *b.* in Edinburgh and *ed.* at Glasgow University and Oxford. After being presented to various livings in England, A. came to Edinburgh as incumbent of St. Paul's Episcopal Chapel, where he attained popularity as a preacher of sermons characterised by quiet beauty of thought and grace of composition. His chief contribution to literature is his *Essay on the Nature and Principles of Taste* (1790), in which the "association" theory is supported.

ALISON, SIR ARCHIBALD (1792-1867).—Historian, *s.* of the above, was *b.* at Kenley, Shropshire, and after studying under a private tutor, and at Edinburgh University, was, in 1814, called to the Bar, at which he ultimately attained some distinction, becoming in 1834 Sheriff of Lanarkshire, in which capacity he rendered valuable service in times of considerable difficulty. It was when travelling in France in 1814 that he conceived the idea of his *History of Europe*, which deals with the period from the outbreak of the French Revolution to the restoration of the Bourbons, and extends, in its original form (1833-42), to 10 vols. The work is one of vast industry, and gives a useful account of an important epoch, but is extremely diffuse and one-sided, and often prosy. Disraeli satirises the author in *Coningsby* as Mr. Wordy, who wrote a history to prove that Providence was on the side of the Tories. It had, however, an enormous sale. A continuation of it (1852-59) brought the story down to the accession of Louis Napoleon. A. was also the author of a life of Marlborough, and of two standard works on the criminal law of Scotland. In his private and official capacities he was highly respected, and was elected Lord Rector successively of Marischal Coll., Aberdeen, and of Glasgow University. He was created a baronet by Lord Derby in 1852.

ALLEN, CHARLES GRANT (1848-1899).—Scientific writer and novelist, *b.* in Canada, to which his *f.*, a clergyman, had emigrated, and *ed.* at Birmingham and Oxford. For a time he was a professor in a college for negroes in Jamaica, but returning to England in 1876 devoted himself to literature. His first books were on scientific subjects, and include *Physiological Æsthetics* (1877) and *Flowers and Their Pedigrees*. After assisting Sir W. W. Hunter in his *Gazeteer of India*, he turned his attention to fiction, and between 1884 and 1899 produced about 30 novels, among which *The Woman Who Did* (1895), promulgating certain startling views on marriage and kindred questions, created some sensation. Another work, *The Evolution of the Idea of God*, propounding a theory of religion on heterodox lines, has the disadvantage of endeavouring to explain everything by one theory. His scientific works also included *Colour Sense*, *Evolutionist at Large*, *Colin Clout's Calendar*, and the *Story of the Plants*, and among his novels may be added *Babylon*, *In all Shades*, *Philistia* (1884), *The Devil's Die*, and *The British Barbarians* (1896).

ALLINGHAM, WILLIAM (1824-1889).—Poet, the *s.* of a banker of English descent, was *b.* at Ballyshannon, entered the customs service, and was ultimately settled in London, where he contributed to *Leigh Hunt's Journal*. Hunt introduced him to Carlyle and other men of letters, and in 1850 he *pub.* a book of poems, which was followed by *Day and Night Songs* (1854), *Laurence Bloomfield in Ireland* (1864) (his most ambitious, though not his most successful work), and *Collected Poems* in 6 vols. (1888-93). He also edited *The Ballad Book* for the *Golden Treasury* series in 1864. In 1870 he retired from the civil service and became sub-editor of *Fraser's Magazine* under Froude, whom he succeeded as editor (1874-79). His verse is clear, fresh, and graceful. He married Helen Paterson, the water colourist, whose idylls have made the name of "Mrs. Allingham" famous also. He *d.* in 1889. Other works are *Fifty Modern Poems* (1865), *Songs, Poems, and Ballads* (1877), *Evil May Day* (1883), *Blackberries* (1884), *Irish Songs and Poems* (1887), and *Varieties in Prose* (1893). A selection from his diaries and autobiography was *pub.* in 1906.

ALLSTON, WASHINGTON (1779-1843).—Painter and poet, *b.* in S. Carolina, became a distinguished painter, and also wrote a good deal of verse including *The Sylphs of the Seasons*, etc. (1813), and *The Two Painters*, a satire. He also produced a novel, *Monaldi*. He was known as "the American Titian."

AMORY, THOMAS (1691(?)-1788).—Eccentric writer, was of Irish descent. ;In 1755 he *publ. Memoirs containing the lives of several ladies of Great Britain, a History of Antiquities and Observations on the Christian Religion*, which was followed by the *Life of John Buncle* (1756), practically a continuation. The contents of these works are of the most miscellaneous description—philology, natural science, theology, and, in fact, whatever occurred to the writer, treated without any system, but with occasional originality and felicity of diction. The author, who was probably more or less insane, is described as having a very peculiar aspect, with the manner of a gentleman, scarcely ever stirring abroad except at dusk. He reached the age of 97.

ANDERSON, ALEXANDER (1845-1909).—Poet, *s.* of a quarrier at Kirkconnel, Dumfriesshire, became a surfaceman on the railway. Spending all his leisure in self-culture, he mastered German, French, and Spanish sufficiently to read the chief masterpieces in these languages. His poetic vein, which was true if somewhat limited in range, soon manifested itself, and his first book, *Songs of Labour*, appeared in 1873, and there followed *Two Angels* (1875), *Songs of the Rail* (1878), and *Ballads and Sonnets* (1879). In the following year he was made assistant librarian in the University of Edinburgh, and after an interval as secretary to the Philosophical Institution there, he returned as Chief Librarian to the university. Thereafter he wrote little. Of a simple and gentle character, he made many friends, including the Duke of Argyll, Carlyle, and Lord Houghton. He generally wrote under the name of "Surfaceman."

ANDREWES, LANCELOT (1555-1626).—Churchman and scholar, was *b.* in London, and *ed.* at Merchant Taylor's School and Cambridge, where he took a fellowship and taught divinity. After receiving various other preferments he became Dean of Westminster, and a chaplain-in-ordinary to Queen Elizabeth, who, however, did not advance him further on account of his opposition to the alienation of ecclesiastical revenues. On the accession, however, of James I., to whom his somewhat pedantic learning and style of preaching recommended him, he rose into great favour, and was made successively Bishop of Chichester, of Ely, and, in 1618, of Winchester. He attended the Hampton Court Conference, and took part in the translation of the Bible, known as the *Authorised Version*, his special work being given to the earlier parts of the Old Testament: he acted, however, as a sort of general editor. He was considered as, next to Ussher, the most learned churchman of his day, and enjoyed a great reputation as an eloquent and impassioned preacher, but the stiffness and artificiality of his style render his sermons unsuited to modern taste. His doctrine was High Church, and in his life he was humble, pious, and charitable.

Ninety-six of his sermons were published in 1631 by command of Charles I.

There are lives by A. T. Russell (1863), and R. L. Ottley (1894); *Devotions* were edited by Rev. Dr. Whyte (1900).

ANSTEY, CHRISTOPHER (1724-1805).—Poet, *s.* of Dr. A., a wealthy clergyman, rector of Brinkley, Cambridgeshire, was *ed.* at Eton and Cambridge. He *pub.* in 1766 a satirical poem of considerable sparkle, *The New Bath Guide*, from which Smollett is said to have drawn largely in his *Humphrey Clinker*. He made many other excursions into literature which are hardly remembered, and ended his days as a country squire at the age of eighty.

D'ARBLAY, FRANCES (BURNEY) (1752-1840).—Novelist, *dau.* of Dr. Charles B., a musician of some distinction, was *b.* at Lynn Regis, where her *f.* was organist. Her mother having died while she was very young, and her *f.*, who had come to London, being too busy to give her any attention, she was practically self-educated. Her first novel, *Evelina, pub.* anonymously in 1778, at once by its narrative and comic power, brought her fame, and, through Mrs. Thrale (*q.v.*), she made the acquaintance of Dr. Johnson, with whom she became a great favourite. Her next literary venture was a comedy, *The Witlings ;* but, by the advice of her *f.*, it was not put upon the stage. In 1782, however, she produced *Cecilia*, which, like its predecessor, had an enormous sale, and which, though not perhaps so popular as *Evelina*, added to her fame. She now became the friend of Burke and other distinguished persons, including Mrs. Delaney, through whom she became known to the royal family, and was offered the appointment of Second Keeper of the Robes, which, with some misgivings, she accepted. This situation did not prove a happy one, the duties being menial, the society uncongenial, and the court etiquette oppressive and injurious to her health, and in 1791 she obtained permission to retire on a pension of £100. She had, during her connection with the court, continued her *Diary*, which she had begun in girlhood, and continued during her whole life, and which during this period contains many interesting accounts of persons and affairs of note. She married (1793) Gen. D'Arblay, a French *emigré*, their only income being her slender pension. This she endeavoured to increase by producing a tragedy, *Edwy and Elvira*, which failed. In 1795 she *pub.* by subscription another novel, *Camilla*, which, though it did not add to her reputation, considerably improved her circumstances, as it is said to have brought her £3000. After some years spent in France, where her husband had obtained employment, she returned to England and *pub.* her last novel, *The Wanderer*, which fell flat. Her only remaining work was a life of her father, written in an extraordinarily grandiloquent style. She died in 1840, aged 87.

ARBUTHNOT, JOHN (1667-1735).—Physician and satirist, was *b.* in Kincardineshire, and after studying at Aberdeen and Oxford, took his degree of M.D. at St. Andrews. Settling in London, he taught mathematics. Being by a fortunate accident at Epsom, he was called in to prescribe for Prince George, who was suddenly taken ill there, and was so successful in his treatment that he was appointed his regular physician. This circumstance made his professional fortune, for his ability enabled him to take full advantage of it, and in 1705 he became physician to the Queen. He became the cherished friend of Swift and Pope, and himself gained a high reputation as a wit and man of letters. His principal works are the *Memoirs of Martinus Scriblerus*, partly by Pope, but to which he was the chief contributor, the *History of John Bull* (1712), mainly against the Duke of Marlborough, *A Treatise concerning the Altercation or Scolding of the Ancients*, and the *Art of Political Lying*. He also wrote various medical treatises, and dissertations on ancient coins, weights, and measures. After the death of Queen Anne, A. lost his court appointments, but this, as well as more serious afflictions with which he was visited, he bore with serenity and dignity. He was an honourable and amiable man, one of the very few who seems to have retained the sincere regard of Swift, whose style he made the model of his own, with such success that writings by the one were sometimes attributed to the other: his *Art of Political Lying* is an example. He has, however, none of the ferocity of S.

ARGYLL, GEORGE JOHN DOUGLAS CAMPBELL, 8TH DUKE OF (1823-1900).—Statesman and writer on science, religion, and politics, succeeded his *f.*, the 7th duke, in 1847. His talents and eloquence soon raised him to distinction in public life. He acted with the Liberal party until its break-up under the Irish policy of Mr. Gladstone, after which he was one of the Unionist leaders. He held the offices of Lord Privy Seal, Postmaster-General, and Indian Secretary. His writings include *The Reign of Law* (1866), *Primeval Man* (1869), *The Eastern Question* (1879), *The Unseen Foundations of Society* (1893), *Philosophy of Belief* (1896), *Organic Evolution Cross-examined* (1898). He was a man of the highest character, honest, courageous, and clear-sighted, and, though regarded by some professional scientists as to a certain extent an amateur, his ability, knowledge, and dialectic power made him a formidable antagonist, and enabled him to exercise a useful, generally conservative, influence on scientific thought and progress.

ARMSTRONG, JOHN, M.D. (1709-1779).—Poet, *s.* of the minister of Castleton, Roxburghshire, studied medicine, which he practised in London. He is remembered as the friend of Thomson, Mallet, and other literary celebrities of the time, and as the author of a poem on *The Art of Preserving Health*, which appeared in 1744, and in which a somewhat unpromising subject for poetic treatment is gracefully and ingeniously handled. His other works, consisting of some poems and prose essays, and a drama, *The Forced Marriage*, are forgotten, with the exception of the four stanzas at the end of the first part of Thomson's *Castle of Indolence*, describing the diseases incident to sloth, which he contributed.

ARNOLD, SIR EDWIN (1832-1904).—Poet, *s.* of a Sussex magistrate, was *b.* at Gravesend, and *ed.* at King's School, Rochester, London, and Oxford. Thereafter he was an assistant master at King Edward's School, Birmingham, and was in 1856 appointed Principal of the Government Deccan College, Poona. Here he received the bias towards, and gathered material for, his future works. In 1861 he returned to England and became connected with *The Daily Telegraph*, of which he was ultimately editor. The literary task which he set before him was the interpretation in English verse of the life and philosophy of the East. His chief work with this object is *The Light of Asia* (1879), a poem on the life and teaching of Buddha, which had great popularity, but whose permanent place in literature must remain very uncertain. In *The Light of the World* (1891), he attempted, less successfully, a similar treatment of the life and teaching of Jesus. Other works are *The Song of Songs of India* (1875), *With Saadi in the Garden*, and *The Tenth Muse*. He travelled widely in the East, and wrote books on his travels. He was made K.C.I.E. in 1888.

ARNOLD, MATTHEW (1822-1888).—Poet and critic, *s.* of Dr. A., of Rugby (*q.v.*), was *b.* at Laleham and *ed.* at Rugby, Winchester, and Balliol Coll., Oxford, becoming a Fellow of Oriel in 1845. Thereafter he was private secretary to Lord Lansdowne, Lord President of the Council, through whose influence he was in 1851 appointed an inspector of schools. Two years before this he had *pub.* his first book of poetry, *The Strayed Reveller*, which he soon withdrew: some of the poems, however, including "Mycerinus" and "The Forsaken Merman," were afterwards republished, and the same applies to his next book, *Empedocles on Etna* (1852), with "Tristram and Iseult." In 1857 he was appointed to the Professorship of Poetry at Oxford, which he held for ten years. After this he produced little poetry and devoted himself to criticism and theology. His principal writings are, in poetry, *Poems* (1853), containing "Sohrab and Rustum," and "The Scholar Gipsy;" *Poems, 2nd Series* (1855), containing "Balder Dead;" *Merope* (1858); *New Poems* (1867), containing "Thyrsis," an elegy on A. H. Clough (*q.v.*), "A Southern Night," "Rugby Chapel," and "The Weary Titan"; in prose he wrote *On Translating Homer* (1861 and 1862), *On the Study of Celtic Literature* (1867), *Essays in Celtic Literature* (1868), *2nd Series* (1888), *Culture and Anarchy* (1869), *St. Paul and Protestantism* (1870), *Friendship's Garland* (1871), *Literature and Dogma* (1873), *God and the Bible* (1875), *Last Essays on Church and Religion* (1877), *Mixed Essays* (1879), *Irish Essays* (1882), and *Discourses in America* (1885). He also wrote some works on the state of education on the Continent. In 1883 he received a pension of £250. The rationalistic tendency of certain of his writings gave offence to many readers, and the sufficiency of his equipment in scholarship for dealing with some of the subjects which he handled was called in question; but he undoubtedly exercised a stimulating influence on his time; his writings are characterised by the finest culture, high purpose, sincerity, and a style of great distinction, and much of his poetry has an exquisite and subtle beauty, though here also it has been doubted whether high culture and wide knowledge of poetry did not sometimes take the place of the true poetic fire.

There is a bibliography of A.'s works by T. B. Smart (1892), and books upon him have been written by Prof. Saintsbury (1899), H. Paul (1902), and G. W. E. Russell (1904), also papers by Sir L. Stephen, F. Harrison, and others.

ARNOLD, THOMAS (1795-1842).—Historian, *s.* of an inland revenue officer in the Isle of Wight, was *ed.* at Winchester and Oxford, and after some years as a tutor, was, in 1828, appointed Head Master of Rugby. His learning, earnestness, and force of character enabled him not only to raise his own school to the front rank of public schools, but to exercise an unprecedented reforming influence on the whole educational system of the country. A liberal in politics, and a zealous church reformer, he was involved in many controversies, educational and religious. As a churchman he was a decided Erastian, and strongly opposed to the High Church party. In 1841 he was appointed Professor of Modern History at Oxford. His chief literary works are his unfinished *History of Rome* (three vols. 1838-42), and his *Lectures on Modern History.* He *d.* suddenly of angina pectoris in the midst of his usefulness and growing influence. His life, by Dean Stanley (*q.v.*), is one of the best works of its class in the language.

ASCHAM, ROGER (1515-1568).—Didactic writer and scholar, *s.* of John A., house-steward in the family of Lord Scrope, was *b.* at Kirby Wiske, Yorkshire, and *ed.* first by Sir Humphrey Wingfield, and then at St. John's Coll., Cambridge, where he devoted himself specially to the study of Greek, then newly revived, and of which, having taken a fellowship, he became a teacher. He was likewise noted for his skill in penmanship, music, and archery, the last of which is the subject of his first work, *Toxophilus*, *pub.* in 1545, and which, dedicated to Henry VIII., gained him the favour of the King, who bestowed a pension upon him. The objects of the book are twofold, to commend the practice of shooting with the long bow as a manly sport and an aid to national defence, and to set the example of a higher style of composition than had yet been attempted in English. Soon afterwards he was made university orator, and master of languages to the Lady (afterwards Queen) Elizabeth. He then went abroad in various positions of trust, returning on being appointed Latin Secretary to Edward VI. This office he likewise discharged to Mary and then to Elizabeth—a testimony to his tact and caution in these changeful times. His principal work, *The Schoolmaster*, a treatise on education, was printed by his widow in 1570. He also *pub.* a book on the political state of Germany.

Editions: of *Toxophilus*, Arber; *Schoolmaster*, Arber, also Mayer (1883); English works, Bennet (1767), with life by Dr. Johnson; whole works, Giles (1864-5).

ASGILL, JOHN (1659-1738).—Eccentric writer, student at the Middle Temple, 1686, and called to the Bar 1692. In 1699 he *pub.* in an unlucky hour a pamphlet to prove that death was not obligatory upon Christians, which, much to his surprise, aroused the public wrath and led to his expulsion from the Irish and English House of Commons successively. A. thereafter fell on evil days, and passed the rest of his life between the Fleet and the King's Bench, where, strange to say, his zeal as a pamphleteer continued unabated. He *d.* in 1738.

ASHMOLE, ELIAS (1617-1692).—Antiquary, was *ed.* at Lichfield, and became a solicitor in 1638. On the breaking out of the Civil War he sided with the royalists; went to Oxford and studied science, including astrology. The result of his studies in this region of mystery was his *Theatrum Chymicum Britannicum*, which gained him great repute and the friendship of John Selden. His last astrological treatise was *The Way to Bliss*, which dealt with the subject of "the philosopher's stone." He also wrote various works on antiquarian subjects, and a *History of the Order of the Garter*. A. held various posts under government, and presented to the University of Oxford a valuable collection of curiosities now known as the Ashmolean Museum. He also bequeathed his library to the University. His wife was a *dau.* of Sir W. Dugdale, the antiquary.

ASSER (*d.* 909?).—Chronicler, a monk of St. David's, afterwards Bishop of Sherborne, was the friend, helper, and biographer of Ælfred. In addition to his life of Ælfred he wrote a chronicle of England from 849 to 887.

ATHERSTONE, EDWIN (1788-1872).—Poet and novelist. His works, which were planned on an imposing scale, attracted some temporary attention and applause, but are now forgotten. His chief poem, *The Fall of Nineveh*, consisting of thirty books, appeared at intervals from 1828 to 1868. He also produced two novels, *The Sea Kings in England* and *The Handwriting on the Wall*.

ATTERBURY, FRANCIS (1662-1732). — Controversialist and preacher, was *b.* near Newport Pagnel, Bucks, and *ed.* at Westminster School and Oxford. He became the leading protagonist on the High Church side in the ecclesiastical controversies of his time, and is believed to have been the chief author of the famous defence of Dr. Sacheverell in 1712. He also wrote most of Boyle's *Examination of Dr. Bentley's Dissertations on the Epistles of Phalaris*, and *pub.* sermons, which, with his letters to Swift, Pope, and other friends, constitute the foundation of his literary reputation. During the reign of the Tories he enjoyed much preferment, having been successively Canon of Exeter, Dean of Christ Church, Dean of Westminster, and Bishop of Rochester. His Jacobite principles, however, and his participation in various plots got him into trouble, and in 1722 he was confined in the Tower, deprived of all his offices, and ultimately banished. He *d.* at Paris, Feb. 15, 1732, and was buried privately in Westminster Abbey.

AUBREY, JOHN (1626-1697).—Antiquary, was a country gentleman who inherited estates in several counties in England, which he lost by litigation and otherwise. He devoted himself to the collection of antiquarian and miscellaneous observations, and gave assistance to Dugdale and Anthony à-Wood in their researches. His own investigations were extensive and minute, but their value is much diminished by his credulity, and want of capacity to weigh evidence. His only publication is his *Miscellanies*, a collection of popular superstitions, etc., but he left various collections, which were edited and *publ.* in the 19th century.

AUSTEN, JANE (1775-1817).—Novelist, *dau.* of a clergyman, was *b.* at the rectory of Steventon near Basingstoke. She received an education superior to that generally given to girls of her time, and took early to writing, her first tale being begun in 1798. Her life was a singularly uneventful one, and, but for a disappointment in love, tranquil and happy. In 1801 the family went to Bath, the scene of many episodes in her writings, and after the death of her *f.* in 1805 to Southampton, and later to Chawton, a village in Hants, where most of her novels were written. A tendency to consumption having manifested itself, she removed in May, 1817, to Winchester for the advantage of skilled medical attendance, but so rapid was the progress of her malady that she died there two months later. Of her six novels, four—*Sense and Sensibility* (1811), *Pride and Prejudice* (1813), *Mansfield Park* (1814) and *Emma* (1816)—were *pub.* anonymously during her life-time; and the others, *Northanger Abbey*—written in 1798—and *Persuasion*, finished in 1816, appeared a few months after her death, when the name of the authoress was divulged. Although her novels were from the first well received, it is only of comparatively late years that her genius has gained the wide appreciation which it deserves. Her strength lies in the delineation of character, especially of persons of her own sex, by a number of minute and delicate touches arising out of the most natural and everyday incidents in the life of the middle and upper classes, from which her subjects are generally taken. Her characters, though of quite ordinary types, are drawn with such wonderful firmness and precision, and with such significant detail as to retain their individuality absolutely intact through their entire development, and they are never coloured by her own personality. Her view of life is genial in the main, with a strong dash of gentle but keen satire: she appeals rarely and slightly to the deeper feelings; and the enforcement of the excellent lessons she teaches is left altogether to the story, without a word of formal moralising. Among her admirers was Sir W. Scott, who said, "That young lady has a talent for describing the involvements of feelings and characters of ordinary life which is to me the most wonderful I ever met with;" others were Macaulay (who thought that in the world there were no compositions which approached nearer to perfection), Coleridge, Southey, Sydney Smith, and E. FitzGerald.

AUSTIN, JOHN (1790-1859).—Jurist, served in the army in Sicily and Malta, but, selling his commission, studied law, and was called to the Bar 1818. He did not long continue to practise, but devoted himself to the study of law as a science, and became Professor of Jurisprudence in London University 1826-32. Thereafter he served on various Royal Commissions. By his works he exercised a profound influence on the views of jurisprudence held in England. These include *The Province of Jurisprudence Determined* (1832), and his *Lectures on Jurisprudence*.

AYTON, SIR ROBERT (1570-1638).—Poet, *s.* of A. of Kinaldie in Fife. After *grad.* at St. Andrews, he studied law at Paris, became ambassador to the Emperor, and held other court offices. He appears to have been well-known to his literary contemporaries in England. He wrote poems in Latin, Greek, and English, and was one of the first Scotsmen to write in the last. His chief poem is

Diophantus and Charidora; Inconstancy Upbraided is perhaps the best of his short poems. He is credited with a little poem, *Old Long Syne*, which probably suggested Burns's famous *Auld Lang Syne*.

AYTOUN, WILLIAM EDMONSTONE (1813-1865).—Poet and humorist, *s.* of Roger A., a Writer to the Signet, was *b.* in Edinburgh and *ed.* there, and was brought up to the law, which, however, as he said, he "followed but could never overtake." He became a contributor to *Blackwood's Magazine* in 1836, and continued his connection with it until his death. In it appeared most of his humorous prose pieces, such as *The Glenmutchkin Railway, How I Became a Yeoman*, and *How I Stood for the Dreepdaily Burghs*, all full of vigorous fun. In the same pages began to appear his chief poetical work, the *Lays of the Scottish Cavaliers*, and a novel, partly autobiographical, *Norman Sinclair*. Other works were *The Bon Gaultier Ballads*, jointly with Theodore Martin, and *Firmilian, a Spasmodic Tragedy*, under the *nom-de-plume* of T. Percy Jones, intended to satirise a group of poets and critics, including Gilfillan, Dobell, Bailey, and Alexander Smith. In 1845 A. obtained the Chair of Rhetoric and Belles Lettres in Edinburgh University, which he filled with great success, raising the attendance from 30 to 150, and in 1852 he was appointed sheriff of Orkney and Shetland. He was married to a *dau.* of Professor Wilson (Christopher North).

BACON, FRANCIS, LORD VERULAM, AND VISCOUNT ST. ALBAN'S (1561-1626).—Philosopher and statesman, was the youngest *s.* of Sir Nicholas B., Lord Keeper, by his second wife, a *dau.* of Sir Anthony Cooke, whose sister married William Cecil, Lord Burghley, the great minister of Queen Elizabeth. He was *b.* at York House in the Strand on Jan. 22, 1561, and in his 13th year was sent with his elder brother Anthony to Trinity Coll., Cambridge. Here he first met the Queen, who was impressed by his precocious intellect, and was accustomed to call him "the young Lord Keeper." Here also he became dissatisfied with the Aristotelian philosophy as being unfruitful and leading only to resultless disputation. In 1576 he entered Gray's Inn, and in the same year joined the embassy of Sir Amyas Paulet to France, where he remained until 1579. The death of his *f.* in that year, before he had completed an intended provision for him, gave an adverse turn to his fortunes, and rendered it necessary that he should decide upon a profession. He accordingly returned to Gray's Inn, and, after an unsuccessful attempt to induce Burghley to give him a post at court, and thus enable him to devote himself to a life of learning, he gave himself seriously to the study of law, and was called to the Bar in 1582. He did not, however, desert philosophy, and *pub.* a Latin tract, *Temporis Partus Maximus* (the Greatest Birth of Time), the first rough draft of his own system. Two years later, in 1584, he entered the House of Commons as member for Melcombe, sitting subsequently for Taunton (1586), Liverpool (1589), Middlesex (1593), and Southampton (1597). In the Parliament of 1586 he took a prominent part in urging the execution of Mary Queen of Scots. About this time he seems again to have approached his powerful uncle, the result of which may possibly be traced in his rapid progress at the Bar, and in his receiving, in 1589, the reversion to the Clerkship of the Star Chamber, a valuable appointment, into the enjoyment of which, however, he did not enter until 1608. About 1591 he formed a friendship with the Earl of Essex, from whom he received many tokens of kindness ill requited. In 1593 the offices of Attorney-general, and subsequently of Solicitor-general became vacant, and Essex used his influence on B.'s behalf, but unsuccessfully, the former being given to Coke, the famous lawyer. These disappointments may have been owing to a speech made by B. on a question of subsidies. To console him for them Essex presented him with a property at Twickenham, which he subsequently sold for £1800, equivalent to a much larger sum now. In 1596 he was made a Queen's Counsel, but missed the appointment of Master of the Rolls, and in the next year (1597), he *pub.* the first edition of his *Essays*, ten in number, combined with *Sarced Meditations* and the *Coulours of Good and Evil.* By 1601 Essex had lost the Queen's favour, and had raised his rebellion, and B. was one of those appointed to investigate the charges against him, and examine witnesess, in connection with which he showed an ungrateful and indecent eagerness in pressing the case against his former friend and benefactor, who was executed on Feb. 25, 1601. This act B. endeavoured to justify in *A Declaration of the Practices and Treasons, etc., of . . . the Earl of Essex, etc.* His circumstances had for some time been bad, and he had been arrested for debt: he had, however, received a gift of a fine of £1200 on one of Essex's accomplices. The accession of James VI. in 1603 gave a favourable turn to his fortunes: he was knighted, and endeavoured to set himself right with the new powers by writing his *Apologie* (defence) of his proceedings in the case of Essex, who had favoured the succession of James. In the first Parliament of the new king he sat for St. Alban's, and was appointed a Commissioner for Union with Scotland. In 1605 he *pub. The Advancement of Learning*, dedicated, with fulsome flattery, to the king. The following year he married Alice Barnham, the *dau.* of a London merchant, and in 1607 he was made Solicitor-General, and wrote *Cogita et Visa*, a first sketch of the *Novum Organum*, followed in 1609 by *The Wisdom of the Ancients.* Meanwhile (in 1608), he had entered upon the Clerkship of the Star Chamber, and was in the enjoyment of a large income; but old debts and present extravagance kept him embarrassed, and he endeavoured to obtain further promotion and wealth by supporting the king in his arbitrary policy. In 1613 he became Attorney-General, and in this capacity prosecuted Somerset in 1616. The year 1618 saw him Lord Keeper, and the next Lord Chancellor and Baron Verulam, a title which, in 1621, he exchanged for that of Viscount St. Albans. Meanwhile he had written the *New Atlantis*, a political romance, and in 1620 he presented to the king the *Novum Organum*, on which he had been engaged for 30 years, and which ultimately formed the main part of the *Instauratio Magna.* In his great office B. showed a failure of character in striking contrast with the majesty of his intellect. He was corrupt alike politically and judicially, and now the hour of retribution arrived. In 1621 a Parliamentary Committee on the administration of the law charged him with corruption under 23 counts; and so clear was the evidence that he made no attempt at defence. To the lords, who sent a committee to inquire whether the confession was really his, he replied, "My lords, it is my act, my hand, and my heart; I beseech your lordships to be merciful to a broken reed." He was sentenced to a fine of £40,000, remitted by the king, to be committed to the Tower during the king's pleasure (which was that he should be released in a few days), and to be incapable of holding office or sitting in parliament. He narrowly escaped being deprived of his titles. Thenceforth he devoted himself to study and writing. In 1622 appeared his *History of Henry VII.*, and the 3rd part of the *Instauratio*; in 1623, *History of Life and Death*, the *De Augmentis Scientarum*, a Latin translation of the *Advancement*, and in 1625 the 3rd edition of the *Essays*, now 58 in number. He also *pub.* *Apophthegms*, and a translation of some of the *Psalms*. His life was now approaching its close. In March, 1626, he came to London, and shortly after, when driving on a snowy day, the idea struck him of making an experiment as to the antiseptic properties of snow, in consequence of which he caught a chill, which ended in his death on 9th April 1626. He left debts to the amount of £22,000. At the time of his death he was engaged upon *Sylva Sylvarum*. The intellect of B. was one of the most powerful and searching ever possessed by man, and his developments of the inductive philosophy revolutionised the future thought of the human race. The most popular of his works is the *Essays*, which convey profound and condensed thought in a style that is at once clear and rich. His moral character was singularly mixed and complex, and bears no comparison with his intellect. It exhibits a singular coldness and lack of enthusiasm, and indeed a bluntness of moral perception and an absence of attractiveness rarely combined with such extraordinary mental endowments. All that was possible to be done in defence of his character and public conduct has been done by his accomplished biographer and editor, Mr. Spedding (*q.v.*). Singular, though of course futile, attempts, supported sometimes with much ingenuity, have been made to claim for B. the authorship of Shakespeare's plays, and have indeed been extended so as to include those of Marlowe, and even the *Essays* of Montaigne.

SUMMARY.—*B.* London 1561, *ed.* Trinity Coll., Cambridge, dissatisfied with Aristotelean philosophy, entered Gray's Inn 1576, in France 1576-79, called to Bar 1582, enters Parliament 1584, became friend of Essex 1591, who presents him with estate 1593, *pub.* 1st ed. of *Essays* 1597, prosecutes Essex 1601, *pub. Advancement of Learning* 1605, Solicitor-Gen. 1607, *pub. Wisdom of the Ancients* 1609, Attorney-Gen. 1613, prosecuted Somerset 1616, Lord Keeper 1618, Lord Chancellor with title of Verulam 1619, Visc. St. Albans 1621, *pub. Novum Organum* 1620, charged with corruption, and retires from public life 1621, *pub. Henry VII.* and 3rd part of *Instauratio* 1622, *d.* 1626.

The standard edition of B.'s works is that of Spedding, Ellis, and Heath (14 vols. 1857-74), including *Life and Letters* by Spedding. See also Macaulay's *Essays*; Dean Church in *Men of Letters Series*; Dr. Abbott's *Life* (1885), etc. For philosophy Fowler's *Novum Organum* (1878).

BACON, ROGER (1214?-1294).—Philosopher, studied at Oxford and Paris. His scientific acquirements, regarded in that age as savouring of witchcraft, and doubtless also his protests against the ignorance and immorality of the clergy, excited the jealousy and hatred of the Franciscans, and he was in consequence imprisoned at Paris for ten years. Clement IV., who had been a sympathiser, desired on his accession to see his works, and in response B. sent him *Opus Majus*, a treatise on the sciences (grammar, logic, mathematics, physics, and philosophy), followed by *Opus Secundum* and *Opus Tertium*. Clement, however, was near death when they arrived. B. was comparatively free from persecution for the next ten years. But in 1278 he was again imprisoned for upwards of ten years. At the intercession of some English noblemen he was at last released, and spent his remaining years at Oxford. He possessed one of the most commanding intellects of his own, or perhaps of any, age, and, notwithstanding all the disadvantages and discouragements to which he was subjected, made many discoveries, and came near to many more. There is still preserved at Oxford a rectified calendar in which he approximates closely to the truth. He received the sobriquet of the "Doctor Mirabilis."

BAGE, ROBERT (1728-1801).—Novelist, *b.* in Derbyshire, was the *s.* of a paper-maker. It was not until he was 53 that he took to literature; but in the 15 years following he produced 6 novels, of which Sir Walter Scott says that "strong mind, playful fancy, and extensive knowledge are everywhere apparent." B., though brought up as a Quaker, imbibed the principles of the French Revolution. He was an amiable and benevolent man, and highly esteemed. *Hermsprong; or, Man as He is Not* (1796) is considered the best of his novels, of which it was the last. The names of the others are *Mount Kenneth* (1781), *Barham Downs* (1784), *The Fair Syrian* (1787), *James Wallace* (1788), and *Man as He is* (1792).

BAGEHOT, WALTER (1826-1877).—Economist, *s.* of a banker, *b.* at Langport, Somerset, *ed.* at University Coll., London, and called to the Bar, but did not practise, and joined his *f.* in business. He wrote for various periodicals, and from 1860 was editor of *The Economist*. He was the author of *The English Constitution* (1867), a standard work which was translated into several languages; *Physics and Politics* (1872), and *Lombard Street* (1873), a valuable financial work. A collection of essays, biographical and economic, was *pub.* after his death.

BAILEY, PHILIP JAMES (1816-1902).—Poet, *s.* of a journalist, *b.* at Nottingham, and *ed.* there and at Glasgow, of which he was made an LL.D. in 1891. His life was a singularly uneventful one. He lived at Nottingham, Jersey, Ilfracombe, London, and again at Nottingham, where he *d.* He travelled a good deal on the Continent. He was by profession a barrister, but never practised, and devoted his whole energies to poetry. His first poem, *Festus* (1839), is, for the daring of its theme and the imaginative power and moral altitude which it displays, one of the most notable of the century; as the work of one little past boyhood it is a prodigy of intellectual precocity. Along with its great qualities it has many faults in execution, and its final place in literature remains to be determined. It was *pub.* anonymously, and had great success, but has fallen into unmerited, but perhaps temporary, neglect. Among its greatest admirers was Tennyson. The subsequent poems of B., *The Angel World* (1850), *The Mystic* (1855), *The Age* (1858), and *The Universal Hymn* (1867), were failures, and the author adopted the unfortunate expedient of endeavouring to buoy them up by incorporating large extracts in the later editions of *Festus*, with the effect only of sinking the latter, which ultimately extended to over 40,000 lines. B. was a man of strikingly handsome appearance, and gentle and amiable character.

BAILLIE, JOANNA (1762-1851).—Dramatist and poetess, *dau.* of the minister of Bothwell, afterwards Professor of Divinity at Glasgow. Her mother was a sister of the great anatomists, William and John Hunter, and her brother was the celebrated physician, Matthew B., of London. She received a thorough education at Glasgow, and at an early age went to London, where the remainder of her long, happy, and honoured, though uneventful, life was passed. In 1798, when she was 36, the first vol. of her *Plays on the Passions* appeared, and was received with much favour, other two vols. followed in 1802 and 1812, and she also produced *Miscellaneous Plays* in 1804, and 3 vols. of *Dramatic Poetry* in 1836. In all her works there are many passages of true and impressive poetry, but the idea underlying her *Plays on the Passions*, that, namely, of exhibiting the principal character as acting under the exclusive influence of one passion, is artificial and untrue to nature.

BAILLIE, LADY GRIZEL (1665-1746).—Poetess, *dau.* of Sir Patrick Home or Hume, afterwards Earl of Marchmont, was married to George Baillie of Jerviswoode. In her childhood she showed remarkable courage and address in the services she rendered to her father and his friend, Robert Baillie of Jerviswoode, the eminent Scottish patriot, when under persecution. She left many pieces both prose and verse in MS., some of which were *pub.* The best known is the beautiful song, *Were na my heart licht I wad die.*

BAILLIE, ROBERT (1599-1662).—Historical writer, *s.* of B. of Jerviston, *ed.* at Glasgow, he entered the Church of Scotland and became minister of Kilwinning in Ayrshire. His abilities soon made him a leading man. He was a member of the historic Assembly of 1638, when Presbyterianism was re-established in Scotland, and also of the Westminster Assembly, 1643. In 1651 he was made Professor of Divinity in Glasgow, and 10 years later Principal. His *Letters and Journals*, edited for the Bannatyne Club by D. Laing (*q.v.*), are of the greatest value for the interesting light they throw on a period of great importance in Scottish history. He was one of the wisest and most temperate churchmen of his time.

BAIN, ALEXANDER (1818-1903).—Philosopher, *b.* at Aberdeen, and graduated at Marischal Coll. there, became in 1860 Professor of Logic in his university, and wrote a number of works on philosophy and psychology, including *The Senses and the Intellect*

(1855), *The Emotions and the Will, Mental and Moral Science* (1868), *Logic* (1870), and *Education as a Science* (1879). In 1881 he was elected Lord Rector of Aberdeen University.

BAKER, SIR RICHARD (1568-1645).—Historian and religious writer, studied law, was knighted in 1603, and was High Sheriff of Oxfordshire 1620. B. was the author of *The Chronicle of the Kings of England* (1643), which was for long held as a great authority among the country gentlemen. It has, however, many errors. B. fell on evil days, was thrown into the Fleet for debt incurred by others, for which he had made himself responsible, and *d.* there. It was during his durance that the *Chronicle* and some religious treatises were composed. The *Chronicle* was continued by Edward Phillips, Milton's nephew, who became a strong Royalist.

BAKER, SIR SAMUEL WHITE (1821-1893).—Traveller, *b.* in London, and after being a planter in Ceylon, and superintending the construction of a railway between the Danube and the Black Sea, went with his wife, a Hungarian lady, in search of the sources of the Nile, and discovered the great lake, Albert Nyanza. B. was knighted in 1866, and was for 4 years Governor-General of the Equatorial Nile Basin. His books, which are all on travel and sport, are well written and include *Albert Nyanza* (1866), *Nile Tributaries of Abyssinia* (1867).

BALE, JOHN (1495-1563).—Historian and controversialist, *b.* at Cove, Suffolk, and *ed.* as a Carmelite friar, but becoming a Protestant, engaged in violent controversy with the Roman Catholics. After undergoing persecution and flying to Flanders, he was brought back by Edward VI. and made Bishop of Ossory. On the death of Edward he was again persecuted, and had to escape from Ireland to Holland, but returned on the accession of Elizabeth, who made him a Prebendary of Canterbury. His chief work is a Latin *Account of the Lives of Eminent Writers of Great Britain* Besides this he wrote some dramas on scriptural subjects, and an account of the trial and death of Sir John Oldcastle. He wrote in all 22 plays, of which only 5 have come down, the names of certain of which give some idea of their nature, *e.g.*, *The Three Leaves of Nature, Moses and Christ*, and *The Temptacyon of Our Lord*.

BALLANTINE, JAMES (1808-1877).—Artist and author, *b.* in Edinburgh, began life as a house painter. He studied art, and became one of the first to revive the art of glass-painting, on which subject he wrote a treatise. He was the author of *The Gaberlunzie's Wallet* (1843), *Miller of Deanhaugh* (1845), *Poems* (1856), 100 *Songs with Music* (1865), and a *Life of David Roberts, R.A.* (1866).

BALLANTYNE, ROBERT MICHAEL (1825-1894).—Writer of tales for boys, *b.* in Edinburgh, was a connection of the well-known printers. As a youth he spent some years in the service of the Hudson's Bay Co., and was then a member of Constable's printing firm. In 1856 he took to literature as a profession, and *pub.* about 80 tales, which, abounding in interesting adventure and information, and characterised by a thoroughly healthy tone, had great popularity. Among them are *The Young Fur Traders* (1856), *The Coral Island, Fighting the Flames, Martin Rattler, The World of Ice, The Dog Crusoe, Erling the Bold,* and *Black Ivory.* B. was also an accomplished water-colour artist, and in all respects lived up to the ideals he sought to instil into his readers. He *d.* at Rome.

BANCROFT, GEORGE (1800-1891).—American historian, *b.* at Worcester, Massachusetts, and after *grad.* at Harvard, studied in Germany, where he became acquainted and corresponded with Goethe, Hegel, and other leaders of German thought. Returning to America he began his *History of the United States* (1834-74). The work covers the period from the discovery of the Continent to the conclusion of the Revolutionary War in 1782. His other great work is *The History of the Formation of the Constitution of the United States* (1882). B. filled various political offices, and was in 1846 Minister Plenipotentiary to England, and in 1867 Minister to Prussia. His writing is clear and vigorous, and his facts generally accurate, but he is a good deal of a partisan.

BANIM, JOHN (1798-1842).—Novelist, began life as a miniature painter, but was led by the success of his first book, *Tales of the O'Hara Family,* to devote himself to literature. The object which he set before himself was to become to Ireland what Scott has been to Scotland, and the influence of his model is distinctly traceable in his writings. His strength lies in the delineation of the characters of the Irish lower classes, and the impulses, often misguided and criminal, by which they are influenced, and in this he has shown remarkable power. The first series of the *O'Hara Tales* appeared in 1825, the second in 1826. Other works are *The Croppy* (1828), *The Denounced* (1830), *The Smuggler* (1831), *The Mayor of Windgap,* and his last, *Father Connell.* Most of these deal with the darker and more painful phases of life, but the feeling shown in the last-named is brighter and tenderer. B. latterly suffered from illness and consequent poverty, which were alleviated by a pension from Government. He also wrote some poems, including *The Celt's Paradise,* and one or two plays. In the *O'Hara Tales,* he was assisted by his brother, MICHAEL BANIM (1796-1874), and there is difficulty in allocating their respective contributions. After the death of John, Michael wrote *Clough Fionn* (1852), and *The Town of the Cascades* (1864).

BANNATYNE, RICHARD (*d.* 1605). — Secretary to John Knox, compiled *Memorials of Transactions in Scotland from* 1569 *to* 1573.

BARBAULD, ANNA LETITIA (1743-1825).—Poetess, etc., *dau.* of Dr. John Aikin (*q.v.*), was *b.* at Kibworth - Hencourt, Leicestershire. Her *f.* kept an academy for boys, whose education she shared, and thus became acquainted with the classics. In 1773 she *pub.* a collection of miscellaneous poems, which was well received, and in the following year she married the Rev. R. Barbauld, a French Protestant and dissenting minister, who also conducted a school near Palgrave in Suffolk. Into this enterprise Mrs. B. threw herself with great energy, and, mainly owing to her talents and reputation, it proved a success and was afterwards carried on at Hampstead and Newington Green. Meantime, she continued her literary occupations, and brought out various devotional works, including her *Hymns in Prose for Children.* These were followed by *Evenings at Home, Selections from the English Essayists, The Letters of Samuel Richardson,* with a life prefixed, and a selection from the British novelists with introductory essay.

BARBOUR, JOHN (1316?-1395).—Poet. Of B.'s youth nothing is certainly known, but it is believed that he was *b.* near Aberdeen, and studied at Oxford and Paris. He entered the Church, and rose to ecclesiastical preferment and Royal favour. He is known to have been Archdeacon of Aberdeen in 1357, when, and again in 1364, he went with some young scholars to Oxford, and he also held various civil offices in connection with the exchequer and the King's household. His principal poem, *The Bruce,* was in progress in 1376. It consists of 14,000 octosyllabic lines, and celebrates the praises of Robert the Bruce and James Douglas, the flowers of Scottish chivalry. This poem is almost the sole authority on the history it deals with, but is much more than a rhyming chronicle; it contains many fine descriptive passages, and sings the praises of freedom. Its style is somewhat bald and severe. Other poems ascribed to B. are *The Legend of Troy,* and *Legends of the Saints,* probably translations. B. devoted a perpetual annuity of 20 shillings, bestowed upon him by the King, to provide for a mass to be sung for himself and his parents, and this was duly done in the church of St. Machar until the Reformation.

The Bruce, edited by C. Innes for Spalding Club (1856), and for Early Engl. Text Soc. by W. W. Skeat, 1870-77; and for Scott. Text Soc. (1894); *The Wallace* and *The Bruce* re-studied, J. T. T. Brown, 1900; G. Neilson in Chambers' Cyc. Eng. Lit. (1903).

BARCLAY, ALEXANDER (1475?-1552).—Poet, probably of Scottish birth, was a priest in England. He is remembered for his satirical poem, *The Ship of Fools* (1509), partly a translation, which is of interest as throwing light on the manners and customs of the times to which it refers. He also translated Sallust's *Bellum Jugurthinum,* and the *Mirrour of Good Manners,* from the Italian of Mancini, and wrote five *Eclogues.* His style is stiff and his verse uninspired.

BARCLAY, JOHN (1582-1621).—Satirist, *s.* of a Scotsman, who was Professor of Law at Pont-à-Mousson, Lorraine, came with his *f.* to England about 1603. He wrote several works in English and Latin, among which are *Euphormionis Satyricon,* against the Jesuits, and *Argenis,* a political romance, resembling in certain respects the *Arcadia* of Sidney, and the *Utopia* of More.

BARCLAY, ROBERT (1648-1690).—Apologist of the Quakers, *s.* of Col. David B. of Ury, *ed.* at the Scots Coll. in Paris, of which his uncle was Rector, made such progress in study as to gain the admiration of his teachers, specially of his uncle, who offered to make him his heir if he would remain in France, and join the Roman Catholic Church. This he refused to do, and, returning to Scotland, he in 1667 adopted the principles of the Quakers as his *f.* had already done. Soon afterwards he began to write in defence of his sect, by *pub.* in 1670 *Truth cleared of Calumnies*, and *a Catechism and Confession of Faith* (1673). His great work, however, is his *Apology for the Quakers*, *pub.* in Latin in 1676, and translated into English in 1678. It is a weighty and learned work, written in a dignified style, and was eagerly read. It, however, failed to arrest the persecution to which the Quakers were exposed, and B. himself, on returning from the Continent, where he had gone with Foxe and Penn, was imprisoned, but soon regained his liberty, and was in the enjoyment of Court favour. He was one of the twelve Quakers who acquired East New Jersey, of which he was appointed nominal Governor. His latter years were spent at his estate of Ury, where he *d.* The essential view which B. maintained was, that Christians are illuminated by an inner light superseding even the Scriptures as the guide of life. His works have often been reprinted.

BARHAM, RICHARD HARRIS (1788-1845).—Novelist and humorous poet, *s.* of a country gentleman, was *b.* at Canterbury, *ed.* at St. Paul's School and Oxford, entered the church, held various incumbencies, and was Divinity Lecturer, and minor canon of St. Paul's. It is not, however, as a churchman that he is remembered, but as the author of the *Ingoldsby Legends*, a series of comic and serio-comic pieces in verse, sparkling with wit, and full of striking and often grotesque turns of expression, which appeared first in *Bentley's Miscellany*. He also wrote, in *Blackwood's Magazine*, a novel, *My Cousin Nicholas*.

BARLOW, JOEL (1754-1812).—Poet, *b.* at Reading, Connecticut, served for a time as an army chaplain, and thereafter betook himself to law, and finally to commerce and diplomacy, in the former of which he made a fortune. He was much less successful as a poet than as a man of affairs. His writings include *Vision of Columbus* (1787), afterwards expanded into the *Columbiad* (1807), *The Conspiracy of Kings* (1792), and *The Hasty Pudding* (1796), a mock-heroic poem, his best work. These are generally pompous and dull. In 1811 he was *app.* ambassador to France, and met his death in Poland while journeying to meet Napoleon.

BARNARD, LADY ANNE (LINDSAY) (1750-1825).—Poet, *e. dau.* of the 5th Earl of Balcarres, married Andrew Barnard, afterwards Colonial Secretary at Cape Town. On the *d.* of her husband in 1807 she settled in London. Her exquisite ballad of *Auld Robin Gray* was written in 1771, and *pub.* anonymously. She confessed the authorship to Sir Walter Scott in 1823.

BARNES, BARNABE (1569?-1609).—Poet, *s.* of Dr. Richard B. Bishop, of Durham, was *b.* in Yorkshire, and studied at Oxford. He wrote *Parthenophil*, a collection of sonnets, madrigals, elegies, and odes, *A Divine Centurie of Spirituall Sonnets*, and *The Devil's Charter*, a tragedy. When at his best he showed a true poetic vein.

BARNES, WILLIAM (1801-1886).—Poet and philologist, *s.* of a farmer, *b.* at Rushay, Dorset. After being a solicitor's clerk and a schoolmaster, he entered the Church, in which he served various cures. He first contributed to a newspaper, *Poems in Dorset Dialect*, separately *pub.* in 1844. *Hwomely Rhymes* followed in 1858, and a collected edition of his poems appeared in 1879. His philological works include *Philological Grammar* (1854), *Se Gefylsta, an Anglo-Saxon Delectus* (1849), *Tiw, or a View of Roots* (1862), and a *Glossary of Dorset Dialect* (1863). B.'s poems are characterised by a singular sweetness and tenderness of feeling, deep insight into humble country life and character, and an exquisite feeling for local scenery.

BARNFIELD, RICHARD (1574-1627).—Poet, *e. s.* of Richard B., gentleman, was *b.* at Norbury, Shropshire, and *ed.* at Oxford. In 1594 he *pub. The Affectionate Shepherd*, a collection of variations in graceful verse of the 2nd Eclogue of Virgil. His next work was *Cynthia, with certain Sonnets and the Legend of Cassandra* in 1595; and in 1598 there appeared a third vol., *The Encomion of Lady Pecunia, etc.*, in which are two songs (" If music and sweet poetrie agree," and " As it fell upon a day ") also included in *The Passionate Pilgrim*, an unauthorised collection, and which were long attributed to Shakespeare. From this time, 1599, B. produced nothing else, and seems to have retired to the life of a country gentleman at Stone in Staffordshire, in the church of which he was buried in 1627. He was for long neglected; but his poetry is clear, sweet, and musical. His gift indeed is sufficiently attested by work of his having passed for that of Shakespeare.

BARROW, ISAAC (1630-1677).—Divine, scholar, and mathematician, *s.* of a linen-draper in London, was *ed.* at Charterhouse, Felsted, Peterhouse, and Trinity Coll., Cambridge, where his uncle and namesake, afterwards Bishop of St. Asaph, was a Fellow. As a boy he was turbulent and pugnacious, but soon took to hard study, distinguishing himself in classics and mathematics. Intending originally to enter the Church, he was led to think of the medical profession, and engaged in scientific studies, but soon reverted to his first views. In 1655 he became candidate for the Greek Professorship at Cambridge, but was unsuccessful, and travelled for four years on the Continent as far as Turkey. On his return he took orders, and, in 1660, obtained the Greek Chair at Cambridge, and in 1662 the Gresham Professorship of Geometry, which he resigned on being appointed first Lucasian Professor of Mathematics in the same university. During his tenure of this chair he *pub.* two mathematical works of great learning and elegance, the first on Geometry and the second on Optics. In 1669 he resigned in favour of his pupil, Isaac Newton, who was long considered his only superior among English mathematicians. About this time also he composed his *Expositions of the Creed, The Lord's Prayer, Decalogue,* and *Sacraments.* He was made a D.D. by royal mandate in 1670, and two years later Master of Trinity Coll., where he founded the library. Besides the works above mentioned, he wrote other important treatises on mathematics, but in literature his place is chiefly supported by his sermons, which are masterpieces of argumentative eloquence, while his treatise on the *Pope's Supremacy* is regarded as one of the most perfect specimens of controversy in existence. B.'s character as a man was in all respects worthy of his great talents, though he had a strong vein of eccentricity. He *d.* unmarried in London at the early age of 47. B.'s theological works were edited by Napier, with memoir by Whewell (9 vols., 1839).

BARTON, BERNARD (1784-1849).—Poet, *b.* of Quaker parentage, passed nearly all his life at Woodbridge, for the most part as a clerk in a bank. He became the friend of Southey, Lamb, and other men of letters. His chief works are *The Convict's Appeal* (1818), a protest against the severity of the criminal code of the time, and *Household Verses* (1845), which came under the notice of Sir R. Peel, through whom he obtained a pension of £100. With the exception of some hymns his works are now nearly forgotten, but he was a most amiable and estimable man—simple and sympathetic. His *dau.* Lucy, who married Edward Fitzgerald, the translator of *Omar Khayyam*, *pub.* a selection of his poems and letters, to which her husband prefixed a biographical introduction.

BAYNES, THOMAS SPENCER (1823-1887).—Philosopher, *s.* of a Baptist minister, *b.* at Wellington, Somerset, intended to study for Baptist ministry, and was at a theological seminary at Bath with that view, but being strongly attracted to philosophical studies, left it and went to Edin., when he became the favourite pupil of Sir W. Hamilton (*q.v.*), of whose philosophical system he continued an adherent. After working as ed. of a newspaper in Edinburgh, and after an interval of rest rendered necessary by a breakdown in health, he resumed journalistic work in 1858 as assistant ed. of the *Daily News*. In 1864 he was appointed Prof. of Logic and English Literature at St. Andrews, in which capacity his mind was drawn to the study of Shakespeare, and he contributed to the *Edinburgh Review* and *Fraser's Magazine* valuable papers (chiefly relating to his vocabulary and the extent of his learning) afterwards collected as *Shakespeare Studies*. In 1873 he was appointed to superintend the ninth ed. of the *Encyclopædia Britannica*, in which, after 1880, he was assisted by W. Robertson Smith (*q.v.*).

BAXTER, RICHARD (1615-1691).—Divine scholar and controversialist, was *b.* of poor, but genteel, parents at Rowton in Shropshire, and although he became so eminent for learning, was not *ed.* at any university. Circumstances led to his turning his attention to a career at court under the patronage of the Master of the Revels, but a short experience of this sufficed; and giving himself to the Christian ministry, he was ordained in 1638, and, after being master of a school at Dudley, exercised his ministry successively at Bridgnorth and Kidderminster. His learning and capacity for business made him the leader of the Presbyterian party. He was one of the greatest preachers of his own day, and consistently endeavoured to exert a moderating influence, with the result that he became the object of attack by extremists of opposing views. Though siding with the Parliament in the Civil War, he opposed the execution of the King and the assumption of supreme power by Cromwell. During the war he served with the army as a chaplain. On the return of Charles II., B. was made one of his chaplains, and was offered the see of Hereford, which he declined, and his subsequent request to be allowed to return to Kidderminster was refused. He subsequently suffered persecution at the hands of Judge Jeffreys. After the Revolution he had a few years of peace and quiet. His literary activity was marvellous in spite of ill-health and outward disturbance. He is said to have written 168 works, the best known of which are *The Saints' Everlasting Rest* (1650), and *Call to the Unconverted* (1657), manuals of practical religion; and, among his controversial writings, *Methodus Theologiæ* (1681), and *Catholic Theology* (1675), in which his theological standpoint—a compromise between Arminianism and Calvinism—is set forth. Dr. Isaac Barrow says that "his practical writings were never mended, and his controversial seldom confuted," and Dean Stanley calls him "the chief English Protestant schoolman." B. left an autobiography, *Reliquiæ Baxterianæ*, which was a favourite book with both Johnson and Coleridge. Other works by him are *The Life of Faith* (1670), *Reasons of the Christian Religion* (1672), and *Christian Directory* (1675). *Practical Works* in 23 vols. (1830) edited with memoirs by W. Orme, also *Lives* by A. B. Grosart (1879), Dean Boyle (1883), and J. H. Davies (1886).

BAYLY, ADA ELLEN (*d.* 1903).—Novelist, wrote several stories under the name of "Edna Lyall," which were very popular. They include *Autobiography of a Slander*, *Donovan*, *Hope the Hermit*, *In the Golden Days*, *To Right the Wrong*, *We Two*, and *Won by Waiting*.

BAYLY, THOMAS HAYNES (1797-1839).—Miscellaneous writer, *s.* of a wealthy lawyer in Bath. Originally intended for the law, he changed his mind and thought of entering the Church, but abandoned this idea also, and gave himself to writing for the stage and the periodical press. He is chiefly known for his songs, of which he wrote hundreds, which, set to the music of Bishop and other eminent composers, found universal acceptance. Some were set to his own music. He also wrote several novels and a number of farces, etc. Although making a large income from his writings, in addition to that of his wife, he fell into embarrassed circumstances. Among the best known of his songs are *I'd be a Butterfly*, *Oh, no, we never mention Her*, and *She wore a Wreath of Roses*. He may be regarded as, excepting Moore, the most popular song writer of his time.

BEACONSFIELD, BENJAMIN DISRAELI, 1ST EARL OF (1804-1881).—Statesman and novelist, was the *s.* of Isaac D. (*q.v.*) Belonging to a Jewish family setttled first in Spain, whence in the 15th century they migrated to Italy, he was *b.* in London in 1804 and privately *ed.* His *f.* destined him for the law, and he was articled to a solicitor. The law was, however, uncongenial, and he had already begun to write. After some journalistic work, he brought himself into general notice by the publication, in 1827, of his first novel, *Vivian Grey*, which created a sensation by its brilliance, audacity, and slightly veiled portraits of living celebrities. After producing a *Vindication of the British Constitution*, and some political pamphlets, he followed up his first success by a series of novels, *The Young Duke* (1831), *Contarini Fleming* (1832), *Alroy* (1833), *Venetia*, and *Henrietta Temple* (1837). During the same period he had also written *The Revolutionary Epic* and three burlesques, *Ixion, The Infernal Marriage,* and *Popanilla.* These works had gained for him a brilliant, if not universally admitted, place in literature. But his ambition was by no means confined to literary achievement; he aimed also at fame as a man of action. After various unsuccessful attempts to enter Parliament, in which he stood, first as a Radical, and then as a Tory, he was in 1837 returned for Maidstone, having for his colleague Mr. Wyndham Lewis, whose widow he afterwards married. For some years after entering on his political career, D. ceased to write, and devoted his energies to parliamentary work. His first speech was a total failure, being received with shouts of laughter, but with characteristic courage and perseverance he pursued his course, gradually rose to a commanding position in parliament and in the country, became leader of his party, was thrice Chancellor of the Exchequer, 1852, 1858-59, and 1866-68, in which last year he became Prime Minister, which office he again held from 1874 till 1880. To return to his literary career, in 1844 he had *pub. Coningsby,* followed by *Sybil* (1845), and *Tancred* (1847), and in 1848 he wrote a life of Lord G. Bentinck, his predecessor in the leadership of the Protectionist party. His last novels were *Lothair* (1870), and *Endymion* (1880). He was raised to the peerage as Earl of Beaconsfield in 1876, and was a Knight of the Garter. In his later years he was the intimate friend as well as the trusted minister of Queen Victoria. The career of D. is one of the most remarkable in English history. With no family or political influence, and with some personal characteristics and the then current prejudices in regard to his race to contend with, he rose by sheer force of will and intellect to the highest honours attainable in this country. His most marked qualities were an almost infinite patience and perseverance, indomitable courage, a certain spaciousness of mind, and depth of penetration, and an absolute confidence in his own abilities, aided by great powers of debate rising occasionally to eloquence. Though the object, first of a kind of contemptuous dislike, then of an intense opposition, he rose to be universally regarded as, at all events, a great political force, and by a large part of the nation as a great statesman. As a writer he is generally interesting, and his books teem with striking thoughts, shrewd maxims, and brilliant phrases which stick in the memory. On the other hand he is often artificial, extravagant, and turgid, and his ultimate literary position is difficult to forecast.

Lives by Froude (1890), Hitchman (1885), see also *Dictionary of Nat. Biog. etc.*

BEATTIE, JAMES (1735-1803).—Poet and philosophical writer, *s.* of a shopkeeper and small farmer at Laurencekirk, Kincardineshire, and *ed.* at Aberdeen; he was, in 1760, appointed Professor of Moral Philosophy there. In the following year he *pub.* a vol. of poems, which attracted attention. The two works, however, which brought him most fame were: (1) his *Essay on Truth* (1770), intended as an answer to Hume, which had great immediate success, and led to an introduction to the King, a pension of £200, and the degree of LL.D. from Oxford; and (2) his poem of *The*

Minstrel, of which the first book was *pub.* in 1771 and the second in 1774, and which constitutes his true title to remembrance. It contains much beautiful descriptive writing. The *Essay on Truth* and his other philosophical works are now forgotten. B. underwent much domestic sorrow in the death of his wife and two promising sons, which broke down his own health and spirits.

BEAUMONT, FRANCIS (1584-1616), AND FLETCHER, JOHN (1579-1625).—Poets and dramatists. As they are indissolubly associated in the history of English literature, it is convenient to treat of them in one place. B. was the *s.* of Francis B., a Judge of the Common Pleas, and was *b.* at the family seat, Grace Dieu, Leicestershire. He was *ed.* at Oxford, but his *f.* dying in 1598, he left without taking his degree. He went to London and entered the Inner Temple in 1600, and soon became acquainted with Ben Jonson, Drayton, and other poets and dramatists. His first work was a translation from Ovid, followed by commendatory verses prefixed to certain plays of Jonson. Soon afterwards his friendship with F. began. They lived in the same house and had practically a community of goods until B.'s marriage in 1613 to Ursula, *dau.* and co-heiress of Henry Isley of Sundridge in Kent, by whom he had two *dau.* He *d.* in 1616, and is buried in Westminster Abbey. F. was the youngest *s.* of Richard F., Bishop of London, who accompanied Mary Queen of Scots to the scaffold. He went to Cambridge, but it is not known whether he took a degree, though he had some reputation as a scholar. His earliest play is *The Woman Hater* (1607). He is said to have died of the plague, and is buried in St. Saviour's Church, Southwark. The plays attributed to B. and F. number 52 and a masque, and much labour has been bestowed by critics in endeavouring to allocate their individual shares. It is now generally agreed that others collaborated with them to some extent—Massinger, Rowley, Shirley, and even Shakespeare. Of those believed to be the joint work of B. and F. *Philaster* and *The Maid's Tragedy* are considered the masterpieces, and are as dramas unmatched except by Shakespeare. *The Two Noble Kinsmen* is thought to contain the work of Shakespeare. As regards their respective powers, B. is held to have had the graver, solider, and more stately genius, while F. excelled in brightness, wit, and gaiety. The former was the stronger in judgment, the latter in fancy. The plays contain many very beautiful lyrics, but are often stained by gross indelicacy. The play of *Henry VIII.* included in Shakespeare's works, is now held to be largely the work of F. and Massinger. Subjoined is a list of the plays with the authorship according to the latest authorities.

(1) BEAUMONT.—*The Masque.* (2) FLETCHER.—*Woman Hater* (1607), *Faithful Shepherdess* (1609), *Bonduca* (*Boädicea*) (1618-19), *Wit without Money* (1614?), *Valentinian* (1618-19), *Loyal Subjects* (1618), *Mad Lover* (1618-19), *Humorous Lieutenant* (1618?), *Women Pleased* (1620?), *Island Princess* (1621), *Pilgrim* (1621), *Wild Goose Chase* (1621), *Woman's Prize* (? *pub.* 1647), *A Wife for a Month* (1624), *Chances* (late, *p.* 1647), perhaps *Monsieur Thomas* (*p.* 1639), and *Sea Voyage* (1622). (3) BEAUMONT and FLETCHER.—*Four Plays in One* (1608), *King and No King* (1611), *Cupid's Revenge*

(1611?), *Knight of Burning Pestle* (1611), *Maid's Tragedy* (1611), *Philaster* (1611), *Coxcomb* (1612-13), *Wits at Several Weapons* (1614), *Scornful Lady* (1616), doubtfully, *Thierry and Theodoret* (1616), and *Little French Lawyer* (1620) perhaps by F. and Massinger, and *Laws of Candy* (?) perhaps by B. and Massinger. (4) FLETCHER and OTHERS.—*Honest Man's Fortune* (1613), F., Mass., and Field; *The Captain* (1613), and *Nice Valour* (*p.* 1647), F. and Middleton (?); *Bloody Brothers* (1616-17), F., Mid., and Rowley or Fielding and B. Jonson (?); *Queen of Corinth* (1618-19), F. and Row. or Mass. and Mid.; *Barneveld* (1619), by F. and Massinger; *Knight of Malta* (1619), *False One* (1620), *A Very Woman* (1621?), *Double Marriage* (1620), *Elder Brother* (*p.* 1637), *Lover's Progress* (*p.* 1647), *Custom of the Country* (1628), *Prophetess* (1622), *Spanish Curate* (1622), by F. and Shakespeare; *Henry VIII.* (1617), and *Two Noble Kinsmen* (*p.* 1634), by F. and Rowley, or Massinger; *Maid of the Mill* (1625-6), *Beggar's Bush* (?) (1622), by F. and Shirley; *Noble Gentleman* (?) *Night Walker* (1633?), *Lover's Pilgrimage* (1623?), *Fair Maid of the Inn* (1625-26), also with Middleton?

The latest ed. is that of Mr. Bullen (11 vols., 1904), and A. R. Waller (7 vols., *pub.* C.U.P., 1909); Dyce (11 vols., 1843-46); *Francis Beaumont*, G. C. Macaulay (1883); *Lyric Poems* of B. and F., E. Rhys (1897); *Bibliography*, A. C. Potter in *Harvard Bibliograph. Contributions*, 1891.

BEAUMONT, SIR JOHN (1582-1627?).—Poet, elder brother of Francis B., the dramatist (*q.v.*). His poems, of which the best known is *Bosworth Field*, *pub.* by his *s.*, 1629. Another, *The Crown of Thorns*, is lost.

BECKFORD, WILLIAM (*c.* 1760-1844).—Miscellaneous writer, only *s.* of William B., Lord Mayor of London, the associate and supporter of John Wilkes, inherited at the age of 9 an enormous fortune. In these circumstances he grew up wayward and extravagant, showing, however, a strong bent towards literature. His education was entrusted to a private tutor, with whom he travelled extensively on the Continent. At the age of 22 he produced his oriental romance, *Vathek* (*c.* 1781), written originally in French and, as he was accustomed to boast, at a single sitting of three days and two nights. There is reason, however, to believe that this was a flight of imagination. It is an impressive work, full of fantastic and magnificent conceptions, rising occasionally to sublimity. His other principal writings are *Memoirs of Extraordinary Painters* (1780), a satirical work, and *Letters from Italy with Sketches of Spain and Portugal* (1835), full of brilliant descriptions of scenes and manners. B.'s fame, however, rests nearly as much upon his eccentric extravagances as a builder and collector as upon his literary efforts. In carrying out these he managed to dissipate his fortune of £100,000 a year, only £80,000 of his capital remaining at his death. He sat in parliament for various constituencies, and one of his two *dau.* became Duchess of Hamilton.

BEDDOES, THOMAS LOVELL (1803-1849).—Dramatic poet and physiologist, *s.* of Dr. Thos. B., an eminent physician, and nephew of Maria Edgeworth. *Ed.* at the Charterhouse and Oxford, he *pub.* in 1821 *The Improvisatore*, which he afterwards endeavoured to suppress. His next venture was *The Bride's Tragedy* (1822), which had considerable success, and won for him the friendship of "Barry Cornwall." Thereafter he went to Göttingen and studied medicine. He then wandered about practising his profession, and expounding democratic theories which got him into trouble. He *d.* at Bale in mysterious circumstances. For some time before his death he had been engaged upon a drama, *Death's Jest Book*, which was published in 1850 with a memoir by his friend, T. F. Kelsall. B. had not the true dramatic instinct, but his poetry is full of thought and richness of diction. Some of his short pieces, *e.g.*: "If there were dreams to sell," and "If thou wilt ease thine heart," are masterpieces of intense feeling exquisitely expressed.

BEDE OR BÆDA (673-735).—Historian and scholar. B., who is sometimes referred to as "the father of English history," was in his youth placed under the care of Benedict Biscop, Abbot of Wearmouth, and of Ceolfrith, afterwards Abbot of Jarrow. Ordained deacon in 692 and priest in 703, he spent most of his days at Jarrow, where his fame as a scholar and teacher of Latin, Greek, and Hebrew brought him many disciples. Here likewise he *d.* and was buried, but his bones were, towards the beginning of the 11th century, removed to Durham. The well-deserved title of "Venerable" usually prefixed to his name first appears in 836. He was the most learned Englishman of his age. His industry was marvellous, and its results remain embodied in about 40 books, of which about 25 are commentaries on books of Scripture. The others are lives of saints and martyrs, and his two great works, *The Ecclesiastical History of England* and the scientific treatise, *De Natura Rerum*. The former of these gives the fullest and best information we have as to the history of England down to the year 731, and the latter is an encyclopædia of the sciences as then known. In the anxious care with which he sought out and selected reliable information, and referred to authorities he shows the best qualities of the modern historian, and his style is remarkable for "a pleasing artlessness."

History of Early Engl. Lit., Stopford Brooke (2 vols., 1892), etc.

BEECHER, HENRY WARD (1813-1887).—Orator and divine, *s.* of Lyman B. and *bro.* of Harriet Beecher Stowe, was one of the most popular of American preachers and platform orators, a prominent advocate of temperance and of the abolition of slavery. His writings, which had a wide popularity, include *Summer in the Soul* and *Life Thoughts*.

BEHN, APHRA (JOHNSTON) (1640-1689).—Novelist and dramatist, *dau.* of a barber named Johnston, but went with a relative whom she called father to Surinam, of which he had been appointed Governor. He, however, *d.* on the passage thither, and her childhood and youth were passed there. She became acquainted with the celebrated slave Oronoko, afterwards the hero of one of her novels. Returning to England in 1658 she *m.* Behn, a Dutch merchant, but was a widow at the age of 26. She then became attached to the Court, and was employed as a political spy at Antwerp. Leaving that city she cultivated the friendship of various playwrights, and produced many plays and novels, also poems and pamphlets. The former are extremely gross, and are now happily little known. She was the first English professional authoress. Among her plays are *The Forced Marriage*, *Abdelazer*, *The Rover*, *The Debauchee*, etc., and her novels include *Oronoko* and *The Nun*. The former of these was the first book to bring home to the country a sense of the horrors of slavery, for which let her have credit.

BELL, HENRY GLASSFORD (1805-1874).—Poet and historian, was a member of the Scottish Bar, and became Sheriff of Lanarkshire. He wrote a *Life of Mary Queen of Scots* (1830), strongly in her defence, and two vols. of poetry, *Summer and Winter Hours* (1831), and *My Old Portfolio*, the latter also containing pieces in prose.

BELLENDEN, OR BALLANTYNE, JOHN (*fl.* 1533-1587?).—Poet, *b.* towards the close of the 15th century, and *ed.* at St. Andrews and Paris. At the request of James V. he translated the *Historia Gentis Scotorum* of Boece. This translation, *Chroniklis of Scotland* is a very free one, with a good deal of matter not in the original, so that it may be almost considered as a new work. It was *pub.* in 1536, and is the earliest existing specimen of Scottish literary prose. He also translated the first five books of Livy. He enjoyed the Royal favour, and was Archdeacon of Moray. He latterly, however, became involved in controversy which led to his going to Rome, where he *d.*, according to one account, about 1550. Another authority, however, states that he was living in 1587.

BENTHAM, JEREMY (1748-1832). — Writer on jurisprudence and politics, *b.* in London, *s.* of a prosperous attorney, *ed.* at Westminster and Oxford, was called to the Bar at Lincoln's Inn, but disliking the law, he made little or no effort to practise, but devoted himself to physical science and the theory of jurisprudence. In 1776 he *pub.* anonymously his *Fragment on Government*, an able criticism of Blackstone's *Commentaries*, which brought him under the notice of Lord Shelburne, and in 1780 his *Introduction to Principles of Morals and Legislation*. Other works were *Panopticon*, in which he suggested improvements on prison discipline, *Discourse on Civil and Penal Legislation* (1802), *Punishments and Rewards* (1811), *Parliamentary Reform Catechism* (1817), and *A Treatise on Judicial Evidence*. By the death of his *f.* he inherited a competency on which he was able to live in frugal elegance, not unmixed with eccentricity. B. is the first and perhaps the greatest of the "philosophical radicals," and his fundamental principle is utilitarianism or "the greatest happiness of the greatest number," a phrase of which he is generally, though erroneously, regarded as the author. The effect of his writings on legislation and the administration of the law has been almost incalculable. He left his body to be dissected; and his skeleton, clothed in his usual attire, is preserved in University College, London.

Life by Bowring in collected works (J. H. Barton, 11 vols., 1844). *Study of Life and Work*, Atkinson, 1903.

BENTLEY, RICHARD (1662-1742).—Theologian, scholar, and critic, *b.* in Yorkshire of humble parentage, went at the age of 14 to Camb., afterwards had charge of a school at Spalding, and then becoming tutor to the *s.* of Dr. Stillingfleet, Dean of St. Paul's, afterwards Bishop of Worcester (*q.v.*), accompanied his pupil to Oxf. After taking his degree at both universities, and entering the Church, he laid the foundation of his reputation as perhaps the greatest scholar England has produced by his letter in Mill's ed. of the *Chronicle of John Malelas*, and his *Dissertation on the Letters of Phalaris* (1699), which spread his fame through Europe. After receiving various preferments, including the Boyle lectureship and the Keepership of the Royal Library, he was, in 1700, appointed Master of Trinity, and afterwards was, largely owing to his own pugnacity and rapacity, which were almost equal to his learning, involved in a succession of litigations and controversies. These lasted for 20 years, and led to the temporary loss of his academic preferments and honours. In 1717, however, he was appointed Regius Prof. of Divinity. During the contentions referred to he continued his literary activity without abatement, and *pub.* various ed. of the classics, including Horace and Terence. He was much less successful in certain emendations of Milton which he attempted. Having incurred the resentment of Pope he was rewarded by being assigned a niche in *The Dunciad!* His style is strong and nervous, and sparkles with wit and sarcasm. His classical controversies called forth Swift's *Battle of the Books*.

Life by Monk (1833). *Life* by Sir R. Jebb in *English Men of Letters* (1882).

BERESFORD, JAMES (1764-1840).—Miscellaneous writer and clergyman. He made translations and wrote religious books, but was chiefly known as the author of a satirical work, *The Miseries of Human Life* (1806-7.)

BERKELEY, GEORGE (1685-1753).—Philosopher, eldest *s.* of William B., a cadet of the noble family of Berkeley, *b.* at Kilcrin near Kilkenny, and *ed.* at the school of his native place and at Trinity Coll., Dublin, where he graduated and took a Fellowship in 1707. His earliest publication was a mathematical one; but the first which brought him into notice was his *Essay towards a New Theory of Vision*, *pub.* in 1709. Though giving rise to much controversy at the time, its conclusions are now accepted as an established part of the theory of optics. There next appeared in 1710 the *Treatise concerning the Principles of Human Knowledge*, which was followed in 1713 by *Dialogues between Hylas* and *Philonous*, in which he propounded his system of philosophy, the leading principle of which is that the world as represented to our senses depends for its existence on being perceived. Of this theory the *Principles* gives the exposition and the *Dialogues* the defence. One of his main objects was to combat the prevailing materialism of the time. A theory so novel was, as might be expected, received with widespread ridicule, though his genius was realised by some of the more elect spirits, such as Dr. S. Clarke. Shortly afterwards B. visited England, and was received into the circle of Addison, Pope, and Steele. He then went to the Continent in various capacities, and on his return was made Lecturer in Divinity and Greek in his university, D.D. in 1721, and Dean of Derry in 1724. In 1725 he formed the project of founding a college in Bermuda for training ministers for the colonies, and missionaries to the Indians, in pursuit of which he gave up his deanery with its income of £1100, and went to America on a salary of £100. Disappointed of promised aid from Government he returned, and was in 1734 appointed Bishop of Cloyne. Soon afterwards he *pub.* *Alciphron, or The Minute Philosopher*, directed against Shaftesbury, and in 1734-37 *The Querist*. His last publications were *Siris*, a treatise on the medicinal virtues of tar-water, and *Further Thoughts on Tar-water*. He *d.* at Oxford in 1753. His affectionate disposition and genial manners made him much beloved. As a thinker his is the greatest name in English philosophy between Locke and Hume. His style is clear and dignified.

The best ed. of B. is Prof. A. C. Fraser's, with Life (4 vols., 1871, and new, 1902); there is also a small work by the same (1881).

BERNERS, BERNES, OR BARNES, JULIANA (*b.* 1388?).—Writer on heraldry and sports. Nothing of her real history is known, but statements more or less mythical have gathered round her name. The work attributed to her is *The Boke of St. Albans* (1486). It consists of four treatises on *Hawking, Hunting, The Lynage of Coote Armiris*, and *The Blasynge of Armis*. She was said to be the *dau.* of Sir James B., and to have been Prioress of Sopwell Nunnery, Herts.

BERNERS, JOHN BOURCHIER, 2ND LORD (1467-1553).—Translator, *b.* at Sherfield, Herts, and *ed.* at Oxf., held various offices of state, including that of Chancellor of the Exchequer to Henry VIII., and Lieutenant of Calais, where he *d.* He translated, at the King's desire, *Froissart's Chronicles* (1523-25), in such a manner as to make a distinct advance in English historical writing, and the *Golden Book of Marcus Aurelius* (1534); also *The History of Arthur of Lytell Brytaine* (Brittany), and the romance of *Huon of Bordeaux*.

BESANT, SIR WALTER (1836-1901).—Novelist and historian of London, *b.* at Portsmouth and *ed.* at King's Coll., London, and Camb., was for a few years a professor in Mauritius, but a breakdown in health compelled him to resign, and he returned to England and took up the duties of Secretary to the Palestine Exploration Fund, which he held 1868-85. He *pub.* in 1868 *Studies in French Poetry*. Three years later he began his collaboration with James Rice (*q.v.*). Among their joint productions are *Ready-money Mortiboy* (1872), and the *Golden Butterfly* (1876), both, especially the latter, very successful. This connection was brought to an end by the death of Rice in 1882. Thereafter B. continued to write voluminously at his own hand, his leading novels being *All in a Garden Fair, Dorothy Forster* (his own favourite), *Children of Gibeon*, and *All Sorts and Conditions of Men*. The two latter belonged to a series in which he endeavoured to arouse the public conscience to a sense of the sadness of life among the poorest classes in cities. In this crusade B. had considerable success, the establishment of The People's Palace in the East of London being one result. In addition to his work in fiction B. wrote largely on the history and topography of London. His plans in this field were left unfinished: among his books on this subject is *London in the 18th Century.*

Other works among novels are *My Little Girl, With Harp and Crown, This Son of Vulcan, The Monks of Thelema, By Celia's Arbour*, and *The Chaplain of the Fleet*, all with Rice; and *The Ivory Gate, Beyond the Dreams of Avarice, The Master Craftsman, The Fourth Generation*, etc., alone. *London under the Stuarts, London under the Tudors* are historical.

BICKERSTAFFE, ISAAC (*c.* 1735-1812?).—Dramatic writer, in early life a page to Lord Chesterfield when Lord Lieutenant of Ireland, produced between 1756 and 1771 many dramatic pieces, which had considerable popularity, the best known of which are *Love in a Village* (1762), and *The Maid of the Mill.* Owing to misconduct he was dismissed from being an officer in the Marines, and had ultimately, in 1772, to fly the country. The remainder of his life seems to have been passed in penury and misery. The date of his death is unknown. He was alive in 1812.

BIRD, ROBERT MONTGOMERY (1803-1854).—Novelist, an American physician, wrote three tragedies, *The Gladiator, Oraloosa,* and *The Broker of Bogota,* and several novels, including *Calavar, The Infidel, The Hawks of Hawk Hollow, Peter Pilgrim,* and *Nick of the Woods,* in the first two of which he gives graphic and accurate details and descriptions of Mexican history.

BISHOP, SAMUEL (1731-1795).—Poet, *b.* in London, and *ed.* at Merchant Taylor's School and Oxf., took orders and became Headmaster of Merchant Taylor's School. His poems on miscellaneous subjects fill two quarto vols., the best of them are those to his wife and *dau.* He also *pub.* essays.

BLACK, WILLIAM (1841-1898).—Novelist. After studying as a landscape painter, he took to journalism in Glasgow. In 1864 he went to London, and soon after *pub.* his first novel, *James Merle,* which made no impression. In the Austro-Prussian War he acted as a war correspondent. Thereafter he began afresh to write fiction, and was more successful; the publication of *A Daughter of Heth* (1871) at once established his popularity, which reached its highest mark in *A Princess of Thule* (1873). Many other books were added before his death in 1898, among which may be mentioned *In Silk Attire* (1869), *The Strange Adventures of a Phæton* (1872), *Macleod of Dare* (1878), *White Wings* (1880), *Shandon Bells* (1882), *Yolande* (1883), *Judith Shakespeare* (1884), *White Heather* (1886), *Stand Fast Craig-Royston!* (1890), *Green Pastures and Piccadilly, Three Feathers, Wild Eelin* (1898).

BLACKIE, JOHN STUART (1809-1895).—Scholar and man of letters, *b.* in Glasgow, and *ed.* at the Universities of Aberdeen and Edin., after which he travelled and studied in Germany and Italy. Returning to Scotland he was, in 1834, admitted to the Scottish Bar, but did not practise. His first work was his translation of *Faust* (1834), which won the approbation of Carlyle. From 1841-52 B. was Prof. of Humanity (Latin) in Aberdeen, and from 1852-82, when he retired, of Greek in Edinburgh. His literary activity was incessant, his works consisting of translations of *Æschylus* and of the *Iliad*, various books of poetry, including *Lays and Legends of Ancient Greece*, and treatises on religious, philosophical, and political subjects, among which may be mentioned *Self-Culture* (1873), *Horæ Hellenicæ*, and a life of Burns. He was an enthusiastic champion of Scottish nationality. Possessed of great conversational powers and general versatility, his picturesque eccentricity made him one of the most notable members of Scottish society. It was owing to his efforts that a Chair of Celtic Language and Literature was established in Edinburgh University.

BLACKLOCK, THOMAS (1721-1791).—Poet, *b.* near Annan of humble parentage, lost his sight by smallpox when 6 months old. He began to write poetry at the age of 12, and studied for the Church. He was appointed Minister of Kirkcudbright, but was objected to by the parishioners on account of his blindness, and gave up the presentation on receiving an annuity. He then retired to Edinburgh, where he took pupils. He *pub.* some miscellaneous poems, which are now forgotten, and is chiefly remembered for having written a letter to Burns, which had the effect of dissuading him from going to the West Indies. He was made D.D. in 1767.

BLACKMORE, SIR RICHARD (*c.* 1650, *d.* 1729).—Poet, one of the Court Physicians to William III. and Anne, wrote several very long and well-intentioned, but dull and tedious, poems, which, though praised by Addison and Johnson, are now utterly forgotten. They include *Prince Arthur*, *Creation*, *Redemption*, *Alfred*. As may be imagined, they were the subject of derision by the profaner wits of the day. B. was a successful physician and an excellent man.

BLACKMORE, RICHARD DODDRIDGE (1825 - 1900). — Novelist and poet, *b.* at Longworth, Berks, *ed.* at Tiverton School and Oxf., practised for a short time as a lawyer but, owing to his health, gave this up, and took to market-gardening and literature at Teddington. His first *pub.* was *Poems by Melanter* (1853), followed by *Epullia* (1855), *The Bugle of the Black Sea* (1855), etc.; but he soon found that fiction, not poetry, was his true vocation. Beginning with *Clara Vaughan* in 1864, he produced fifteen novels, all of more than average, and two or three of outstanding merit. Of these much the best in the opinion of the public, though not of the author, is *Lorna Doone* (1869), the two which rank next to it being *The Maid of Sker* (1872) (the author's favourite) and *Springhaven* (1887). Others are *Cradock Nowell* (1866), *Alice Lorraine* (1875), *Cripps the Carrier* (1876), *Mary Anerley* (1880), and *Christowell* (1882). One of the most striking features of B.'s writings is his marvellous eye for, and sympathy with, Nature. He may be said to have done for Devonshire what Scott did for the Highlands. He has been described as "proud, shy, reticent, strong-willed, sweet-tempered, and self-centred."

BLACKSTONE, SIR WILLIAM (1723-1780).—Legal Writer, posthumous *s.* of a silk mercer in London, was *ed.* at Charterhouse School and Oxf., and entered the Middle Temple in 1741. His great work is his *Commentaries on the Laws of England*, in 4 vols.

(1765-1769), which still remains the best general history of the subject. It had an extraordinary success, and is said to have brought the author £14,000. B. was not a man of original mind, nor was he a profound lawyer; but he wrote an excellent style, clear and dignified, which brings his great work within the category of general literature. He had also a turn for neat and polished verse, of which he gave proof in *The Lawyer's Farewell to his Muse.*

BLAIR, HUGH (1718-1800).—Divine, and man of letters, *b.* and *ed.* at Edin. After being minister at Collessie in Fife, he was translated to Edinburgh, where he filled various pulpits, latterly that of the High Church. In 1759 he commenced a series of lectures on composition, and soon after the Chair of Rhetoric and Belles Lettres was founded, to which he was appointed. His *Lectures* were *pub.* on his resignation of the chair in 1783. His chief fame, however, rests upon his *Sermons*, in 4 vols., which had an extraordinary popularity, and obtained for him a pension of £200. Time has not sustained the opinion of his contemporaries: they have been described as feeble in thought though elegant in style, and even as "a bucket of warm water." B. was amiable, kind to young authors, and remarkable for a harmless, but rather ridiculous vanity and simplicity.

BLAIR, ROBERT (1699-1746).—Poet, *b.* at Edin., where his *f.* was a clergyman, became minister of Athelstaneford, Haddingtonshire. His sole work was *The Grave*, a poem in blank verse extending to 767 lines of very various merit, in some passages rising to great sublimity, and in others sinking to commonplace. It was illustrated by William Blake (*q.v.*) B.'s *s.*, Robert, was a very distinguished Scottish judge and Lord President of the Court of Session; and his successor in his ministerial charge was Home, the author of *Douglas*.

BLAKE, WILLIAM (1757-1827).—Poet and painter, *b.* in London, was from earliest youth a seer of visions and a dreamer of dreams, seeing "Ezekiel sitting under a green bough," and "a tree full of angels at Peckham," and such he remained to the end of his days. His teeming imagination sought expression both in verse and in drawing, and in his 14th year he was apprenticed to James Basire, an eminent engraver, and thereafter studied at the Royal Academy. Among his chief artistic works were illustrations for Young's *Night Thoughts*, Blair's *Grave*, "Spiritual Portraits," and his finest work, "Inventions to the Book of Job," all distinguished by originality and imagination. In literature his *Songs of Innocence* appeared in 1789, *Songs of Experience* in 1794. These books were literally made by Blake and his heaven-provided wife; poems and designs alike being engraved on copper by B. and bound by Mrs. B. In like fashion were produced his mystical books, *The Book of Thel* (1789), *The Marriage of Heaven and Hell* (1790), *The Gates of Paradise, Visions of the Daughters of Albion, Europe, The Book of Urizen* (1794), *The Book of Los* and *The Book of Ahania* (1795). His last books were *Jerusalem* and *Milton*. His earlier and shorter pieces, *e.g.* "The Chimney-Sweeper," "Holy Thursday," "The Lamb," "The Sunflower," "The Tiger," etc., have an exquisite simplicity arising from directness and intensity of feeling—sometimes tender, sometimes sublime—always individual. A truly pious and loving soul, neglected and misunderstood by the world, but appreciated by an elect few, he led a cheerful and contented life of poverty illumined by visions and celestial inspirations.

BLAMIRE, SUSANNA (1747-1794).—Poetess, was of good Cumberland family, and received the sobriquet of "The Muse of Cumberland." Her poems, which were not collected until 1842, depict Cumbrian life and manners with truth and vivacity. She also wrote some fine songs in the Scottish dialect, including "Ye shall walk in Silk Attire," and "What ails this Heart o' Mine."

BLESSINGTON, MARGARET (POWER), COUNTESS OF (1789-1849).—Married as her second husband the 1st Earl of B., with whom she travelled much on the Continent, where she met Lord Byron, her *Conversations* with whom she *pub.* in 1834. This is the only one of her books which has any value. The others were slight works on Travel, such as *The Idler in Italy*, annuals, and novels. She became bankrupt and went to Paris, where she lived under the protection of the Count d'Orsay.

BLIND HARRY OR HENRY THE MINSTREL (*fl.* 1470-1492).—Is spoken of by John Major in his *History of Scotland* as a wandering minstrel, skilled in the composition of rhymes in the Scottish tongue, who "fabricated" a book about William Wallace, and gained his living by reciting it to his own accompaniment on the harp at the houses of the nobles. Harry claims that it was founded on a Latin *Life of Wallace* written by Wallace's chaplain, John Blair, but the chief sources seem to have been traditionary. Harry is often considered inferior to Barbour as a poet, and has little of his moral elevation, but he surpasses him in graphic power, vividness of description, and variety of incident. He occasionally shows the influence of Chaucer, and is said to have known Latin and French.

BLIND, MATHILDE (1841-1896).—Poetess, *b.* at Mannheim, but settled in London about 1849, and *pub.* several books of poetry, *The Prophecy of St. Oran* (1881), *The Heather on Fire* (1886), *Songs and Sonnets* (1893), *Birds of Passage* (1895), etc. She also translated Strauss's *Old Faith and New*, and other works, and wrote Lives of George Eliot and Madame Roland. Her own name was Cohen, but she adopted that of her stepfather, Karl Blind.

BLOOMFIELD, ROBERT (1766-1823).—Poet, *b.* at Honington in Suffolk, lost his *f.* when he was a year old, and received the rudiments of education from his mother, who kept the village school. While still a boy he went to London, and worked as a shoemaker under an elder brother, enduring extreme poverty. His first and chief poem, *The Farmer's Boy*, was composed in a room where half a dozen other men were at work, and the finished lines he carried in his head until there was time to write them down. The manuscript, after passing through various hands, fell into those of Capel Lofft, a Suffolk squire of literary tastes, by whose exertions it was *pub.*

in 1800. It had a signal success, twenty-six thousand copies having been sold in three years. The Duke of Grafton obtained for him an appointment in the Seal Office, and when, through ill-health, he was obliged to resign this, allowed him a pension of 1s. a day. Other works were *Rural Tales* (1802), *Wild Flowers* (1806), *The Banks of Wye* (1811), and *May Day with the Muses* (1822). An attempt to carry on business as a bookseller failed, his health gave way, his reason was threatened, and he *d.* in great poverty at Shefford in 1823. B.'s poetry is smooth, correct, and characterised by taste and good feeling, but lacks fire and energy. Of amiable and simple character, he was lacking in self-reliance.

BODENHAM, JOHN (*fl.* 1600).—Anthologist, is stated to have been the ed. of some of the Elizabethan anthologies, viz., *Politeuphuia* (*Wits' Commonwealth*) (1597), *Wits' Theater* (1598), *Belvidere, or the Garden of the Muses* (1600), and *England's Helicon* (1600). Mr. Bullen says that B. did not himself ed. any of the Elizabethan miscellanies attributed to him by bibliographers: but that he projected their publication, and he befriended the editors.

BOECE, OR BOETHIUS, HECTOR (1465?-1536).—Historian, probably *b.* at Dundee, and *ed.* there and at Paris, where he was a regent or professor, 1492 to 1498. While there he made the acquaintance of Erasmus. Returning to Scotland he co-operated with Elphinstone, Bishop of Aberdeen, in founding the univ. there of which he was the first Principal. His literary fame rests on two works, his *Lives of the Bishops of Mortlach and Aberdeen*, in which his friend Elphinstone figures prominently, and his *History of Scotland* to the accession of James III. These works were, of course, composed in Latin, but the *History* was translated into Scottish prose by John Bellenden, 1530 to 1533, and into English for Hollinshed's *Chronicle*. The only predecessor of the work was the compendium of Major, and as it was written in a flowing and pleasing style it became very popular, and led to ecclesiastical preferment and Royal favour. B. shared in the credulity of his age, but the charge of inventing his authorities formerly brought against him has been shown to be, to some extent at any rate, unfounded.

BOKER, GEORGE HENRY (1823-90).—Poet, was in the American Diplomatic Service. Among his dramas, generally tragedies, are *Anne Boleyn*, *The Betrothed*, and *Francesca da Rimini*, and among his books of poetry, *Street Lyrics*, *Kōnigsmark*, and *The Book of the Dead*. His dramas combine poetic merit with adaptability for acting.

BOLINGBROKE, HENRY ST. JOHN, 1ST VISCOUNT (1678-1751.—Statesman and philosopher, *s.* of Sir Henry St. J., *b.* at Battersea, and *ed.* at Eton and perhaps Oxf., was during his youth noted chiefly for dissipation, but entering Parliament in 1701 as a supporter of Harley, soon made himself a name by his eloquence and talent. He held office as War and Foreign Sec. successively, became a peer in 1712, intrigued successfully against Harley, and formed an administration during the last days of Queen Anne, with the intention of bringing back the Stuarts, which was frustrated by the Queen's death. On the arrival of George I. and the accession to power of the Whigs, B. was impeached, and his name erased from the Roll of Peers. He went to France, and became Sec. of State to the Pretender James, who, however, dismissed him in 1716, after which he devoted himself to philosophy and literature. In 1723 he was pardoned and returned to England, and an act was passed in 1725 restoring his forfeited estates, but still excluding him from the House of Lords. He thereupon retired to his house, Dawley, near Uxbridge, where he enjoyed the society of Swift and Pope, on the latter of whom he exerted a strong influence. After some ineffectual efforts to regain a position in political life, he returned to France in 1735, where he remained for 7 years, and wrote most of his chief works.

B. was a man of brilliant and versatile talents, but selfish, insincere, and intriguing, defects of character which led to his political ruin. His writings, once so much admired, reflect his character in their glittering artificiality, and his pretensions to the reputation of a philosopher have long been exploded; the chief of them are *Reflections upon Exile*, *Letters on the Study of History* (in which he attacked Christianity), *Letters on the Spirit of Patriotism*, and *Idea of a Patriot King*. He left his MSS. to David Mallet (*q.v.*), who *pub.* a complete ed. of his works in 5 vols. (1753-54).

BONAR, HORATIUS (1808-1889).—Divine and poet, *s.* of James B., Solicitor of Exise for Scotland, *b.* and *ed.* in Edin., entered the Ministry of the Church of Scotland, and was settled at Kelso. He joined the Free Church at the Disruption in 1843, and in 1866 was translated to Edin. In 1853 he was made D.D. of Aberdeen. He was a voluminous and highly popular author, and in addition to many books and tracts wrote a number of hymns, many of which, *e.g.*, "I heard the voice of Jesus say," are known all over the English-speaking world. A selection of these was *pub.* as *Hymns of Faith and Hope* (3 series). His last vol. of poetry was *My Old Letters*.

BOORDE, OR BORDE, ANDREW (1490?-1549).—Traveller, *b.* near Cuckfield, Sussex, was brought up as a Carthusian, and held ecclesiastical appointments, then practised medicine at various places, including Glasgow, and was employed in various capacities by T. Cromwell. He travelled widely, going as far as Jerusalem, and wrote descriptions of the countries he had visited. His *Dyetary* is the first English book of domestic medicine. The *Boke of the Introduction of Knowledge* describes his journeys on the Continent. Other works are *The Boke of Berdes* (Beards), *Handbook of Europe*, and *Itinerary of England*.

BORROW, GEORGE (1803-1881).—Philologist and miscellaneous author, and traveller, *b.* at East Dereham, Norfolk, *s.* of a recruiting officer, had a somewhat wandering childhood. He received most of his education in Edin., and showed a peculiar talent for acquiring languages. After being for a short time in the office of a solicitor in Norwich, he travelled widely on the Continent and in the East, acquainting himself with the people and languages of the various countries he visited. He specially attached himself to the

Gipsies, with whose language he became so familiar as to *pub.* a dictionary of it. His learning was shown by his publishing at St. Petersburg *Targum*, a work containing translations from 30 languages. B. became a travelling agent of the Bible Society, and his book, *The Bible in Spain* (1843), giving an account of his remarkable adventures in that country, made his literary reputation. It was followed by *Lavengro* (1851), and its sequel, *Romany Rye* (1857), and *Wild Wales* (1862), which, though works of originality and extreme interest, and now perhaps his most popular books, were received with less public favour. The two first give a highly coloured picture of his own story. He translated the New Testament into Manchu. In his latter years he settled at Oulton Broad, Norfolk, where he *d.* B. was a man of striking appearance and great vigour and originality of character and mind. His writings hold a unique place in English literature.

BOSTON, THOMAS (1677-1732).—Scottish divine, was successively schoolmaster at Glencairn, and minister of Simprin in Berwickshire, and Ettrick in Selkirkshire. In addition to his best-known work, *The Fourfold State*, one of the religious classics of Scotland, he wrote an original little book, *The Crook in the Lot*, and a learned treatise on the Hebrew points. He also took a leading part in the Courts of the Church in what was known as the "Marrow Controversy," regarding the merits of an English work, *The Marrow of Modern Divinity*, which he defended against the attacks of the "Moderate" party in the Church. B., if unduly introspective, was a man of singular piety and amiability. His autobiography is an interesting record of Scottish life, full of sincerity and tenderness, and not devoid of humorous touches, intentional and otherwise.

BOSWELL, SIR ALEXANDER (1775-1822).—Antiquary and song writer, *s.* of James B., of Auchinleck, Johnson's biographer, was interested in old Scottish authors, some of whose works he reprinted at his private press. He wrote some popular Scotch songs, of which *Jenny's Bawbee* and *Jenny dang the Weaver* are the best known. B. *d.* in a duel with Mr. Stuart of Dunearn.

BOSWELL, JAMES (1740-1795).—Biographer, *s.* of Alexander B. of Auchinleck, Ayrshire, one of the judges of the Supreme Courts of Scotland, was *ed.* at the High School and Univ. of Edin., and practised as an advocate. He travelled much on the Continent and visited Corsica, where he became acquainted with the patriot General Paoli. Fortunately for posterity he was in 1763 introduced to Dr. Johnson, and formed an acquaintance with him which soon ripened into friendship, and had as its ultimate fruit the immortal *Life*. He was also the author of several works of more or less interest, including an *Account of Corsica* (1768), and *Journal of Tour to the Hebrides* (in the company of Johnson) (1786). Vain and foolish in an exceptional degree, and by no means free from more serious faults, B. has yet produced the greatest biography in the language. *The Life of Samuel Johnson, LL.D.* appeared in 1791, and at once commanded an admiration which has suffered no diminution since. But by this time a cloud had fallen upon the author. He had lost his excellent wife, his health had given way, the intemperance to which he had always been subject had mastered him, and he *d.* four years after the appearance of his great work. B. was called to the English as well as to the Scottish Bar, but his various foibles prevented his reaching any great success, and he had also vainly endeavoured to enter on a political career. The question has often been raised how a man with the characteristics of B. could have produced so unique a work, and has been discussed at length by Macaulay and by Carlyle, the former paradoxically arguing that his supreme folly and meanness themselves formed his greatest qualifications; the latter, with far deeper insight, that beneath these there lay the possession of an eye to discern excellence and a heart to appreciate it, intense powers of accurate observation and a considerable dramatic faculty. His letters to William Temple were discovered at Boulogne, and *pub.* 1857.

BOUCICAULT, DION (1820-90).—Actor and dramatist, *b.* in Dublin and *ed.* in London, joined Macready while still young, and made his first appearance upon the stage with Benj. Webster at Bristol. Soon afterwards he began to write plays, occasionally in conjunction, of which the first, *London Assurance* (1841) had an immediate success. He was an excellent actor, especially in pathetic parts. His plays are for the most part adaptations, but are often very ingenious in construction, and have had great popularity. Among the best known are *The Colleen Bawn*, *Arrah-na-Pogue*, *Faust and Marguerite*, and *The Shaughraun*. B. *d.* in America.

BOWDLER, THOMAS (1754-1825).—Editor of *The Family Shakespeare*, *b.* near Bath, *s.* of a gentleman of independent fortune, studied medicine at St. Andrews and at Edin., where he took his degree in 1776, but did not practise, devoting himself instead to the cause of prison reform. In 1818 he *pub.* his *Family Shakespeare* in 10 vols., "in which nothing is added to the original text, but those words and expressions are omitted which cannot with propriety be read aloud in a family." The work had considerable success, 4 editions having been *pub.* before 1824, and others in 1831, 1853, and 1861. It was, however, subjected to some criticism and ridicule, and gave rise to the expression "bowdlerise," always used in an opprobrious sense. On the other hand, Mr. Swinburne has said, "More nauseous and foolish cant was never chattered than that which would deride the memory or depreciate the merits of B. No man ever did better service to Shakespeare than the man who made it possible to put him into the hands of intelligent and imaginative children." B. subsequently essayed a similar enterprise in regard to Gibbon, which, however, was not so successful.

BOWER, ARCHIBALD (1686-1766).—Historian, *b.* at Dundee, and *ed.* at the Scots Coll., Douay, became a Jesuit, but afterwards joined the Church of England, and again became a Jesuit. He wrote a *History of Rome* (1735-44), a *History of the Popes* (1748-66). These works are ill-proportioned and inaccurate. His whole life appears to have been a very discreditable one.

BOWER, OR BOWMAKER, WALTER (*d.* 1449).—Was Abbot of Inchcolm, and continued and enlarged Fordun's *Scotichronicon*.

BOWLES, WILLIAM LISLE (1762-1850).—Poet and antiquary, *b.* at King's Sutton, Northamptonshire, of which his *f.* was vicar, and *ed.* at Winchester and Oxf., was for the most of his life Vicar of Bremhill, Wilts, and became Prebendary and Canon Residentiary of Salisbury. His first work, *pub.* in 1789, was a little vol. containing 14 sonnets, which was received with extraordinary favour, not only by the general public, but by such men as Coleridge and Wordsworth. It may be regarded as the harbinger of the reaction against the school of Pope, in which these poets were soon to bear so great a part. B. *pub.* several other poems of much greater length, of which the best are *The Spirit of Discovery* (1805), and *The Missionary of the Andes* (1815), and he also enjoyed considerable reputation as an antiquary, his principal work in that department being *Hermes Britannicus* (1828). In 1807 he *pub.* a *Life of Pope*, in the preface to which he expressed some views on poetry which resulted in a rather fierce controversy with Byron, Campbell, and others. He also wrote a *Life of Bishop Ken.* B. was an amiable, absent-minded, and rather eccentric man. His poems are characterised by refinement of feeling, tenderness, and pensive thought, but are deficient in power and passion.

Other works are *Coombe Ellen and St. Michael's Mount* (1798), *The Battle of the Nile* (1799), *The Sorrows of Switzerland* (1801), *St. John in Patmos* (1833), etc.

BOWRING, SIR JOHN (1792-1872).—Linguist, writer, and traveller, was *b.* at Exeter. His talent for acquiring languages enabled him at last to say that he knew 200, and could speak 100. He was appointed editor of the *Westminster Review* in 1824; travelled in various countries with the view of reporting on their commercial position; was an M.P. 1835-37 and 1841-49, and held various appointments in China. His chief literary work was the translation of the folk-songs of most European nations, and he also wrote original poems and hymns, and works on political and economic subjects. B. was knighted in 1854. He was the literary executor of Jeremy Bentham (*q.v.*).

BOYD, ANDREW KENNEDY HUTCHISON (1825-1899).—Miscellaneous writer, *s.* of Rev. Dr. B. of Glasgow, was originally intended for the English Bar, but entered the Church of Scotland, and was minister latterly at St. Andrews, wrote in *Fraser's Magazine* a series of light, chirping articles subsequently collected as the *Recreations of a Country Parson,* also several books of reminiscences, etc., written in a pleasant chatty style, and some sermons. He was D.D. and LL.D.

BOYD, ZACHARY (1585-1653).—Divine, belonged to the family of B. of Pinkhill, Ayrshire, was *ed.* at Glasgow and at Saumur. He translated many parts of Scripture into uncouth verse. Among his works are *The Garden of Zion* and *Zion's Flowers.*

BOYLE, THE HON. ROBERT (1627-1691).—Natural Philosopher and chemist, 7th *s.* of the 1st Earl of Cork, was *b.* at Lismore, Co. Waterford, and *ed.* at Eton and by private tutors, after which he pursued his studies on the Continent. On his return to England he devoted himself to the study of science, especially natural philosophy and chemistry. He was one of the founders of the Royal Society, and, by his experiments and observations added to existing knowledge, especially in regard to pneumatics. He at the same time devoted much study to theology; so much indeed that he was strongly urged by Lord Clarendon to enter the Church. Thinking, however, that he could serve the cause of religion better as a layman, he declined this advice. As a director of the East India Co. he did much for the propagation of Christianity in the East, and for the dissemination of the Bible. He also founded the "Boyle Lectures" in defence of Christianity. He declined the offer of a peerage. B. was a man of great intellectual acuteness, and remarkable for his conversational powers. Among his writings are *Origin of Forms and Qualities*, *Experiments touching Colour*, *Hydrostatical Paradoxes*, and *Observations on Cold;* in theology, *Seraphic Love*. His complete works were *pub.* in 5 vols. in 1744.

BRADLEY, EDWARD (1827-1889).—Novelist, was a clergyman. He wrote under the name of "Cuthbert Bede" a few novels and tales, *Fairy Fables* (1858), *Glencraggan* (1861), *Fotheringhay* (1885), etc.; but his most popular book was *Verdant Green, an Oxford Freshman*, which had great vogue.

BRADWARDINE, THOMAS (1290?-1349).—Theologian, was at Oxf., where he became Prof. of Divinity and Chancellor, and afterwards Chaplain to Edward III., whom he attended in his French wars. He was twice elected Archbishop of Canterbury by the monks, and on the second occasion accepted, but *d.* of the plague within 40 days. He wrote on geometry, but his great work was *De Causa Dei* (on the Cause of God against Pelagius), in which he treated theology mathematically, and which earned for him from the Pope the title of the Profound Doctor.

BRAITHWAITE, OR BRATHWAITE, RICHARD (1588-1673).—Poet, *b.* near Kendal, and *ed.* at Oxf., is believed to have served with the Royalist army in the Civil War. He was the author of many works of very unequal merit, of which the best known is *Drunken Barnaby's Four Journeys*, which records his pilgrimages through England in rhymed Latin (said by Southey to be the best of modern times), and doggerel English verse. *The English Gentleman* (1631) and *English Gentlewoman* are in a much more decorous strain. Other works are *The Golden Fleece* (1611) (poems), *The Poet's Willow*, *A Strappado for the Devil* (a satire), and *Art Asleepe, Husband?*

BRAMSTON, JAMES (*c.* 1694-1744).—Satirist, *ed.* at Westminster School and Oxf., took orders and was latterly Vicar of Hastings. His poems are *The Art of Politics* (1729), in imitation of Horace, and *The Man of Taste* (1733), in imitation of Pope. He also parodied Phillips's *Splendid Shilling* in *The Crooked Sixpence*. His verses have some liveliness.

BRAY, ANNA ELIZA (1790-1883).—Novelist, *dau.* of Mr. J. Kempe, was married first to C. A. Stothard, *s.* of the famous R.A., and himself an artist, and secondly to the Rev. E. A. Bray. She wrote about a dozen novels, chiefly historical, and *The Borders of the Tamar and Tavy* (1836), an account of the traditions and superstitions of the neighbourhood of Tavistock in the form of letters to Southey, of whom she was a great friend. This is probably the most valuable of her writings. Among her works are *Branded, Good St. Louis and his Times, Trelawney,* and *White Hoods.*

BRETON, NICHOLAS (1545-1626).—Poet and novelist. Little is known of his life. He was the *s.* of William B., a London merchant, was perhaps at Oxf., and was a rather prolific author of considerable versatility and gift. Among his poetical works are *A Floorish upon Fancie, Pasquil's Mad-cappe* (1626), *The Soul's Heavenly Exercise,* and *The Passionate Shepherd.* In prose he wrote *Wit's Trenchmour, The Wil of Wit* (1599), *A Mad World, my Masters, Adventures of Two Excellent Princes, Grimello's Fortunes* (1604), *Strange News out of Divers Countries* (1622), etc. His mother married E. Gascoigne, the poet (*q.v.*). His lyrics are pure and fresh, and his romances, though full of conceits, are pleasant reading, remarkably free from grossness.

BREWSTER, SIR DAVID (1781-1868).—Man of science and writer, *b.* at Jedburgh, originally intended to enter the Church, of which, after a distinguished course at the Univ. of Edin., he became a licentiate. Circumstances, however, led him to devote himself to science, of which he was one of the most brilliant ornaments of his day, especially in the department of optics, in which he made many discoveries. He maintained his habits of investigation and composition to the very end of his long life, during which he received almost every kind of honorary distinction open to a man of science. He also made many important contributions to literature, including a *Life of Newton* (1831), *The Martyrs of Science* (1841), *More Worlds than One* (1854), and *Letters on Natural Magic* addressed to Sir W. Scott, and he also edited, in addition to various scientific journals, *The Edinburgh Encyclopædia* (1807-29). He likewise held the offices successively of Principal of the United Coll. of St. Salvator and St. Leonard, St. Andrews (1838), and of the Univ. of Edin. (1859). He was knighted in 1831. Of high-strung and nervous temperament, he was somewhat irritable in matters of controversy; but he was repeatedly subjected to serious provocation. He was a man of highly honourable and fervently religious character.

BROKE, OR BROOKE, ARTHUR (*d.* 1563).—Translator, was the author of *The Tragicall Historie of Romeus and Juliett,* from which Shakespeare probably took the story of his *Romeo and Juliet.* Though indirectly translated, through a French version, from the Italian of Bandello, it is so much altered and amplified as almost to rank as an original work. The only fact known regarding him is his death by shipwreck when crossing to France.

BROME, RICHARD (*d.* 1652?).—Dramatist, the servant and friend of Ben Jonson, produced upwards of 20 plays, some in conjunction with Dekker and others. Among them are *A Fault in Friendship, Late Lancashire Witches* (with Heywood and Dekker),

A Jovial Crew (1652), *The Northern Lass* (1632), *The Antipodes* (1646), *City Wit* (1653), *Court Beggar* (1653), etc. He had no original genius, but knew stage-craft well.

BRONTÉ, CHARLOTTE (1816-1855).—Novelist, *dau.* of the Rev. Patrick B., a clergyman of Irish descent and of eccentric habits who embittered the lives of his children by his peculiar theories of education. Brought up in a small parsonage close to the graveyard of a bleak, windswept village on the Yorkshire moors, and left motherless in early childhood, she was " the motherly friend and guardian of her younger sisters," of whom two, Emily and Anne, shared, but in a less degree, her talents. After various efforts as schoolmistresses and governesses, the sisters took to literature and *pub.* a vol. of poems under the names of Currer, Ellis, and Acton Bell, which, however, fell flat. Charlotte then wrote her first novel, *The Professor*, which did not appear until after her death, and began *Jane Eyre*, which, appearing in 1847, took the public by storm. It was followed by *Shirley* in 1849, and *Villette* in 1852. In 1854 she was married to her father's curate, the Rev. A. Nicholls, but after a short though happy married life she *d.* in 1855. ANNE B. (1820-1849) was the authoress of *The Tenant of Wildfell Hall* and *Agnes Grey* (1848). She had not the intellectual force of her sisters. The novels of Charlotte especially created a strong impression from the first, and the *pub.* of *Jane Eyre* gave rise to much curiosity and speculation as to its authorship. Their strength and originality have retained for them a high place in English fiction which is likely to prove permanent. There is a biography of Charlotte by Mrs. Gaskell (*q.v.*).

BRONTÉ, EMILY (1818-1848).—Novelist and poet. Sister to CHARLOTTE and ANNE. Wrote a story of extraordinary reality and imagination in *Wuthering Heights;* in whose pages the Yorkshire moors are given a wild and tragic personal reality. The same emotional force marks the best of her poems, though written with an apparently heedless pen for her own relief.

BROOKE, FULKE GREVILLE, LORD (1554-1628).—Poet and statesman, *b.* at Beauchamp Court, Warwickshire, and *ed.* at Shrewsbury and Camb., was a Privy Councillor, and held various important offices of state, including that of Chancellor of the Exchequer (1614-21). In the latter year he was created a peer. He was murdered by a servant. His works, which were chiefly *pub.* after his death, consist of tragedies and sonnets, and poems on political and moral subjects, including *Cælica* (109 sonnets). He also wrote a Life of Sir P. Sidney, whose friend he was. His style is grave and sententious. He is buried in the church at Warwick, and the inscription on his tomb, written by himself, is a compendious biography. It runs: " Fulke Greville, servant to Queen Elizabeth, counsellor to King James, friend to Sir Philip Sidney."

BROOKE, HENRY (1703-1783).—Novelist and dramatist, *b.* in Ireland, *s.* of a clergyman, studied law, but embraced literature as a career. He wrote poems, dramas, and novels; but the only work which has kept its place is *The Fool of Quality* (5 vols. 1766-70), which was a favourite book with John Wesley. His now forgotten poem, *Universal Beauty* (1735), was admired by Pope. His *dau.*, CHARLOTTE, the only survivor of 22 children, tended him to his last days of decay, and was herself a writer, her principal work being *Reliques of Irish Poetry* (1789). She *d.* 1793.

BROOKS, CHARLES WILLIAM SHIRLEY (1816-1874).—Journalist and novelist, *b.* in London, began life in a solicitor's office. He early, however, took to literature, and contributed to various periodicals. In 1851 he joined the staff of *Punch*, to which he contributed "Essence of Parliament," and on the death of Mark Lemon (*q.v.*) he succeeded him as editor. He *pub.* a few novels, including *Aspen Court* and *The Gordian Knot*.

BROOKS, MARIA (GOWAN) (1795?-1845).—American poetess, was early *m.* to a merchant, who lost his money, and left her a young widow, after which she wrote highly romantic and impassioned poetry. Her chief work, *Zophiël or The Bride of Swen*, was finished under the auspices of Southey, who called her "Maria del Occidente," and regarded her as "the most impassioned and imaginative of all poetesses," but time has not sustained this verdict.

BROOME, WILLIAM (1689-1745).—Poet and translator, *b.* at Haslington, Cheshire, and *ed.* at Eton and Camb., entered the Church, and held various incumbencies. He translated the *Iliad* in prose along with others, and was employed by Pope, whom he excelled as a Greek scholar, in translating the *Odyssey*, of which he Englished the 8th, 11th, 12th, 16th, 18th, and 23rd books, catching the style of his master so exactly as almost to defy identification, and thus annoying him so as to earn a niche in *The Dunciad*. He *pub.* verses of his own of very moderate poetical merit.

BROUGHAM AND VAUX, HENRY, 1ST LORD (1778-1868).—*S.* of Henry B. of Brougham Hall, Westmoreland, *b.* in Edin., and *ed.* at the High School and Univ. there, where he distinguished himself chiefly in mathematics. He chose a legal career, and was called to the Scottish Bar in 1800, and to the English Bar in 1808. His chief forensic display was his defence of Queen Caroline in 1822. In 1810 he entered Parliament, where his versatility and eloquence soon raised him to a foremost place. The questions on which he chiefly exerted himself were the slave trade, commercial, legal, and parliamentary reform, and education, and in all of these he rendered signal service. When, in 1830, the Whigs, with whom he had always acted, attained power, B. was made Lord Chancellor; but his arrogance, selfishness, and indiscretion rendered him a dangerous and unreliable colleague, and he was never again admitted to office. He turned fiercely against his former political associates, but continued his efforts on behalf of reform in various directions. He was one of the founders of London Univ. and of the Society for the Diffusion of Useful Knowledge. In literature he has a place as one of the original projectors of and most voluminous contributers to *The Edinburgh Review*, and as the author of a prodigious number of treatises on science, philosophy, and history, including *Dialogues on Instinct*, Lives of Statesmen, Philosophers, and Men of Science of the Time of George III., Natural Theology, etc., his last work being an autobiography written in his 84th year, and *pub.* 1871. His writings were far too numerous and far too diverse in subject to be of permanent value. His fame now rests chiefly on his services to political and specially to legal reform, and to the diffusion of useful literature, which are his lasting monuments.

BROUGHTON, JOHN CAM HOBHOUSE, 1ST LORD (1786-1869).—Eldest *s.* of Sir Benjamin H., *b.* at Redland near Bristol, *ed.* at Westminster School and at Camb., where he became intimate with Byron, and accompanied him in his journeys in the Peninsula, Greece, and Turkey, and acted as his "best man." In 1816 he was with him after his separation from his wife, and contributed notes to the fourth canto of *Childe Harold*, which was dedicated to him. On his return he threw himself into politics with great energy as an advanced Radical, and wrote various pamphlets, for one of which he was in 1819 imprisoned in Newgate. In the following year he entered Parliament, sitting for Westminster. After the attainment of power by the Whigs he held various offices, including those of Sec. at War, Chief Sec. for Ireland, and Pres. of the Board of Control. He *pub.* *Journey through Albania* (1813), *Historical Illustrations of the Fourth Canto of Childe Harold* (1818), and *Recollections of a Long Life* (1865), for private circulation, and he left in MS. *Diaries, Correspondence, and Memoranda, etc., not to be opened till* 1900, extracts from which were *pub.* by his *dau.*, Lady Dorchester, also under the title of *Recollections from a Long Life* (1909).

BROWN, CHARLES BROCKDEN (1771-1810).—Novelist, *b.* in Philadelphia, belonged to a Quaker family, became a lawyer, but exchanged law for literature, and has the distinction of being the first American to adopt a purely literary career. He wrote several novels, including *Wieland* (1798), *Ormond* (1799), *Arthur Mervyn* (1800-1), and his last, *Jane Talbot* (1801). With a good deal of crudeness and sentimentality he has occasional power, but dwells too much on the horrible and repulsive, the result, perhaps, of the morbidity produced by the ill-health from which he all his life suffered.

BROWN, GEORGE DOUGLAS (1869-1902).—Novelist, wrote *The House with the Green Shutters*, which gives a strongly outlined picture of the harder and less genial aspects of Scottish life and character. It may be regarded as a useful supplement and corrective to the more roseate presentations of the kail-yard school of J. M. Barrie and "Ian Maclaren." It made a considerable impression. The author *d.* almost immediately after its publication. There is an ed. with a memoir by Mr. Andrew Lang.

BROWN, DR. JOHN (1810-1882).—Physician and essayist, *s.* of John B., D.D., a distinguished dissenting minister in Edin. *B.* at Biggar, he was *ed.* at the High School and Univ. of Edin., where practically the whole of his uneventful life was spent as a physician, and where he was revered and beloved in no common degree, and he was the cherished friend of many of his most distinguished contemporaries, including Thackeray. He wrote comparatively little; but all he did write is good, some of it perfect, of its kind. His essays, among which are *Rab and his Friends*, *Pet Marjorie*, *Our Dogs*, *Minchmoor*, and *The Enterkine*, were collected along with papers on art, and medical history and biography, in *Horæ Subsecivæ* (Leisure Hours), 3 vols. In the mingling of tenderness and delicate humour he has much in common with Lamb; in his insight into dog-nature he is unique. His later years were clouded with occasional fits of depression.

BROWN, THOMAS (1778-1820).—Metaphysician, *s.* of the Rev. Samuel B., minister of Kirkmabreck, practised for some time as a physician in Edin., but his tastes and talents lying in the direction of literature and philosophy, he devoted himself to the cultivation of these, and succeeded Dugald Stewart as Professor of Moral Philosophy in the Univ. of Edin., in which position he had remarkable popularity as a lecturer. His main contribution to literature is his *Lectures*, *pub.* after his death. B. was a man of attractive character and considerable talents, but as a philosopher he is now largely superseded. He also wrote poetry, which, though graceful, lacked force, and is now forgotten.

BROWN, THOMAS EDWARD (1830-1897).—Poet, *b.* at Douglas, Isle of Man, *s.* of a clergyman, and *ed.* there and at Oxf., entered the Church and held various scholastic appointments, including a mastership at Clifton. His later years were spent in his native island. He had a true lyrical gift, and much of his poetry was written in Manx dialect. His poems include *Fo'c'sle Yarns* (1881), *The Doctor* (1887), *The Manx Witch* (1889), and *Old John* (1893). He was also an admirable letter-writer, and 2 vols. of his letters have been *pub.*

BROWN, TOM (1663-1704).—Satirist, was *ed.* at Oxf., and there composed the famous epigram on Dr. Fell. He was for a few years schoolmaster at Kingston-on-Thames, but owing to his irregularities lost the appointment, and went to London, where he wrote satires, epigrams, and miscellaneous pieces, generally coarse and scurrilous.

BROWNE, CHARLES FARRAR (1834-1867).—Humorist (Artemus Ward), *b.* in Maine, U.S., worked as a compositor and reporter, and became a highly popular humorous writer, his books being *Artemus Ward his Book*, *A. W. His Panorama*, *A. W. among the Mormons*, and *A. W. in England*.

BROWNE, ISAAC HAWKINS (1705-1760).—Is remembered as the author of some clever imitations of contemporary poets on the theme of *A Pipe of Tobacco*, somewhat analogous to the *Rejected Addresses* of a later day. He also wrote a Latin poem on the immortality of the soul. B., who was a country gentleman and barrister, had great conversational powers. He was a friend of Dr. Johnson.

BROWNE, SIR THOMAS (1605-1682).—Physician and miscellaneous and metaphysical writer, *s.* of a London merchant, was *ed.* at Winchester and Oxf., after which he studied medicine at various Continental univs., including Leyden, where he *grad.* He ultimately settled and practised at Norwich. His first and perhaps best known work, *Religio Medici* (the Religion of a Physician) was *pub.* in 1642. Other books are *Pseudodoxia Epidemica: Enquiries into Vulgar Errors* (1646), *Hydriotaphia, or Urn-burial* (1658); and *The Garden of Cyrus* in the same year. After his death were *pub.* his *Letter to a Friend* and *Christian Morals.* B. is one of the most original writers in the English language. Though by no means free from credulity, and dealing largely with trivial subjects of inquiry, the freshness and ingenuity of his mind invest everything he touches with interest; while on more important subjects his style, if frequently rugged and pedantic, often rises to the highest pitch of grave and stately eloquence. In the Civil War he sided with the King's party, and was knighted in 1671 on the occasion of a Royal visit to Norwich. In character he was simple, cheerful, and retiring. He has had a profound if indirect influence on succeeding literature, mainly by impressing master-minds such as Lamb, Coleridge, and Carlyle.

There is an ed. of B.'s works by S. Wilkin (4 vols., 1835-6), *Religio Medici* by Dr. Greenhill, 1881. *Life* by Gosse in Men of Letters Series, 1903.

BROWNE, WILLIAM (1590?-1645?).—Poet, *b.* at Tavistock, *ed.* at Oxf., after which he entered the Inner Temple. His poems, which are mainly descriptive, are rich and flowing, and true to the phenomena of nature, but deficient in interest. Influenced by Spenser, he in turn had an influence upon such poets as Milton and Keats. His chief works were *Britannia's Pastorals* (1613), and *The Shepheard's Pipe* (1614).

BROWNING, ELIZABETH BARRETT (1806-1861).—Poetess, was the *dau.* of Edward Barrett Moulton Barrett, who assumed the last name on succeeding to the estates of his grandfather in Jamaica. She was *b.* at Coxhoe Hall, Durham, but spent her youth at Hope End, near Great Malvern. While still a child she showed her gift, and her *f. pub.* 50 copies of a juvenile epic, on the Battle of Marathon. She was *ed.* at home, but owed her profound knowledge of Greek and much mental stimulus to her early friendship with the blind scholar, Hugh Stuart Boyd, who was a neighbour. At the age of 15 she met with an injury to her spine which confined her to a recumbent position for several years, and from the effects of which she never fully recovered. In 1826 she *pub.* anonymously *An Essay on Mind and Other Poems.* Shortly afterwards the abolition of slavery, of which he had been a disinterested supporter, considerably reduced Mr. B.'s means: he accordingly disposed of his estate and removed with his family first to Sidmouth and afterwards to London. At the former Miss B. wrote *Prometheus Bound* (1835). After her removal to London she fell into delicate health, her lungs being threatened. This did not, however, interfere with her literary labours, and she contributed to various periodicals *The Romaunt of Margaret, The Romaunt of the Page, The Poet's Vow,* and other pieces. In 1838 appeared *The Seraphim and Other Poems* (including "Cowper's Grave.") Shortly thereafter the death, by drowning, of her favourite brother gave a serious shock to her already fragile health, and for a time she hovered between life and death. Eventually, however, she regained strength, and meanwhile her fame was growing. The *pub.* about 1841 of *The Cry of the Children* gave it a great impulse, and about the same time she contributed some critical papers in prose to R. H. Horne's *New Spirit of the Age*. In 1844 she *pub.* two vols. of *Poems*, which comprised "The Drama of Exile," "Vision of Poets," and "Lady Geraldine's Courtship." In 1845 she met for the first time her future husband, Robert Browning (*q.v.*). Their courtship and marriage, owing to her delicate health and the extraordinary objections entertained by Mr. B. to the marriage of any of his children, were carried out under somewhat peculiar and romantic circumstances. After a private marriage and a secret departure from her home, she accompanied her husband to Italy, which became her home almost continuously until her death, and with the political aspirations of which she and her husband both thoroughly indentified themselves. The union proved one of unalloyed happiness to both, though it was never forgiven by Mr. Barrett. In her new circumstances her strength greatly increased. Her husband and she settled in Florence, and there she wrote *Casa Guidi Windows* (1851)—by many considered her strongest work—under the inspiration of the Tuscan struggle for liberty. *Aurora Leigh*, her largest, and perhaps the most popular of her longer poems, appeared in 1856. In 1850 *The Sonnets from the Portuguese*—the history of her own love-story, thinly disguised by its title—had appeared. In 1860 she issued a *coll.* ed. of her poems under the title, *Poems before Congress*. Soon thereafter her health underwent a change for the worse; she gradaully lost strength, and *d.* on June 29, 1861. She is generally considered the greatest of English poetesses. Her works are full of tender and delicate, but also of strong and deep, thought. Her own sufferings, combined with her moral and intellectual strength, made her the champion of the suffering and oppressed wherever she found them. Her gift was essentially lyrical, though much of her work was not so in form. Her weak points are the lack of compression, an occasional somewhat obtrusive mannerism, and frequent failure both in metre and rhyme. Though not nearly the equal of her husband in force of intellect and the higher qualities of the poet, her works had, as might be expected on a comparison of their respective subjects and styles, a much earlier and wider acceptance with the general public. Mrs. B. was a woman of singular nobility and charm, and though not beautiful, was remarkably attractive. Miss Mitford (*q.v.*) thus describes her as a young woman: "A slight, delicate figure, with a shower of dark curls falling on each side of a most expressive face; large, tender eyes, richly fringed by dark eyelashes, and a smile like a sunbeam."

Life by J. H. Ingram (1889); *Letters of R. Browning and E. B. Browning* (1889). *Coll.* ed. of her works, *see* above.

BROWNING, ROBERT (1812-1889).—Poet, only *s.* of Robert B., a man of fine intellect and equally fine character, who held a position in the Bank of England, was *b.* in Camberwell. His mother, to whom he was ardently attached, was the *dau.* of a German shipowner who had settled in Dundee, and was alike intellectually and morally worthy of his affection. The only other member of the family was a younger sister, also highly gifted, who was the sympathetic companion of his later years. In his childhood he was distinguished by his love of poetry and natural history. At 12 he had written a book of poetry which he destroyed when he could not find a publisher. After being at one or two private schools, and showing an insuperable dislike to school life, he was *ed.* by a tutor, and thereafter studied Greek at Univ. Coll., London. Through his mother he inherited some musical talent, and composed settings for various songs. His first *pub.* was *Pauline,* which appeared anonymously in 1833, but attracted little attention. In 1834 he paid his first visit to Italy, in which so much of his future life was to be passed. The publication of *Paracelsus* in 1835, though the poem had no general popularity, gained the notice of Carlyle, Wordsworth, and other men of letters, and gave him a reputation as a poet of distinguished promise. Two years later his drama of *Strafford* was performed by his friend Macready and Helen Faucit, and in 1840 the most difficult and obscure of his works, *Sordello,* appeared; but, except with a select few, did little to increase his reputation. It was followed by *Bells and Pomegranates* (containing *Pippa Passes*) (1841), *A Blot in the 'Scutcheon* (drama) (1843), *Luria* and *A Soul's Tragedy* (1846). In this year he married Miss Elizabeth Barrett (*q.v.*), the poetess, a union of ideal happiness. Thereafter his home until his wife's death in 1861 was in Italy, chiefly at Florence. In 1850 he wrote *Christmas Eve and Easter Day,* and in 1855 appeared *Men and Women.* After the death of Mrs. Browning he returned to England, paying, however, frequent visits to Italy. Settling in London he published successively *Dramatis Personæ* (1864), *The Ring and the Book* (1868-69), his greatest work, *Balaustion's Adventure,* and *Prince Hohenstiel-Schwangau* (1871), *Fifine at the Fair* (1872), *Red Cotton Night-cap Country* (1873), *The Inn Album* (1875), *Pacchiarotto* (1876), translation of *Agamemnon* (1879), *La Saisiaz,* etc. (1878), *Dramatic Idylls* (1879 and 1880), *Asolando* (1889) appeared on the day of his death. To the great majority of readers, probably, B. is best known by some of his short poems, such as, to name a few, "Rabbi Ben Ezra," "How they brought the good News to Aix," "Evelyn Hope," "The Pied Piper of Hammelin," "A Grammarian's Funeral," "A Death in the Desert." It was long before England recognised that in B. she had received one of the greatest of her poets, and the causes of this lie on the surface. His subjects were often recondite and lay beyond the ken and sympathy of the great bulk of readers; and owing, partly to the subtle links connecting the ideas and partly to his often extremely condensed and rugged expression, the treatment of them was not seldom difficult and obscure. Consequently for long he appealed to a somewhat narrow circle. As time went on, however, and work after work was added, the circle widened, and the marvellous depth and variety of thought and intensity of feeling told with increasing force. Societies began to be formed for the study of the poet's work. Critics became more and more appreciative, and he at last reaped the harvest of admiration and honour which was his due. Many distinctions came to him. He was made LL.D. of Edin., a life Governor of London Univ., and had the offer of the Lord Rectorship of Glasgow. He *d.* in the house of his son at Venice, and was buried in Westminster Abbey. The keynote of his teaching is a wise and noble optimism. His poems were collected in 2 vols. in 1896. Some vols. of his correspondence with Mrs. B. were also *pub.*

Uniform ed. of Works (17 vols. 1888-90); Furnivall's *Browning Bibliography* (1883), *Lives* by Mrs. Sutherland Orr (1891); Gosse (1890); Dowden (1904), G. K. Chesterton (English Men of Letters), etc.; *Poetry of Robert Browning* by Stopford Brooke, 1902, etc.

SUMMARY.—*B.* 1812, *pub. Paracelsus* 1835, *Sordello* 1840, *Bells and Pomegranates* 1841, *m.* to E. B. B. 1846, lives chiefly in Italy till her *d.*, 1861, when he returned to England and continued to write until his *d.*, *pub. Dramatis Personæ*, *Ring and Book* 1868-9, *Asolando* 1889, *d.* 1889.

BRUCE, JAMES (1730-1794).—Traveller, was *b.* at the family seat of Kinnaird, Perthshire, and *ed.* at Harrow. After various travels in Europe he set out in 1768 on his expedition to Abyssinia, and in 1770 reached the source of the Blue Nile. He returned to England in 1774, and in 1790 *pub.* his *Travels* in 5 quarto vols. His notorious vanity, the singular adventures he related, and the generally embellished character which he imparted to his narrative excited some degree of scepticism, and he was subjected to a good deal of satire, to which, though much annoyed, he did not reply. It is, however, generally allowed that he had shown great daring, perseverance, and zeal in his explorations, and that he made a real addition to the geographical knowledge of his day.

BRUCE, MICHAEL (1746-1767).—Poet, *s.* of a poor weaver at Kinnesswood, Kinross-shire, as a child herded cattle, but received a good education, including 4 sessions at the Univ. of Edin., and for a short time kept a school. His longest poem, *Loch Leven*, shows the influence of Thomson. His best is his *Elegy*. His promising career was cut short by consumption in 1767. The authorship of the beautiful *Ode to the Cuckoo* beginning "Hail, beauteous stranger of the grove" is contested, some authorities claiming it for B. and others for the Rev. John Logan (*q.v.*), who ed. B.'s works, adding some of his own, and who claimed the *Ode* as his.

BRUNTON, MARY (BALFOUR) (1778-1818).—Novelist, *dau.* of Col. Balfour of Elwick, and *m.* to the Rev. Dr. Brunton, Prof. of Oriental Languages in the Univ. of Edin., was the authoress of two novels, *Self-Control* (1811) and *Discipline* (1814), which were popular in their day.

BRYANT, JACOB (1715-1804).—Scholar, *ed.* at Eton and Camb., wrote learnedly, but paradoxically, on mythological and Homeric subjects. His chief works were *A New System or Analysis of Ancient Mythology* (1774-76), *Observations on the Plain of Troy* (1795), and *Dissertation concerning the Wars of Troy* (1796). In the last two he endeavoured to show that the existence of Troy and the Greek expedition were fabulous. Though so sceptical on these points he was an implicit believer in the authenticity of the Rowley authorship of Chatterton's fabrications. He also wrote on theological subjects.

BRYANT, WILLIAM CULLEN (1794-1878).—Poet, was *b.* at Cummington, Massachusetts, the *s.* of a doctor. His ancestors on both sides came over in the *Mayflower*. His first poem was *Thanatopsis* (1817), which was greeted as the best poem produced in America up to that time. After being a lawyer for some time he was induced to exchange law for journalism, and acted as ed. of various periodicals. Among his best known poems are *Lines to a Water-fowl, The Rivulet, The West Wind, The Forest Hymn, The Fringed Gentian,* etc. His muse is tender and graceful, pervaded by a contemplative melancholy, and a love of solitude and the silence of the woods. Though he was brought up to admire Pope, and in his early youth imitated him, he was one of the first American poets to throw off his influence. He had a high sense of duty, was a prominent and patriotic citizen, and enjoyed the esteem and even the reverence of his fellow-countrymen. B. also produced a blank-verse translation of the *Iliad* and the *Odyssey*.

BRYDGES, SIR SAMUEL EGERTON (1762-1837).—Bibliographer and genealogist, *ed.* at Camb., was called to the Bar in 1787. He wrote some novels and poems, now forgotten, but rendered valuable service by his bibliographical publications, *Censura Literaria, Titles and Opinions of Old English Books* (10 vols. 1805-9), his editions of E. Phillips's *Theatrum Poetarum Anglicanorum* (1800) Collin's *Peerage of England* (1812), and of many rare Elizabethan authors. He was made a baronet in 1814. He *d.* at Geneva.

BUCHANAN, GEORGE (1506-1582).—Historian and scholar *b.* at Killearn, Stirlingshire, of poor parents, was sent in 1519, with the help of an uncle, to the Univ. of Paris, where he first came in contact with the two great influences of the age, the Renaissance and the Reformation. His uncle having died, he had to leave Paris, and after seeing some military service, returned to Scotland, and in 1524 went to St. Andrews, where he studied under John Major (*q.v.*). Two years later he found means to return to Paris, where he graduated at the Scots Coll. in 1528, and taught grammar in the Coll. of St. Barbe. Returning to Scotland in 1536 with a great reputation for learning he was made by James V. tutor to one of his illegitimate sons, and incited by him to satirise the vices of the clergy, which he did in two Latin poems, *Somnium* and *Franciscanus*. This stirred the wrath of the ecclesiastical powers to such a heat that, the King withholding his protection, he was obliged in 1539 to save himself by flight first to England and then to France, where he remained until 1547 teaching Latin at Bordeaux and Paris. In the latter year he was invited to become a prof. at Coimbra, where he was imprisoned by the Inquisition as a heretic from 1549-51, and wrote the greater part of his magnificent translation of the Psalms into Latin verse, which has never been excelled by any modern. He returned to England in 1552, but soon re-crossed to France and taught in the Coll. of Boncourt. In 1561 he came back to his native country, where he remained for the rest of his life. Hitherto, though a supporter of the new learning and a merciless exposer of the vices of the clergy, he had remained in the ancient faith, but he now openly joined the ranks of the Reformers. He held the Principalship of St. Leonard's Coll., St. Andrews, was a supporter of the party of the Regent Moray, produced in 1571 his famous *Detectio Mariæ Reginæ*, a scathing exposure of the Queen's relations to Darnley and the circumstances leading up to his death, was tutor, 1570-78, to James VI., whom he brought up with great strictness, and to whom he imparted the learning of which the King was afterwards so vain. His chief remaining works were *De Jure Regni apud Scotos* (1579), against absolutism, and his *History of Scotland*, which was *pub.* immediately before his death. Though he had borne so great a part in the affairs of his country, and was the first scholar of his age, he *d.* so poor that he left no funds to meet the expenses of his interment. His literary masterpiece is his *History*, which is remarkable for the power and richness of its style. Its matter, however, gave so much offence that a proclamation was issued calling in all copies of it, as well as of the *De Jure Regni*, that they might be purged of the "offensive and extraordinary matters" which they contained. B. holds his great and unique place in literature not so much for his own writings as for his strong and lasting influence on subsequent writers.

BUCHANAN, ROBERT (1841-1901).—Poet and novelist, *b.* at Caverswall, Staffordshire, the *s.* of a Scottish schoolmaster and socialist, and *ed.* at Glasgow, was the friend of David Gray (*q.v.*) and with him went to London in search of fame, but had a long period of discouragement. His first work, a collection of poems, *Undertones* (1863), had, however, some success, and was followed by *Idylls of Inverburn* (1865), *London Poems* (1866), and others, which gave him a growing reputation, and raised high hopes of his future. Thereafter he took up prose fiction and the drama, not always with success, and got into trouble owing to some drastic criticism of his contemporaries, culminating in his famous article on the *Fleshly School of Poetry*, which appeared in the *Contemporary Review* (Oct. 1871), and evoked replies from Rossetti (*The Stealthy School of Criticism*), and Swinburne (*Under the Microscope*). Among his novels are *A Child of Nature* (1879), *God and the Man* (1881), and among his dramas *A Nine Days' Queen*, *A Madcap Prince*, and *Alone in London.* His latest poems, *The Outcast* and *The Wandering Jew*, were directed against certain aspects of Christianity. B. was unfortunate in his latter years; a speculation turned out ruinously; he had to sell his copyrights, and he sustained a paralytic seizure, from the effects of which he *d.* in a few months. He ultimately admitted that his criticism of Rossetti was unjustifiable.

BUCKINGHAM, GEORGE VILLIERS, 2ND DUKE OF (1628-1687).—Dramatist, *s.* of the 1st Duke, who was in 1628 assassinated by Felton. His life was full of adventure and change of fortune. The Restoration gave him back his already twice lost estates, which he again squandered by a life of wild extravagance and profligacy at Court. He was a member of the "Cabal" and intrigued against Clarendon. He wrote pamphlets, lampoons, and plays, but his chief contribution to literature was *The Rehearsal*, a comedy, in which he satirised the heroic drama of Dryden and others. It is believed that S. Butler had a hand in it. Dryden had his revenge in his picture of B. as *Zimri* in *Absalom and Achitophel.*

BUCKINGHAM AND NORMANBY, JOHN SHEFFIELD, 1ST DUKE OF (1648-1721).—*S.* of the 2nd Earl of Mulgrave, served in his youth as a soldier under Prince Rupert and Turenne, and is also said to have made love to the Princess, afterwards Queen, Anne. He was a Privy Councillor under James II., William and Mary, and Anne, with the last of whom he remained a favourite. His magnificent mansion was purchased and pulled down to make way for Buckingham Palace. He wrote *An Account of the Revolution*, *An Essay on Satire*, and *An Essay on Poetry*. He also remodelled Shakespeare's *Julius Cæsar*.

BUCKINGHAM, JAMES SILK (1786-1855).—Journalist and traveller, wrote many books of travel, both on the Old and New World. He established, and for a year or two ed., *The Athenæum*, and produced many pamphlets on political and social subjects.

BUCKLAND, FRANCIS TREVELYAN (1826-80).—Naturalist, *b.* and *ed.* at Oxf., where his *f.* was Dean of Christchurch. He studied medicine and was assistant-surgeon in the Life Guards. An enthusiastic lover of natural history, he wrote largely upon it, among his works being *Curiosities of Natural History* (4 vols. 1857-72), *Log Book of a Fisherman and Zoologist* (1876), *Natural History of British Fishes* (1881). He also founded and ed. *Land and Water.* He was for a time Inspector of Salmon Fisheries, and served on various commissions. Though observant, he was not always strictly scientific in his methods and modes of expression, and he was a strong opponent of Darwin.

BUCKLE, HENRY THOMAS (1821-1862).—Historical writer, *s.* of a wealthy shipowner in London, was *b.* at Lee in Kent. Though never at a univ. and little at school, he received a high degree of education privately, and inheriting an ample fortune and a large library, he devoted himself to travel and study, with the view of preparing for a great work which he had projected, *The History of Civilisation in England.* As an introduction to this he entered upon the consideration of the state of civilisation in various other countries, but this he had scarcely completed when his death took place at Damascus in 1862. The first vol. was *pub.* in 1857, and the second in 1861. In these the results of a vast amount of reading are shown; but they are not free from one-sided views and generalisations resting on insufficient data. He has, however, the credit of having contributed a new idea of history and the method of writing it. The completed work was to have extended to 14 vols. B. was one of the greatest chess-players in Europe.

BUDGELL, EUSTACE (1686-1737).—Miscellaneous writer, *ed.* at Oxf., was a cousin of Addison, who took him to Ireland and got him appointed to a lucrative office, which, however, he was foolish enough to throw away by lampooning the Viceroy. He assisted A. in the *Spectator*, of which he wrote 37 numbers signed X. In these he imitates A.'s style with some success. B., who was vain and vindictive, fell on evil days, lost a fortune in the South Sea Bubble, was accused of forging a will, and committed suicide by throwing himself out of a boat at London Bridge.

Bull, George (1634-1710).—Theologian, *b.* at Wells, *ed.* at Tiverton and Oxf., took orders, was ordained by an ejected bishop in 1658, and received the living of Suddington near Bristol. He was a strong Royalist, and was privy to a scheme for bringing back the Royal family. After the Restoration he obtained further preferment, and became in 1704 Bishop of St. David's at an age when his strength had become unequal to any very active discharge of the duties of his see. He has a high place among Anglican theologians, and as a defender of the doctrine of the Trinity was held in high esteem even by Continental Romanist controversialists. Among his works are *Harmonia Apostolica* (1669-70) in which he endeavoured to reconcile alleged discrepancies between the teaching of St. Paul and St. James on the relation between faith and works, in which he assigned to the latter the higher authority, *Defensio Fidei Nicænæ* (1685) and *Corruptions of the Church of Rome.*

Bulwer, E. L. (*See* Lytton.)

Bunyan, John (1628-1688).—*B.* at Elstow, near Bedford, the *s.* of a poor tinker, was *ed.* at a free school, after which he worked at his father's trade. At 17 he was drafted as a soldier in the Civil War, and served for two years at Newport Pagnell. At 19 he *m.* a pious young woman, whose only dowry appears to have been two books, the *Plain Man's Pathway to Heaven* and the *Practice of Piety*, by which he was influenced towards a religious life. In his autobiographical book, *Grace Abounding*, B. describes himself as having led an abandoned life in his youth; but there appears to be no evidence that he was, outwardly at any rate, worse than the average of his neighbours: the only serious fault which he specifies is profanity, others being dancing and bell-ringing. The overwhelming power of his imagination led him to contemplate acts of impiety and profanity, and to a vivid realisation of the dangers these involved. In particular he was harassed by a curiosity in regard to the "unpardonable sin," and a prepossession that he had already committed it. He continually heard voices urging him to "sell Christ," and was tortured by fearful visions. After severe spiritual conflicts he escaped from this condition, and became an enthusiastic and assured believer. In 1657 he joined the Baptist Church, began to preach, and in 1660 was committed to Bedford Jail, at first for three months, but on his refusing to conform, or to desist from preaching, his confinement was extended with little interval for a period of nearly 12 years, not always, however, very rigorous. He supported his family (wife and four children, including a blind girl) by making tagged laces, and devoted all the time he could spare from this to studying his few books and writing. During this period he wrote among other things, *The Holy City* and *Grace Abounding*. Under the Declaration of Indulgence he was released in 1672, and became a licensed preacher. In 1675 the Declaration was cancelled, and he was, under the Conventicle Act, again imprisoned for six months, during which he wrote the first part of *The Pilgrim's Progress*, which appeared in 1678, and to which considerable additions were made in subsequent editions. It was followed by the *Life and Death of Mr. Badman* (1680), *The Holy War* (1682), and the second part of *The Pilgrim's Progress* (1684). B. was now widely known as a popular preacher and author, and exercised a wide influence. In 1688 he set out on a journey to mediate between a father and son, in which he was successful. On the return journey he was drenched with rain, caught a chill and *d.* in London on August 31. He is buried in Bunhill Fields. B. has the distinction of having written, in *The Pilgrim's Progress*, probably the most widely read book in the English language, and one which has been translated into more tongues than any book except the Bible. The charm of the work, which makes it the joy of old and young, learned and ignorant, and of readers of all possible schools of thought and theology, lies in the interest of a story in which the intense imagination of the writer makes characters, incidents, and scenes alike live in that of his readers as things actually known and remembered by themselves, in its touches of tenderness and quaint humour, its bursts of heart-moving eloquence, and its pure, nervous, idiomatic English, Macaulay has said, " Every reader knows the straight and narrow path as well as he knows a road on which he has been backwards and forwards a hundred times," and he adds that " In England during the latter half of the seventeenth century there were only two minds which possessed the imaginative faculty in a very eminent degree. One of these minds produced the *Paradise Lost*, the other *The Pilgrim's Progress*." B. wrote about 60 books and tracts, of which *The Holy War* ranks next to *The Pilgrim's Progress* in popularity, while *Grace Abounding* is one of the most interesting pieces of biography in existence.

There are numerous Lives, the most complete being that by Dr. John Brown of Bedford (1885 new 1888): others are Southey's (1830), on which Macaulay's *Essay* is based, Offor (1862), Froude (1880). On *The Pilgrim's Progress, The People of the Pilgrimage*, by J. Kerr Bain, D.D. *Bunyan Characters*, by Principal Whyte, D.D.

BURCKHARDT, JOHN LEWIS (1784-1817).—Traveller, *b.* at Lausanne and *ed.* in Germany, came to England in 1806 and wrote his books of travel in English. He travelled widely in Africa and in Syria, and the adjoining countries, became a great oriental scholar, and, disguising himself, made the pilgrimage to Mecca, and obtained access to places not open to Christians. He wrote accounts of his travels, and a book on Arabic proverbs. He *d.* of dysentery at Cairo when about to start on a new journey into the interior of Africa.

BURKE, EDMUND (1729-1797).—Statesman, orator, and political philosopher, was the *s.* of an attorney in Dublin, where he was *b.* His *f.* was a Protestant, but his mother, whose maiden name was Nagle, was a Roman Catholic. He received his early *ed.* at a Quaker school at Ballitore, and in 1743 proceeded to Trinity Coll., Dublin, where he graduated in 1748. His *f.* wished him to study for the law, and with this object he, in 1750, went to London and entered the Middle Temple. He, however, disliked law and spent more time in literary pursuits than in legal study. In 1756 his first *pub.* work appeared, *A Vindication of Natural Society*, a satire on the views of Bolingbroke, but so close was the imitation of that writer's style, and so grave the irony, that its point as a satire was largely missed.

In the same year he *pub.* his famous treatise *On the Sublime and Beautiful*, which attracted universal attention, and three years later (1759) he projected with Dodsley the publisher *The Annual Register*, for which he continued to write the yearly Survey of Events until 1788. About the same time he was introduced to W. G. Hamilton (known as Single-speech H.) then about to go to Ireland as Chief Sec., and accompanied him in the capacity of private sec., in which he remained for three years. In 1765 he became private sec. to the Marquis of Rockingham, the Whig statesman, then Prime Minister, who became his fast friend until his death. At the same time he entered Parliament as member for Wendover, and began his brilliant career as an orator and philosophic statesman. The first great subject in which he interested himself was the controversy with the American colonies, which soon developed into war and ultimate separation, and in 1769 he *pub.*, in reply to G. Grenville, his pamphlet on *The Present State of the Nation*. In the same year he purchased the small estate of Gregories near Beaconsfield. His speeches and writings had now made him famous, and among other effects had brought about the suggestion that he was the author of the *Letters of Junius*. It was also about this time that he became one of the circle which, including Goldsmith, Garrick, etc., had Johnson for its central luminary. In 1770 appeared *Thoughts on the Causes of the Present Discontent*, directed against the growth of the Royal power on the one hand, and of faction on the other. In 1774 he was elected member for Bristol, and continued so until 1780, when differences with his constituency on the questions of Irish trade and Catholic emancipation led to his resignation, after which he sat for Malton until his final retirement from public life. Under the administration of Lord North (1770-1782) the American war went on from bad to worse, and it was in part owing to the splendid oratorical efforts of B. that it was at last brought to an end. To this period belong two of his most brilliant performances, his speech on *Conciliation with America* (1775), and his *Letter to the Sheriffs of Bristol* (1777). The fall of North led to Rockingham being recalled to power, which, however, he held for a few months only, dying in the end of 1782, during which period B. held the office of Paymaster of the Forces, and was made a Privy Councillor. Thereafter he committed the great error of his political life in supporting Fox in his coalition with North, one of the most flagitious, as it was to those concerned in it, one of the most fatal, political acts in our parliamentary history. Under this unhappy combination he continued to hold during its brief existence the office of Paymaster, and distinguished himself in connection with Fox's India Bill. The coalition fell in 1783, and was succeeded by the long administration of Pitt, which lasted until 1801. B. was accordingly for the remainder of his political life in opposition. In 1785 he made his great speech on *The Nabob of Arcot's Debts*, and in the next year (1786) he moved for papers in regard to the Indian government of Warren Hastings, the consequence of which was the impeachment of that statesman, which, beginning in 1787, lasted until 1794, and of which B. was the leading promoter. Meanwhile, the events in France were in progress which led to the Revolution, and culminated in the death of the King and Queen. By these B.

was profoundly moved, and his *Reflections on the French Revolution* (1790) electrified England, and even Europe. Its success was enormous. The same events and the differences which arose regarding them in the Whig party led to its break up, to the rupture of B's friendship with Fox, and to his *Appeal from the New to the Old Whigs*. In 1794 a terrible blow fell upon him in the loss of his son Richard, to whom he was tenderly attached, and in whom he saw signs of promise, which were not patent to others, and which in fact appear to have been non-existent. In the same year the Hastings trial came to an end. B. felt that his work was done and indeed that he was worn out; and he took leave of Parliament. The King, whose favour he had gained by his attitude on the French Revolution, wished to make him Lord Beaconsfield, but the death of his son had deprived such an honour of all its attractions, and the only reward he would accept was a pension of £2500. Even this modest reward for services so transcendent was attacked by the Duke of Bedford, to whom B. made a crushing reply in the *Letter to a Noble Lord* (1796). His last *pub.* was the *Letter on a Regicide Peace* (1796), called forth by negotiations for peace with France. When it appeared the author was dead.

B. was one of the greatest political thinkers whom England has produced, and all his writings, like his speeches, are characterised by the welding together of knowledge, thought, and feeling. Unlike most orators he is more successful as a writer than as a speaker. He rose too far above the heads of his audience, which the continued splendour of his declamation, his inordinate copiousness, and his excessive vehemence, often passing into fury, at length wearied, and even disgusted: but in his writings are found some of the grandest examples of a fervid and richly elaborated eloquence. Though he was never admitted to the Cabinet, he guided and influenced largely the policy of his party, while by his efforts in the direction of economy and order in administration at home, and on behalf of kindly and just government in India, as well as by his contributions to political philosophy, he laid his country and indeed the world under lasting obligations.

There are *Lives* by Prior (1824 and 1854); J. Morley (1867), and various ed. of his works have appeared. *Select Works* by Payne (3 vols. 1874-78).

SUMMARY.—*B.* 1729, *ed.* Trinity Coll., Dublin, enters Middle Temple 1750, *pub.* treatise *On the Sublime and Beautiful* 1756, became friend of Rockingham 1765, enters Parliament and engages in American controversy, *pub.* speech on *Conciliation with America* 1775, Paymaster of Forces and P. C. 1782, joined coalition of Fox and North 1782, leads in prosecution of W. Hastings 1787-94, *pub.* *Reflections on French Revolution* 1790 and breaks with Fox party, *pub.* *Letter on a Regicide Peace* 1796, *d.* 1797.

BURNET, GILBERT (1643-1715).—Theologian and historian, *s.* of a Royalist and Episcopalian lawyer, who became a judge, and of the sister of Johnston of Warristoun, a leader of the Covenanters, was *b.* in Edin., and *ed.* at Aberdeen and at Amsterdam, where he studied Hebrew under a Rabbi. Returning to Scotland, he was successively Episcopal minister at Saltoun and Prof. of

Divinity in Glasgow (1669), and was then offered, but declined, a Scotch bishopric. His energetic and bustling character led him to take an active part in the controversies of the time, and he endeavoured to bring about a reconciliation between Episcopacy and Presbytery. Going to London he was in some favour with Charles II., from whom he received various preferments. His literary reputation was greatly enhanced by the publication in 1679 of the first vol. of his *History of the Reformation of the Church of England*, for which he received the thanks of Parliament, and which was completed by other two vols., in 1682 and 1714. On account of a letter of reproof which he ventured to write to the King, he lost favour at Court, and the policy pursued by James II. being very repugnant to him, he betook himself in 1687 to Holland, where he became one of the advisers of the Prince of Orange. Returning to England at the Revolution, he was made Bishop of Salisbury, which office he adorned by liberal views and a zealous discharge of duty. The work by which his fame is chiefly sustained, his *History of my Own Times*, was, by his direction, not to be *pub.* until 6 years after his death. It appeared in 1723. It gives a sketch of the history of the Civil Wars and Commonwealth, and a detailed account of the immediately succeeding period down to 1713. While not free from egotism and some party feeling, it is written with a sincere desire for accuracy and fairness, and it has largely the authority of an eye-witness. The style, if somewhat lacking in dignity, is lively and picturesque. Among his other writings are a *History of the Dukes of Hamilton*, and an *Exposition of the 39 Articles*.

BURNET, THOMAS (1635?-1715).—Theologian and writer on cosmogony, was *b.* at Croft near Darlington, and *ed.* at Camb., and became Master of Charterhouse and Clerk of the Closet to William III. His literary fame rests on his *Telluris Theoria Sacra, or Sacred Theory of the Earth, pub.* about 1692, first in Latin and afterwards in English, a work which, in absence of all scientific knowledge of the earth's structure, was necessarily a mere speculative cosmogony. It is written, however, with much eloquence. Some of the views expressed in another work, *Archæolgiæ Philosophicæ*, were, however, so unacceptable to contemporary theologians that he had to resign his post at Court.

BURNEY, FRANCES (*see* D'ARBLAY under "A").

BURNS, ROBERT (1759-1796).—Poet, was *b.* near Ayr, the *s.* of William Burness or Burns, a small farmer, and a man of considerable force of character and self-culture. His youth was passed in poverty, hardship, and a degree of severe manual labour which left its traces in a premature stoop and weakened constitution. He had little regular schooling, and got much of what education he had from his father, who taught his children reading, writing, arithmetic, geography, and history, and also wrote for them "A Manual of Christian Belief." With all his ability and character, however, the elder B. was consistently unfortunate, and migrated with his large family from farm to farm without ever being able to improve his circumstances. In 1781 Robert went to Irvine to become a flax-dresser, but, as the result of a New Year carousal of the workmen, including himself, the shop took fire and was burned to the ground. This venture accordingly came to an end. In 1784 the *f.* died, and B. with his brother Gilbert made an ineffectual struggle to keep on the farm; failing in which they removed to Mossgiel, where they maintained an uphill fight for 4 years. Meanwhile, his love affair with Jean Armour had passed through its first stage, and the troubles in connection therewith, combined with the want of success in farming, led him to think of going to Jamaica as book-keeper on a plantation. From this he was dissuaded by a letter from Dr. Thomas Blacklock (*q.v.*), and at the suggestion of his brother *pub.* his poems. This first ed. was brought out at Kilmarnock in June 1786, and contained much of his best work, including "The Twa Dogs," "The Address to the Deil," "Hallowe'en," "The Cottar's Saturday Night," "The Mouse," "The Daisy," etc., many of which had been written at Mossgiel. Copies of this ed. are now extremely scarce, and as much as £550 has been paid for one. The success of the work was immediate, the poet's name rang over all Scotland, and he was induced to go to Edin. to superintend the issue of a new ed. There he was received as an equal by the brilliant circle of men of letters which the city then boasted—Dugald Stewart, Robertson, Blair, etc., and was a guest at aristocratic tables, where he bore himself with unaffected dignity. Here also Scott, then a boy of 15, saw him and describes him as of "manners rustic, not clownish. His countenance . . . more massive than it looks in any of the portraits . . . a strong expression of shrewdness in his lineaments; the eye alone indicated the poetical character and temperament. It was large, and of a dark cast, and literally glowed when he spoke with feeling or interest." The results of this visit outside of its immediate and practical object, included some life-long friendships, among which were those with Lord Glencairn and Mrs. Dunlop. The new ed. brought him £400. About this time the episode of Highland Mary occurred. On his return to Ayrshire he renewed his relations with Jean Armour, whom he ultimately married, took the farm of Ellisland near Dumfries, having meanwhile taken lessons in the duties of an exciseman, as a line to fall back upon should farming again prove unsuccessful. At Ellisland his society was cultivated by the local gentry. And this, together with literature and his duties in the excise, to which he had been appointed in 1789, proved too much of a distraction to admit of success on the farm, which in 1791 he gave up. Meanwhile he was writing at his best, and in 1790 had produced *Tam o' Shanter*. About this time he was offered and declined an appointment in London on the staff of the *Star* newspaper, and refused to become a candidate for a newly-created Chair of Agriculture in the Univ. of Edin., although influential friends offered to support his claims. After giving up his farm he removed to Dumfries. It was at this time that, being requested to furnish words for *The Melodies of Scotland*, he responded by contributing over 100 songs, on which perhaps his claim to immortality chiefly rests, and which placed him in the front rank of lyric poets. His worldly prospects were now perhaps better than they had ever been; but he was entering upon the last and darkest period of his career. He had become soured, and moreover had alienated many of his best friends by too freely expressing sympathy with the French Revolution, and the then unpopular advocates of reform at home. His health began to give way; he became prematurely old, and fell into fits of despondency; and the habits of intemperance, to which he had always been more or less addicted, grew upon him. He *d.* on July 21, 1797.

The genius of B. is marked by spontaneity, directness, and sincerity, and his variety is marvellous, ranging from the tender intensity of some of his lyrics through the rollicking humour and blazing wit of *Tam o' Shanter* to the blistering satire of *Holy Willie's Prayer* and *The Holy Fair*. His life is a tragedy, and his character full of flaws. But he fought at tremendous odds, and as Carlyle in his great Essay says, "Granted the ship comes into harbour with shrouds and tackle damaged, the pilot is blameworthy . . . but to know *how* blameworthy, tell us first whether his voyage has been round the Globe or only to Ramsgate and the Isle of Dogs."

The books about Burns, his life and writings, are innumerable. Among the Lives are those by Currie (1800); Allan Cunningham (1834); J. G. Lockhart (1828), on which is based Carlyle's memorable *Essay* (which *see*). Among the famous ed. of the *Poems* may be mentioned the first (Kilmarnock 1786), Edin. (1787), and the *Centenary* (1896), by W. E. Henley and T. F. Henderson.

SUMMARY.—*B.* 1759, flax-dresser at Irvine 1781, farms at Mossgiel, has love affair with Jean Armour, *pub.* first ed. of poems 1786, visits Edin. 1786, goes to Ellisland, became exciseman 1789, *pub.* songs, *c.* 1791, *d.* 1797.

BURTON, JOHN HILL (1809-1881).—Historian, was *b.* and *ed.* at Aberdeen, was in 1831 called to the Bar, but had little practice, and in 1854 was appointed Sec. to the Prison Board of Scotland, and in 1877 a Commissioner of Prisons. He became at an early period of his life a contributor to *Blackwood's Magazine* and other periodicals, and in 1846 *pub.* a life of Hume, which attracted considerable attention, and was followed by Lives of Lord Lovat and Lord President Forbes. He began his career as an historian by the publication in 1853 of *History of Scotland from the Revolution to the Extinction of the last Jacobite Insurrection*, to which he added (1867-70) *History of Scotland from Agricola's Invasion to the Revolution*, in 7 vols., thus completing a continuous narrative. Subsequently he *pub.* a *History of the Reign of Queen Anne* (1880). Other works of a lighter kind were *The Book-Hunter* (1862), and *The Scot Abroad* (1864). B.'s historical works display much research and a spirit of candour and honesty, and have picturesque and spirited passages, but the style is unequal, and frequently lacks dignity. On the whole, however, his is regarded as the most generally trustworthy and valuable history of Scotland at present existing.

BURTON, SIR RICHARD FRANCIS (1821-1890).—Explorer and scholar, *s.* of an officer in the army, was *b.* at Barham House, Herts, and after a somewhat desultory education abroad as well as at home, entered upon a life of travel, adventure, and military and civil service in almost every quarter of the world, including India, Africa, the nearer East, and North and South America, in the course of which he mastered 35 languages. As an official his masterful ways and spirit of adventure frequently brought him into collision with superior powers, by whom he not seldom considered himself ill-used. He was the author of upwards of 50 books on a great variety of subjects, including travels, novels, and translations, among which are *Personal Narrative of a Journey to Mecca* (1855), *First Footprints in East Africa* (1856), *Lake Regions of Equatorial Africa* (1860), *The Nile Basin*, a translation and life of Camoens, an absolutely literal translation of the *Arabian Nights*, with notes and commentaries, of which his accomplished wife *pub.* an expurgated edition. Lady B., who was the companion of his travels after 1861, also wrote books on Syria, Arabia, and other eastern countries, as well as a life of her husband, a number of whose manuscripts she destroyed.

BURTON, ROBERT (1577-1640).—Miscellaneous writer, *b.* at Lindley, Leicestershire, and *ed.* at Oxf., took orders, and became Vicar of St. Thomas, Oxf., 1616, and Rector of Segrave, Leicestershire, 1630. Subject to depression of spirits, he wrote as an antidote the singular book which has given him fame. *The Anatomy of Melancholy*, in which he appears under the name of *Democritus Junior*, was *pub.* in 1621, and had great popularity. In the words of Warton, " The author's variety of learning, his quotations from rare and curious books, his pedantry sparkling with rude wit and shapeless elegance . . . have rendered it a repertory of amusement and information." It has also proved a store-house from which later authors have not scrupled to draw without acknowledgment. It was a favourite book of Dr. Johnson. B. was a mathematician and dabbled in astrology. When not under depression he was an amusing companion, " very merry, facete, and juvenile," and a person of " great honesty, plain dealing, and charity."

The best ed. is that of Rev. A. R. Shilleto, with introduction by A. H. Bullen (3 vols. 1893).

BURY, LADY CHARLOTTE (1775-1861).—Novelist, *dau.* of the 5th Duke of Argyll, and *m.* first to Col. J. Campbell, and second to Rev. E. J. Bury, wrote a number of novels—*Flirtation*, *Separation*, *The Divorced*, etc., but is chiefly remembered in connection with a *Diary illustrative of the Times of George IV.* (1838), a somewhat scandalous work generally, and probably correctly, ascribed to her. She also wrote some poems and two devotional works. She held for some time an appointment in the household of the Princess of Wales.

BURY, RICHARD DE (1281-1345).—*S.* of Sir Richard Aungerville, *b.* at Bury St. Edmunds, studied at Oxf., and was a Benedictine monk, became tutor to Edward III. when Prince of Wales, and Bishop of Durham, and held many offices of State. He was a patron of learning, and one of the first English collectors of books, and he wrote his work, *Philobiblon*, in praise of books, and founded a library at Durham.

BUTLER, JOSEPH (1692-1752).—Theologian, *b.* at Wantage, *s.* of a Presbyterian linen-draper, was destined for the ministry of that Church, but in 1714 he decided to enter the Church of

England, and went to Oxf. After holding various other preferments he became rector of the rich living of Stanhope, Bishop of Bristol (1738), and Bishop of Durham (1750), and was said to have refused the Primacy. In 1726 he *pub. Fifteen Sermons*, and in 1736 *The Analogy of Religion.* These two books are among the most powerful and original contributions to ethics and theology which have ever been made. They depend for their effect entirely upon the force of their reasoning, for they have no graces of style. B. was an excellent man, and a diligent and conscientious churchman. Though indifferent to general literature, he had some taste in the fine arts, especially architecture. B.'s works were ed. by W. E. Gladstone (2 vols. 1896), and there are Lives by Bishop W. Fitzgerald, Spooner (1902), and others, *see* also *History of English Thought in 18th Century*, by Leslie Stephen.

BUTLER, SAMUEL (1612-1680).—Satirist, was the *s.* of a Worcestershire farmer. In early youth he was page to the Countess of Kent, and thereafter clerk to various Puritan justices, some of whom are believed to have suggested characters in *Hudibras.* After the Restoration he became Sec. to the Lord Pres. of Wales, and about the same time *m.* a Mrs. Herbert, a widow with a jointure, which, however, was lost. In 1663 the first part of *Hudibras* was *pub.*, and the other two in 1664 and 1668 respectively. This work, which is to a certain extent modelled on *Don Quixote*, stands at the head of the satirical literature of England, and for wit and compressed thought has few rivals in any language. It is directed against the Puritans, and while it holds up to ridicule the extravagancies into which many of the party ran, it entirely fails to do justice to their virtues and their services to liberty, civil and religious. Many of its brilliant couplets have passed into the proverbial commonplaces of the language, and few who use them have any idea of their source. Butler, notwithstanding the popularity of his work, was neglected by the Court, and *d.* in poverty.

Ed. of B.'s works have been issued by Bell (3 vols., 1813), and Johnson (2 vols., 1893).

BUTLER, SAMUEL (1825-1902).—Miscellaneous writer, *ed.* at Shrewsbury and Camb., wrote two satirical books, *Erewhon* (nowhere) (1872), and *Erewhon Revisited* (1901). He translated the *Iliad* and *Odyssey* in prose, and mooted the theory that the latter was written by a woman. Other works were *The Fair Haven, Life and Habit, The Way of all Flesh* (a novel) (1903), etc., and some sonnets. He also wrote on the Sonnets of Shakespeare.

BYRON, GEORGE GORDON, 6TH LORD BYRON (1788-1824). —Poet, was *b.* in London, the *s.* of Captain John B. and of Catherine Gordon, heiress of Gight, Aberdeenshire, his second wife, whom he *m.* for her money and, after squandering it, deserted. He was also the grand-nephew of the 5th, known as the "wicked" Lord B. From his birth he suffered from a malformation of the feet, causing a slight lameness, which was a cause of lifelong misery to him, aggravated by the knowledge that with proper care it might have been cured. After the departure of his *f.* his mother went to Aberdeen, where she lived on a small salvage from her fortune. She was a capricious woman of violent temper, with no fitness for guiding her volcanic son, and altogether the circumstances of his early life explain, if they do not excuse, the spirit of revolt which was his life-long characteristic. In 1794, on the death of a cousin, he became heir-presumptive to the title and embarrassed estates of the family, to which, on the death of his great-uncle in 1798, he succeeded. In 1801 he was sent to Harrow, where he remained until 1805, when he proceeded to Trinity Coll., Camb., where he read much history and fiction, lived extravagantly, and got into debt. Some early verses which he had *pub.* in 1806 were suppressed. They were followed in 1807 by *Hours of Idleness*, which was savagely attacked in the *Edinburgh Review*. In reply he sent forth *English Bards and Scotch Reviewers* (1809), which created considerable stir and shortly went through 5 ed. Meanwhile, he had settled at Newstead Abbey, the family seat, where with some of his cronies he was believed to have indulged in wild and extravagant orgies, the accounts of which, however, were probably greatly exaggerated. In 1809 he left England, and passing through Spain, went to Greece. During his absence, which extended over two years, he wrote the first two cantos of *Childe Harold*, which were *pub.* after his return in 1812, and were received with acclamation. In his own words, "he awoke one morning and found himself famous." He followed up his success with some short poems, *The Corsair*, *Lara*, etc. About the same time began his intimacy with his future biographer, Thomas Moore (*q.v.*), and about 1815 he married Anne Isabella Milbanke, who had refused him in the previous year, a union which, owing to the total incompatibility of the parties, and serious provocations on the part of B., proved unhappy, and was in 1816 dissolved by a formal deed of separation. The only fruit of it was a *dau.*, Augusta Ada. After this break-up of his domestic life, followed as it was by the severe censure of society, and by pressure on the part of his creditors, which led to the sale of his library, B. again left England, as it turned out, for ever, and, passing through Belgium and up the Rhine, went to Geneva, afterwards travelling with Shelley through Switzerland, when he wrote the third canto of *Childe Harold*. He wintered in Venice, where he formed a connection with Jane Clairmont, the *dau.* of W. Godwin's second wife (*q.v.*). In 1817 he was in Rome, whence returning to Venice he wrote the fourth canto of *Childe Harold*. In the same year he sold his ancestral seat of Newstead, and about the same time *pub.* *Manfred*, *Cain*, and *The Deformed Transformed*. The first five cantos of *Don Juan* were written between 1818 and 1820, during which period he made the acquaintance of the Countess Guiccioli, whom he persuaded to leave her husband. It was about this time that he received a visit from Moore, to whom he confided his MS. autobiography, which Moore, in the exercise of the discretion left to him, burned in 1824. His next move was to Ravenna, where he wrote much, chiefly dramas, including *Marino Faliero*. In 1821-22 he finished *Don Juan* at Pisa, and in the same year he joined with Leigh Hunt in starting a short-lived newspaper, *The Liberal*, in the first number of which appeared *The Vision of Judgment*. His last Italian home was Genoa, where he was still accompanied by the Countess, and where he lived until 1823, when he offered himself as an ally to the Greek insurgents. In July of that year he started for Greece, spent some months in Cephalonia waiting for the Greeks to form some definite plans. In January, 1824, he landed at Missolonghi, but caught a malarial fever, of which he *d.* on April 19, 1824.

The final position of B. in English literature is probably not yet settled. It is at present undoubtedly lower than it was in his own generation. Yet his energy, passion, and power of vivid and richly-coloured description, together with the interest attaching to his wayward and unhappy career, must always make him loom large in the assembly of English writers. He exercised a marked influence on Continental literature, and his reputation as poet is higher in some foreign countries than in his own.

Among ed. of the works of B. may be mentioned Murray's (13 vols. 1898-1904). Moore's *Life* (1830), Lady Blessington's *Conversations with Lord Byron* (1834, new, 1894).

SUMMARY.—*B.* 1788, spent childhood in Aberdeen, *ed.* Harrow and Camb., *pub. English Bards etc.*, 1809, *Childe Harold* first two cantos 1812, married 1815, separated 1816, owing to this and financial difficulties leaves England, meets Shelley, *pub.* third canto of *Childe Harold* 1816, fourth canto 1817, writes *Don Juan* cantos 1-4 1818-20, lives at various places in Italy 1816-24 with Countess Guiccioli, finished *Don Juan* 1822, goes to Greece 1823 to assist insurgents, *d.* 1824.

BYRON, HENRY JAMES (1834-1884).—Dramatist, *b.* at Manchester, entered the Middle Temple, but soon took to writing for the stage, and produced many popular burlesques and extravaganzas. He also wrote for periodicals, and was the first editor of *Fun.* Among his best dramatic pieces are *Cyril's Success* (1868), *Our Boys* (1875), and *The Upper Crust.*

CÆDMON (*d.* 680).—The first English poet of whom we have any knowledge. Originally employed as cowherd at the Abbey of Whitby, he became a singer when somewhat advanced in life. The story of how the gift of song came to him is given by Bede, how having fallen asleep in the stable he dreamed that one came to him desiring a song, and on his asking "What shall I sing?" replied "Sing to me of the beginning of created things." Therefore he began to sing and, on awaking, remembered his song and added to it. Thereafter he told what had befallen him to the bailiff who was over him, who repeated the tale to the Abbess Hilda. She having called together certain learned and pious persons, C. was brought before them, told his story, and recited his verses. A part of Scripture was read to him, which he was asked to turn into verse; and this being done he was received into the Abbey where, for the rest of his life, he lived as a monk, and continued to make his holy songs. Much that was formerly attributed to C. is now held to be of later date. All that is known to be his is a Northumbrian version of Bede's Latin paraphrases of C.'s first song: although by some the authorship of "The Dream of the Holy Rood," and of a fragment on "The Temptation and Fall of Man" is claimed for him.

English Literature from Beginning to Norman Conquest, Stopford Brooke (1898), and *History of Early English Literature*, by the same (1892).

CAIRD, EDWARD (1835-1908).—Philosopher, younger brother of John C. (*q.v.*), was *b.* at Greenock, and *ed.* at Glasgow and Oxf., where he became Fellow and Tutor of Merton Coll. In 1866 he was appointed to the Chair of Moral Philosophy at Glasgow, which he held until 1893, when he became Master of Balliol Coll., from which he retired in 1907. He has written *Critical Philosophy of Kant* (1877), *Hegel* (1883), *Evolution of Religion, Social Philosophy and Religion of Comte* (1885), *Evolution of Theology in the Greek Philosophers* (1904).

CAIRD, JOHN (1820-1898).—Theologian, *b.* at Greenock, and *ed.* at Glasgow, entered the Church of Scotland, of which he became one of the most eloquent preachers. After being a minister in the country and in Edinburgh, he was translated to Glasgow, becoming in 1862 Prof. of Divinity in the Univ. of that city, and in 1873 Principal. A sermon on *Religion in Common Life*, preached before Queen Victoria, made him known throughout the Protestant world. He wrote an *Introduction to the Philosophy of Religion* (1880), and a vol. on *Spinoza* (1888).

CALAMY, EDMUND (1600-1666).—Puritan Divine, *b.* in London, and *ed.* at Camb., was one of the principal authors of a famous controversial work bearing the title *Smectymnuus*, made up of the initials of the various writers, and *pub.* in 1641 in reply to Bishop Hall's *Divine Right of Episcopacy*. His other chief work is *The Godly Man's Ark*. A Presbyterian, he was a supporter of monarchy, and favoured the Restoration, after which he was offered, but declined, the see of Coventry and Lichfield. He was a member of the Savoy Conference. The passing of the Act of Uniformity led to his retiring from ministerial work. He is said to have *d.* of melancholy caused by the great fire of London.

CALDERWOOD, DAVID (1575-1650).—Scottish Church historian, belonged to a good family, and about 1604 became minister of Crailing, Roxburghshire. Opposing the designs of James VI. for setting up Episcopacy, he was imprisoned 1617, and afterwards had to betake himself to Holland, where his controversial work, *Altare Damascenum*, against Episcopacy, was *pub.* In 1625 he returned to Scotland, and began his great work, *The Historie of the Kirk of Scotland*, which was *pub.* in an abridged form (1646). The complete work was printed (1841-49) for the Woodrow Society. C. became minister of Pencaitland, East Lothian, about 1640, and was one of those appointed to draw up *The Directory for Public Worship in Scotland*.

CALVERLEY, CHARLES STUART (1831-1884).—Poet and translator, *s.* of the Rev. H. Blayds (who assumed the name of Calverley), was *ed.* at Harrow, Oxf., and Camb. He was called to the Bar in 1865, and appeared to have a brilliant career before him, when a fall on the ice in 1866 changed him from a distinguished athlete to a life-long invalid. Brilliant as a scholar, a musician, and a talker, he is perhaps best known as one of the greatest of parodists. He *pub.* *Verses and Translations* (1862), and *Fly-leaves* (1872). He also translated *Theocritus* (1869).

CAMDEN, WILLIAM (1551-1623).—Antiquary and historian, *b.* in London, and *ed.* at Christ's Hospital, St. Paul's School, and Oxf., was in 1575 appointed Second Master in Westminster School, and Head Master in 1593, and spent his vacations in travelling over England collecting antiquarian information. His great work, *Britannia,* was *pub.* in 1586, and at once brought him fame both at home and abroad. It is a work of vast labour and erudition, written in elegant Latin. In 1597 C. was made Clarencieux King-at-Arms which, setting him free from his academic duties, enabled him to devote more time to his antiquarian and historical labours. His other principal works are *Annals of the Reign of Elizabeth* (printed 1615-1623), *Monuments and Inscriptions in Westminster Abbey* (1600), and a *coll.* of *Ancient English Historians.* He was buried in Westminster Abbey. The Camden Society for historical research, founded in 1838, is named after him.

CAMPBELL, GEORGE (1719-1796).—Theologian and philosopher, was a minister of the Church of Scotland at Aberdeen, and Principal and Prof. of Divinity in Marischal Coll. there. His *Dissertation on Miracles* (1763), in answer to Hume, was in its day considered a masterly argument, and was admitted to be so by Hume himself. His other principal works were *The Philosophy of Rhetoric* (1776), which is still a standard work, and *A Translation of the Four Gospels with Notes.*

CAMPBELL, JOHN, 1ST LORD CAMPBELL (1779-1861).—Lawyer and biographer, *s.* of the minister of Cupar-Fife, had a highly successful career as a lawyer, and held the offices successively of Solicitor and Attorney-General, Lord Chancellor of Ireland, Lord Chief Justice, and Lord Chancellor. His contributions to literature were *Lives of the Chancellors* and *Lives of the Chief Justices.* These works, though deficient in research and accuracy, often unfair in judgments of character, and loose and diffuse in style, are interesting and full of information.

CAMPBELL, JOHN FRANCIS (1822-1885).—Celtic scholar, *ed.* at Eton and Edin., was afterwards Sec. to the Lighthouse Commission. He was an authority on Celtic folk-lore, and *pub. Popular Tales of the West Highlands* (4 vols., 1860-62), and various Gaelic texts.

CAMPBELL, LEWIS (1830-1908).—Scholar, *s.* of a naval officer, *ed.* at Edin., Glasgow, and Oxf., took orders, and was Vicar of Milford, Hants, until 1863, when he was appointed Prof. of Greek at St. Andrews. He brought out ed. of Sophocles and other works on the Greek classics, and in conjunction with E. Abbott *The Life and Letters of Prof. Jowett* (*q.v.*), with whom he had collaborated in editing the *Republic of Plato.* He also ed. the poems of Thomas Campbell, to whom he was related.

CAMPBELL, THOMAS (1777-1844).—Poet, was the youngest *s.* of Alexander C., a merchant in Glasgow, where he was *b.* After leaving the Univ. of that city, where he gained some distinction by his translations from the Greek, and acting for some time as a tutor, he went to Edin. to study law, in which, however, he did not make much progress, but gained fame by producing in 1799, at the age of 21, his principal poem, *The Pleasures of Hope.* In spite of some of the faults of youth, the vigour of thought and description, and power of versification displayed in the poem, as well as its noble feeling for liberty, made it a marvellous performance for so young a man. His other larger poems are *Gertrude of Wyoming* (1809), *O'Connor's Child,* and *Theodric* (1824). It is not, however, for these that he will be chiefly remembered, but for his patriotic and war lyrics, *Ye Mariners of England, Hohenlinden,* and *The Battle of the Baltic,* which are imperishable. C. was also distinguished as a critic, and his *Specimens of the British Poets* (1819) is prefaced by an essay which is an important contribution to criticism. C. resided in London from 1803 until the year of his death, which took place at Boulogne, whither he had repaired in search of health. In addition to the works mentioned he wrote various compilations, including *Annals of Great Britain,* covering part of the reign of George III. In 1805 he received a Government pension, and he was Lord Rector of Glasgow Univ. 1826-29. He is buried in Westminster Abbey.

Life and Letters, Beattie (1840); Poems, *Aldine* ed. (1875, new, 1890).

CAMPION, THOMAS (*c.* 1575-1620).—Poet and musician, *b.* at Witham, Essex, and *ed.* at Camb., and on the Continent, studied law at Gray's Inn, but discarding it, practised medicine in London. He wrote masques, and many fine lyrics remarkable for their metrical beauty, of which "Cherry Ripe" and "Lesbia" are well known. He also wrote *Epigrams* in Latin, and *Observations on the Arte of Poesie* (1602). He composed the music for most of his songs.

CANNING, GEORGE (1770-1827).—Statesman, was *b.* in London, the *s.* of a lawyer. He lost his *f.* while still an infant, and was brought up by an uncle, who sent him to Eton and Oxf. In 1793 he entered Parliament as a supporter of Pitt, and soon became one of the most brilliant debaters in the House. After filling various offices, including that of Foreign Sec., with striking ability, he was in 1827 appointed Prime Minister, but *d.*, deeply mourned by the nation, a few months later. He has a place in literature as the leading spirit in the *Anti-Jacobin,* a paper started during the French Revolution, in support of the English Constitution, and which, with Gifford for ed., had many of the most eminent men of the day as contributors. C. wrote the *Needy Knife-grinder, The Loves of the Triangles,* parts II. and III., a parody on E. Darwin's *Loves of the Plants, The Progress of Man,* etc. His *coll. Poems* were *pub.* 1823.

CAPGRAVE, JOHN (1393-1464).—Historian and theologian, *b.* at Lynn, became an Augustinian Friar, and at length Provincial of the Order in England. He studied probably at Camb., visited Rome, and was a client of Humphrey, Duke of Gloucester, whose life he wrote. He was the author of numerous theological and historical works, some of which are of considerable importance, including in Latin, *Nova Legenda Angliæ, De Illustribus Henricis:* lives of German Emperors, English Kings, etc., of the name of Henry, and in English, monotonous and dull, lives of St. Gilbert and St. Katharine, and a *Chronicle* reaching to 1417.

CAREW, RICHARD (1555-1620).—Translator and antiquary, a county gentleman of Cornwall, *ed.* at Oxf., made a translation of the first five cantos of Tasso's *Jerusalem Delivered* (1594), more correct than that of Fairfax. Other works were *A Survey of Cornwall* (1602), and an *Epistle concerning the Excellencies of the English Tongue* (1605).

CAREW, THOMAS (1594?-1639).—Poet, *s.* of Sir Matthew C., was *ed.* at Oxf., entered the Middle Temple, and was one of the first and best of the courtly poets who wrote gracefully on light themes of Court life and gallantry. C.'s poems have often much beauty and even tenderness. His chief work is *Coelum Britannicum.* He lived the easy and careless life of a courtier of the day, but is said to have *d.* in a repentant frame. His poems, consisting chiefly of short lyrics, were *coll.* and *pub.* after his death. One of the most beautiful and best known of his songs is that beginning " He that loves a rosy cheek."

CAREY, HENRY (*d.* 1743).—Dramatist and song-writer, was believed to be an illegitimate *s.* of George Savile, Marquis of Halifax. He wrote innumerable burlesques, farces, songs, etc., often with his own music, including *Chrononhotonthologos* (1734), a burlesque on the mouthing plays of the day, and *The Dragon of Wantley* (1744?). His poem, *Namby Pamby,* in ridicule of Ambrose Phillips (*q.v.*), added a word to the language, and his *Sally in our Alley* is one of our best-known songs. *God Save the King* was also claimed for him, but apparently without reason.

CARLETON, WILLIAM (1794-1869).—Novelist, *s.* of a poor Irish cottar, *b.* and brought up among the Irish peasantry, acquired an insight into their ideas and feelings which has never been equalled. His finest work is in his short stories, collected under the title of *Traits and Stories of the Irish Peasantry,* of which two series were *pub.* in 1830 and 1832 respectively. He also wrote several longer novels, of which the best is *Fardorougha the Miser* (1837), a work of great power. Others are *The Misfortunes of Barny Branagan* (1841), *Valentine M'Clutchy* (1845), *Rody the Rover* (1847), *The Squanders of Castle Squander* (1854), and *The Evil Eye.* C. received a pension of £200 from Government.

CARLYLE, ALEXANDER (1722-1805).—Autobiographer, *s.* of the Minister of Cummertrees, Dumfriesshire, was *ed.* at Edin. and Leyden, and entering the Church became Minister of Inveresk, and was associated with Principal Robertson as an ecclesiastical leader. Hs was a man of great ability, shrewdness, and culture, and the friend of most of the eminent literary men in Scotland of his day. He left an autobiography in MS., which was ed. by Hill Burton, and *pub.* in 1860, and which is one of the most interesting contemporary accounts of his time. His stately appearance gained for him the name of " Jupiter " C.

CARLYLE, THOMAS (1795-1881).—Historian and essayist, was *b.* at Ecclefechan in Dumfriesshire. His *f.*, James C., was a stonemason, a man of intellect and strong character, and his mother was, as he said, "of the fairest descent, that of the pious, the just, and the wise." His earliest education was received at the parish school of Ecclefechan (the Entepfuhl of *Sartor Resartus*). Thence he went to the Grammar School of Annan, and in 1809 to the Univ. of Edin., the 90 miles to which he travelled on foot. There he read voraciously, his chief study being mathematics. After completing his "Arts" course, he went on to divinity with the view of entering the Church, but about the middle of his course found that he could not proceed. He became a schoolmaster first at Annan and then at Kirkcaldy, where he formed a profound friendship with Edward Irving (*q.v.*), and met Margaret Gordon, afterwards Lady Bannerman, believed by some to be the prototype of *Blumine* in *Sartor*. Returning in 1819 to Edin. he for a time studied law and took pupils; but his health was bad, he suffered from insomnia and dyspepsia, and he tired of law. He was also sorely bestead by mental and spiritual conflicts, which came to a crisis in Leith Walk in June 1821 in a sudden uprising of defiance to the devil and all his works, upon which the clouds lifted. For the next two years, 1822-24, he acted as tutor to Charles Buller (whose promising political career was cut short by his premature death) and his brother. On the termination of this engagement he decided upon a literary career, which he began by contributing articles to the *Edinburgh Encyclopædia*. In 1824 he translated Legendre's *Geometry* (to which he prefixed an essay on Proportion), and Goethe's *Wilhelm Meister;* he also wrote for the *London Magazine* a *Life of Schiller*. About this time he visited Paris and London, where he met Hazlitt, Campbell, Coleridge, and others. Thereafter he returned to Dumfriesshire. In the following year (1826) he *m.* Jane Baillie Welsh, and settled in Edin. Here his first work was *Specimens of German Romance* (4 vols.) A much more important matter was his friendship with Jeffrey and his connection with the *Edinburgh Review*, in which appeared, among others, his essays on *Richter*, *Burns*, *Characteristics*, and *German Poetry*. In 1828 C. applied unsuccessfully for the Chair of Moral Philosophy in St. Andrews, and the same year he went to Craigenputtock, a small property in Dumfriesshire belonging to Mrs. C., where they remained for several years, and where many of his best essays and *Sartor Resartus* were written, and where his correspondence with Goethe began. In 1831 he went to London to find a publisher for *Sartor*, but was unsuccessful, and it did not appear in book form until 1838, after having come out in *Fraser's Magazine* in 1833-34. The year last mentioned found him finally in London, settled in Cheyne Row, Chelsea, his abode for the rest of his life. He immediately set to work on his *French Revolution*. While it was in progress he in 1835 lent the MS. to J. S. Mill, by whose servant nearly the whole of the first vol. was burned, in spite of which misfortune the work was ready for publication in 1837. Its originality, brilliance, and vividness took the world by storm, and his reputation as one of the foremost men of letters in the country was at once and finally established. In the same year he appeared as a public lecturer, and delivered four courses on *German Literature*, *Periods of European Culture*, *Revolutions of Modern Europe*, and *Heroes and Hero-Worship*, the last of which was *pub.* as a book in 1841. Although his writings did not yet produce a large income, his circumstances had become comfortable, owing to Mrs. C. having succeeded to her patrimony in 1840. Books now followed each other rapidly, *Chartism* had appeared in 1839, *Past and Present* came out in 1843, and *Letters and Speeches of Oliver Cromwell* in 1845, the last named being perhaps the most successful of his writings, inasmuch as it fully attained the object aimed at in clearing Cromwell from the ignorant or malevolent aspersions under which he had long lain, and giving him his just place among the greatest of the nation. In 1850 he *pub.* his fiercest blast, *Latter Day Pamphlets*, which was followed next year by his biography of his friend John Sterling (*q.v.*). It was about this time, as is shown by the *Letters and Memoirs* of Mrs. C., that a temporary estrangement arose between his wife and himself, based apparently on Mrs. C.'s part upon his friendship with Lady Ashburton, a cause of which C. seems to have been unconscious. In 1851 he began his largest, if not his greatest work, *Frederick the Great*, which occupied him from that year until 1865, and in connection with which he made two visits to Germany in 1852 and 1858. It is a work of astonishing research and abounds in brilliant passages, but lacks the concentrated intensity of *The French Revolution*. It is, however, the one of his works which enjoys the highest reputation in Germany. In 1865 he was elected Lord Rector of the Univ. of Edin., and delivered a remarkable address to the students by whom he was received with enthusiasm. Almost immediately afterwards a heavy blow fell upon him in the death of Mrs. C., and in the discovery, from her diary, of how greatly she had suffered, unknown to him, from the neglect and want of consideration which, owing to absorption in his work and other causes, he had perhaps unconsciously shown. Whatever his faults, of which the most was made in some quarters, there can be no doubt that C. and his wife were sincerely attached to each other, and that he deeply mourned her. In 1866 his *Reminiscences* (*pub.* 1881) were written. The Franco-German War of 1870-71 profoundly interested him, and evoked a plea for Germany. From this time his health began to give way more and more. In 1872 hs right hand became paralysed. In 1874 he received the distinction of the Prussian Order of Merit, as the biographer of its founder, and in the same year, Mr. Disraeli offered him the choice of the Grand Cross of the Bath or a baronetcy and a pension, all of which he declined. The completion of his 80th year in 1875 was made the occasion of many tributes of respect and veneration, including a gold medal from some of his Scottish admirers. He *d.* on February 5, 1881. Burial in Westminster Abbey was offered, but he had left instructions that he should lie with his kindred. He bequeathed the property of Craigenputtock to the Univ. of Edin.

C. exercised a very powerful influence upon the thought of his age, not only by his own writings and personality, but through the many men of distinction both in literature and active life whom he imbued with his doctrines; and perhaps no better proof of this exists than the fact that much that was new and original when first propounded by him has passed into the texture of the national ideas. His style is perhaps the most remarkable and individual in our literature, intensely strong, vivid, and picturesque, but utterly unconventional, and often whimsical or explosive. He had in a high degree the poetic and imaginative faculty, and also irresistible humour, pungent sarcasm, insight, tenderness, and fierce indignation.

All the works of C. shed light on his personality, but *Sartor Resartus* especially may be regarded as autobiographical. Froude's *Thomas Carlyle . . . First* 40 *Years of his Life* (1882), *Thomas Carlyle . . . His Life in London*, by the same (1884), *Letters and Memories of Jane Welsh Carlyle* (1883), various *Lives* and *Reminiscences* by Prof. Masson and Nichol, etc.

SUMMARY.—*B.* 1795, *ed.* Edin., studies for Church but gives it up, tries law, then tutor, takes to literature and writes for encyclopædias and magazines, and translates, *m.* 1826 Jane Welsh, settles in Edin., writes essays in *Edinburgh Review*, goes to Craigenputtock 1828, writes *Sartor* and corresponds with Goethe, *Sartor* appears in *Fraser's Magazine* 1833-4, settles in London 1834, *pub. French Revolution* 1837, lectures, *pub. Heroes*, and *Chartism* and *Sartor* as a book 1839, *Past and Present* 1843, *Oliver Cromwell* 1845, *Latter Day Pamphlets* 1850, writes *Frederick the Great* 1851-65, Lord Rector of Edin. Univ. 1865, Mrs. C. *d.* 1865, writes *Reminiscences* 1866 (*pub.* 1881), *d.* 1881.

CARRUTHERS, ROBERT (1799-1878).—Journalist and miscellaneous writer, *b.* in Dumfriesshire, was for a time a teacher in Huntingdon, and wrote a *History of Huntingdon* (1824). In 1828 he became ed. of the *Inverness Courier*, which he conducted with great ability. He ed. Pope's works with a memoir (1853), and along with Robert Chambers (*q.v.*) ed. the first ed. of *Chambers's Cyclopædia of English Literature* (1842-44). He received the degree of LL.D. from Edin.

CARTE, THOMAS (1686-1754).—Historian, *b.* near Rugby, and *ed.* at Oxf., took orders, but resigned his benefice at Bath when required to take the oath of allegiance to George I. He was sec. to Francis Atterbury (*q.v.*), and was involved in the consequences of his conspiracy, but escaped to France, where he remained until 1728. After his return he *pub.* a life of the Duke of Ormonde (1736), and a *History of England to* 1654 in 4 vols. (1747-54), the latter a work of great research, though dry and unattractive in style.

CARTER, ELIZABETH (1717-1806).—Miscellaneous writer, *b.* at Deal, *dau.* of a clergyman. Originally backward, she applied herself to study with such perseverance that she became perhaps the most learned Englishwoman of her time, being mistress of Latin, Greek, Hebrew, and Arabic, besides several modern European languages. She was also well read in science. She translated Epictetus 1758, and wrote a small vol. of poems. She was the friend of Dr. Johnson and many other eminent men. She was of agreeable and unassuming manners.

CARTWRIGHT, WILLIAM (1611-1643).—Dramatist, *s.* of a gentleman of Gloucestershire, who had run through his fortune and kept an inn at Cirencester, *ed.* at Westminster School and Oxf., entered the Church, was a zealous Royalist, and an eloquent preacher, and lecturer in metaphysics. He also wrote spirited lyrics and four plays. He was the friend of Ben Jonson, H. Vaughan, and Izaak Walton. He *d.* at Oxf. of camp fever. Among his plays are *The Royal Slave*, *The Siege*, and *The Lady Errant*. His virtues, learning, and charming manners made him highly popular in his day.

CARY, ALICE (1820-1871), and PHŒBE (1824-1871).—Were the *dau.* of a farmer near Cincinnati. The former wrote *Clovernook Papers* and *Clovernook Children*, and other tales, and some poems. The latter wrote poems and hymns. Both sisters attained considerable popularity.

CARY, HENRY FRANCIS (1772-1844).—Translator, was *b.* at Gibraltar, and *ed.* at Oxf., where he was distinguished for his classical attainments. His great work is his translation of the *Divina Commedia* of Dante (1805-1814), which is not only faithful to the original, but full of poetic fire, and rendered into such fine English as to be itself literature apart from its merits as a translation. He also translated from the Greek. C., who was a clergyman, received a pension in 1841.

CATLIN, GEORGE (1796-1872).—Painter and writer, *b.* at Wilkesbarre, Pennsylvania, practised for some time as a lawyer, but yielding to his artistic instincts he took to painting. He spent the 7 years, 1832-39, among the Indians of North America, of whom he painted about 500 portraits. He became thoroughly acquainted with their life, and *pub.* an interesting work, *Illustrations of the Manners, etc., of the North American Indians* (1857). His later years were spent chiefly in Europe.

CAVE, EDWARD (1691-1754).—Publisher, *b.* near Rugby, started in 1731 *The Gentleman's Magazine*, for which Dr. Johnson was parliamentary reporter from 1740. He *pub.* many of Johnson's works.

CAVENDISH, GEORGE (1500-1561).—Biographer, was Gentleman Usher to Cardinal Wolsey, to whom he was so much attached that he followed him in his disgrace, and continued to serve him until his death. He left in MS. a life of his patron, which is the first separate biography in English, and is the main original authority of the period. Admitting Wolsey's faults, it nevertheless presents him in an attractive light. The simple yet eloquent style gives it a high place as a biography.

CAXTON, WILLIAM (1422-1491).—Printer and translator, *b.* in the Weald of Kent, was apprenticed to a London mercer. On his master's death in 1441 he went to Bruges, and lived there and in various other places in the Low Countries for over 30 years, engaged apparently as head of an association of English merchants trading in foreign parts, and in negotiating commercial treaties between England and the Dukes of Burgundy. His first literary labour was a translation of a French romance, which he entitled *The Recuyell of the Historyes of Troye*, and which he finished in 1471. About this time he learned the art of printing, and, after being in the service of

Margaret Duchess of Burgundy, an English princess, returned to his native country and set up at Westminster in 1476 his printing press, the first in England. His *Recuyell* and *The Game and Playe of Chesse* had already been printed—the first books in English—on the Continent. Here was produced the first book printed in England, *The Dictes and Sayings of the Philosophers* (1477). C. obtained Royal favour, printed from 80 to 100 separate works—many of them translations of his own—and *d.* almost with pen in hand in 1491. His style is clear and idiomatic.

CENTLIVRE, MRS. SUSANNA (1667-1723).—Dramatist and actress, was the *dau.* of a gentleman of the name of either Rawkins or Freeman, who appears to have belonged either to Lincolnshire or Ireland, or was perhaps connected with both, and who suffered at the hands of the Stuarts. She *m.* at 16, lost her husband in a year, then *m.* an officer, who fell in a duel in 18 months, and finally, in 1706, *m.* Joseph C., cook to Queen Anne, with whom she lived happily for the rest of her days. She wrote 18 or 19 plays, well constructed and amusing, among which may be mentioned *The Perjured Husband* (1700), *The Busybody* (1709), *The Warder* (1714), and *A Bold Stroke for a Wife* (1717). She was a strong Whig, and sometimes made her plays the medium of expressing her political opinions.

CHALKHILL, JOHN (*fl.* 1600).—Poet, mentioned by Izaak Walton as having written a pastoral poem, *Thealma and Clearchus*. As nothing else is known of him it has been held by some that the name was a *nom-de-plume* of W. himself. It has been shown, however, that a gentleman of the name existed during the reign of Elizabeth. W. says he was a friend of Spenser, and that his life was "useful, quiet, and virtuous."

CHALMERS, GEORGE (1742-1825).—Antiquary, *b.* at Fochabers, Elginshire, emigrated to America and practised law in Baltimore; but on the outbreak of the Revolutionary War returned to Britain, and settled in London as a clerk in the Board of Trade. He *pub.* in 1780 a *History of the United Colonies*, and wrote lives of Sir David Lyndsay, De Foe, and Mary Queen of Scots. His great work, however, is his *Caledonia*, of which 3 vols. had been *pub.* at his death. It was to have been a complete *coll.* of the topography and antiquities of Scotland; and, as it stands, is a monument of industry and research, though not always trustworthy in disputed points. Besides those mentioned, C. was the author of many other works on political, historical, and literary subjects, and had projected several which he was unable to carry out.

CHALMERS, THOMAS (1780-1847).—Divine, economist, and philanthropist, *b.* at Anstruther, Fife, *s.* of a shipowner and merchant, studied at St. Andrews and, entering the ministry of the Church of Scotland, was first settled in the small parish of Kilmeny, Fife, but, his talents and eloquence becoming known, he was, in 1815, translated to Glasgow, where he was soon recognised as the most eloquent preacher in Scotland, and where also he initiated his schemes for the management of the poor. In 1823 he became Prof. of Moral Philosophy at St. Andrews, and in 1828 of Divinity in Edin. In 1834 he began his great scheme of Church extension, the result of which was that in seven years £300,000 had been raised, and 220 churches built. In the same year, 1834, began the troubles and controversies in regard to patronage and the relations of Church and State, which in 1843 ended in the disruption of the Church, when 470 ministers with C. at their head, resigned their benefices, and founded the Free Church of Scotland. C. was chosen its first Moderator and Principal of its Theological Coll. in Edin. The remaining four years of his life were spent in organising the new Church, and in works of philanthropy. He was found dead in bed on the morning of May 30, 1847. His chief works, which were *coll.* and *pub.* in 34 vols., relate to natural theology, evidences of Christianity, political economy, and general theology and science. Those which perhaps attracted most attention were his *Astronomical Discourses* and his *Lectures on Church Establishments,* the latter delivered in London to audiences containing all that was most distinguished in rank and intellect in the country. The style of C. is cumbrous, and often turgid, but the moral earnestness, imagination, and force of intellect of the writer shine through it and irradiate his subjects. And yet the written is described by contemporaries to have been immeasurably surpassed by the spoken word, which carried away the hearer as in a whirlwind. And the man was even greater than his achievements. His character was one of singular simplicity, nobility, and lovableness, and produced a profound impression on all who came under his influence. The character of his intellect was notably practical, as is evidenced by the success of his parochial administration and the "Sustentation Fund," devised by him for the support of the ministry of the Free Church. He was D.D., LL.D., D.C.L. (Oxon.), and a Corresponding Member of the Institute of France.

Memoirs (Hanna, 4 vols.). Smaller works by Prof. Blaikie (1897), Mrs. Oliphant (1893), and many others.

CHAMBERLAYNE, WILLIAM (1619-1689).—Poet, practised medicine at Shaftesbury. On the outbreak of the Civil War he joined the Royalists and fought at the second battle of Newbury. He wrote a play, *Love's Victory* (1658), and an epic *Pharonnida* (1659). With occasional beauties he is, in the main, heavy and stiff, and is almost forgotten. He influenced Keats.

CHAMBERS, ROBERT (1802-1871).—Historical and scientific writer, was *b.* at Peebles. Early dependent on his own exertions, he started business as a bookseller in Edin. at the age of 16, devoting all his spare time to study, to such purpose that in 1824 he *pub. Traditions of Edinburgh,* a work in which he had the assistance of Sir W. Scott. Thereafter he poured forth a continuous stream of books and essays on historical, social, antiquarian, and scientific subjects. He joined his brother William (*q.v.*) in establishing the publishing firm of W. and R. Chambers, and in starting *Chambers's Journal,* to which he was a constant contributor. Later ventures were *The Cyclopædia of English Literature* (1842-44), of which several ed. have appeared (last 1903-6), and *Chambers's Cyclopædia* (10 vols. 1859-68; new 1888-92). Among his own works may be mentioned *Vestiges of Creation, pub.* anonymously (1844), a precursor of Darwinism, *A Life of Burns* (1851), *Popular Rhymes of Scotland* (1847), *History of the Rebellions in Scotland, Domestic Annals of Scotland* (1859-61), *Ancient Sea Margins* (1848), *Dictionary of Eminent Scotsmen* and *The Book of Days* (1863). He was LL.D. of St. Andrews.

CHAMBERS, WILLIAM (1800-1883).—Publisher and miscellaneous author, *b.* at Peebles, started in 1832 with his brother Robert (*q.v.*) *Chambers's Journal*, and soon after joined him in the firm of W. and R. Chambers. Besides contributions to the *Journal* he wrote several books, including a *History of Peeblesshire* (1864), and an autobiography of himself and his brother. C. was a man of great business capacity, and, though of less literary distinction than his brother, did much for the dissemination of cheap and useful literature. He was Lord Provost of Edin. 1865-69, and was an LL.D. of the Univ. of that city. He restored the ancient church of St. Giles there.

CHAMIER, FREDERICK (1796-1870).—Novelist, was in the navy, in which he rose to the rank of Captain. Retiring in 1827, he wrote several sea novels somewhat in the style of Marryat, including *Life of a Sailor* (1832), *Ben Brace, Jack Adams*, and *Tom Bowling* (1841). He also continued James's *Naval History*, and wrote books of travel.

CHANNING, WILLIAM ELLERY (1780-1842).—American Divine, *b.* at Newport, Rhode Island, was for a time a minister in the Congregationalist Church, but became the leader of the Unitarians in New England. He had a powerful influence on the thought and literature of his time in America, and was the author of books on Milton and Fénelon, and on social subjects. The elevation and amiability of his character caused him to be held in high esteem. He did not class himself with Unitarians of the school of Priestley, but claimed to "stand aloof from all but those who strive and pray for clearer light."

CHAPMAN, GEORGE (1559-1634).—Dramatist and translator, was *b.* near Hitchin, and probably *ed.* at Oxf. and Camb. He wrote many plays, including *The Blind Beggar of Alexandria* (1596), *All Fools* (1599), *A Humerous Daye's Myrthe* (1599), *Eastward Hoe* (with Jonson), *The Gentleman Usher, Monsieur d'Olive*, etc. As a dramatist he has humour, and vigour, and occasional poetic fire, but is very unequal. His great work by which he lives in literature is his translation of Homer. The *Iliad* was *pub.* in 1611, the *Odyssey* in 1616, and the *Hymns*, etc., in 1624. The work is full of energy and spirit, and well maintains its place among the many later translations by men of such high poetic powers as Pope and Cowper, and others: and it had the merit of suggesting Keats's immortal Sonnet, in which its name and memory are embalmed for many who know it in no other way. C. also translated from Petrarch, and completed Marlowe's unfinished *Hero and Leander*.

CHAPONE, HESTER (MULSO) (1727-1801).—Miscellaneous writer, *dau.* of a gentleman of Northamptonshire, was *m.* to a solicitor, who *d.* a few months afterwards. She was one of the learned ladies who gathered round Mrs. Montague (*q.v.*), and was the author of *Letters on the Improvement of the Mind* and *Miscellanies.*

CHARLETON, WALTER (1619-1707).—Miscellaneous writer, *ed.* at Oxf., was titular physician to Charles I. He was a copious writer on theology, natural history, and antiquities, and *pub. Chorea Gigantum* (1663) to prove that Stonehenge was built by the Danes. He was also one of the "character" writers, and in this kind of literature wrote *A Brief Discourse concerning the Different Wits of Men* (1675).

CHATTERTON, THOMAS (1752-1770).—Poet, *b.* at Bristol, posthumous *s.* of a schoolmaster, who had been a man of some reading and antiquarian tastes, after whose death his mother maintained herself and her boy and girl by teaching and needlework. A black-letter Bible and an illuminated music-book belonging to her were the first things to give his mind the impulse which led to such mingled glory and disaster. Living under the shadow of the great church of St. Mary Redcliffe, his mind was impressed from infancy with the beauty of antiquity, he obtained access to the charters deposited there, and he read every scrap of ancient literature that came in his way. At 14 he was apprenticed to a solicitor named Lambert, with whom he lived in sordid circumstances, eating in the kitchen and sleeping with the foot-boy, but continuing his favourite studies in every spare moment. In 1768 a new bridge was opened, and C. contributed to a local newspaper what purported to be a contemporary account of the old one which it superseded. This attracted a good deal of attention. Previously to this he had been writing verses and imitating ancient poems under the name of Thomas Rowley, whom he feigned to be a monk of the 15th century. Hearing of H. Walpole's collections for his *Anecdotes of Painting in England*, he sent him an "ancient manuscript" containing biographies of certain painters, not hitherto known, who had flourished in England centuries before. W. fell into the trap, and wrote asking for all the MS. he could furnish, and C. in response forwarded accounts of more painters, adding some particulars as to himself, on which W., becoming suspicious, submitted the whole to T. Gray and Mason (*q.v.*), who pronounced the MS. to be forgeries. Some correspondence, angry on C.'s part, ensued, and the whole budget of papers was returned. C. thereafter, having been dismissed by Lambert, went to London, and for a short time his prospects seemed to be bright. He worked with feverish energy, threw off poems, satires, and political papers, and meditated a history of England; but funds and spirits failed, he was starving, and the failure to obtain an appointment as ship's surgeon, for which he had applied, drove him to desperation, and on the morning of August 25, 1770, he was found dead from a dose of arsenic, surrounded by his writings torn into small pieces. From childhood C. had shown a morbid familiarity with the idea of suicide, and had written a last will and testament, "executed in the presence of Omniscience," and full of wild and profane wit. The magnitude of his tragedy is only realised when it is considered not only that the poetry he left was of a high order of originality and imaginative power, but that it was produced at an age at which our greatest poets, had they died, would have remained unknown. Precocious not only in genius but in dissipation, proud and morose as he was, an unsympathetic age confined itself mainly to awarding blame to his literary and moral delinquencies. Posterity has weighed him in a juster balance, and laments the early quenching of so brilliant a light. His *coll.* works appeared in 1803, and another ed. by Prof. Street in 1875. Among these are *Elinoure and Juga, Balade of Charitie, Bristowe Tragedie, Ælla,* and *Tragedy of Godwin.*

The best account of his life is the Essay by Prof. Masson.

CHAUCER, GEOFFREY (1340?-1400).—Poet, was *b.* in London, the *s.* of John C., a vintner of Thames Street, who had also a small estate at Ipswich, and was occasionally employed on service for the King (Edward III.), which doubtless was the means of his son's introduction to the Court. The acquaintance which C. displays with all branches of the learning of his time shows that he must have received an ample education; but there is no evidence that he was at either of the Univ. In 1357 he appears as a page to the Lady Elizabeth, wife of Lionel Duke of Clarence, and in 1359 he first saw military service in France, when he was made a prisoner. He was, however, ransomed in 1360. About 1366 he was married to Philippa, *dau.* of Sir Payne Roet, one of the ladies of the Duchess of Lancaster, whose sister Katharine, widow of Sir Hugh Swynford, became the third wife of John of Gaunt. Previous to this he had apparently been deeply in love with another lady, whose rank probably placed her beyond his reach; his disappointment finding expression in his *Compleynt to Pité.* In 1367 he was one of the valets of the King's Chamber, a post always held by gentlemen, and received a pension of 20 marks, and he was soon afterwards one of the King's esquires. In 1369 Blanche, the wife of John of Gaunt, died, which gave occasion for a poem by C. in honour of her memory, *The Dethe of Blaunche the Duchesse.* In the same year he again bore arms in France, and during the next ten years he was frequently employed on diplomatic missions. In 1370 he was sent to Genoa to arrange a commercial treaty, on which occasion he may have met Petrarch, and was rewarded by a grant in 1374 of a pitcher of wine daily. In the same year he got from the corporation of London a lease for life of a house at Aldgate, on condition of keeping it in repair; and soon after he was appointed Comptroller of the Customs and Subsidy of Wool, Skins, and Leather in the port of London; he also received from the Duke of Lancaster a pension of £10. In 1375 he obtained the guardianship of a rich ward, which he held for three years, and the next year he was employed on a secret service. In 1377 he was sent on a mission to Flanders to treat of peace with the French King. After the accession of Richard II. in that year, he was sent to France to treat for the marriage of the King with the French Princess Mary, and thereafter to Lombardy, on which occasion he appointed John Gower (*q.v.*) to act for him in his absence in any legal proceedings which might arise. In 1382 he became Comptroller of the Petty Customs of the port of London, and in 1385 was allowed to appoint a deputy, which enabled him to devote more time to writing. He had in 1373 begun his *Canterbury Tales*, on which he was occupied at intervals for the rest of his life. In 1386 C. was elected Knight of the Shire for Kent, a county with which he appears to have had some connection, and where he may have had property. His fortunes now suffered some eclipse. His patron, John of Gaunt, was abroad, and the government was presided over by his brother Gloucester, who was at feud with him. Owing probably to this cause, C. was in December, 1386, dismissed from his employments, leaving him with no income beyond his pensions, on which he was obliged to raise money. His wife also died at the same time. In 1389, however, Richard took the government into his own hands, and prosperity returned to C., whose friends were now in power, and he was appointed Clerk of the King's works. This office, however, he held for two years only, and again fell into poverty, from which he was rescued in 1394 by a pension from the King of £20. On the accession of Henry IV. (1399) an additional pension of 40 marks was given him. In the same year he took a lease of a house at Westminster, where he probably *d.*, October 25, 1400. He is buried in Poets' Corner, Westminster Abbey, where a monument to him was erected by Nicholas Brigham, a minor poet of the 16th century. According to some authorities he left two sons, Thomas, who became a man of wealth and importance, and Lewis, who died young, the little ten-year-old boy to whom he addressed the treatise on the *Astrolabe*. Others see no evidence that Thomas was any relation of the poet. An Elizabeth C., placed in the Abbey of Barking by John of Gaunt, was probably his *dau.* In person C. was inclined to corpulence, "no poppet to embrace," of fair complexion with "a beard the colour of ripe wheat," an "elvish" expression, and an eye downcast and meditative.

Of the works ascribed to C. several are, for various reasons, of greater or less strength, considered doubtful. These include *The Romaunt of the Rose*, *Chaucer's Dream*, and *The Flower and the Leaf*. After his return from Italy about 1380 he entered upon his period of greatest productiveness: *Troilus and Criseyde* (1382?), *The Parlement of Foules* (1382?), *The House of Fame* (1384?), and *The Legende of Goode Women* (1385), belong to this time. The first of them still remains one of the finest poems of its kind in the language. But the glory of C. is, of course, the *Canterbury Tales*, a work which places him in the front rank of the narrative poets of the world. It contains about 18,000 lines of verse, besides some passages in prose, and was left incomplete. In it his power of story-telling, his humour, sometimes broad, sometimes sly, his vivid picture-drawing, his tenderness, and lightness of touch, reach their highest development. He is our first artist in poetry, and with him begins modern English literature. His character — genial, sympathetic, and pleasure-loving, yet honest, diligent, and studious—is reflected in his writings.

SUMMARY.—*B.* 1340, fought in France 1359, by his marriage in 1366 became connected with John of Gaunt, employed on diplomatic missions 1369-79, Controller of Customs, etc., *c.* 1374, began *Canterbury Tales* 1373, elected to Parliament 1386, loses his appointments 1386, Clerk of King's Works 1389-91, pensioned by Richard II. and Henry IV., *d. c.* 1400.

The best ed. of C. is *The Complete Works of Geoffrey Chaucer* (6 vols. 1894), ed. by Prof. Skeat. Others are Thos. Wright's for the Percy Society (1842), and Richard Morris's in Bell's Aldine Classics (1866).

CHERRY, ANDREW (1762-1812).—Dramatist, *s.* of a bookseller at Limerick, was a successful actor, and managed theatres in the provinces. He also wrote some plays, of which *The Soldier's Daughter* is the best. His chief claim to remembrance rests on his three songs, *The Bay of Biscay, The Green Little Shamrock*, and *Tom Moody*.

CHESTERFIELD, PHILIP DORMER STANHOPE, 4TH EARL OF (1694-1773).—Statesman and letter-writer, was the eldest *s.* of the 3rd Earl. After being at Trinity Coll., Camb., he sat in the House of Commons until his accession to the peerage in 1726. He filled many high offices, including those of Ambassador to Holland, Lord Lieutenant of Ireland, and Sec. of State. He was distinguished for his wit, conversational powers, and grace of manner. His place in literature is fixed by his well-known *Letters* addressed to his natural son, Philip Dormer Stanhope. Though brilliant, and full of shrewdness and knowledge of the world, they reflect the low tone of morals prevalent in the age when they were written. He was the recipient of Johnson's famous letter as to his "patronage."

CHETTLE, HENRY (1565-1607?).—Dramatist. Very little is known of him. He ed. R. Greene's *Groat's-worth of Wit* (1592), is believed to have written 13 and collaborated in 35 plays. He also wrote two satires, *Kind Harts Dreame* (1593), and *Pierre Plainnes Prentship* (1595). He was imprisoned for debt 1599.

Among his own plays, which have considerable merit, is *Hoffmann*, which has been reprinted, and he had a hand in *Patient Grissill* (1603) (which may have influenced Shakespeare in the *Merry Wives of Windsor*), *The Blind Beggar of Bethnal Green*, and *Jane Shore*.

CHILD, FRANCIS J. (1825-1896).—English scholar, *b.* at Boston, Mass., was a prof. at Harvard, one of the foremost students of early English, and especially of ancient ballads in America. He ed. the American ed. of English Poets in 130 vols., and English and Scottish Ballads. He was also a profound student of Chaucer, and *pub. Observations on the Language of Chaucer*, and *Observations on the Language of Gower's Confessio Amantis*.

CHILD, MRS. LYDIA MARIA (FRANCIS) (1802-1880).—Was the author of many once popular tales, *Hobomok, The Rebels, Philothes*, etc.

CHILLINGWORTH, WILLIAM (1602-1644).—Theologian and controversialist, *b.* and *ed.* at Oxf., was god-son of Archbishop Laud. Falling into theological doubts. he subsequently became a convert to Roman Catholicism, and studied at the Jesuit Coll. at Douay, 1630. In the following year he returned to Oxf., and after further consideration of the points at issue, he rejoined the Church of England, 1634. This exposed him to violent attacks on the part of the Romanists, in reply to which he *pub.* in 1637 his famous polemic, *The Religion of the Protestants a Safe Way to Salvation,* characterised by clear style and logical reasoning. For a time he refused ecclesiastical preferment, but ultimately his scruples were overcome, and he became Prebendary and Chancellor of Salisbury. C. is regarded as one of the ablest controversialists of the Anglican Church.

CHURCH, RICHARD WILLIAM (1815-1890).—Divine, historian, and biographer, was *b.* at Lisbon, and *ed.* at Oxf., where he became a friend of J. H. Newman (*q.v.*). He took orders, and became Rector of Whatley, Somerset, and in 1871 Dean of St. Paul's. He was a leading member of the High Church party, but was held in reverence by many who did not sympathise with his ecclesiastical views. Among his writings are *The Beginning of the Middle Ages* (1877), and a memoir on *The Oxford Movement* (1891), *pub.* posthumously. He also wrote Lives of Anselm, Dante, Spenser, and Bacon.

CHURCHILL, CHARLES (1731-1764).—Satirist, *s.* of a clergyman, was *ed.* at Westminster School, and while still a schoolboy made a clandestine marriage. He entered the Church, and on the death of his *f.* in 1758 succeeded him in the curacy and lectureship of St. John's, Westminster. In 1761 he *pub.* the *Rosciad,* in which he severely satirised the players and managers of the day. It at once brought him both fame and money; but he fell into dissipated habits, separated from his wife, and outraged the proprieties of his profession to such an extent that he was compelled to resign his preferments. He also incurred the enmity of those whom he had attacked, which led to the publication of two other satirical pieces, *The Apology* and *Night.* He also attacked Dr. Johnson and his circle in *The Ghost,* and the Scotch in *The Prophecy of Famine.* He attached himself to John Wilkes, on a visit to whom, at Boulogne, he *d.* of fever.

CHURCHYARD, THOMAS (1520?-1604).—Poet and miscellaneous writer, began life as a page to the Earl of Surrey, and subsequently passed through many vicissitudes as a soldier in Scotland, Ireland, France, and the Low Countries. He was latterly a hanger-on at Court, and had a pension of eighteenpence a day from Queen Elizabeth, which was not, however, regularly paid. He wrote innumerable pamphlets and broadsides, and some poems, of which the best are *Shore's Wife* (1563), *The Worthiness of Wales* (1587) *repub.* by the Spenser Society (1871), and *Churchyard's Chips* (1575), an autobiographical piece.

CIBBER, COLLEY (1671-1757).—Actor and dramatist, *b.* in London, *s.* of a Danish sculptor, and *ed.* at Grantham School. Soon after his return to London he took to the stage. Beginning with tragedy, in which he failed, he turned to comedy, and became popular in eccentric *rôles.* In 1696 he brought out his first play, *Love's Last Shift,* and produced in all about 30 plays, some of which were very successful. In 1730 he was made Poet Laureate, and wrote some forgotten odes of no merit, also an entertaining autobiography. Pope made him the hero of the *Dunciad.*

Among other plays are *The Nonjuror* (1717), *Woman's Wit, She*

Would and She Would Not, The Provoked Husband (1728) (with Vanbrugh).

CLARE, JOHN (1793-1864).—Poet, *s.* of a cripple pauper, was *b.* at Helpstone near Peterborough. His youth is the record of a noble struggle against adverse circumstances. With great difficulty he managed to save one pound, with which he was able to have a prospectus of his first book of poems printed, which led to an acquaintance with Mr. Drury, a bookseller in Stamford, by whose help the poems were *pub.*, and brought him £20. The book, *Poems descriptive of Rural Life* (1820), immediately attracted attention. Various noblemen befriended him and stocked a farm for him. But unfortunately C. had no turn for practical affairs, and got into difficulties. He, however, continued to produce poetry, and in addition to *The Village Minstrel*, which had appeared in 1821, *pub. The Shepherd's Calendar* (1827), and *Rural Muse* (1835). Things, however, went on from bad to worse; his mind gave way, and he *d.* in an asylum. C. excels in description of rural scenes and the feelings and ideas of humble country life.

CLARENDON, EDWARD HYDE, EARL OF (1608-1674).—Lawyer, statesman, and historian, *s.* of a country gentleman of good estate in Wiltshire, was *b.* at Dinton in that county, and *ed.* at Oxf. Destined originally for the Church, circumstances led to his being sent to London to study law, which he did under his uncle, Sir Nicholas H., Chief Justice of the King's Bench. In early life he was the friend of all the leading men of the day. Entering Parliament in 1640 he at first supported popular measures, but, on the outbreak of the Civil War, attached himself to the King, and was the author of many of his state papers. From 1648 until the Restoration C. was engaged in various embassies and as a counsellor of Charles II., who made him in 1658 his Lord Chancellor, an office in which he was confirmed at the Restoration, when he also became Chancellor of the Univ. of Oxf., and was likewise raised to the peerage. His power and influence came to an end, however, in 1667, when he was dismissed from all his offices, was impeached, and had to fly to France. The causes of his fall were partly the miscarriage of the war with Holland, and the sale of Dunkirk, and partly the jealousy of rivals and the intrigues of place hunters, whose claims he had withstood. In his enforced retirement he engaged himself in completing his great historic work, *The History of the Rebellion and Civil Wars in England*, which he had begun in 1641, and which was not *pub.* until 1702-4. C.'s style is easy, flowing, diffuse, and remarkably modern, with an occasional want of clearness owing to his long and involved sentences. His great strength is in character-painting, in which he is almost unrivalled. The *History* was followed by a supplementary *History of the Civil War in Ireland* (1721). C. also wrote an autobiography, *The Life of Edward Earl of Clarendon* (1759), a reply to the *Leviathan* of Hobbes, and *An Essay on the Active and Contemplative Life*, in which the superiority of the former is maintained. C. *d.* at Rouen. He was a man of high personal character, and great intellect and sagacity, but lacking in the firmness and energy necessary for the troublous times in which he lived. His *dau.* Anne married the

Duke of York, afterwards James II., a connection which involved him in much trouble and humiliation.

CLARKE, CHARLES COWDEN (1787-1877).—Writer on Shakespeare, etc., friend of Keats, and a publisher in London. Latterly he lived in France and Italy. His wife, MARY C.-C. (1809-1898), *dau.* of V. Novello, musician, compiled a complete *Concordance to Shakespeare* (1844-45), and wrote *The Shakespeare Key* (1879) and, with her husband, *Recollections of Writers* (1878).

CLARKE, MARCUS (1846-1881).—Novelist, *b.* in London, went to Australia, where he took to journalism. He wrote two novels, *Long Odds* and *For the Term of his Natural Life* (1874), the latter dealing in a powerful and realistic manner with transportation and convict labour. He also wrote *Lower Bohemia in Melbourne*, *The Humbug Papers*, *The Future Australian Race*.

CLARKE, SAMUEL (1675-1729).—Divine and metaphysician, *b.* at Norwich, was *ed.* at Camb., where he became the friend and disciple of Newton, whose System of the Universe he afterwards defended against Leibnitz. In 1704-5 he delivered the Boyle lectures, *The Being and Attributes of God*, assuming an intermediate position between orthodoxy and Deism. In 1712 he *pub.* views on the doctrine of the Trinity which involved him in trouble, from which he escaped by a somewhat unsatisfactory explanation. He was, however, a powerful opponent of the freethinkers of the time. C. also *pub.* an ed. of the *Iliad*, a Latin translation of the *Optics* of Newton, on whose death he was offered the Mastership of the Mint, which, however, he declined.

CLEMENS, SAMUEL LANGHORNE ("MARK TWAIN") (1835-1910).—American Humourist, *b.* at Florida, Missouri. After working as a printer and as a Mississippi pilot, he became a journalist in San Francisco. The result of a tour to the Mediterranean was *The Innocents Abroad* (1869). Other works were *The Jumping Frog* (1867), *Adventures of Tom Sawyer* (1876), *A Tramp Abroad* (1880), *Life on the Mississippi* (1883), *Huckleberry Finn* (1885), *The £1,000,000 Bank Note* (1893), *Pudd'nhead Wilson* (1894), *The Man that Corrupted Hadleyburg* (1900), and *Christian Science* (1907). In the midst of his success he was overtaken by a heavy financial disaster through the failure of a publishing firm of which he had become a partner. He however set himself to work off his liabilities. Though his humour was often rather mechanical or rough, it was often keen, subtle, and based on serious principles. In 1907 he visited England, and was received with enthusiasm, and among other distinctions received from Oxford the degree of LL.D.

CLEVELAND, JOHN (1613-1658).—Poet, *s.* of an usher in a charity school, was *b.* at Loughborough, and *ed.* at Camb., where he became coll. tutor and lecturer on rhetoric at St. John's, and was much sought after. A staunch Royalist, he opposed the election of Oliver Cromwell as member for Camb. in the Long Parliament, and was in consequence ejected from his coll. in 1645. Joining the King, by whom he was welcomed, he was appointed to the office of Judge Advocate at Newark. In 1646, however, he was deprived of this, and wandered about the country dependent on the bounty of the Royalists. In 1655 he was imprisoned at Yarmouth, but released by Cromwell, to whom he appealed, and went to London, where he lived in much consideration till his death. His best work is satirical, giving a faint adumbration of *Hudibras;* his other poems, with occasional passages of great beauty, being affected and artificial. The *Poems* were *pub.* in 1656.

CLINTON, HENRY FYNES (1781-1852).—Chronologist, *b.* at Gamston, Notts, *ed.* at Southwell, Westminster, and Oxf., where he devoted himself chiefly to the study of Greek. Brought into Parliament by the Duke of Newcastle in 1806, he took no active part in political life, and retired in 1826. He bought in 1810 the estate of Welwyn, and there he entered upon wide and profound studies bearing upon classical chronology, and wrote various important treatises on the subject, viz., *Fasti Hellenici, Civil and Literary Chronology of Greece,* part i. (1824), part ii. (1827), part iii. (1830), part iv. (1841), *Fasti Romani, Civil and Literary Chronology of Rome and Constantinople,* vol. i. (1850), vol. ii. (1851), *An Epitome of the Civil and Literary Chronology of Greece* (1851), the same for Rome (1853). He also wrote a tragedy, *Solyman,* which was a failure.

CLOUGH, ARTHUR HUGH (1819-1861).—Poet, *s.* of a cotton merchant in Liverpool, he spent his childhood in America, but was sent back to England for his education, which he received at Rugby and Oxf. While at the Univ., where he was tutor and Fellow of Oriel, he fell under the influence of Newman, but afterwards became a sceptic and resigned his Fellowship in 1848. In the same year he *pub.* his poem, *The Bothie of Tober-na-Vuolich,* written in hexameters. After travelling on the Continent for a year, he was in 1849 appointed Warden of Univ. Hall, London. In 1849 appeared *Amours de Voyage,* a rhymed novelette, and the more serious work, *Dipsychus.* In 1854 he was appointed an examiner in the Education Office, and married. His last appointment was as Sec. of a Commission on Military Schools, in connection with which he visited various countries, but was seized with illness, and *d.* at Florence. C. was a man of singularly sincere character, with a passion for truth. His poems, though full of fine and subtle thought, are, with the exception of some short lyrics, deficient in form, and the hexameters which he employed in *The Bothie* are often rough, though perhaps used as effectively as by any English verse-writer. M. Arnold's *Thyrsis* was written in memory of C.

COBBE, FRANCES POWER (1822-1904).—Theological and social writer, was *b.* near Dublin. Coming under the influence of Theodore Parker, she became a Unitarian. Her first work, *pub.* anonymously, was on *The Intuitive Theory of Morals* (1855). She travelled in the East, and *pub. Cities of the Past* (1864). Later she became interested in social questions and philanthropic work, and wrote many books on these and kindred subjects, including *Criminals, Idiots, Women* and *Minors* (1869), *Darwinism in Morals* (1872), and *Scientific Spirit of the Age* (1888). She was a strong opponent of vivisection.

COBBETT, WILLIAM (1762-1835).—Essayist and political writer, *b.* at Farnham, Surrey, *s.* of a small farmer, his youth was spent as a farm labourer, a clerk, and in the army, in which his good conduct and intelligence led to his promotion to the rank of sergeant-major. After moving about between England and America, and alternating between journalism and agriculture, in the former of which his daring opposition to men in power got him into frequent trouble and subjected him to heavy fines in both countries, he settled down in England in 1800, and continued his career as a political writer, first as a Tory and then as a Radical. His violent changes of opinion, and the force and severity with which he expressed himself naturally raised up enemies in both camps. In 1817 he went back to America, where he remained for two years. Returning he stood, in 1821, for a seat in Parliament, but was unsuccessful. In 1832, however, he was returned for Oldham, but made no mark as a speaker. C. was one of the best known men of his day. His intellect was narrow, but intensely clear, and he was master of a nervous and idiomatic English style which enabled him to project his ideas into the minds of his readers. His chief writings are *English Grammar, Rural Rides, Advice to Young Men and Women.* His *Weekly Political Register* ran from 1802 until his death.

COCKBURN, HENRY (1779-1854).—Scottish judge and biographer, *b.* (probably) and *ed.* in Edin., became a distinguished member of the Scottish Bar, and ultimately a judge. He was also one of the leaders of the Whig party in Scotland in its days of darkness prior to the Reform Act of 1832. The life-long friend of Francis Jeffrey, he wrote his life, *pub.* in 1852. His chief literary work, however, is his *Memorials of his Time* (1856), continued in his *Journal* (1874). These constitute an autobiography of the writer interspersed with notices of manners, public events, and sketches of his contemporaries, of great interest and value.

COLENSO, JOHN WILLIAM (1814-1883).—Mathematician and Biblical critic, *b.* at St. Austell, Cornwall, and *ed.* at St. John's Coll., Camb., where he was a tutor, entered the Church, and *pub.* various mathematical treatises and *Village Sermons.* In 1853 he was appointed first Bishop of Natal. He mastered the Zulu language, introduced printing, wrote a Zulu grammar and dictionary, and many useful reading-books for the natives. His *Commentary on the Romans* (1861) excited great opposition from the High Church party, and his *Critical Examination of the Pentateuch* (1862-1879), by its then extreme views, created great alarm and excitement. He was in 1863 deposed and excommunicated by Bishop Gray of Cape Town, but confirmed in his see by the Courts of Law.

COLERIDGE, HARTLEY (1796-1849).—Poet, eldest *s.* of Samuel T. C. (*q.v.*), *b.* at Clevedon, spent his youth at Keswick among the "Lake poets." His early education was desultory, but he was sent by Southey to Oxf. in 1815. His talents enabled him to win a Fellowship, but the weakness of his character led to his being deprived of it. He then went to London and wrote for magazines. From 1823 to 1828 he tried keeping a school at Ambleside, which failed, and he then led the life of a recluse at Grasmere until his death. Here he wrote *Essays*, *Biographia Borealis* (lives of worthies of the northern counties) (1832), and a *Life of Massinger* (1839). He is remembered chiefly for his *Sonnets*. He also left unfinished a drama, *Prometheus*.

COLERIDGE, MARY ELIZABETH (1861–1907).—Great-niece of S. T. Coleridge, made her reputation in 1897 with a historical romance *The King with Two Faces*. But she is chiefly remembered for her poems, which appeared anonymously in volume form in 1896–7–8 and in periodicals from 1900–7. A posthumous collection was published in 1907 (*Poems, Old and New*).

COLERIDGE, SAMUEL TAYLOR (1772-1834).—Poet, philosopher, and critic, *s.* of the Rev. John C., vicar and schoolmaster of Ottery St. Mary, Devonshire, was *b.* there in 1772, the youngest of 13 children. He was at Christ's Hospital from 1782 to 1790, and had Charles Lamb for a schoolfellow, and the famous scholar and disciplinarian, James Boyer, for his master. Thence he proceeded to Jesus Coll., Camb., in 1791, where he read much, but desultorily, and got into debt. The troubles arising thence and also, apparently, a disappointment in love, led to his going to London and enlisting in the 15th Dragoons under the name of Silas Tomkyn Comberbacke. He could not, however, be taught to ride, and through some Latin lines written by him on a stable door, his real condition was discovered, his friends communicated with, and his release accomplished, his brothers buying him off. After this escapade he returned (1794) to Camb. He had by this time imbibed extreme democratic or, as he termed them, pantisocratic principles, and on leaving Camb. in the same year he visited Oxf., where he made the acquaintance of Southey, and discussed with him a project of founding a "pantisocracy" on the banks of the Susquehanna, a scheme which speedily fell through, owing firstly to want of funds, and secondly to the circumstance of the two projectors falling in love simultaneously with two sisters, Sarah and Edith Fricker, of whom the former became, in 1795, the wife of C., and the latter of Southey. C. had spent one more term at Camb., and there in Sept. 1794 his first work, *The Fall of Robespierre*, a drama, to which Southey contributed two acts, the second and third, was *pub.* After his marriage he settled first at Clevedon, and thereafter at Nether Stowey, Somerset, where he had Wordsworth for a neighbour, with whom he formed an intimate association. About 1796 he fell into the fatal habit of taking laudanum, which had such disastrous effects upon his character and powers of will. In the same year *Poems on various Subjects* appeared, and a little later *Ode to the Departing Year*. While at Nether Stowey he was practically supported by Thomas Poole, a tanner, with whom he had formed a friendship. Here he wrote *The Ancient Mariner*, the first part of *Christabel* and *Kubla Khan*, and here he joined with Wordsworth in producing the *Lyrical Ballads*. Some time previously he had become a Unitarian, and was much engaged as a preacher in that body, and for a short time acted as a minister at Shrewsbury. Influenced by Josiah and Thomas Wedgwood, who each in 1798 gave him an annuity of £75 on condition of his devoting himself to literature, he resigned this position, and soon afterwards went to Germany, where he remained for over a year, an experience which profoundly influenced the future development of his intellect. On his return he made excursions with Southey and Wordsworth, and at the end of 1799 went to London, where he wrote and reported for the *Morning Post*. His great translation of Schiller's *Wallenstein* appeared in 1800. In the same year he migrated to Greta Hall, near Keswick, where he wrote the second part of *Christabel*. Soon after this his health gave way, and he suffered much; and, whether as the cause or the consequence of this, he had become a slave to opium. In 1804 he went to Malta in search of health, and there became the friend of the governor, Sir Alexander Ball, who appointed him his sec., in which position he showed remarkable capacity for affairs. Resigning this occupation, of which he had become tired, he travelled in Italy, and in the beginning of 1806 reached Rome, where he enjoyed the friendship of Tieck, Humboldt, and Bunsen. He returned to England in the end of 1806, and in 1808 delivered his first course of lectures on Shakespeare at the Royal Institution, and thereafter (1809), leaving his family at Keswick, he went to live with Wordsworth at Grasmere. Here he started *The Friend*, a philosophical and theological periodical, which lasted for 9 months. That part of his annuity contributed by T. Wedgwood had been confirmed to him by will in 1805, and this he allowed to his wife, but in 1811 the remaining half was stopped. He delivered a second course of lectures in London, and in 1813 his drama, *Remorse*, was acted at Drury Lane with success. Leaving his family dependent upon Southey, he lived with various friends, first, from 1816 to 1819, with John Morgan at Calne. While there he *pub. Christabel* and *Kubla Khan* in 1816, and in 1817 *Biographia Literaria, Sybilline Leaves*, and an autobiography. In 1818 he appeared for the last time as a lecturer. He found in 1819 a final resting-place in the household of James Gillman, a surgeon, at Highgate. His life thenceforth was a splendid wreck. His nervous system was shattered, and he was a constant sufferer. Yet these last years were, in some respects, his best. He maintained a struggle against opium which lasted with his life, and though he ceased to write much, he became the revered centre of a group of disciples, including such men as Sterling, Maurice, and Hare, and thus indirectly continued and increased his influence in the philosophic and theological thought of his time. He returned to Trinitarianism, and a singular and childlike humility became one of his most marked characteristics. In 1824 he was elected an Assoicate of the Royal Society of Literature, which brought him a pension of 100 guineas. His latest publications were *Aids to Reflection* (1825) and *The Constitution of Church and State*. After his death there were *pub.*, among other works, *Table Talk* (1835), *Confessions of an Enquiring Spirit* (1840), *Letters* and *Anima Poetæ* (1895).

Endowed with an intellect of the first order, and an imagination at once delicate and splendid, C., from a weakness of moral constitution, and the lamentable habit already referred to, fell far short of the performance which he had planned, and which included various epic poems, and a complete system of philosophy, in which all knowledge was to be co-ordinated. He has, however, left enough poetry of such excellence as to place him in the first rank of English poets, and enough philosophic, critical, and theological matter to constitute him one of the principal intellectually formative forces of his time. His knowledge of philosophy, science, theology, and literature was alike wide and deep, and his powers of conversation, or rather monologue, were almost unique. A description of him in later life tells of "the clerical-looking dress, the thick, waving, silver hair, the youthful coloured cheek, the indefinable mouth and lips, the quick, yet steady and penetrating greenish-grey eye, the slow and continuous enunciation, and the everlasting music of his tones."

SUMMARY.—*B.* 1772, *ed.* Christ's Hospital and Camb., enlists 1794 but bought off, became intimate with Southey, and proposes to found pantisocracy, settles at Clevedon and Nether Stowey 1795, and became friend of Wordsworth, began to take opium 1796, writes *Ancient Mariner*, and joins W. in *Lyrical Ballads*, became Unitarian preacher, visits Germany 1798, *pub.* translation of *Wallenstein* 1800, settles at Greta Hall and finishes *Christabel*, goes to Malta 1804, lectures on Shakespeare 1808, leaves his family and lives with W. 1809, and thereafter with various friends, latterly with Gillman at Highgate, returned to Trinitarianism, *pub.* various works 1808-1825, *d.* 1834.

S. T. Coleridge, a Narrative, J. D. Campbell (1893), also H. D. Traill (Men of Letters Series, 1884), also Pater's *Appreciations*, De Quincey's Works, Principal Shairp's *Studies in Poetry and Philosophy* (1868).

COLERIDGE, SARA (1802-1852).—Miscellaneous writer, the only *dau.* of the above, *m.* her cousin, Henry Nelson C. She translated Dobrizhöffer's *Account of the Abipones*, and *The Joyous and Pleasant History . . . of the Chevalier Bayard*. Her original works are *Pretty Lessons in Verse*, etc. (1834), which was very popular, and a fairy tale, *Phantasmion*. She also ed. her father's works, to which she added an essay on Rationalism.

COLET, JOHN (1467-1519).—Scholar and theologian, was *b.* in London, the *s.* of a wealthy citizen, who was twice Lord Mayor. The only survivor of a family of 22, he went to Oxf. and Paris, and thence to Italy, where he learned Greek. He entered the Church, and held many preferments, including the Deanery of St. Paul's. He continued to follow out his studies, devoting himself chiefly to St. Paul's epistles. He was outspoken against the corruptions of the Church, and would have been called to account but for the protection of Archbishop Warham. He devoted his great fortune to founding and endowing St. Paul's School. Among his works are a treatise on the Sacraments and various devotional writings. It is rather for his learning and his attitude to the advancement of knowledge than for his own writings that he has a place in the history of English literature.

COLLIER, JEREMY (1650-1726).—Church historian and controversialist, *b.* at Stow, Cambridgeshire, *ed.* at Ipswich and Camb., entered the Church, and became Rector of Ampton, Suffolk, lecturer of Gray's Inn, London, and ultimately a nonjuring bishop. He was a man of war from his youth, and was engaged in controversies almost until his death. His first important one was with Gilbert Burnet, and led to his being imprisoned in Newgate. He was, however, a man of real learning. His chief writings are his *Ecclesiastical History of Great Britain* (1708-1714), and especially his *Short View of the Immorality and Profaneness of the English Stage* (1699), on account of which he was attacked by Congreve and Farquhar, for whom, however, he showed himself more than a match. The work materially helped towards the subsequent purification of the stage.

COLLINS, JOHN (*d.* 1808).—Actor and writer, was a staymaker, but took to the stage, on which he was fairly successful. He also gave humorous entertainments and *pub. Scripscrapologia*, a book of verses. He is worthy of mention for the little piece, *Tomorrow*, beginning "In the downhill of life when I find I'm declining," characterised by Palgrave as "a truly noble poem."

COLLINS, JOHN CHURTON (1848-1908).—Writer on literature and critic, *b.* in Gloucestershire, and *ed.* at King Edward's School, Birmingham, and Oxf., became in 1894 Prof. of English Literature at Birmingham. He wrote books on *Sir J. Reynolds* (1874), *Voltaire in England* (1886), *Illustrations of Tennyson* (1891), and also on Swift and Shakespeare, various collections of essays, *Essays and Studies* (1895), and *Studies in Poetry and Criticism* (1905), etc., and he issued ed. of the works of C. Tourneur, Greene, Dryden, Herbert of Cherbury, etc.

COLLINS, MORTIMER (1827-1876).—Novelist, *s.* of a solicitor at Plymouth, was for a time a teacher of mathematics in Guernsey. Settling in Berkshire he adopted a literary life, and was a prolific author, writing largely for periodicals. He also wrote a good deal of occasional and humorous verse, and several novels, including *Sweet Anne Page* (1868), *Two Plunges for a Pearl* (1872), *Mr. Carrington* (1873), under the name of "R. T. Cotton," and *A Fight with Fortune* (1876).

COLLINS, WILLIAM (1721-1759).—Poet, *s.* of a respectable hatter at Chichester, where he was *b.* He was *ed.* at Chichester, Winchester, and Oxf. His is a melancholy career. Disappointed with the reception of his poems, especially his Odes, he sank into despondency, fell into habits of intemperance, and after fits of melancholy, deepening into insanity, *d.* a physical and mental wreck. Posterity has signally reversed the judgment of his contemporaries, and has placed him at the head of the lyrists of his age. He did not write much, but all that he wrote is precious. His first publication was a small vol. of poems, including the *Persian* (afterwards called *Oriental*) *Eclogues* (1742); but his principal work was his *Odes* (1747), including those to *Evening* and *The Passions*, which will live as long as the language. When Thomson died in 1748 C., who had been his friend, commemorated him in a beautiful ode. Another—left unfinished—that on the *Superstitions of the Scottish Highlands*, was for many years lost sight of, but was discovered by Dr. Alex.

Carlyle (*q.v.*). C.'s poetry is distinguished by its high imaginative quality, and by exquisitely felicitous descriptive phrases.

Memoirs prefixed to Dyce's ed. of Poems (1827), Aldine ed., Moy Thomas, 1892.

COLLINS, WILLIAM WILKIE (1824-1889).—Novelist, *s.* of William C., R.A., entered Lincoln's Inn, and was called to the Bar 1851, but soon relinquished law for literature. His first novel was *Antonina* (1850), a historical romance. He found his true field, however, in the novel of modern life, in which his power lies chiefly in the construction of a skilful plot, which holds the attention of the reader and baffles his curiosity to the last. In Count Fosco, however, he has contributed an original character to English fiction. Among his numerous novels two, *The Woman in White* (1860), and *The Moonstone* (1868), stand out pre-eminent. Others are *The Dead Secret* (1857), *Armadale* (1866), *No Name* (1862), *After Dark*, "*I say No*," etc. He collaborated with Dickens in *No Thoroughfare*.

COLMAN, GEORGE, THE ELDER (1732-1794).—Dramatist, *b.* at Florence, where his *f.* was British Envoy, he was a friend of Garrick, and took to writing for the stage with success. He wrote more than 30 dramatic pieces, of which the best known are *The Jealous Wife* (1761), and *The Clandestine Marriage* (1766). C. was also manager and part proprietor of various theatres. He was a scholar and translated Terence and the *De Arte Poetica* of Horace, wrote essays, and ed. Beaumont and Fletcher and B. Jonson.

COLMAN, GEORGE, THE YOUNGER (1762-1836).—Dramatist, *s.* of the preceding, wrote or adapted numerous plays, including *The Heir at Law* and *John Bull*. He was Examiner of Plays (1824-1836). Many of his plays are highly amusing, and keep their place on the stage. His wit made him popular in society, and he was a favourite with George IV.

COLTON, CHARLES CALEB (1780-1832).—Miscellaneous writer, *ed.* at Eton and Camb., took orders and held various livings. He was an eccentric man of talent, with little or no principle, took to gaming, and had to leave the country. He *d.* by his own hand. His books, mainly collections of epigrammatic aphorisms and short essays on conduct, etc., though now almost forgotten, had a phenomenal popularity in their day. Among them are *Lacon, or Many Things in Few Words*, and a few poems.

COMBE, GEORGE (1788-1858).—Writer on phrenology and education, *b.* in Edin., where for some time he practised as a lawyer. Latterly, however, he devoted himself to the promotion of phrenology, and of his views on education, for which he in 1848 founded a school. His chief work was *The Constitution of Man* (1828).

COMBE, WILLIAM (1741-1823).—Miscellaneous writer. His early life was that of an adventurer, his later was passed chiefly within the "rules" of the King's Bench prison. He is chiefly remembered as the author of *The Three Tours of Dr. Syntax*, a comic poem (?). His cleverest piece of work was a series of imaginary letters, supposed to have been written by the second, or "wicked" Lord Lyttelton. Of a similar kind were his letters between Swift and Stella. He also wrote the letterpress for various illustrated books, and was a general hack.

CONGREVE, WILLIAM (1670-1729). Dramatist, was *b.* in Yorkshire. In boyhood he was taken to Ireland, and *ed.* at Kilkenny and at Trinity Coll., Dublin. In 1688 he returned to England and entered the Middle Temple, but does not appear to have practised, and took to writing for the stage. His first comedy, *The Old Bachelor*, was produced with great applause in 1693, and was followed by *The Double Dealer* (1693), *Love for Love* (1695), and *The Way of the World* (1700), and by a tragedy, *The Mourning Bride* (1697). His comedies are all remarkable for wit and sparkling dialogue, but their profanity and licentiousness have driven them from the stage. These latter qualities brought them under the lash of Jeremy Collier (*q.v.*) in his *Short View of the English Stage*. Congreve rushed into controversy with his critic who, however, proved too strong for him. C. was a favourite at Court, and had various lucrative offices conferred upon him. In his latter years he was blind; otherwise his life was prosperous, and he achieved his chief ambition of being admired as a fine gentleman and gallant.

Life, Gosse (1888). *Works*, ed. by Henley (1895), also Mermaid Series (1888).

CONINGTON, JOHN (1825-1869).—Translator, *s.* of a clergyman at Boston, Lincolnshire, where he was *b.*, *ed.* at Rugby, and Magdalen and Univ. Coll., Oxf., and began the study of law, but soon relinquished it, and devoting himself to scholarship, became Prof. of Latin at Oxf. (1854-1869). His chief work is his translation of Virgil's *Æneid* in the octosyllabic metre of Scott (1861-68). He also translated the *Satires* and *Epistles* of Horace in Pope's couplets, and completed Worsley's *Iliad* in Spenserian stanza. He also brought out valuable ed. of Virgil and Perseus. C. was one of the greatest translators whom England has produced.

CONSTABLE, HENRY (1562-1613).—Poet, *s.* of Sir Robert C., *ed.* at Camb., but becoming a Roman Catholic, went to Paris, and acted as an agent for the Catholic powers. He *d.* at Liège. In 1592 he *pub. Diana*, a collection of sonnets, and contributed to *England's Helicon* four poems, including *Diaphenia* and *Venus and Adonis*. His style is characterised by fervour and richness of colour.

COOKE, JOHN ESTEN (1830-1886).—Novelist, *b.* in Virginia, illustrated the life and history of his native state in the novels, *The Virginia Comedians* (1854), and *The Wearing of the Gray*, a tale of the Civil War, and more formally in an excellent History of the State. His style was somewhat high-flown.

COOPER, JAMES FENIMORE (1789-1851).—Novelist, *b.* at Burlington, New Jersey, and *ed.* at Yale Coll., he in 1808 entered the U.S. Navy, in which he remained for 3 years, an experience which was of immense future value to him as an author. It was not until 1821 that his first novel, *Precaution*, appeared. Its want of success did not discourage him, and in the next year (1822), he produced *The Spy*, which at once gained him a high place as a story-teller. He wrote over 30 novels, of which may be mentioned *The Pioneers* (1823), *The Pilot* (1823), *The Last of the Mohicans* (1826), *The Prairie* (1826), *The Red Rover* (1831), *The Bravo* (1840), *The Pathfinder*, *The Deerslayer* (1841), *The Two Admirals* (1842), and *Satanstoe* (1845). He also wrote a *Naval History of the United States* (1839). C. was possessed of remarkable narrative and descriptive powers, and could occasionally delineate character. He had the merit of opening up an entirely new field, and giving expression to the spirit of the New World, but his true range was limited, and he sometimes showed a lack of judgment in choosing subjects with which he was not fitted to deal. He was a proud and combative but honest and estimable man.

COOPER, THOMAS (1805-1892).—Chartist poet, was *b.* at Leicester, and apprenticed to a shoemaker. In spite of hardships and difficulties, he *ed.* himself, and at 23 was a schoolmaster. He became a leader and lecturer among the Chartists, and in 1842 was imprisoned in Stafford gaol for two years, where he wrote his *Purgatory of Suicides*, a political epic. At the same time he adopted sceptical views, which he continued to hold until 1855, when he became a Christian, joined the Baptists, and was a preacher among them. In his latter years he settled down into an old-fashioned Radical. His friends in 1867 raised an annuity for him, and in the last year of his life he received a government pension. In addition to his poems he wrote several novels. Somewhat impulsive, he was an honest and sincere man.

CORBET, RICHARD (1582-1635).—Poet, *s.* of a gardener, was *ed.* at Westminster School and Oxf., and entered the Church, in which he obtained many preferments, and rose to be Bishop successively of Oxf. and Norwich. He was celebrated for his wit, which not seldom passed into buffoonery. His poems, which are often mere doggerel, were not *pub.* until after his death. They include *Journey to France*, *Iter Boreale*, the account of a tour from Oxf. to Newark, and the *Farewell to the Fairies*.

CORNWALL, BARRY, *see* PROCTER, B. W.

CORY, WILLIAM JOHNSON (1823-1892).—Poet, *b.* at Torrington, and *ed.* at Eton, where he was afterwards a master. He was a brilliant writer of Latin verse. His chief poetical work is *Ionica*, containing poems in which he showed a true lyrical gift.

CORYATE, OR CORYATT, THOMAS (1577-1617).—Poet, *b.* at Odcombe, Somerset, and *ed.* at Westminster and Oxf., entered the household of Prince Henry. In 1608 he made a walking tour in France, Italy, and Germany, walking nearly 2000 miles in one pair of shoes, which were, until 1702, hung up in Odcombe Church, and known as "the thousand mile shoes." He gave an amusing account of this in his *Coryate's Crudities hastily cobbled up* (1611), prefixed to which were commendatory verses by many contemporary poets. A sequel, *Coryate's Crambé*, or *Colewort twice Sodden* followed. Next year (1612) C. bade farewell to his fellow-townsmen, and set out on another journey to Greece, Egypt, and India, from which he never returned. He *d.* at Surat. Though odd and conceited, C. was a close observer, and took real pains in collecting information as to the places he visited.

COSTELLO, LOUISA STUART (1799-1877).—Poet and novelist, *b.* in Ireland, lived chiefly in Paris, where she was a miniature-painter. In 1815 she *pub. The Maid of the Cyprus Isle*, etc. (poems). She also wrote books of travel, which were very popular, as were her novels, chiefly founded on French history. Another work, *pub.* in 1835, is *Specimens of the Early Poetry of France.*

COTTON, CHARLES (1630-1687).—Poet and translator, succeeded to an embarrassed estate, which his happy-go-lucky methods did not improve, wrote burlesques on *Virgil* and *Lucian*, and made an excellent translation of *Montaigne's Essays*, also a humorous *Journey to Ireland.* C. was the friend of Izaak Walton, and wrote a second part of *The Complete Angler.* He was apparently always in difficulties, always happy, and always a favourite.

COTTON, SIR ROBERT BRUCE (1571-1631).—Antiquary, *b.* at Denton, Hunts, and *ed.* at Camb., was a great collector of charters and records throwing light upon English history, and co-operated with Camden (*q.v.*). Among his works are a history of the *Raigne of Henry III.* (1627). He was the collector of the Cottonian library, now in the British Museum, and was the author of various political tracts.

COUSIN, ANNE ROSS (CUNDELL) (1824-1906).—Poetess, only *dau.* of D. R. Cundell, M.D., Leith, *m.* 1847 Rev. Wm. Cousin, minister of the Free Church of Scotland, latterly at Melrose. Some of her hymns, especially "The Sands of Time are sinking," are known and sung over the English-speaking world. A collection of her poems, *Immanuel's Land and Other Pieces*, was *pub.* in 1876 under her initials A. R. C., by which she was most widely known.

COVERDALE, MILES (1488-1568).—Translator of the Bible, *b.* in Yorkshire, and *ed.* at Camb. Originally an Augustinian monk, he became a supporter of the Reformation. In 1535 his translation of the Bible was *pub.*, probably at Zurich. It bore the title, *Biblia, the Bible: that is the Holy Scripture of the Olde and New Testament faithfully and newly translated out of the Doutche and Latyn into English.* C. was made Bishop of Exeter in 1551, but, on the accession of Mary, he was imprisoned for two years, at the end of which he was released and went to Denmark and afterwards to Geneva. On the death of Mary he returned to England, but the views he had imbibed in Geneva were adverse to his preferment. He ultimately, however, received a benefice in London, which he resigned before his death. Besides the Bible he translated many treatises of the Continental Reformers.

COWLEY, ABRAHAM (1618-1667).—Poet, *s.* of a grocer or stationer in London, where he was *b.* In childhood he was greatly influenced by reading Spenser, a copy of whose poems was in the possession of his mother. This, he said, made him a poet. His first book, *Poetic Blossoms* (1633), was *pub.* when he was only 15. After being at Westminster School he went to Camb., where he was distinguished for his graceful translations. On the outbreak of the Civil War he joined the Royalists, was turned out of his college, and in 1646 followed the Queen to Paris, where he remained for 10 or 12 years, during which he rendered unwearied service to the royal family. At the Restoration he wrote some loyal odes, but was disappointed by being refused the Mastership of the Savoy, and retired to the country. He received a lease of Crown lands, but his life in the country did not yield him the happiness he expected. He is said by Pope to have *d.* of a fever brought on by lying in the fields after a drinking-bout. The drinking-bout, however, is perhaps an ill-natured addition. C.'s fame among his contemporaries was much greater than that which posterity has accorded to him. His poems are marred by conceits and a forced and artificial brilliancy. In some of them, however, he sings pleasantly of gardens and country scenes. They comprise *Miscellanies, The Mistress, or Love Poems* (1647), *Pindaric Odes*, and *The Davideis*, an epic on David (unfinished). He is at his best in such imitations of Anacreon as *The Grasshopper*. His prose, especially in his Essays, though now almost unread, is better than his verse; simple and manly, it sometimes rises to eloquence. C. is buried in Westminster Abbey near Spenser.

Ed., Grosart (1881), Waller (1903).

COWPER, WILLIAM (1731-1800).—Poet, was the *s.* of the Rev. John C., Rector of Great Berkhampstead, Herts, and Chaplain to George II. His grandfather was a judge, and he was the grand-nephew of the 1st Earl C., the eminent Lord Chancellor. A shy and timid child, the death of his mother when he was 6 years old, and the sufferings inflicted upon him by a bullying schoolfellow at his first school, wounded his tender and shrinking spirit irrecoverably. He was sent to Westminster School, where he had for schoolfellows Churchill, the poet (*q.v.*), and Warren Hastings. The powerful legal influence of his family naturally suggested his being destined for the law, and at 18 he entered the chambers of a solicitor, where he had for a companion Thurlow, the future Chancellor, a truly incongruous conjunction; the pair, however, seem to have got on well together, and employed their time chiefly in "giggling and making giggle." He then entered the Middle Temple, and in 1754 was called to the Bar. This was perhaps the happiest period of his life, being enlivened by the society of two cousins, Theodora and Harriet C. With the former he fell in love; but his proposal of marriage was opposed by her *f.*, who had observed symptoms of morbidity in him, and he never met her again. The latter, as Lady Hesketh, was in later days one of his most intimate friends. In 1759 he received a small sinecure appointment as Commissioner of Bankrupts, which he held for 5 years, and in 1763, through the influence of a relative, he received the offer of the desirable office of Clerk of the Journals to the House of Lords. He accepted the appointment, but the dread of having to make a formal appearance before the House so preyed upon his mind as to induce a temporary loss of reason, and he was sent to an asylum at St. Albans, where he remained for about a year. He had now no income beyond a small sum inherited from his *f.*, and no aims in life; but friends supplemented his means sufficiently to enable him to lead with a quiet mind the life of retirement which he had resolved to follow. He went to Huntingdon, and there made the acquaintance of the Unwins, with whom he went to live as a boarder. The acquaintance soon ripened into a close friendship, and on the death, from an accident (1767), of Mr. U., C. accompanied his widow (the "Mary" of his poems) to Olney, where the Rev. John Newton (*q.v.*) was curate. N. and C. became intimate friends, and collaborated in producing the well-known *Olney Hymns*, of which 67 were composed by C. He became engaged to Mary Unwin, but a fresh attack of his mental malady in 1773 prevented their marriage. On his recovery he took to gardening, and amused himself by keeping pets, including the hares "Tiny" and "Puss," and the spaniel "Beau," immortalised in his works. The chief means, however, which he adopted for keeping his mind occupied and free from distressing ideas was the cultivation of his poetic gift. At the suggestion of Mrs. U., he wrote *The Progress of Error; Truth, Table Talk, Expostulation, Hope, Charity, Conversation,* and *Retirement* were added, and the whole were *pub.* in one vol. in 1782. Though not received with acclamation, its signal merits of freshness, simplicity, graceful humour, and the pure idiomatc English in which it was written gradually obtained recognition, and the fame of the poet-recluse began to spread. His health had now become considerably re-established, and he enjoyed an unwonted measure of cheerfulness, which was fostered by the friendship of Lady Austin, who had become his neighbour. From her he received the story of John Gilpin, which he forthwith turned into his immortal ballad. Hers also was the suggestion that he should write a poem in blank verse, which gave its origin to his most famous poem, *The Task.* Before it was *pub.*, however, the intimacy had, apparently owing to some little feminine jealousies, been broken off. *The Task* was *pub.* in 1785, and met with immediate and distinguished success. Although not formally or professedly, it was, in fact, the beginning of an uprising against the classical school of poetry, and the founding of a new school in which nature was the teacher. As Dr. Stopford Brooke points out, "Cowper is the first of the poets who loves Nature entirely for her own sake," and in him "the idea of Mankind as a whole is fully formed." About this time he resumed his friendship with his cousin, Lady Hesketh, and, encouraged by her, he began his translation of *Homer*, which appeared in 1791. Before this he had removed with Mrs. U. to the village of Weston Underwood. His health had again given way; and in 1791 Mrs. U. became paralytic, and the object of his assiduous and affectionate care. A settled gloom with occasional brighter intervals was now falling upon him. He strove to fight it by engaging in various translations, and in revising his *Homer*, and undertaking a new ed. of Milton, which last was, however, left unfinished. In 1794 a pension of £300 was conferred upon him, and in 1795 he removed with Mrs. U., now a helpless invalid, to East Dereham. Mrs. U. *d.* in the following year, and three years later his own death released him from his heavy burden of trouble and sorrow. His last poem was *The Castaway*, which, with its darkness almost of despair, shows no loss of intellectual or poetic power. In addition to his reputation as a poet C. has that of being among the very best of English letter-writers, and in this he shows, in an even easier and more unstudied manner, the same command of pure idiomatic English, the same acute observation, and the same mingling of gentle humour and melancholy. In literature C. is the connecting link between the classical school of Pope and the natural school of Burns, Crabbe, and Wordsworth, having, however, much more in common with the latter.

SUMMARY.—*B.* 1731, *ed.* Westminster School, entered Middle Temple and called to the Bar, 1754, appointed Clerk of Journals of House of Lords, but mind gave way 1763, lives with the Unwins, became intimate with J. Newton and with him writes *Olney Hymns*, *pub. Poems* (*Progress of Error*, etc.), 1782, *Task* 1785, *Homer* 1791, *d.* 1731.

The standard ed. of C.'s works is Southey's, with memoir (15 vols. 1834-37). Others are the Aldine (1865), the Globe (1870). There are *Lives* by Hayley (2 vols., 1805), Goldwin Smith (Men of Letters Series), and T. Wright.

COXE, WILLIAM (1747-1828).—Historian, was *b.* in London, and *ed.* at Eton and Camb. As tutor to various young men of family he travelled much on the Continent, and *pub.* accounts of his journeys. His chief historical work is his *Memoirs of the House of Austria* (1807), and he also wrote lives of Walpole, Marlborough, and others. He had access to valuable original sources, and his books, though somewhat heavy, are on the whole trustworthy, notwithstanding a decided Whig bias. He was a clergyman, and *d.* Archdeacon of Wilts.

CRABBE, GEORGE (1754-1832).—Poet, *b.* at Aldborough, Suffolk, where his *f.* was collector of salt dues, he was apprenticed to a surgeon, but, having no liking for the work, went to London to try his fortune in literature. Unsuccessful at first, he as a last resource wrote a letter to Burke enclosing some of his writings, and was immediately befriended by him, and taken into his own house, where he met Fox, Reynolds, and others. His first important work, *The Library*, was *pub.* in 1781, and received with favour. He took orders, and was appointed by the Duke of Rutland his domestic chaplain, residing with him at Belvoir Castle. Here in 1783 he *pub.* *The Village*, which established his reputation, and about the same time he was presented by Lord Thurlow to two small livings. He was now secured from want, made a happy marriage, and devoted himself to literary and scientific pursuits. The *Newspaper* appeared in 1785, and was followed by a period of silence until 1807, when he came forward again with *The Parish Register*, followed by *The Borough* (1810), *Tales in Verse* (1812), and his last work, *Tales of the Hall* (1817-18). In 1819 Murray the publisher gave him £3000 for the last named work and the unexpired copyright of his other poems. In 1822 he visited Sir Walter Scott at Edinburgh. Soon afterwards his health began to give way, and he *d.* in 1832. C. has been called "the poet of the poor." He describes in simple, but strong and vivid, verse their struggles, sorrows, weaknesses, crimes, and pleasures, sometimes with racy humour, oftener in sombre hues.

His pathos, sparingly introduced, goes to the heart; his pictures of crime and despair not seldom rise to the terrific, and he has a marvellous power of painting natural scenery, and of bringing out in detail the beauty and picturesqueness of scenes at first sight uninteresting, or even uninviting. He is absolutely free from affectation or sentimentality, and may be regarded as one of the greatest masters of the realistic in our literature. With these merits he has certain faults, too great minuteness in his pictures, too frequent dwelling upon the sordid and depraved aspects of character, and some degree of harshness both in matter and manner, and not unfrequently a want of taste.

CRAIGIE, MRS. PEARL MARY TERESA (RICHARDS) (1867-1906). *Dau.* of John Morgan, R. *b.* in Boston, Massachusetts. Most of her education was received in London and Paris, and from childhood she was a great reader and observer. At 19 she *m.* Mr. R. W. Craigie, but the union did not prove happy and was, on her petition, dissolved. In 1902 she became a Roman Catholic. She wrote, under the pseudonym of "John Oliver Hobbes," a number of novels and dramas, distinguished by originality of subject and treatment, brightness of humour, and finish of style, among which may be mentioned *Some Emotions and a Moral*, *The Gods, Some Mortals and Lord Wickenham* (1895), *The Herb Moon* and *The School for Saints* (1897), and *Robert Orange* (1900), *The Dream and The Business* (1907). Her dramas include *The Ambassador* and *The Bishop's Move.*

CRAIK, GEORGE LILLIE (1798-1866).—Writer on English literature, etc., *b.* at Kennoway, Fife, and *ed.* at St. Andrews, went to London in 1824, where he wrote largely for the "Society for the Promotion of Useful Knowledge." In 1849 he was appointed Prof. of English Literature and History at Belfast. Among his books are *The Pursuit of Knowledge under Difficulties* (1831), *History of British Commerce* (1844), and *History of English Literature and the English Language* (1861). He was also joint author of *The Pictorial History of England*, and wrote books on Spenser and Bacon.

CRANE, STEPHEN (1871–1900).—American novelist, *b.* at Newark, New Jersey. After some work as a journalist sprang into fame with *The Red Badge of Courage* (1895), showing special gifts for the position of a war correspondent, which he became. Wrote some excellent short stories (*The Open Boat*), and was a precursor of the free-verse school.

CRANMER, THOMAS (1489-1556).—Theologian and Churchman, *b.* at Aslacton, Notts, *ed.* at Camb., and became an eminent classical and biblical scholar. He supported Henry VIII. in his divorce proceedings against Queen Catherine, gained the King's favour, and obtained rapid preferment, ending with the Primacy. He was one of the chief promoters of the Reformation in England. On the accession of Mary, he was committed to the Tower, and after a temporary failure of courage and constancy, suffered martyrdom at the stake. It is largely to C. that we owe the stately forms of the Book of Common Prayer.

CRASHAW, RICHARD (1613?-1649).—Poet, *s.* of William C., a Puritan divine, was *b.* in London, and *ed.* at Charterhouse and Camb., where he became a Fellow of Peterhouse, from which, however, he was, in 1643, ejected for refusing to take the Solemn League and Covenant. Thereafter he went to France, and joined the Roman communion. He suffered great straits, being almost reduced to starvation, but was, through the influence of Queen Henrietta Maria, appointed Sec. to Cardinal Palotta. About 1649 he went to Italy, and in the following year became a canon of the Church of Loretto. He *d.* the same year. C. is said to have been an eloquent preacher, and was a scholar as well as a poet of a high order in the ecstatic and transcendental style. His chief work is *Steps to the Temple* (1646), consisting mainly of religious poems somewhat in the style of Herbert; his *Weeping of the Magdalen* is full of the most extravagant conceits, a fondness for which is, indeed, his besetting sin as a poet. His friend Cowley commemorated him in a beautiful ode.

CRAWFORD, FRANCIS MARION (1854-1909).—Novelist and historian, *s.* of Thomas C., an American sculptor, *b.* at Bagni di Lucca, Italy, and *ed.* in America, at Camb., and in Germany, he went to India and ed. *The Indian Herald* (1879-80). Thereafter he settled in Italy, living chiefly at Sorrento, and becoming a Roman Catholic. His principal historical works are *Ave Roma Immortalis* (1898), *The Rulers of the South* (reprinted as *Sicily, Calabria, and Malta*, 1904), and *Venetian Gleanings* (1905), but his reputation rests mainly on his novels, of which he wrote between 30 and 40, the best known of which are perhaps *Mr. Isaacs* (1882), *Dr. Claudius* (1883), *A Roman Singer* (1884), *Marzio's Crucifix* (1887), *Saracinesca* (1887), *A Cigarette-maker's Romance* (1890), generally considered his masterpiece, *Don Orsino* (1892), *Pietro Ghisleri* (1893), and *The Heart of Rome* (1903). His one play is *Francesca da Rimini*. His novels are all interesting, and written in a style of decided distinction. His historical works, though full of information, lack spirit.

CREASY, SIR EDWARD SHEPHERD (1812-1878).—Historian, *ed.* at Eton and Camb., and called to the Bar in 1837, he became in 1840 Prof. of History, London Univ., and in 1860 Chief Justice of Ceylon, when he was knighted. His best known contribution to literature is his *Fifteen Decisive Battles of the World* (1852). Other works are *Historical and Critical Account of the Several Invasions of England* (1852), *History of the Ottoman Turks*, and *Imperial and Colonial Institutions of the British Empire* (1872).

CREECH, THOMAS (1659-1700).—Translator, *b.* near Sherborne, *ed.* at Oxf., became Head Master of Sherborne School. He translated *Lucretius* in verse (1682), for which he received a Fellowship at Oxf., also Horace, Theocritus, and other classics. Owing to a disappointment in love and pecuniary difficulties he hanged himself.

CREIGHTON, MANDELL (1843-1901).—Churchman and historian, *b.* at Carlisle, and *ed.* at Durham Grammar School and Merton Coll., Oxf., he took orders, and was presented to the living of Embleton, Northumberland, in 1875, where, in addition to zealous discharge of pastoral duties, he pursued the historical studies on the results of which his reputation chiefly rests. In 1882 the first two vols. of his *History of the Papacy* appeared, followed by two more in 1887, and a fifth in 1894. In 1884 he was appointed first Dixie Prof. of Ecclesiastical History at Camb. He ed. the *English Historical Review* (1886-91). In 1891, after having held canonries at Worcester and Windsor, he became Bishop of Peterborough, from which he was in 1897 translated to London. His duties as Bishop of London made the completion of his great historical work an impossibility. He wrote in addition to it various text-books on history, a life of Queen Elizabeth, a memoir of Sir George Grey, and many articles and reviews. He was recognised as a leading authority on the department of history to which he had specially devoted himself, and he made his mark as a Churchman.

CROKER, JOHN WILSON (1780-1857).—Politician and miscellaneous writer. *Ed.* at Trinity Coll., Dublin, he entered Parliament as a Tory, and was appointed to various offices, including the Secretaryship of the Admiralty, which he held for 20 years. He was one of the founders of the *Quarterly Review*, and wrote some of its most violent political articles and reviews. He *pub.* in 1831 an ed. of *Boswell's Life of Johnson*. He also wrote some historical essays and satirical pieces.

CROKER, THOMAS CROFTON (1798-1854).—Irish Antiquary, *b.* at Cork, for some years held a position in the Admiralty. He devoted himself largely to the collection of ancient Irish poetry and folk-lore. Among his publications are *Researches in the South of Ireland* (1824), *Fairy Legends and Traditions of the South of Ireland* (1825-27), *Popular Songs of Ireland* (1837), *Daniel O'Rourke* (1829), and *Barney Mahoney* (1832). He assisted in founding the "Camden" and "Percy" Societies.

CROLY, GEORGE (1780-1860).—Poet, novelist, historian, and divine, *b.* at Dublin, and *ed.* at Trinity Coll. there, he took orders and became Rector of St. Stephen's, Walbrook, and had a high reputation as a preacher. He wrote poems, dramas, satires, novels, history, and theological works, and attained some measure of success in all. Perhaps his best known works are his novels, *Salathiel* (1829), founded on the legend of "the wandering Jew," and *Mareton* (1846). His chief contribution to theological literature is an exposition of the Apocalypse.

CROWE, CATHERINE (STEVENS) (1800-1876).—Wrote dramas, children's books, and one or two novels, including *Susan Hopley* (1841), and *Lilly Dawson* (1847), but is chiefly remembered for her *Night-side of Nature* (1848), a collection of stories of the supernatural. Though somewhat morbid she had considerable talent.

CROWE, EYRE EVANS (1799-1868).—Historian and novelist, *s.* of an officer in the army, *b.* near Southampton, and *ed.* at Trinity Coll., Dublin. He wrote several novels, including *Vittoria Colonna, To-day in Ireland* (1825), *The English in France* (1828), and *Charles Dalmer* (1853). Among his historical works are a *History of France* in *Lardner's Cabinet Encyclopædia*, afterwards enlarged and separately *pub.*, and a *History of Louis XVIII. and Charles X.*

CROWE, SIR JOSEPH ARCHER (1825-1896).—Writer on art, *s.* of the above, was *b.* in London. Most of his childhood was spent in France, and on his return to England in 1843 he became a journalist. He was then for some years engaged in educational work in India, and was afterwards war correspondent for the *Times* on various occasions, and filled various important consular posts, for which he was in 1890 made K.C.M.G. In collaboration with G. B. Cavalcasselle, an Italian refugee, he was the author of several authoritative works on art, including *The Early Flemish Painters* (1856), *A New History of Painting in Italy* (1864-68), *A History of Painting in North Italy* (1871), *Titian, His Life and Times* (1877), and *Raphael, His Life and Works* (1883-85). The actual writing of all these was the work of C.

CROWE, WILLIAM (1745-1829).—Poet, *b.* at Midgham, Berks, the *s.* of a carpenter, was *ed.* as a foundationer at Winchester, whence he proceeded to Oxf., where he became Public Orator. He wrote a smooth, but somewhat conventional poem, *Lewesdon Hill* (1789), ed. Collins's Poems (1828), and lectured on poetry at the Royal Institution. His poems were *coll.* in 1827. C. was a clergyman and Rector of Alton Barnes, Wilts.

CROWNE, JOHN (1640?-1703).—Dramatist, returned from Nova Scotia, to which his *f.*, a Nonconformist minister, had emigrated, and became gentleman usher to a lady of quality. His first play, *Juliana*, appeared in 1671. He wrote in all about 17 dramatic pieces, of which the best is *Sir Courtly Nice* (1685), adapted from the Spanish. It is amusing, and enjoyed a long continued vogue. In general, however, C. is dull.

CUDWORTH, RALPH (1617-1688).—Divine and philosopher, *b.* at Aller, Somerset, and *ed.* at Camb., where, after being a tutor, he became Master of Clare Hall 1645, Prof. of Hebrew (1645-88), and Master of Christ's Coll., 1654. His great work is *The True Intellectual System of the Universe* (1678). A work of vast learning and acuteness, it is directed against the infidelity of the age. C.'s candour in his statement of the opposing position was so remarkable that Dryden remarked "that he raised such strong objections against the being of a God and Providence that many thought he had not answered them." He also left in MS. a *Treatise concerning Eternal and Immutable Morality*, *pub.* in 1731.

CUMBERLAND, RICHARD (1732-1811).—Novelist and dramatist, *ed.* at Westminster and Camb., entered the diplomatic service, and filled several government appointments. His best play is *The West Indian.* His novels do not rise much above mediocrity. Along with Sir J. B. Burges he wrote an epic entitled *The Exodiad*, and he also made some translations from the Greek.

CUMMINS, MARIA SUSANNA (1827-1866).—*B.* at Salem, Mass., was well-known as the authoress of *The Lamplighter*, a somewhat sentimental tale which had very wide popularity. She wrote others, including *Mabel Vaughan*, none of which had the same success.

CUNNINGHAM, ALLAN (1784-1842).—Poet and miscellaneous writer, *b.* near Dalswinton, Dumfriesshire, in his youth knew Burns, who was a friend of his father's. He was apprenticed to a stonemason, but gave his leisure to reading and writing imitations of old Scottish ballads, which he contributed to Cromek's *Remains of Nithsdale and Galloway Song*, *pub.* in 1810, and which gained for him the friendship of Scott and Hogg. Thereafter he went to London, and became a parliamentary reporter, and subsequently assistant to Chantrey, the sculptor, but continued his literary labours, writing three novels, a life of Sir D. Wilkie, and *Lives of Eminent British Painters, Sculptors, and Architects*, besides many songs, of which the best is *A wet sheet and a flowing Sea*. He also brought out an ed. of Burns's Works. He had four sons, all of whom rose to important positions, and inherited in some degree his literary gifts.

CURTIS, GEORGE WILLIAM (1824-1892). — American essayist, editor, and journalist, contributed to *New York Tribune*, and to *Putnam's* and *Harper's* monthlies, in which most of his books first appeared. Among these are *Trumps*, a story of New York life, *Prue and I*, *Lotus-eating*, and the *Potiphar Papers*. C. was also one of the finest American orators of his day.

CYNEWULF (*fl.* 750).—Anglo-Saxon poet. He was probably a Northumbrian, though sometimes thought to have been a Mercian. His poems, and some others, more or less doubtfully attributed to him, are contained in the Exeter Book and the Vercelli Book. The poems which are considered to be certainly his are the *Riddles*, from hints and allusions in which is derived nearly all that is known of him, or at least of the earlier part of his life, which appears to have been that of a joyous and poetical nature, rejoicing in the beauty of the world. His next poem, *Juliana*, the legend of a virgin-martyr, indicates a transition in his spiritual life; sorrow and repentance are its predominant notes, and in these respects another poem, *St. Guthlac*, resembles it. In the *Crist* (Christ), C. has passed through the clouds to an assured faith and peace. *The Phœnix*, and the second part of *Guthlac*, though not certainly his, are generally attributed to him. *The Fates of the Apostles* and *Elene* (the legend of St. Helena) are his; the *Andreas* and *The Dream of the Roode* are still in some respects the subject of controversy. In several of the poems the separate letters of C.'s name are introduced in a peculiar manner, and are regarded as an attesting signature. *Juliana*, *Crist*, *The Apostles*, and *Elene* are thus said to be signed. The Exeter and Vercelli Books are collections of ancient English poems, and they are named from the places where they were found.

DALLING AND BULWER, WILLIAM HENRY LYTTON EARLE BULWER, 1ST LORD (1801-1872).—Elder brother of Lord Lytton (*q.v.*), and a distinguished diplomatist. He represented England at Madrid, Washington (where he concluded the Bulwer-Clayton Treaty), Florence, Bucharest, and Constantinople, and was raised to the peerage in 1871. He was the author of a number of books of travel and biography, including *An Autumn in Greece* (1826), a *Life of Byron* (1835), *Historical Characters* (1868-70), and an unfinished life of Lord Palmerston.

DAMPIER, WILLIAM (1652-1715).—Discoverer and buccaneer, *b.* near Yeovil. After various seafaring adventures, and leading a semi-piratical life, he was in 1688 marooned on Nicobar Island, but escaped to Acheen, returned to England in 1691. He *pub.* his *Voyage Round the World* (1697), and *A Discourse of Winds* (1699). He was then employed by government on a voyage of survey and discovery (1699-1700), in the course of which he explored the north-west coast of Australia and the coasts of New Guinea and New Britain. In 1701 he was wrecked upon Ascension Island, from which he was rescued by an East Indiaman. He was afterwards court-martialled for cruelty, and wrote an angry but unconvincing vindication. His *Voyage* is written in a style plain and homely, but is perspicuous and interesting.

DANA, RICHARD HENRY (1787-1879).—Novelist and critic, *b.* at Camb., Mass., was called to the Bar in 1817. Among his novels are *Tom Thornton* and *Paul Felton*, both somewhat violent and improbable tales, and his poems, which are better, include *The Buccaneer* (1827), and *The Dying Raven*. He is, however, stronger as a critic than as a writer. He wrote largely in *The North American Review*, and for a time conducted a paper, *The Idle Man*, which contains some of his best work.

DANA, RICHARD HENRY, JR. (1815-1882).—Miscellaneous writer, *s.* of the above, *ed.* at Harvard, but on his eyesight giving way shipped as a common sailor, and gave his experiences in *Two Years before the Mast* (1840). Called to the Bar in 1840, he became an authority on maritime law. Other books by him are *The Seaman's Friend* (1841), and *Vacation Voyage to Cuba* (1859).

DANIEL, SAMUEL (1562-1619).—Poet, *s.* of a music master, was *b.* near Taunton, and *ed.* at Oxf., but did not graduate. He attached himself to the Court as a kind of voluntary laureate, and in the reign of James I. was appointed "Inspector of the children of the Queen's revels," and a groom of the Queen's chamber. He is said to have enjoyed the friendship of Shakespeare and Marlowe, but was "at jealousies" with Ben Jonson. In his later years he retired to a farm which he owned in Somerset, where he *d.* D. bears the title of the "well-languaged," his style is clear and flowing, with a remarkably modern note, but is lacking in energy and fire, and is thus apt to become tedious. His works include sonnets, epistles, masques, and dramas. The most important of them is *The History of the Civil Wars between York and Lancaster* in 8 books, *pub.* in 1604. His *Epistles* are generally considered his best work, and his sonnets have had some modern admirers. Among his poems may be mentioned the *Complaynt of Rosamund*, *Tethys Festival* (1610), and *Hymen's Triumph* (1615), a masque, and *Musophilus*, a defence of learning, *Defence of Rhyme* (1602).

DARLEY, GEORGE (1795-1846).—Poet, novelist, and critic, *b.* at Dublin, and *ed.* at Trinity Coll. there, he early decided to follow a literary career, and went to London, where he brought out his first poem, *Errors of Ecstasie* (1822). He also wrote for the *London Magazine*, under the pseudonym of John Lacy. In it appeared his best story, *Lilian of the Vale*. Various other books followed, including *Sylvia, or The May Queen*, a poem (1827). Thereafter he joined the *Athenæum*, in which he showed himself a severe critic. He was also a dramatist and a profound student of old English plays, editing those of Beaumont and Fletcher in 1840. So deeply was he imbued with the spirit of the 17th century that his poem, "It is not beauty I desire," was included by F. T. Palgrave in the first ed. of his *Golden Treasury* as an anonymous lyric of that age. He was also a mathematician of considerable talent, and *pub.* some treatises on the subject. D. fell into nervous depression and *d.* in 1846.

DARWIN, CHARLES ROBERT (1809-1882).—Naturalist, *s.* of a physician, and grandson of Dr. Erasmus D. (*q.v.*), and of Josiah Wedgwood, the famous potter, was *b.* and was at school at Shrewsbury. In 1825 he went to Edin. to study medicine, but was more taken up with marine zoology than with the regular curriculum. After two years he proceeded to Camb., where he *grad.* in 1831, continuing, however, his independent studies in natural history. In the same year came the opportunity of his life, his appointment to accompany the *Beagle* as naturalist on a survey of South America. To this voyage, which extended over nearly five years, he attributed the first real training of his mind, and after his return *pub.* an account of it, *Zoology of the Voyage of the Beagle* (1840). After spending a few years in London arranging his collections and writing his *Journal*, he removed to Down, a retired village near the Weald of Kent, where, in a house surrounded by a large garden, his whole remaining life was passed in the patient building up, from accurate observations, of his theory of Evolution, which created a new epoch in science and in thought generally. His industry was marvellous, especially when it is remembered that he suffered from chronic bad health. After devoting some time to geology, specially to coral reefs, and exhausting the subject of barnacles, he took up the development of his favourite question, the transformation of species. In these earlier years of residence at Down he *pub.* *The Structure and Distribution of Coral Reefs* (1842), and two works on the geology of volcanic islands, and of South America. After he had given much time and profound thought to the question of evolution by natural selection, and had written out his notes on the subject, he received in 1858 from Mr. A. R. Wallace (*q.v.*) a manuscript showing that he also had reached independently a theory of the origin of species similar to his own. This circumstance created a situation of considerable delicacy and difficulty, which was ultimately got over by the two discoverers presenting a joint paper, *On the Tendency of Species to form Varieties*, and *On the Perpetuation of Varieties and Species by Natural Means of Selection*. The publication in 1859 of *The Origin of Species* gave D. an acknowledged place among the greatest men of science, and the controversies which, along with other of his works, it raised, helped to carry his name all over the civilised world. Among his numerous subsequent writings may be mentioned *The Fertilisation of Orchids* (1862), *Variation of Plants and Animals under Domestication* (1868), *The Descent of Man, and Selection in relation to Sex* (1871), *The Expression of the Emotions in*

Man and Animals (1872), *Insectivorous Plants* (1875), *Climbing Plants* (1875), *Different Forms of Flowers* (1877), *The Power of Movement in Plants* (1880), and *The Formation of Vegetable Mould through the Action of Worms* (1881). D., with a modesty which was one of his chief characteristics, disclaimed for himself the possession of any remarkable talents except "an unusual power of noticing things which easily escape attention, and of observing them carefully." In addition, however, to this peculiar insight, he had a singular reverence for truth and fact, enormous industry, and great self-abnegation: and his kindliness, modesty, and magnanimity attracted the affection of all who knew him.

Life and Letters, by his son, F. Darwin, 3 vols., 1887; *C. Darwin and the Theory of Natural Selection*, E. B. Poulton, 1896; various short Lives by Grant Allen and others.

DARWIN, ERASMUS (1731-1802).—Poet, physician, and scientist, was *b.* at Elston, Notts, and *ed.* at Camb. and at Edin., where he took his degree of M.D. He ultimately settled in Lichfield as a physician, and attained a high professional reputation, so much so that he was offered, but declined, the appointment of physician to George III. In 1778 he formed a botanical garden, and in 1789 *pub.* his first poem, *The Loves of the Plants*, followed in 1792 by *The Economy of Vegetation*, which combined form *The Botanic Garden*. Another poem, *The Temple of Nature*, was *pub.* posthumously. He also wrote various scientific works in prose. The poems of D., though popular in their day, are now little read. Written in polished and sonorous verse, they glitter with startling similes and ingenious, though often forced, analogies, but have little true poetry or human interest.

DASENT, SIR GEORGE WEBBE (1817-1896).—Scandinavian scholar, *b.* in the island of St. Vincent, of which his *f.* was Attorney-general, *ed.* at Westminster School, King's Coll., London, and Oxf., he entered the diplomatic service, and was for several years Sec. to the British Embassy at Stockholm, where he became interested in Scandinavian literature and mythology. Returning to England he was appointed Assistant Ed. of *The Times* (1845-1870). In 1852 he was called to the Bar, and in the following year was appointed Prof. of English Literature and Modern History at King's Coll., London, an office which he held for 13 years. He was knighted in 1876. His principal writings have to do with Scandinavian language, mythology, and folk-lore, and include an *Icelandic Grammar*, *The Prose or Younger Edda* (1842), *Popular Tales from the Norse* (1859), *The Saga of Burnt Njal* (1861), and *The Story of Gisli the Outlaw* (1866), mostly translated from the Norwegian of Asbjörnsen. He also translated the Orkney and Hacon Sagas for the Rolls Series, and wrote four novels, *Annals of an Eventful Life*, *Three to One*, *Half a Life*, and *The Vikings of the Baltic*. His style is pointed and clear.

DAVENANT, OR D'AVENANT, SIR WILLIAM (1606-1668).—Poet and dramatist, was *b.* at Oxf., where his *f.* kept an inn, which Shakespeare was in the habit of visiting. This had some influence on the future poet, who claimed to be Shakespeare's natural son. D., *ed.* at Lincoln Coll., was afterwards in the service of Lord Brooke, became involved in the troubles of the Civil War, in which he took the Royalist side, and was imprisoned in the Tower, escaped to France, and after returning was, in 1643, knighted. Later D. was employed on various missions by the King and Queen, was again in the Tower from 1650 to 1652, when he *pub.* his poem *Gondibert.* He is said to have owed his release to the interposition of Milton. In 1656 he practically founded the English Opera by his *Siege of Rhodes* (1656). In 1659 he was again imprisoned, but after the Restoration he seems to have enjoyed prosperity and Royal favour, and established a theatre, where he was the first habitually to introduce female players and movable scenery. D. wrote 25 dramatic pieces, among which are *Albovine, King of the Lombards* (1629), *Platonick Lovers* (1636), *The Wits* (1633), *Unfortunate Lovers* (1643), *Love and Honour* (1649). None of them are now read; and the same may be said of *Gondibert,* considered a masterpiece by contemporaries. D. succeeded Ben Jonson as Poet Laureate, and collaborated with Dryden in altering (and debasing) *The Tempest.* He *coll.* his miscellaneous verse under the title of *Madagascar.* He is said to have had the satisfaction of repaying in kind the good offices of Milton when the latter was in danger in 1660. He joined with Waller and others in founding the classical school of English poetry.

DAVIDSON, JOHN (1837-1909).—Poet and playwright, *b.* at Barrhead, Renfrewshire, *s.* of a Dissenting minister, entered the chemical department of a sugar refinery in Greenock in his 13th year, returning after one year to school as a pupil teacher. He was afterwards engaged in teaching at various places, and having taken to literature went in 1890 to London. He achieved a reputation as a writer of poems and plays of marked individuality and vivid realism. His poems include *In a Music Hall* (1891), *Fleet Street Eclogues* (1893), *Baptist Lake* (1894), *New Ballads* (1896), *The Last Ballad* (1898), *The Triumph of Mammon* (1907), and among his plays are *Bruce* (1886), *Smith: a Tragic Farce* (1888), *Godfrida* (1898). D. disappeared on March 27, 1909, under circumstances which left little doubt that under the influence of mental depression he had committed suicide. Among his papers was found the MS. of a new work, *Fleet Street Poems,* with a letter containing the words, "This will be my last book." His body was discovered a few months later.

DAVIES, JOHN (1565?-1618).—Called "the Welsh Poet," was a writing-master, wrote very copiously and rather tediously on theological and philosophical themes. His works include *Mirum in Modum, Microcosmus* (1602), and *The Picture of a Happy Man* (1612), *Wit's Bedlam* (1617), and many epigrams on his contemporaries which have some historical interest.

DAVIES, SIR JOHN (1569-1626).—Lawyer and poet, *s.* of a lawyer at Westbury, Wiltshire, was *ed.* at Winchester and Oxf., and became a barrister of the Middle Temple, 1595. He was a member successively of the English and Irish Houses of Commons, and held various legal offices. In literature he is known as the writer of two poems, *Orchestra : a Poem of Dancing* (1594), and *Nosce Teipsum* (Know Thyself), in two elegies (1) Of Humane Knowledge (2) Of the Immortality of the Soul. The poem consists of quatrains, each containing a complete and compactly expressed thought. It was *pub.* in 1599. D. was also the author of treatises on law and politics.

DAVIS, OR DAVYS, JOHN (1550?-1605).—Navigator, known as D. of Sandridge to distinguish him from another of the same name. He was one of the most enterprising of the Elizabethan sailors, who devoted themselves to the discovery of the North-west Passage. Davis Strait was discovered by, and named after, him. He made many voyages, in the last of which he met his death at the hands of a Japanese pirate. He was the author of a book, now very scarce, *The World's Hydrographical Description*, and he also wrote a work on practical navigation, *The Seaman's Secrets*, which had great repute.

DAVIS, THOMAS OSBORNE (1814-1845).—Poet, *b.* at Mallow, *ed.* at Trinity Coll., Dublin, and called to the Irish Bar 1838. He was one of the founders of *The Nation* newspaper, and of the Young Ireland party. He wrote some stirring patriotic ballads, originally contributed to *The Nation*, and afterwards republished as *Spirit of the Nation*, also a memoir of Curran the great Irish lawyer and orator, prefixed to an ed. of his speeches; and he had formed many literary plans which were brought to naught by his untimely death.

DAVY, SIR HUMPHREY (1778-1829).—Chemist and man of letters, *s.* of a wood-carver, was *b.* at Penzance. He early showed an enthusiasm for natural science, and continued to pursue his studies when apprenticed in 1795 to a surgeon. He became specially interested in chemistry, to which in 1797 he began more exclusively to devote himself. Thereafter he assisted Dr. Beddoes in his laboratory at Bristol, and entered upon his brilliant course of chemical discovery. His *Researches, Chemical, and Philosophical* (1799), led to his appointment as Director of the Chemical Laboratory at the Royal Institution, where he also delivered courses of scientific lectures with extraordinary popularity. Thereafter his life was a succession of scientific triumphs and honours. His great discovery was that of the metallic bases of the earths and alkalis. He also discovered various metals, including sodium, calcium, and magnesium. In 1812 he was knighted, and *m.* a wealthy widow. Thereafter he investigated volcanic action and fire-damp, and invented the safety lamp. In 1818 he was *cr.* a baronet, and in 1820 became Pres. of the Royal Society, to which he communicated his discoveries in electro-magnetism. In addition to his scientific writings, which include *Elements of Agricultural Chemistry* (1813), and *Chemical Agencies of Electricity*, he wrote *Salmonia, or Days of Fly Fishing* (1828), somewhat modelled upon Walton, and *Consolations in Travel* (1830), dialogues on ethical and religious questions. D. sustained an apoplectic seizure in 1826, after which his health was much impaired, and after twice wintering in Italy, he *d.* at Geneva, where he received a public funeral. Though not attached to any Church, D. was a sincerely religious man, strongly opposed to materialism and scepticism. He holds a foremost place among scientific discoverers.

DAY, JOHN (*b.* 1574).—Dramatist, *s.* of a Norfolk yeoman, was at Camb., 1592-3. It is only since 1881 that his works have been identified. He collaborated with Dekker and others in plays, and was the author of *The Isle of Gulls* (1606), *Law Trickes* (1608), and *Humour out of Breath* (1608), also of an allegorical masque, *The Parliament of Bees.*

DAY, THOMAS (1748-1789).—Miscellaneous writer, was *b.* in London, *ed.* at the Charterhouse and at Oxf., and called to the Bar 1775, but having inherited in infancy an independence, he did not practise. He became a disciple of Rousseau in his social views, and endeavoured to put them in practice in combination with better morality. He was a benevolent eccentric, and used his income, which was increased by his marriage with an heiress, in schemes of social reform as he understood it. He is chiefly remembered as the author of the once universally-read *History of Sandford and Merton.*

DEFOE, DANIEL (1661?-1731).—Journalist and novelist, *s.* of a butcher in St. Giles, where he was *b.* His *f.* being a Dissenter, he was *ed.* at a Dissenting coll. at Newington with the view of becoming a Presbyterian minister. He joined the army of Monmouth, and on its defeat was fortunate enough to escape punishment. In 1688 he joined William III. Before settling down to his career as a political writer, D. had been engaged in various enterprises as a hosier, a merchant-adventurer to Spain and Portugal, and a brick-maker, all of which proved so unsuccessful that he had to fly from his creditors. Having become known to the government as an effective writer, and employed by them, he was appointed Accountant in the Glass-Duty Office, 1695-1699. Among his more important political writings are an *Essay on Projects* (1698), and *The True-born Englishman* (1701), which had a remarkable success. In 1702 appeared *The Shortest Way with the Dissenters,* written in a strain of grave irony which was, unfortunately for the author, misunderstood, and led to his being fined, imprisoned, and put in the pillory, which suggested his *Hymns to the Pillory* (1704). Notwithstanding the disfavour with the government which these disasters implied, D.'s knowledge of commercial affairs and practical ability were recognised by his being sent in 1706 to Scotland to aid in the Union negotiations. In the same year *Jure Divino,* a satire, followed by a *History of the Union* (1709), and *The Wars of Charles XII.* (1715). Further misunderstandings and disappointments in connection with political matters led to his giving up this line of activity, and, fortunately for posterity, taking to fiction. The first and greatest of his novels, *Robinson Crusoe,* appeared in 1719, and its sequel (of greatly inferior interest) in 1720. These were followed by *Captain Singleton* (1720), *Moll Flanders, Colonel Jacque,* and *Journal of the Plague Year* (1722), *Memoirs of a Cavalier* (1724), *A New Voyage Round the World* (1725), and *Captain Carlton* (1728). Among his miscellaneous works are *Political History of the Devil* (1726), *System of Magic* (1727), *The Complete English Tradesman* (1727), and *The Review,* a paper which he ed. In all he *pub.*, including pamphlets, etc., about 250 works. All D.'s writings are distinguished by a clear, nervous style, and his works of fiction by a minute verisimilitude and naturalness of incident which has never been equalled except perhaps by Swift, whose genius his, in some other respects, resembled. The only description of his personal appearance is given in an advertisement intended to lead to his apprehension, and runs, "A middle-sized, spare man about forty years old, of a brown complexion, and dark brown-coloured hair, but wears a wig; a hooked nose, a sharp chin, grey eyes, and a large mole near his mouth." His mind was a peculiar amalgam of imagination and matter-of-fact, seeing strongly and clearly what he did see, but little conscious, apparently, of what lay outside his purview

Lives by Chalmers (1786), H. Morley (1889), T. Wright (1894), and others; shorter works by Lamb, Hazlitt, L. Stephens, and Prof. Minto, Bohn's *British Classics*, etc.

DEKKER, THOMAS (1570?-1641?).—Dramatist and miscellaneous writer, was *b.* in London. Few details of D.'s life have come down to us, though he was a well-known writer in his day, and is believed to have written or contributed to over 20 dramas. He collaborated at various times with several of his fellow-dramatists, including Ben Jonson. Ultimately Jonson quarrelled with Marston and D., satirising them in *The Poetaster* (1601),to which D. replied in *Satiromastix* (1602). D.'s best play is *Old Fortunatus* (1606), others are *The Shoemaker's Holiday* (1600), *Honest Whore* (1604), *Roaring Girl* (1611), *The Virgin Martyr* (1622) (with Massinger), and *The Witch of Edmonton* (1658) (with Ford and Rowley), *History of Sir Thomas Wyat*, *Westward Ho*, and *Northward Ho*, all with Webster. His prose writings include *The Gull's Hornbook* (1609), *The Seven Deadly Sins of London*, and *The Belman of London* (1608), satirical works which give interesting glimpses of the life of his time. His life appears to have been a somewhat chequered one, alternating between revelry and want. He is one of the most poetical of the older dramatists. Lamb said he "had poetry enough for anything."

DE LOLME, JOHN LOUIS (1740?-1807).—Political writer, *b.* at Geneva, has a place in English literature for his well-known work, *The Constitution of England*, written in French, and translated into English in 1775. He also wrote a comparison of the English Government with that of Sweden, a *History of the Flagellants* (1777), and *The British Empire in Europe* (1787). He came to England in 1769, lived in great poverty, and having inherited a small fortune, returned to his native place in 1775.

DELONEY, THOMAS (1543-1600).—Novelist and balladist, appears to have worked as a silk-weaver in Norwich, but was in London by 1586, and in the course of the next 10 years is known to have written about 50 ballads, some of which involved him in trouble, and caused him to lie *perdue* for a time. It is only recently that his more important work as a novelist, in which he ranks with Greene and Nash, has received attention. He appears to have turned to this new field of effort when his original one was closed to him for the time. Less under the influence of Lyly and other preceding writers than Greene, he is more natural, simple, and direct, and writes of middle-class citizens and tradesmen with a light and pleasant humour. Of his novels, *Thomas of Reading* is in honour of clothiers, *Jack of Newbury* celebrates weaving, and *The Gentle Craft* is dedicated to the praise of shoemakers. He "dy'd poorely," but was "honestly buried."

DE MORGAN, AUGUSTUS (1806-1871).—Mathematician, *b.* in India, and *ed.* at Camb., was one of the most brilliant of English mathematicians. He is mentioned here in virtue of his *Budget of Paradoxes*, a series of papers originally *pub.* in *The Athenæum*, in which mathematical fallacies are discussed with sparkling wit, and the keenest logic.

DENHAM, SIR JOHN (1615-1669).—Poet, *s.* of the Chief Baron of Exchequer in Ireland, was *b.* in Dublin, and *ed.* at Oxf. He began his literary career with a tragedy, *The Sophy* (1641), which seldom rises above mediocrity. His poem, *Cooper's Hill* (1642), is the work by which he is remembered. It is the first example in English of a poem devoted to local description. D. received extravagant praise from Johnson; but the place now assigned him is a much more humble one. His verse is smooth, clear, and agreeable, and occasionally a thought is expressed with remarkable terseness and force. In his earlier years D. suffered for his Royalism; but after the Restoration enjoyed prosperity. He, however, made an unhappy marriage, and his last years were clouded by insanity. He was an architect by profession, coming between Inigo Jones and Wren as King's Surveyor.

DENNIS, JOHN (1657-1734).—Critic, etc., *s.* of a saddler, was *b.* in London, and *ed.* at Harrow and Caius Coll., Camb., from the latter of which he was expelled for stabbing a fellow-student, and transferred himself to Trinity Hall. He attached himself to the Whigs, in whose interest he wrote several bitter and vituperative pamphlets. His attempts at play-writing were failures; and he then devoted himself chiefly to criticising the works of his contemporaries. In this line, while showing some acuteness, he aroused much enmity by his ill-temper and jealousy. Unfortunately for him, some of those whom he attacked, such as Pope and Swift, had the power of conferring upon him an unenviable immortality. Embalmed in *The Dunciad*, his name has attained a fame which no work of his own could have given it. Of Milton, however, he showed a true appreciation. Among his works are *Rinaldo and Armida* (1699), *Appius and Virginia* (1709), *Reflections Critical and Satirical* (1711), and *Three Letters on Shakespeare*. He *d.* in straitened circumstances.

DE QUINCEY, THOMAS (1785-1859).—Essayist and miscellaneous writer, *s.* of a merchant in Manchester, was *b.* there. The aristocratic "De" was assumed by himself, his *f.*, whom he lost while he was still a child, having been known by the name of Quincey, and he claimed descent from a Norman family. His *Autobiographic Sketches* give a vivid picture of his early years at the family residence of Greenheys, and show him as a highly imaginative and over-sensitive child, suffering hard things at the hands of a tyrannical elder brother. He was *ed.* first at home, then at Bath Grammar

School, next at a private school at Winkfield, Wilts, and in 1801 he was sent to the Manchester Grammar School, from which he ran away, and for some time rambled in Wales on a small allowance made to him by his mother. Tiring of this, he went to London in the end of 1802, where he led the strange Bohemian life related in *The Confessions.* His friends, thinking it high time to interfere, sent him in 1803 to Oxf., which did not, however, preclude occasional brief interludes in London, on one of which he made his first acquaintance with opium, which was to play so prominent and disastrous a part in his future life. In 1807 he became acquainted with Coleridge, Wordsworth, and Southey, and soon afterwards with C. Lamb. During the years 1807-9 he paid various visits to the Lakes, and in the latter year he settled at Townend, Grasmere, where Wordsworth had previously lived. Here he pursued his studies, becoming gradually more and more enslaved by opium, until in 1813 he was taking from 8000 to 12,000 drops daily. John Wilson (Christopher North), who was then living at Elleray, had become his friend, and brought him to Edinburgh occasionally, which ended in his passing the latter part of his life in that city. His marriage to Margaret Simpson, *dau.* of a farmer, took place in 1816. Up to this time he had written nothing, but had been steeping his mind in German metaphysics, and out-of-the-way learning of various kinds; but in 1819 he sketched out *Prolegomena of all future Systems of Political Economy*, which, however, was never finished. In the same year he acted as ed. of the *Westmoreland Gazette.* His true literary career began in 1821 with the publication in the *London Magazine* of *The Confessions of an English Opium-Eater.* Thereafter he produced a long series of articles, some of them almost on the scale of books, in *Blackwood's* and *Tait's* magazines, the *Edinburgh Literary Gazette*, and *Hogg's Instructor.* These included *Murder considered as one of the Fine Arts* (1827), and in his later and more important period, *Suspiria De Profundis* (1845), *The Spanish Military Nun* (1847), *The English Mail-Coach, and Vision of Sudden Death* (1849). In 1853 he began a *coll.* ed. of his works, which was the main occupation of his later years. He had in 1830 brought his family to Edinburgh, which, except for two years, 1841-43, when he lived in Glasgow, was his home till his death in 1859, and in 1837, on his wife's death, he placed them in the neighbouring village of Lasswade, while he lived in solitude, moving about from one dingy lodging to another.

De Q. stands among the great masters of style in the language. In his greatest passages, as in the *Vision of Sudden Death* and the *Dream Fugue*, the cadence of his elaborately piled-up sentences falls like cathedral music, or gives an abiding expression to the fleeting pictures of his most gorgeous dreams. His character unfortunately bore no correspondence to his intellectual endowments. His moral system had in fact been shattered by indulgence in opium. His appearance and manners have been thus described: "A short and fragile, but well-proportioned frame; a shapely and compact head; a face beaming with intellectual light, with rare, almost feminine beauty of feature and complexion; a fascinating courtesy of manner, and a fulness, swiftness, and elegance of silvery speech." His own works give very detailed information regarding himself.

See also Page's *Thomas De Quincey: his Life and Writings* (1879), Prof. Masson's *De Quincey* (English Men of Letters). *Collected Writings* (14 vols. 1889-90).

DERMODY, THOMAS (1775-1802).—Poet, *b.* at Ennis, showed great capacity for learning, but fell into idle and dissipated habits, and threw away his opportunities. He *pub.* two books of poems, which after his death were *coll.* as *The Harp of Erin.*

DE VERE, AUBREY THOMAS (1814-1902).—Poet, *s.* of Sir Aubrey de V., himself a poet, was *b.* in Co. Limerick, and *ed.* at Trinity Coll., Dublin. In early life he became acquainted with Wordsworth, by whom he was greatly influenced. On the religious and ecclesiastical side he passed under the influence of Newman and Manning, and in 1851 was received into the Church of Rome. He was the author of many vols. of poetry, including *The Waldenses* (1842), *The Search for Proserpine* (1843), etc. In 1861 he began a series of poems on Irish subjects, *Inisfail, The Infant Bridal, Irish Odes*, etc. His interest in Ireland and its people led him to write prose works, including *English Misrule and Irish Misdeeds* (1848); and to criticism he contributed *Essays chiefly on Poetry* (1887). His last work was his *Recollections* (1897). His poetry is characterised by lofty ethical tone, imaginative power, and grave stateliness of expression.

DIBDIN, CHARLES (1745-1814).—Dramatist and song-writer, *b.* at Southampton, began his literary career at 16 with a drama, *The Shepherd's Artifice.* His fame, however, rests on his sea songs, which are unrivalled, and include *Tom Bowling, Poor Jack*, and *Blow High Blow Low.* He is said to have written over 1200 of these, besides many dramatic pieces and two novels, *Hannah Hewitt* (1792), and *The Younger Brother* (1793), and a *History of the Stage* (1795).

DICKENS, CHARLES (1812-1870).—Novelist, *b.* at Landport, near Portsmouth, where his *f.* was a clerk in the Navy Pay-Office. The hardships and mortifications of his early life, his want of regular schooling, and his miserable time in the blacking factory, which form the basis of the early chapters of *David Copperfield*, are largely accounted for by the fact that his *f.* was to a considerable extent the prototype of the immortal Mr. Micawber; but partly by his being a delicate and sensitive child, unusually susceptible to suffering both in body and mind. He had, however, much time for reading, and had access to the older novelists, Fielding, Smollett, and others. A kindly relation also took him frequently to the theatre, where he acquired his life-long interest in, and love of, the stage. After a few years' residence in Chatham, the family removed to London, and soon thereafter his *f.* became an inmate of the Marshalsea, in which by-and-by the whole family joined him, a passage in his life which furnishes the material for parts of *Little Dorrit.* This period of family obscuration happily lasted but a short time: the elder D. managed to satisfy his creditors, and soon after retired from his official duties on a pension. About the same time D. had two years of continuous schooling, and shortly afterwards he entered a law office. His leisure he devoted to reading and learning shorthand, in which he became very expert. He then acted as parliamentary reporter, first for *The True Sun*, and from 1835 for the *Morning Chronicle*. Meanwhile he had been contributing to the *Monthly Magazine* and the *Evening Chronicle* the papers which, in 1836, appeared in a *coll.* form as *Sketches by Boz;* and he had also produced one or two comic burlettas. In the same year he *m*. Catherine Hogarth; and in the following year occurred the opportunity of his life. He was asked by Chapman and Hall to write the letterpress for a series of sporting plates to be done by Robert Seymour who, however, *d.* shortly after, and was succeeded by Hablot Browne (Phiz), who became the illustrator of most of D.'s novels. In the hands of D. the original plan was entirely altered, and became the *Pickwick Papers* which, appearing in monthly parts during 1837-39, took the country by storm. Simultaneously *Oliver Twist* was coming out in *Bentley's Miscellany*. Thenceforward D.'s literary career was a continued success, and the almost yearly publication of his works constituted the main events of his life. *Nicholas Nickleby* appeared in serial form 1838-39. Next year he projected *Master Humphrey's Clock*, intended to be a series of miscellaneous stories and sketches. It was, however, soon abandoned, *The Old Curiosity Shop* and *Barnaby Rudge* taking its place. The latter, dealing with the Gordon Riots, is, with the partial exception of the *Tale of Two Cities*, the author's only excursion into the historical novel. In 1841 D. went to America, and was received with great enthusiasm, which, however, the publication of *American Notes* considerably damped, and the appearance of *Martin Chuzzlewit* in 1843, with its caustic criticisms of certain features of American life, converted into extreme, though temporary, unpopularity. The first of the Christmas books—the *Christmas Carol*—appeared in 1843, and in the following year D. went to Italy, where at Genoa he wrote *The Chimes*, followed by *The Cricket on the Hearth*, *The Battle of Life*, and *The Haunted Man*. In January, 1846, he was appointed first ed. of *The Daily News*, but resigned in a few weeks. The same year he went to Switzerland, and while there wrote *Dombey and Son*, which was *pub.* in 1848, and was immediately followed by his masterpiece, *David Copperfield* (1849-50). Shortly before this he had become manager of a theatrical company, which performed in the provinces, and he had in 1849 started his magazine, *Household Words*. *Bleak House* appeared in 1852-53, *Hard Times* in 1854, and *Little Dorrit* 1856-57. In 1856 he bought Gadshill Place, which, in 1860, became his permanent home. In 1858 he began his public readings from his works, which, while eminently successful from a financial point of view, from the nervous strain they entailed on him gradually broke down his constitution, and hastened his death. In the same year he separated from his wife, and consequent upon the controversy which arose thereupon he brought *Household Words* to an end, and started *All the Year Round*, in which appeared *A Tale of Two Cities* (1859), and *Great Expectations* (1860-61). *Our Mutual Friend* came out in numbers (1864-65). D. was now in the full tide of his readings, and decided to give a course of them in America. Thither accordingly he went in the end of 1867, returning in the following May. He had a magnificent reception, and his profits amounted to £20,000; but the effect on his health was such that he was obliged, on medical advice, finally to abandon all appearances of the kind. In 1869 he began his last work, *The Mystery of Edwin Drood*, which was interrupted by his death from an apoplectic seizure on June 8, 1870.

One of D.'s most marked characteristics is the extraordinary wealth of his invention as exhibited in the number and variety of the characters introduced into his novels. Another, especially, of course, in his earlier works, is his boundless flow of animal spirits. Others are his marvellous keenness of observation and his descriptive power. And the English race may well, with Thackeray, be "grateful for the innocent laughter, and the sweet and unsullied pages which the author of *David Copperfield* gives to [its] children." On the other hand, his faults are obvious, a tendency to caricature, a mannerism that often tires, and almost disgusts, fun often forced, and pathos not seldom degenerating into mawkishness. But at his best how rich and genial is the humour, how tender often the pathos. And when all deductions are made, he had the laughter and tears of the English-speaking world at command for a full generation while he lived, and that his spell still works is proved by a continuous succession of new editions.

SUMMARY.—*B.* 1812, parliamentary reporter *c.* 1835, *pub. Sketches by Boz* 1836, *Pickwick* 1837-39, and his other novels almost continuously until his death, visited America 1841, started *Household Words* 1849, and *All the Year Round* 1858, when also he began his public readings, visiting America again in 1867, *d.* 1870.

Life by John Foster (1872), *Letters* ed. by Miss Hogarth (1880-82). Numerous Lives and Monographs by Sala, F. T. Marzials (Great Writers Series), A. W. Ward (Men of Letters Series), F. G. Kitton, G. K. Chesterton, etc.

DICKINSON, EMILY (1830–1886).—American poetess, *b.* Dec. 10 at Amherst, Mass. She was *ed.* at the Amherst Academy and the Mount Holyoke Female Seminary. In 1853–1854 she visited Washington and Philadelphia and at the latter city became involved in an unfortunate love affair. She gave up her lover either because of parental opposition or because of another woman (probably both), and returned to her home at Amherst to live the life of a recluse until her death. She wrote a quantity of lyric poetry, but only two or three poems were published in her lifetime. Between 1890 and 1896 three series of her poems were published which were extremely successful, but her complete poems were not published until 1924; her *Letters* were published in the same year. She *d.* May 16.

DIGBY, SIR KENELM (1603-1665).—Miscellaneous writer, *b.* near Newport Pagnell, *s.* of Sir Everard D., one of the Gunpowder Plot conspirators, was *ed.* at Oxf., travelled much, and was engaged in sea-fighting. Brought up first as a Romanist, then as a Protestant, he in 1636 joined the Church of Rome. During the Civil War he was active on the side of the King, and on the fall of his cause was for a time banished. He was the author of several books on religious and quasi-scientific subjects, including one on the *Choice of a Religion*, on the *Immortality of the Soul*, *Observations on*

Spenser's Faery Queen, and a criticism on Sir T. Browne's *Religio Medici*. He also wrote a *Discourse on Vegetation*, and one *On the Cure of Wounds* by means of a sympathetic powder which he imagined he had discovered.

DILKE, CHARLES WENTWORTH (1789-1864).—Critic and writer on literature, served for many years in the Navy Pay-Office, on retiring from which he devoted himself to literary pursuits. He had in 1814-16 made a continuation of Dodsley's *Collection of English Plays*, and in 1829 he became part proprietor and ed. of *The Athenæum*, the influence of which he greatly extended. In 1846 he resigned the editorship, and assumed that of *The Daily News*, but contributed to *The Athenæum* his famous papers on *Pope*, *Burke*, *Junius*, etc., and shed much new light on his subjects. His grandson, the present Sir C. W. Dilke, *pub.* these writings in 1875 under the title, *Papers of a Critic*.

DISRAELI, B. (*see* BEACONSFIELD).

D'ISRAELI, ISAAC (1766-1848).—Miscellaneous writer, was decended from a Jewish family which had been settled first in Spain, and afterwards at Venice. *Ed.* at Amsterdam and Leyden, he devoted himself to literature, producing a number of interesting works of considerable value, including *Curiosities of Literature*, in 3 series (1791-1823), *Dissertation on Anecdotes* (1793), *Calamities of Authors* (1812), *Amenities of Literature* (1841); also works dealing with the lives of James I. and Charles I. D. was latterly blind. He was the *f.* of Benjamin D., Earl of Beaconsfield (*q.v.*).

DIXON, WILLIAM HEPWORTH (1821-1879).—Historian and traveller, *b.* near Manchester, went to London in 1846, and became connected with *The Daily News*, for which he wrote articles on social and prison reform. In 1850 he *pub.* *John Howard and the Prison World of Europe*, which had a wide circulation, and about the same time he wrote a *Life of Peace* (1851), in answer to Macaulay's onslaught. Lives of *Admiral Blake* and *Lord Bacon* followed, which received somewhat severe criticisms at the hands of competent authorities. D. was ed. of *The Athenæum*, 1853-69, and wrote many books of travel, including *The Holy Land* (1865), *New America* (1867), and *Free Russia* (1870). His later historical works include *Her Majesty's Tower*, and *The History of Two Queens* (Catherine of Arragon and Anne Boleyn). He was one of the founders of the Palestine Exploration Fund, and was a member of the first School Board for London (1870).

DOBELL, SYDNEY THOMPSON (1824-1874).—Poet, *b.* at Cranbrook, Kent, *s.* of a wine-merchant, who removed to Cheltenham, where most of the poet's life was passed. His youth was precocious (he was engaged at 15 and *m.* at 20). In 1850 his first work, *The Roman*, appeared, and had great popularity. *Balder, Part I.* (1854), *Sonnets on the War*, jointly with Alexander Smith (*q.v.*) (1855), and *England in Time of War* (1856) followed. His later years were passed in Scotland and abroad in search of health, which, however, was damaged by a fall while exploring some ruins at Pozzuoli. D.'s poems exhibit fancy and brilliancy of diction, but want simplicity, and sometimes run into grandiloquence and other faults of the so-called Spasmodic School to which he belonged.

DODD, WILLIAM (1729-1777).—Divine and forger, *ed.* at Camb., became a popular preacher in London, and a Royal Chaplain, but, acquiring expensive habits, got involved in hopeless difficulties, from which he endeavoured to escape first by an attempted simoniacal transaction, for which he was disgraced, and then by forging a bond for £4200, for which, according to the then existing law, he was hanged. Great efforts were made to obtain a commutation of the sentence, and Dr. Johnson wrote one of the petitions, but on D.'s book, *Thoughts in Prison*, appearing posthumously, he remarked that " a man who has been canting all his days may cant to the last." D. was the author of a collection of *Beauties of Shakespeare, Reflections on Death*, and a translation of the *Hymns of Callimachus*.

DODDRIDGE, PHILIP (1702 - 1751). — Nonconformist divine and writer of religious books and hymns, *b.* in London, and *ed.* for the ministry at a theological institution at Kibworth, became minister first at Market Harborough, and afterwards at Northampton, where he also acted as head of a theological academy. D., who was a man of amiable and joyous character, as well as an accomplished scholar, composed many standard books of religion, of which the best known is *The Rise and Progress of Religion in the Soul* (1745). In 1736 he received the degree of D.D. from Aberdeen. He *d.* at Lisbon, whither he had gone in search of health. Several of his hymns, *e.g., Ye Servants of the Lord, O Happy Day*, and *O God of Bethel*, are universally used by English-speaking Christians, and have been translated into various languages.

DODGSON, CHARLES LUTWIDGE ("LEWIS CARROLL") (1832-1898).—Mathematician and writer of books for children, *s.* of a clergyman at Daresbury, Cheshire, was *ed.* at Rugby and Oxf. After taking orders he was appointed lecturer on mathematics, on which subject he *pub.* several valuable treatises. His fame rests, however, on his books for children, full of ingenuity and delightful humour, of which *Alice's Adventures in Wonderland*, and its sequel, *Through the Looking-glass*, are the best.

DODSLEY, ROBERT (1703-1764).—Poet, dramatist, and bookseller, *b.* near Mansfield, and apprenticed to a stocking-weaver, but not liking this employment, he ran away and became a footman. While thus engaged he produced *The Muse in Livery* (1732). This was followed by *The Toy Shop*, a drama, which brought him under the notice of Pope, who befriended him, and assisted him in starting business as a bookseller. In this he became eminently successful, and acted as publisher for Pope, Johnson, and Akenside. He projected and *pub. The Annual Register*, and made a collection of *Old English Plays*, also of *Poems by Several Hands* in 6 vols. In addition to the original works above mentioned he wrote various plays and poems, including *The Blind Beggar of Bethnal Green* (1741), and *Cleone* (1758).

DONNE, JOHN (1573-1631).—Poet and divine, *s.* of a wealthy ironmonger in London, where he was *b.* Brought up as a Roman Catholic, he was sent to Oxf. and Camb., and afterwards entered Lincoln's Inn with a view to the law. Here he studied the points of controversy between Romanists and Protestants, with the result that he joined the Church of England. The next two years were somewhat changeful, including travels on the Continent, service as a private sec., and a clandestine marriage with the niece of his patron, which led to dismissal and imprisonment, followed by reconciliation. On the suggestion of James I., who approved of *Pseudo-Martyr* (1610), a book against Rome which he had written, he took orders, and after executing a mission to Bohemia, he was, in 1621, made Dean of St. Paul's. D. had great popularity as a preacher. His poetical works consist of elegies, satires, epigrams, and religious pieces, in which, with some conceits, there is much noble poetry and imagination of a high order. Among his writings may be noted *An Anatomy of the World* (1611), an elegy; also his fine *Epithalamium* (1613), *Progress of the Soul* (1601), and *Divine Poems.* Collections of his poems appeared in 1633 and 1649. He exercised a strong influence on literature for over half a century after his death; an influence that shows signs of reviving. Early folios of his remarkable sermons appeared, 1640, 1649, 1660.

DORAN, JOHN (1807-1878).—Miscellaneous writer, of Irish parentage, wrote a number of works dealing with the lighter phases of manners, antiquities, and social history, often bearing punning titles, *e.g., Table Traits with Something on Them* (1854), and *Knights and their Days.* He also wrote *Lives of the Queens of England of the House of Hanover* (1855), and *A History of Court Fools* (1858), and ed. Horace Walpole's *Journal of the Reign of George III.* His books contain much curious and out-of-the-way information. D. was for a short time ed. of *The Athenæum.*

DORSET, CHARLES SACKVILLE, 6TH EARL OF (1638-1706).—Poet, was one of the dissolute and witty courtiers of Charles II., and a friend of Sir C. Sedley (*q.v.*), in whose orgies he participated. He was, however, a patron of literature, and a benefactor of Dryden in his later and less prosperous years. He wrote a few satires and songs, among the latter being the well-known, *To all you Ladies now on Land.* As might be expected, his writings are characterised by the prevailing indelicacy of the time.

DORSET, THOMAS SACKVILLE, 1ST EARL OF, AND LORD BUCKHURST (1536-1608).—Poet and statesman, was *b.* at Buckhurst, Sussex, the only *s.* of Sir Richard S., and *ed.* at Oxf. and Camb. He studied law at the Inner Temple, and while there wrote, in conjunction with Thomas Norton, *Ferren and Porrex* or *Gerboduc* (1561-2), the first regular English tragedy. A little later he planned *The Mirror for Magistrates,* which was to have been a series of narratives of distinguished Englishmen, somewhat on the model of Boccaccio's *Falls of Princes.* Finding the plan too large, he handed it over to others—seven poets in all being engaged upon it—and himself contributed two poems only, one on *Buckingham,* the confederate, and afterwards the victim, of Richard III., and an *Induction* or introduction, which constitute nearly the whole value of the work. In these poems S. becomes the connecting link between Chaucer and Spenser. They are distinguished by strong invention and imaginative power, and a stately and sombre grandeur of style. S. played a prominent part in the history of his time, and held many high offices, including those of Lord Steward and Lord Treasurer, the latter of which he held from 1599 till his death. It fell to him to announce to Mary Queen of Scots the sentence of death.

DOUCE, FRANCIS (1757-1834).—Antiquary, *b.* in London, was for some time in the British Museum. He *pub.* *Illustrations of Shakespeare* (1807), and a dissertation on *The Dance of Death* (1833).

DOUGLAS, GAVIN (1474?-1522).—Poet, 3rd *s.* of the 5th Earl of Angus, was *b.* about 1474, and *ed.* at St. Andrews for the Church. Promotion came early, and he was in 1501 made Provost of St. Giles, Edin., and in 1514 Abbot of Aberbrothock, and Archbishop of St. Andrews. But the times were troublous, and he had hardly received these latter preferments when he was deprived of them. He was, however, named Bishop of Dunkeld in 1514 and, after some difficulty, and undergoing imprisonment, was confirmed in the see. In 1520 he was again driven forth, and two years later *d.* of the plague in London. His principal poems are *The Palace of Honour* (1501), and *King Hart*, both allegorical; but his great achievement was his translation of the *Æneid* in ten-syllabled metre, the first translation into English of a classical work. D.'s language is more archaic than that of some of his predecessors, his rhythm is rough and unequal, but he had fire, and a power of vivid description, and his allegories are ingenious and felicitous.

Coll. ed. of works by John Small, LL.D., 4 vols., 1874.

DOYLE, SIR FRANCIS HASTINGS (1810-1888).—Poet, belonged to a military family which produced several distinguished officers, including his *f.*, who bore the same name. He was *b.* near Tadcaster, Yorkshire, and *ed.* at Eton and Oxf. Studying law he was called to the Bar in 1837, and afterwards held various high fiscal appointments, becoming in 1869 Commissioner of Customs. In 1834 he *pub.* *Miscellaneous Verses*, followed by *Two Destinies* (1844), *Œdipus, King of Thebes* (1849), and *Return of the Guards* (1866). He was elected in 1867 Prof. of Poetry at Oxf. D.'s best work is his ballads, which include *The Red Thread of Honour*, *The Private of the Buffs*, and *The Loss of the Birkenhead*. In his longer poems his genuine poetical feeling was not equalled by his power of expression, and much of his poetry is commonplace.

DRAKE, JOSEPH RODMAN (1795-1820).—Poet, *b.* at New York, studied medicine, *d.* of consumption. He collaborated with F. Halleck in the *Croaker Papers*, and wrote "The Culprit Fay" and "The American Flag."

DRAPER, JOHN WILLIAM (1811-1882).—Historian, *b.* at St. Helen's, Lancashire, emigrated to Virginia, and was a prof. in the Univ. of New York. He wrote *History of the American Civil War* (1867-70), *History of the Intellectual Development of Europe* (1863), and *History of the Conflict between Science and Religion* (1874), besides treatises on various branches of science.

DRAYTON, MICHAEL (1563-1631).—Poet, *b.* in Warwickshire, was in early life page to a gentleman, and was possibly at Camb. or Oxf. His earliest poem, *The Harmonie of the Church*, was destroyed. His next was *The Shepherd's Garland* (1593), afterwards reprinted as *Eclogues*. Three historical poems, *Gaveslon* (1593), *Matilda* (1594), and *Robert, Duke of Normandie* (1596) followed, and he then appears to have collaborated with Dekker, Webster, and others in dramatic work. His *magnum opus*, however, was *Polyolbion* (1613?), a topographical description of England in twelve-syllabled verse, full of antiquarian and historical details, so accurate as to make the work an authority on such matters. The rushing verse is full of vigour and gusto. Other poems of D. are *The Wars of the Barons* (1603), *England's Heroical Epistles* (1598) (being imaginary letters between Royal lovers such as Henry II. and Rosamund), *Poems, Lyric and Heroic* (1606) (including the fine ballad of "Agincourt"), *Nymphidia*, his most graceful work, *Muses Elizium*, and *Idea's Mirrour*, a collection of sonnets, Idea being the name of the lady to whom they were addressed. Though often heavy, D. had the true poetic gift, had passages of grandeur, and sang the praises of England with the heart of a patriot.

DRUMMOND, HENRY (1851-1897).—Theological and scientific writer, *b.* at Stirling, and *ed.* at Edin., he studied for the ministry of the Free Church. Having a decided scientific bent he gave himself specially to the study of geology, and made a scientific tour in the Rocky Mountains with Sir A. Geikie. Some years later he undertook a geological exploration of Lake Nyassa and the neighbouring country for the African Lakes Corporation, and brought home a valuable Report. He also *pub. Tropical Africa*, a vivid account of his travels. He became much associated with the American evangelist, D. L. Moody, and became an extremely effective speaker on religious subjects, devoting himself specially to young men. His chief contribution to literature was his *Natural Law in the Spiritual World*, which had extraordinary popularity. *The Ascent of Man* was less successful. D. was a man of great personal fascination, and wrote in an interesting and suggestive manner, but his reasoning in his scientific works was by no means unassailable.

DRUMMOND, WILLIAM (1585-1649).—Poet, was descended from a very ancient family, and through Annabella D., Queen of Robert III., related to the Royal House. *Ed.* at Edin. Univ., he studied law on the Continent, but succeeding in 1610 to his paternal estate of Hawthornden, he devoted himself to poetry. *Tears on the Death of Meliades* (Prince Henry) appeared in 1613, and in 1616 *Poems, Amorous, Funerall, Divine, etc.* His finest poem, *Forth Feasting* (1617), is addressed to James VI. on his revisiting Scotland. D. was also a prose-writer, and composed a *History of the Five Jameses, Kings of Scotland from* 1423-1524, and *The Cypress Grove*, a meditation on death. He was also a mechanical genius, and patented 16 inventions. D., though a Scotsman, wrote in the classical English of the day, and was the friend of his principal literary contemporaries, notably of Ben Jonson, who visited him at Hawthornden, on which occasion D. preserved notes of his conversations, not always flattering. For this he has received much blame, but it must be remembered that he did not *pub.* them. As a poet he belonged to the school of Spenser. His verse is sweet, flowing, and harmonious. He excelled as a writer of sonnets, one of which, on *John the Baptist*, has a suggestion of Milton.

Life by Prof. Masson (1873), *Three Centuries of Scottish Literature*, Walker, 1893. *Maitland Club* ed. of *Poems* (1832).

DRYDEN, JOHN (1631-1700).—Poet, dramatist, and satirist, was *b.* at Aldwincle Rectory, Northamptonshire. His *f.*, from whom he inherited a small estate, was Erasmus, 3rd *s.* of Sir Erasmus Driden; his mother was Mary Pickering, also of good family; both families belonged to the Puritan side in politics and religion. He was *ed.* at Westminster School and Trinity Coll., Camb., and thereafter, in 1657, came to London. While at coll. he had written some not very successful verse. His *Heroic Stanzas on the Death of Oliver Cromwell* (1658) was his first considerable poem. It was followed, in 1660, by *Astræa Redux*, in honour of the Restoration. The interval of 18 months had been crowded with events, and though much has been written against his apparent change of opinion, it is fair to remember that the whole cast of his mind led him to be a supporter of *de facto* authority. In 1663 he *m.* Lady Elizabeth Howard, *dau.* of the Earl of Berkshire. The Restoration introduced a revival of the drama in its most debased form, and for many years D. was a prolific playwright, but though his vigorous powers enabled him to work effectively in this department, as in every other in which he engaged, it was not his natural line, and happily his fame does not rest upon his plays, which are deeply stained with the immorality of the age. His first effort, *The Wild Gallant* (1663), was a failure; his next, *The Rival Ladies*, a tragi-comedy, established his reputation, and among his other dramas may be mentioned *The Indian Queene*, *Amboyna* (1673), *Tyrannic Love* (1669), *Almanzar and Almahide* (ridiculed in Buckingham's *Rehearsal*) (1670), *Arungzebe* (1675), *All for Love* (an adaptation of Shakespeare's *Antony and Cleopatra*) (1678). During the great plague, 1665, D. left London, and lived with his father-in-law at Charleton. On his return he *pub.* his first poem of real power, *Annus Mirabilis*, of which the subjects were the great fire, and the Dutch War. In 1668 appeared his *Essay on Dramatic Poetry* in the form of a dialogue, fine alike as criticism and as prose. Two years later (1670) he became Poet Laureate and Historiographer Royal with a pension of £300 a year. D. was now in prosperous circumstances, having received a portion with his wife, and besides the salaries of his appointments, and his profits from literature, holding a valuable share in the King's play-house. In 1671 G. Villiers, Duke of Buckingham, produced his *Rehearsal*, in ridicule of the overdone heroics of the prevailing drama, and satirising D. as Mr. Bayes. To this D. made no immediate reply, but bided his time. The next years were devoted to the drama. But by this time public affairs were assuming a critical aspect. A large section of the nation was becoming alarmed at the prospect of the succession of the Duke of York, and a restoration of popery, and Shaftesbury was supposed to be promoting the claims of the Duke of Monmouth. And now D. showed his full powers. The first part of *Absalom and Achitophel* appeared in 1681, in which Charles figures as "David," Shaftesbury as "Achitophel," Monmouth as "Absalom," Buckingham as "Zimri," in the short but crushing delineation of whom the attack of the *Rehearsal* was requited in the most ample measure. The effect of the poem was tremendous. Nevertheless the indictment against Shaftesbury for high treason was ignored by the Grand Jury at the Old Bailey, and in honour of the event a medal was struck, which gave a title to D.'s next stroke. His *Medal* was issued in 1682. The success of these wonderful poems raised a storm round D. Replies were forthcoming in Elkanah Settle's *Absalom and Achitophel Transposed*, and Pordage's *Azaria and Hushai*. These compositions, especially Pordage's, were comparatively moderate. Far otherwise was Shadwell's *Medal of John Bayes*, one of the most brutal and indecent pieces in the language. D.'s revenge—and an ample one—was the publication of *MacFlecknoe*, a satire in which all his opponents, but especially Shadwell, were held up to the loathing and ridicule of succeeding ages, and others had conferred upon them an immortality which, however unenviable, no efforts of their own could have secured for them. Its immediate effect was to crush and silence all his assailants. The following year, 1683, saw the publication of *Religio Laici* (the religion of a layman). In 1686 D. joined the Church of Rome, for which he has by some been blamed for time-serving of the basest kind. On the other hand his consistency and conscientiousness have by others been as strongly maintained. The change, which was announced by the publication in 1687 of *The Hind and the Panther, a Defence of the Roman Church*, at all events did not bring with it any worldly advantages. It was parodied by C. Montague and Prior in the *Town and Country Mouse*. At the Revolution D. was deprived of all his pensions and appointments, including the Laureateship, in which he was succeeded by his old enemy Shadwell. His latter years were passed in comparative poverty, although the Earl of Dorset and other old friends contributed by their liberality to lighten his cares. In these circumstances he turned again to the drama, which, however, was no longer what it had been as a source of income. To this period belong *Don Sebastian*, and his last play, *Love Triumphant*. A new mine, however, was beginning to be opened up in the demand for translations which had arisen. This gave D. a new opportunity, and he produced, in addition to translations from Juvenal and Perseus, his famous "Virgil" (1697). About the same time appeared *The Ode for St. Cecilia's Day*, and *Alexander's Feast*, and in 1700, the year of his death, the *Fables*, largely adaptations from Chaucer and Boccaccio. In his own line, that of argument, satire, and declamation, D. is without a rival in our literature: he had little creative imagination and no pathos. His dramas, which in bulk are the greatest part of his work, add almost nothing to his fame; in them he was meeting a public demand, not following the native bent of his genius. In his satires, and in such poems as *Alexander's Feast*, he rises to the highest point of his powers in a verse swift and heart-stirring. In prose his style is clear, strong, and nervous. He seems to have been almost insensible to the beauty of Nature.

SUMMARY.—*B.* 1631, *ed.* Westminster and Camb., became prolific playwright, *pub. Annus Mirabilis c.* 1666, Poet Laureate 1667, *pub. Absalom and Achitophel* (part 1) 1681, *Medal* 1682, *MacFlecknoe* 1682, *Religio Laici* 1683, joined Church of Rome 1686, *pub. Hind and Panther* 1687, deprived of offices and pensions at Revolution 1688, *pub.* translations including "Virgil" 1697, *St. Cecilia's Day* and *Alexander's Feast c.* 1697, and *Fables* 1700, when he *d.*

Sir W. Scott's ed. with *Life* 1808, re-edited in 18 vols. by Prof. Saintsbury (1883-93); Aldine ed. (5 vols., 1892), Johnson's *Lives of the Poets*, etc.

DUFF, SIR MOUNTSTUART E. GRANT (1829-1906).—Miscellaneous writer, was M.P. for the Elgin Burghs, and Lieut.-Governor of Madras. He *pub. Studies of European Politics*, books on Sir H. Maine, Lord de Tabley, and Renan, and a series of *Notes from a Diary*, perhaps his most interesting work.

DUFFERIN, HELEN SELINA (SHERIDAN), COUNTESS OF (1807-1867).—Eldest *dau.* of Tom S., grand-daughter of Richard Brinsley S. (*q.v.*), and sister of Mrs. Norton (*q.v.*). She and her two sisters were known as "the three Graces," the third being the Duchess of Somerset. She shared in the family talent, and wrote a good deal of verse, her best known piece being perhaps *The Lament of the Irish Emigrant*, beginning "I'm sittin' on the stile, Mary." She also wrote *Lispings from Low Latitudes, or Extracts from the Journal of the Hon. Impulsia Gushington, Finesse, or a Busy Day at Messina*, etc.

DUFFY, SIR CHARLES GAVAN (1816-1903).—Poet, *b.* in Monaghan, early took to journalism, and became one of the founders of the *Nation* newspaper, and one of the leaders of the Young Ireland movement. Thereafter he went to Australia, where he became a leading politician, and rose to be Premier of Victoria. His later years were spent chiefly on the Continent. He did much to stimulate in Ireland a taste for the national history and literature, started *The Library of Ireland*, and made a collection, *The Ballad Poetry of Ireland*, which was a great success. He also *pub.* an autobiography, *My Life in Two Hemispheres*.

DUGDALE, SIR WILLIAM (1605-1686).—Herald and antiquary, was *b.* at Coleshill, Warwickshire, and *ed.* at Coventry School. From early youth he showed a strong bent towards heraldic and antiquarian studies, which led to his appointment, in 1638, as a Pursuivant-extraordinary, from which he rose to be Garter-King-at-Arms. In 1655, jointly with Roger Dodsworth, he brought out the first vol. of *Monasticon Anglicanum* (the second following in 1661, and the third in 1673), containing the charters of the ancient monasteries. In 1656 he *pub.* the *Antiquities of Warwickshire*, which maintains a high place among county histories, and in 1666 *Origines Judiciales.* His great work, *The Baronage of England*, appeared in 1675-6. Other works were a *History of Imbanking and Drayning*, and a *History of St. Paul's Cathedral.* All D.'s writings are monuments of learning and patient investigation.

DU MAURIER, GEORGE LOUIS PALMELLA BUSSON (1834-1896).—Artist and novelist, *b.* and *ed.* in Paris, in 1864 succeeded John Leech on the staff of *Punch.* His three novels, *Peter Ibbetson* (1891), *Trilby* (1894), and *The Martian* (1896), originally appeared in *Harper's Magazine.*

DUNBAR, WILLIAM (1465?-1530?).—Poet, is believed to have been *b.* in Lothian, and *ed.* at St. Andrews, and in his earlier days he was a Franciscan friar. Thereafter he appears to have been employed by James IV. in some Court and political matters. His chief poems are *The Thrissil and the Rois* (*The Thistle and the Rose*) (1503), *The Dance of the Seven Deadly Sins,* a powerful satire, *The Golden Targe,* an allegory, and *The Lament for the Makaris* (poets) (*c.* 1507). In all these there is a vein of true poetry. In his allegorical poems he follows Chaucer in his setting, and is thus more or less imitative and conventional: in his satirical pieces, and in the *Lament,* he takes a bolder flight and shows his native power. His comic poems are somewhat gross. The date and circumstances of his death are uncertain, some holding that he fell at Flodden, others that he was alive so late as 1530. Other works are *The Merle* and *The Nightingale,* and the *Flyting* (scolding) of Dunbar and Kennedy. Mr. Gosse calls D. " the largest figure in English literature between Chaucer and Spenser." He has bright strength, swiftness, humour, and pathos, and his descriptive touch is vivid and full of colour.

DUNLOP, JOHN COLIN (*c.* 1785-1842).—Historian, *s.* of a Lord Provost of Glasgow, where and at Edin. he was *ed.*, was called to the Bar in 1807, and became Sheriff of Renfrewshire. He wrote a *History of Fiction* (1814), a *History of Roman Literature to the Augustan Age* (1823-28), and *Memoirs of Spain during the Reigns of Philip IV. and Charles II.* (1834). He also made translations from the Latin Anthology.

DUNS SCOTUS, JOHANNES (1265?-1308?).—Schoolman. The dates of his birth and death and the place of his birth are alike doubtful. He may have been at Oxf., is said to have been a regent or prof. at Paris, and was a Franciscan. He was a man of extraordinary learning, and received the sobriquet of Doctor Subtilis. Among his many works on logic and theology are a philosophic grammar, and a work on metaphysics, *De Rerum Principio* (of the beginning of things). His great opponent was Thomas Aquinas, and schoolmen of the day were divided into Scotists and Thomists, or realists and nominalists.

D'URFEY, THOMAS (1653-1723).—Dramatist and song-writer, was a well-known man-about-town, a companion of Charles II., and lived on to the reign of George I. His plays are now forgotten, and he is best known in connection with a collection of songs entitled, *Pills to Purge Melancholy.* Addison describes him as a " diverting companion," and " a cheerful, honest, good-natured man." His writings are nevertheless extremely gross. His plays include *Siege of Memphis* (1676), *Madame Fickle* (1677), *Virtuous Wife* (1680), and *The Campaigners* (1698).

DWIGHT, TIMOTHY (1752-1817).—Theologian and poet, *b.* at Northampton, Mass., was a grandson of Jonathan Edwards, became a Congregationalist minister, Prof. of Divinity, and latterly Pres. of Yale. His works include, besides theological treatises and sermons, the following poems, *America* (1772), *The Conquest of Canaan* (1785), and *The Triumph of Infidelity*, a satire, admired in their day, but now unreadable.

DYCE, ALEXANDER (1798-1869).—Scholar and critic, *s.* of Lieut.-General Alexander D., was *b.* in Edin., and *ed.* there and at Oxf. He took orders, and for a short time served in two country curacies. Then, leaving the Church and settling in London, he betook himself to his life-work of ed. the English dramatists. His first work, *Specimens of British Poetesses*, appeared in 1825; and thereafter at various intervals ed. of Collins's *Poems*, and the dramatic works of *Peele, Middleton, Beaumont and Fletcher, Marlowe, Greene, Webster*, and others. His great ed. of *Shakespeare* in 9 vols. appeared in 1857. He also ed. various works for the Camden Society, and *pub. Table Talk of Samuel Rogers.* All D.'s work is marked by varied and accurate learning, minute research, and solid judgment.

DYER, SIR EDWARD (1545?-1607).—Poet, *b.* at Sharpham Park, Somerset, and *ed.* at Oxf., was introduced to the Court by the Earl of Leicester, and sent on a mission to Denmark, 1589. He was in 1596 made Chancellor of the Order of the Garter, and knighted. In his own day he had a reputation for his elegies among such judges as Sidney and Puttenham. For a long time there was doubt as to what poems were to be attributed to him, but about a dozen pieces have now been apparently identified as his. The best known is that on contentment beginning, "My mind to me a kingdom is."

DYER, JOHN (1700-1758).—Poet, was *b.* in Caermarthenshire. In his early years he studied painting, but finding that he was not likely to attain a satisfactory measure of success, entered the Church. He has a definite, if a modest, place in literature as the author of three poems, *Grongar Hill* (1727), *The Ruins of Rome* (1740), and *The Fleece* (1757). The first of these is the best, and the best known, and contains much true natural description; but all have passages of considerable poetical merit, delicacy and precision of phrase being their most noticeable characteristic. Wordsworth had a high opinion of D. as a poet, and addressed a sonnet to him.

EARLE, JOHN (1601-1665).—Divine and miscellaneous writer, *b.* at York, and *ed.* at Oxf., where he was a Fellow of Merton. He took orders, was tutor to Charles II., a member of the Assembly of Divines at Westminster, 1643, Chaplain and Clerk of the Closet to Charles when in exile. On the Restoration he was made Dean of Westminster, in 1662 Bishop of Worcester, and the next year Bishop of Salisbury. He was learned and eloquent, witty and agreeable in society, and was opposed to the "Conventicle" and "Five Mile" Acts, and to all forms of persecution. He wrote *Hortus Mertonensis* (the Garden of Merton) in Latin, but his chief work was *Microcosmographie, or a Piece of the World dis-*

covered in Essays and Characters (1628), the best and most interesting of all the "character" books.

EASTLAKE, ELIZABETH, LADY (RIGBY) (1809-1893).—*dau.* of Dr. Edward Rigby of Norwich, a writer on medical and agricultural subjects, spent her earlier life on the Continent and in Edin. In 1849 she *m.* Sir Charles L. Eastlake, the famous painter, and Pres. of the Royal Academy. Her first work was *Letters from the Shores of the Baltic* (1841). From 1842 she was a frequent contributor to the *Quarterly Review*, in which she wrote a very bitter criticism of *Jane Eyre*. She also wrote various books on art, and Lives of her husband, of Mrs. Grote, and of Gibson the sculptor.

ECHARD, LAURENCE (*c.* 1670-1730).—Historian, *b.* at Barsham, Suffolk, and *ed.* at Camb., took orders and became Archdeacon of Stow. He translated Terence, part of Plautus, D'Orleans' *History of the Revolutions in England*, and made numerous compilations on history, geography, and the classics. His chief work, however, is his *History of England* (1707-1720). It covers the period from the Roman occupation to his own times, and continued to be the standard work on the subject until it was superseded by translations of Rapin's French *History of England*.

EDGAR, JOHN GEORGE (1834-1864).—Writer for Boys, *s.* of Rev. John E. Hutton, Berwickshire. Among his books are *Boyhood of Great Men* (1853), *Runnymede and Lincoln Fair* (1866), *Footprints of Famous Men, Cressy and Poictiers*. He was also the first editor of *Every Boy's Magazine*.

EDGEWORTH, MARIA (1767-1849).—Novelist, *dau.* of Rich. Lovell E., of Edgeworthstown, Co. Longford, was *b.* near Reading. Her *f.*, who was himself a writer on education and mechanics, bestowed much attention on her education. She showed early promise of distinction, and assisted her *f.* in his literary labours, especially in *Practical Education* and *Essay on Irish Bulls* (1802). She soon discovered that her strength lay in fiction, and from 1800, when her first novel, *Castle Rackrent*, appeared, until 1834, when her last, *Helen*, was *pub.*, she continued to produce a series of novels and tales characterised by ingenuity of invention, humour, and acute delineation of character, notwithstanding a tendency to be didactic, and the presence of a "purpose" in most of her writings. It was the success of Miss E. in delineating Irish character that suggested to Sir W. Scott the idea of rendering a similar service to Scotland. Miss E., who had great practical ability, was able to render much aid during the Irish famine. In addition to the works above mentioned, she wrote *Moral Tales* and *Belinda* (1801), *Leonora* (1806), *Tales of Fashionable Life* (1809 and 1812), and a Memoir of her *f.*

EDWARDS, JONATHAN (1702?-1758).—Theologian, *s.* of a minister, was *b.* at East Windsor, Connecticut, *ed.* at Yale Coll., and licensed as a preacher in 1722. The following year he was appointed as tutor at Yale, a position in which he showed exceptional capacity. In 1726 he went to Northampton, Conn., as minister of a church there, and remained for 24 years, exercising his ministry with unusual earnestness and diligence. At the end of that time, however, he was in 1750 dismissed by his congregation, a disagreement having arisen on certain questions of discipline. Thereafter he acted as a missionary to the Indians of Massachusetts. While thus engaged he composed his famous treatises, *On the Freedom of the Will* (1754), and *On Original Sin* (1758). Previously, in 1746, he had produced his treatise, *On the Religious Affections*. In 1757 he was appointed Pres. of Princeton Coll., New Jersey, but was almost immediately thereafter stricken with small-pox, of which he *d.* on March 22, 1757. E. possessed an intellect of extraordinary strength and clearness, and was capable of sustaining very lengthened chains of profound argument. He is one of the ablest defenders of the Calvinistic system of theology, which he developed to its most extreme positions. He was a man of fervent piety, and of the loftiest and most disinterested character.

EDWARDS, RICHARD (1523?-1566).—Poet, was at Oxf., and went to Court, where he was made a Gentleman of the Chapel Royal, and master of the singing boys. He had a high reputation for his comedies and interludes. His *Palamon and Arcite* was acted before Elizabeth at Oxf. in 1566, when the stage fell and three persons were killed and five hurt, the play nevertheless proceeding. *Damon and Pythias* (1577), a comedy, is his only extant play.

EGAN, PIERCE (1772-1849).—Humorist, *b.* in London, he satirised the Prince Regent in *The Lives of Florizel and Perdita* (1814), but is best remembered by *Life in London: or the Day and Night Scenes of Jerry Hawthorn and his elegant friend, Corinthian Tom*, a collection of sketches which had great success at the time, and which gives a picture of the sports and amusements of London in the days of the Regency. It was illustrated by George Cruikshank.

EGGLESTON, EDWARD (1837-1902).—Novelist, *b.* at Vevay, Indiana, was a Methodist minister. He wrote a number of tales, some of which, specially the "Hoosier" series, attracted much attention, among which are *The Hoosier Schoolmaster, The Hoosier Schoolboy, The End of the World, The Faith Doctor, Queer Stories for Boys and Girls*, etc.

"ELIOT, GEORGE," *see* EVANS.

ELIZABETH, QUEEN (1533-1603).—Was one of the scholar-women of her time, being versed in Latin, Greek, French, and Italian. Her translation of Boethius shows her exceptional art and skill. In the classics Roger Ascham was her tutor. She wrote various short poems, some of which were called by her contemporaries "sonnets," though not in the true sonnet form. Her original letters and despatches show an idiomatic force of expression beyond that of any other English monarch.

ELLIOT, MISS JEAN (1727-1805).—Poetess, *dau.* of Sir Gilbert Elliot of Minto, has a small niche in literature as the authoress of the beautiful ballad, *The Flowers of the Forest*, beginning, "I've heard the lilting at our yowe-milking." Another ballad with the same title beginning, "I've seen the smiling of fortune beguiling" was written by Alicia Rutherford, afterwards Mrs. Cockburn.

ELLIOT, EBENEZER (1781-1849).—Poet, *b.* at Masborough, Yorkshire, in his youth worked in an iron-foundry, and in 1821 took up the same business on his own account with success. He is best known by his poems on behalf of the poor and oppressed, and especially for his denunciations of the Corn Laws, which gained for him the title of the Corn Law Rhymer. Though now little read, he had considerable poetic gift. His principal poems are *Corn Law Rhymes* (1831), *The Ranter*, and *The Village Patriarch* (1829).

ELLIS, GEORGE (1753-1815).—Miscellaneous writer, *s.* of a West Indian planter, gained some fame by *Poetical Tales by Sir Gregory Gander* (1778). He also had a hand in the *Rolliad*, a series of Whig satires which appeared about 1785. Changing sides he afterwards contributed to the *Anti-Jacobin*. He accompanied Sir J. Harris on his mission to the Netherlands, and there *coll.* materials for his *History of the Dutch Revolution* (1789). He ed. *Specimens of the Early English Poets* (1790), and *Specimens of the Early English Romances*, both works of scholarship. He was a friend of Scott, who dedicated the fifth canto of *Marmion* to him.

ELLWOOD, THOMAS (1639-1713).—A young Quaker who was introduced to Milton in 1662, and devoted much of his time to reading to him. It is to a question asked by him that we owe the writing of *Paradise Regained*. He was a simple, good man, ready to suffer for his religious opinions, and has left an autobiography of singular interest alike for the details of Milton's later life, which it gives, and for the light it casts on the times of the writer. He also wrote *Davideis* (1712), a sacred poem, and some controversial works.

ELPHINSTONE, MOUNTSTUART (1779-1859).—Fourth *s.* of the 11th Lord E., was *ed.* at Edin., and entered the Bengal Civil Service in 1795. He had a very distinguished career as an Indian statesman, and did much to establish the present system of government and to extend education. He was Governor of Bombay (1819-1827), and prepared a code of laws for that Presidency. In 1829 he was offered, but declined, the position of Governor-General of India. He wrote a *History of India* (1841), and *The Rise of the British Power in the East*, *pub.* in 1887.

ELWIN, WHITWELL (1816-1900).—Critic and editor, *s.* of a country gentlemen of Norfolk, studied at Camb., and took orders. He was an important contributor to the *Quarterly Review*, of which he became editor in 1853. He undertook to complete Croker's ed. of Pope, and brought out 5 vols., when he dropped it, leaving it to be finished by Mr. Courthope. As an ed. he was extremely autocratic, and on all subjects had pronounced opinions, and often singular likes and dislikes.

ELYOT, SIR THOMAS (1490-1546).—Diplomatist, physician, and writer, held many diplomatic appointments. He wrote *The Governor* (1531), a treatise on education, in which he advocated gentler treatment of schoolboys, *The Castle of Health* (1534), a medical work, and *A Defence of Good Women* (1545). He also in 1538 *pub.* the first *Latin and English Dictionary*, and made various translations.

EMERSON, RALPH WALDO (1803-1882).—Philosopher, was *b.* at Boston, Massachusetts. His *f.* was a minister there, who had become a Unitarian, and who *d.* in 1811, leaving a widow with six children, of whom Ralph, then aged 8, was the second. Mrs. E. was, however, a woman of energy, and by means of taking boarders managed to give all her sons a good education. E. entered Harvard in 1817 and, after passing through the usual course there, studied for the ministry, to which he was ordained in 1827, and settled over a congregation in his native city. There he remained until 1832, when he resigned, ostensibly on a difference of opinion with his brethren on the permanent nature of the Lord's Supper as a rite, but really on a radical change of view in regard to religion in general, expressed in the maxim that "the day of formal religion is past." About the same time he lost his young wife, and his health, which had never been robust, showed signs of failing. In search of recovery he visited Europe, where he met many eminent men and formed a life-long friendship with Carlyle. On his return in 1834 he settled at Concord, and took up lecturing. In 1836 he *pub.* *Nature*, a somewhat transcendental little book which, though containing much fine thought, did not appeal to a wide circle. *The American Scholar* followed in 1837. Two years previously he had entered into a second marriage. His influence as a thinker rapidly extended, he was regarded as the leader of the transcendentalists, and was one of the chief contributors to their organ, *The Dial*. The remainder of his life, though happy, busy, and influential, was singularly uneventful. In 1847 he paid a second visit to England, when he spent a week with Carlyle, and delivered a course of lectures in England and Scotland on "Representative Men," which he subsequently *pub.* *English Traits* appeared in 1856. In 1857 *The Atlantic Monthly* was started, and to it he became a frequent contributor. In 1874 he was nominated for the Lord Rectorship of the Univ. of Glasgow, but was defeated by Disraeli. He, however, regarded his nomination as the greatest honour of his life. After 1867 he wrote little. He *d.* on April 27, 1882. His works were *coll.* in 11 vols., and in addition to those above mentioned include *Essays* (two series), *Conduct of Life, Society and Solitude, Natural History of Intellect*, and *Poems*. The intellect of E. was subtle rather than robust, and suggestive rather than systematic. He wrote down the intuitions and suggestions of the moment, and was entirely careless as to whether these harmonised with previous statements. He was an original and stimulating thinker and writer, and wielded a style of much beauty and fascination. His religious views approached more nearly to Pantheism than to any other known system of belief. He was a man of singular elevation and purity of character.

ERCILDOUN, THOMAS OF, OR "THOMAS THE RHYMER" (*fl.* 1220-1297).—A minstrel to whom is ascribed *Sir Tristrem*, a rhyme or story for recitation. He had a reputation for prophecy, and is reported to have foretold the death of Alexander III., and various other events.

ERIGENA, OR SCOTUS, JOHN (*fl.* 850).—Philosopher, *b.* in Scotland or Ireland, was employed at the Court of Charles the

Bald, King of France. He was a pantheistic mystic, and made translations from the Alexandrian philosophers. He was bold in the exposition of his principles, and had both strength and subtlety of intellect. His chief work is *De Divisione Naturæ*, a dialogue in which he places reason above authority.

ERSKINE, RALPH (1685-1752).—Scottish Divine and poet, was *b.* near Cornhill, Northumberland, where his *f.*, a man of ancient Scottish family, was, for the time, a nonconforming minister. He became minister of Dunfermline, and, with his brother Ebenezer, was involved in the controversies in the Church of Scotland, which led to the founding of the Secession Church in 1736. He has a place in literature as the writer of devotional works, especially for his *Gospel Sonnets* (of which 25 ed. had appeared by 1797), and *Scripture Songs* (1754).

ERSKINE, THOMAS (1788-1870).—Theologian, *s.* of David E., of Linlathen, to which property he succeeded, his elder brother having *d.* He was called to the Bar in 1810, but never practised. Having come under unusually deep religious impressions he devoted himself largely to the study of theology, and *pub.* various works, including *The Internal Evidence for the Truth of Revealed Religion* (1820), *Unconditional Freeness of the Gospel*, and *The Spiritual Order*. He was a man of singular charm of character, and wielded a great influence on the religious thought of his day. He enjoyed the friendship of men of such different types as Carlyle, Chalmers, Dean Stanley, and Prévost Paradol. His *Letters* were ed. by Dr. W. Hanna (1877-78).

ETHEREGE, SIR GEORGE (1635?-1691).—Dramatist, was at Camb., travelled, read a little law, became a man-about-town, the companion of Sedley, Rochester, and their set. He achieved some note as the writer of three lively comedies, *Love in a Tub* (1664), *She would if she Could* (1668), and *The Man of Mode* (1676), all characterised by the grossness of the period. He was sent on a mission to Ratisbon, where he broke his neck when lighting his guests downstairs after a drinking bout.

EVANS, MARY ANN OR MARIAN ("GEORGE ELIOT") (1819-1880).—Novelist, was *b.* near Nuneaton, Warwickshire, *dau.* of Robert E., land agent, a man of strong individuality. Her education was completed at a school in Coventry, and after the death of her mother in 1836, and the marriage of her elder sister, she kept house for her *f.* until his death in 1849. In 1841 they gave up their house in the country, and went to live in Coventry. Here she made the acquaintance of Charles Bray, a writer on phrenology, and his brother-in-law Charles Hennell, a rationalistic writer on the origin of Christianity, whose influence led her to renounce the evangelical views in which she had been brought up. In 1846 she engaged in her first literary work, the completion of a translation begun by Mrs. Hennell of Strauss's *Life of Jesus*. On her *f.'s* death she went abroad with the Brays, and, on her return in 1850, began to write for the *Westminster Review*, of which from 1851-53 she was assistant-editor. In this capacity she was much thrown into the society of Herbert Spencer and George Henry Lewes (*q.v.*), with the latter of whom she in 1854 entered into an irregular connection which lasted until his death. In the same year she translated Feuerbach's *Essence of Christianity*, the only one of her writings to which she attached her real name. It was not until she was nearly 40 that she appears to have discovered the true nature of her genius; for it was not until 1857 that *The Sad Fortunes of the Rev. Amos Barton* appeared in *Blackwood's Magazine*, and announced that a new writer of singular power had arisen. It was followed by *Mr. Gilfil's Love Story* and *Janet's Repentance*, all three being reprinted as *Scenes from Clerical Life* (1857); *Adam Bede* was *pub.* in 1859, *The Mill on the Floss*, in its earlier chapters largely autobiographical, in 1860, *Silas Marner*, perhaps the most artistically constructed of her books, in 1861. In 1860 and 1861 she visited Florence with the view of preparing herself for her next work, *Romola*, a tale of the times of Savonarola, which appeared in 1863 in the *Cornhill Magazine*. *Felix Holt the Radical* followed in 1866. Miss E. now for a time abandoned novel-writing and took to poetry, and between 1868 and 1871 produced *The Spanish Gipsy*, *Agatha*, *The Legend of Jubal*, and *Armgart*. These poems, though containing much fine work, did not add to her reputation, and in fact in writing them she had departed from her true vocation. Accordingly, she returned to fiction, and in *Middlemarch*, which appeared in parts in 1871-72, she was by many considered to have produced her greatest work. *Daniel Deronda*, which came out in 1874-76, was greatly inferior, and it was her last novel. In 1878 she *pub.* *The Impressions of Theophrastus Such*, a collection of miscellaneous essays. In the same year Mr. Lewes *d.*, an event which plunged her into melancholy, which was, however, alleviated by the kindness of Mr. John Cross, who had been the intimate friend of both L. and herself, and whom she *m.* in March, 1880. The union was a short one, being terminated by her death on December 22 in the same year.

George Eliot will probably always retain a high place among writers of fiction. Her great power lies in the minute painting of character, chiefly among the lower middle classes, shopkeepers, tradesmen, and country folk of the Midlands, into whose thoughts and feelings she had an insight almost like divination, and of whose modes of expression she was complete mistress. Her general view of life is pessimistic, relieved by a power of seizing the humorous elements in human stupidity and ill-doing. There is also, however, much seriousness in her treatment of the phases of life upon which she touches, and few writers have brought out with greater power the hardening and degrading effects of continuance in evil courses, or the inevitable and irretrievable consequences of a wrong act. Her descriptions of rural scenes have a singular charm.

Life, ed. by J. W. Cross (1885-6). Books on her by Oscar Browning, 1890, and Sir Leslie Stephen (Men of Letters), 1902.

EVELYN, JOHN (1620-1706).—Diarist, and miscellaneous writer, was of an old Surrey family, and was *ed.* at a school at Lewes and at Oxf. He travelled much on the Continent, seeing all that was best worth seeing in the way of galleries and collections, both public and private, of which he has given an interesting account in his *Diary*. He was all his life a staunch Royalist, and joined the King as a volunteer in 1642, but soon after repaired again to the Continent. After 1652 he was at home, settled at Sayes Court, near Deptford, where his gardens were famous. After the Restoration he was employed in various matters by the Government, but his lofty and pure character was constantly offended by the manners of the Court. In addition to his *Diary*, kept up from 1624-1706, and which is full of interesting details of public and private events, he wrote upon such subjects as plantations, *Sylva* (1664), gardening, *Elysium Britannicum* (*unpub.*), architecture, prevention of smoke in London, engraving, *Sculptura* (1662), and he was one of the founders of the Royal Society, of which he was for a time sec. The dignity and purity of E'.s character stand forth in strong relief against the laxity of his times.

EWING, MRS. JULIANA HORATIA (GATTY) (1842-1885).—Writer of children's stories, *dau.* of Mrs. Alfred Gatty (*q.v.*), also a writer for children. Among her tales, which have hardly been excelled in sympathetic insight into child-life, and still enjoy undiminished popularity, are: *A Flat Iron for a Farthing*, *Jackanapes*, *Jan of the Windmill*, *Mrs. Overtheway's Remembrances*, and *The Story of a Short Life*.

FABER, FREDERICK WILLIAM (1814-1863).—Theologian and hymn-writer, was *b.* at Calverley, Yorkshire, and *ed.* at Harrow and Oxf., where he came under the influence of Newman, whom he followed into the Church of Rome. He wrote various theological treatises, but has a place in literature for his hymns, which include *The Pilgrims of the Night*, *My God how wonderful thou art*, and *Sweet Saviour, bless us ere we go*.

FABYAN, ROBERT (*d.* 1513).—Chronicler, was *b.* in London, of which he became an Alderman and Sheriff. He kept a diary of notable events, which he expanded into a chronicle, which he entitled, *The Concordance of Histories*. It covers the period from the arrival of Brutus in England to the death of Henry VII., and deals mainly with the affairs of London. It was not printed until 1515, when it appeared under the title of *The New Chronicles of England and France*.

FAIRFAX, EDWARD (1580?-1635).—Translator, natural *s.* of Sir Thomas F., lived at Fuystone, near Knaresborough, in peace and prosperity. His translation of Tasso's *Jerusalem Delivered*, on which his fame is founded, is a masterpiece, one of the comparatively few translations which in themselves are literature. It was highly praised by Dryden and Waller. The first ed. appeared in 1600, and was dedicated to Queen Elizabeth. F. also wrote a treatise on *Demonology*, in which he was a devout believer.

FALCONER, WILLIAM (1732-1769).—Poet, *s.* of a barber in Edin., where he was *b.*, became a sailor, and was thus thoroughly competent to describe the management of the storm-tossed vessel, the career and fate of which are described in his poem, *The Shipwreck* (1762), a work of genuine, though unequal, talent. The efforts which F. made to improve the poem in the successive ed. which followed the first were not entirely successful. The work gained for him the patronage of the Duke of York, through whose influence he obtained the position of purser on various warships. Strangely enough, his own death occurred by shipwreck. F. wrote other poems, now forgotten, besides a useful *Nautical Dictionary*.

FANSHAWE, CATHERINE MARIA (1765-1834).—Poetess, *dau.* of a Surrey squire, wrote clever occasional verse. Her best known production is the famous *Riddle on the Letter H*, beginning "'Twas whispered in heaven, 'twas muttered in hell" often attributed to Lord Byron.

FANSHAWE, SIR RICHARD (1608-1666).—Diplomatist, translator, and poet, *b.* at Ware Park, Herts, and *ed.* at Camb., travelled on the Continent, and when the Civil War broke out sided with the King and was sent to Spain to obtain money for the cause. He acted as Latin Sec. to Charles II. when in Holland. After the Restoration he held various appointments, and was Ambassador to Portugal and Spain successively. He translated Guarini's *Pastor Fido*, *Selected Parts of Horace*, and *The Lusiad* of Camoens. His wife, *née* Anne Harrison, wrote memoirs of her own life.

FARADAY, MICHAEL (1791-1867).—Natural philosopher, *s.* of a blacksmith, was *b.* in London, and apprenticed to a bookbinder. He early showed a taste for chemistry, and attended the lectures of Sir H. Davy (*q.v.*), by whom he was, in 1813, appointed his chemical assistant in the Royal Institution. He became one of the greatest of British discoverers and popularisers of science, his discoveries being chiefly in the department of electro-magnetism. He had an unusual power of making difficult subjects clearly understood. Among his writings are *History of the Progress of Electro-Magnetism* (1821), *The Non-metallic Elements*, *The Chemical History of a Candle*, and *The Various Forces in Nature*. F. was a man of remarkable simplicity and benevolence of character, and deeply religious.

FARMER, RICHARD (1735-1797).—Shakespearian scholar, *b.* at Leicester, and *ed.* at Camb., where he ultimately became Master of Emanuel Coll. He wrote an *Essay on the Learning of Shakespeare* (1767), in which he maintained that Shakespeare's knowledge of the classics was through translations, the errors of which he reproduced. It is a production of great ability. F. was a clergyman, and held a prebend in St. Paul's.

FARQUHAR, GEORGE (1678-1707).—Dramatist, *b.* at Londonderry, *s.* of a clergyman, and *ed.* at Trinity Coll., Dublin, on leaving which he took to the stage, but had no great success as an actor. This, together with an accident in which he wounded a fellow-actor with a sword, led to his relinquishing it, and giving himself to writing plays instead of acting them. Thereafter he joined the army. *Love and a Bottle* (1698) was his first venture, and others were *The Constant Couple* (1700), *Sir Harry Wildair* (1701), *The Inconstant* (1703), *The Recruiting Officer* (1706), and *The Beau's Stratagem* (1707). F.'s plays are full of wit and sparkle and, though often coarse, have not the malignant pruriency of some of his predecessors. He made an unfortunate marriage, and *d.* in poverty.

FARRAR, FREDERIC WILLIAM (1831-1903).—Theological writer, *b.* in Bombay, and *ed.* at London Univ. and Camb., was for some years a master at Harrow, and from 1871-76 Head Master of Marlborough School. He became successively Canon of Westminster and Rector of St. Margaret's, Archdeacon of Westminster and Dean of Canterbury. He was an eloquent preacher and a voluminous author, his writings including stories of school life, such as *Eric* and *St. Winifred's*, a *Life of Christ*, which had great popularity, a *Life of St. Paul*, and two historical romances.

FAWCETT, HENRY (1833-1884).—Statesman and economist, *b.* at Salisbury, and *ed.* at Camb., where he became Fellow of Trinity Hall. In 1858 he was blinded by a shooting accident, in spite of which he continued to prosecute his studies, especially in economics, and in 1863 *pub.* his *Manual of Political Economy*, becoming in the same year Prof. of Political Economy in Camb. Having strong political views he desired to enter upon a political career, and after repeated defeats was elected M.P. for Brighton. He soon attained a recognised position, devoting himself specially to parliamentary reform and Indian questions, and was in 1880 appointed Postmaster-General, in which office he approved himself a capable administrator. His career was, however, cut short by his premature death, but not before he had made himself a recognised authority on economics, his works on which include *The Economic Position of the British Labourer* (1871), *Labour and Wages*, etc. In 1867 he *m.* Miss Millicent Garrett, a lady highly qualified to share in all his intellectual interests, who collaborated with him in some of his publications. Mrs. Fawcett has written independently *Some Eminent Women of our Times*, *Janet Doncaster* (a novel), and *Political Economy for Beginners*. There is a life of Fawcett by Sir L. Stephen.

FAWKES, FRANCIS (1721-1777).—Poet and translator, *b.* near Doncaster, and *ed.* at Camb., after which he took orders. He translated Anacreon, Sappho, and other classics, modernised parts of the poems of Gavin Douglas, and was the author of the song, *The Brown Jug*, and two poems, *Bramham Park* and *Partridge Shooting*.

FELTHAM, OWEN (1602?-1668).—Religious writer, author of a book entitled *Resolves, Divine, Moral, and Political* (*c.* 1620), containing 146 short essays. It had great popularity in its day. Though sometimes stiff and affected in style, it contains many sound, if not original or brilliant, reflections, and occasional felicities of expression. F. was for a time in the household of the Earl of Thomond as chaplain or sec., and *pub.* (1652), *Brief Character of the Low Countries*.

FENTON, ELIJAH (1683-1730).—Poet and translator, *ed.* at Camb., for a time acted as sec. to the Earl of Orrery in Flanders, and was then Master of Sevenoaks Grammar School. In 1707 he *pub.* a book of poems. He is best known, however, as the assistant of Pope in his translation of the *Odyssey*, of which he Englished the first, fourth, nineteenth, and twentieth books, catching the manner of his master so completely that it is hardly possible to distinguish between their work; while thus engaged he *pub.* (1723) a successful tragedy, *Marianne.* His latest contributions to literature were a *Life of Milton*, and an ed. of *Waller's Poems* (1729).

FERGUSON, ADAM (1723-1816). Philosopher and historian, *s.* of the parish minister of Logierait, Perthshire, studied at St. Andrews and Edin. Univ., in the latter of which he was successively Professor of Mathematics, and Moral Philosophy (1764-1785). As a young man he was chaplain to the 42nd Regiment, and was present at the Battle of Fontenoy. In 1757 he was made Keeper of the Advocates' Library. As a Prof. of Philosophy he was highly successful, his class being attended by many distinguished men no longer students at the Univ. In 1778-9 he acted as sec. to a commission sent out by Lord North to endeavour to reach an accommodation with the American colonists. F.'s principal works are *Essay on the History of Civil Society* (1765), *Institutes of Moral Philosophy* (1769), *History of the Progress and Termination of the Roman Republic* (1782), and *Principles of Moral and Political Science* (1792), all of which have been translated into French and German. F. spent his later years at St. Andrews, where he *d.* in 1816 at the age of 92. He was an intimate friend of Sir Walter Scott. The French philosopher Cousin gave F. a place above all his predecessors in the Scottish school of philosophy.

FERGUSON, SIR SAMUEL (1810-1886).—Poet and antiquary, *b.* at Belfast, the *s.* of parents of Scottish extraction, he was *ed.* at Trinity Coll., Dublin, from which he received in 1865 the honorary degree of LL.D. He practised with success as a barrister, became Q.C. in 1859, and Deputy Keeper of the Irish Records 1867, an appointment in which he rendered valuable service, and was knighted in 1878. He was a contributor to *Blackwood's Magazine*, in which appeared his best known poem, *The Forging of the Anchor*, and was one of the chief promoters of the Gaelic revival in Irish literature. His *coll.* poems appeared under the title of *Lays of the Western Gael* (1865), *Congal, an epic poem* (1872), and his prose tales posthumously (1887), as *Hibernian Nights' Entertainments.* His principal antiquarian work was *Ogham Inscriptions in Ireland, Wales, and Scotland.*

FERGUSSON, JAMES (1808-1886).—Writer on architecture, *b.* at Ayr, was engaged in commercial pursuits in India, where he became interested in the architecture of the country, and *pub.* his first work, *Picturesque Illustrations of Ancient Architecture in Hindustan* (1840), which was followed by *An Historical Inquiry into the True Principles of Beauty in Art* (1849), and *A History of Architecture in all Countries from the Earliest Times to the Present Day* (1865-67). He also wrote *Fire and Serpent Worship*, etc., and a book on the use of earthworks in fortification.

FERGUSSON, ROBERT (1750-1774).—Scottish poet, *s.* of a bank clerk, was *ed.* at the Univ. of St. Andrews. His *f.* dying, he became a copying clerk in an Edin. lawyer's office. Early displaying a talent for humorous descriptive verse, he contributed to *Ruddiman's Weekly Magazine*, then the principal Scottish receptacle for fugitive poetry. His verses, however, attracted attention by their merit, and he *pub.* some of them in a *coll.* form. Unfortunately he fell into dissipated habits, under which his delicate constitution gave way, and he *d.* insane in his 24th year. His poems influenced Burns, who greatly admired them.

FERRIER, JAMES FREDERICK (1808-1864).—Metaphysician, *b.* in Edin., and *ed.* there and at Oxf., he was called to the Scottish Bar in 1832, but devoted himself to literature and philosophy. In 1842 he was appointed Prof. of History in Edin., and in 1845 translated to the Chair of Moral Philosophy and Political Economy at St. Andrews. He *pub.* in 1854 *Institutes of Metaphysics,* and ed. the *coll.* works of his father-in-law, Prof. Wilson (" Christopher North.")

FERRIER, SUSAN EDMONSTOUNE (1782-1854).—Novelist, *dau.* of James F., one of the principal clerks of the Court of Session, in which office he was the colleague of Sir Walter Scott. Miss F. wrote three excellent novels, *Marriage* (1818), *The Inheritance* (1824), and *Destiny* (1831), all characterised by racy humour and acute character-painting. Her cheerful and tactful friendship helped to soothe the last days of Sir W. Scott.

FIELD, NATHANIEL (1587-1633).—Dramatist and actor, was one of " the children of the Queen's Revels," who performed in Ben Jonson's *Cynthia's Revels* in 1600. He wrote *A Woman's a Weathercock* (1612), *Amends for Ladies* (1618), and (with Massinger) *The Fatal Dowry* (1632).

FIELDING, HENRY (1707-1754).—Novelist, was *b.* at Sharpham Park, near Glastonbury. His father was General Edmund F., descended from the Earls of Denbigh and Desmond, and his mother was the *dau.* of Sir Henry Gould of Sharpham Park. His childhood was spent at East Stour, Dorset, and his education was received at first from a tutor, after which he was sent to Eton. Following a love affair with a young heiress at Lyme Regis he was sent to Leyden to study law, where he remained until his *f.*, who had entered into a second marriage, and who was an extravagant man, ceased to send his allowance. Thrown upon his own resources, he came to London and began to write light comedies and farces, of which during the next few years he threw off nearly a score. The drama, however, was not his true vein, and none of his pieces in this kind have survived, unless *Tom Thumb,* a burlesque upon his contemporary playwrights, be excepted. About 1735 he *m.* Miss Charlotte Cradock, a beautiful and amiable girl to whom, though he gave her sufficient cause for forbearance, he was devotedly attached. She is the prototype of his " Amelia " and " Sophia." She brought him £1500, and the young couple retired to East Stour, where he had a small house inherited from his mother. The little fortune was, however, soon dissipated; and in a year he was back in London, where he formed a company of comedians, and managed a small theatre in the Haymarket. Here he produced successfully *Pasquin, a Dramatic Satire on the Times,* and *The Historical Register for 1736,* in which Walpole was satirised. This enterprise was brought to an end by the passing of the Licensing Act, 1737, making the *imprimatur* of the Lord Chamberlain necessary to the production of any play. F. thereupon read law at the Middle Temple, was called to the Bar in 1740, and went the Western Circuit. The same year saw the publication of Richardson's *Pamela*, which inspired F. with the idea of a parody, thus giving rise to his first novel, *Joseph Andrews*. As, however, the characters, especially Parson Adams, developed in his hands, the original idea was laid aside, and the work assumed the form of a regular novel. It was *pub.* in 1742, and though sharing largely in the same qualities as its great successor, *Tom Jones*, its reception, though encouraging, was not phenomenally cordial. Immediately after this a heavy blow fell on F. in the death of his wife. The next few years were occupied with writing his *Miscellanies*, which contained, along with some essays and poems, two important works, *A Journey from this World to the Next*, and *The History of Jonathan Wild the Great*, a grave satire; and he also conducted two papers in support of the Government, *The True Patriot* and *The Jacobite Journal*, in consideration of which he was appointed Justice of the Peace for Middlesex and Westminster, and had a pension conferred upon him. In 1746 he set convention at defiance by marrying Mary MacDaniel, who had been his first wife's maid, and the nurse of his children, and who proved a faithful and affectionate companion. F. showed himself an upright, diligent, and efficient magistrate, and his *Inquiry into the Increase of Robbers* (1751), with suggested remedies, led to beneficial results. By this time, however, the publication of his great masterpiece, *The History of Tom Jones, a Foundling* (1749), had given him a place among the immortals. All critics are agreed that this book contains passages offensive to delicacy, and some say to morality. This is often excused on the plea of the coarser manners of the age; but a much stronger defence is advanced on the ground that, while other novelists of the time made immorality an incentive to merriment, F.'s treatment of such subjects, as Lowell has said, "shocks rather than corrupts," and that in his pages evil is evil. On the other hand, there is universal agreement as to the permanent interest of the types of character presented, the profound knowledge of life and insight into human nature, the genial humour, the wide humanity, the wisdom, and the noble and masculine English of the book. His only other novel, *Amelia*, which some, but these a small minority, have regarded as his best, was *pub.* in 1751. His health was now thoroughly, broken, and in 1753, as a forlorn hope, he went in search of restoration to Lisbon, where he *d.* on October 8, and was buried in the English cemetery. His last work was a *Journal* of his voyage. Though with many weaknesses and serious faults, F. was fundamentally a man of honest and masculine character, and though improvident and reckless in his habits, especially in earlier life, he was affectionate in his domestic relations, and faithful and efficient in the performance of such public duties as he was called to discharge. Thackeray thus describes his appearance, "His figure was tall and stalwart, his face handsome, manly, and noble-looking; to the last days of his life he retained a grandeur of air; and, though worn down by disease, his aspect and presence imposed respect upon people round about him."

SUMMARY.—*B.* 1707, *ed.* Eton, studied law at Leyden, came to London and wrote dramas, called to Bar 1740, *pub. Joseph Andrews* 1742, became journalist, appointed a magistrate for Middlesex, etc., and *pub. Inquiry into Increase of Robbers* 1751, *pub. Tom Jones* 1749, *Amelia* 1751, *d.* at Lisbon 1754.

His works are included in Ballantyne's Novelists' Library with a biography by Scott (1821). An ed. in 10 vols. with a study by L. Stephen was *pub.* by Smith, Elder and Co. (1882); another in 12 vols. by Prof. Saintsbury, Dent and Co. (1893), and various others. There are various Lives by Watson (1807), Lawrence (1855), and A. Dobson (Men of Letters, 1883).

FIELDING, SARAH (1710-1768).—Novelist, was the sister of the above, who had a high opinion of her talents. She wrote several novels, including *David Simple* (1744), *The Governess,* and *The Countess* of *Dellwyn.* She also translated Xenophon's *Memorabilia* and *Apologia* (1762).

FILMER, SIR ROBERT (*d.* 1653 ?).—Political writer, *s.* of Sir Edward F., of East Sutton, Kent, was *ed.* at Camb. He was an enthusiastic Royalist, was knighted by Charles I. and, in 1671, was imprisoned in Leeds Castle, Kent. He is notable as the defender, in its most extreme form, of the doctrine of the divine right of kings, which he expounded in a succession of works, of which the latest and best known, *Patriarcha,* appeared in 1679. His theory is founded on the idea that the government of a family by the father is the original and method of all government. His doctrines were afterwards attacked by Locke in his *Treatise on Government.* He was opposed to the persecution of old women for supposed witchcraft.

FINLAY, GEORGE (1799-1875).—Historian, of Scottish descent, was *b.* at Faversham, Kent, where his *f.*, an officer in the army, was inspector of government powder mills. Intended for the law, he was *ed.* at Glasgow, Göttingen, and Edin., but becoming an enthusiast in the cause of Greece, he joined Byron in the war of independence, and thereafter bought a property near Athens, where he settled and busied himself with schemes for the improvement of the country, which had little success. His *History of Greece,* produced in sections between 1843 and 1861, did not at first receive the recognition which its merits deserved, but it has since been given by students in all countries, and specially in Germany, a place among works of permanent value, alike for its literary style and the depth and insight of its historical views. It was re-issued in 1877 as *A History of Greece from the Roman Conquest to the Present Time* (146 B.C. *to* 1864).

FISHER, JOHN (*c.* 1469-1535).—Controversialist and scholar, *b.* at Beverley, and *ed.* at Camb., entered the Church, and became in 1504 Bishop of Rochester. He wrote in Latin against the doctrines of the Reformation, but was a supporter of the New Learning, and endeavoured to get Erasmus to teach Greek at Camb. Through his influence the Lady Margaret Professorship of Divinity were founded at both the Univ. by Margaret Countess of Richmond, and in 1502 he became first prof. at Camb., where he was also (1505-8) Head of Queen's Coll. He was also instrumental in founding Christ's and St. John's Coll. For opposing the divorce proceedings of Henry VIII. he was burned. Made a cardinal in 1535, he was beatified in 1886.

FISKE, JOHN (1842-1901).—Miscellaneous writer, was *b.* at Hartford, Connecticut. The family name was Green; but this he dropped, and adopted that of his mother's family. After being at Harvard he studied for, and was admitted to, the Bar, but did not practise. He wrote on a variety of subjects, including mythology, history, and evolution. Among his books on these subjects are, *Myths and Mythmakers* (1872), *Cosmic Philosophy, Darwinism, The Idea of God, Origin of Evil.* He was also the author of many works on America. These include *Old Virginia, New France and New England, The American Revolution,* and *Discovery of America* (1892).

FITZGERALD, EDWARD (1809-1883).—Translator and letter-writer, was *b.* near Woodbridge, Suffolk, *s.* of John Purcell, who took his wife's surname on the death of her *f.* in 1818. He was *ed.* at Bury St. Edmunds and Camb. Thereafter he lived in retirement and study with his parents until 1838, when he took a neighbouring cottage. In 1856 he *m.* a *dau.* of Bernard Barton, the poet, from whom, however, he soon separated. Afterwards he lived at various places in the East of England, continuing his studies, with yachting for his chief recreation. By this time, however, he had become an author, having written a life of his father-in-law prefixed to his *coll.* poems (1849), *Euphranor,* a dialogue on youth (1851), and *Polonius, a Collection of Wise Saws and Modern Instances* (1852). Becoming interested in Spanish literature, he *pub.* translations of *Six Dramas of Calderon.* Thereafter turning his attention to Persian, he produced (1859), anonymously, his famous translation of the *Rubaiyat of Omar Khayyám.* He also *pub.* translations of the *Agamemnon* of Æschylus, and the *Œdipus Tyrannus* and *Œdipus Coloneus* of Sophocles. In his translations F. aimed not so much at a mere literal reproduction of the sense of the original, as at reproducing its effect on the reader, and in this he was extraordinarily successful. In the department of letter-writing also he attained an excellence perhaps unequalled in his day.

FITZSTEPHEN, WILLIAM (*d.* 1190).—Was a servant of Thomas à Becket, witnessed his murder, and wrote his biography, which contains an interesting account of London in the 12th century.

FLAVEL, JOHN (1627-1691).—Divine, *b.* at Bromsgrove, studied at Oxf., was a Presbyterian, and was settled at Dartmouth, but ejected from his living in 1662, continuing, however, to preach there secretly. He was a voluminous and popular author. Among his works are *Husbandry Spiritualised* and *Navigation Spiritualised,* titles which suggest some of his characteristics as an expositor.

FLECKNOE, RICHARD (*d.* 1678).—Poet, said to have been an Irish priest. He wrote several plays, now forgotten, also miscellaneous poems, some of them sacred, and a book of travels. His name has been preserved in Dryden's satire, *MacFlecknoe,* as "throughout the realms of nonsense absolute;" but according to some authorities his slighter pieces were not wanting in grace and fancy.

FLETCHER, ANDREW (1655-1716).—Scottish statesman and political writer, *s.* of Sir Robert F. of Saltoun, East Lothian, to which estate he succeeded at an early age. He was *ed.* under the care of Bishop Burnet, who was then minister of Saltoun. Being firmly opposed to the arbitrary measures of the Duke of York, afterwards James II., he went to Holland, where he joined Monmouth, whom he accompanied on his ill-starred expedition. Happening to kill, in a quarrel, one Dare, another of the Duke's followers, he fled to the Continent, travelled in Spain and Hungary, and fought against the Turks. After the Revolution he returned to Scotland, and took an active part in political affairs. He opposed the Union, fearing the loss of Scottish independence, and advocated federation rather than incorporation. He introduced various improvements in agriculture. His principal writings are *Discourse of Government* (1698), *Two Discourses concerning the Affairs of Scotland* (1698), *Conversation concerning a right Regulation of Government for the Common Good of Mankind* (1703), in which occurs his well-known saying, "Give me the making of the songs of a nation, and I care not who makes its laws."

FLETCHER, GILES, AND PHINEAS (1588?-1623) (1582-1650).—Poets, were the sons of Giles F., himself a minor poet, and Envoy to Russia. Phineas, the elder, was *ed.* at Eton and Camb., and entered the Church, becoming Rector of Hilgay, Norfolk. He wrote *The Purple Island* (1633), a poem in 10 books, giving an elaborate allegorical description of the body and mind of man, which, though tedious and fanciful, contains some fine passages, recalling the harmonious sweetness of Spenser, whose disciple the poet was. He was also the author of *Piscatory Dialogues*. GILES, the younger, was also *ed.* at Camb., and, like his brother, became a country parson, being Rector of Alderton. His poem, *Christ's Victory and Triumph* (1610), which, though it contains passages rising to sublimity, is now almost unknown except to students of English literature, is said to have influenced Milton.

Both brothers, but especially Giles, had a genuine poetic gift, but alike in the allegorical treatment of their subjects and the metre they adopted, they followed a style which was passing away, and thus missed popularity. They were cousins of John F., the dramatist.

FLORENCE OF WORCESTER (*d.* 1118).—Chronicler, was a monk of Worcester. His work is founded upon that of Marianus, an Irish chronicler, supplemented by additions taken from the *Anglo-Saxon Chronicle*, Bede's *Lives of the Saints*, and Asser's *Life of Alfred*. After his death it was brought down to 1295.

FLORIO, JOHN (1553?-1625).—Translator, *s.* of an Italian preacher, exiled for his Protestantism, but who appears to have lost credit owing to misconduct, *b.* in London, was, about 1576, a private tutor of languages at Oxf. In 1581 he was admitted a member of

Magdalen Coll., and teacher of French and Italian. Patronised by various noblemen, he became in 1603 reader in Italian to Anne of Denmark, Queen of James I. He *pub. First Fruites* (1578), *Second Fruites* (1591), consisting of Italian and English Dialogues, and his great Italian dictionary entitled *A World of Wonder*, in 1598. His chief contribution to pure literature is his famous translation of *The Essays of Montaigne*, in stately if somewhat stiff Elizabethan English.

FONBLANQUE, ALBANY WILLIAM (1793-1872).—Journalist and political writer, was of Huguenot descent, the *s.* of a Commissioner in Bankruptcy. He was bred to the law, but deserted it for journalism, in which he took a high place. He wrote much for *The Times*, and *Westminster Review*, and subsequently became ed. and proprietor of the *Examiner*. His best articles were republished as *England under Seven Administrations* (1837). He also wrote *How we are Governed*. In 1847 he was appointed Statistical Sec. to the Board of Trade.

FOOTE, SAMUEL (1720-1777).—Actor and dramatist, *b.* at Truro of a good family, and *ed.* at Oxf., succeeded by his extravagance and folly in running through two fortunes. To repair his finances he turned to the stage, and began with tragedy, in which he failed. He then took to comedy, and the mimetic representation of living characters, for which his extraordinary comic powers highly qualified him. He also became a prolific author of dramatic pieces. He wrote 20 plays, and claimed to have added 16 original characters to the stage. Several of his pieces, owing to the offence they gave to persons of importance, were suppressed, but were usually revived in a slightly modified form. His conversation was agreeable and entertaining in the highest degree. Among his best works are *An Auction of Pictures*, *The Liar*, and *The Mayor of Garratt* (1763), *The Lame Lover* (1770), *The Knights* (1749), *Author* (suppressed) 1757, *Devil upon Two Sticks* (1768), *The Nabob* (1779), *The Capuchin* (1776).

FORBES, JAMES DAVID (1809-1868).—Natural Philosopher, *s.* of Sir William F., of Pitsligo, was *b.* and *ed.* at Edin. He studied law, and was called to the Bar, but devoted himself to science, in which he gained a great reputation both as a discoverer and teacher. He was Prof. of Natural Philosophy at Edin., 1833-1859, when he succeeded Sir D. Brewster, as Principal of the United Coll. at St. Andrews. He was one of the founders of the British Association in 1831. His scientific investigations and discoveries embraced the subjects of heat, light, polarisation, and specially glaciers. In connection with the last of these he wrote *Travels through the Alps* (1843), *Norway and its Glaciers* (1853), *Tour of Mont Blanc and Monte Rosa* (1855), and *Papers on the Theory of Glaciers*.

FORD, JOHN (*c.* 1586?).—Dramatist, *b.* probably at Ilsington, Devonshire, was admitted to the Middle Temple in 1602, and appears to have practised as a lawyer. His chief plays are *The Lover's Melancholy* (1629), *'Tis Pity*, *The Broken Heart*, and *Love's Sacrifice* (1633), *Perkin Warbeck* (1634), *The Lady's Trial* (1639), and *Fancies Chaste and Noble* (1638). He also collaborated with

Dekker and Rowley in *The Witch of Edmonton* (1624). F. has a high position as a dramatist, though rather for general intellectual power and austere beauty of thought than for strictly dramatic qualities. C. Lamb says, "F. was of the first order of poets." He had little humour; his plays, though the subjects are painful, and sometimes horrible, are full of pensive tenderness expressed in gently flowing verse. The date of his death is uncertain.

FORD, PAUL LEICESTER (1865-1902).—Novelist and biographer, was *b.* in Brooklyn. He wrote Lives of Washington, Franklin, and others, ed. the works of Jefferson, and wrote a number of novels, which had considerable success, including *Peter Sterling* (1894), *Story of an Untold Love*, *Janice Meredith*, *Wanted a Matchmaker*, and *Wanted a Chaperone*. He *d.* by violence.

FORD, RICHARD (1796-1858).—Writer on art and travel, *ed.* at Winchester and Camb., and travelled for several years in Spain, becoming intimately acquainted with the country and people. He wrote a *Handbook for Travellers in Spain* (1845), which is much more than a mere guide-book, and *Gatherings from Spain* (1846). An accomplished artist and art critic, he was the first to make the great Spanish painter, Velasquez, generally known in England.

FORDUN, JOHN (*d.* 1384?).—Chronicler, said to have been a chantry priest and Canon of Aberdeen. He began the *Scotichronicon*, for which he prepared himself, it is said, by travelling on foot through Britain and Ireland in search of materials. He also compiled *Gesta Annalia*, a continuation. He brought the history down to 1153, leaving, however, material to the time of his own death, which was subsequently worked up by Walter Bower (*q.v.*).

FORSTER, JOHN (1812-1876).—Historian and biographer, *b.* at Newcastle, *ed.* at the Grammar School there, and at Univ. Coll., London, became a barrister of the Inner Temple, but soon relinquished law for literature. In 1834 he accepted the post of assistant ed. of the *Examiner*, and was ed. 1847-55. In this position F. exercised a marked influence on public opinion. He also ed. the *Foreign Quarterly Review* 1842-3, the *Daily News* in 1846, and was Sec. to the Lunacy Commission and a Commissioner 1861-72. His historical writings were chiefly biographies, among which are *Statesmen of the Commonwealth of England* (1836-9), *Life of Goldsmith* (1854), *Biographical and Historical Essays* (1859), *Sir John Eliot* (1864), *Lives of Walter S. Landor* (1868), and *Charles Dickens* (1871-4). He also left the first vol. of a Life of Swift. F., who was a man of great decision and force of character, concealed an unusually tender heart under a somewhat overbearing manner.

FORTESCUE, SIR JOHN (1394?-1476?).—Political writer, was descended from a Devonshire family. He was an eminent lawyer, and held the office of Lord Chief Justice of the King's Bench (1442). During the Wars of the Roses he was a staunch Lancastrian. On the triumph of Edward IV. at Towton he was attainted, and followed the fortunes of the fallen Lancastrians, accompanying Queen Margaret to Scotland and Flanders. He fought at Tewkesbury, was captured, but pardoned on condition of writing in support of the Yorkish claims, which he did, considering that his own party appeared to be hopelessly ruined. He is said to have been at one time Lord Chancellor; but it is probable that this was only a titular appointment given him by the exiled family. His works are various defences of the Lancastrian title to the crown, and two treatises, *De Laudibus Legum Angliæ* (1537) (in praise of the laws of England), and *On the Governance of the Kingdom of England*, not printed till 1714, the former for the instruction of Edward, Prince of Wales.

FOSTER, JOHN (1770-1843).—Essayist, was *b.* at Halifax, and *ed.* at Bristol for the Baptist ministry. Though a man of powerful and original mind he did not prove popular as a preacher, and devoted himself mainly to literature, his chief contribution to which is his four Essays (1) *On a Man's Writing Memoirs of Himself*, (2) *On Decision of Character*, (3) *On the Epithet "Romantic,"* (4) *On Evangelical Religion, etc.*, all of which attracted much attention among the more thoughtful part of the community, and still hold their place. These Essays were *pub.* in 1805, and in 1819. F. added another on the *Evils of Popular Ignorance*, in which he advocated a national system of education.

FOSTER, STEPHEN COLLINS (1826-1864).—Song-writer, was *b.* in Pittsburgh. He wrote over 100 songs, many of which had extraordinary popularity, among which may be mentioned *The Old Folks at Home, Nelly Bly, Old Dog Tray, Camp Town Races, Massa's in de cold, cold Ground*, and *Come where my Love lies Dreaming*. He composed the music to his songs.

FOX, CHARLES JAMES (1749-1806).—Statesman and historian, *s.* of Henry F., 1st Lord Holland, was one of the greatest orators who have ever sat in the House of Commons. His only serious literary work was a fragment of a proposed *History of the Reign of James the Second*. An introductory chapter sketching the development of the constitution from the time of Henry VII., and a few chapters conducting the history up to the execution of Monmouth are all which he completed.

FOX, GEORGE (1624-1691).—Religious enthusiast, and founder of the Society of Friends, *b.* at Drayton, Leicestershire, was in youth the subject of peculiar religious impressions and trances, and adopted a wandering life. The protests which he conceived himself bound to make against the prevailing beliefs and manners, and which sometimes took the form of interrupting Divine service, and the use of uncomplimentary forms of address to the clergy, involved him in frequent trouble. The clergy, the magistrates, and the mob alike treated him with harshness amounting to persecution. None of these things, however, moved him, and friends, many of them influential, among them Oliver Cromwell, extended favour towards him. From 1659 onwards he made various missionary journeys in Scotland, Ireland, America, and Holland. Later he was repeatedly imprisoned, again visited the Continent, and *d.* in 1691. F.'s literary works are his *Journal, Epistles*, and *Doctrinal Pieces*. He was not a man of strong intellect, and the defence of his doctrines was undertaken by the far more competent hand of his follower, Barclay (*q.v.*). The *Journal*, however, is full of interest as a sincere transcript of the singular experiences, religious and others, of a spiritual enthusiast and mystic.

The best Life is that by Hodgkin, 1896. *Journal* (reprint, 1885).

FOXE, JOHN (1516-1587).—Martyrologist, was *b.* at Boston, Lincolnshire, and *ed.* at Oxf., where he became a Fellow of Magdalen Coll. While there he gave himself to the study of the theological questions then in debate, and ended by becoming a Protestant, in consequence of which he in 1545 left his coll. He then became tutor in the family of Sir T. Lucy of Charlecote, and afterwards to the children of the recently executed Earl of Surrey. During the reign of Mary he retired to the Continent, and *pub.*, at Strasburg, his *Commentarii* (the first draft of the *Acts and Monuments*). Removing to Basel he was employed as a reader for the press by the famous printer Oporinus, who *pub.* some of his writings. On the accession of Elizabeth, F. returned to England, was received with kindness by the Duke of Norfolk, one of his former pupils, and soon afterwards (1563) *pub.* the work on which his fame rests, the English version of the *Acts and Monuments*, better known as *The Book of Martyrs*. Received with great favour by the Protestants, it was, and has always been, charged by the Roman Catholics with gross and wilful perversion of facts. The truth of the matter appears to be that while Foxe was not, as in the circumstances he could hardly have been, free from party spirit or from some degree of error as to facts, he did not intentionally try to mislead; and comparison of his citations from authorities with the originals has shown him to have been careful and accurate in that matter. F., who had been ordained a priest in 1560, became Canon of Salisbury in 1563. He wrote sundry other theological works, and *d.* in 1587. There is a memoir of him attributed to his *s.*, but of doubtful authenticity. Some of his papers, used by Strype (*q.v.*), are now in the British Museum.

FRANCIS, SIR PHILIP (1740-1818).—Reputed author of *The Letters of Junius*, *s.* of the Rev. Philip F., a scholar of some note, was *b.* in Dublin. On the recommendation of Lord Holland he received an appointment in the office of the Sec. of State, and was thereafter private sec. to Lord Kinnoull in Portugal, and to Pitt in 1761-2. He was then transferred to the War Office, where he remained from 1762-72, during which period he contributed to the press under various pseudonyms. His next appointment was that of a member of Council of Bengal, which he held from 1773-80. While in India he was in continual conflict with the Governor-General, Warren Hastings, by whom he was wounded in a duel in 1779. He returned to England in 1780 with a large fortune, and entered Parliament as a Whig. In 1787 he was associated with Burke in the impeachment of Hastings, against whom he showed extraordinary vindictiveness. Later he was a sympathiser with the French Revolution, and a member of the association of the Friends of the People. He retired from public life in 1807, and *d.* in 1818. He was the author of about 20 political pamphlets, but the great interest attaching to him is his reputed authorship of the *Letters of*

Junius. These letters which, partly on account of the boldness and implacability of their attacks and the brilliance of their literary style, and partly because of the mystery in which their author wrapped himself, created an extraordinary impression, and have ever since retained their place as masterpieces of condensed sarcasm. They appeared in *The Public Advertiser*, a paper *pub.* by Woodfall, the first on January 21, 1769, and the last on the corresponding day of 1772, and were chiefly directed against the Dukes of Grafton and Bedford, and Lord Mansfield; but even the king himself did not escape. Not only were the public actions of those attacked held up to execration, but every circumstance in their private lives which could excite odium was dragged into the light. Their authorship was attributed to many distinguished men, *e.g.* Burke, Lord Shelburne, J. Wilkes, Horne Tooke, and Barré, and recently to Gibbon; but the evidence appears to point strongly to F., and, in the opinion of Macaulay, would "support a verdict in a civil, nay, in a criminal trial." It rests upon such circumstances as the similarity of the MS. to what is known to be the disguised writing of F., the acquaintance of the writer with the working of the Sec. of State's Office and the War Office, his denunciation of the promotion of a Mr. Chamier in the War Office, which was a well-known grievance of F., his acquaintance with Pitt, and the existence of a strong tie to Lord Holland, the silence of Junius when F. was absent, and resemblances in the style and the moral character of the writer to those of F.

FRANKLIN, BENJAMIN (1706-1790).—American statesman, philosopher, and writer, was one of a numerous family. His *f.* was a soap-boiler at Boston, where F. was *b.* He was apprenticed at the age of 13 to his brother, a printer, who treated him harshly. After various changes, during which he lived in New York, London, and Philadelphia, he at last succeeded in founding a successful business as a printer. He also started a newspaper, *The Gazette*, which was highly popular, *Poor Richard's Almanac*, and the *Busybody Papers*, in imitation of the *Spectator*. After holding various minor appointments, he was made deputy Postmaster-General for the American Colonies. In 1757 he went to London on some public business in which he was so successful that various colonies appointed him their English agent. In the midst of his varied avocations he found time for scientific investigation, especially with regard to electricity. For these he became known over the civilised world, and was loaded with honours. In 1762 he returned to America, and took a prominent part in the controversies which led to the Revolutionary War and the independence of the Colonies. In 1776 he was U.S. Minister to France, and in 1782 was a signatory of the treaty which confirmed the independence of the States. He returned home in 1785, and, after holding various political offices, retired in 1788, and *d.* in 1790. His autobiography is his chief contribution to literature, and is of the highest interest.

Works (10 vols., Bigelow, 1887-9), Autobiography (1868), Lives by M'Master (1887), and Morse (1889).

FREEMAN, EDWARD AUGUSTUS (1823-1892).—Historian, *s.* of John F., was *b.* at Harborne, Staffordshire. He lost both his parents in childhood, and was brought up by his paternal grandmother. He was *ed.* at private schools, and as a private pupil of the Rev. R. Gutch, whose *dau.* he afterwards *m.* In 1841 he was elected to a scholarship at Oxf. He had inherited an income sufficient to make him independent of a profession, and a prepossession in favour of the celibacy of the clergy disinclined him to enter the Church, of which he had at one time thought. He settled ultimately at Somerleaze, near Wells, where he occupied himself in study, writing for periodicals, and with the duties of a magistrate. He was a strong Liberal, and on one occasion stood unsuccessfully as a candidate for Parliament. He was also twice unsuccessful as an applicant for professional chairs, but ultimately, in 1884, succeeded Stubbs as Prof. of Modern History at Oxf. He had always been an enthusiastic traveller, and it was when on a tour in Spain that he took ill and *d.* on May 16, 1892. F. was a voluminous author, and a keen controversialist. His first book was a *History of Architecture* (1849), and among the very numerous publications which he issued the most important were *History of Federal Government* (1863), *The History of the Norman Conquest* (6 vols., 1867-79), *The Historical Geography of Europe* (1881-2), *The Reign of William Rufus* (1882), and an unfinished *History of Sicily.* Besides these he wrote innumerable articles in periodicals, many of which were separately *pub.* and contain much of his best work. He was laborious and honest, but the controversial cast of his mind sometimes coloured his work. His short books, such as his *William I.*, and his *General Sketch of European History,* are marvels of condensation, and show him at his best. His knowledge of history was singularly wide, and he sometimes showed a great power of vivid presentation.

FRENEAU, PHILIP (1752-1832).—Poet, *b.* in New York, produced two vols. of verse (1786-8), the most considerable contribution to poetry made up to that date in America. He fought in the Revolutionary War, was taken prisoner, and confined in a British prison-ship, the arrangements of which he bitterly satirised in *The British Prison Ship* (1781). He also wrote vigorous prose, of which *Advice to Authors* is an example. Amid much commonplace and doggerel, F. produced a small amount of genuine poetry in his short pieces, such as *The Indian Burying Ground,* and *The Wild Honeysuckle.*

FRERE, JOHN HOOKHAM (1769 - 1846). — Diplomatist, translator, and author, eldest *s.* of John F., a distinguished antiquary, was *b.* in London, and *ed.* at Eton and Camb. He became a clerk in the Foreign Office, and subsequently entering Parliament was appointed Under Foreign Sec. In 1800 he was Envoy to Portugal, and was Ambassador to Spain 1802-4, and again 1808-9. In 1818 he retired to Malta, where he *d.* He was a contributor to the *Anti-Jacobin,* to Ellis's *Specimens of the Early English Poets* (1801), and to Southey's *Chronicle of the Cid.* He also made some masterly translations from *Aristophanes ;* but his chief original contribution to literature was a burlesque poem on *Arthur and the Round Table,* purporting to be by William and Robert Whistlecraft. All F.'s writings are characterised no less by scholarship than by wit.

FROUDE, JAMES ANTHONY (1818-1894).—Historian and essayist, 3rd *s.* of the Archdeacon of Totnes, Devonshire, near which he was *b.*, and brother of Richard Hurrell F., one of the leaders of the Tractarian party, was *ed.* at Westminster School and Oxf., where for a short time he came under the influence of Newman, and contributed to his *Lives of the English Saints*, and in 1844 he took Deacon's orders. The connection with Newman was, however, short-lived; and the publication in 1848 of *The Nemesis of Faith* showed that in the severe mental and spiritual conflict through which he had passed, the writer had not only escaped from all Tractarian influences, but was in revolt against many of the fundamental doctrines of Christianity. One result of the book was his resignation of his Fellowship at Oxf.: another was his loss of an appointment as Head Master of the Grammar School of Hobart Town, Tasmania. In the same year began his friendship with Carlyle, and about the same time he became a contributor to the *Westminster Review* and to *Fraser's Magazine*, of which he was ed. from 1860-74. These papers were afterwards *coll.* and *pub.* in the 4 vols. of *Short Studies on Great Subjects*. In 1856 he *pub.* the first 2 vols. of the great work of his life, *The History of England from the Fall of Cardinal Wolsey to the Spanish Armada*, which extended to 12 vols., the last of which appeared in 1870. As literature this work has a place among the greatest productions of the century; but in its treatment it is much more dramatic, ethical, and polemical than historical in the strict sense; and indeed the inaccuracy in matters of fact to which F. was liable, combined with his tendency to idealise and to colour with his own prejudices the characters who figure in his narrative, are serious deductions from the value of his work considered as history. *The English in Ireland in the Eighteenth Century* appeared in 1872-4. On the death of Carlyle in 1881, F. found himself in the position of his sole literary executor, and in that capacity *pub.* successively the *Reminiscences* (1881), *History of the First Forty Years of Carlyle's Life* (1882), *Letters and Memorials of Jane Welsh Carlyle* (1883), *History of Carlyle's Life in London* (1884). The opinion is held by many that in the discharge of the duties entrusted to him by his old friend and master he showed neither discretion nor loyalty; and his indiscreet revelations and gross inaccuracies evoked a storm of controversy and protest. F. did not confine his labours to purely literary effort. In 1874-5 he travelled as a Government Commissioner in South Africa with the view of fostering a movement in favour of federating the various colonies there; in 1876 he served on the Scottish Univ. Commission; in 1884-5 he visited Australia, and gave the fruit of his observations to the world in *Oceana* (1886), and in 1886-7 he was in the West Indies, and *pub. The English in the West Indies* (1888). The year 1892 saw his appointment as Prof. of Modern History at Oxf., and his lectures there were *pub.* in his last books, *Life and Letters of Erasmus* (1894), *English Seamen in the Sixteenth Century* (1895), and *The Council of Trent* (1896). F. was elected in 1869 Lord Rector of the Univ. of St. Andrews, and received the degree of LL.D. from Edinburgh in 1884. By his instructions no Biography was to be written.

FULLER, SARAH MARGARET (1810-1850).—Was *b.* in Massachusetts, *dau.* of a lawyer, who encouraged her in overworking herself in the acquisition of knowledge with life-long evil results to her health. On his death she supported a large family of brothers and sisters by teaching. Her early studies had made her familiar with the literature not only of England but of France, Spain, and Italy; she had become imbued with German philosophy and mysticism, and she co-operated with Theodore Parker in his revolt against the Puritan theology till then prevalent in New England, and became the conductor of the Transcendentalist organ, *The Dial*, from 1840-2. She made various translations from the German, and *pub.* *Summer on the Lakes* (1844), and *Papers on Literature and Art* (1846). In the same year she went to Europe, and at Rome met the Marquis Ossoli, an Italian patriot, whom she *m.* in 1847. She and her husband were in the thick of the Revolution of 1848-9, and in the latter year she was in charge of a hospital at Rome. After the suppression of the Revolution she escaped with her husband from Italy, and took ship for America. The voyage proved most disastrous: small-pox broke out on the vessel, and their infant child *d.*, the ship was wrecked on Fire Island, near New York, and she and her husband were lost. Destitute of personal attractions, she was possessed of a singular power of conciliating sympathy. She was the intimate friend of Emerson, Hawthorn, Channing, and other eminent men.

FULLER, THOMAS (1608-1661).—Divine and antiquary, *s.* of a clergyman of the same name, was *b.* at Aldwinkle, Northamptonshire. Possessed of exceptional intelligence and a wonderful memory, he became a good scholar, and distinguished himself at Camb., where he was sent. Entering the Church, he obtained rapid preferment, including the lectureship at the Savoy, and a chaplaincy to Charles II. He was a voluminous author, his works dealing with theology, morals, history, and antiquities. Among the chief are *History of the Holy War, i.e.* the Crusades (1643), *The Holy State and the Profane State* (1642), *A Pisgah Sight of Palestine* (1650), *Church History of Britain, History of Cambridge University* (1655), *Worthies of England* (1662), and *Good Thoughts in Bad Times*. The outstanding characteristic of F.'s writings is shrewd observation conveyed in a style of quaint humour. Lamb says, "His conceits are oftentimes deeply steeped in human feeling and passion." But in addition there is much wisdom and a remarkable power of casting his observations into a compact, aphoristic form. The *Worthies*, though far from being a systematic work, is full of interesting biographical and antiquarian matter which, but for the pains of the author, would have been lost. Coleridge says of him, "He was incomparably the most sensible, the least prejudiced great man in an age that boasted a galaxy of great men." F., who was of a singularly amiable character, was a strong Royalist, and suffered the loss of his preferments during the Commonwealth. They were, however, given back to him at the Restoration.

Lives by Russell (1844), J. E. Bailey (1874), and M. Fuller (1886).

FULLERTON, LADY GEORGIANA (LEVESON-GOWER) (1812-1885).—Novelist, *dau.* of the 1st Earl Granville, and sister of the eminent statesman. She wrote a number of novels, some of which had considerable success. They include *Ellen Middleton* (1844),

Grantley Manor (1847), and *Too Strange not to be True* (1864). She also *pub.* two vols. of verse. She joined the Church of Rome in 1846.

GAIMAR, GEOFFREY (*fl.* 1140?).—Chronicler, translated the chronicle of Geoffrey of Monmouth into French verse for the wife of his patron, Ralph Fitz-Gilbert, and added a continuation dealing with the Saxon Kings. His work is entitled *L'Estoire des Engles.*

GALT, JOHN (1779-1839).—Novelist and miscellaneous writer, *s.* of the captain of a West Indiaman, was *b.* at Irvine, Ayrshire, but while still a young man he went to London and formed a commercial partnership, which proved unfortunate, and he then entered Lincoln's Inn to study law. A little before this he had produced his first book, a poem on the Battle of Largs, which, however, he soon suppressed. He then went to various parts of the Continent in connection with certain commercial schemes, and met Lord Byron, with whom he travelled for some time. Returning home he *pub. Letters from the Levant,* which had a favourable reception, and some dramas, which were less successful. He soon, however, found his true vocation in the novel of Scottish country life, and his fame rests upon the *Ayrshire Legatees* (1820), *The Annals of the Parish* (1821), *Sir Andrew Wylie* (1822), *The Entail* (1824), and *The Provost.* He was not so successful in the domain of historical romance, which he tried in *Ringan Gilbaize, The Spae-wife, The Omen,* etc., although these contain many striking passages. In addition to his novels G. produced many historical and biographical works, including a *Life of Wolsey* (1812), *Life and Studies of Benjamin West* (1816), *Tour of Asia, Life of Byron* (1830), *Lives of the Players,* and an Autobiography (1834). In addition to this copious literary output, G. was constantly forming and carrying out commercial schemes, the most important of which was the Canada Company, which, like most of his other enterprises, though conducted with great energy and ability on his part, ended in disappointment and trouble for himself. In 1834 he returned from Canada to Greenock, broken in health and spirits, and *d.* there in 1839 of paralysis. G. was a man of immense talent and energy, but would have held a higher place in literature had he concentrated these qualities upon fewer objects. Most of his 60 books are forgotten, but some of his novels, especially perhaps *The Annals of the Parish,* have deservedly a secure place. The town of Galt in Canada is named after him.

GARDINER, SAMUEL RAWSON (1829-1902).—Historian, *b.* at Alresford, Hants, was *ed.* at Winchester and Oxf. In 1855 he *m.* Isabella, *dau.* of Edward Irving (*q.v.*), the founder of the Catholic Apostolic Church, which he joined, and in which he ultimately held high office. About the time of his leaving Oxf. he had planned his great work, *The History of England from the Accession of James I. to the Restoration,* and the accomplishment of this task he made the great object of his life for more than 40 years. The first two vols. appeared in 1863 as *The History of England from the Accession of James I. to the Disgrace of Chief Justice Cooke,* and subsequent instalments appeared under the following titles: *Prince Charles and*

The Spanish Marriage (1867), *England under Buckingham and Charles I.* (1875), *Personal Government of Charles I.* (1877), *The Fall of the Government of Charles I.* (1881); these were in 1883-4 re-issued in a consolidated form entitled *History of England from the Accession of James I. to the Outbreak of the Civil War.* The second section of the work, *History of the Great Civil War*, followed in three vols. *pub.* in 1886, 1889, and 1891 respectively, and three more vols., *History of the Commonwealth and Protectorate* in 1894, 1897, and 1901, brought the story down to 1656, when the health of the indefatigable writer gave way, and he *d.* in 1902. In addition to this monumental work G. wrote many school and college historical text-books, and contributed to the Epochs of Modern History Series, *The Thirty Years' War* (1874), and *The First Two Stuarts* (1876); he also wrote *Outlines of English History*, three parts (1881-3), and *Students' History of England*, three parts (1891). From 1871-85 he was Prof. of History at King's Coll., London, and lecturer on history for the London Society for the Extension of Univ. Teaching. He also ed. many of the historical documents which he unearthed in his investigations, and many of those issued by the "Camden," "Clarendon," and other societies. He was ed. of *The English Historical Review*, and contributed largely to the *Dictionary of National Biography*. The sober and unadorned style of G.'s works did little to commend them to the general reader, but their eminent learning, accuracy, impartiality, and the laborious pursuit of truth which they exhibited earned for him, from the first, the respect and admiration of scholars and serious students of history; and as his great work advanced it was recognised as a permanent contribution to historical literature. In 1882 he received a civil list pension, and was elected to Research Fellowships, first by All Souls' Coll., and subsequently by Merton. He held honorary degrees from the Univ. of Oxford, Gottingen, and Edinburgh.

GARNETT, RICHARD (1835-1906).—Biographer and writer on literature, *s.* of Richard G., an assistant keeper of Printed Books in the British Museum. *B.* at Lichfield, and *ed.* at a school in Bloomsbury, he entered the British Museum in 1851 as an assistant librarian. There he remained for nearly 50 years, and rose to be Keeper of Printed Books. He acquired a marvellous knowledge of books, and of everything connected with pure literature. He made numerous translations from the Greek, German, Italian, Spanish, and Portuguese, and wrote books of graceful verse, *The Twilight of the Gods and other Tales* (1888), various biographical works on Carlyle, Milton, Blake, and others, *The Age of Dryden*, a *History of Italian Literature*, and contributed many articles to encyclopædias, and to the *Dictionary of National Biography*.

GARRICK, DAVID (1717-1779).—Actor and dramatist, *b.* at Hereford, but got most of his education at Lichfield, to which his *f.* belonged. He was also one of the three pupils who attended Johnson's School at Edial. With his great preceptor, whom he accompanied to London, he always remained on friendly terms. He took to the stage, and became the greatest of English actors. He also wrote various plays, and adaptations, and did not scruple to undertake "improved" versions of some of Shakespeare's greatest plays, including *Cymbeline*, *The Taming of the Shrew*, and *The Winter's Tale*, performing the same service for Jonson and Wycherley, in the last case with much more excuse. Of his original plays *The Lying Valet* and *Miss in her Teens* are perhaps the best.

GARRISON, WILLIAM LLOYD (1805-1879).—Orator, was *b.* at Newburyport, Mass. Though chiefly known for his eloquent advocacy of negro emancipation, he is also remembered for his *Sonnets and other Poems* (1847).

GARTH, SIR SAMUEL (1661-1719).—Physician and poet, *b.* at Bolam in the county of Durham, and *ed.* at Camb., he settled as a physician in London, where he soon acquired a large practice. He was a zealous Whig, the friend of Addison and, though of different political views, of Pope, and he ended his career as physician to George I., by whom he was knighted in 1714. He is remembered as the author of *The Dispensary*, a satire, which had great popularity in its day, and of *Claremont*, a descriptive poem. He also ed. a translation of Ovid's *Metamorphoses*, to which Addison, Pope, and others contributed. Perhaps, however, the circumstance most honourable to him is his intervention to procure an honourable burial for Dryden, over whose remains he pronounced a eulogy.

GASCOIGNE, GEORGE (1525 or 1535-1577).—Poet and dramatist, *s.* of Sir John G., and descended from Sir William G., the famous Chief Justice to Henry IV., he was *ed.* at Camb., and entered Gray's Inn 1555. While there he produced two plays, both translations, *The Supposes* (1566) from Ariosto, and *Jocasta* (1566) from Euripides. Disinherited on account of his prodigality, he *m.*, in order to rehabilitate his finances, a widow, the mother of Nicholas Breton (*q.v.*). He had, nevertheless, to go to Holland to escape from the importunities of his creditors. While there he saw service under the Prince of Orange, and was taken prisoner by the Spaniards. Released after a few months, he returned to England, and found that some of his poems had been surreptitiously *pub.* He thereupon issued an authoritative ed. under the title of *An Hundred Sundrie Floures bound up in one Poesie* (1572). Other works are *Notes of Instruction*, for making English verse, *The Glasse of Government* (1575), and *The Steele Glasse* (1576), a satire. He also contributed to the entertainments in honour of Queen Elizabeth at Kenilworth and appears to have had a share of Court favour. G. was a man of originality, and did much to popularise the use of blank verse in England.

GASKELL, ELIZABETH CLEGHORN (STEVENSON) (1810-1865).—Novelist, *dau.* of William Stevenson, a Unitarian minister, and for some time Keeper of the Treasury Records. She *m.* William G., a Unitarian minister, at Manchester, and in 1848 *pub.* anonymously her first book, *Mary Barton*, in which the life and feelings of the manufacturing working classes are depicted with much power and sympathy. Other novels followed, *Lizzie Leigh* (1855), *Mr. Harrison's Confessions* (1865), *Ruth* (1853), *Cranford* (1851-3), *North and South* (1855), *Sylvia's Lovers* (1863), etc. Her last work was *Wives and Daughters* (1865), which appeared in the *Cornhill*

Magazine, and was left unfinished. Mrs. G. had some of the characteristics of Miss Austen, and if her style and delineation of character are less minutely perfect, they are, on the other hand, imbued with a deeper vein of feeling. She was the friend of Charlotte Bronté (*q.v.*), to whom her sympathy brought much comfort, and whose *Life* she wrote. Of *Cranford* Lord Houghton wrote, "It is the finest piece of humoristic description that has been added to British literature since Charles Lamb."

GATTY, MRS. ALFRED (MARGARET SCOTT) (1809-1873).—*Dau.* of Rev. A. J. Scott, D.D., a navy chaplain, who served under, and was the trusted friend of, Nelson. She *m.* the Rev. Alfred Gatty, D.D., Ecclesfield, Yorkshire, and became a highly useful and popular writer of tales for young people. Among her books may be mentioned *Parables from Nature*, *Worlds not Realised*, *Proverbs Illustrated*, and *Aunt Judy's Tales*. She also conducted *Aunt Judy's Magazine*, and wrote a book on British sea-weeds. Juliana Ewing (*q.v.*) was her daughter.

GAUDEN, JOHN (1605-1662).—Theologian, *b.* at Mayfield in Essex, and *ed.* at Camb. His claim to remembrance rests on his being the reputed author of *Eikon Basiliké* (the Royal Image), a book purporting to be written by Charles I. during his imprisonment, and containing religious meditations and defences of his political acts. *Pub.* immediately after the King's execution, it produced an extraordinary effect, so much so that Charles II. is reported to have said that, had it been *pub.* a week earlier, it would have saved his father's life. There seems now to be little doubt that Gauden was the author. At all events he claimed to be recompensed for his services, and was made Bishop successively of Exeter and Worcester, apparently on the strength of these claims. The work passed through 50 ed. within a year, and was answered by Milton in his *Iconoclastes* (the Image-breaker).

GAY, JOHN (1685-1732).—Poet and dramatist, *b.* near Barnstaple of a good but decayed family. His parents dying while he was a child he was apprenticed to a silk-mercer in London, but not liking the trade, was released by his master. In 1708 he *pub.* a poem, *Wine*, and in 1713 *Rural Sports*, which he dedicated to Pope, whose friendship he obtained. A little before this he had received an appointment as sec. in the houseohld of the Duchess of Monmouth. His next attempts were in the drama, in which he was not at first successful; but about 1714 he made his first decided hit in *The Shepherd's Week*, a set of six pastorals designed to satirise Ambrose Philips, which, however, secured public approval on their own merits. These were followed by *Trivia* (1716), in which he was aided by Swift, an account in mock heroic verse of the dangers of the London streets, and by *The Fan*. G. had always been ambitious of public employment, and his aspirations were gratified by his receiving the appointment of sec. to an embassy to Hanover, which, however, he appears to have resigned in a few months. He then returned to the drama in *What d'ye call It*, and *Three Hours after Marriage*, neither of which, however, took the public fancy. In 1720 he *pub.* a collection of his poems, which brought him £1000, but soon after lost all his means in the collapse of the South Sea Company. After producing another drama, *The Captive*, he *pub.* his *Fables* (1727), which added to his reputation, and soon after, in 1728, achieved the great success of his life in *The Beggar's Opera*, a Newgate pastoral, suggested by Swift, in which the graces and fantasticalities of the Italian Opera were satirised. A sequel, *Polly*, was suppressed by the Lord Chamberlain as reflecting upon the Court, but was *pub.* and had an enormous sale. The last few years of his life were passed in the household of the Duke of Queensberry, who had always been his friend and patron. He *d.* after three days' illness, aged 47. G. was an amiable, easy-going man, who appears to have had the power of attracting the strong attachments of his friends, among whom were Pope and Swift. He seems to have been one of the very few for whom the latter had a sincere affection. He is buried in Westminster Abbey. Of all he has written he is best remembered by one or two songs, of which the finest is *Black-eyed Susan*.

GEDDES, ALEXANDER (1737-1802).—Theologian and scholar, of Roman Catholic parentage, was *b.* at Ruthven, Banffshire, and *ed.* for the priesthood at the local seminary of Scalan, and at Paris, and became a priest in his native county. His translation of the *Satires* of Horace made him known as a scholar, but his liberality of view led to his suspension. He then went to London, where he became known to Lord Petre, who enabled him to proceed with a new translation of the Bible for English Roman Catholics, which he carried on as far as Ruth, with some of the Psalms, and which was *pub.* in 3 vols. (1792-6). This was followed by *Critical Remarks on the Hebrew Scriptures*, in which he largely anticipated the German school of criticism. The result of this publication was his suspension from all ecclesiastical functions. G. was also a poet, and wrote *Linton: a Tweedside Pastoral*, *Carmen Seculare pro Gallica Gente* (1790), in praise of the French Revolution. He *d.* without recanting, but received absolution at the hands of a French priest, though public mass for his soul was forbidden by the ecclesiastical powers.

GEOFFREY OF MONMOUTH (1100?-1154).—Chronicler, was probably a Benedictine monk, and became Bishop of St. Asaph. He wrote a Latin *History of British Kings*. *Merlin's Prophecies*, long attributed to him, is now held to be not genuine. The history is rather a historical romance than a sober history, and gave scandal to some of the more prosaic chroniclers who followed him. It was subsequently translated into Anglo-Norman by Gaimar and Wace, and into English by Layamon.

GERARD, ALEXANDER (1728-1795).—Philosophical writer, *s.* of Rev. Gilbert G., was *ed.* at Aberdeen, where he became Prof., first of Natural Philosophy, and afterwards of Divinity, and one of the ministers of the city. As a prof. he introduced various reforms. In 1756 he gained the prize for an *Essay on Taste* which, together with an *Essay on Genius*, he subsequently *pub.* These treatises, though now superseded, gained for him considerable reputation.

GIBBON, EDWARD (1737-1794).—Historian, was *b.* at Putney of an ancient Kentish family. His *f.* was Edward G., and his mother Judith Porten. He was the only one of a family of seven who survived infancy, and was himself a delicate child with a precocious love of study. After receiving his early education at home he was sent to Westminster School, and when 15 was entered at Magdalen Coll., Oxf., where, according to his own account, he spent 14 months idly and unprofitably. Oxf. was then at its lowest ebb, and earnest study or effort of any kind had little encouragement. G., however, appears to have maintained his wide reading in some degree, and his study of Bossuet and other controversialists led to his becoming in 1753 a Romanist. To counteract this his *f.* placed him under the charge of David Mallet (*q.v.*), the poet, deist, and ed. of Bolingbroke's works, whose influence, not unnaturally, failed of the desired effect, and G. was next sent to Lausanne, and placed under the care of a Protestant pastor, M. Pavilliard. Various circumstances appear to have made G. not unwilling to be re-converted to Protestantism; at all events he soon returned to the reformed doctrines. At Lausanne he remained for over four years, and devoted himself assiduously to study, especially of French literature and the Latin classics. At this time also he became engaged to Mademoiselle Suzanne Curchod; but on the match being peremptorily opposed by his *f.* it was broken off. With the lady, who eventually became the wife of Necker, and the mother of Madame de Staël, he remained on terms of friendship. In 1758 G. returned to England, and in 1761 *pub. Essai sur l'Etude de la Littérature*, translated into English in 1764. About this time he made a tour on the Continent, visiting Paris, where he stayed for three months, and thence proceeding to Switzerland and Italy. There it was that, musing amid the ruins of the Capitol at Rome on October 15, 1764, he formed the plan of writing the history of the Decline and Fall of the Roman Empire. He returned to England in 1765, and in 1770 his *f. d.*, leaving him the embarrassed estate of Buriton, which had been his usual home when in England. With a view to recovering his affairs, he left his estate and lived in London where, in 1772, he seriously set himself to realise the great plan which, since its conception, had never been out of his thoughts. The first chapter was written three times, and the second twice before he could satisfy himself that he had found the style suited to his subject. The progress of the work was delayed by the fact that G. had meanwhile (1774) entered the House of Commons, where, as member for Liskeard, he was a steady, though silent, supporter of Lord North in his American policy. He subsequently sat for Lymington, and held office as a Commissioner of Trade and Plantations 1779-82. The first vol. of the *Decline and Fall* appeared in 1776, and was received with acclamation, and it was not until some time had elapsed that the author's treatment of the rise of Christianity excited the attention and alarm of the religious and ecclesiastical world. When, however, the far-reaching nature of his views was at length realised, a fierce and prolonged controversy arose, into which G. himself did not enter except in one case where his fidelity as an historian was impugned. The second and third vols. appeared in 1781, and thereafter (1783) G. returned to Lausanne, where he lived tranquilly with an early friend, M. Deyverdun, devoting his mornings to the completion of his history, and his evenings to society. At length, on the night of June 27, 1787, in the summer-house of his garden, the last words were penned, and the great work of his life completed. Of the circumstances, and of his feelings at the moment, he has himself given an impressive account. The last three vols. were issued in 1788, G. having gone to London to see them through the press. This being done he returned to Lausanne where, within a year, his beloved friend Deyverdun *d.* His last years were clouded by ill-health, and by anxieties with regard to the French Revolution. In 1793, though travelling was a serious matter for him, he came to England to comfort his friend Lord Sheffield on the death of his wife, took ill, and *d.* suddenly in London on January 16, 1794.

The place of G. among historians is in the first rank, and if the vast scale of his work and the enormous mass of detail involved in it are considered along with the learning and research employed in accumulating the material, and the breadth of view, lucidity of arrangement, and sense of proportion which have fused them into a distinct and splendid picture, his claims to the first place cannot be lightly dismissed. His style, though not pure, being tinged with Gallicisms, is one of the most noble in our literature, rich, harmonious, and stately; and though sources of information not accessible to him have added to our knowledge, and have shown some of his conclusions to be mistaken, his historical accuracy has been comparatively little shaken, and his work is sure of permanence. As a man G. seems to have been somewhat calm and cool in his feelings, though capable of steady and affectionate friendships, such as those with Deyverdun and the Sheffields, which were warmly reciprocated, and he appears to have been liked in society, where his brilliant conversational powers made him shine. He was vain, and affected the manners of the fine gentleman, which his unattractive countenance and awkward figure, and latterly his extreme corpulence, rendered somewhat ridiculous. He left an interesting *Autobiography.*

SUMMARY.—*B.* 1737, *ed.* Westminster and Oxf., became Romanist and sent to Lausanne 1753, where he returned to Protestantism, *pub. Essay on Study of Literature* 1761, visited Rome 1764 and resolved to write his *Decline and Fall of Roman Empire*, began to write it 1772, *pub.* 1776-87, *d.* 1794.

Decline and Fall (Sir W. Smith, 8 vols., 1854-55), another (J. B. Bury, 7 vols., 1896-1900). *Autobiography* (Lord Sheffield, 1796), often reprinted.

GIFFORD, RICHARD (1725-1807).—Poet, was *ed.* at Oxford and took orders. He was the author of a poem, *Contemplation.* He also wrote theological and controversial works.

GIFFORD, WILLIAM (1756-1826).—Critic and poet, was *b.* of humble parentage at Ashburton, Devonshire, and after being for a short time at sea, was apprenticed to a cobbler. Having, however, shown signs of superior ability, and a desire for learning, he was befriended and *ed.*, ultimately at Oxf., where he *grad.* Becoming known to Lord Grosvenor, he was patronised by him, and in course of time produced his first poem, *The Baviad* (1794), a satire directed against the Della Cruscans, a clique of very small and sentimental poets, which at once quenched their little tapers. This was followed by another satire, *The Mæviad*, against some minor dramatists. His last effort in this line was his *Epistle to Peter Pindar* (Dr. Walcot), inspired by personal enmity, which evoked a reply, *A Cut at a Cobbler*. These writings had established the reputation of G. as a keen, and even ferocious critic, and he was appointed in 1797 ed. of the *Anti-Jacobin*, which Canning and his friends had just started, and of the *Quarterly Review* (1809-24). He also brought out ed. of Massinger, Ben Jonson, and Ford. As a critic he had acuteness; but he was one-sided, prejudiced, and savagely bitter, and much more influenced in his judgments by the political opinions than by the literary merits of his victims. In his whole career, however, he displayed independence and spirit in overcoming the disadvantages of his early life, as well as gratitude to those who had served him. He held various appointments which placed him above financial anxiety.

GILDAS (516?-570?).—British historian, was a monk who is believed to have gone to Brittany about 550, and founded a monastery. He wrote a history, *De Excidio Britanniæ* (concerning the overthrow of Britain). It consists of two parts, the first from the Roman invasion until the end of the 4th century, and the second a continuation to the writer's own time. It is obscure and wordy, and not of much value.

GILDER, RICHARD WATSON (1844-1909).—Poet, *b.* at Borderstown, New Jersey, was successively a lawyer, a soldier, and a journalist, in which last capacity he ed. *Scribner's* (afterwards the *Century*) *Magazine*. He holds a high place among American poets as the author of *The New Day* (1875), *The Celestial Passion, The Great Remembrance, Five Books of Song* (1894), *In Palestine* (1898), *In the Heights* (1905), *A Book of Music* (collection) (1906), etc.

GILDON, CHARLES (1665-1724).—Critic and dramatist, belonged to a Roman Catholic family, and was an unsuccessful playwright, a literary hack, and a critic of little acumen or discrimination. He attacked Pope as "Sawny Dapper," and was in return embalmed in *The Dunciad*. He also wrote a Life of Defoe.

GILFILLAN, GEORGE (1813-1878).—Poet and critic, *s.* of a dissenting minister at Comrie, Perthshire, studied at Glasgow Univ., and was ordained minister of a church in Dundee. He was a voluminous author. Among his writings are *Gallery of Literary Portraits*, and a Series of British Poets with introductions and notes in 48 vols. He also wrote Lives of Burns, Scott, and others, and *Night* (1867), a poem in nine books. His style was somewhat turgid, and his criticism rather sympathetic than profound.

GILFILLAN, ROBERT (1798-1850).—Poet, *b.* at Dunfermline, was latterly Collector of Police Rates in Leith. He wrote a number of Scottish songs, and was favourably mentioned in *Noctes Ambrosianæ* (see Wilson, J.). He was the author of the beautiful song, *Oh, why left I my Hame?*

GILLESPIE, GEORGE (1613-1648).—Scottish Theologian, was *b.* at Kirkcaldy, and studied at St. Andrews. He became one of the ministers of Edin., and was a member of the Westminster Assembly, in which he took a prominent part. A man of notable intellectual power, he exercised an influence remarkable in view of the fact that he *d.* in his 36th year. He was one of the most formidable controversialists of a highly controversial age. His best known work is *Aaron's Rod Blossoming*, a defence of the ecclesiastical claims of the high Presbyterian party.

GILLIES, JOHN (1747-1836).—Historian, *b.* at Brechin and *ed.* there and at Glasgow, wrote a *History of Greece* (1786) from a strongly anti-democratic standpoint, a *History of the World from Alexander to Augustus* (1807), and a *View of the Reign of Frederick II. of Prussia.* He also made various translations from the Greek. He succeeded Principal Robertson as Historiographer Royal for Scotland.

GIRALDUS CAMBRENSIS (literary name of GERALD DE BARRI) (1146?-1220?).—Geographer and historian, was *b.* of a Norman family settled in Wales, which intermarried with the Royal family of that country. He was an eminent scholar and Churchman, whose object of ambition was the Bishopric of St. David's, to which he was twice elected by the chapter, but from which he was kept out by the opposition of the King. When travelling in Ireland with Prince John (1185) he wrote *Topographia Hibernica*, a valuable descriptive account of the country, and in 1188 he wrote *Itinerarium Cambriæ*, a similar work on Wales. He left several other works, including an autobiography, *De Rebus a se Gestis* (concerning his own doings).

GISSING, GEORGE (1857-1903).—Novelist, *b.* at Wakefield. In his novels he depicted the environment and struggles of the lower and lower middle classes with a somewhat pessimistic and depressing realism, although his last work, *The Private Papers of Henry Ryecroft*, seemed to usher in the dawn of a somewhat brighter outlook. His other novels include *Demos* (1886), *Thyrza* (1887), *The Nether World* (1889), *New Grub Street* (1891), *Born in Exile* (1892), *In the Year of Jubilee* (1894), and *The Town Traveller* (1898). He *d.* at St. Jean de Luz in the Pyrenees.

GLADSTONE, WILLIAM EWART (1809-1898).—Statesman, scholar, and man of letters, fourth *s.* of Sir John G., a merchant in Liverpool, was of Scottish ancestry. He was *ed.* at Eton and Christ Church, Oxf. From his youth he was deeply interested in religious and ecclesiastical questions, and at one time thought of entering the Church. In 1832 he entered Parliament as a Tory, and from the first gave evidence of the splendid talents for debate and statesmanship, especially in the department of finance, which raised him to the position of power and influence which he afterwards attained. After holding the offices of Pres. of the Board of Trade, Colonial Sec., and Chancellor of the Exchequer, he attained the position of Prime Minister, which he held four times 1868-74, 1880-85, 1885-86, and 1892-93. His political career was one of intense energy and activity in every department of government, especially after he became Prime Minister, and while it gained him the enthusiastic applause and devotion of a large portion of the nation, it exposed him to a correspondingly intense opposition on the part of another. The questions which involved him in the greatest conflicts of his life and evoked his chief efforts of intellect were the disestablishment of the Irish Church, the foreign policy of his great rival Disraeli, and Home Rule for Ireland, on the last of which the old Liberal party was finally broken up. In the midst of political labours which might have been sufficient to absorb even his tireless energy, he found time to follow out and write upon various subjects which possessed a life-long interest for him. His first book was *The State in its Relations with the Church* (1839), which formed the subject of one of Macaulay's essays. *Studies on Homer and the Homeric Age* (1858), *Juventus Mundi* (1869), and *Homeric Synchronism* (1876), *The Impregnable Rock of Holy Scripture* (1890), *The Vatican Decrees and Vaticanism* (1874-75), and *Gleanings of Past Years* (1897), 8 vols., were his other principal contributions to literature. G.'s scholarship, though sound and even brilliant, was of an old-fashioned kind, and his conclusions on Homeric questions have not received much support from contemporary scholars. In his controversies with Huxley and others his want of scientific knowledge and of sympathy with modern scientific tendencies placed him at a disadvantage. His character was a singularly complex one, and his intellect possessed a plasticity which made it possible to say of him that he never *was* anything, but was always *becoming* something. His life was a singularly noble and stainless one, and he must probably ever remain one of the great figures in the history of his country.

Life by J. Morley (3 vols.), others by J. M'Carthy, Sir Wemyss Reid, and many others.

GLANVILL, JOSEPH (1636-1680).—Controversialist and moral writer, *b.* at Plymouth, and *ed.* at Oxf., took orders, and held various benefices, including the Rectory of Bath Abbey and a prebend at Worcester. He came under the influence of the Camb. Platonists, especially of Henry More (*q.v.*). His contendings were chiefly with the English Nonconformists, against whom (with the exception of Baxter whom he held in great esteem) he exhibited great bitterness. His chief work is the *Vanity of Dogmatizing* (1661) which contains the story of "The Scholar Gipsy," in later days turned to such fine account by Matthew Arnold. G. wrote a fine literary style, at its best recalling that of Sir Thomas Browne.

GLAPTHORNE, HENRY (*fl.* 1640).—Dramatist, had a high reputation among his contemporaries, though now almost forgotten. He wrote two comedies, three tragedies, and a book of poems, which were all reprinted in two vols. in 1874. His best work is *Argalus and Parthenia* (1639), based upon Sidney's *Arcadia*. Others were *The Hollander*, *Wit is a Constable*, and *The Ladies' Privilege* (all 1640).

GLASCOCK, WILLIAM NUGENT (1787-1847).—Novelist. He saw a good deal of service in the navy with credit, and from this drew the inspiration of his vigorous and breezy sea-stories, which include *Sailors and Saints* (1829), *Tales of a Tar* (1836), and *Land Sharks and Sea Gulls* (1838).

GLEIG, GEORGE ROBERT (1796-1888).—*S.* of George G., Bishop of Brechin, entered the army, and served in the Peninsula and America. In 1820 he took orders, and after serving various cures *bec.*, in 1834, Chaplain of Chelsea Hospital, and in 1844 Chaplain-General of the Forces, which office he held until 1875. He was a frequent contributor to reviews and magazines, especially *Blackwood's*, in which his best known novel, *The Subaltern*, appeared, and he was also the author of Lives of Warren Hastings, Clive, *and* Wellington, *Military Commanders*, *Chelsea Pensioners*, and other works.

GLEN, WILLIAM (1789-1826).—Poet, *b.* in Glasgow, was for some years in the West Indies. He *d.* in poverty. He wrote several poems, but the only one which has survived is his Jacobite ballad, *Wae's me for Prince Charlie.*

GLOVER, RICHARD (1712-1785).—Poet and dramatist, was a London merchant, and M.P. for Weymouth. A scholarly man with a taste for literature, he wrote two poems in blank verse, *Leonidas* (1737), and *The Athenaid* (1787). Though not without a degree of dignity, they want energy and interest, and are now forgotten. He also produced a few dramas, which had little success. He is best remembered by his beautiful ballad, *Hosier's Ghost*, beginning "As near Portobello lying." G. had the reputation of a useful and public-spirited citizen.

GODWIN, MRS. MARY (WOLLSTONECRAFT) (1759-1797).—Miscellaneous writer, was of Irish extraction. Her *f.* was a spendthrift of bad habits, and at 19 Mary left home to make her way in the world. Her next ten years were spent as companion to a lady, in teaching a school at Newington Green, and as governess in the family of Lord Kingsborough. In 1784 she assisted her sister to escape from a husband who ill-treated her. In 1788 she took to translating, and became literary adviser to Johnson the publisher. through whom she became known to many of the literary people of the day, as well as to certain Radicals, including Godwin, Paine, Priestly, and Fuseli, the painter. She then, 1792, went to Paris, where she met Captain Imlay, with whom she formed a connection, the fruit of which was her daughter Fanny. Captain Imlay having deserted her, she tried to commit suicide at Putney Bridge, but was rescued. Thereafter she resumed her literary labours, and lived with W. Godwin, who married her in 1797. Their *dau.*, Mary, whose birth she did not survive, became the second wife of Shelley. Her chief original writings are a *Reply* to Burke's *Reflections on the French Revolution* (1791), *Vindication of the Rights of Women* (1792), and *Original Stories for Children*, illustrated by W. Blake. Her *Vindication* received much adverse criticism on account of its extreme positions and over-plainness of speech.

GODWIN, WILLIAM (1756-1836).—Philosopher and novelist, *b.* at Wisbeach, and *ed.* at a school in Norwich, to which city his *f.*, a Presbyterian minister, had removed, and subsequently at a Presbyterian coll. at Hoxton, with a view to the ministry.

From 1778 to 1783 he acted as minister of various congregations near London; but his theological views having undergone important changes, he resigned his pastorate, and devoted himself to a literary career. His first work, a series of historical sketches in the form of sermons, failed. He then found employment as one of the principal writers in the *New Annual Register*, and became otherwise prominent as an advocate of political and social reform. Many of his views were peculiar and extreme, and even tended, if fully carried out in practice, to subvert morality; but they were propounded and supported by their author with a whole-hearted belief in their efficacy for the regeneration of society: and the singular circumstances of his connection with and ultimate marriage to Mary Wollstonecraft showed at least that he had the courage of his opinions. His *Enquiry concerning Political Justice* (1793) made him famous. A year later he *pub.* his masterpiece, *Caleb Williams*, a novel exhibiting a sombre strength rarely equalled. The next few years were occupied in political controversy, for which G. was, by his sincerity and his masculine style, well fitted; and it was in the midst of these—in 1797—that his first marriage, already alluded to, and the death of his wife, of whom he *pub.* a singular but interesting Life, occurred. In 1799 his second great novel, *St. Leon*, based upon the philosopher's stone and the elixir of life, appeared. His other novels, *Fleetwood* (1804), *Mandeville* (1817), and *Cloudesley* (1830), are much inferior. In addition to these works G. brought out an elaborate *Life of Chaucer* in 2 vols. (1803), *An Essay on Sepulchres* (1808), containing much fine thought finely expressed, *A History of the Commonwealth*, an Essay against the theories of Malthus (*q.v.*), and his last work, *Lives of the Necromancers*. For some time he engaged in the publishing business, in which, however, he ultimately proved unsuccessful. In his later years he had the office of Yeoman Usher of the Exchequer conferred upon him. G. entered in 1801 into a second marriage with a widow, Mrs. Clairmont, by whom he had a *dau.* This lady had already a *s.* and *dau.*, the latter of whom had an irregular connection with Byron. His *dau.* by his first marriage—Mary Wollstonecraft G.,—became in 1816 the wife of Shelley. G. was a man of simple manners and imperturbable temper.

GOLDING, ARTHUR (1535?-1605?).—Translator, *s.* of a gentleman of Essex, was perhaps at Camb., and was diligent in the translation of theological works by Calvin, Beza, and others, but is chiefly remembered for his versions of Cæsar's *Commentaries* (1565), and specially of Ovid's *Metamorphoses* (1565-67), the latter in ballad metre. He also translated Justin's *History*, and part of Seneca.

GOLDSMITH, OLIVER (1728-1774).—Poet, dramatist, and essayist, *s.* of an Irish clergyman, was *b.* at Pallasmore in Co. Longford. His early education was received at various schools at Elphin, Athlone, and Edgeworthstown. At the age of 8 he had a severe attack of smallpox which disfigured him for life. In 1744 he went to Trinity Coll., Dublin, whence, having come into collision with one of the coll. tutors, he ran away in 1746. He was, however, induced to return, and *grad.* in 1749. The Church was chosen for him as a profession—against his will be it said in justice to him He presented himself before the Bishop of Elphin for examination

—perhaps as a type of deeper and more inward incongruencies—in scarlet breeches, and was rejected. He next figured as a tutor; but had no sooner accumulated £30 than he quitted his employment and forthwith dissipated his little savings. A long-suffering uncle named Contarine, who had already more than once interposed on his behalf, now provided means to send him to London to study law. He, however, got no farther than Dublin, where he was fleeced to his last guinea, and returned to the house of his mother, now a widow with a large family. After an interval spent in idleness, a medical career was perceived to be the likeliest opening, and in 1752 he steered for Edin., where he remained on the usual happy-go-lucky terms until 1754, when he proceeded to Leyden. After a year there he started on a walking tour, which led him through France, Germany, Switzerland, and Italy. How he lived it is hard to say, for he left Leyden penniless. It is said that he disputed at Univ., and played the flute, and thus kept himself in existence. All this time, however, he was gaining the experiences and knowledge of foreign countries which he was afterwards to turn to such excellent account. At one of the Univ. visited at this time, he is believed to have secured the medical degree, of which he subsequently made use. Louvain and Padua have both been named as the source of it. He reached London almost literally penniless in 1756, and appears to have been occupied successively as an apothecary's journeyman, a doctor of the poor, and an usher in a school at Peckham. In 1757 he was writing for the *Monthly Review*. The next year he applied unsuccessfully for a medical appointment in India; and the year following, 1759, saw his first important literary venture, *An Enquiry into the State of Polite Learning in Europe*. It was *pub.* anonymously, but attracted some attention, and brought him other work. At the same time he became known to Bishop Percy, the collector of the *Reliques of Ancient Poetry*, and he had written *The Bee*, a collection of essays, and was employed upon various periodicals. In 1761 began his friendship with Johnson, which led to that of the other great men of that circle. His *Chinese Letters*, afterwards republished as *The Citizen of the World*, appeared in *The Public Ledger* in 1762. *The Traveller*, the first of his longer poems, came out in 1764, and was followed in 1766 by *The Vicar of Wakefield*. In 1768 he essayed the drama, with *The Good-natured Man*, which had considerable success. The next few years saw him busily occupied with work for the publishers, including *The History of Rome* (1769), Lives of Parnell the poet, and Lord Bolingbroke (1770), and in the same year *The Deserted Village* appeared; *The History of England* was *pub.* in 1771. In 1773 he produced with great success his other drama, *She Stoops to Conquer*. His last works were *The Retaliation*, *The History of Greece*, and *Animated Nature*, all *pub.* in 1774. In that year, worn out with overwork and anxiety, he caught a fever, of which he *d.* April 4. With all his serious and very obvious faults—his reckless improvidence, his vanity, and, in his earlier years at any rate, his dissipated habits—G. is one of the most lovable characters in English literature, and one whose writings show most of himself—his humanity, his bright and spontaneous humour, and "the kindest heart in the world." His friends included some of the best and greatest men in England, among them

Johnson, Burke, and Reynolds. They all, doubtless, laughed at and made a butt of him, but they all admired and loved him. At the news of his death Burke burst into tears, Reynolds laid down his brush and painted no more that day, and Johnson wrote an imperishable epitaph on him. The poor, the old, and the outcast crowded the stair leading to his lodgings, and wept for the benefactor who had never refused to share what he had (often little enough) with them. Much of his work—written at high pressure for the means of existence, or to satisfy the urgency of duns—his histories, his *Animated Nature*, and such like, have, apart from a certain charm of style which no work of his could be without, little permanent value; but *The Traveller* and *The Deserted Village*, *She Stoops to Conquer*, and, above all, *The Vicar of Wakefield*, will keep his memory dear to all future readers of English.

SUMMARY.—*B.* 1728, *ed.* Trinity Coll., Dublin, went to Edin. 1752, and to Leyden 1754, travelled on foot over large part of Continent, reached London 1756, and wrote for magazines, etc., and after publishing various other works produced *The Citizen of the World* in 1762, *pub. Vicar of Wakefield* 1766, *Deserted Village* 1770, and *She Stoops to Conquer* 1773, *d.* 1774.

There are many ed. of G.'s works by Prior, 1837, Cunningham, 1854, Prof. Masson (Globe), 1869, Gibb (Bohn's Standard Library), 1885. Biographies by Prior, 1837, Foster, 1848-71, Washington Irving, and others. *See* also Boswell's *Johnson*, and Thackeray's *English Humorists*.

GOODALL, WALTER (1706?-1766).—Historical writer, *b.* in Banffshire, and *ed.* King's Coll., Aberdeen, became assistant librarian to the Advocates' Library in Edin. In 1754 he *pub.* an *Examination of the Letters said to have been written by Mary Queen of Scots*, in which he combats the genuineness of the "Casket Letters." He also ed., among other works, Fordun's *Scotichronicon* (1759).

GOODWIN, THOMAS (1600-1680).—Divine, was *b.* in Norfolk, and *ed.* at Camb., where he was Vicar of Trinity Church. Becoming an Independent, he ministered to a church in London, and thereafter at Arnheim in Holland. Returning to England he was made Chaplain to Cromwell's Council of State, and Pres. of Magdalen Coll., Oxf. At the Restoration he was deprived, but continued to preach in London. He was the author of various commentaries and controversial pamphlets, was a member of the Westminster Assembly, and assisted in drawing up the amended Confession, 1658. He attended Oliver Cromwell on his deathbed.

GOOGE, BARNABE (1540-1594).—Poet and translator, *b.* at Lincoln, studied at both Camb. and Oxf. He was a kinsman of Cecil, who gave him employment in Ireland. He translated from the Latin of Manzolli *The Zodiac of Life*, a satire against the Papacy, and *The Popish Kingdome* by T. Kirchmayer, a similar work; also *The Foure Bookes of Husbandrie* of Conrad Heresbach. In 1563 he *pub.* a vol. of original poems, *Eglogs*, *Epytaphes*, and *Sonnettes*.

GORDON, ADAM LINDSAY (1833-1870).—Poet, was *b.* in the Azores, the *s.* of an officer in the army. He went to Australia, where he had a varied career in connection with horses and riding, for which he had a passion. He betook himself to the Bush, got into financial trouble, and *d.* by his own hand. In the main he derives his inspiration (as in the *Rhyme of Joyous Garde*, and *Britomarte*) from mediæval and English sources, not from his Australian surroundings. Among his books are *Sea-spray and Smoke-drift* (1867), *Bush Ballads* (containing *The Sick Stock-rider*) (1870), *Ashtaroth* (1867). In many of his poems, *e.g. An Exile's Farewell*, and *Whispering in the Wattle Boughs*, there is a strong vein of sadness and pathos.

GORE, MRS. CATHERINE GRACE FRANCES (MOODY) (1799-1861).—Novelist, *dau.* of a wine merchant at Retford, where she was *b.* She *m.* a Captain Gore, with whom she resided mainly on the Continent, supporting her family by her voluminous writings. Between 1824 and 1862 she produced about 70 works, the most successful of which were novels of fashionable English life. Among these may be mentioned *Manners of the Day* (1830), *Cecil, or the Adventures of a Coxcomb* (1841), and *The Banker's Wife* (1843). She also wrote for the stage, and composed music for songs.

GOSSON, STEPHEN (1554-1624).—Poet, actor, and satirist, *b.* in Kent, and *ed.* at Oxf., he went to London, and wrote plays, which are now lost, and pastorals; but, moved by a sermon preached at Paul's Cross in 1577 during a plague, he deserted the theatre, and became one of its severest critics in his prose satire, *The School of Abrose* (1579), directed against "poets, pipers, players, jesters, and such-like Caterpillars of a Commonwealth." Dedicated to Sir P. Sidney, it was not well received by him, and is believed to have evoked his *Apologie for Poetrie* (1595). G. entered the Church, and *d* Rector of St. Botolph's, London.

GOUGH, RICHARD (1735-1809).—Antiquary, was *b.* in London, and studied at Camb. For many years he made journeys over England in pursuit of his antiquarian studies. He *pub.* about 20 works, among which are *British Topography* (1768), *Sepulchral Monuments of Great Britain* (1786-99), an ed. of Camden's *Britannia*, a translation of *The Arabian Nights* (1798), and various other treatises on archæology, topography, and numismatics.

GOWER, JOHN (1325?-1408).—Poet. Although few details of his life have come down to us, he appears to have been a man of wealth and importance, connected with Kent, well known at Court, and in possession of more than one estate. He was the friend of Chaucer, who gives him the title of "the moral Gower," which has clung to him ever since. His first principal work was *Speculum Meditantis* (the Mirror of one meditating) written in French on the subject of married life. It was long believed to have been lost. It was followed by *Vox Clamantis* (the Voice of one crying) written in Latin, giving an account of the peasants' revolt of 1381, and attacking the misgovernment and social evils which had led to it. His third, and only English poem, was *Confessio Amantis* (Lover's Confession), a work of 30,000 lines, consisting of tales and meditations on love, written at the request of Richard II. It is the earliest large collection of tales in the English tongue. In his old age G. became blind. He had, when about 70, retired to the Priory of St. Mary Overies, the chapel of which is now the Church of St. Saviour, Southwark, where he spent his last years, and to which he was a liberal benefactor. G. represented the serious and cultivated man of his time, in which he was reckoned the equal of Chaucer, but as a poet he is heavy and prolix.

GRAFTON, RICHARD (*d.* 1572).—Printer and chronicler, printed various ed. of the Bible and Prayer-book; also the Proclamation of the Accession of Lady Jane Grey, for which he was cast into prison, where he compiled an *Abridgement of the Chronicles of England* (1563). To this he added in 1568 *A Chronicle at Large.* Neither holds a high place as authorities.

GRAHAME, JAMES (1765-1811).—Poet, *s.* of a lawyer, was *b.* and *ed.* in Glasgow. After spending some time in a law office in Edin., he was called to the Scottish Bar. His health being delicate, and his circumstances easy, he early retired from practice, and taking orders in the Church of England in 1809, was appointed curate successively of Shipton, Gloucestershire, and Sedgefield, Durham. He wrote several pleasing poems, of which the best is *The Sabbath* (1804). He *d.* on a visit to Glasgow in his 47th year. His poems are full of quiet observation of country sights expressed in graceful verse.

GRAHAME, SIMON OR SIMION (1570-1614).—*B.* in Edin., led a dissolute life as a traveller, soldier, and courtier on the Continent. He appears to have been a good scholar, and wrote the *Passionate Sparke of a Relenting Minde,* and *Anatomy of Humours,* the latter of which is believed to have suggested to Burton his *Anatomy of Melancholie.* He became an austere Franciscan.

GRAINGER, JAMES (1721-1766).—Poet, of a Cumberland family, studied medicine at Edin., was an army surgeon, and on the peace settled in practice in London, where he became the friend of Dr. Johnson, Shenstone, and other men of letters. His first poem, *Solitude,* appeared in 1755. He subsequently went to the West Indies (St. Kit's), where he made a rich marriage, and *pub.* his chief poem, *The Sugar-Cane* (1764).

GRANGER, JAMES (1723-1776).—Biographer, was at Oxf. and, entering the Church, became Vicar of Shiplake, Oxon. He *pub.* a *Biographical History of England from Egbert the Great to the Revolution* (1769). He insisted on the importance of collecting engravings of portraits and himself gathered 14,000, and gave a great impulse to the practice of making such collections.

GRANT, MRS. ANNE (M'VICAR) (1755-1838).—Was *b.* in Glasgow, and in 1779 *m.* the Rev. James Grant, minister of Laggan, Inverness-shire. She *pub.* in 1802 a vol. of poems. She also wrote *Letters from the Mountains,* and *Essays on the Superstitions of the Highlands.* After 1810 she lived in Edin., where she was the friend of Sir W. Scott and other eminent men, through whose influence a pension of £100 was bestowed upon her.

GRANT, JAMES (1822-1887).—Novelist, was the *s.* of an officer in the army, in which he himself served for a short time. He wrote upwards of 50 novels in a brisk, breezy style, of which the best known are perhaps *The Romance of War* (1845), *Adventures of an Aide-de-Camp*, *Frank Hilton*, *Bothwell*, *Harry Ogilvie*, and *The Yellow Frigate*. He also wrote biographies of *Kirkcaldy of Grange*, *Montrose*, and others which, however, are not always trustworthy from an historical point of view.

GRANT, JAMES AUGUSTUS (1827-1892).—Traveller, was an officer in the army, and was sent by the Royal Geographical Society along with Captain JOHN HANNING SPEKE (1827-1864), to search for the equatorial lakes of Africa. Grant wrote *A Walk across Africa*, *The Botany of the Speke and Grant Expedition*, and *Khartoum as I saw it in* 1863. Speke wrote *Journal of the Discovery of the Source of the Nile* (1863), and *What led to the Discovery of the Source of the Nile* (1864).

GRATTAN, THOMAS COLLEY (1792-1864).—Miscellaneous writer, *b.* in Dublin, and *ed.* for the law, but did not practise. He wrote a few novels, including *The Heiress of Bruges* (4 vols., 1830); but his best work was *Highways and Byways*, a description of his Continental wanderings, of which he *pub.* three series. He also wrote a history of the Netherlands and books on America. He was for some time British Consul at Boston, U.S.

GRAY, DAVID (1838-1861).—Poet, *s.* of a hand-loom weaver at Kirkintilloch, Dumbartonshire. He gave early promise at school, was destined for the service of the Church, and was for 4 years at Glasgow Univ. while he maintained himself by teaching. His first poems appeared in the *Glasgow Citizen*. In 1860, however, he went with his friend Robert Buchanan to London, where he soon fell into consumption. He was befriended by Mr. Monckton Milnes, afterwards Lord Houghton, but after a sojourn in the South of England, returned home to die. His chief poem, *The Luggie* (the river of his birthplace) contains much beautiful description; but his genius reached its highest expression in a series of 30 sonnets written in full view of an early death and blighted hopes, and bearing the title, *In the Shadow*. They breathe a spirit of the deepest melancholy unrelieved by hope.

GRAY, THOMAS (1716-1771).—Poet, was *b.* in London, the *s.* of a scrivener, who, though described as "a respectable citizen," was of so cruel and violent a temper that his wife had to separate from him. To his mother and her sister, who carried on a business, G. was indebted for his liberal education at Eton (where he became a friend of Horace Walpole), and Camb. After completing his Univ. course he accompanied Walpole to France and Italy, where he spent over two years, when a difference arising G. returned to England, and went back to Camb. to take his degree in law without, however, any intention of practising. He remained at Camb. for the rest of his life, passing his time in the study of the classics, natural science, and antiquities, and in visits to his friends, of whom Walpole was again one. It was in 1747 that his first poem, the *Ode on a Distant*

Prospect of Eton College, appeared, and it was followed between 1750 and 1757 by his *Pindaric Odes*, including *The Progress of Poesy*, and *The Bard*, which were, however, somewhat coldly received. Nevertheless he had, on the death of Colley Cibber, the offer of the laureateship, which he declined; but in 1768 he accepted the Professorship of Modern History in his Univ., worth £400 a year. Having been drawn to the study of Icelandic and Celtic poetry he produced *The Fatal Sisters*, and *The Descent of Odin*, in which are apparent the first streaks of the dawn of the Romantic Revival. G.'s poems occupy little space, but what he wrote he brought to the highest perfection of which he was capable, and although there is a tendency on the part of some modern critics to depreciate him, it is probable that his place will always remain high among all but the first order of poets. Probably no poem has had a wider acceptance among all classes of readers than his *Elegy in a Country Churchyard*. In addition to his fame as a poet, he enjoys that of one of the greatest of English letter-writers, and of a really great scholar. He *d.* at Camb. after a short illness following upon a gradually declining state of health.

Life by Gosse (Men of Letters Series, 1882).

GREELEY, HORACE (1811-1872).—Journalist and miscellaneous writer, was the *s.* of a small farmer in New Hampshire. His early life was passed first as a printer, and thereafter in editorial work. He started in 1841, and conducted until his death, the *New York Tribune*. He was long a leader in American politics, and in 1872 was an unsuccessful candidate for the Presidency. His writings, which are chiefly political and economical, include *Essays on Political Economy* (1870), and *Recollections of a Busy Life* (1868).

GREEN, JOHN RICHARD (1837-1883).—Historian, was the *s.* of a tradesman in Oxf., where he was *ed.*, first at Magdalen Coll. School, and then at Jesus Coll. He entered the Church, and served various cures in London, under a constant strain caused by delicate health. Always an enthusiastic student of history, his scanty leisure was devoted to research. In 1869 he finally gave up clerical work, and received the appointment of librarian at Lambeth. He had been laying plans for various historical works, including a History of the English Church as exhibited in a series of Lives of the Archbishops of Canterbury, and, what he proposed as his *magnum opus*, A History of England under the Angevin Kings. The discovery, however, that his lungs were affected, necessitated the abridgment of all his schemes, and he concentrated his energies on the preparation of his *Short History of the English People*, which appeared in 1874, and at once gave him an assured place in the first rank of historical writers. In 1877 he *m.* Miss Alice Stopford, by whose talents and devotion he was greatly assisted in carrying out and completing such work as his broken health enabled him to undertake during his few remaining years. Abandoning his proposed history of the Angevins, he confined himself to expanding his *Short History* into *A History of the English People* in 4 vols. (1878-80), and writing *The Making of England*, of which one vol. only, coming down to 828, had appeared when he *d.* at Mentone in March 1883. After his death appeared *The Conquest of England*. The *Short*

History may be said to have begun a new epoch in the writing of history, making the social, industrial, and moral progress of the people its main theme. To infinite care in the gathering and sifting of his material G. added a style of wonderful charm, and an historical imagination which has hardly been equalled.

GREEN, MATTHEW (1696-1737).—Poet, is known as the author of *The Spleen*, a lively and original poem in octosyllabic verse on the subject of low spirits and the best means of prevention and cure. It has life-like descriptions, sprightliness, and lightness of touch, and was admired by Pope and Gray. The poem owes its name to the use of the term in the author's day to denote depression. G., who held an appointment in the Customs, appears to have been a quiet, inoffensive person, an entertaining companion, and a Quaker.

GREEN, THOMAS HILL (1836-1882).—Philosopher, was *b.* at Birken Rectory, Yorkshire, and *ed.* at Rugby and Balliol Coll., Oxf., where he became Whyte Prof. of Moral Philosophy and, by his character, ability, and enthusiasm on social questions, exercised a powerful influence. His chief works are an *Introduction to Hume's Treatise on Human Nature* (Clarendon Press ed.), in which he criticised H.'s philosophy severely from the idealist standpoint, and *Prolegomena to Ethics*, *pub.* posthumously.

GREENE, ROBERT (1560?-1592).—Poet, dramatist, and pamphleteer, was *b.* at Norwich, and studied at Camb., where he *grad.* A.B. He was also incorporated at Oxf. in 1588. After travelling in Spain and Italy, he returned to Camb. and took A.M. Settling in London he was one of the wild and brilliant crew who passed their lives in fitful alternations of literary production and dissipation, and were the creators of the English drama. He has left an account of his career in which he calls himself "the mirror of mischief." During his short life about town, in the course of which he ran through his wife's fortune, and deserted her soon after the birth of her first child, he poured forth tales, plays, and poems, which had great popularity. In the tales, or pamphlets as they were then called, he turns to account his wide knowledge of city vices. His plays, including *The Scottish History of James IV.* and *Orlando Furioso*, which are now little read, contain some fine poetry among a good deal of bombast; but his fame rests, perhaps, chiefly on the poems scattered through his writings, which are full of grace and tenderness. G. *d.* from the effects of a surfeit of pickled herrings and Rheinish wine. His extant writings are much less gross than those of many of his contemporaries, and he seems to have given signs of repentance on his deathbed, as is evidenced by his last work, *A Groat's-worth of Wit bought with a Million of Repentance*. In this curious work occurs his famous reference to Shakespeare as "an upstart crow beautified with our feathers." Among his other works may be mentioned *Euphues' censure to Philautus*, *Pandosto, the Triumph of Time* (1588), from which Shakespeare borrowed the plot of *The Winter's Tale*, *A Notable Discovery of Coosnage*, *Arbasto, King of Denmark*, *Penelope's Web*, *Menaphon* (1589), and *Coney Catching*. His plays, all *pub.*

posthumously, include *Friar Bacon and Friar Bungay, Alphonsus, King of Aragon*, and *George-a-Greene, the Pinner of Wakefield.* His tales are written under the influence of Lyly, whence he received from Gabriel Harvey the nickname of "Euphues' Ape."

Plays ed. by Dyce (2 vols., 1831, new ed., 1861). His works are included in Grosart's "Huth Library."

GREG, WILLIAM RATHBONE (1809-1881).—Essayist, *b.* in Manchester, and *ed.* at Bristol and Edin., was for some years engaged in his father's business as a millowner at Bury. Becoming deeply interested in political and social questions he contributed to reviews and magazines many papers and essays on these subjects, which were *repub.* in three collections, viz., *Essays on Political and Social Science* (1854), *Literary and Social Judgments* (1869), and *Miscellaneous Essays* (1884). Other works of his are *Enigmas of Life* (1872), *Rocks Ahead* (1874), and *Mistaken Aims, etc.* (1876). In his writings he frequently manifested a distrust of democracy and a pessimistic view of the future of his country. He held successively the appointments of Commissioner of Customs and Controller of H.M. Stationery Office.

GREVILLE, CHARLES CAVENDISH FULKE (1794-1865).—Political annalist, *ed.* at Eton and Oxf., was a page to George III., sec. to Earl Bathurst, and afterwards held the sinecure office of Sec. of Jamaica. In 1821 he became Clerk to the Privy Council, an office which brought him into close contact with the leaders of both political parties, and gave him unusual opportunities of becoming acquainted with all that was passing behind the scenes. The information as to men and events thus acquired he fully utilised in his *Journal of the Reigns of George IV., William IV., and Queen Victoria*, which, ed. by Henry Reeve, of the *Edinburgh Review*, was *pub.* in three series between 1874 and 1887. The *Journal* covers the period from 1820-60, and constitutes an invaluable contribution to the history of the time.

GRIFFIN, BARTHOLOMEW? (*fl.* 1596).—Poet, of whom almost nothing is known, *pub.* in 1596 a collection of 62 sonnets under the title of *Fidessa*, of which some are excellent.

GRIFFIN, GERALD (1803-1840).—Dramatist, novelist, and poet, *s.* of a tradesman, *b.* and *ed.* in Limerick, he went in 1823 to London, where most of his literary work was produced. In 1838 he returned to Ireland and, dividing his property among his brothers, devoted himself to a religious life by joining the Teaching Order of the Christian Brothers. Two years thereafter he *d.*, worn out by self-inflicted austerities. His chief novel, *The Collegians*, was adapted by Boucicault as *The Colleen Bawn*, and among his dramas is *Gisippus*. His novels depict southern Irish life.

GRIMOALD, NICHOLAS (1519-1562).—Poet, was at Camb. and Oxf., and was chaplain to Bishop Ridley. He contributed to Tottel's *Songs and Sonnettes* (1557), wrote two dramas in Latin, *Archi-propheta* and *Christus Redivivus*, and made translations.

GROOME, FRANCIS HINDES (1851-1902).—Miscellaneous writer, *s.* of a clergyman, wrote for various encyclopædias, etc. He was a student of the gipsies and their language, and *pub. In Gypsy Tents* (1880), *Gypsy Folk Tales* (1899), and an ed. of Borrow's *Lavengro* (1900). Other works were *A Short Border History* (1887), *Kriegspiel* (1896), a novel, and *Two Suffolk Friends* (his *f.* and Edward Fitzgerald, *q.v.*).

GROSART, ALEXANDER BALLOCH (1827-1899).—Was a minister of the English Presbyterian Church. He wrote Lives of various Puritan divines, ed. their works, and also issued ed., with Lives, of the poems of Michael Bruce (*q.v.*) and Robert Fergusson (*q.v.*). But his chief service to literature was his reprints, with notes, of rare Elizabethan and Jacobean literature, including *Fuller's Worthies Library*, 39 vols. (1868-76), *Occasional Issues of Unique and Very Rare Books*, 38 vols. 1875-81, *Huth Library*, 33 vols. (1886), Spenser's *Works*, 10 vols., *Daniel's Works*, etc.

GROSE, FRANCIS (1731-1791).—Antiquary and lexicographer, of Swiss extraction, was Richmond Herald 1755-63. He *pub. Antiquities of England and Wales* (1773-87), which was well received, and thereafter, 1789, set out on an antiquarian tour through Scotland, the fruit of which was *Antiquity of Scotland* (1789-91). He afterwards undertook a similar expedition to Ireland, but *d.* suddenly at Dublin. In addition to the works above mentioned he wrote *A Classical Dictionary of the Vulgar Tongue* (1785), *A Provincial Glossary* (1787), a *Treatise on Ancient Armour and Weapons*, etc. He was an accomplished draughtsman, and illustrated his works.

GROSSETESTE, ROBERT (*d.* 1253).—Theologian and scholar, was *b.* of poor parents at Stradbrook, Suffolk, and studied at Oxf. and possibly Paris. His abilities and learning procured him many preferments; but after an illness he refused to be longer a pluralist, and resigned all but a prebend at Lincoln. Later he was a strenuous and courageous reformer, as is shown by his refusing in 1253 to induct a nephew of the Pope to a canonry at Lincoln, of which he had been Bishop since 1235. He was equally bold in resisting the demand of Henry III. for a tenth of the Church revenues. Amid his absorbing labours as a Churchman, he found time to be a copious writer on a great variety of subjects, including husbandry, physical and moral philosophy, as also sermons, commentaries, and an allegory, the *Chateau d'Amour*. Roger Bacon was a pupil of his, and testifies to his amazing variety of knowledge.

GROTE, GEORGE (1794-1871).—Historian, *s.* of a wealthy banker in London, was *b.* at Beckenham, and *ed.* at Charterhouse School. In 1810 he entered the bank, of which he became head in 1830. In 1832 he was elected one of the members of Parliament for the City of London. In 1841 he retired from Parliament, and in 1843 from the bank, thenceforth devoting his whole time to literature, which, along with politics, had been his chief interest from his youth. He early came under the influence of Bentham and the two Mills, and was one of the leaders of the group of theorists known as "philosophical Radicals." In 1820 he *m.* Miss Harriet Lewin who, from her intellectual powers, was fitted to be his helper in his literary and political interests. In 1826 he contributed to the *Westminster Review* a severe criticism of Mitford's *History of Greece*, and in 1845 *pub.* the first 2 vols. of his own, the remaining 6 vols. appearing at intervals up to 1856. G. belongs to the school of philosophical historians, and his *History*, which begins with the legends, ends with the fall of the country under the successors of Alexander the Great. It is one of the standard works on the subject, which his learning enabled him to treat in a full and thorough manner; the style is clear and strong. It has been repeatedly re-issued, and has been translated into French and German. G. also *pub.*, in 1865, *Plato and other Companions of Socrates*, and left unfinished a work on *Aristotle*. In political life G. was, as might be expected, a consistent and somewhat rigid Radical, and he was a strong advocate of the ballot. He was one of the founders of the first London Univ., a Trustee of the British Museum, D.C.L. of Oxf., LL.D. of Camb., and a Foreign Associate of the Académie des Sciences. He was offered, but declined, a peerage in 1869, and is buried in Westminster Abbey.

GRUB, GEORGE (1812-1892).—Historian, was *b.* in Old Aberdeen, and *ed.* at King's Coll. there. He studied law, and was admitted in 1836 to the Society of Advocates, Aberdeen, of which he was librarian from 1841 until his death. He was appointed Lecturer on Scots Law in Marischal Coll., and was Prof. of Law in the Univ. (1881-91). He has a place in literature as the author of an *Ecclesiastical History of Scotland* (1861), written from the standpoint of a Scottish Episcopalian, which, though dry, is concise, clear, fair-minded, and trustworthy. G. also ed. (along with Joseph Robertson) Gordon's *Scots Affairs* for the Spalding Club, of which he was one of the founders.

GUEST, LADY CHARLOTTE (BERTIE) (1812-1895).—*Dau.* of the 9th Earl of Lindsey, *m.* in 1833 Sir Josiah J. Guest, a wealthy ironmaster, after whose death in 1852 she managed the works. She was an enthusiastic student of Welsh literature, and aided by native scholars translated with consummate skill the *Mabinogion*, the manuscript of which in Jesus Coll., Oxf., is known as the *Red Book of Hergest*, and which is now a recognised classic of mediæval romance. She also prepared a 'Boys' *Mabinogion* containing the earliest Welsh tales of Arthur. She was also noted as a collector of china, fans, and playing cards, on which subjects she wrote several volumes. She entered into a second marriage in 1855 with Dr. C. Schreiber, but in literature she is always referred to under her first married name.

GUTHRIE, THOMAS (1803-1873).—Divine and philanthropist, *b.* at Brechin, studied for the Church, and became a minister in Edin. Possessed of a commanding presence and voice, and a remarkably effective and picturesque style of oratory, he became perhaps the most popular preacher of his day in Scotland, and was associated with many forms of philanthropy, especially temperance and ragged schools, of the latter of which he was the founder. He was one of the leaders of the Free Church, and raised over £100,000 for manses for its ministers. Among his writings are *The Gospel in Ezekiel*, *Plea for Ragged Schools*, and *The City, its Sins and Sorrows*.

HABINGTON, WILLIAM (1605-1654).—Poet, *s.* of a Worcestershire Roman Catholic gentleman, was *ed.* at St. Omer's, but refused to become a Jesuit. He *m.* Lucia, *dau.* of Lord Powis, whom he celebrated in his poem *Castara* (1634), in which he sang the praises of chaste love. He also wrote a tragi-comedy, *The Queen of Arragon* (1640), and a *Historie of Edward IV*. His verse is graceful and tender.

HAILES, DALRYMPLE DAVID, LORD (1726-1792).—Scottish judge and historical writer, was *b.* at Edin. Belonging to a family famous as lawyers, he was called to the Bar in 1748, and raised to the Bench in 1766. An excellent judge, he was also untiring in the pursuit of his favourite studies, and produced several works of permanent value on Scottish history and antiquities, including *Annals of Scotland* (1776), and *Canons of the Church of Scotland* (1769). He was a friend and correspondent of Dr. Johnson.

HAKE, THOMAS GORDON (1809-1895).—Poet, *b.* at Leeds, *ed.* at Christ's Hospital, was a physician, and practised at various places. His books include *Madeline* (1871), *Parables and Tales* (1873), *The Serpent Play* (1883), *New Day Sonnets* (1890), and *Memoirs of Eighty Years* (1893).

HAKLUYT, RICHARD (1553?-1616).—Collector of voyages, belonged to a good Herefordshire family of Dutch descent, was *b.* either at Eyton in that county or in London, and *ed.* at Westminster School and Oxf. The sight of a map of the world fired his imagination and implanted in his mind the interest in geography and the lives and adventures of our great navigators and discoverers, which became the ruling passion of his life; and in order to increase his knowledge of these matters he studied various foreign languages and the art of navigation. He took orders, and was chaplain of the English Embassy in Paris, Rector of Witheringsett, Suffolk, 1590, Archdeacon of Westminster, 1602, and Rector of Gedney, Lincolnshire, 1612. After a first collection of voyages to America and the West Indies he compiled, while at Paris, his great work, *The Principal Navigations, Voyages . . . and Discoveries of the English Nation made by Sea or over Land to the Remote and Farthest Distant Quarters of the Earth . . . within the Compass of these* 1500 *Years.* It appeared in its final form (three folio vols.) in 1599. Besides it he *pub. A Discourse of Western Planting*, and he left a vast mass of MS. afterwards used (in far inferior style) by S. Purchas (*q.v.*). In all his work H. was actuated not only by the love of knowledge, but by a noble patriotism: he wished to see England the great sea-power of the world, and he lived to see it so. His work, as has been said, is "our English epic." In addition to his original writings he translated various works, among them being *The Discoveries of the World*, from the Portuguese of Antonio Galvano.

HALE, SIR MATTHEW (1609-1676).—Jurist and miscellaneous writer, has left a great reputation as a lawyer and judge. Steering a neutral course during the political changes of his time, he served under the Protectorate and after the Restoration, and rose to be Chief Justice of the King's Bench. He is mentioned here as the author of several works on science, divinity, and law. Among them are *The Primitive Origination of Mankind*, and *Contemplations, Moral and Divine*. His legal works are still of great authority. Though somewhat dissipated in early youth, he has handed down a high reputation for wisdom and piety.

HALES, JOHN (1584-1656).—Theologian, *b.* at Bath, and *ed.* there and at Oxf., became one of the best Greek scholars of his day, and lectured on that language at Oxf. In 1616 he accompanied the English ambassador to the Hague in the capacity of chaplain, and attended the Synod of Dort, where he was converted from Calvinism to Arminianism. A lover of quiet and learned leisure, he declined all high and responsible ecclesiastical preferment, and chose and obtained scholarly retirement in a Fellowship of Eton, of which his friends Sir Henry Savile and Sir Henry Wotton were successively Provost. A treatise on *Schism and Schismatics* (1636?) gave offence to Laud, but H. defended himself so well that Laud made him a Prebendary of Windsor. Refusing to acknowledge the Commonwealth, he was deprived, fell into poverty, and had to sell his library. Afteı his death his writings were *pub.* in 1659 as *The Golden Remains of the Ever-Memorable Mr. John Hales of Eton College.*

HALIBURTON, THOMAS CHANDLER (1796-1865).—*B.* at Windsor, Nova Scotia, was a lawyer, and rose to be Judge of the Supreme Court of the Colony. He was the author of *The Clockmaker, or Sayings and Doings of Samuel Slick of Slickville*, and a continuation, *The Attaché, or Sam Slick in England.* In these he made a distinctly original contribution to English fiction, full of shrewdness and humour. He may be regarded as the pioneer of the American school of humorists. He wrote various other works, including *The Old Judge, Nature and Human Nature, A Historical and Statistical Account of Nova Scotia*, etc. In 1856 he settled in England, and sat in the House of Commons for Launceston.

HALIFAX, CHARLES MONTAGU, 1ST EARL OF (1661-1715). —A famous wit, statesman, and patron of literature, was *ed.* at Westminster School and Trinity Coll., Camb. Entering Parliament he became Chancellor of the Exchequer in 1694, and First Lord of the Treasury 1697. Vain and arrogant, he soon lost popularity and power. His chief literary effort was his collaboration with Prior in *The Town and Country Mouse* (1687), a parody of and reply to Dryden's *Hind and Panther*. H. was the friend and patron of Addison, Steele, Congreve, and many other of the classical writers of his day. He became a peer in 1701.

HALL, MRS. ANNA MARIA (FIELDING) (1800-1881).—Novelist, was *b.* in Dublin, but left Ireland at the age of 15. Nevertheless, that country gave her the motive of several of her most successful books, such as *Sketches of Irish Character* (1829), *Lights and Shadows of Irish Character* (1838), *Marian* (1839), and *The White Boy* (1845). Other works are *The Buccaneer*, and *Midsummer Eve*, a fairy tale, and many sketches in the *Art Journal*, of which her husband, SAMUEL CARTER HALL (1800-1889), was ed. With him she also collaborated in a work entitled *Ireland, its Scenery, Character*, *etc.* Mrs. H. was a very voluminous writer; her descriptive talents were considerable, as also was her power of depicting character. Her husband was likewise a writer of some note, chiefly on art.

HALL, BASIL (1788-1844).—Traveller, *s.* of Sir James H., an eminent man of science, was in the navy, and rose to be captain. He was one of the first to visit Corea, and wrote *Voyage of Discovery to Corea* (1818), also *Travels in North America in* 1827-28, a lively work which gave some offence in the U.S., *Fragments of Voyages and Travels* (1831-40), and some tales and romances. He was latterly insane.

HALL, OR HALLE, EDWARD (1499?-1547).—Chronicler, *b.* in London, studied successively at Camb. and Oxf. He was a lawyer, and sat in Parliament for Bridgnorth, and served on various Commissions. He wrote a history of *The Union of the two Noble and Illustre Families of Lancastre and Yorke*, commonly called *Hall's Chronicle*. It was *pub.* after the author's death by Richard Grafton, and was prohibited by Queen Mary.

HALL, JOSEPH (1574-1656).—Divine, *b.* at Ashby-de-la-Zouche, and *ed.* at Camb., he entered the Church, and became in 1627 Bishop of Exeter, and in 1641 Bishop of Norwich. He had a chequered career. He accompanied James I. to Scotland in 1617, and was a Deputy to the Synod of Dort. Accused of Puritanism, and at enmity with Laud, he fell on troublous days, and was, in 1641, imprisoned in the Tower for joining those bishops who protested against the validity of laws passed during their exclusion (owing to tumult in the streets) from Parliament. Returning to Norwich he found that his revenues had been sequestrated, and his private property seized. In 1647 he retired to a small farm near Norwich, where he passed the remainder of his life. Among his works are *Contemplations, Characters of Virtues and Vices* (1614), and his *Virgidemiarum, or Satires* (1597-8), the last written before he was in orders, and condemned by Archbishop Whitgift to be burned. Pope, however, thought them "the best poetry and truest satire in the English language." H.'s *Divine Right of Episcopacy* gave rise to much controversy, in which Archbishop Ussher, Milton, and the writers who called themselves "Smectymnuus" (a combination of their initials) took part.

HALL, ROBERT (1764-1831).—Divine, *b.* at Arnsby, Leicestershire, the *s.* of a Baptist minister of some note, was *ed.* at a Baptist Academy, and at the Univ. of Aberdeen, from which he received the degree of D.D. in 1817. He ministered to congregations at Bristol, Cambridge, Leicester, and again at Bristol, and became one of the greatest pulpit orators of his day. His most famous sermon was that on the *Death of the Princess Charlotte* (1817). Another which created a great impression was that on *Modern Infidelity*. H. was a life-long sufferer, and was occasionally insane, yet his intellectual activity was unceasing. After his death a collection of 50 of his sermons was *pub.* (1843), and *Miscellaneous Works and Remains* (1846).

HALLAM, HENRY (1777-1859).—Historian, *s.* of a Dean of Wells, was *b.* at Windsor, and *ed.* at Eton and Oxf. He was called to the Bar at the Inner Temple, and appointed a Commissioner of Stamps. Among his earliest writings were papers in the *Edinburgh Review;* but in 1818 he leaped into a foremost place among historical writers by the publication of his *View of the State of Europe during the Middle Ages.* This was followed in 1827 by *The Constitutional History of England from the Accession of Henry VII. to the Death of George II.*, and his third great work, *Introduction to the Literature of Europe in the 15th, 16th, and 17th Centuries,* in 4 vols., appeared in 1837-39. All these, which have gone through several ed., and have been translated into the principal languages of Europe, are characterised by wide and profound learning, indefatigable research, and judicial impartiality. They opened a new field of investigation in which their author has had few, if any, superiors. In politics H. was a Whig; but he took no active share in party warfare. He had two sons of great promise, both of whom predeceased him. Of these the elder, ARTHUR HENRY, is the subject of Tennyson's *In Memoriam,* and of him his *f.* wrote a touching memoir prefixed to his literary remains.

HALLECK, FITZGREENE (1790-1867).—Poet, *b.* at Guilford, Conn., wrote, with Rodman Drake, a young poet who *d.* at 25, *The Croaker Papers,* a series of satirical and humorous verses, and *Fanny,* also a satire. In 1822 he visited Europe, and the traces of this are found in most of his subsequent poetry, *e.g.* his lines on Burns, and on Alnwick Castle.

HALLIWELL-PHILLIPS, JAMES ORCHARD (1820-1889).—Archæologist and Shakespearian scholar, *ed.* at Camb., was the author of a *Life of Shakespeare* (1848), *New Boke about Shakespeare and Stratford upon Avon* (1850), *Folio Edition of Shakespeare* (1853-65), and various other works relative to him, also *Dictionary of Old English Plays* (1860). He also ed. works for the Camden and Percy Societies, and compiled a *Dictionary of Archaic and Provincial Words.* In 1872 he added his wife's name of Phillips to his own.

HAMERTON, PHILIP GILBERT (1834-1894).—Artist and writer on æsthetics, *s.* of a solicitor, was *b.* near Oldham. Originally intended for the Church, he decided for art and literature. After working as an artist in the Highlands with his wife, who was a Frenchwoman, he settled in France, and devoted himself to writing on art. Among his works are *Etching and Etchers, etc.* (1868), *Painting in France after the Decline of Classicism* (1869), *The Intellectual Life* (1873), *Human Intercourse* (1884), *The Graphic Arts* (1882), *Landscape* (1885), some of which were magnificently illustrated. He also left an autobiography. His writings had a great influence upon artists, and also in stimulating and diffusing the love of art among the public.

HAMILTON, ALEXANDER (1757-1804).—Statesman and political writer, *b.* in the West Indies, was one of the framers of the Constitution of the United States, and was the first Sec. of the national Treasury. He was one of the greatest of American statesmen, and has also a place in literature as the principal writer in the *Federalist,* a periodical founded to expound and defend the new

Constitution, which was afterwards *pub.* as a permanent work. H. contributed 51 of its 85 articles.

HAMILTON, ELIZABETH (1758-1816).—Wrote *The Cottagers of Glenburnie,* a tale which had much popularity in its day, and perhaps had some effect in the improvement of certain aspects of humble domestic life in Scotland. She also wrote *Letters on Education, Essays on the Human Mind,* and *The Hindoo Rajah.*

HAMILTON, THOMAS (1789-1842).—Novelist, brother of Sir William Hamilton (*q.v.*), wrote a novel, *Cyril Thornton* (1827), which was received with great favour. He was an officer in the army, and, on his retirement, settled in Edin., and became a contributor to *Blackwood.* He was also the author of *Annals of the Peninsular Campaign* (1829), and *Men and Manners in America* (1833).

HAMILTON, WILLIAM (OF BANGOUR) (1704-1754).—Poet, was *b.* at the family seat in Linlithgowshire. Cultivated and brilliant, he was a favourite of society, and began his literary career by contributing verses to Allan Ramsay's *Tea Table Miscellany.* He joined the Pretender in 1745, and celebrated the Battle of Prestonpans in *Gladsmuir.* After Culloden he wandered in the Highlands, where he wrote his *Soliloquy,* and escaped to France. His friends, however, succeeded in obtaining his pardon, and he returned to his native country. In 1750, on the death of his brother, he succeeded to the family estate, which, however, he did not long live to enjoy. He is best remembered for his fine ballad of *The Braes of Yarrow.* He also wrote *The Episode of the Thistle.* He *d.* at Lyons.

HAMILTON, WILLIAM (OF GILBERTFIELD) (1665?-1751) — Poet, served in the army, from which he retired with the rank of Lieutenant. He wrote poetical *Epistles* to Allan Ramsay, and an abridgment in modern Scotch of Blind Harry's *Life of Sir William Wallace.*

HAMILTON, SIR WILLIAM (1788-1856).—Metaphysician, *b.* in Glasgow, in the Univ. of which his *f.* and grandfather successively filled the Chair of Anatomy and Botany, *ed.* there and at Balliol Coll., Oxf., was called to the Scottish Bar, at which he attained little practice, but was appointed Solicitor of Teinds. In 1816 he established his claim to the baronetcy of H. of Preston. On the death of Dr. Thomas Brown in 1820, he was an unsuccessful candidate for the Chair of Moral Philosophy in Edin., but in the following year he was appointed Prof. of History. It was not until 1829 that he gave full proof of his remarkable powers and attainments as a philosopher in a famous article in the *Edinburgh Review,* a critique of Victor Cousin's doctrine of the Infinite. This paper carried his name over Europe, and won for him the homage of continental philosophers, including Cousin himself. After this H. continued to contribute to the *Review,* many of his papers being translated into French, German, and Italian. In 1852 they were *coll.* with notes and additions, and *pub.* as *Discussions in Philosophy and Literature, etc.* In 1836 H. was elected Professor of Logic and Metaphysics at Edinburgh, which office he held with great reputation until his death, after which the lectures he had delivered were edited and *pub.* by Prof. Mansel and Veitch. His *magnum opus* was his edition of the *Works of Dr. Thomas Reid*, left unfinished, and completed by Mansel. H. was the last, and certainly the most learned and accomplished, of the Scottish school of philosophy, which he considered it his mission to develop and correlate to the systems of other times and countries. He also made various important contributions to the science of logic. During his later years he suffered from paralysis of one side, which, though it left his mind unaffected, impaired his powers of work. A Memoir of H. by Prof. Veitch appeared in 1869.

HANNA, WILLIAM (1808-1882).—Divine and biographer, *s.* of Samuel H., Prof. of Divinity in the Presbyterian Coll., Belfast, was *b.* there, became a distinguished minister of the Free Church of Scotland, and colleague of Dr. T. Guthrie (*q.v.*). He wrote an admirable *Life of Dr. Chalmers*, whose son-in-law he was, and ed. his works. He also ed. the *Letters of Thomas Erskine of Linlathen* (*q.v.*), and wrote various theological works.

HANNAY, JAMES (1827-1873).—Novelist and journalist, was *b.* at Dumfries, and after serving for some years in the navy took to literature, and became ed. of the *Edinburgh Courant*. He wrote two novels, *Singleton Fontenoy* (1850), and *Eustace Conyers* (1855); also *Lectures on Satire and Satirists*, and *Studies on Thackeray*. For the last five years of his life he was British Consul at Barcelona.

HARE, AUGUSTUS JOHN CUTHBERT (1834 - 1903). — Youngest *s.* of Francis H., and nephew of Aug. and Julius H. (*q.v.*), *b.* at Rome, practically adopted by his aunt, the widow of Aug. H., and *ed.* at Harrow. He was the author of a large number of books, which fall into two classes: biographies of members and connections of his family, and descriptive and historical accounts of various countries and cities. To the first belong *Memorials of a Quiet Life* (his adoptive mother's), *Story of Two Noble Lives* (Lady Canning and Lady Waterford), *The Gurneys of Earlham*, and an inordinately extended autobiography; to the second, *Walks in Rome*, *Walks in London*, *Wanderings in Spain*, *Cities of Northern, Southern, and Central Italy* (separate works), and many others. His writings are all interesting and informing, but in general suffer from his tendency to diffuseness.

HARE, AUGUSTUS WILLIAM (1792-1834).—Was the *s.* of Francis Hare-Naylor, who *m.* a cousin of the famous Duchess of Devonshire, and was the author of a history of Germany. He was sent by the widow of Sir W. Jones, whose godson he was, to Winchester, and New Coll., Oxf., in the latter of which he was for some time a tutor. Entering the Church he became incumbent of the rural parish of Alton Barnes where, leading an absolutely unselfish life, he was the father and friend of his parishioners. In addition to writing in conjunction with his brother Julius (*q.v.*), *Guesses at Truth*, a work containing short essays on multifarious subjects, which attracted much attention, he left two vols. of sermons.

HARE, JULIUS CHARLES (1795-1855).—Essayist, etc., younger brother of the above, was *b.* at Vicenza. When two years old his parents left him to the care of Clotilda Tambroni, female Prof. of Greek at Bologna. *Ed.* at Charterhouse and Camb., he took orders and, in 1832, was appointed to the rich family living of Hurstmonceau, which Augustus had refused. Here he had John Sterling (*q.v.*) for curate, and Bunsen for a neighbour. He was also Archdeacon of Lewes and a Chaplain to the Queen. His first work was *Guesses at Truth* (1827), jointly with his brother, and he also *pub.*, jointly with Thirlwall (*q.v.*), a translation of Niebuhr's *History of Rome*, wrote *The Victory of Faith* and other theological books and pamphlets on Church and other questions, *A Life of Sterling*, and a *Vindication of Luther*. H., though a lovable, was an eccentric, man of strong antipathies, unmethodical, and unpunctual.

HARINGTON, SIR JOHN (1561-1612).—Miscellaneous writer, and translator, *b.* at Kelston Park near Bath, and *ed.* at Eton and Camb., became a courtier of Queen Elizabeth, whose godson he was. In 1599 he served in Ireland under Essex, by whom he was knighted on the field, a stretch of authority which was much resented by the Queen. While there he wrote *A Short View of the State of Ireland*, first *pub.* 1880. He was in repute for his epigrams, of which some have wit, but others are only indelicate. His translation of the *Orlando Furioso* of Ariosto, in the metre of the original, is a somewhat free paraphrase, and is now superseded. It first appeared in the form of extracts, which were handed in MS. about the Court until they reached the Queen, who reprimanded the translator for corrupting the morals of her ladies by translating the most unedifying passages, and banished him to his country seat until he should have translated the whole poem. His most valuable work is one which was *pub.* in 1769 by a descendant, under the title of *Nugæ Antiquæ* (Old-time Trifles), a miscellaneous collection from his writings and papers, containing many things of interest, *e.g.*, a minute account of the Queen's last illness, and letters and verses by her and other eminent persons.

HARLAND, HENRY (1861-1905).—Novelist, *b.* of American parentage at St. Petersburg, and *ed.* at Rome. Thereafter he went to Paris, and thence to America, where he graduated at Harvard, and settled in New York. His literary career falls into two distinctly marked sections, very diverse in character. During the first of these he produced, under the pseudonym of "Sidney Luska," a series of highly sensational novels, thrown off with little regard to literary quality, and which it was his wish should be forgotten; but about 1890 his aspirations underwent a complete change, and he became an enthusiast in regard to style and the *mot propre*. The first novels of this new era, *Mademoiselle Miss* (1893), *Grey Roses* (1895), and *Comedies and Errors* (1898), though obtaining the approval of the literary elect, had little general popularity; but the tide turned with the appearance of *The Cardinal's Snuff-box* (1900), which was widely admired. It was followed by *The Lady Paramount* (1901), and *My Friend Prospero* (1903). H. *d.* at San Remo after a prolonged illness.

HARRINGTON, JAMES (1611-1677).—Political theorist, *s.* of Sir Sapcotes H., was *b.* at Upton, Northamptonshire, and *ed.* at

Oxf., where he was a pupil of Chillingworth. After leaving the university he travelled on the Continent, visiting, among other places, The Hague and Venice, where he imbibed republican principles. He was for some time a groom of the bedchamber to Charles I. On the outbreak of the Civil War he sided with the Parliament, but disapproved of the execution of the King, for whom he appears, notwithstanding his political theories, to have cherished a personal attachment. Thereafter he withdrew from active life, and devoted himself to composing his political romance (as it may be called) of *Oceana*, which he *pub.* in 1656, and in which Oceana represents England, Marpesia Scotland, and Panopæa Ireland. In this work he propounds the theory that the natural element of power in states is property, of which land is the most important. He further endeavoured to propagate his views by establishing a debating society called the Rota, and by his conversations with his friends. After the Restoration he was confined in the Tower, and subsequently at Plymouth. He issued several defences of *Oceana*, and made translations from Virgil. In his later years he laboured under mental delusions. Aubrey describes him as of middle stature, strong, well-set, with quick, fiery hazel eyes, and thick curly hair.

HARRIS, JAMES (1709-1780).—Grammarian, was a wealthy country gentleman and member of Parliament, who held office in the Admiralty and the Treasury. He was the author of a singular and learned work entitled *Hermes, or a Philosophical Inquiry concerning Universal Grammar*. For the purpose which it had in view it is useless; but it contains much curious matter. His *s.* was the eminent diplomatist, James H., 1st Earl of Malmesbury.

HARRIS, JOEL CHANDLER (1848-1908).—Writer of tales, etc., *b.* at Eatonton, Georgia, was successively printer, lawyer, and journalist. He struck out an original line in his stories of animal life as it presents itself to the mind of the Southern negro, in whose dialect they are written. These not only achieved and retain an exceptional popularity among children, to whom they were in the first instance addressed, but attracted the attention of students of folklore and anthology. Among his writings are *Uncle Remus* (1880), *Nights with Uncle Remus* (1884), *Mr. Rabbit at Home* (1895), *Aaron in the Wild Woods* (1897), *Chronicles of Aunt Minervy Ann* (1899), etc.

HARTE, FRANCIS BRET (1839-1902).—American humorist, *b.* in Albany, N.Y., but when still a boy went to California. He had a somewhat varied career as a teacher, miner, and journalist, and it is as a realistic chronicler of the gold-field and an original humorist that his chief literary triumphs were achieved. Among his best known writings are *Condensed Novels*, in which he showed great skill as a parodist, *The Luck of Roaring Camp*, *The Idyll of Red Gulch*, and *The Heathen Chinee*. In 1880 he came to Glasgow as U.S. Consul, and from 1885 he lived in London. His writings often show the tenderness and fine feeling that are allied to the higher forms of humour, and he may be said to have created a special form of short story in his Californian tales and prose idylls.

HARTLEY, DAVID (1705-1757).—Philosopher, *b.* at Luddenden, Yorkshire, and *ed.* at Camb., studied for the Church, but owing to theological difficulties turned to medicine as a profession, and practised with success at various places, including London and Bath. He also attained eminence as a writer on philosophy, and indeed may be said to have founded a school of thought based upon two theories, (1) the Doctrine of Vibrations, and (2) that of Association of Ideas. These he developed in an elaborate treatise, *Observations on Man, his Frame, his Duty, and his Expectations.* Though his system has long been discarded, its main ideas have continued to influence thought and investigation.

HARVEY, GABRIEL (1545?-1630).—Poet, *s.* of a ropemaker, was *b.* at Saffron Walden, *ed.* at Camb., and became the friend of Spenser, being the Hobbinol of *The Shepheard's Calendar.* He wrote various satirical pieces, sonnets, and pamphlets. Vain and ill-tempered, he was a remorseless critic of others, and was involved in perpetual controversy, specially with Greene and Nash, the latter of whom was able to silence him. He wrote treatises on rhetoric, claimed to have introduced hexameters into English, was a foe to rhyme, and persuaded Spenser temporarily to abandon it.

HAWES, STEPHEN (*d.* 1523?).—Poet; very little concerning him is known with certainty. He is believed to have been *b.* in Suffolk, and may have studied at Oxf. or Camb. He first comes clearly into view as a Groom of the Chamber in 1502, in which year he dedicated to Henry VII. his *Pastyme of Pleasure,* first printed in 1509 by Wynkyn de Worde. In the same year appeared the *Convercyon of Swerers* (1509), and *A Joyful Meditacyon of all England* (1509), on the coronation of Henry VIII. He also wrote the *Exemple of Vertu.* H. was a scholar, and was familiar with French and Italian poetry. No great poet, he yet had a considerable share in regularising the language.

HAWKER, ROBERT STEPHEN (1804-1875).—Poet and antiquary, *ed.* at Cheltenham and Oxf., became parson of Morwenstow, a smuggling and wrecking community on the Cornish coast, where he exercised a reforming and beneficent, though extremely unconventional, influence until his death, shortly before which he was received into the Roman Catholic Church. He wrote some poems of great originality and charm, *Records of the Western Shore* (1832-36), and *The Quest of the Sangraal* (1863) among them, besides short poems, of which perhaps the best known is *Shall Trelawny Die?* which, based as it is on an old rhyme, deceived both Scott and Macaulay into thinking it an ancient fragment. He also *pub.* a collection of papers, *Footprints of Former Men in Cornwall* (1870).

HAWTHORNE, NATHANIEL (1804-1864).—Novelist, *b.* at Salem, Massachusetts, *s.* of a sea captain, who *d.* in 1808, after which his mother led the life of a recluse. An accident when at play conduced to an early taste for reading, and from boyhood he cherished literary aspirations. His education was completed at Bowdoin Coll., where he had Longfellow for a fellow-student. After graduating, he obtained a post in the Custom-House, which, however, he did not find congenial, and soon gave up, betaking himself to literature, his earliest efforts, besides a novel, *Fanshawe,* which had no success, being short tales and sketches, which, after appearing in periodicals, were *coll.* and *pub.* as *Twice-told Tales* (1837), followed by a second series in 1842. In 1841 he joined for a few months the socialistic community at Brook Farm, but soon tired of it, and in the next year he *m.* and set up house in Concord in an old manse, formerly tenanted by Emerson, whence proceeded *Mosses from an Old Manse* (1846). It was followed by *The Snow Image* (1851), *The Scarlet Letter* (1850), his most powerful work, *The House of Seven Gables*, and *The Blithedale Romance* (1852), besides his children's books, *The Wonder Book*, and *The Tanglewood Tales*. Such business as he had occupied himself with had been in connection with Custom-House appointments at different places; but in 1853 he received from his friend Franklin Pierce, on his election to the Presidency, the appointment of United States Consul at Liverpool, which he retained for four years, when, in consequence of a threatened failure of health, he went to Italy and began his story of *The Marble Faun*, *pub.* in England in 1860 under the title of *The Transformation.* The last of his books *pub.* during his lifetime was *Our Old Home* (1863), notes on England and the English. He had returned to America in 1860, where, with failing health and powers, he passed his remaining four years. After his death there were *pub. The Ancestral Footstep*, *Septimus Felton*, *Dr. Grimshawe's Secret*, and *The Dolliver Romance*, all more or less fragmentary. Most of H.'s work is pervaded by a strong element of mysticism, and a tendency to dwell in the border-land between the seen and the unseen. His style is characterised by a distinctive grace and charm, rich, varied, suggestive, and imaginative. On the whole he is undoubtedly the greatest imaginative writer yet produced by America.

There are several ed. of the *Works*, *e.g.* Little Classics, 25 vols.; Riverside, 15 vols.; Standard Library, 15 vols.; the two last have biographies. *Lives* by his son Julian, H. James (English Men of Letters, 1850), M. D. Conway (Great Writers, 1890), etc.

HAY, JOHN (1838-1906).—Diplomatist and poet, *b.* at Salem, Indiana, *ed.* at Brown Univ., and called to the Illinois Bar, served in the army, and was one of President Lincoln's secs. He then held diplomatic posts at Paris, Madrid, and Vienna, was Ambassador to Great Britain, and was in 1898 appointed Sec. of State. He has a place in literature by virtue of his *Pike County Ballads*, and *Castilian Days* (1871).

HAYLEY, WILLIAM (1745-1820).—Poet and biographer, was *b.* at Chichester, and *ed.* at Eton and Camb. Though overstrained and romantic, he had some literary ability, and was a good conversationalist. He was the friend of Cowper, whose Life he wrote; and it was to his influence with Pitt that the granting of a pension to the poet was due. He was the author of numerous poems, including *The Triumph of Temper*, and of *Essays* on *History* and *Epic Poetry*, and, in addition to his biography of Cowper, wrote a *Life of Milton.* On the death of Thos. Warton in 1790 he was offered, but declined, the Laureateship. Of him Southey said, "Everything about that man is good except his poetry."

HAYNE, PAUL HAMILTON (1830-1886).—Poet, *b.* at Charleston, S. Carolina, of an old family, contributed to various magazines, and *pub.* *Poems* (1885), containing "Legends and Lyrics." His graceful verses show the influence of Keats. His sonnets are some of his best work.

HAYWARD, ABRAHAM (1802-1884).—Miscellaneous writer, belonged to an old Wiltshire family and was *ed.* at Tiverton School. He studied law at the Inner Temple, and was called to the Bar 1832. He had a great reputation as a *raconteur* and sayer of good things, and he was a copious contributor to periodicals, especially the *Quarterly Review.* Many of his articles were reprinted as *Biographical and Critical Essays,* and *Eminent Statesmen and Writers;* he also wrote Lives of George Selwyn and Lord Chesterfield, and books on Whist, Junius, and *The Art of Dining.* His *Select Correspondence* appeared posthumously.

HAYWARD, SIR JOHN (1564?-1627).—Historian, *b.* at Felixstowe, was the author of various historical works, the earliest of which, *The First Part of the Life and Reign of King Henry IV.*, was *pub.* in 1599, and gave such offence to Queen Elizabeth that the author was imprisoned. He, however, managed to ingratiate himself with James I. by supporting his views of kingly prerogative. He also, at the request of Prince Henry, wrote a *History of the three Norman Kings of England* (William I., William II., and Henry I.) *The Life and Reign of Edward VI.* was *pub.* posthumously in 1630.

HAYWOOD, MRS. ELIZA (FOWLER) (1693-1756).—Dramatist and novelist, *b.* in London, was early *m.* to a Mr. H., but the union turning out unhappily, she took to the stage, upon which she appeared in Dublin about 1715. She afterwards settled in London, and produced numerous plays and novels, into which she introduced scandalous episodes regarding living persons whose identity was very thinly veiled, a practice which, along with her political satires, more than once involved her in trouble, and together with certain attacks upon Pope, made in concert with Curll the bookseller, procured for her a place in *The Dunciad.* Her enemies called her reputation in question, but nothing very serious appears to have been proved. She is repeatedly referred to by Steele, and has been doubtfully identified with his "Sappho." Some of her works, such as *The History of Jemmy and Jenny Jessamy* had great popularity. Others were *The Fair Captive* (1721), *Idalia* (1723), *Love in Excess* (1724), *Memoirs of a Certain Island adjacent to Utopia* (anonymously) (1725), *Secret History of Present Intrigues at the Court of Caramania* (anonymously) (1727). She also conducted *The Female Spectator*, and other papers.

HAZLITT, WILLIAM (1778-1830).—Essayist and critic, *b.* at Maidstone, was the *s.* of a Unitarian minister. At his father's request he studied for the ministry at a Unitarian Coll. at Hackney. His interests, however, were much more philosophical and political than theological. The turning point in his intellectual development was his meeting with Coleridge in 1798. Soon after this he studied art with the view of becoming a painter, and devoted himself specially to portraiture, but though so good a judge as his friend, J. Northcote, R.A., believed he had the talent requisite for success, he could not satisfy himself, and gave up the idea, though always retaining his love of art. He then definitely turned to literature, and in 1805 *pub.* his first book, *Essay on the Principles of Human Action*, which was followed by various other philosophical and political essays. About 1812 he became parliamentary and dramatic reporter to the *Morning Chronicle;* in 1814 a contributor to the *Edinburgh Review;* and in 1817 he *pub.* a vol. of literary sketches, *The Round Table.* In the last named year appeared his *Characters of Shakespeare's Plays*, which was severely attacked in the *Quarterly Review* and *Blackwood's Magazine*, to which his democratic views made him obnoxious. He defended himself in a cutting *Letter to William Gifford*, the ed. of the former. The best of H.'s critical work—his three courses of Lectures, *On the English Poets*, *On the English Comic Writers*, and *On the Dramatic Literature of the Age of Queen Elizabeth*—appeared successively in 1818, 1819, and 1820. His next works were *Table Talk*, in which he attacked Shelley (1821-22), and *The Spirit of the Age* (1825), in which he criticised some of his contemporaries. He then commenced what he intended to be his chief literary undertaking, a life of *Napoleon Buonaparte*, in 4 vols. (1828-30). Though written with great literary ability, its views and sympathies were unpopular, and it failed in attaining success. His last work was a *Life of Titian*, in which he collaborated with Northcote. H. is one of the most subtle and acute of English critics, though, when contemporaries came under review, he sometimes allowed himself to be unduly swayed by personal or political feeling, from which he had himself often suffered at the hands of others. His chief principle of criticism as avowed by himself was that "a genuine criticism should reflect the colour, the light and shade, the soul and body of a work." In his private life he was not happy. His first marriage, entered into in 1807, ended in a divorce in 1822, and was followed by an amour with his landlady's *dau.*, which he celebrated in *Liber Amoris*, a work which exposed him to severe censure. A second marriage with a Mrs. Bridgewater ended by the lady leaving him shortly after. The fact is that H. was possessed of a peculiar temper, which led to his quarrelling with most of his friends. He was, however, a man of honest and sincere convictions. There is a *coll.* ed. of his works, the "Winterslow," by A. R. Waller and A. Glover, 12 vols., with introduction by W. E. Henley, etc.

HEAD, SIR FRANCIS BOND (1793-1875).—Traveller, essayist, and biographer, served in the Engineers, went to South America as manager of a mining company, which failed, and then turned to literature, and made considerable reputation by a book of travels, *Rapid Journeys across the Pampas and among the Andes* (1827), which was followed by *Bubbles from the Brunnens of Nassau* (1834). He was Governor of Upper Canada 1835-37, but was not a great success. Thereafter he contributed to the *Quarterly Review*, and *repub.* his articles as *Stokers and Pokers—Highways and Byways*, and wrote a *Life* of Bruce, the Abyssinian traveller. He was made a Baronet in 1836.

HEARN, LAFCADIO (1850–1904).—Journalist and writer on Japan, *s.* of an Irish Army surgeon and of a Greek lady, *b.* in

Leucadia, Ionian Islands, lost his parents early, and was sent home to be taken charge of by an aunt in Wales, a Roman Catholic. On her death, when he was still a boy, he was left penniless, delicate, and half blind, and after experiencing great hardships, in spite of which he *ed.* himself, he took to journalism. Going to New Orleans he attained a considerable reputation as a writer with a distinctly individual style. He came under the influence of Herbert Spencer, and devoted himself largely to the study of social questions. After spending three years in the French West Indies, he was in 1890 sent by a publisher to Japan to write a book on that country, and there he remained, becoming a naturalised subject, taking the name of Yakomo Koizumi, and marrying a Japanese lady. He lectured on English literature in the Imperial Univ. at Tokio. Though getting nearer than, perhaps, any other Western to an understanding of the Japanese, he felt himself to the end to be still an alien. Among his writings, which are distinguished by acute observation, imagination, and descriptive power of a high order, are *Stray Leaves from Strange Literature* (1884), *Some Chinese Ghosts* (1887), *Gleanings in Buddha Fields* (1897), *Ghostly Japan, Kokoro, Hints and Echoes of Japanese Inner Life*, etc. He was also an admirable letter-writer.

HEARNE, THOMAS (1678-1735).—Antiquary, *b.* at White Waltham, Berkshire, and *ed.* at Oxf., where in 1712 he became second keeper of the Bodleian Library. A strong Jacobite, he was deprived of his post in 1716, and afterwards he refused, on political grounds, the chief librarianship. He *pub.* a large number of antiquarian works, including *Reliquiæ Bodleianæ* (1703), and ed. of Leland's *Itinerary* and *Collectanea*, Camden's *Annals*, and Fordun's *Scotochronicon*. Some of his own collections were *pub.* posthumously.

HEBER, REGINALD (1783-1826).—Poet, *s.* of the Rector of Malpas, a man of family and wealth, and half-brother of Richard H., the famous book-collector, was *ed.* at Oxf., where he gained the Newdigate prize for his poem, *Palestine*, and was elected in 1805 Fellow of All Souls. After travelling in Germany and Russia, he took orders in 1807, and became Rector of the family living of Hodnet. In 1822, after two refusals, he accepted the Bishopric of Calcutta, an office in which he showed great zeal and capacity. He *d.* of apoplexy in his bath at Trichinopoly in 1826. In addition to *Palestine* he wrote *Europe*, a poem having reference specially to the Peninsular War, and left various fragments, including an Oriental romance based on the story of Bluebeard. H.'s reputation now rests mainly on his hymns, of which several, *e.g.*, *From Greenland's Icy Mountains*, *Brightest and Best of the Sons of the Morning*, and *Holy, holy, holy, Lord God Almighty*, are sung wherever the English language is known. He also wrote a *Life of Jeremy Taylor* (1822). H. was a scholar and wit as well as a devoted Christian and Churchman.

HELPS, SIR ARTHUR (1813-1875).—Essayist and historian, was *b.* at Streatham, Surrey, and *ed.* at Eton and Camb. After leaving the Univ. he was private sec. to various public men, and in 1841, his circumstances rendering him independent of employment, he retired to Bishop's Waltham, and devoted himself for 20 years to study and writing. Appointed, in 1860, Clerk to the Privy Council, he became known to, and a favourite of, Queen Victoria, who entrusted him with the task of editing the *Speeches and Addresses of the Prince Consort* (1862), and her own book, *Leaves from the Journal of our Life in the Highlands* (1868). Of his own publications the first was *Thoughts in the Cloister and the Crowd* (1835), a series of aphorisms, and there followed, among others, *Essays written in the Intervals of Business* (1841), *Friends in Council*, 4 series (1847-59), *Realmah* (1869), and *Conversations on War and General Culture* (1871). In history H. wrote *The Conquerors of the New World* (1848-52), and *The Spanish Conquests in America*, 4 vols. (1855-61). He also wrote a *Life of Thos. Brassey*, and, as the demand for his historical works fell off, he *repub.* parts of them as individual biographies of Las Casas, Columbus, Pizarro, and Cortez. He also tried the drama, but without success. His essays are his most successful work, containing as they do the thoughts and opinions of a shrewd, experienced, and highly cultivated man, written in what Ruskin called "beautiful quiet English." They have not, however, any exceptional depth or originality.

HEMANS, FELICIA DOROTHEA (BROWNE) (1793-1835).—Poetess, *dau.* of a Liverpool merchant, who, owing to reverses, retired to North Wales. While yet little more than a child she *pub.* her first poems, the reception of which was not encouraging. In the same year, 1808, a further publication appeared which drew a letter from Shelley. Her first important work, *The Domestic Affections*, appeared in 1812, in which year she was *m.* to Captain Hemans, an Irish officer. The union, however, was not a happy one, and her husband practically deserted her and her five sons in 1818. Her literary activity was continued during the whole of her short life, and her works include, *The Vespers of Palermo*, a drama, which was not successful, *The Forest Sanctuary* (1826), her best poem, *Records of Woman*, *Lays of Leisure Hours*, *Songs of the Affections*, *Hymns for Childhood*, and *Thoughts during Sickness* (1834), her last effort. In 1829 she visited Scotland, where she was the guest of Scott, who held her in affectionate regard. She also enjoyed the friendship of Wordsworth. Always somewhat delicate, her health latterly entirely gave way, and she *d.* of a decline in 1835. Her shorter pieces enjoyed much popularity, and still, owing to their grace and tenderness, retain a certain place, but her long poems are lacking in energy and depth, and are forgotten.

HENLEY, WILLIAM ERNEST (1849-1903).—Poet and critic, *b.* at Gloucester, made the acquaintance of Robert Louis Stevenson (*q.v.*), and collaborated with him in several dramas, including *Deacon Brodie*, and *Robert Macaire*. He engaged in journalism, and became ed. of *The Magazine of Art*, *The National Observer*, and *The New Review*, compiled *Lyra Heroica*, an anthology of English poetry for boys, and, with Mr. Farmer, ed. a *Dictionary of Slang*. His poems, which include *Hospital Rhymes*, *London Voluntaries*, *The Song of the Sword*, *For England's Sake*, and *Hawthorn and Lavender*, are very unequal in quality, and range from strains of the purest music to an uncouth and unmusical realism of no poetic worth. He wrote with T. F. Henderson a *Life of Burns*, in which the poet is set forth as a "lewd peasant of genius."

HENRY VIII. (1491-1547).—Besides writing songs including *The King's Ballad*, was a learned controversialist, and contended against Luther in *Assertio Septem Sacramentorum* (Defence of the Seven Sacraments), a treatise which gained for him the title of Defender of the Faith.

HENRY OF HUNTINGDON (1084-1155).—Historian, was Archdeacon of Huntingdon from 1109. His *Historia Anglorum* (History of the English) comes down to 1154. He also wrote a treatise, *De Contemptu Mundi* (on Contempt of the World).

HENRY, MATTHEW (1662-1714).—Commentator, *s.* of Philip H., a learned Nonconformist divine, was *b.* in Flintshire. He was originally destined for the law, and studied at Gray's Inn, but turned his mind to theology, and in 1687, became minister of a Nonconformist church at Chester. He wrote many religious works, but is chiefly remembered by his *Exposition of the Old and New Testaments*, which he did not live to complete beyond the Acts.

HENRY, O. (real name WILLIAM SYDNEY PORTER) (1862–1910).—American humorist, *b.* in N. Carolina; after a varied beginning, became employed in a bank and took to writing humorous articles. Imprisoned for embezzling bank funds in 1898; began writing in earnest and in a few years had achieved fame as a short story writer under his *nom de plume*. *Cabbages and Things* (1904), *The Four Million* (1906), *Complete Writings* (1917).

HENRY, ROBERT (1718-1790).—Historian, *b.* at St. Ninians, Stirlingshire, entered the Church of Scotland, becoming one of the ministers of Edin. He wrote the *History of Great Britain on a New Plan* (1771-93), in 6 vols., covering the period from the Roman invasion until the reign of Henry VIII. The novelty consisted in dividing the subjects into different heads, civil history, military, social, and so on, and following out each of them separately. The work was mainly a compilation, having no critical qualities, and is now of little value. Notwithstanding the persistent and ferocious attacks of Dr. Gilbert Stewart (*q.v.*), it had a great success, and brought the author over £3000, and a government pension of £100.

HENRY, THE MINSTREL (*see* BLIND HARRY).

HENRYSON, ROBERT (1430?-1506?).—Scottish poet. Few details of his life are known, even the dates of his birth and death being uncertain. He appears to have been a schoolmaster, perhaps in the Benedictine Convent, at Dunfermline, and was a member of the Univ. of Glasgow in 1462. He also practised as a Notary Public, and may have been in orders. His principal poems are *The Moral Fables of Esope the Phrygian*, *The Testament of Cresseide*, a sequel to the *Troilus and Cressida* of Chaucer, to whom it was, until 1721, attributed, *Robene and Makyne*, the first pastoral, not only in Scottish vernacular, but in the English tongue, *The Uplandis Mous and The Burges Mous* (Country and Town Mouse), and the *Garmond of Gude Ladeis.* H., who was versed in the learning and general culture of his day, had a true poetic gift. His verse is strong and swift, full of descriptive power, and sparkling with wit. He is the first Scottish lyrist and the introducer of the pastoral to English literature.

HENTY, GEORGE ALFRED (1832-1902).—Boys' novelist, wrote over 80 books for boys, which had great popularity. Among them are *By England's Aid, Dash for Khartoum, Facing Death, In Freedom's Cause, Out on the Pampas,* etc., all full of adventure and interest, and conveying information as well as amusement.

HERAUD, JOHN ABRAHAM (1799-1887).—Poet, *b.* in London, of Huguenot descent, he contributed to various periodicals, and *pub.* two poems, which attracted some attention, *The Descent into Hell* (1830), and *The Judgment of the Flood* (1834). He also produced a few plays, miscellaneous poems, books of travel, etc.

HERBERT, OF CHERBURY, EDWARD, 1ST LORD (1583-1648). —Philosopher and historian, was the eldest *s.* of Richard H., of Montgomery Castle, and was *b.* there or at Eyton, Shropshire. He was at Oxf., and while there, at the age of 16, he *m.* a kinswoman four years his senior, the *dau.* of Sir William H. Thereafter he returned to the Univ. and devoted himself to study, and to the practice of manly sports and accomplishments. At his coronation in 1603 James I. made him a Knight of the Bath, and in 1608 he went to the Continent, where for some years he was engaged in military and diplomatic affairs, not without his share of troubles. In 1624 he was *cr.* an Irish, and a few years later, an English, peer, as Baron H., of Cherbury. On the outbreak of the Civil War he sided, though somewhat half-heartedly, with the Royalists, but in 1644 he surrendered to the Parliament, received a pension, held various offices, and *d.* in 1648. It was in 1624 that he wrote his treatise, *De Veritate,* "An empirical theory of knowledge," in which truth is distinguished from (1) revelation, (2) the probable, (3) the possible, (4) the false. It is the first purely metaphysical work written by an Englishman, and gave rise to much controversy. It was reprinted in 1645, when the author added two treatises, *De Causis Errorum* (concerning the Causes of Errors), and *De Religione Laici* (concerning the Religion of a Layman). His other chief philosophical work was *De Religione Gentilium* (1663), of which an English translation appeared in 1705, under the title of *The Ancient Religion of the Gentiles and Cause of their Errors considered.* It has been called "the charter of the Deists," and was intended to prove that "all religions recognise five main articles—(1) a Supreme God, (2) who ought to be worshipped, (3) that virtue and purity are the essence of that worship, (4) that sin should be repented of, and (5) rewards and punishments in a future state. Among his historical works are *Expeditio Buckinghamii Ducis* (1656), a vindication of the Rochelle expedition, a *Life of Henry VIII.* (1649), extremely partial to the King, his *Autobiography,* which gives a brilliant picture of his contemporaries, and of the manners and events of his time, and a somewhat vainglorious account of himself and his doings. He was also the author of some poems of a metaphysical cast. On the whole his is one of the most shining and spirited figures of the time.

Autobiography ed. by S. Lee (1886). Poems ed. by J. Churton Collins, etc.

HERBERT, GEORGE (1593-1633).—Poet, brother of above, was *ed.* at Westminster School and Trinity Coll., Camb., where he took his degree in 1616, and was public orator 1619-27. He became the friend of Sir H. Wotton, Donne, and Bacon, the last of whom is said to have held him in such high esteem as to submit his writings to him before publication. He acquired the favour of James I., who conferred upon him a sinecure worth £120 a year, and having powerful friends, he attached himself for some time to the Court in the hope of preferment. The death of two of his patrons, however, led him to change his views, and coming under the influence of Nicholas Ferrar, the quietist of Little Gidding, and of Laud, he took orders in 1626 and, after serving for a few years as prebendary of Layton Ecclesia, or Leighton Broomswold, he became in 1630 Rector of Bemerton, Wilts, where he passed the remainder of his life, discharging the duties of a parish priest with conscientious assiduity. His health, however, failed, and he *d.* in his 40th year. His chief works are *The Temple, or Sacred Poems and Private Ejaculations* (1634), *The Country Parson* (1652), and *Jacula Prudentium*, a collection of pithy proverbial sayings, the two last in prose. Not *pub.* until the year after his death, *The Temple* had immediate acceptance, 20,000 copies, according to I. Walton, who was H.'s biographer, having been sold in a few years. Among its admirers were Charles I., Cowper, and Coleridge. H. wrote some of the most exquisite sacred poetry in the language, although his style, influenced by Donne, is at times characterised by artificiality and conceits. He was an excellent classical scholar, and an accomplished musician.

Works with *Life* by Izaak Walton, ed. by Coleridge, 1846, etc.

HERBERT, SIR THOMAS (1606-1682).—Traveller and historian, belonged to an old Yorkshire family, studied at Oxf. and Camb., and went in connection with an embassy to Persia, of which, and of other Oriental countries, he *pub.* a description. On the outbreak of the Civil War he was a Parliamentarian, but was afterwards taken into the household of the King, to whom he became much attached, was latterly his only attendant, and was with him on the scaffold. At the Restoration he was made a Baronet, and in 1678 *pub. Threnodia Carolina*, an account of the last two years of the King's life.

HERD, DAVID (1732-1810).—Scottish anthologist, *s.* of a farmer in Kincardineshire, was clerk to an accountant in Edin., and devoted his leisure to collecting old Scottish poems and songs, which he first *pub.* in 1769 as *Ancient Scottish Songs, Heroic Ballads, etc.* Other and enlarged ed. appeared in 1776 and 1791. Sir W. Scott made use of his MS. collections in his *Minstrelsy of the Scottish Border.*

HERRICK, ROBERT (1591-1674).—Poet, *b.* in London, was apprenticed as a goldsmith to his uncle, Sir William H., with whom he remained for 10 years. Thereafter he went to Camb., took orders, and was in 1629 presented by Charles I. to the living of Dean Prior, a remote parish in Devonshire, from which he was ejected in 1647, returning in 1662. In the interval he appears to have lived in Westminster, probably supported, more or less, by the gifts of wealthy Royalists. His *Noble Numbers or Pious Pieces* was *pub.* in 1647, his *Hesperides or Works both Human and Divine* in 1648, and the two together in one vol. in the latter year. Over 60, however, of the lighter poems included in *Hesperides* had previously appeared anonymously in a collection entitled *Wit's Recreations.* H.'s early life in London had been a free one, and his secular poems, in which he appears much more at ease than in his sacred, show him to have been a thorough Epicurean, though he claims that his life was not to be judged by his muse. As a lyric poet H. stands in the front rank for sweetness, grace, and true poetic fire, and some of his love songs, *e.g. Anthea*, and *Gather ye Rose-buds*, are unsurpassed in their kind; while in such exquisite little poems as *Blossoms, Daffodils*, and others he finds a classic expression for his love of nature and country life. In his epigrams, however, he falls much below himself. He has been described as "the most frankly pagan of English poets."

Poems ed. by Nutt (1810), Grosart (1876), Pollard (preface by Swinburne, 1891).

HERSCHEL, SIR JOHN FREDERICK WILLIAM (1792-1871).—*S.* of Sir William H., the eminent astronomer and discoverer of the planet Uranus, was *b.* at Slough, and *ed.* at Camb., where he was Senior Wrangler and first Smith's prizeman. He became one of the greatest of English astronomers. Among his writings are treatises on Sound and Light, and his *Astronomy* (1831) was for long the leading manual on the subject. He also *pub. Popular Lectures* and *Collected Addresses*, and made translations from Schiller, and from the *Iliad*.

HERVEY, JAMES (1714-1758).—Religious writer, Rector of Weston Favell, Northants, was the author of *Meditations among the Tombs* (1745-47), *Theron and Aspasio*, and other works, which had a great vogue in their day. They are characterised by overwrought sentiment, and overloaded with florid ornament. H. was a devout and unselfish man, who by his labours broke down a delicate constitution.

HERVEY, JOHN, LORD (1696-1743).—Writer of memoirs, was a younger *s.* of the 1st Earl of Bristol. Entering Parliament he proved an able debater, and held various offices, including that of Lord Privy Seal. He was a favourite with Queen Caroline, and a dexterous and supple courtier. He wrote *Memoirs of the Reign of George II.*, which gives a very unfavourable view of the manners and morals of the Court. It is written in a lively, though often spiteful style, and contains many clever and discriminating character sketches. He was satirised by Pope under the name of "Sporus" and "Lord Fanny."

HEYLIN, PETER (1600-1662).—Ecclesiastical writer, *b.* at Burford, Oxon., was one of the clerical followers of Charles I., who suffered for his fidelity, being deprived under the Commonwealth of his living of Alresford, and other preferments. After the Restoration he was made sub-Dean of Westminster, but the failure of his health prevented further advancement. He was a voluminous writer, and a keen and acrimonious controversialist against the Puritans. Among his works are a *History of the Reformation*, and a Life of Laud (*Cyprianus Anglicanus*) (1668).

HEYWOOD, JOHN (1497?-1580?).—Dramatist and epigrammatist, is believed to have been *b.* at North Mimms, Herts. He was a friend of Sir Thomas More, and through him gained the favour of Henry VIII., and was at the Court of Edward VI. and Mary, for whom, as a young Princess, he had a great regard. Being a supporter of the old religion, he enjoyed her favour, but on the accession of Elizabeth, he left the country, and went to Mechlin, where he *d.* He was famous as a writer of interludes, a species of composition intermediate between the old "moralities" and the regular drama, and displayed considerable constructive skill, and a racy, if somewhat broad and even coarse, humour. Among his interludes are *The Play of the Wether* (1532), *The Play of Love* (1533), and *The Pardoner and the Frere*. An allegorical poem is *The Spider and the Flie* (1556), in which the Spider stands for the Protestants, and the Flie for the Roman Catholics. H. was likewise the author of some 600 epigrams, whence his title of "the old English epigrammatist."

HEYWOOD, THOMAS (*d.* 1650).—Dramatist. Few facts about him have come down, and these are almost entirely derived from his own writings. He appears to have been *b.* in Lincolnshire, and was a Fellow of Peterhouse, Camb., and an ardent Protestant. His literary activity extends from about 1600 to 1641, and his production was unceasing; he claims to have written or "had a main finger in" 220 plays, of which only a small proportion (24) are known to be in existence, a fact partly accounted for by many of them having been written upon the backs of tavern bills, and by the circumstance that though a number of them were popular, few were *pub.* Among them may be mentioned *The Four Prentices of London* (1600) (ridiculed in Fletcher's *Knight of the Burning Pestle*), *Edward IV.* (2 parts) in 1600 and 1605, *The Royal King and the Loyal Subject* (1637), *A Woman Killed with Kindness* (1603), *Rape of Lucrece* (1608), *Fair Maid of the Exchange* (1607), *Love's Mistress* (1636), and *Wise Woman of Hogsdon* (1638). H. also wrote an *Apology for Actors* (1612), a poem, *Hierarchy of the Blessed Angels* (1635), and made various translations. He was thoroughly English in his subjects and treatment, and had invention, liveliness, and truth to nature, but lacked the higher poetic sense, and of course wrote far too much to write uniformly well.

HIGDEN, RANULF OR RALPH (*d.* 1364).—Chronicler, is believed to have been *b.* in the West of England, took the monastic vow (Benedictine), at Chester in 1299, and seems to have travelled over the North of England. His fame rests on his *Polychronicon*, a universal history reaching down to contemporary events. The work is divided into 7 books and, though of no great value as an authority, has an interest as showing the state of historical and geographical knowledge at the time. Written in Latin, it was translated into English by John of Trevisa (*q.v.*) (1387), and printed by Caxton (1482), and by others. Another translation of the 15th century was issued in the Rolls Series. For two centuries it was an approved work. H. wrote various other treatises on theology and history.

HILL, AARON (1685-1750).—Dramatist and miscellaneous writer, *s.* of a country gentleman of Wiltshire, was *ed.* at Westminster School, and thereafter made a tour in the East. He was the author of 17 dramatic pieces, some of them, such as his versions of Voltaire's *Zaire* and *Merope*, being adaptations. He also wrote a quantity of poetry, which, notwithstanding some good passages, is as a general rule dull and pompous. Having written some satiric lines on Pope he received in return a niche in *The Dunciad*, which led to a controversy, in which H. showed some spirit. Afterwards a reconciliation took place. He was a friend and correspondent of Richardson, whose *Pamela* he highly praised. In addition to his literary pursuits H. was a great projector, but his schemes were usually unsuccessful. He was a good and honourable man, but over-impressed with his own importance.

HINTON, JAMES (1822-1875).—Writer on sociology and psychology, *s.* of a Baptist minister, became a successful aurist, but his attention being arrested by social questions, he gave more and more of his time to the consideration and exposition of these. Open-minded and altruistic, his books are full of thought and suggestion. Among his writings may be mentioned *Man and his Dwelling-place* (1859), *The Mystery of Pain* (1866), *The Law of Human Life* (1874), *Chapters on the Art of Thinking* (1879), and *Philosophy and Religion* (1881).

HOADLEY, BENJAMIN (1676-1761).—Theologian and controversialist, *ed.* at Camb., entered the Church, and became Bishop successively of Bangor, Hereford, Salisbury, and Winchester. He was a great supporter of the Revolution, and controvertor of the doctrines of divine right and passive obedience. His works were generally either the causes of controversy or elicited by it. One of his sermons, *On the Nature of the Kingdom or Church of Christ* was the originating cause of what was known as the Bangorian controversy, which raged for a long time with great bitterness.

HOBBES, THOMAS (1588-1679).—Philosopher, was *b.* at Malmesbury, the *s.* of a clergyman, and *ed.* at Oxf. Thereafter he travelled as tutor through France, Italy, and Germany, with William Lord Cavendish, afterwards 2nd Earl of Devonshire, with whom he remained as sec. after the completion of the tour. While engaged in this capacity he became acquainted with Bacon (whose amanuensis he is said to have been), Herbert of Cherbury, and Ben Jonson. In 1629 he *pub.* a translation of *Thucydides*. After the death of his patron, which took place in 1626, he went in 1628 to Paris, where he remained for 18 months, and in 1631 he assumed the position of tutor to his *s.*, afterwards the 3rd Earl, with whom he went in 1634 to France, Italy, and Savoy. When in Italy he was the friend of

Galileo, Gassendi, and other eminent men. Returning to England he remained in the Earl's service, and devoted himself to his studies on philosophy and politics. The commotions of the times, however, disturbed him; and his Royalist principles, expounded in his treatise, *De Corpore Politico*, led to his again, in 1641, leaving England and going to Paris, where he remained until 1652. While there, he entered into controversy on mathematical subjects with Descartes, *pub.* some of his principal works, including *Leviathan*, and received, in 1647, the appointment of mathematical tutor to the Prince of Wales, afterwards Charles II., who was then in that city. The views expressed in his works, however, brought him into such unpopularity that the Prince found it expedient to break the connection, and H. returned to England. In 1653 he resumed his relations with the Devonshire family, living, however, in London in habits of intimacy with Selden, Cowley, and Dr. Harvey. On the Restoration the King conferred upon him a pension of £100, but like most of the Royal benefactions of the day, it was but irregularly paid. His later years were spent in the family of his patron, chiefly at Chatsworth, where he continued his literary activity until his death, which occurred in 1679, in his 91st year. H. was one of the most prominent Englishmen of his day, and has continued to influence philosophical thought more or less ever since, generally, however, by evoking opposition. His fundamental proposition is that all human action is ultimately based upon selfishness (more or less enlightened), allowing no place to the moral or social sentiments. Similarly in his political writings man is viewed as a purely selfish being who must be held in restraint by the strong hand of authority. His chief philosophical works are *De Corpore Politico*, already mentioned, *pub.* in 1640; *Philosophical Rudiments concerning Government and Society*, originally in Latin, translated into English in 1650; *Leviathan, or the Matter, Form, and Power of a Commonwealth, Ecclesiastical and Civil* (1651); *Treatise on Human Nature* (1650); and *Letters upon Liberty and Necessity* (1654). Generally speaking, all his works led him into controversy, one of his principal opponents being Clarendon. The *Letters upon Liberty and Necessity*, which is one of the ablest of them, and indeed one of the ablest ever written on the subject, brought him into collision with Bramhall, Bishop of Londonderry, whom he completely overthrew. He was not, however, so successful in his mathematical controversies, one of the chief of which was on the Quadrature of the Circle. Here his antagonist was the famous mathematician Wallis, who was able easily to demonstrate his errors. In 1672, when 84, H. wrote his autobiography in Latin verse, and in the same year translated 4 books of the *Odyssey*, which were so well received that he completed the remaining books, and also translated the whole of the *Iliad*. Though accurate as literal renderings of the sense, these works fail largely to convey the beauties of the original, notwithstanding which three ed. were issued within 10 years, and they long retained their popularity. His last work was *Behemoth*, a history of the Civil War, completed just before his death, which occurred at Hardwick Hall, one of the seats of the Devonshire family. Although a clear and bold thinker, and a keen controversialist, he was characterised by a certain constitutional timidity believed to have been caused by the alarm of his mother near the time of his birth at the threatened descent of the Spanish Armada. Though dogmatic and impatient of contradiction, faults which grew upon him with age, H. had the courage of his opinions, which he did not trim to suit the times.

SUMMARY.—*B.* 1588, *ed.* Oxf., became acquainted with Bacon, went to Paris 1628, in Italy 1634, *pub. De Corpore Politico* (1640), again in Paris 1641-52, and while there was in controversy with Descartes, and *pub. Leviathan* (1651), appointed mathematical tutor to Charles II. 1647, returned to England 1652, pensioned at Restoration, later years spent at Chatsworth, *pub. Human Nature* 1650, *Liberty and Necessity* 1654, controversy with Bramhall and Wallis, writes autobiography 1672, translates *Homer, pub. Behemoth* 1679, *d.* 1679.

Works ed. by Sir W. Molesworth (16 vols. 1839-46), monograph by Croom Robertson. *Life* by L. Stephen (English Men of Letters Series).

HOBY, SIR THOMAS (1530-1566).—Translator, *b.* at Leominster, and *ed.* at Camb., translated Bucer's *Gratulation to the Church of England*, and *The Courtyer of Count Baldessar Castilio*, the latter of which had great popularity. H. *d.* in Paris while Ambassador to France.

HOCCLEVE, OR OCCLEVE, THOMAS (1368?-1450?).—Poet, probably *b.* in London, where he appears to have spent most of his life, living in Chester's Inn in the Strand. Originally intended for the Church, he received an appointment in the Privy Seal Office, which he retained until 1424, when quarters were assigned him in the Priory of Southwick, Hants. In 1399 a pension of £10, subsequently increased to £13, 6s. 8d., had been conferred upon him, which, however, was paid only intermittently, thus furnishing him with a perpetual grievance. His early life appears to have been irregular, and to the end he was a weak, vain, discontented man. His chief work is *De Regimine Principum* or *Governail of Princes*, written 1411-12. The best part of this is an autobiographical prelude *Mal Regle de T. Hoccleve*, in which he holds up his youthful follies as a warning. It is also interesting as containing, in the MS. in the British Museum, a drawing of Chaucer, from which all subsequent portraits have been taken.

HOFFMAN, CHARLES FENNO (1806-1884).—Poet, etc., *b.* in New York, *s.* of a lawyer, was bred to the same profession, but early deserted it for literature. He wrote a successful novel, *Greyslaer*, and much verse, some of which displayed more lyrical power than any which had preceded it in America.

HOGG, JAMES (THE ETTRICK SHEPHERD) (1770-1835).—Poet, and writer of tales, belonged to a race of shepherds, and began life by herding cows until he was old enough to be trusted with a flock of sheep. His imagination was fed by his mother, who was possessed of an inexhaustible stock of ballads and folk-lore. He had little schooling, and had great difficulty in writing out his earlier poems, but was earnest in giving himself such culture as he could. Entering the service of Mr. Laidlaw, the friend of Scott, he was by him introduced to the poet, and assisted him in collecting material for his *Border Minstrelsy*. In 1796 he had begun to write his songs, and when on a visit to Edin. in 1801 he *coll.* his poems under the title of *Scottish Pastorals, etc.*, and in 1807 there followed *The Mountain Bard*. A treatise on the diseases of sheep brought him £300, on the strength of which he embarked upon a sheep-farming enterprise in Dumfriesshire which, like a previous smaller venture in Harris, proved a failure, and he returned to Ettrick bankrupt. Thenceforward he relied almost entirely on literature for support. With this view he, in 1810, settled in Edin., *pub. The Forest Minstrel*, and started the *Spy*, a critical journal, which ran for a year. In 1813 *The Queen's Wake* showed his full powers, and finally settled his right to an assured place among the poets of his country. He joined the staff of *Blackwood*, and became the friend of Wilson, Wordsworth, and Byron. Other poems followed, *The Pilgrims of the Sun* (1815), *Madoc of the Moor, The Poetic Mirror*, and *Queen Hynde* (1826); and in prose *Winter Evening Tales* (1820), *The Three Perils of Man* (1822), and *The Three Perils of Woman*. In his later years his home was a cottage at Altrive on 70 acres of moorland presented to him by the Duchess of Buccleuch, where he *d.* greatly lamented. As might be expected from his almost total want of regular education, H. was often greatly wanting in taste, but he had real imagination and poetic faculty. Some of his lyrics like *The Skylark* are perfect in their spontaneity and sweetness, and his *Kilmeny* is one of the most exquisite fairy tales in the language. Hogg was vain and greedy of praise, but honest and, beyond his means, generous. He is a leading character, partly idealised, partly caricatured, in Wilson's *Noctes Ambrosianæ*.

HOGG, THOMAS JEFFERSON (1792-1862).—Biographer, *s.* of John H., a country gentleman of Durham, *ed.* at Durham Grammar School, and Univ. Coll., Oxf., where he made the acquaintance of Shelley, whose lifelong friend and biographer he became. Associated with S. in the famous pamphlet on *The Necessity of Atheism*, he shared in the expulsion from the Univ. which it entailed, and thereafter devoted himself to the law, being called to the Bar in 1817. In 1832 he contributed to Bulwer's *New Monthly Magazine* his *Reminiscences of Shelley*, which was much admired. Thereafter he was commissioned to write a biography of the poet, of which he completed 2 vols., but in so singular a fashion that the material with which he had been entrusted was withdrawn. The work, which is probably unique in the annals of biography, while giving a vivid and credible picture of S. externally, shows no true appreciation of him as a poet, and reflects with at least equal prominence the humorously eccentric personality of the author, which renders it entertaining in no common degree. Other works of H. were *Memoirs of Prince Alexy Haimatoff*, and a book of travels, *Two Hundred and Nine Days* (1827). He *m.* the widow of Williams, Shelley's friend, who was drowned along with him.

HOLCROFT, THOMAS (1745-1809).—Dramatist, *s.* of a small shoemaker in London, passed his youth as a pedlar, and as a Newmarket stable boy. A charitable person having given him some education he became a schoolmaster, but in 1770 went on the provincial stage. He then took to writing plays, and was the first to introduce the melodrama into England. Among his plays, *The Road to Ruin* (1792) is the best, and is still acted; others were *Duplicity* (1781), and *A Tale of Mystery*. Among his novels are *Alwyn* (1780), and *Hugh Trevor*, and he wrote the well-known song, *Gaffer Gray*. H. was a man of stern and irascible temper, industrious and energetic, and a sympathiser with the French Revolution.

HOLINSHED, OR HOLLINGSHEAD, RAPHAEL OR RALPH *d.* 1580?). — Belonged to a Cheshire family, and is said by Anthony Wood to have been at one of the Univ., and to have been a priest. He came to London, and was in the employment of Reginald Wolf, a German printer, making translations and doing hack-work. His *Chronicles of Englande, Scotlande, and Irelande*, from which Shakespeare drew much of his history, was based to a considerable extent on the collections of Leland, and he had the assistance of W. Harrison, R. Stanyhurst, and others. The introductory description of England and the English was the work of Harrison, Stanyhurst did the part relating to Ireland, and H. himself the history of England and Scotland, the latter being mainly translated from the works of Boece and Major. *Pub.* in 1577 it had an eager welcome, and a wide and lasting popularity. A later ed. in 1586 was ed. by J. Hooker and Stow. It is a work of real value—a magazine of useful and interesting information, with the authorities cited. Its tone is strongly Protestant, its style clear.

HOLLAND, JOSIAH GILBERT (1819-1881).—Novelist and poet, *b.* in Massachusetts, helped to found and ed. *Scribner's Monthly* (afterwards the *Century Magazine*), in which appeared his novels, *Arthur Bonnicastle*, *The Story of Sevenoaks*, *Nicholas Minturn*. In poetry he wrote *Bitter Sweet* (1858), *Kathrina*, etc.

HOLLAND, PHILEMON (1552-1637).—Translator, *b.* at Chelmsford, and *ed.* at Camb., was master of the free school at Coventry, where he also practised medicine. His chief translations, made in good Elizabethan English, are of Pliny's *Natural History*, Plutarch's *Morals*, Suetonius, Xenophon's *Cyropædia*, and Camden's *Britannia*. There are passages in the second of these which have hardly been excelled by any later prose translator of the classics. His later years were passed in poverty.

HOLMES, OLIVER WENDELL (1809-1894).—Essayist, novelist, and poet, was *b.* of good Dutch and English stock at Camb., Massachusetts, the seat of Harvard, where he graduated in 1829. He studied law, then medicine, first at home, latterly in Paris, whence he returned in 1835, and practised in his native town. In 1838 he was appointed Prof. of Anatomy and Physiology at Dartmouth Coll., from which he was in 1847 transferred to a similar chair at Harvard. Up to 1857 he had done little in literature: his first book of poems, containing "The Last Leaf," had been *pub.* But in that year the *Atlantic Monthly* was started with Lowell for ed., and H. was engaged as a principal contributor. In it appeared the trilogy by which he is best known, *The Autocrat of the Breakfast Table* (1857), *The Professor*, *The Poet* (1872), all graceful, allusive, and pleasantly egotistical. He also wrote *Elsie Venner* (1861), which has been called "the snake story of literature," and *The Guardian Angel*. By many readers he is valued most for the poems which lie imbedded in his books, such as "The Chambered Nautilus," "The Last Leaf," "Homesick in Heaven," "The Voiceless," and "The Boys."

HOME, JOHN (1722-1808).—Dramatist, *s.* of the Town-Clerk of Leith, where he was *b.*, *ed.* there and at Edin., and entered the Church. Before doing so, however, he had fought on the Royalist side in the '45, and had, after the Battle of Falkirk, been a prisoner in Doune Castle, whence he escaped. His ministerial life, which was passed at Athelstaneford, East Lothian, was brought to an end by the action of the Church Courts on his producing the play of *Douglas*. This drama, which had been rejected by Garrick, but brought out in Edin. in 1756, created an immense sensation, and made its appearance in London the following year. H. then became private sec. to the Earl of Bute, who gave him the sinecure of Conservator of Scots Privileges at Campvere in Holland. Thereafter he was tutor to the Prince of Wales (George III.), who on his accession conferred upon him a pension of £300. Other plays were *The Siege of Aquileia*, *The Fatal Discovery* (1769), *Alonzo*, and *Alfred* (1778), which was a total failure. He also wrote a *History of the Rebellion*. In 1778 he settled in Edin., where he was one of the brilliant circle of literary men of which Robertson was the centre. He supported the claims of Macpherson to be the translator of Ossian.

HONE, WILLIAM (1780-1842).—Miscellaneous writer, *b.* at Bath, in his youth became a convinced and active democrat. His zeal in the propagation of his views, political and philanthropic, was so absorbing as to lead to a uniform want of success in his business undertakings. He *pub.* many satirical writings, which had immense popularity, among which were *The Political House that Jack Built* (1819), *The Man in the Moon* (1820), *The Political Showman* (1821), and *The Apocryphal New Testament*. For one of his earliest satires, *The Political Litany*, *pub.* in 1817, he was prosecuted, but acquitted. Later he brought out *Ancient Mysteries* (1823), *Every Day Book* (1826-27), *Table Book* (1827-28), and *Year Book* (1828). These works, in which he had the assistance of other writers, are full of curious learning on miscellaneous subjects, such as ceremonies, dress, sports, customs, etc. His last literary enterprise was an ed. of *Strutt's Sports and Pastimes* (1830). Always a self-sacrificing and honest man, he was originally an unbeliever, but in his atter years he became a sincere Christian.

HOOD, THOMAS (1799-1845).—Poet and comic writer, *s.* of a bookseller in London, where he was *b.*, was put into a mercantile office, but the confinement proving adverse to his health, he was sent to Dundee, where the family had connections, and where he obtained some literary employment. His health being restored, he returned to London, and entered the employment of an uncle as an engraver. Here he acquired an acquaintance with drawing, which he afterwards turned to account in illustrating his comic writings.

After working for a short time on his own account he became, at the age of 22, sub-editor of the *London Magazine*, and made the acquaintance of many literary men, including De Quincey, Lamb, and Hazlitt. His first separate publication, *Odes and Addresses to Great People*, appeared in 1825, and had an immediate success. Thus encouraged he produced in the next year *Whims and Oddities*, and in 1829, he commenced *The Comic Annual*, which he continued for 9 years, and wrote in *The Gem* his striking poem, *Eugene Aram*. Meanwhile he had *m.* in 1824, a step which, though productive of the main happiness and comfort of his future life, could not be considered altogether prudent, as his health had begun to give way, and he had no means of support but his pen. Soon afterwards the failure of his publisher involved him in difficulties which, combined with his delicate health, made the remainder of his life a continual struggle. The years between 1834 and 1839 were the period of most acute difficulty, and for a part of this time he was obliged to live abroad. In 1840 friends came to his assistance, and he was able to return to England. His health was, however, quite broken down, but his industry never flagged. During the five years which remained to him he acted as ed. first of the *New Monthly Magazine*, and then of *Hood's Monthly Magazine*. In his last year a Government pension of £100 was granted to his wife. Among his other writings may be mentioned *Tylney Hall*, a novel which had little success, and *Up the Rhine*, in which he satirised the English tourist. Considering the circumstances of pressure under which he wrote, it is little wonder that much of his work was ephemeral and beneath his powers, but in his particular line of humour he is unique, while his serious poems are instinct with imagination and true pathos. A few of them, such as *The Song of the Shirt*, and *The Bridge of Sighs* are perfect in their kind.

Life by his *s.* and *dau.* Ed. of *Works* by same (7 vols. 1862). Selections, with Biography, by Ainger, 1897.

HOOK, THEODORE EDWARD (1788-1841).—Dramatist and novelist, *s.* of James H., music-hall composer, was *b.* in London, and *ed.* at Harrow. As a boy he wrote words for his father's comic dramas. In 1805 he produced a comic opera, *The Soldier's Return*, which was followed by *Catch Him who Can*. Both of them were highly successful, and were followed by many others. His marvellous powers as a conversationalist and *improvisatore* made him a favourite in the highest circles. In 1812 he received the appointment of Accountant-General of Mauritius, which he held for 5 years, when serious irregularities were discovered, and he was sent home in disgrace, prosecuted by Government for a claim of £12,000, and imprisoned. It subsequently appeared that the actual peculation had been the work of a subordinate, and that H. himself was only chargeable with gross neglect of duty, but though he was released the claims against him were not departed from. He then became ed. of *John Bull*, a journal of high Tory and aristocratic proclivities, which he conducted with great ability; he also ed. the *New Monthly Magazine*, and wrote many novels, among which were *Sayings and Doings* (3 series), *Gilbert Gurney*, and *Jack Brag*. Though making a large income, he was always in difficulties, and, after a long struggle with broken health and spirits, he *d.* at Fulham in 1841.

HOOK, WALTER FARQUHAR (1798-1875).—Biographer, *s.* of James H., Dean of Worcester, *b.* at Worcester, and *ed.* at Winchester and Oxf. Entering the Church, he held various benefices, and became Vicar of Leeds (where, largely owing to his exertions, 20 new churches and many schools were built), and afterwards Dean of Chichester. Besides his labours as a churchman he was a voluminous author, his works including *Church Dictionary* (1842), *Dictionary of Ecclesiastical Biography* (1845-52), and *Lives of the Archbishops of Canterbury* (1860-75), on which he was still engaged at his death, and which he had brought down to Juxon, vol. xi. His sermon *Hear the Church* (1838), in which he affirmed the Apostolical succession of the Anglican episcopate, attracted much attention.

HOOKER, RICHARD (1554?-1600).—Theologian, *b.* near Exeter, of a family the original name of which was Vowell. His ability and gentleness as a schoolboy recommended him to the notice of Bishop Jewel, who sent him to Corpus Christi Coll., Oxf., where he graduated and became a Fellow in 1577. His proficiency in Hebrew led to his appointment in 1579 as Deputy Prof. Two years later, 1581, he took orders, and soon thereafter advantage was taken of his simplicity to entrap him into an unsuitable marriage with a woman named Joan Churchman, whose mother had nursed him in an illness. As might have been expected, the connection turned out unhappily, his wife being a scold, and, according to Anthony Wood, "a silly, clownish woman." His fate may, however, have been mitigated by the fact that his own temper was so sweet that he is said never to have been seen angry. Some doubt, moreover, has been cast on some of the reported details of his domestic life. In 1584 he received the living of Drayton-Beauchamp, in Bucks, and in the following year was appointed Master of the Temple. Here he had for a colleague as evening lecturer Walter Travers, a man of mark among the Puritans. Though both men were of the finest moral character, their views on ecclesiastical questions were widely different, and as neither was disposed to conceal his opinions, it came to be said that in the Temple "the pulpit spake pure Canterbury in the morning and Geneva in the afternoon." Things developed into an animated controversy, in which H. was considered to have triumphed, and the Archbishop (Whitgift) suspended Travers. The position, however, had become intolerable for H. who respected his opponent in spite of their differences, and he petitioned Whitgift that he might retire to the country and find time and quiet to complete his great work, the *Ecclesiastical Polity*, on which he was engaged. He was accordingly, in 1591, presented to the living of Boscombe near Amesbury, and made sub-Dean and a minor Prebendary of Salisbury. Here he finished *The Four Books of the Lawes of Ecclesiastical Polity*, *pub.* in 1594. The following year he was presented by Queen Elizabeth to the living of Bishopsbourne, Kent. Here the fifth book was *pub.* (1597), and here he *d.* in 1600. The sixth and eighth books were not *pub.* until 1648, and the seventh only appeared in 1662. The *Ecclesiastical Polity* is one of the greatest achievements alike in English theology and English literature, a masterpiece of reasoning and eloquence, in a style stately and sonorous, though often laborious and involved. Hallam considered that no English writer had better displayed the capacities of the language. The argument is directed against the Romanists on the one hand and the Puritans on the other, and the fundamental idea is "the unity and all embracing character of law as the manifestation of the divine order of the universe." The distinguishing note of H.'s character was what Fuller calls his "dove-like simplicity." Izaak Walton, his biographer, describes him as "an obscure, harmless man, in poor clothes, of a mean stature and stooping . . . his body worn out, not with age, but study, and holy mortification, his face full of heat-pimples . . . and tho' not purblind, yet short, or weak, sighted." In his calling as a parish priest he was faithful and diligent. In preaching "his voice was low . . . gesture none at all, standing stone-still in the pulpit." The sixth book of the *Ecclesiastical Polity* has been considered of doubtful authority, and to have no claim to its place, and the seventh and eighth are believed to have been put together from rough notes. Some of his MSS. were destroyed after his death by his wife's relatives. The epithet "judicious" attached to his name first appears in the inscription on his monument at Bishopsbourne.

Works, ed. by Keble (1836); new ed. revised by Church, etc. (1888). It includes the *Life* by I. Walton.

HOPE, THOMAS (1770-1831).—Novelist and writer on art, was a wealthy merchant of Amsterdam, of Scotch descent, his family having emigrated to Holland in the 17th century. In early life he spent much time in travel, studying architecture, and collecting objects of art. Returning, he settled in London, and occupied himself in arranging his vast collections. In 1807 he *pub.* a work on *Household Furniture and Decoration*, which had a great effect in improving the public taste in such matters. This was followed by two magnificent works, *On the Costume of the Ancients* (1809), and *Designs of Modern Costumes* (1812). Up to this time his reputation had been somewhat that of a transcendent upholsterer, but in 1819 he astonished the literary world by his novel, *Anastasius ; or, Memoirs of a Modern Greek*, a work full of imagination, descriptive power, and knowledge of the world. This book, which was *pub.* anonymously, was attributed to Byron, and only credited to the author on his avowing it in *Blackwood's Magazine*. H. also wrote a treatise on the *Origin and Prospects of Man*, and *Essays on Architecture*. He was a munificent and discerning patron of rising artists.

HOPKINS, GERARD MANLEY (1844–1889).—*Ed.* at Highgate and Oxf., entered Jesuit novitiate in 1868, Greek Professor at Dublin Univ. 1884. Wrote a number of short poems, but they were only collected and published in 1918 (reissued, with additions, 1930). Robert Bridges was a great admirer of Hopkins and was responsible for the poems' publication.

HORNE, RICHARD HENRY OR HENGIST (1803-1884).—Eccentric poet, was *b.* in London, and *ed.* at Sandhurst for the East India Company Service, but failed to get a nomination. After a youth of adventure, partly in the Mexican Navy, he returned to England, and began in 1828 a highly combative literary career with a poem, *Hecatompylos*, in the *Athenæum*. His next appearance, *The False Medium* (1833), an exposition of the obstacles thrown in the way of "men of genius" by literary middlemen, raised a nest of hornets; and *Orion*, an "epic poem," *pub.* 1843 at the price of one farthing, followed. His plays, which include *Cosmo de Medici* (1837), *The Death of Marlowe* (1837), and *Judas Iscariot*, did not add greatly to his reputation. In *The New Spirit of the Age* (1844), he had the assistance of Mrs. Browning. Though a writer of talent, he was not a poet.

HORNE, THOMAS HARTWELL (1780-1862).—Theologian, *ed.* at Christ's Hospital, was for a time in the law, but became a great biblical scholar, and in 1818 *pub. Introduction to the Critical Study and Knowledge of the Holy Scriptures* (1818), in consideration of which he was admitted to orders without the usual preliminaries, and in 1833 obtained a benefice in London and a prebend in St. Paul's, and was senior assistant in the printed books department of the British Museum (1824-60). He wrote an *Introduction to the Study of Bibliography* (1814), and various other works, but he is chiefly remembered in connection with that first mentioned, which was frequently reprinted, and was very widely used as a text-book both at home and in America.

HOUGHTON, RICHARD MONCKTON MILNES, 1ST LORD (1809-1885).—Poet, *s.* of Robert (known as "single-speech") M., *b.* in London, and *ed.* privately and at Camb. He sat in the House of Commons for Pontefract from 1837-63, when he was raised to the Peerage. His interests were, however, mainly literary and philanthropic, and it was said of him that he "knew everybody worth knowing at home and abroad;" and his sympathies being of the widest, he was able to bring together the most opposite extremes of life and opinion. He championed the cause of oppressed nationalities, and of the slave. He *pub.* many vols. of poetry, among which were *Poetry for the People* (1840), and *Palm Leaves* (1848). He also wrote a Life of Keats, and various books of travels. Though he had not the depth of mind or intensity of feeling to make a great poet, his verse is the work of a man of high culture, graceful and refined, and a few of his shorter poems—such as *The Beating of my own Heart*, and *Strangers Yet*, strike a true note which gained for them wide acceptance.

HOWARD, EDWARD (*d.* 1841).—Novelist, a sea-comrade of Captain Marryat, and as sub-ed. assisted him in conducting the *Metropolitan Magazine*. He wrote several sea novels, of which *Rattlin the Reefer*, sometimes attributed to Marryat, is the best known. Others were *Outward Bound* and *Jack Ashore*.

HOWARD, SIR ROBERT (1626-1698).—Dramatist, *s.* of the Earl of Berkshire, and brother-in-law of Dryden. On the outbreak of the Civil War he was of the King's party, and was imprisoned during the Commonwealth. After the Restoration, however, he was in favour with the Court, and held many important posts. He wrote some plays, of which the best was *The Committee*, and collaborated with Dryden in *The Indian Queen*. He was at odds with him, however, on the question of rhyme, the use of which he wrote against in very indifferent blank verse.

HOWE, JOHN (1630-1705).—Puritan divine, *b.* at Loughborough, of which his *f.* was curate, studied at Camb., and became, in 1652, minister of Great Torrington, Devonshire, where he was famous for the unusual length of his sermons and prayers. In 1657 Oliver Cromwell made him his resident chaplain at Whitehall, a position which he retained under Richard C., so long as the latter held the office of Protector. On the Restoration H. returned to Great Torrington, from which, however, he was ejected in 1662. Thereafter he wandered from place to place, preaching in secret until 1671, when he went to Ireland as chaplain to Lord Massareene, and in 1675 he became minister of a dissenting congregation in London. In 1685 he travelled with Lord Wharton on the Continent, but returned in 1687 to London, where he *d.* in 1705. H. was the author of many excellent works of practical divinity, among which are *The Living Temple, Inquiry into the Doctrine of the Trinity*, and *The Divine Presence*. The substance of his writings is better than their style, which is involved and extremely diffuse, and evinces much vigour of mind. H. is described as of a fine presence and dignified manners.

HOWELL, JAMES (1594?-1666).—Miscellaneous writer, *s.* of a clergyman at Abernant, Caermarthenshire, was at Oxf. and spent the greater part of his earlier life travelling in various Continental countries, including the Low Countries, France, Spain, and Italy, on various matters of business, during which he became versed in many languages, and amassed stores of information and observations on men and manners. He was a keen Royalist, and was on this account imprisoned in the Fleet, 1643-51. He wrote a large number of books, including *Dodona's Grove*, a political allegory, *Instructions for Foreign Travel* (1642), *England's Tears for the Present Wars, A Trance, or News from Hell*, and above all, *Epistolæ Ho-Elianæ, or Familiar Letters*, chiefly written in the Fleet to imaginary correspondents, but no doubt based upon notes of his own travels. It is one of the most interesting and entertaining books in the language.

HOWIE, JOHN (1735-1793).—Biographer, a Renfrewshire farmer, who claimed descent from an Albigensian refugee, wrote Lives of the martyrs of Scotland from Patrick Hamilton, the first, to James Renwick, the last, under the title of *Scots Worthies*. The work of an unlettered man, it has considerable merit as regards both matter and style, and was long a classic among the Scottish peasantry as well as higher orders of the people.

HOWITT, WILLIAM (1792-1879), HOWITT, MARY (BOTHAM) (1799-1888).—Miscellaneous writers. William H. was *b.* at Heanor, Derbyshire, and was apprenticed to a builder; Mary was *b.* at Coleford, Gloucestershire; they *m.* in 1821, and settled at Hanley, where they carried on business as chemists. Two years later they removed to Nottingham, where they remained for 12 years, and where much of their literary work was accomplished. Thereafter they lived successively at Esher, London, Heidelberg, and Rome, at the last of which they both *d.* Their literary work, which was very voluminous, was done partly in conjunction, partly independently, and covered a considerable variety of subjects—poetry, fiction, history, translations, and social and economical subjects. Useful and pleasing in its day, little of it is likely to survive. William's works include *A History of Priestcraft* (1833), *Rural Life in England* (1837), *Visits to Remarkable Places, Homes and Haunts of the Poets, Land, Labour, and Gold* (1855), *Rural Life in Germany, History of the Supernatural,* and *History of Discovery in Australia.* Mary translated the Swedish novels of Frederica Bremer, H. C. Andersen's *Improvisatore,* and wrote novels, including *Wood Leighton* and *The Cost of Caergwyn,* many successful tales and poems for children, and a *History of the United States.* Their joint productions include *The Forest Minstrel, Book of the Seasons,* and *Ruined Abbeys and Castles of Great Britain.* Both brought up as Quakers, they left that communion in 1847, and became believers in spiritualism; and in 1882 Mary joined the Church of Rome.

HUCHOWN, or SIR HUGH OF EGLINTON (*fl.* 14th cent.).—Unless identified with Sir Hugh, Huchown is shrouded in mystery. He was a writer of alliterative verse, referred to by Andrew of Wyntoun. If he be identified with Sir Hugh, he was an Ayrshire nobleman related to Robert II., *b. c.* 1300-20, Chamberlain of Cunningham, Justiciar of Lothian, and Commissioner for the Borders. He also held office under David II. In that case also he is believed by some scholars to have translated the poems bearing the titles *The Destruction of Troy* and *The Wars of Alexander.*

HUGHES, JOHN (1677-1720).—Essayist and dramatist, was a clerk in the Ordnance Office, then sec. for the Commission of the Peace. He contributed to the *Spectator, Tatler,* and *Guardian,* ed. Spenser, and wrote several dramas, of which the best is *The Siege of Damascus.* It was his last, he having *d.* on the first night of its performance. Addison thought so well of his dramatic talent that he requested him to write the conclusion of *Cato.* He, however, finished it himself. H. was a highly respectable person, and is affectionately commemorated by Sir Richard Steele.

HUGHES, THOMAS (1823?-1896).—Novelist and biographer, *s.* of a Berkshire squire, was *ed.* at Rugby and Oxf., and called to the Bar in 1848. Much the most successful of his books was *Tom Brown's School-days* (1856), which had an immense popularity, and perhaps remains the best picture of English public-school life in the language. Its sequel, *Tom Brown at Oxford* (1861), was a comparative failure, but his *Scouring of the White Horse* deals in a charming way with his own countryside. He also wrote Lives of Alfred the Great, Bishop Fraser, and D. Macmillan, the publisher. H. devoted much attention to philanthropic work in conjunction with Kingsley and Maurice. In 1882 he was appointed a County Court Judge.

HUME, ALEXANDER (1560-1609).—Poet, *s.* of Patrick, 5th Lord Polwarth, *ed.* at St. Andrews, and on the Continent, was originally destined for the law, but devoted himself to the service of the Church, and was minister of Logie in Stirlingshire. He *pub.* in 1599 *Hymns and Sacred Songs*, including the beautiful "Day Estival," descriptive of a summer day.

HUME, DAVID, (1711-1776).—Philosopher and historian, second *s.* of Joseph H., of Ninewells, Berwickshire, was *b.* and *ed.* in Edin., and was intended for the law. For this, however, he had no aptitude, and commercial pursuits into which he was initiated in a counting-house in Bristol proving equally uncongenial, he was permitted to follow out his literary bent, and in 1734 went to France, where he passed three years at Rheims and La Flèche in study, living on a small allowance made him by his *f.* In 1739 he *pub.* anonymously his *Treatise on Human Nature*, which attracted little attention. Having returned to Scotland, he wrote at Ninewells his *Essays, Moral and Philosophical* (1741-42). He now became desirous of finding some employment which would put him in a position of independence, and having been unsuccessful in his candidature for the Chair of Moral Philosophy in Edin., he became in 1745 governor to the Marquis of Annandale, a nobleman whose state was little removed from insanity. Two years later he accepted the more congenial appointment of Judge-Advocate-General to General St. Clair on his expedition to Port L'Orient, and in 1748 accompanied him on a diplomatic mission to France, whence he passed on to Vienna and Turin. About the same time he produced his *Philosophical Essays* (1748), including the famous *Essay in Miracles*, which gave rise to so much controversy. These were followed in 1751 by his *Enquiry into the Principles of Morals*, which he considered his best work; and in 1752 by his *Political Discourses*, which alone of his works had an immediate success. In the same year he applied unsuccessfully for the Chair of Logic in Glasgow, but was appointed Keeper of the Advocates' Library in Edin. The access to books and original authorities which this position gave him appears to have suggested to his mind the idea of writing a history, and the first vol. of his *History of England*, containing the reigns of James I. and Charles I., was *pub.* in 1754. Its reception was not favourable, and the disappointment of the author was so great that, had it not been for the state of war between the two countries, he would have left his native land, changed his name, and settled permanently in France. The second vol., which appeared in 1757, dealing with the Commonwealth, and the reigns of Charles II. and James II., had a better reception, and had the effect of "buoying up its unfortunate brother." Thereafter the tide completely turned, and the remaining four vols., 1759 and 1762, in which he turned back and finished the history from the invasion of Julius Cæsar to the accession of Henry VII., attained a vast popularity, which extended to the whole work. During the progress of the history H. *pub.* in 1757 *Four Dissertations: the Natural History of Religion; of the Passions; of Tragedy; of the Standard of Taste.* Two others on *Suicide* and on *The Immortality of the Soul* were cancelled, but *pub.* posthumously. In 1763 H. accompanied

Lord Hertford to Paris, and for a few months acted as *Chargé d'Affaires*. While there he was introduced to the brilliant literary society for which the French capital was then famous. Among other acquaintances which he made was that of Rousseau, whom he persuaded to accompany him on his return home, and for whom he procured a pension. The suspicious and fickle character of R., however, soon brought the friendship to an end. Soon after his return H. received a pension, and from 1767-68 he was under-sec. to General Conway, then Sec. of State. In 1769 he retired, and returned to Edin. with an income of £1000 a year which, time and place considered, was an ample competence, and there he spent the remainder of his days, the recognised head of the intellectual and literary society of the city.

The mind of H. was one of the most original and operative of his age. His philosophy was largely a questioning of the views of previous metaphysicians, and he occupied towards mind, considered as a self-subsisting entity, a position analogous to that assumed by Berkeley towards matter similarly considered. He profoundly influenced European thought, and by indirectly calling into being the philosophy of Kant on the one hand, and that of the Scottish School on the other, created a new era of thought. As a historian he showed the same originality. He introduced a new and higher method of writing history than had previously been practised. Until his time chronicles and contemporary memoirs had, generally speaking, been all that had been produced; and though his great work cannot, from its frequent inaccuracies and the fact that it is not based upon original documents, claim the character of an authority, its clear, graceful, and spirited narrative style, and its reflection of the individuality of the writer, constitute it a classic, and it must always retain a place among the masterpieces of historical literature. In character H. was kindly, candid, and good-humoured, and he was beloved as a man even by many who held his views in what was little short of abhorrence.

SUMMARY.—*B.* 1711, *ed.* at Edin., tries law and commerce, but decides for literature, goes to France 1734-37, *pub. Human Nature* 1739, *Essays Moral and Philosophical* 1741-2, governor to M. of Annandale 1745, accompanies expedition to L'Orient, engaged diplomatically 1748, *pub. Philosophical Essays*, including *Miracles* 1748, *Enquiry into Principles of Morals* 1751, *Political Discourses* 1752, Keeper of Advocates' Library 1752, *pub. History of England* 1754-62, *Four Dissertations* 1757, *Chargé d'Affaires* at Paris 1763, became acquainted with Rousseau, under-sec. of State 1767-8, retires and settles in Edin. 1769.

Life by Hill Burton (2 vols., 1846), shorter ones by Huxley, Knight, and Calderwood. *Works* ed. by Green and Grose (4 vols., 1874). *History* often reprinted with Smollett's continuations.

HUNNIS, WILLIAM (*d.* 1597).—Poet, was a gentleman of the Chapel Royal to Edward VI., imprisoned during the reign of Mary, but after the accession of Elizabeth was released, and in 1566 made "master of the children" of the Chapel Royal. He wrote metrical versions of the Psalms, and some vols. of verse, *A Hiveful of Honey*, and *A Handful of Honeysuckles*.

HUNT, JAMES HENRY LEIGH (1784-1859).—Essayist and poet, was *b.* at Southgate, and *ed.* at Christ's Hospital. A selection of his earliest poems was *pub.* by his *f.* in 1801 under the title of *Juvenilia.* In 1805 he joined his brother John in conducting a paper, the *News*, which the latter had started. Thereafter the brothers embarked upon the *Examiner*, a paper of pronounced Radical views. The appearance in this journal of an article on the Prince Regent in which he was described in words which have been condensed into "a fat Adonis of fifty," led to H. being fined £500, and imprisoned for two years. With his customary genial philosophy, however, the prisoner made the best of things, turned his cell into a study, with bookcases and a piano, and his yard into a garden. He had the sympathy of many, and received his friends, including Byron, Moore, and Lamb. On his release he *pub.* his poem, *The Story of Rimini.* Two other vols. of poetry followed, *The Feast of the Poets* and *Foliage*, in 1814 and 1818 respectively. In the latter year he started the *Indicator*, a paper something in the style of the *Spectator* or *Tatler*, and after this had run its course the *Companion*, conceived on similar lines, took its place in 1828. In 1822 H. went to Italy with Byron, and there established the *Liberal*, a paper which did not prove a success. Disillusioned with Byron, H. returned home, and *pub.* in 1828 *Lord Byron and his Contemporaries*, a work which gave great offence to Byron's friends, who accused the author of ingratitude. In 1834 H. started the *London Journal*, which he ed. for two years. Among his later works are *Captain Sword and Captain Pen* (1835), *The Palfrey*, a poem, *A Legend of Florence* (drama), *Imagination and Fancy* (1844), *Wit and Humour* (1846), *A Jar of Honey from Mount Hybla* (1848), *The Old Court Suburb* (1855), *The Town*, *Sir Ralph Esher*, a novel, and his Autobiography (1850). Although his poems have considerable descriptive power and brightness, he had not the depth and intensity to make a poet, and his reputation rests rather upon his essays, which are full of a genial philosophy, and display a love of books, and everything pleasant and beautiful. He did much to popularise the love of poetry and literature in general among his fellow-countrymen.

HURD, RICHARD (1720-1808).—Divine, and miscellaneous writer, *b.* at Congreve, Staffordshire, was *ed.* at Camb., and entering the Church, became Bishop successively of Lichfield and Worcester. He produced an ed. of the *Ars Poetica* of Horace, *Dissertations on Poetry*, *Dialogues on Sincerity*, *Letters on Chivalry and Romance*, and *An Introduction to the Prophecies.* He was in 1783 offered, but declined, the Primacy.

HUTCHESON, FRANCIS (1694-1746).—Philosopher, *b.* in Ireland, and *ed.* for the Presbyterian ministry at Glasgow Univ. After keeping an academy at Dublin for some years he *pub.* his *Enquiry into Beauty and Virtue*, which won for him a great reputation. In 1729 he became Prof. of Moral Philosophy at Glasgow, where he exercised a great influence over his students, and also upon the Scottish system of philosophy. In his philosophical views he was to some extent a disciple of Shaftesbury. He introduced the term, "moral sense," which he defined as a power of perceiving moral attributes in action. His *System of Moral Philosophy* appeared posthumously in two vols.

HUTCHINSON, MRS. LUCY (*b.* 1620).—Biographer, *dau.* of Sir Allan Apsley, Lieutenant of the Tower of London, *m.* in 1638 John, afterwards Colonel, Hutchinson, one of those who signed the death-warrant of Charles I., but who afterwards protested against the assumption of supreme power by Cromwell. She has a place in literature for her Life of her husband, one of the most interesting biographies in the language, not only on account of its immediate subject, but of the light which it throws upon the characteristics and conditions of the life of Puritans of good family. Originally intended for her family only, it was printed by a descendant in 1806, and did much to clear away the false impressions as to the narrowness and austerity of the educated Puritans which had prevailed. Colonel H. and his wife were noble representatives of their class.

HUTTON, RICHARD HOLT (1826-1897).—Essayist and miscellaneous writer, was brought up as a Unitarian, and for some time was a preacher of that body, but coming under the influence of F. D. Maurice and others of his school, joined the Church of England. He was a frequent contributor to various magazines and reviews, and assisted Walter Bagehot in ed. the *National Review*. In 1861 he became joint-proprietor and ed. of the *Spectator*. Among his other writings may be mentioned *Essays, Theological and Literary* (1871), *Modern Guides of English Thought* (1887), and *Contemporary Thought and Thinkers* (1894), which were more or less reprints or expansions of his work in periodicals, and a memoir of Bagehot prefixed to an ed. of his works.

HUXLEY, THOMAS HENRY (1825-1895).—Scientific writer, *s.* of an assistant master in a public school, was *b.* at Ealing. From childhood he was an insatiable reader. In his 13th year he became a medical apprentice, and in 1842 entered Charing Cross Hospital. Thereafter he was for a few months surgeon on board the *Victory* at Haslar, and was then appointed surgeon on H.M.S. *Rattlesnake*, which was sent to make surveys at Torres Strait. While in this position he made numerous observations, which he communicated to the Linnæan Society. In 1851 he became a Fellow of the Royal Society, and in 1854 Prof. of Natural History at the School of Mines. Henceforth his life was a very full one, divided between scientific investigation and public work. He was recognised as the foremost English biologist, and was elected Pres. of the Royal Society 1883. He served on the London School Board and on various Royal Commissions. His writings are in the main distinguished by a clearness, force, and charm which entitle them to a place in literature; and besides the addition which they made to the stock of human knowledge, they did much to diffuse a love and study of science. H. was a keen controversialist, contending for the strictly scientific view of all subjects as distinguished from the metaphysical or theological, and accordingly encountered much opposition, and a good deal of abuse. Nevertheless, he was not a materialist, and was in sympathy with the moral and tender aspects of Christianity. He was a strong supporter of the theory of evolution. Among the more eminent of his opponents were Bishop Wilberforce and Mr. Gladstone. His *pub.* works, including scientific communications, are very numerous. Among the more important are those on the *Medusæ, Zoological Evidences of Man's Place in Nature* (1863), *Elementary Lessons on Physiology* (1866), *Evolution and Ethics* (1893), *Collected Essays* (9 vols. 1893-4). He was also an admirable letter-writer, as appears from the *Life and Letters*, ed. by his son, and to him we owe the word, and almost the idea, "Agnostic."

INCHBALD, MRS. ELIZABETH (SIMPSON) (1753-1821).—Novelist and dramatist, *dau.* of a Suffolk farmer. In a romantic fit she left her home at the age of 16, and went to London, where she became acquainted with Inchbald the actor, who *m.* her in 1772. Seven years later her husband *d.*, and for the next ten years she was on the stage, chiefly in Scotland and Ireland. She produced many plays, including *Mogul Tale* (1784), *I'll Tell you What* (1785), *Appearance is against Them* (1785), *Such Things Are, The Married Man, The Wedding Day*, and two novels, *A Simple Story* (1791), and *Nature and Art* (1796), which have been frequently reprinted. She also made a collection of plays, *The Modern Theatre*, in 10 vols. Her life was remarkable for its simplicity and frugality, and a large part of her earnings was applied in the maintenance of a delicate sister. Though of a somewhat sentimental and romantic nature, she preserved an unblemished reputation.

INGELOW, JEAN (1820-1897).—Poetess and novelist, *dau.* of a banker at Boston, Lincolnshire, *pub.* three vols. of poems, of which perhaps the best known individual piece is "The High Tide on the Coast of Lincolnshire," and several successful novels, including *Off the Skelligs* (1872), *Fated to be Free* (1875), and *Sarah de Berenger* (1879). She also wrote excellent stories for children, *Mopsa the Fairy, Stories told to Children*, etc. Her poems show a considerable lyric gift.

INNES, COSMO (1798-1874).—Historian and antiquary, was called to the Scottish Bar in 1822, and was appointed Prof. of Constitutional Law and History in the Univ. of Edin. in 1846. He was the author of *Scotland in the Middle Ages* (1860), and *Sketches of Early Scottish History* (1861). He also ed. many historical MSS. for the Bannatyne and other antiquarian clubs. Much learning is displayed in his works.

INNES, THOMAS (1662-1744).—Historian, was descended from an old Roman Catholic family in Aberdeenshire. He studied in Paris at the Scots Coll., of which he became Principal. He was the author of two learned works, *Critical Essay on the Ancient Inhabitants of the Northern Parts of Britain* (1729), and *Civil and Ecclesiastical History of Scotland*, 80 *to* 818 (*pub.* by the Spalding Club, 1853).

IRELAND, WILLIAM HENRY (1777-1835).—Forger of Shakespeare manuscripts, *s.* of an antiquarian bookseller in London. He claimed to have discovered the MSS. in the house of a gentleman of fortune. The forgeries included various deeds, a Protestant confession of faith by Shakespeare, letters to Ann Hathaway,

Southampton, and others, a new version of *King Lear*, and a complete drama, *Vortigern and Rowena*. He completely deceived his *f.* and various men of letters and experts, but was detected by Malone, and the representation of *Vortigern* on the stage completed the exposure. I. then tried novel-writing, in which he failed. He *pub.* a confession in regard to the forgeries, in which he asserted that his *f.* had no part in the imposture, but had been completely deceived by it.

IRVING, EDWARD (1792-1834).—Theologian and orator, *b.* at Annan, Dumfriesshire, and *ed.* at Edin. Univ., for some years thereafter was engaged in teaching at Kirkcaldy. Ordained to the ministry of the Church of Scotland he became, in 1819, assistant to Dr. Chalmers in Glasgow, after which he went to the Scotch Church in Hatton Gardens, London, where he had an almost unprecedented popularity, his admirers including De Quincey, Coleridge, Canning, Scott, and others. The effect of his spoken oratory is not preserved in his writings, and was no doubt in a considerable degree due to his striking appearance and fine voice. He is described as "a tall, athletic man, with dark, sallow complexion and commanding features; long, glossy black hair, and an obvious squint." Soon after removing to a new church in Regent Square he began to develop his views relative to the near approach of the Second Advent; and his *Homilies on the Sacraments* involved him in a charge of heretical views on the person of Christ, which resulted in his ejection from his church, and ultimately in his deposition from the ministry. Thereafter his views as to the revival, as in the early Church, of the gifts of healing and of tongues, to which, however, he made no personal claim, underwent rapid development, and resulted in the founding of a new communion, the Catholic Apostolic Church, the adherents of which are commonly known as "Irvingites." Whether right or mistaken in his views there can be no doubt of the personal sincerity and nobility of the man. His *pub.* writings include *For the Oracles of God*, *For Judgment to Come*, and *The Last Days*, and contain many passages of majestic eloquence.

IRVING, WASHINGTON (1783-1859).—Essayist and historian, *b.* in New York, *s.* of William I. who had emigrated from Scotland. He was in his youth delicate, and his education was somewhat desultory, but his *f.* had a fine library, of which he had the run, and he was an omnivorous reader. In 1799 he entered a law office, but a threatening of consumption led to his going, in 1804, on a European tour in search of health. On his return in 1806 he was admitted to the Bar. He did not, however, prosecute law, but joined his brothers in business as a sleeping partner, while he devoted himself to literature. In 1807 he conducted *Salmagundi*, an amusing miscellany, and in 1809 appeared *A History of New York by Diedrich Knickerbocker*, a burlesque upon the old Dutch settlers, which has become a classic in America. He made in 1815 a second visit to Europe, from which he did not return for 17 years. In England he was welcomed by Thomas Campbell, the poet, who introduced him to Scott, whom he visited at Abbotsford in 1817. The following year the firm with which he was connected failed, and he had to look to literature for a livelihood. He produced *The Sketch-Book* (1819), which was, through the influence of Scott, accepted by

Murray, and had a great success on both sides of the Atlantic. In 1822 he went to Paris, where he began *Bracebridge Hall*, followed in 1824 by *Tales of a Traveller*. In 1826 Everett, the American minister at Madrid, invited him to come and assist him by making translations relative to Columbus, which opened up to him a new field hitherto little cultivated. The result was a series of fascinating historical and romantic works, beginning with *History of the Life and Voyages of Columbus* (1828), and including *The Conquest of Granada* (1829), *Voyages of the Companions of Columbus* (1831), *The Alhambra* (1832), *Legends of the Conquest of Spain* (1835), and *Mahomet and his Successors* (1849). Meanwhile he had returned to England in 1829, and to America in 1832. In 1842 he was appointed Minister to Spain, and in 1846 he finally returned to America. In the same year he *pub.* a *Life of Goldsmith*, and his great work, the *Life of Washington*, came out 1855-59, *Wolfert's Roost*, a collection of tales and essays, appeared in 1855. I. was never *m.*: in his youth he had been engaged to a girl who *d.*, and whose memory he faithfully cherished. His last years were spent at Sunnyside, an old Dutch house near his "sleepy hollow," and there he *d.* suddenly on Nov. 28, 1859. Though not, perhaps, a writer of commanding power or originality, I., especially in his earlier works, imparted by his style and treatment a singular charm to every subject he touched, and holds a high place among American men of letters, among whom he is the first who has produced what has, on its own merits, living interest in literature. He was a man of high character and amiable disposition.

JAMES I., KING OF SCOTLAND (1394-1437).—Poet, the third *s.* of Robert III., was *b.* at Dunfermline. In 1406 he was sent for safety and education to France, but on the voyage was taken prisoner by an English ship, and conveyed to England, where until 1824 he remained confined in various places, but chiefly in the Tower of London. He was then ransomed and, after his marriage to Lady Jane or Joan Beaufort, *dau.* of the Duke of Somerset, and the heroine of *The King's Quhair* (or Book), crowned at Scone. While in England he had been carefully *ed.*, and on his return to his native country endeavoured to reduce its turbulent nobility to due subjection, and to introduce various reforms. His efforts, however, which do not appear to have been always marked by prudence, ended disastrously in his assassination in the monastery of the Black Friars, Perth, in February, 1437. J. was a man of great natural capacity both intellectual and practical—an ardent student and a poet of no mean order. In addition to *The King's Quhair*, one of the finest love poems in existence, and *A Ballad of Good Counsel*, which are very generally attributed to him, he has been more doubtfully credited with *Peeblis to the Play* and *Christis Kirke on the Greene*.

JAMES, GEORGE PAYNE RAINSFORD (1801-1860).—Novelist and historical writer, *s.* of a physician in London, was for many years British Consul at various places in the United States and on the Continent. At an early age he began to write romances, and continued his production with such industry that his works reach to 100 vols. This excessive rapidity was fatal to his permanent reputation; but his books had considerable immediate popularity. Among them are *Richelieu* (1829), *Philip Augustus* (1831), *The Man at Arms* (1840), *The Huguenot* (1838), *The Robber, Henry of Guise* (1839), *Agincourt* (1844), *The King's Highway* (1840). In addition to his novels he wrote *Memoirs of Great Commanders*, a *Life of the Black Prince*, and other historical and biographical works. He held the honorary office of Historiographer Royal.

JAMESON, MRS. ANNA BROWNELL (MURPHY) (1794-1860).—Writer on art, *dau.* of Denis B. M., a distinguished miniature painter, *m.* Robert Jameson, a barrister (afterwards Attorney-General of Ontario). The union, however, did not turn out happily: a separation took place, and Mrs. J. turned her attention to literature, and specially to subjects connected with art. Among many other works she produced *Loves of the Poets* (1829), *Celebrated Female Sovereigns* (1831), *Beauties of the Court of Charles II.* (1833), *Rubens* (translated from the German), *Hand Book to the Galleries of Art, Early Italian Painters, Sacred and Legendary Art* (1848), etc. Her works show knowledge and discrimination and, though now in many respects superseded, still retain interest and value.

JEBB, SIR RICHARD CLAVERHOUSE (1841-1905).—*B.* at Dundee, and *ed.* at St. Columba's Coll., Dublin, Charterhouse, and Camb., at the last of which he lectured on the classics, and was in 1869 elected Public Orator. After being Prof. of Greek at Glasgow, he held from 1889 the corresponding chair at Camb., and for a time represented the Univ. in Parliament. He was one of the founders of the British School of Archæology at Athens. Among his works are *The Attic Orators, An Introduction to Homer, Lectures on Greek Poetry, Life of Richard Bentley* (English Men of Letters Series), and he ed. the works of Sophocles, and the Poems and Fragments of Bacchylides, discovered in 1896. J. was one of the most brilliant of modern scholars.

JEFFERIES, RICHARD (1848-1887).—Naturalist and novelist, *s.* of a farmer, was *b.* at Swindon, Wilts. He began his literary career on the staff of a local newspaper, and first attracted attention by a letter in the *Times* on the Wiltshire labourer. Thereafter he wrote for the *Pall Mall Gazette*, in which appeared his *Gamekeeper at Home*, and *Wild Life in a Southern County* (1879), both afterwards *repub.* Both these works are full of minute observation and vivid description of country life. They were followed by *The Amateur Poacher* (1880), *Wood Magic* (1881), *Round about a Great Estate* (1881), *The Open Air* (1885), and others on similar subjects. Among his novels are *Bevis*, in which he draws on his own childish memories, and *After London, or Wild England* (1885), a romance of the future, when London has ceased to exist. *The Story of My Heart* (1883) is an idealised picture of his inner life. J. *d.* after a painful illness, which lasted for six years. In his own line, that of depicting with an intense sense for nature all the elements of country and wild life, vegetable and animal, surviving in the face of modern civilisation, he has had few equals. Life by E. Thomas.

JEFFREY, FRANCIS (1773-1850).—Critic and political writer, *s.* of a legal official, *b.* in Edinburgh, *ed.* at the High School there, and at Glasgow and Oxf., where, however, he remained for a few months only. Returning to Edinburgh he studied law, and was called to the Bar in 1794. Brought up as a Tory, he early imbibed Whig principles, and this, in the then political state of Scotland, together with his strong literary tendencies, long hindered his professional advancement. Gradually, however, his ability, acuteness, and eloquence carried him to the front of his profession. He was elected Dean of the Faculty of Advocates in 1829 and, on the accession to power of the Whigs in 1830, became Lord Advocate, and had a large share in passing the Reform Bill, in so far as it related to Scotland. In 1832 he was elected M.P. for Edinburgh, and was raised to the Bench as Lord Jeffrey in 1834. His literary fame rests on his work in connection with the *Edinburgh Review*, which he edited from its commencement in 1802 until 1829, and to which he was a constant contributor. The founding of this periodical by a group of young men of brilliant talents and liberal sympathies, among whom were Brougham, Sydney Smith, and F. Horner, constituted the opening of a new epoch in the literary and political progress of the country. J.'s contributions ranged over literary criticism, biography, politics, and ethics and, especially in respect of the first, exercised a profound influence; he was, in fact, regarded as the greatest literary critic of his age, and although his judgments have been far from universally supported either by the event or by later critics, it remains true that he probably did more than any of his contemporaries to diffuse a love of literature, and to raise the standard of public taste in such matters. A selection of his papers, made by himself, was *pub.* in 4 vols. in 1844 and 1853. J. was a man of brilliant conversational powers, of vast information and sparkling wit, and was universally admired and beloved for the uprightness and amiability of his character.

JERROLD, DOUGLAS WILLIAM (1803-1857).—Dramatist and miscellaneous writer, *s.* of an actor, himself appeared as a child upon the stage. From his 10th to his 12th year he was at sea. He then became apprentice to a printer, devoting all his spare time to self-education. He early began to contribute to periodicals, and in his 18th year he was engaged by the Coburg Theatre as a writer of short dramatic pieces. In 1829 he made a great success by his drama of *Black-eyed Susan*, which he followed up by *The Rent Day*, *Bubbles of the Day*, *Time works Wonders*, etc. In 1840 he became ed. of a publication, *Heads of the People*, to which Thackeray was a contributor, and in which some of the best of his own work appeared. He was one of the leading contributors to *Punch*, in which *Mrs. Caudle's Curtain Lectures* came out, and from 1852 he ed. *Lloyd's Weekly Newspaper*. Among his novels are *St. Giles and St. James*, and *The Story of a Feather*. J. had a great reputation as a wit, was a genial and kindly man, and a favourite with his fellow *littérateurs*, who raised a fund of £2000 for his family on his death.

JESSE, JOHN HENEAGE (1815-1874).—Historical writer, *ed.* at Eton, was a clerk in the Admiralty. He wrote *Memoirs* of the

Court of England, of G. Selwyn and his contemporaries (1843), of the Pretender (1845), etc., and *Celebrated Etonians* (1875).

JEVONS, WILLIAM STANLEY (1835-1882).—Logician and economist, *b.* in Liverpool, *s.* of an iron merchant, his mother was the *dau.* of W. Roscoe (*q.v.*). He was *ed.* at the Mechanics Institute High School, Liverpool, and at University Coll., London. After studying chemistry for some time he received in 1853 the appointment of assayer to the mint at Sydney, where he remained until 1859, when he resigned his appointment, and came home to study mathematics and economics. While in Australia he had been a contributor to the *Empire* newspaper, and soon after his return home he *pub.* *Remarks on the Australian Goldfields*, wrote in various scientific periodicals, and from time to time *pub.* important papers on economical subjects. The position which he had attained as a scientific thinker and writer was recognised by his being appointed in 1863 tutor, and in 1866, Prof. of Logic, Political Economy, and Mental and Moral Philosophy in Owen's Coll., Manchester. In 1864 he *pub.* *Pure Logic* and *The Coal Question;* other works were *Elementary Lessons in Logic* (1870), *Principles of Science* (1874), and *Investigations in Currency and Finance* (1884), posthumously. His valuable and promising life was brought to a premature close by his being drowned while bathing. His great object in his writings was to place logic and economics in the position of exact sciences, and in all his work he showed great industry and care combined with unusual analytical power.

JEWSBURY, GERALDINE ENDSOR (1812-1880).—Novelist, wrote several novels, of which *Zoe*, *The Half-Sisters*, and *Constance Herbert* may be mentioned. She also wrote stories for children, and was a contributor to various magazines.

JOHN OF SALISBURY (1120?-1180?).—*B.* at Salisbury, studied at Paris. He became sec. to Theobald Archbishop of Canterbury, and retained the office under Becket. In 1176 he was made Bishop of Chartres. He wrote in Latin, in 8 books, *Polycraticus, seu De Nugis Curialium et Vestigiis Philosophorum* (on the Trifles of the Courtiers, and the Footsteps of the Philosophers). In it he treats of pastimes, flatterers, tyrannicide, the duties of kings and knights, virtue and vice, glory, and the right of the Church to remove kings if in its opinion they failed in their duty. He also wrote a Life of Anselm. He was one of the greatest scholars of the Middle Ages.

JOHNSON, LIONEL (1867-1902).—Poet and critic. *Ireland and other Poems* (2 vols.) (1897), *The Art of Thomas Hardy*, and miscellaneous critical works.

JOHNSON, SAMUEL (1649-1703).—Political writer, sometimes called "the Whig" to distinguish him from his great namesake. Of humble extraction, he was *ed.* at St. Paul's School and Camb., and took orders. He attacked James II. in *Julian the Apostate* (1682), and was imprisoned. He continued, however, his attacks on the Government by pamphlets, and did much to influence the public mind in favour of the Revolution. Dryden gave him a place in *Absalom and Achitophel* as "Benjochanan." After the Revolution he received a pension, but considered himself insufficiently rewarded by a Deanery, which he declined.

JOHNSON, SAMUEL (1709-1784).—Moralist, essayist, and lexicographer, *s.* of a bookseller at Lichfield, received his early education at his native town, and went in 1728 to Oxf., but had, owing to poverty, to leave without taking a degree. For a short time he was usher in a school at Market Bosworth, but found the position so irksome that he threw it up, and gained a meagre livelihood by working for a publisher in Birmingham. In 1735, being then 26, he *m.* Mrs. Porter, a widow of over 40, who brought him £800, and to whom he was sincerely attached. He started an academy at Ediol, near Lichfield, which, however, had no success, only three boys, one of whom was David Garrick (*q.v.*), attending it. Accordingly, this venture was given up, and J. in 1737 went to London accompanied by Garrick. Here he had a hard struggle with poverty, humiliation, and every kind of evil, always, however, quitting himself like the true man he was. He contributed to the *Gentleman's Magazine*, furnishing the parliamentary debates in very free and generally much improved form, under the title of "Debates of the Senate of Lilliput." In 1738 appeared *London*, a satire imitated from Juvenal which, *pub.* anonymously, attracted immediate attention, and the notice of Pope. His next work was the life of his unfortunate friend Savage (*q.v.*) (1744); and in 1747 he began his great *English Dictionary*. Another satire, *The Vanity of Human Wishes*, appeared in 1749, and in the same year *Irene*, a tragedy. His next venture was the starting of the *Rambler*, a paper somewhat on the lines of the *Spectator*; but, sententious and grave, it had none of the lightness and grace of its model, and likewise lacked its popularity. It was almost solely the work of J. himself, and was carried on twice a week for two years. In 1752 his wife, "his dear Tetty" *d.*, and was sincerely mourned; and in 1755 his *Dictionary* appeared. The patronage of Lord Chesterfield (*q.v.*), which he had vainly sought, was then offered, but proudly rejected in a letter which has become a classic. The work made him famous, and Oxf. conferred upon him the degree of M.A. He had become the friend of Reynolds and Goldsmith; Burke and others were soon added. The *Idler*, a somewhat less ponderous successor of the *Rambler*, appeared in 1758-60, and *Rasselas*, his most popular work, was written in 1759 to meet the funeral expenses of his mother, who then *d.* at the age of 90. At last the tide of his fortunes turned. A pension of £300 was conferred upon him in 1762, and the rest of his days were spent in honour, and such comfort as the melancholy to which he was subject permitted. In 1763 he made the acquaintance, so important for posterity, of James Boswell; and it was probably in the same year that he founded his famous "literary club." In 1764 he was introduced to Mr. Thrale, a wealthy brewer, and for many years spent much of his time, an honoured guest, in his family. The kindness and attentions of Mrs. T., described by Carlyle as "a bright papilionaceous creature, whom the elephant loved to play with, and wave to and fro upon his trunk," were a refreshment and solace to him. In 1765 his ed. of Shakespeare came out, and his last great work was the *Lives of the Poets*, in 10 vols. (1779-81). He had in 1775 *pub.* his *Journey to the Western Isles of Scotland*, an account of a tour made in the company of Boswell. His last years were darkened by the loss of friends such as Goldsmith and Thrale, and by an estrangement from Mrs. T., on her marriage with Piozzi, an Italian musician. Notwithstanding a lifelong and morbid fear of death, his last illness was borne with fortitude and calmness, soothed by the pious attentions of Reynolds and Burke, and he *d.* peacefully on December 13, 1784. He was buried in Westminster Abbey, and a monument in St. Paul's was erected by the "club." Statues of him were also erected in Lichfield and Uttoxeter. He had received from Oxf. and Dublin the degree of LL.D.

Though of rough and domineering manners, J. had the tenderest of hearts, and his house was for years the home of several persons, such as Mrs. Williams and Levett, the surgeon, who had no claim upon him but their helplessness and friendlessness. As Goldsmith aptly said, he "had nothing of the bear but his skin." His outstanding qualities were honesty and courage, and these characterise all his works. Though disfigured by prejudice and, as regards matters of fact, in many parts superseded, they remain, as has been said, "some excellent, all worthy and genuine works;" and he will ever stand one of the greatest and most honourable figures in the history of English literature. Boswell's marvellous *Life* has made J.'s bodily appearance, dress, and manners more familiar to posterity than those of any other man—the large, unwieldy form, the face seamed with scrofula, the purblind eyes, the spasmodic movements, the sonorous voice, even the brown suit, metal buttons, black worsted stockings, and bushy wig, the conversation so full of matter, strength, sense, wit, and prejudice, superior in force and sparkle to the sounding, but often wearisome periods of his written style. Of his works the two most important are the *Dictionary*, which, long superseded from a philological point of view, made an epoch in the history of the language, and the *Lives of the Poets*, many of them deformed by prejudice and singularly inadequate criticism, others, almost perfect in their kind, and the whole written in a style less pompous and more natural and lively than his earlier works.

SUMMARY.—*B.* 1709, *ed.* Oxf., usher and hack writer, starts academy at Ediol, goes to London 1737, reports parliamentary debates, *pub. London* 1738, *Life of Savage* 1744, began *Dictionary* 1747, *pub. Vanity of Human Wishes* and *Irene* 1749, conducts *Rambler* 1750-52, *pub. Dictionary* 1755, *Idler* appears 1758-60, *pub. Rasselas* 1759, receives pension 1762, became acquainted with Boswell 1763, *pub.* ed. of *Shakespeare* 1765, and *Lives of Poets* 1779-81, *d.* 1784.

Recollections, etc., by Mrs. Piozzi, Reynolds, and others, also *Johnsoniana* (Mrs. Napier, 1884), Boswell's *Life*, various ed., including that of Napier, 1884, and Birkbeck Hill, 1889.

JOHNSTON, ARTHUR (*c.* 1587-1641).—Poet in Latin, *b.* near Aberdeen, studied medicine at Padua, where he graduated. After living for about 20 years in France, he returned to England, became physician to Charles I., and was afterwards Rector of King's Coll.,

Aberdeen. He attained a European reputation as a writer of Latin poetry. Among his works are *Musæ Aulicæ* (1637), and a complete translation of the Psalms, and he ed. *Deliciæ Poetarum Scotorum*, a collection of Latin poetry by Scottish authors.

JOHNSTONE, CHARLES (1719?-1800).—Novelist. Prevented by deafness from practising at the Irish Bar, he went to India, where he was proprietor of a newspaper. He wrote one successful book, *Chrysal, or the Adventures of a Guinea*, a somewhat sombre satire, and some others now utterly forgotten.

JONES, EBENEZER (1820-1860).—Poet, wrote a good deal of poetry of very unequal merit, but at his best shows a true poetic vein. He was befriended by Browning and Rossetti. His chief work was *Studies of Sensation and Event* (1843). His most widely appreciated poems were "To the Snow," "To Death," and "When the World is Burning." He made an unhappy marriage, which ended in a separation.

JONES, ERNEST CHARLES (1819-1869).—Poet, novelist, and Chartist, *s.* of Major J., equerry to the Duke of Cumberland, afterwards King of Hanover, was *b.* at Berlin. He adopted the views of the Chartists in an extreme form, and was imprisoned for two years for seditious speeches, and on his release conducted a Chartist newspaper. Afterwards, when the agitation had died down, he returned to his practice as a barrister, which he had deserted, and also wrote largely. He produced a number of novels, including *The Maid of Warsaw, Woman's Wrongs*, and *The Painter of Florence*, also some poems, *The Battle Day* (1855), *The Revolt of Hindostan* (1857), and *Corayda* (1859). Some of his lyrics, such as *The Song of the Poor, The Song of the Day Labourers*, and *The Factory Slave*, were well known.

JONES, SIR WILLIAM (1746-1794).—Orientalist and jurist, was *b.* in London, and *ed.* at Harrow and Oxf. He lost his *f.*, an eminent mathematician, at 3 years of age. He early showed extraordinary aptitude for acquiring languages, specially those of the East, and learned 28. Devoting himself to the study of law he became one of the most profound jurists of his time. He was appointed one of the Judges in the Supreme Court of Bengal, knighted in 1783, and started for India, whence he never returned. While there, in addition to his judicial duties, he pursued his studies in Oriental languages, from which he made various translations. Among his original works are *The Enchanted Fruit*, and *A Treatise on the Gods of Greece, Italy, and India*. He founded the Bengal Asiatic Society. He left various works unfinished which, with his other writings, were *coll.* and ed. by Lord Teignmouth. He *d.* universally beloved and honoured at the early age of 48. His chief legal work was *The Institutes of Hindu Law or the Ordinances of Manu.*

JONSON, BEN OR BENJAMIN (1573-1637).—Poet and dramatist, was probably *b.* in Westminster. His *f.*, who *d.* before Ben was four, seems to have come from Carlisle, and the family to have originally belonged to Annandale. He was sent to Westminster School, for which he seems to have been indebted to the kindness of W. Camden (*q.v.*), who was one of the masters. His mother, meanwhile, had *m.* a bricklayer, and he was for a time put to that trade, but disliking it, he ran away and joined the army, fighting against the Spaniards in the Low Countries. Returning to England about 1592 he took to the stage, both as an actor and as a playwright. In the former capacity he was unsuccessful. In 1598, having killed a fellow-actor in a duel, he was tried for murder, but escaped by benefit of clergy. About the same time he joined the Roman Catholic Church, in which he remained for 12 years. It was in 1598 also that his first successful play, *Every Man in his Humour*, was produced, with Shakespeare as one of the players. *Every Man out of his Humour* (1599), *Cynthia's Revels* (1600), and *The Poetaster* (1601), satirising the citizens, the courtiers, and the poets respectively, followed. The last called forth several replies, the most notable of which was the *Satiromastix* (Whip for the Satirist) of Dekker (*q.v*), a severe, though not altogether unfriendly, retort, which J. took in good part, announcing his intention of leaving off satire and trying tragedy. His first work in this kind was *Sejanus* (1603), which was not very favourably received. It was followed by *Eastward Ho*, in which he collaborated with Marston and Chapman. Certain reflections on Scotland gave offence to James I., and the authors were imprisoned, but soon released. From the beginning of the new reign J. devoted himself largely to the writing of Court masques, in which he excelled all his contemporaries, and about the same time entered upon the production of the three great plays in which his full strength is shown. The first of these, *Volpone, or the Fox*, appeared in 1605; *Epicœne, or the Silent Woman* in 1609, and *The Alchemist* in 1610. His second and last tragedy, *Catiline*, was produced in 1611. Two years later he was in France as companion to the son of Sir W. Raleigh, and on his return he held up hypocritical Puritanism to scorn in *Bartholomew Fair*, which was followed in 1616 by a comedy, *The Devil is an Ass*. In the same year he *coll.* his writings—plays, poems, and epigrams—in a folio entitled his *Works*. In 1618 he journeyed on foot to Scotland, where he was received with much honour, and paid his famous visit to Drummond (*q.v.*) at Hawthornden. His last successful play, *The Staple of Newes*, was produced in 1625, and in the same year he had his first stroke of palsy, from which he never entirely recovered. His next play, *The New Inn*, was driven from the stage, for which in its rapid degeneracy he had become too learned and too moral. A quarrel with Inigo Jones, the architect, who furnished the machinery for the Court masques, lost him Court favour, and he was obliged, with failing powers, to turn again to the stage, for which his last plays, *The Magnetic Lady* and *The Tale of a Tub*, were written in 1632 and 1633. Town and Court favour, however, turned again, and he received a pension of £100; that of the best poets and lovers of literature he had always kept. The older poets were his friends, the younger were proud to call themselves, and be called by him, his sons. In 1637, after some years of gradually failing health, he *d.*, and was buried in Westminster Abbey. An admirer caused a mason to cut on the slab over his grave the well-known inscription, "O Rare Ben Jonson." He left a fragment, *The Sad Shepherd*. His works include a number of epigrams and translations, collections of poems (*Underwoods* and *The Forest*); in prose a book of short essays and notes on various subjects, *Discoveries*.

J. was the founder of a new style of English comedy, original, powerful, and interesting, but lacking in spontaneity and nature. His characters tend to become mere impersonations of some one quality or "humour," as he called it. Thus he is the herald, though a magnificent one, of decadence. He painted in general with a powerful, but heavy hand; in his masques, however, he often shows a singular gracefulness, especially in the lyrics which he introduces. His character, as given by Drummond, is not a particularly attractive one, "a great lover and praiser of himself, a contemner and scorner of others, given rather to lose a friend than a jest, jealous of every word and action of those about him, especially after drink . . . a dissembler of ill parts which reign in him, a bragger of some good that he wanteth . . . passionately kind and angry . . . oppressed with fantasy which hath ever mastered his reason." There must, however, have been far other qualities in a man who could command, as J. undoubtedly did, the goodwill and admiration of so many of the finest minds of his time. In person he was tall, swarthy, marked with small-pox, and in later years burly.

SUMMARY.—*B.* 1573, *ed.* Westminster School, serves in Low Countries, returns to England 1592, and takes to stage, kills actor in brawl 1598, a Romanist *c.* 1598-*c.* 1610, *Every Man in his Humour* 1598, *Every Man out of his Humour* 1599, and other plays till 1633, *coll.* works *pub.* 1616, visits Drummond 1618, loses and recovers Court favour, *d.* 1637.

Among the ed. of J.'s works may be mentioned those of Gifford (9 vols., 1816), re-issued (1875), selected plays Mermaid Series (3 vols., 1893-5), Morley (1884), and Symonds (1886). Lives and studies by Symonds (English Worthies), and Swinburne (1890).

JORTIN, JOHN (1698-1770).—Ecclesiastical historian, *ed.* at Camb., and entering the Church held various benefices, becoming in 1764 Archdeacon of London. He *pub.* *Remarks on Ecclesiastical History* (1751-54), a Life of Erasmus, and various miscellaneous pamphlets and tracts; 7 vols. of sermons appeared after his death. All his works show learning, and are written in a lively style.

JOWETT, BENJAMIN (1817-1893).—Scholar, was *b.* at Camberwell, and *ed.* at St. Paul's School and Balliol Coll., where he had a distinguished career, becoming Fellow 1838, Tutor 1840, and Master 1870. He held the Regius Professorship of Greek 1855-93 though for the first 10 years he was, owing to the opposition of his theological opponents in the Univ., deprived of a large part of the usual emoluments. He was a keen and formidable controversialist, and was usually found on what was, for the time, the unpopular side. His contribution (an essay on *The Interpretation of Scripture*) to the famous *Essays and Reviews*, which appeared in 1860, brought him into strong collision with powerful sections of theological opinion, to which he had already given offence by his commentaries on the *Epistles to the Thessalonians, Galatians, and Romans*. His views were, indeed, generally considered to be extremely latitudinarian. Latterly he exercised an extraordinary influence in the Univ., and was held in reverence by his pupils, many of whom have risen to eminence. His chief works are translations, with learned introductions, of *The Dialogues* of Plato, of Thucydides, and of the *Politics* of Aristotle. He also, in conjunction with Prof. Campbell, brought out an ed. of *The Republic* of Plato. He held the degree of LL.D. from the Univ. of Edin. (1884), and Camb. (1890), and Doctor of Theology of Leyden (1875).

JUDD, SYLVESTER (1813-1853).—Novelist, *b.* at Westhampton, Mass., studied for the ministry at Yale, and became a Unitarian pastor. He *pub.* *Philo,* a religious poem, followed by *Margaret, a Tale of the Real and the Ideal* (1845), *Richard Edney, A Rus-Urban Tale* (1850). He also produced some theological works. His work is very unequal, but often, as in *Margaret,* contains fine and true descriptive passages both of nature and character.

KAMES, HENRY HOME, LORD (1696-1782).—Miscellaneous writer, *s.* of Geo. H., of Kames, Berwickshire, was admitted an advocate in 1723, and raised to the Bench in 1752. In 1748 he *pub.* a collection of Decisions of the Court of Session. It is, however, on his philosophical and historical writings that his literary fame rests. His writings include *Essays on the Principles of Morality and Natural Religion* (1751), *The Elements of Criticism* (1762), in which he sought for principles based on the elements of human nature; *Sketches of the History of Man* (1774), and *Loose Hints on Education,* in which many modern views are anticipated. In all these works, while the style is stiff and crabbed, there is much original thought. Lord K. was also an eminent authority upon agriculture, on which he in 1777 *pub.* a work entitled *The Gentleman Farmer.*

KAVANAGH, JULIA (1824-1877).—Novelist, *dau.* of Morgan K., poet, and philologist, wrote many novels, of which the scene is usually in France, among which are *Madeleine* (1848), *Adèle,* and *Daisy Burns;* also biographical works, *Woman in France in the 18th Century* (1850), etc.

KAYE, SIR JOHN WILLIAM (1814-1876).—Historian and biographer, *s.* of a London solicitor, was *ed.* at Eton and Addiscombe. After serving for some time in the Bengal Artillery, he succeeded J. S. Mill as sec. to the political and secret department in the East India Office. His first literary work was a novel *pub.* in 1845, and he then began his valuable series of histories and biographies illustrative of the British occupation of India, including *The War in Afghanistan* (1851), and *The Sepoy War in India,* which he did not live to finish, and which was completed by G. B. Malleson as *The History of the Indian Mutiny* (6 vols., 1890); also histories of the East India Company and of Christianity in India, and Lives of Sir John Malcolm and other Indian soldiers and statesmen. All his writings are characterised by painstaking research, love of truth, and a style suited to the importance of his subjects. He was made K.C.S.I. in 1871.

KEARY, ANNIE (1825-1879).—Novelist, wrote some good novels, including *Castle Daly, A Doubting Heart,* and *Oldbury,* also books for children and educational works.

KEATS, JOHN (1795-1821).—Poet, *s.* of the chief servant at an inn in London, who *m.* his master's *dau.*, and *d.* a man of some substance. He was sent to a school at Enfield, and having meanwhile become an orphan, was in 1810 apprenticed to a surgeon at Edmonton. In 1815 he went to London to walk the hospitals. He was not, however, at all enthusiastic in his profession, and having become acquainted with Leigh Hunt, Hazlitt, Shelley, and others, he gave himself more and more to literature. His first work—some sonnets—appeared in Hunt's *Examiner*, and his first book, *Poems*, came out in 1817. This book, while containing much that gave little promise of what was to come, was not without touches of beauty and music, but it fell quite flat, finding few readers beyond his immediate circle. *Endymion*, begun during a visit to the Isle of Wight, appeared in 1818, and was savagely attacked in *Blackwood* and the *Quarterly Review*. These attacks, though naturally giving pain to the poet, were not, as was alleged at the time, the cause of his health breaking down, as he was possessed of considerable confidence in his own powers, and his claim to immortality as a poet. Symptoms of hereditary consumption, however, began to show themselves and, in the hope of restored health, he made a tour in the Lakes and Scotland, from which he returned to London none the better. The death soon after of his brother Thomas, whom he had helped to nurse, told upon his spirits, as did also his unrequited passion for Miss Fanny Brawne. In 1820 he *pub. Lamia and Other Poems*, containing *Isabella*, *Eve of St. Agnes*, *Hyperion*, and the odes to the *Nightingale* and *The Grecian Urn*, all of which had been produced within a period of about 18 months. This book was warmly praised in the *Edinburgh Review*. His health had by this time completely given way, and he was likewise harassed by narrow means and hopeless love. He had, however, the consolation of possessing many warm friends, by some of whom, the Hunts and the Brawnes, he was tenderly nursed. At last in 1821 he set out, accompanied by his friend Severn, on that journey to Italy from which he never returned. After much suffering he *d.* at Rome, and was buried in the Protestant cemetery there. The character of K. was much misunderstood until the publication by R. M. Milnes, afterwards Lord Houghton (*q.v.*), of his *Life and Letters*, which gives an attractive picture of him. This, together with the accounts of other friends, represent him as "eager, enthusiastic, and sensitive, but humorous, reasonable, and free from vanity, affectionate, a good brother and friend, sweet-tempered, and helpful." In his political views he was liberal, in his religious, indefinite. Though in his life-time subjected to much harsh and unappreciative criticism, his place among English poets is now assured. His chief characteristics are intense, sensuous imagination, and love of beauty, rich and picturesque descriptive power, and exquisitely melodious versification.

Life, Letters, etc., by R. M. Milnes (1848), *Poems and Letters* (Forman, 5 vols., 1900). Keats (Men of Letters Series, Colvin, 1887), etc. *Poems* (1817), *Endymion* (1818), *Lamia and Other Poems* (1820).

KEBLE, JOHN (1792-1866).—Poet and divine, *s.* of the Rev. John K., Vicar of Coln St. Aldwyn's, Gloucestershire, *b.* at Fairford in the same county, *ed.* by his *f.* and at Oxf., where he was elected a Fellow of Oriel Coll., and was for some years tutor and examiner in the Univ. His ideal life, however, was that of a country clergyman, and having taken orders in 1815, he became curate to his *f.* Meantime he had been writing *The Christian Year*, which appeared in 1827, and met with an almost unparalleled acceptance. Though at first anonymous, its authorship soon became known, with the result that K. was in 1831 appointed to the Chair of Poetry at Oxf., which he held until 1841. In 1833 his famous sermon on "national apostasy" gave the first impulse to the Oxf. movement of which, after the secession of Newman to the Church of Rome, he, along with Pusey, was regarded as the leader, and in connection with which he contributed several of the more important "tracts" in which were enforced "deep submission to authority, implicit reverence for Catholic tradition, firm belief in the divine prerogatives of the priesthood, the real nature of the sacraments, and the danger of independent speculation." His *f.* having *d.*, K. became in 1836 Vicar of Hursley, near Winchester, where he remained until his death. In 1846 he *pub.* another book of poems, *Lyra Innocentium.* Other works were a Life of Wilson, Bishop of Sodor and Man, and an ed. of the Works of Hooker. After his death appeared *Letters of Spiritual Counsel*, and 12 vols. of *Parish Sermons.* The literary position of K. must mainly rest upon *The Christian Year, Thoughts in Verse for the Sundays*, and *Holidays throughout the Year*, the object of which was, as described by the author, to bring the thoughts and feelings of the reader into unison with those exemplified in the Prayer Book. The poems, while by no means of equal literary merit, are generally characterised by delicate and true poetic feeling, and refined and often extremely felicitous language; and it is a proof of the fidelity to nature with which its themes are treated that the book has become a religious classic with readers far removed from the author's ecclesiastical standpoint and general school of thought. K. was one of the most saintly and unselfish men who ever adorned the Church of England, and, though personally shy and retiring, exercised a vast spiritual influence upon his generation.

Life by J. D. Coleridge (1869), another by Rev. W. Lock (1895).

KEIGHTLEY, THOMAS (1789-1872).—Historian, *ed.* at Trinity Coll., Dublin, wrote works on mythology and folklore, and at the request of Dr. Arnold of Rugby, a series of text-books on English, Greek, and other histories. His *History of Greece* was translated into modern Greek. Among his other books are *Fairy Mythology* (1850), and *Mythology of Ancient Greece and Italy*, and a work on Popular Tales and their transmission from one country to another.

KEITH, ROBERT (1681-1757).—Historian, *b.* in Kincardineshire, belonged to the family of the Earls Marischal, and was Bishop of Fife in the Scottish Episcopal Church. He was deeply versed in Scottish antiquities, and *pub. History of the Affairs of Church and State in Scotland* during the Reformation. He also compiled *A Catalogue of the Bishops of Scotland* (1755).

KELLY, HUGH (1739-1777).—Dramatist, *s.* of a Dublin publican, worked in London as a staymaker, 1760, and after ed.

various journals, wrote *Memoirs of a Magdalen* (1767). His play, *False Delicacy* (1768), had an extraordinary success, and was translated into French, German, and Portuguese. His other plays had no great success. He left off writing for the stage in 1774, and endeavoured to practise as a barrister, but without success. He also wrote political pamphlets, for which he received a pension from Government.

KEN, THOMAS (1637-1711).—Religious writer, *s.* of an attorney, was *b.* at Little Berkhampstead, *ed.* at Winchester and Oxf., and entering the Church received the living of Brightstone, Isle of Wight, where he composed his *Morning, Evening, and Midnight Hymns*, perhaps the most widely known of English hymns. These he was accustomed to sing daily to the lute. After holding other benefices he became Bishop of Bath and Wells, and a Chaplain to Charles II. He was one of the "Seven Bishops" sent to the Tower by James II. Refusing to take the oaths to William and Mary, he was deprived, and spent his later years in comparative poverty, though he found an asylum at Longleat with Lord Weymouth. Izaak Walton was his brother-in-law. K. wrote a manual of prayers for Winchester School, and other devotional works.

KENNEDY, JOHN PENDLETON (1795-1870).—Novelist, *b.* in Baltimore, was distinguished as a lawyer and politician. He wrote three novels, *Swallow Barn* (1832), *Horse Shoe Robinson* (1835), and *Rob of the Bowl* (1838), which give a vivid presentation of life in the Southern States.

KENNEDY, WALTER (*fl.* 1500).—*S.* of Lord K., was *ed.* at Glasgow, and is perhaps best known as Dunbar's antagonist in the *Flyting of Dunbar and Kennedy*. Other poems are *Praise of Aige* (Age), *Ane Ballat in Praise of Our Lady*, and *The Passion of Christ*. Most of his work is probably lost.

KILLIGREW, THOMAS (1612-1683).—Dramatist, *s.* of Sir Robert K., of Hanworth, was a witty, dissolute courtier of Charles II., and wrote nine plays, each in a different city. Of them the best known is *The Parson's Wedding*.

KING, HENRY (1592-1669).—Poet, *s.* of a Bishop of London, was *ed.* at Westminster School and Oxf. He entered the Church, and rose in 1642 to be Bishop of Chichester. The following year he was deprived, but was reinstated at the Restoration. He wrote many elegies on Royal persons and on his private friends, who included Donne and Ben Jonson. A selection from his *Poems and Psalms* was *pub.* in 1843.

KINGLAKE, ALEXANDER WILLIAM (1809-1891).—*B.* near Taunton, *ed.* at Eton and Camb., was called to the Bar in 1837, and acquired a considerable practice, which in 1856 he abandoned in order to devote himself to literature and public life. His first literary venture had been *Eothen*, a brilliant and original work of Eastern travel, *pub.* in 1844; but his *magnum opus* was his *Invasion of the Crimea*, in 8 vols. (1863-87), which is one of the most effective works of its class. It has, however, been charged with being too favourable to Lord Raglan, and unduly hostile to Napoleon III., for whom the author had an extreme aversion. Its great length is also against it.

KINGSFORD, WILLIAM (1819-1898).—Historian, *b.* in London, served in the army, and went to Canada, where he was engaged in surveying work. He has a place in literature for his *History of Canada* in 10 vols., a work of careful research, though not distinguished for purely literary merits.

KINGSLEY, CHARLES (1819-1875).—Novelist and historian, *s.* of a clergyman, was *b.* at Holne Vicarage near Dartmoor, but passed most of his childhood at Barnack in the Fen country, and Clovelly in Devonshire, *ed.* at King's Coll., London, and Camb. Intended for the law, he entered the Church, and became, in 1842, curate, and two years later rector, of Eversley, Hampshire. In the latter year he *pub.* *The Saints' Tragedy*, a drama, of which the heroine is St. Elizabeth of Hungary. Two novels followed, *Yeast* (1848) and *Alton Locke* (1850), in which he deals with social questions as affecting the agricultural labouring class, and the town worker respectively. He had become deeply interested in such questions, and threw himself heart and soul, in conjunction with F. D. Maurice and others, into the schemes of social amelioration, which they supported under the name of Christian socialism, contributing many tracts and articles under the signature of "Parson Lot." In 1853 appeared *Hypatia*, in which the conflict of the early Christians with the Greek philosophy of Alexandria is depicted; it was followed in 1855 by *Westward Ho*, perhaps his most popular work; in 1857 by *Two Years Ago*, and in 1866 by *Hereward the Wake*. *At Last* (1870), gave his impressions of a visit to the West Indies. His taste for natural history found expression in *Glaucus, or the Wonders of the Shore* (1855), and other works. *The Water Babies* is a story for children written to inspire love and reverence of Nature. K. was in 1860 appointed to the Professorship of Modern History at Camb., which he held until 1869. The literary fruit of this was *Roman and Teuton* (1864). In the same year he was involved in a controversy with J. H. Newman, which resulted in the publication by the latter of his *Apologia*. K., who had in 1869 been made a Canon of Chester, became Canon of Westminster in 1873. Always of a highly nervous temperament, his over-exertion resulted in repeated failures of health, and he *d.* in 1875. Though hot-tempered and combative, he was a man of singularly noble character. His type of religion, cheerful and robust, was described as "muscular Christianity." Strenuous, eager, and keen in feeling, he was not either a profoundly learned, or perhaps very impartial, historian, but all his writings are marked by a bracing and manly atmosphere, intense sympathy, and great descriptive power.

KINGSLEY, HENRY (1830-1876).—Novelist, brother of the above, *ed.* at King's Coll., London, and Oxf., which he left without graduating, and betook himself to the Australian gold-diggings, being afterwards in the mounted police. On his return in 1858 he devoted himself industriously to literature, and wrote a number of novels of much more than average merit, including *Geoffrey*

Hamlyn (1859), *The Hillyars and the Burtons* (1865), *Ravenshoe* (1861), and *Austin Elliot* (1863). Of these *Ravenshoe* is generally regarded as the best. In 1869 he went to Edinburgh to ed. the *Daily Review*, but he soon gave this up, and became war correspondent for his paper during the Franco-German War.

KINGSLEY, MARY HENRIETTA (1862-1900).—Traveller, *dau.* of George Henry K. (himself a traveller, and author of *South Sea Bubbles*, a very successful book), and niece of Charles K. (*q.v.*). She travelled in West Africa, where she made valuable observations and collections. Her *Travels in West Africa* is one of the most original and stimulating books of its class. Miss K. had a singular power of viewing the religious rites of savage peoples from their point of view. She was about to undertake another journey, but stopped to nurse Boer prisoners, and *d.* of fever.

KINGSTON, WILLIAM HENRY GILES (1814-1880).—Writer of tales for boys, *b.* in London, but spent much of his youth in Oporto, where his *f.* was a merchant. His first book, *The Circassian Chief*, appeared in 1844. His first book for boys, *Peter the Whaler*, was *pub.* in 1851, and had such success that he retired from business and devoted himself entirely to the production of this kind of literature, in which his popularity was deservedly great; and during 30 years he wrote upwards of 130 tales, including *The Three Midshipmen* (1862), *The Three Lieutenants* (1874), *The Three Commanders* (1875), *The Three Admirals* (1877), *Digby Heathcote*, etc. He also conducted various papers, including *The Colonist*, and *Colonial Magazine and East India Review*. He was also interested in emigration, volunteering, and various philanthropic schemes. For services in negotiating a commercial treaty with Portugal he received a Portuguese knighthood, and for his literary labours a Government pension.

KIRKLAND, JOSEPH (1830-1894).—Novelist, *b.* in New York State, was a lawyer in Chicago, then served in the war. He is remembered as the author of two very vivid and life-like novels of pioneer life in the Far West, *Illinois Zury* and *The McVeys*. Other works are *The Captain of Company K.* and *The Story of Chicago*.

KITTO, JOHN (1804-1854).—Biblical scholar, *s.* of a Cornish stonemason, was *b.* at Plymouth. At the age of 12 a fall led to his becoming totally deaf. From poverty and hardship he was rescued by friends, to whom his mental powers had become known, and the means of education were placed within his reach. By these he profited so remarkably that he became a valuable contributor to Biblical scholarship. He travelled much in the East in the pursuit of his favourite studies. Among his works are *Scripture Lands*, *Daily Bible Illustrations*, and *The Lost Senses* in 2 vols., one dealing with Deafness and the other with Blindness. He also ed. *The Pictorial Bible*, *The Journal of Sacred Literature*, *The Cyclopædia of Bible Literature*, and contributed to various periodicals. He received a pension of £100 from Government. In 1844 the Univ. of Giessen conferred upon him the degree of D.D.

KNIGHT, CHARLES (1791-1873).—Publisher and writer, *b.* at Windsor, where his *f.* was a bookseller. After serving his apprenticeship with him he went to London, and in 1823 started business as a publisher, and co-operated effectively with Brougham and others in connection with The Society for Diffusing Useful Knowledge. He was publisher for the Society, and issued *The Penny Magazine*, *Penny Cyclopædia*, *Pictorial History of England*, etc. He ed. with success *The Pictorial Shakespeare*, and was the author of a vol. of essays, *Once upon a Time*, an autobiography, *Passages from a Working Life* (1863), a *History of the Thirty Years' Peace*, which was completed by Miss Harriet Martineau, and various other works.

KNIGHT, HENRY GALLY (1786-1846).—A country gentleman of Yorkshire, *ed.* at Eton and Camb., was the author of several Oriental tales, *Ilderim, a Syrian Tale* (1816), *Phrosyne, a Grecian Tale*, and *Alashtar, an Arabian Tale* (1817). He was also an authority on architecture, and wrote various works on the subject, including *The Ecclesiastical Architecture of Italy*, and *The Normans in Sicily*, which brought him more reputation than his novels.

KNOLLES, RICHARD (1550?-1610).—Historian, *b.* at Coldashby, Northamptonshire, and *ed.* at Oxf., *pub.* in 1603 *The History of the Turks*, which went through many ed. Its principal value now is as a piece of fine English of its time, for which it is ranked high by Hallam. K. was master of a school at Sandwich. The History was continued by Sir Paul Rycaut (1628-1700).

KNOWLES, HERBERT (1798-1817).—Poet, author of the well-known *Stanzas written in Richmond Churchyard*, which gave promise of future excellence. But he *d.* a few weeks after he had been enabled, through the help of Southey to whom he had sent some of his poems, to go to Camb.

KNOWLES, JAMES SHERIDAN (1784-1862).—Dramatist, *s.* of James K., schoolmaster and lexicographer, was *b.* at Cork. He was the author of a ballad, *The Welsh Harper*, which had great popularity, and gained for him the notice of Hazlitt and others. For some years he studied medicine, which, however, he abandoned for literature, and produced several plays, including *Caius Gracchus* (1815), *Virginius* (1820), *The Hunchback* (1832), and *The Love Chase* (1837), in some of which he acted. He gave up the stage in 1843, became a preacher in connection with the Baptist communion, and enjoyed great popularity. He *pub.* two polemical works, *The Rock of Rome*, and *The Idol demolished by its own Priests*.

KNOX, JOHN (1505?-1572).—Reformer and historian, was *b.* near Haddington, and *ed.* at the Grammar School there and at Glasgow. He is believed to have had some connection with the family of K. of Ranfurly in Renfrewshire. The year of his birth was long believed to be 1505, but of late some writers have found reason to hold that he was really *b.* some years later, 1510 or even 1513. At Glasgow he was the pupil of John Major (*q.v.*), and became distinguished as a disputant. He is believed to have been ordained a priest about 1530, after which he went to St. Andrews and taught. About this time, however, there is a gap of 12 years or more, during which almost nothing is known of his life. About 1545 he came under the influence of George Wishart, who was burned as a heretic at St. Andrews in the following year, and embraced the Reformation principles, of which he became a champion on the Continent, in England, and finally and especially in Scotland. He joined the reforming party in St. Andrews in 1547, and was, much against his will, elected their minister. The next year he was made prisoner, sent to France, and condemned to the galleys, where he remained for nearly two years. For the next five years he was in England, chiefly at Newcastle and Berwick, where he was zealously engaged in propagating and defending the reformed doctrines. On the accession of Mary in 1553 K. escaped to the Continent, where he remained—at Dieppe, Frankfort on the Maine, and Geneva—until 1559. During this period, in addition to his pastoral and ecclesiastical activities, he wrote copiously, the best known of his works of that time being his *First Blast of the Trumpet against the Monstrous Regiment [government] of Women.* The first, it proved also the last, as he never produced the other two which he promised or threatened. He finally returned to Scotland in 1559, and was at once the chief actor and the chief narrator of the crowded and pregnant events which culminated in the abdication of Queen Mary and the establishment of Protestantism in Scotland. As minister of the High Church of Edin. K. was at the centre of events, which he probably did more to mould than any other man. As Carlyle says, "He is the one Scotchman to whom, of all others, his country and the world owe a debt." Here, after his long battle with principalities and powers, and spiritual wickedness in high places, his triumphs, and disappointments, after growing weakness and becoming "weary of the world," he *d.* on November 24, 1572. His place in literature he has by virtue of his *Historie of the Reformation in Scotland.* It extends from 1558-67. Its language is much more English than that spoken and written in Scotland at the time. It is of the highest historical value, and in style terse, vigorous, with flashes of a quiet, somewhat saturnine humour, and of vivid description—the writing of a great man of action dealing with the events in which he had been the leading actor. His own figure and that of the Queen are those round which the drama turns. The leading features of his character were courage and intense earnestness. "Here," said the Regent Morton, "lies a man who never feared the face of man." And with all his sternness there was in him a vein of cordial friendliness and humour. He has been accused of intolerance, and of harshness in his dealings with the Queen. But as Carlyle has said, as regards the second accusation, "They are not so coarse, these speeches; they seem to me about as fine as the circumstances would permit. It was unfortunately not possible to be polite with the Queen of Scotland unless one proved untrue to the nation."

Lives by M'Crie (1812), and Prof. Hume Brown (1895). *Works* ed. by D. Laing.

KNOX, VICESIMUS (1752-1821).—Essayist, etc., *ed.* at Oxf., took orders, and became Head Master of Tunbridge School. He *pub. Essays Moral and Literary* (1778), and compiled the formerly well-known *Elegant Extracts*, often reprinted.

KNOX, WILLIAM (1789-1825).—Poet, *s.* of a farmer in Roxburghshire, wrote several books of poetry, *The Lonely Hearth, Songs of Israel, Harp of Zion,* etc., which gained him the friendship of Scott. He fell into dissipated habits, was latterly a journalist in Edin., and *d.* at 36.

KYD, THOMAS (1558-1595).—Dramatist, *s.* of a London scrivener, *ed.* at Merchant Taylor's School, appears to have led the life of hardship so common with the dramatists of his time, was for a short time imprisoned for "treasonable and Atheistic views," and made translations from the French and Italian. His drama, *The Spanish Tragedy* (1594), had extraordinary popularity, and was translated into Dutch and German. Some of the scenes are believed to have been contributed by another hand, probably by Ben Jonson. He also produced a play on the story of Hamlet, not now in existence, and he may have written the first draft of *Titus Andronicus.* Other plays which have been attributed to him are *The First Part of Jeronimo* (1605), *Cornelia* (1594), *The Rare Triumphs of Love and Fortune,* and *The Tragedye of Solyman and Perseda* (1599). But, although one of the best known dramatists in his day, very little is now certain either as to his personal history or his works.

LAIDLAW, WILLIAM (1780-1845).—Poet, *s.* of a border farmer, became steward and amanuensis to Sir W. Scott, and was the author of the beautiful and well-known ballad, *Lucy's Flittin'.*

LAING, DAVID (1793-1878).—Antiquary, *s.* of a bookseller in Edin., with whom he was in partnership until his appointment, in 1837, as librarian of the Signet Library. He ed. many of the publications of the Bannatyne Club, of which he was sec. (1823-61). He was also Honorary Prof. of Antiquities to the Royal Scottish Academy. Among the more important works which he ed. were *Baillie's Letters and Journals* (1841-2), *John Knox's Works* (1846-64), and the poems of Sir D. Lyndsay, Dunbar, and Henryson.

LAING, MALCOLM (1762-1818).—Was a country gentleman in Orkney. He completed Henry's *History of Great Britain,* and wrote a *History of Scotland from the Union of the Crowns to the Union of the Kingdoms* (1802). He was an assailant of the authenticity of the Ossianic poems, and wrote a dissertation on the Participation of Mary Queen of Scots in the Murder of Darnley. He did much to improve the agriculture of Orkney.

LAMB, LADY CAROLINE (1785-1828).—Novelist, *dau.* of 3rd Earl of Bessborough, *m.* the Hon. William Lamb, afterwards Lord Melbourne and Prime Minister. She wrote three novels, which, though of little literary value, attracted much attention. The first of these, *Glenarvon* (1816), contained a caricature portrait of Lord Byron, with whom the authoress had shortly before been infatuated. It was followed by *Graham Hamilton* (1822), and *Ada Reis* (1823). Happening to meet the hearse conveying the remains of Byron, she became unconscious, and fell into mental alienation, from which she never recovered.

LAMB, CHARLES (1775-1834).—Essayist and poet, was *b.* in London, his *f.* being confidential clerk to Samuel Salt, one of the benchers of the Inner Temple. After being at a school in the neighbourhood, he was sent by the influence of Mr. Salt to Christ's Hospital, where he remained from 1782-89, and where he formed a lifelong friendship with Coleridge. He was then for a year or two in the South Sea House, where his elder brother John was a clerk. Thence he was in 1792 transferred to the India House, where he remained until 1825, when he retired with a pension of two-thirds of his salary. Mr. Salt *d.* in 1792, and the family, consisting of the *f.*, mother, Charles, and his sister Mary, ten years his senior, lived together in somewhat straitened circumstances, John, comparatively well off, leaving them pretty much to their own resources. In 1796 the tragedy of L.'s life occurred. His sister Mary, in a sudden fit of insanity, killed her mother with a table-knife. Thenceforward, giving up a marriage to which he was looking forward, he devoted himself to the care of his unfortunate sister, who became, except when separated from him by periods of aberration, his lifelong and affectionate companion—the "Cousin Bridget" of his essays. His first literary appearance was a contribution of four sonnets to Coleridge's *Poems on Various Subjects* (1796). Two years later he *pub.*, along with his friend Charles Lloyd, *Blank Verse*, the little vol. including *The Old Familiar Faces*, and others of his best known poems, and his romance, *Rosamund Gray*, followed in the same year. He then turned to the drama, and produced *John Woodvil*, a tragedy, and *Mr. H.*, a farce, both failures, for although the first had some echo of the Elizabethan music, it had no dramatic force. Meantime the brother and sister were leading a life clouded by poverty and by the anxieties arising from the condition of the latter, and they moved about from one lodging to another. L.'s literary ventures so far had not yielded much either in money or fame, but in 1807 he was asked by W. Godwin (*q.v.*) to assist him in his "Juvenile Library," and to this he, with the assistance of his sister, contributed the now famous *Tales from Shakespeare*, Charles doing the tragedies and Mary the comedies. In 1808 they wrote, again for children, *The Adventures of Ulysses*, a version of the *Odyssey*, *Mrs. Leicester's School*, and *Poetry for Children* (1809). About the same time he was commissioned by Longman to ed. selections from the Elizabethan dramatists. To the selections were added criticisms, which at once brought him the reputation of being one of the most subtle and penetrating critics who had ever touched the subject. Three years later his extraordinary power in this department was farther exhibited in a series of papers on Hogarth and Shakespeare, which appeared in Hunt's *Reflector*. In 1818 his scattered contributions in prose and verse were *coll.* as *The Works of Charles Lamb*, and the favour with which they were received led to his being asked to contribute to the *London Magazine* the essays on which his fame chiefly rests. The name "Elia" under which they were written was that of a fellow-clerk in the India House. They appeared from 1820-25. The first series was printed in 1823, the second, *The Last Essays of Elia*, in 1833. In 1823 the L.s had left London and taken a cottage at Islington, and had practically adopted Emma Isola, a young orphan, whose presence brightened their lives until her marriage in 1833 to E. Moxon, the publisher. In 1825 L. retired, and lived at Enfield and Edmonton. But his health was impaired, and his sister's attacks of mental alienation were ever becoming more frequent and of longer duration. During one of his walks he fell, slightly hurting his face. The wound developed into erysipelas, and he *d.* on December 29, 1834. His sister survived until 1847.

The place of L. as an essayist and critic is the very highest. His only rival in the former department is Addison, but in depth and tenderness of feeling, and richness of fancy L. is the superior. In the realms of criticism there can be no comparison between the two. L. is here at once profound and subtle, and his work led as much as any other influence to the revival of interest in and appreciation of our older poetry. His own writings, which are self-revealing in a quite unusual and always charming way, and the recollections of his friends, have made the personality of Lamb more familiar to us than any other in our literature, except that of Johnson. His weaknesses, his oddities, his charm, his humour, his stutter, are all as familiar to his readers as if they had known him, and the tragedy and noble self-sacrifice of his life add a feeling of reverence for a character we already love.

Life and Letters and Final Memorials by Talfourd, also Memoir by B. W. Proctor and A. Ainger prefixed to ed. of *Works* (1883-88). Life, Works, and Letters of Charles and Mary Lamb, in 9 vols., E. V. Lucas, and 12 vols. ed. W. Macdonald.

LANDON, LETITIA ELIZABETH (1802-1838).—Poetess, *dau.* of an army agent, was *b.* in London. She was a prolific and, in her day, remarkably popular writer, but she wrote far too easily and far too much for permanent fame. Many of her poems appeared in the *Literary Gazette*, and similar publications, but she *pub.* separately *The Fate of Adelaide* (1821), *The Improvisatrice* (1824), *The Troubadour* (1825), *The Venetian Bracelet* (1829), etc. She also wrote a few novels, of which *Ethel Churchill* was the best, and a tragedy *Castruccio Castracani* (1837). She *m.* a Mr. Maclean, Governor of one of the West African Colonies, where, shortly after her arrival, she was found dead from the effects of an overdose of poison, which it was supposed she had taken as a relief from spasms to which she was subject. She was best known by her initials, L. E. L., under which she was accustomed to write.

LANDOR, WALTER SAVAGE (1775-1864).—Poet and miscellaneous author, *s.* of a physician, was *b.* at Ipsley Court, Warwick, the property of his mother, and *ed.* at Rugby and Oxf., where he earned the nickname of "the mad Jacobin," and whence he was rusticated. His whole long life thereafter was a series of quarrels, extravagances, and escapades of various kinds, the result of his violent prejudices, love of paradox, and ungovernable temper. He quarrelled with his *f.*, his wife, most of his relations, and nearly all his friends, ran through a large fortune, and ended his days in Italy supported by a pension granted by his brothers. Yet he was not devoid of strong affections and generosity. His earliest publication was *Poems* (1795); *Gebir* (1798), an epic, had little success, but won for him the friendship of Southey. In 1808 he went to Spain to take part in the war against Napoleon, and saw some service. His first work to attract attention was his powerful tragedy of *Don Julian* (1811). About the same time he *m.* Miss Julia Thuillier—mainly, as would appear, on account of her "wonderful golden hair"—and purchased the estate of Llantony Abbey, Monmouthshire, whence, after various quarrels with the local authorities, he went to France. After a residence of a year there, he went in 1815 to Italy, where he lived until 1818 at Como, which, having insulted the authorities in a Latin poem, he had to leave. At Florence, which was his residence for some years, he commenced his famous *Imaginary Conversations*, of which the first two vols. appeared 1824, the third 1828, fourth and fifth 1829. Other works were *The Examination of W. Shakespeare touching Deer-stealing* (1834), *Pericles and Aspasia* (1836), *Pentameron* (1837), *Hellenics* (1847), and *Poemata et Inscriptiones* (1847). He quarrelled finally with his wife in 1835, and returned to England, which, however, he had to leave in 1858 on account of an action for libel arising out of a book, *Dry Sticks Fagoted.* He went to Italy, where he remained, chiefly at Florence, until his death. L. holds one of the highest places among the writers of English prose. His thoughts are striking and brilliant, and his style rich and dignified.

Works ed. C. G. Crump, 10 vols.

LANE, EDWARD WILLIAM (1801-1876).—Arabic scholar, *s.* of a prebendary of Hereford, where he was *b.*, began life as an engraver, but going to Egypt in search of health, devoted himself to the study of Oriental languages and manners, and adopted the dress and habits of the Egyptian man of learning. He *pub. Manners and Customs of the Modern Egyptians* (1836), which remains a standard authority, and a translation of *The Thousand and One Nights* (1838-40) (Arabian Nights). What was intended to be the great work of his life, his *Arabic Lexicon*, was left unfinished at his death, but was completed by his nephew, Prof. S. L. Poole. L. was regarded as the chief European Orientalist of his day.

LANGHORNE, JOHN (1735-1779).—Poet, *s.* of a clergyman, was *b.* at Kirkby Stephen; having taken orders, he was for two years a curate in London, and from 1776 Rector of Blagdon, Somerset, and Prebendary of Wells. He is chiefly remembered as being the translator, jointly with his brother, Rev. William L., of *Plutarch's Lives*, but in his day he had some reputation as a poet, his chief work in poetry being *Studley Park* and *Fables of Flora.* In his *Country Justice* (1774-77) he dimly foreshadows Crabbe, as in his descriptive poems he dimly foreshadows Wordsworth. He was twice married, and both of his wives *d.* in giving birth to a first child.

LANGLAND, WILLIAM (OR WILLIAM OF LANGLEY) (1330?-1400?).—Poet. Little can be gleaned as to his personal history, and of that little part is contradictory. In a note of the 15th century written on one MS. he is said to have been *b.* in Oxfordshire, the *s.* of a freeman named Stacy de Rokayle, while Bale, writing in the 16th century, makes his name Robert (certainly an error), and says he was *b.* at Cleobury Mortimer in Shropshire. From his great poem, *Piers the Plowman*, it is to be gathered that he was bred to the Church, and was at one time an inmate of the monastery at Great Malvern. He *m.*, however, and had a *dau.*, which, of course, precluded him from going on to the priesthood. It has further been inferred from his poem that his *f.*, with the help of friends, sent him to school, but that on the death of these friends the process of education came to an end, and he went to London, living in a little house in Cornhill and, as he says, not only *in* but *on* London, supporting himself by singing *requiems* for the dead. "The tools I labour with . . . [are] *Paternoster*, and my primer *Placebo*, and *Dirige*, and my *Psalter*, and my seven Psalms." References to legal terms suggest that he may have copied for lawyers. In later life he appears to have lived in Cornwall with his wife and *dau.* Poor himself, he was ever a sympathiser with the poor and oppressed. His poem appears to have been the great interest of his life, and almost to the end he was altering and adding to, without, however, improving it. The full title of the poem is *The Vision of Piers Plowman.* Three distinct versions of it exist, the first *c.* 1362, the second *c.* 1377, and the third 1393 or 1398. It has been described as "a vision of Christ seen through the clouds of humanity." It is divided into nine dreams, and is in the unrhymed, alliterative, first English manner. In the allegory appear such personifications as Meed (worldly success), Falsehood, Repentance, Hope, etc. Piers Plowman, first introduced as the type of the poor and simple, becomes gradually transformed into the Christ. Further on appear Do-well, Do-bet, Do-best. In this poem, and its additions, L. was able to express all that he had to say of the abuses of the time, and their remedy. He himself stands out as a sad, earnest, and clear-sighted onlooker in a time of oppression and unrest. It is thought that he may have been the author of a poem, *Richard the Redeless:* if so he was, at the time of writing, living in Bristol, and making a last remonstrance to the misguided King, news of whose death may have reached him while at the work, as it stops in the middle of a paragraph. He is not much of an artist, being intent rather on delivering his message than that it should be in a perfect dress. Prof. Manley, in the *Cambridge History of English Literature*, advances the theory that *The Vision* is not the work of one, but of several writers, W. L. being therefore a dramatic, not a personal name. It is supported on such grounds as differences in metre, diction, sentence structure, and the diversity of view on social and ecclesiastic matters expressed in different parts of the poem.

LANIER, SIDNEY (1842-1881).—Miscellaneous writer, *s.* of a lawyer of Huguenot descent, was *b.* at Macon, Georgia. He had a varied career, having been successively soldier, shopman, teacher, lawyer, musician, and prof. His first literary venture was a novel, *Tiger Lilies* (1867). Thereafter he wrote mainly on literature, his works including *The Science of English Verse* (1881), *The English Novel* (1883), and *Shakespeare and his Forerunners* (1902); also some poems which have been greatly admired, including "Corn," "The Marshes of Glynn," and "The Song of the Chattahoochee"; ed. of Froissart, and the Welsh *Mabinogion* for children. He worked under the shadow of serious lung trouble, which eventually brought about his death.

LARDNER, DIONYSIUS (1793-1859).—Scientific writer, *s.* of a solicitor in Dublin, and *b.* there, was intended for the law, but having no taste for it, he entered Trinity Coll., Dublin, and took orders, but devoted himself to literary and scientific pursuits, and became a contributor to the *Edinburgh Review*, and various Encyclopædias. In 1827 he was appointed Prof. of Natural Philosophy and Astronomy in the Univ. of London (afterwards Univ. Coll.), and in 1829 began his great work, *The Cabinet Cyclopædia*, which was finished in 133 vols. 20 years later. In his literary undertakings, which included various other schemes of somewhat similar character, he was eminently successful, financially and otherwise. He lived in Paris from 1845 until his death.

LATIMER, HUGH (1485-1555).—Reformer and divine, *s.* of a Leicestershire yeoman, went to Camb. in 1500, and became Fellow of Clare Hall. Taking orders, he was at first a defender of the ancient faith, but convinced by the arguments of Bilney, embraced the reformed doctrines. He was called to appear before Wolsey, but dismissed on subscribing certain articles. His opposition to the Pope, and his support of the King's supremacy, brought him under the notice of Henry, and he was appointed chaplain to Anne Boleyn, and in 1535 Bishop of Worcester. For preaching in favour of the reformed doctrines he was twice imprisoned in the Tower, 1539 and 1546, and on the former occasion resigned his bishopric, which he declined to resume on the accession of Edward VI. On the accession of Mary he was with Ridley, Bishop of London, thrown into prison (1554), and on October 16, 1555, burned at Oxf. His words of encouragement to his fellow-martyr are well known, "Be of good comfort, Master Ridley, and play the man; we shall this day light such a candle by God's grace in England as I trust shall never be put out." He holds his place in English literature by virtue of his sermons—especially that on *The Ploughers*—which, like himself, are outspoken, homely, and popular, with frequent touches of kindly humour.

LAUDER, SIR THOMAS DICK (1784-1848).—Novelist and miscellaneous writer, *s.* of a Scottish baronet, wrote two novels, *Lochandhu* (1825), and *The Wolf of Badenoch* (1827), but is best known for his *Account of the Great Floods in Morayshire in* 1829. He also wrote *Legendary Tales of the Highlands*, and contributed to scientific journals and magazines.

LAW, WILLIAM (1686-1761).—Divine, *s.* of a grocer at Kingscliffe, Northamptonshire, was *ed.* at Camb., and in 1727 became tutor to the *f.* of Edward Gibbon, the historian. About 1728 he *pub.* his best known book, *A Serious Call to a Devout and Holy Life*, a work which has had a profound influence upon the religious life of England, largely owing to the impression which it produced upon such minds as those of Dr. Johnson, the Wesleys, and others. In 1737 he became a student of the works of Jacob Bœhmen, the German mystic, and devoted himself largely to the exposition of his views.

The theological position of L. was a complicated one, combining High Churchism, mysticism, and Puritanism: his writings are characterised by vigorous thought, keen logic, and a lucid and brilliant style, relieved by flashes of bright, and often sarcastic, humour. His work attacking Mandeville's *Fable of the Bees* (1723) is perhaps that in which these qualities are best displayed in combination. He retired in 1740 to Kingscliffe, where he had founded a school for 14 girls.

LAWRENCE, GEORGE ALFRED (1827-1876).—Novelist, was a barrister. He wrote several novels, of which one—*Guy Livingstone* (1857)—had great popularity. On the outbreak of the American Civil War he went to America with the intention of joining the Confederate Army, but was taken prisoner and only released on promising to return to England.

LAYAMON (*fl.* 1200).—Metrical historian, the *s.* of Leovenath. All that is known of him is gathered from his own writings. He was a priest at Ernley (now Areley Regis), Worcestershire. In his day the works of Geoffrey of Monmouth and Wace, in French, were the favourite reading of the educated, and "it came to him in mind" that he would tell the story of *Brut* in English verse. He set out in search of books and, founding his poem on the earlier writers, he added so much from his own knowledge of Welsh and West of England tradition that while Wace's poem consists of 15,000 lines, his extends to 32,000. Among the legends he gives are those of *Locrine*, *Arthur*, and *Lear*. The poem is in the old English unrhymed, alliterative verse, and "marks the revival of the English mind and spirit."

LAYARD, SIR AUSTIN HENRY (1817-1894).—Explorer of Nineveh, *b.* at Paris, *s.* of a Ceylon civilian. After spending some years in the office of a London solicitor, he set out in search of employment in Ceylon, but passing through Western Asia, became interested in the work of excavating the remains of ancient cities. Many of his finds—human-headed bulls, etc.—were sent to the British Museum. Two books—*Nineveh and its Remains* (1848-49), and *The Ruins of Nineveh and Babylon* (1853)—brought him fame, and on his return home he received many honours, including the freedom of the City of London, the degree of D.C.L. from Oxf., and the Lord Rectorship of Aberdeen Univ. He entered Parliament, where he sat as a Liberal. He held the offices of Under-Foreign Sec. (1861-66), and Chief Commissioner of Works (1868-69), and was Ambassador to Spain 1869, and Constantinople 1877; and on his retirement in 1878 he was made G.C.B. He was a very successful excavator, and described his work brilliantly, but he was no great linguist, and most of the deciphering of the inscriptions was done by Sir H. Rawlinson. His last work was *Early Adventures in Persia, etc.*, and he left an autobiography, *pub.* in 1903. He also wrote on Italian art.

LEAR, EDWARD (1812-1888).—Artist and miscellaneous author, *b.* in London, and settled in Rome as a landscape painter. He was an indefatigable traveller, and wrote accounts, finely illustrated, of his journeys in Italy, Greece, and Corsica. His best known works are, however, his *Book of Nonsense* (1840) (full of wit and *good* sense), *More Nonsense Rhymes* (1871), and *Laughable Lyrics* (1876). L. had also a remarkable faculty for depicting birds.

LECKY, WILLIAM EDWARD HARTPOLE (1838-1903).—Historian, the *s.* of a landed gentleman of Carlow, was *b.* near Dublin, and *ed.* at Cheltenham and Trinity Coll., Dublin. Originally intended for the Church, he devoted himself to a literary career. His first work of importance was *Leaders of Public Opinion in Ireland* (1861) (essays on Swift, Flood, Grattan, and O'Connell). The study of Buckle's *History of Civilisation* to some extent determined the direction of his own writings, and resulted in the production of two important works, *History of the Rise and Influence of the Spirit of Rationalism in Europe* (1865), and *History of European Morals from Augustus to Charlemagne* (1869), both remarkable for learning, clearness, and impartiality. Both, however, gave rise to considerable controversy and criticism. His principal work is *The History of England in the Eighteenth Century* (1878-90). Characterised by the same sterling qualities as his preceding books, it deals with a subject more generally interesting, and has had a wide acceptance. His view of the American war, and the controversies which led to it, is more favourable to the English position than that of some earlier historians. Other works are *Democracy and Liberty* (1896), and *The Map of Life* (1899). Though of warm Irish sympathies, L. was strongly opposed to Home Rule. He sat in Parliament for his Univ. from 1895 until his death. He received many academical distinctions, and was a Corresponding Member of the Institute of France, and one of the original members of the Order of Merit.

LEE, NATHANIEL (1653?-1692).—Dramatist, *s.* of a clergyman at Hatfield, was *ed.* at Westminster School and Camb. After leaving the Univ. he went to London, and joined the stage both as actor and author. He was taken up by Rochester and others of the same dissolute set, led a loose life, and drank himself into Bedlam, where he spent four years. After his recovery he lived mainly upon charity, and met his death from a fall under the effects of a carouse. His tragedies, which, with much bombast and frequent untrained flights of imagination, have occasional fire and tenderness, are generally based on classical subjects. The principal are *The Rival Queens, Theodosius*, and *Mithridates.* He also wrote a few comedies, and collaborated with Dryden in an adaptation of *Œdipus*, and in *The Duke of Guise.*

LEE, SOPHIA (1750-1824), LEE, HARRIET (1757-1851).—Novelists and dramatists, *dau.* of John L., an actor, were the authors of various dramatic pieces and novels. By far their most memorable work was *The Canterbury Tales*, 5 vols. (1797-1805) which, with the exception of two, *The Young Lady's* and *The Clergyman's*, were all by Harriet. The most powerful of them, *Kruitzner*, fell into the hands of Byron in his boyhood, and made so profound an impression upon him that, in 1821, he dramatised it under the title of *Werner, or the Inheritance.* The authoress also adapted it for the stage as *The Three Strangers.* The tales are in general remarkable for the ingenuity of their plots. Harriet lived to the age of 94.

preserving to the last her vigour of mind and powers of conversation. Godwin made her an offer of marriage to which, however, his religious opinions presented an insuperable barrier. Sophia's chief work was *The Chapter of Accidents*, a comedy, which had a great run, the profits of which enabled the sisters to start a school at Bath, which proved very successful, and produced for them a competence on which they were able to retire in their later years.

LE FANU, JOSEPH SHERIDAN (1814-1873).—Novelist, *s.* of a Dean of the Episcopal Church of Ireland, and grand-nephew of Richard Brinsley Sheridan, was *ed.* at Trinity Coll., Dublin, and became a contributor and ultimately proprietor of the *Dublin University Magazine*, in which many of his novels made their first appearance. Called to the Bar in 1839, he did not practise, and was first brought into notice by two ballads, *Phaudrig Croohoore* and *Shamus O'Brien*, which had extraordinary popularity. His novels, of which he wrote 12, include *The Cock and Anchor* (1845), *Torlough O'Brien* (1847), *The House by the Churchyard* (1863), *Uncle Silas* (perhaps the most popular) (1864), *The Tenants of Malory* (1867), *In a Glass Darkly* (1872), and *Willing to Die* (posthumously). They are generally distinguished by able construction, ingenuity of plot, and power in the presentation of the mysterious and supernatural. Among Irish novelists he is generally ranked next to Lever.

LEIGHTON, ROBERT (1611-1684).—Divine, was the *s.* of Alexander L., physician, and writer on theology, who, on account of his anti-prelatic books, was put in the pillory, fined, and had his nose slit and his ears cut off. Robert was *ed.* at Edin., after which he resided for some time at Douay. Returning to Scotland he received Presbyterian ordination, and was admitted minister of Newbattle, near Edin. In 1653 he was appointed Principal and Prof. of Divinity in the Univ. of Edin., which offices he held until 1662 when, having separated himself from Presbyterianism, he was appointed Bishop of Dunblane, under the new Episcopal establishment. He repeatedly but unsuccessfully endeavoured to bring about an ecclesiastical union in Scotland on the basis of combining the best elements in each system. Discouraged by his lack of success in his well-meant efforts, he offered in 1665 to resign his see, but was persuaded by Charles II. to remain in it, and in 1669 was promoted to be Archbishop of Glasgow, from which position, wearied and disappointed, he finally retired in 1674, and lived with his widowed sister, Mrs. Lightmaker, at Broadhurst Manor, Sussex. On a visit to London he was seized with a fatal illness, and *d.* in the arms of his friend, Bishop Burnet, who says of him, " he had the greatest elevation of soul, the largest compass of knowledge, the most mortified and heavenly disposition that I ever saw in mortal." His sermons and commentaries, all *pub.* posthumously, maintain a high place among English religious classics, alike for thought and style. They consist of his *Commentary on St. Peter*, *Sermons*, and *Spiritual Exercises*, *Letters*, *etc.* His *Lectures and Addresses* in Latin were also *pub.*

LELAND, CHARLES GODFREY (1824-1903).—American humorist, *b.* at Philadelphia, was *ed.* at Princeton, and in Europe. In his travels he made a study of the gipsies, on whom he wrote more than one book. His fame rests chiefly on his *Hans Breitmann Ballads* (1871), written in the *patois* known as Pennsylvania Dutch. Other books of his are *Meister Karl's Sketch-book* (1855), *Legends of Birds* (1864), *Algonquin Legends* (1884), *Legends of Florence* (1895), and *Flaxius, or Leaves from the Life of an Immortal.*

LELAND OR LEYLAND, JOHN (1506-1552).—Antiquary, *b.* in London, and *ed.* at St. Paul's School and at Camb., Oxf., and Paris. He was a good linguist, and one of the first Englishmen to acquire Greek, and he was likewise acquainted with French, Italian, Spanish, Welsh, and Anglo-Saxon. He became chaplain and librarian to Henry VIII., from whom he received the Rectory of Poppeling, near Calais, and in 1533 the appointment of King's Antiquary. Soon afterwards he was permitted to do his work in France by deputy, and was commissioned to go over England in search of documents and antiquities; and on the strength of this made his famous tour, which lasted for about six years. He was able to do something to stem the destruction of manuscripts on the dissolution of the monasteries, and made vast collections of documents and information regarding the monuments and general features of the country, which, however, he was unable fully to digest and set in order. They formed, nevertheless, an almost inexhaustible quarry in which succeeding workers in the same field, such as Stow, Camden, and Dugdale, wrought. In his last years he was insane, and hence none of his collections appeared in his lifetime. His *Itinerary* was, however, at length *pub.* by T. Hearne in 9 vols. (1710-12), and his *Collectanea* in 6 vols. (1715).

LEMON, MARK (1809-1870).—Journalist and humorist, *b.* in London, wrote many theatrical pieces, and a few novels, of which the best is *Falkner Lyle*, others being *Leyton Hall*, and *Loved at Last.* He also wrote stories for children, lectured and gave public readings, and contributed to various periodicals. He is best known as one of the founders and, from 1843 until his death, the ed. of *Punch.* His *Jest Book* appeared in 1864.

LENNOX, CHARLOTTE (RAMSAY) (1720-1804).—Was *b.* in New York, of which her *f.*, Colonel Ramsay, was Governor. She wrote a novel, *The Female Quixote* (1752), which had considerable vogue in its day. Her other writings—novels, translations, and a play—are now forgotten. She was befriended by Dr. Johnson. Mrs. Thrale (*q.v.*) said that "everybody admired Mrs. L., but nobody liked her."

LESLIE, OR LESLEY, JOHN (1527-1596).—Historian, studied at Aberdeen and Paris, at the former of which he became, in 1562, Prof. of Canon Law. He was a Privy Councillor 1565, and Bishop of Ross 1566, and was the confidential friend of Queen Mary, who made him her ambassador to Queen Elizabeth. He was thrown into the Tower for his share in promoting a marriage between Mary and the Duke of Norfolk, whence being released on condition of leaving England, he went first to Paris and then to Rome, where he busied himself on behalf of his mistress. He became Vicar-General of the diocese of Rouen in 1579, and *d.* at the monastery of Guirtenburg near Brussels. While in England he wrote in Scots vernacular his

History of Scotland from the death of James I. (where Boece left off) to his own time. At Rouen he rewrote and expanded it in Latin (1575), from which it was re-translated into Scots by James Dalrymple in 1596.

L'ESTRANGE, SIR ROGER (1616-1704).—Journalist and pamphleteer, youngest *s.* of a Norfolk baronet, was probably at Camb., and in 1638 took arms for the King. Six years later he was captured, imprisoned in Newgate, and condemned to death. He, however, escaped, endeavoured to make a rising in Kent, and had to flee to Holland, where he was employed in the service of Charles II. On receiving a pardon from Cromwell he returned to England in 1653. In view of the Restoration he was active in writing on behalf of monarchy, and in 1663 *pub. Considerations and Proposals in order to Regulating of the Press*, for which he was appointed Surveyor of Printing-Presses and Licenser of the Press, and received a grant of the sole privilege of printing public news. His first newspaper, *The Intelligencer*, appeared in the same year, and was followed by *The News* and the *City Mercury, or Advertisements concerning Trade.* Thereafter his life was spent in ed. newspapers and writing political pamphlets in support of the Court and against the Whigs and Dissenters. In 1685 he was knighted. His controversies repeatedly got him into trouble, and after the Revolution he lost his appointments, and was more than once imprisoned. In addition to his political writings he translated *Æsop's Fables*, Seneca's *Morals*, and Cicero's *Offices*. His *Æsop* contains much from other authors, including himself. In his writings he was lively and vigorous, but coarse and abusive.

LEVER, CHARLES JAMES (1806-1872).—Novelist, *b.* at Dublin, and *ed.* at Trinity Coll. there. He studied medicine at Göttingen, and practised at various places in Ireland. In 1837 he contributed to the *Dublin University Magazine* his first novel, *Harry Lorrequer*, and the immediate and wide acceptance which it found decided him to devote himself to literature. He accordingly followed it with *Charles O'Malley* (1840), his most popular book. After this scarcely a year passed without an addition to the list of his light-hearted, breezy, rollicking stories, among which may be mentioned *Jack Hinton* (1842), *Tom Burke of Ours*, *Arthur O'Leary*, and *The Dodd Family Abroad*. *The O'Donoghue* and *The Knight of Gwynne* (1847) are more in the nature of historical romances. In 1864 he contributed to *Blackwood's Magazine* a series of miscellaneous papers, *Cornelius O'Dowd on Men, Women, and Things in General.* L.'s life was largely spent abroad. After practising his profession in Brussels 1840-42 he returned to Dublin to ed. the *Dublin University Magazine*, which he did until 1845, after which he went to Italy, settled at Florence, and thereafter was British Consul successively at Spezzia and Trieste, at the latter of which he *d.* He continued to produce novels up to the end of his life. Among the later ones are *Sir Brooke Fosbrooke*, *The Bramleighs of Bishop's Folly*, and *Lord Kilgobbin* (1872).

LEWES, GEORGE HENRY (1817-1878).—Philosopher and miscellaneous writer, *b.* in London, and *ed.* at Greenwich, and in

Jersey and Brittany. His early life was varied; he tried law, commerce, and medicine successively, and was then for two years in Germany, on returning from which he tried the London stage, and eventually settled down to journalism, writing for the *Morning Chronicle*, for the *Penny Encyclopædia*, and various periodicals. Thereafter he ed. the *Leader* (1851-54), and the *Fortnightly Review* (which he founded) (1865-66). His articles deal with an extraordinary variety of subjects—criticism, the drama, biography, and science, both physical and mental. His chief works are *The History of Philosophy from Thales to Comte*, *Comte's Philosophy of the Sciences* (1853), *The Psychology of Common Life* (1859), *Studies in Animal Life* (1862), *Problems of Life and Mind* (1873-79). L. was an exceptionally able dramatic critic, and in this department he produced *Actors and the Art of Acting* (1875), and a book on the Spanish Drama. By far his greatest work, however, is his *Life and Works of Goethe* (1855), which remains the standard English work on the subject, and which by the end of the century had, in its German translation, passed into 16 ed. He also wrote two novels, *Ranthorpe* (1847), and *Rose, Blanche, and Violet* (1848), neither of which attained any success. In his writings he is frequently brilliant and original; but his education and training, whether in philosophy or biology, were not sufficiently thorough to give him a place as a master in either. L.'s life was in its latter section influenced by his irregular connection with Miss Evans ("George Eliot"), with whom he lived for the last 24 years of it, in close intellectual sympathy. To his appreciation and encouragement were largely due her taking up prose fiction.

LEWIS, SIR GEORGE CORNEWALL (1806-1863).—Scholar and statesman, *s.* of Sir Thomas F. L., a Radnorshire baronet, was *ed.* at Eton and Oxf. He studied law, was called to the Bar in 1831, and entered Parliament in 1847, where his intellect and character soon gained him great influence. After serving on various important commissions and holding minor offices, he became Chancellor of the Exchequer 1855-58, Home Sec. 1859-61, and War Sec. 1861-63. His official labours did not prevent his entering into profound and laborious studies, chiefly in regard to Roman history, and the state of knowledge among the ancients. In his *Inquiry into the Credibility of Ancient Roman History* (1855), he combated the methods and results of Niebuhr. Other works are *On the Use and Abuse of Political Terms*, *Authority in Matters of Opinion*, *The Astronomy of the Ancients*, and a *Dialogue on the best Form of Government*. The somewhat sceptical turn of his mind led him to sift evidence minutely, and the labour involved in his wide range of severe study and his public duties no doubt shortened his valuable life.

LEWIS, MATTHEW GREGORY (1775-1818).—Novelist, *s.* of Matthew L., Deputy Sec. in the War Office, was *ed.* at Westminster and Oxf. Thereafter he went to Germany. From his childhood tales of witchcraft and the supernatural had a powerful fascination for him, and in Germany he had ample opportunities for pursuing his favourite study, with the result that at the age of 20 he became the author of *The Monk*, a tale in which the supernatural and the horrible predominate to an unprecedented extent, and from which he is known as "Monk L." The same characteristic appears in all his works, among which may be mentioned *Tales of Terror* (1779), *Tales of Wonder* (to which Sir W. Scott contributed), and *Romantic Tales* (1808). Though affected and extravagant in his manners, L. was not wanting in kindly and generous feelings, and in fact an illness contracted on a voyage to the West Indies to inquire into and remedy some grievances of the slaves on his estates there was the cause of his death.

LEYDEN, JOHN (1775-1811).—Poet and Orientalist, *b.* at Denholm, Roxburghshire, gave early evidence of superior ability, and his *f.*, who was a shepherd, destined him for the Church. He accordingly entered the Univ. of Edin., where he had a brilliant career, showing a special aptitude for languages and natural history. In 1800 he became a licentiate of the Church, but continued his scientific and linguistic studies, and also began to write. In 1799 he had *pub.* a sketch of the *Discoveries and Settlements of the Europeans in Northern and Western Africa*, and he contributed to Scott's *Minstrelsy of the Scottish Border*, and to "Monk" Lewis's *Tales of Wonder*. His enthusiasm for Oriental learning led to application being made on his behalf to Government for some situation which would make his acquirements available for the public service, but the only opening which could be obtained was that of a ship's surgeon. By extraordinary exertions L. qualified himself for this in a few months, and set sail for the East, after finishing his poem, *Scenes of Infancy*. Soon after his arrival at Madras his health gave way, and after some time passed in Prince of Wales Island he visited the Malay Peninsula, and some of the East Indian Islands, collecting vast stores of linguistic and ethnographical information, on which was founded his great *Dissertation on the Indo-Persian, Indo-Chinese, and Dekkan Languages* (1807). Soon after this L. was appointed a prof. in the Bengal Coll., and a little later a judge in Calcutta. In 1811 he accompanied the Governor-General, Lord Minto, to Java. His health, however, had been undermined by his almost superhuman exertions, and immediately after landing he contracted a fever, of which he *d.* in three days at the early age of 36. Two Oriental works translated by him, *Sejârah Malâyu* (Malay Annals) and *Commentaries of Baber* were *pub.* respectively in 1821 and 1826.

LIDDELL, HENRY GEORGE (1811-1898).—Historian, etc. *Ed.* at Charterhouse and Christ Church, Oxf., of which in 1855 he became Dean. He wrote a *History of Ancient Rome* (1855), and, along with R. Scott, *pub.* a *Greek-English Lexicon* (1843).

LIDDON, HENRY PARRY (1829-1890).—Divine, *s.* of a captain in the navy, was *b.* at North Stoneham, Hants, and *ed.* at King's Coll. School, London, and Oxf. He took orders 1853, was Vice-Principal of Cuddesdon Theological Coll. 1854-59, Prebendary of Salisbury 1864, and Canon of St. Paul's 1870. He was also Ireland Prof. of Exegesis at Oxf. 1870-82. In 1866 he delivered his Bampton Lectures on *The Divinity of Our Lord*, and came to be recognised as one of the ablest and most eloquent representatives of the High Church party. His sermons in St. Paul's were among the leading features of the religious life of London. L. was an ardent protagonist in the various controversies of his time bearing upon ecclesiastical and moral questions.

LIGHTFOOT, JOSEPH BARBER (1828-1889).—Theologian and scholar, *b.* at Liverpool, and *ed.* at King Edward's School, Birmingham, and Camb., entered the Church, and was successively Hulsean Prof. of Divinity 1861, Chaplain to Queen Victoria 1862, member of the New Testament Company of Revisers 1870-80, Margaret Prof. of Divinity, Camb., 1875, and Bishop of Durham 1879. He was probably the greatest scholar of his day in England, especially as a grammarian and textual critic. Among his works are *Commentaries* on several of the minor Pauline epistles, a fragmentary work on the Apostolic Fathers, *Leaders in the Northern Church* (1890), and *The Apostolic Age* (1892).

LILLO, GEORGE (1693-1739).—Dramatist, of Dutch descent, was *b.* in London, succeeded his *f.* in business as a jeweller, in which he had good speed, and devoted his leisure to the composition of plays in the line of what was known as the "domestic drama." He wrote in all seven of these, among which are *The London Merchant, or the History of George Barnewell*, acted 1731, *The Christian Hero* (1735), and *Fatal Curiosity* (1736). He was a friend of Fielding, who said of him that "he had the spirit of an old Roman joined to the innocence of a primitive Christian."

LINDSAY, OR LYNDSAY, SIR DAVID (1490-1555).—Scottish poet and satirist, *s.* of David L. of Garmylton, near Haddington, was *b.* either there or at The Mount in Fife, and *ed.* at St. Andrews. Early in life he was at the Court of James IV., and on the King's death was appointed to attend on the infant James V., whose friend and counsellor he remained, though his advice was, unhappily for his country, not always given heed to. In 1529 he was knighted and made Lyon King at Arms. He was employed on various missions to the Emperor Charles V., and to Denmark, France, and England. He was always in sympathy with the people as against the nobles and the clergy, and was their poet, with his words in their mouths. He favoured the Reformers, and was one of those who urged Knox to become a preacher. He did not, however, adhere to the reformed congregation, and *d.* at least nominally in the Roman Church. Yet he lashed the vices of the clergy as they had never been lashed before, and only escaped their vengeance by the protection of the King, who also condoned the severities directed against himself. His latter days were spent at The Mount, where he *d.* His chief writings are *The Dreme*, written 1528, *The Complaynt to the King* (1529), *The Testament and Complaynt of our Soverane Lord's Papyngo* (Parrot) (1530), *Ane Pleasant Satyre of the Three Estaitis*, *A Dialogue betwixt Experience and a Courtier* (1552), *The Monarchy* (1554), and *The History of Squyer Meldrum*. L. was a true poet, gifted with fancy, humour, and a powerful satiric touch and a love of truth and justice. He had a strong influence in turning the minds of the common people in favour of the Reformation.

Works ed. by Chalmers (3 vols., 1806), and D. Laing (3 vols., 1879).

LINDSAY, OR LINDESAY, ROBERT (1500?-1565?).—Historian, Laird or tenant of Pitscottie, Fife, wrote a history entitled *The Chronicles of Scotland*, intended as a continuation of that of Boece. It deals with the period 1436-1515, and though often inaccurate in detail, is often vivid and quaint.

LINGARD, JOHN (1771-1851).—Historian, *b.* at Winchester of humble Roman Catholic parentage, was in 1782 sent to the English Coll. at Douay, whence he escaped from the revolutionaries in 1793, and returning to England, went to Crookhall Coll., near Durham, and afterwards to Ushaw. Ordained a priest in 1795, he became Vice-Pres. and Prof. of Philosophy at the latter coll. In 1806 he *pub. The Antiquities of the Anglo-Saxon Church*, and while a missioner at Hornby, Lancashire, began his *History of England to the Accession of William and Mary* (8 vols., 1819-30). In the preparation of this work L. had access to material hitherto *unpub.*, and not available for Protestant historians, such as documents in the Vatican and other Roman Catholic sources, and was consequently able to throw new light on various parts of his subject. The work was attacked by various writers from the Protestant standpoint. L. replied to his critics with the result that it is now generally admitted that the history, while in parts coloured by the theological and political point of view of the author, is generally an impartial and valuable work, and it remains a leading authority on the Reformation period viewed from the side of the enlightened Roman Catholic priesthood. This opinion is supported by the fact that the Ultramontane party among the Roman Catholics regarded the book as a dangerous one in respect of the interests of their Church.

LINTON, MRS. ELIZA LYNN (1822-1898).—Novelist and miscellaneous writer, *dau.* of a clergyman, settled in London in 1845, and next year produced her first novel, *Azeth, the Egyptian; Amymone* (1848), and *Realities* (1851), followed. None of these had any great success, and she then joined the staff of the *Morning Chronicle*, and *All the Year Round*. In 1858 she *m.* W. J. Linton, an eminent wood-engraver, who was also a poet of some note, a writer upon his craft, and a Republican. In 1867 they separated in a friendly way, the husband going to America, and the wife devoting herself to novel-writing, in which she attained wide popularity. Her most successful works were *The True History of Joshua Davidson* (1872), *Patricia Kemball* (1874), and *Christopher Kirkland*. She was a severe critic of the "new woman."

LISTER, THOMAS HENRY (1800-1842).—Novelist, *ed.* at Westminster and Camb., was latterly the first Registrar-General for England and Wales. He wrote several novels, among which are *Granby* (1826), *Herbert Lacy* (1828), *Arlington* (1832). He was also the author of a Life of Clarendon.

LITHGOW, WILLIAM (1582-1645).—Traveller, *b.* at Lanark, claimed at the end of his various peregrinations to have tramped 36,000 miles on foot. Previous to 1610 he had visited Shetland, Switzerland, and Bohemia. In that year he set out for Palestine and Egypt. His next journey, 1614-16, was in Tunis and Fez; but his last, 1619-21, to Spain, ended unfortunately in his apprehension at Malaga and torture as a spy. He gave an account of his travels in *Rare Adventures and Paineful Peregrinations*, and wrote *The Siege of Breda, The Siege of Newcastle*, and *Poems*.

LIVINGSTONE, DAVID (1813-1873).—Missionary explorer, *b.* at Blantyre, Lanarkshire, spent the years between 10 and 24 as an operative in a cotton mill there. Becoming interested in foreign missions he qualified himself, and entering the service of the London Missionary Society, set out in 1846 to South Africa. He subsequently made journeys into the interior, which ultimately developed into his great pioneering and exploration expeditions, in which he discovered Lake Ngami 1849, and the river Zambesi 1851. In 1856 he visited England, *pub.* his *Missionary Travels* (1857), and retired from the service of the London Missionary Society. He was Consul at Quilimane 1858-64, and in 1858 commanded an expedition for exploring Eastern and Central Africa, in the course of which he discovered Lakes Shirwa and Nyassa 1859. Again visiting England he *pub.* his second book, *The Zambesi and its Tributaries* (1865). Returning to Africa he organised an expedition to the Nile basin, discovered Lake Bangweolo, explored the cannibal country, enduring terrible sufferings and dangers, from which he was rescued just in time by H. M. Stanley. His last journey was to discover the sources of the Nile, but it proved fatal, as he *d.* at a village in Ilala. His remains were brought home and buried in Westminster Abbey. L. was a man of indomitable courage, and of a simple nobility of character. His writings are plain, unadorned statements of his work and experiences. He ranks among the greatest explorers and philanthropists. The diary which he kept was *pub.* as *Last Journals of David Livingstone in Central Africa* (1874). His view of his duty in the circumstances in which he found himself was to be a pioneer opening up new ground, and leaving native agents to work it up.

LLOYD, ROBERT (1733-1764).—Poet, *ed.* at Westminster and Camb., *pub. The Actor* (1760), a poem which had considerable popularity, some miscellaneous verses, and a comic opera, *The Conscious Lovers* (1764). He was a friend of Churchill, who showed him much kindness in his frequent misfortunes; and on hearing of C.'s death he took to bed, and soon *d.*, apparently of a broken heart.

LOCKE, DAVID ROSS (PETROLEUM V. NASBY) (1833-1888).—Humorist, *b.* in New York State. His political satires really influenced opinion during the war. He was a printer and then a journalist, and his writings include *Swingin' round the Cirkle, Struggles of P. V. Nasby, Nasby in Exile*, and two novels, *A Paper City* and *The Demagogue*.

LOCKE, JOHN (1632-1704).—Philosopher, *s.* of a land-steward, was *b.* at Wrington, near Bristol, and *ed.* at Westminster School and Oxf. In 1660 he became lecturer on Greek, in 1662 on Rhetoric, and in 1664 he went as sec. to an Embassy to Brandenburg. While a student he had turned from the subtleties of Aristotle and the schoolmen, had studied Descartes and Bacon, and becoming attracted to experimental science, studied medicine, and practised a little in Oxf. At the same time his mind had been much exercised by questions of morals and government, and in 1667 he wrote his *Essay on Toleration.* In the same year he became known to Lord Ashley (afterwards 1st Earl of Shaftesbury), in whose house he went to reside. Here he made the acquaintance of Buckingham, Halifax, and other leading men of the time, and was entrusted by Ashley with the education of his *s.*, and afterwards of his grandson, the famous 3rd Earl of Shaftesbury (*q.v.*). He was also employed by him to draw up a constitution for the new colony of Carolina, the provisions of which in regard to religion were regarded as too liberal and were, at the instance of the Established Church, departed from. In 1672 when Ashley became Chancellor he bestowed upon L. the office of Sec. of Presentations, and afterwards a post at the Board of Trade. In 1675 L. graduated M.B., and in the same year went for the benefit of his health, which had always been delicate, to Montpelier, where there was then a celebrated medical school, and subsequently to Paris, where he became acquainted with most of the eminent Frenchmen of the day. Recalled by Shaftesbury in 1679 he returned to England but, his patron having in 1682 been obliged to take refuge in Holland from a prosecution for high treason, he followed him there. In consequence of this he became obnoxious to the Government, and was in 1684 deprived of his studentship at Christ Church. Shaftesbury having *d.* in Holland, L. remained there until the Revolution, when he returned to England in the fleet which carried the Princess of Orange. He was now in favour with Government, and had the offer of diplomatic employment which, on account of his health, he declined, but was appointed a Commissioner of Appeals. In 1698 he was an adviser of the Government on the question of the coinage, and was made a member of the newly instituted Council on Trade, which position he resigned in 1700. During his last years he lived with Sir Francis and Lady Masham at Oates in Essex, where Lady M., who was a *dau.* of Ralph Cudworth (*q.v.*), and an old friend, assiduously tended his last years. The services of L. to his country in civil and religious matters were various and great; but it is upon his philosophical writings, and chiefly on his *Essay on the Human Understanding* (1690) that his fame rests. It is divided into four books, of which the first treats of innate ideas (the existence of which he denies), the second traces the origin of ideas, the third deals with language, and the fourth lays down the limits of the understanding. Other works of his are *Thoughts concerning Education* (1693), *On the Conduct of the Understanding* (*pub.* posthumously), *The Reasonableness of Christianity* (1695), *Treatise on Government*, and *Letters on Toleration.* If not a very profound or original philosopher L. was a calm, sensible, and reasonable writer, and his books were very influential on the English thought of his day, as well as on the French philosophy of the next century. His style is plain and clear, but lacking in brightness and variety.

Lives by Lord King (1829), and Bourne (1876). *Works* ed. by Prof. A. C. Fraser (1894). *See* also T. H. Green's Introduction to Hume (1874).

LOCKER-LAMPSON, FREDERICK (1821-1895).—Poet, *s.* of the sec. of Greenwich Hospital, held appointments in Somerset House and the Admiralty. He wrote a number of clever *vers de societé*, which were *coll.* as *London Lyrics* (1857). He also compiled *Lyra Elegantiarum*, an anthology of similar verse by former authors, and *Patchwork*, a book of extracts, and wrote an autobiography, *My Confidences* (1896).

LOCKHART, JOHN GIBSON (1794-1854).—Novelist and biographer, *s.* of a minister of the Church of Scotland of good family, was *b.* at Cambusnethan, Lanarkshire, and *ed.* at Glasgow and Oxf. He studied law at Edin., and was called to the Scottish Bar in 1816, but had little taste for the profession. Having, however, already tried literature (he had translated Schlegel's *Lectures on the History of Literature*), he devoted himself more and more to a literary life. He joined John Wilson, and became one of the leading contributors to *Blackwood's Magazine*. After bringing out *Peter's Letters to his Kinsfolk* (1819), sketches mainly of Edinburgh society, he produced four novels, *Valerius* (1821), *Adam Blair* (1822), *Reginald Dalton* (1824), and *Matthew Wald* (1824). His *Life of Burns* appeared in 1828. He was ed. of the *Quarterly Review* 1824-53. In 1820 he had *m.* Sophia, *dau.* of Sir Walter Scott, which led to a close friendship with the latter, and to his writing his famous *Life of Scott*, undoubtedly one of the greatest biographies in the language. His later years were overshadowed with deep depression caused by the death of his wife and children. A singularly reserved and cold manner led to his being regarded with dislike by many, but his intimate friends were warmly attached to him.

LODGE, THOMAS (1558?-1625).—Poet and dramatist, *s.* of Sir Thomas L., Lord Mayor of London, was *ed.* at Merchant Taylor's School and Oxf. He was a student of Lincoln's Inn, but abandoned law for literature, ultimately studied medicine, and took M.D. at Oxf. 1603; having become a Roman Catholic, he had a large practice, chiefly among his co-religionists. In 1580 he *pub.* *A Defence of Plays* in reply to Gosson's *School of Abuse*; and he wrote poems, dramas, and romances. His principal dramatic works are *The Wounds of Civil War*, and (in conjunction with Greene, *q.v.*) *A Looking-glass for London and England*. Among his romances may be mentioned *Euphues' Shadow*, *Forbonius and Prisceria* (1584), and *Rosalynde, Euphues' Golden Legacie* (1590). His poems include *Glaucus and Scilla* (1589), *Phillis honoured with Pastoral Sonnets, Elegies, and Amorous Delights* (1593). *Rosalynde*, his best known work, and the source from which Shakespeare is said to have drawn *As you like It*, was written to beguile the tedium of a voyage to the Canaries. *Robin the Divell* and *William Longbeard* are historical romances. L. was also a voluminous translator. He was one of the founders of the regular English drama, but his own plays are heavy and tedious. His romances, popular in their day, are sentimental and over-refined in language, but are enlivened by lyrical pieces in which he is far more successful than in his dramatic work.

LOGAN, JOHN (1748-1788).—Poet, *s.* of a small farmer at Soutra, Midlothian, was destined for the ministry of a small Dissenting sect to which his *f.* belonged, but attached himself to the Church of Scotland, and became minister of South Leith in 1773. He read lectures on the philosophy of history in Edin., and was the author of a vol. of poems. He also ed. those of his friend, Michael Bruce (*q.v.*), in such a way, however, as to lead to a controversy, still unsettled, as to the authorship of certain of the pieces inserted. L., in fact, suppressed some of Bruce's poems and introduced others of his own. Unfortunately for the reputation of both poets the disputed authorship extends to the gem of the collection, the exquisite *Ode to the Cuckoo*, beginning "Hail, beauteous stranger of the grove," which Burke considered the most beautiful lyric in the language. L. fell into dissipated habits, resigned his ministerial charge, and went to London, where he took an active part in the controversy regarding the impeachment of Warren Hastings.

LONG, GEORGE (1800-1879).—Classical scholar, *ed.* at Camb. He was Prof. of Ancient Languages in the Univ. of Virginia, Charlottesville, 1824-28, of Greek at University Coll., London, 1828-31, and of Latin there, 1842-46. He did much for the diffusion of education, was one of the founders and sec. of the Royal Geographical Society, and ed. of the *Penny Cyclopædia*. He translated Marcus Aurelius (1862), and *The Discourses of Epictetus* (1877), and wrote *Two Discourses on Roman Law* (1847), a subject on which he was the greatest English authority.

LONGFELLOW, HENRY WADSWORTH (1807-1882).—Poet, was *b.* at Portland, Maine, the *s.* of Stephen L., a lawyer. From childhood he cared little for games, but was always devoted to reading. In 1822 he was sent to Bowdoin Coll., of which his *f.* was a Trustee, and after graduating was appointed to a new Chair of Modern Languages, which the coll. had decided to establish, and with the view of more completely qualifying him for his duties, he was sent to Europe for a three years' course of study. He accordingly went to France, Spain, and Italy. Returning in 1829 he commenced his professional duties, writing also in the *North American Review*. In 1831 he entered into his first marriage, and in 1833 he *pub.* his first books, a translation from the Spanish, followed by the first part of *Outre Mer*, an account of his travels. At the end of the year L. was invited to become Prof. of Modern Languages at Harvard, an offer which he gladly accepted. He paid a second visit to Europe accompanied by his wife, who, however, *d.* at Amsterdam. He returned to his duties in 1836, and in 1838 appeared *Voices of the Night*, containing the "Psalm of Life" and "Excelsior," which had extraordinary popularity, and gave him a place in the affections of his countrymen which he held until his death. The same year saw the publication of *Hyperion*. His next work was *Ballads and other Poems*, containing "The Wreck of the Hesperus" and "The Village Blacksmith." In 1843 he *m.* his second wife, and in the same year appeared *The Spanish Student*, a drama. The *Belfry of Bruges* and *Evangeline* (1847), generally considered his masterpiece, followed. In 1849 he *pub.* *Kavanagh*, a novel which added nothing to his reputation, and in 1851 *Seaside and Fireside*, and *The Golden Legend*. Having now a sufficient and secure income from his writings, he resigned his professorship, and devoted himself entirely to literature. *Hiawatha* appeared in 1855, and *The Courtship of Miles Standish* in 1858. In 1861 he lost his wife under tragic circumstances, a blow which told heavily upon him. His latest works were a translation of Dante's *Divina Commedia, Tales of a Wayside Inn, The New England Tragedies,* and *The Divine Tragedy,* the last two of which he combined with *The Golden Legend* into a trilogy, which he named *Christus.* In 1868 he paid a last visit to England, where he was received with the highest honour. Later works were *Three Books of Song, Aftermath,* and *Ultima Thule.* He *d.* on March 14, 1882. L. lacked the intensity of feeling and power of imagination to make him a great poet; but few poets have appealed to a wider circle of readers. If he never soars to the heights or sounds the deeps of feeling he touches the heart by appealing to universal and deep-seated affections. He was a man of noble and chivalrous character.

Lives by S. Longfellow in Riverside ed. of works (11 vols. 1886-90), Robertson (Great Writers Series), and Higginson (American Men of Letters).

LOVELACE, RICHARD (1618-1658).—Poet, *b.* at Woolwich, *s.* of Sir William L., was *ed.* at Oxf., where he is described by Anthony Wood as "the most amiable and beautiful person that eye ever beheld." He was an enthusiastic Royalist, and spent his whole fortune in support of that cause. For presenting "the Kentish petition" in favour of the King, he was imprisoned in 1642, when he wrote his famous song, *When Love with unconfinèd wings.* After his release he served in the French army, and was wounded at Dunkirk. Returning, he was again imprisoned, 1648, and produced his *Lucasta : Epodes, Odes,* etc. He lives in literature by a few of his lyrics which, though often careless, are graceful and tender. He *d.* in poverty.

LOVER, SAMUEL (1797-1868).—Song-writer and novelist, was a painter of portraits, chiefly miniatures. He produced a number of Irish songs, of which several—including *The Angel's Whisper, Molly Bawn,* and *The Four-leaved Shamrock*—attained great popularity. He also wrote some novels, of which *Rory O'More* (in its first form a ballad), and *Handy Andy* are the best known, and short Irish sketches, which, with his songs, he combined into a popular entertainment called *Irish Nights.* He joined with Dickens in founding *Bentley's Magazine.*

LOWELL, JAMES RUSSELL (1819-1891).—Poet and essayist, *b.* at Camb., Massachusetts, *s.* of a Unitarian minister, was *ed.* at Harvard. He began active life as a lawyer, but soon abandoned business, and devoted himself mainly to literature. In 1841 he *pub.* a vol. of poems, *A Year's Life,* and in 1843 a second book of verses appeared. He also wrote at this time political articles in the *Atlantic* and *North American Review.* In 1848 he *pub.* a third vol. of *Poems, A Fable for Critics, The Biglow Papers,* and *The Vision of Sir Launfal;* and he was in 1855 appointed Professor of Modern Languages at Harvard in succession to Longfellow. *Among my Books* appeared in 2 series, in 1870 and 1876. His later poems included various *Odes* in celebration of national events, some of which were *coll.* in *Under the Willows, The Cathedral,* and *Heartsease and Rue.* In 1877 he was appointed United States minister to Spain, and he held a similar appointment in England 1880-85. He *d.* at

Elmwood, the house in which he was *b.* L. was a man of singularly varied gifts, wit, humour, scholarship, and considerable poetic power, and he is the greatest critic America has yet produced. He was a strong advocate of the abolition of slavery.

LOWTH, ROBERT (1710-1787).—Theologian and scholar, *s.* of William L., Prebendary of Winchester, and author of a *Commentary on the Prophets*, was *b.* at Winchester, and *ed.* there and at Oxf. Entering the Church he became Bishop successively of St. David's, Oxf., and London. In 1753 he *pub. De Sacra Poesi Hebræorum.* He also wrote a *Life of William of Wykeham,* the founder of Winchester Coll., and made a new translation of Isaiah.

LYDGATE, JOHN (1370?-1451?).—Poet, *b.* in Suffolk, was ordained a priest in 1397. After studying at Oxf., Paris, and Padua, he taught literature in his monastery at Bury St. Edmunds. He appears to have been a bright, clear-minded, earnest man, with a love of the beautiful, and a faculty of pleasant, flowing verse. He wrote copiously and with tiresome prolixity whatever was required of him, moral tales, legends of the saints, and histories, and his total output is enormous, reaching 130,000 lines. His chief works are *Troy Book* (1412-20), written at the request of Henry V. when Prince of Wales, *The Falls of Princes* (1430-38), and *The Story of Thebes* (*c.* 1420). These books were first *printed* in 1513, 1494, and *c.* 1500 respectively. L. also wrote many miscellaneous poems. He was for a time Court poet, and was patronised by Humphrey, Duke of Gloucester; but the greater part of his life was spent in the monastery at Bury St. Edmunds. He was an avowed admirer of Chaucer, though he largely follows the French romancists previous to him.

LYELL, SIR CHARLES (1797-1875).—Geologist and writer, *s.* of Charles L., of Kinnordy, Forfarshire (a distinguished botanist and student of Dante), was brought up near the New Forest. After going to school at various places in England, he was sent to Oxf., where under Buckland he imbibed a taste for science. He studied law, and was called to the Bar, but soon devoted himself to geology, and made various scientific tours on the Continent, the results of his investigations being *pub.* chiefly in the Transactions of the Geological Society, of which he was afterwards repeatedly Pres. His two chief works are *The Principles of Geology* (1830-33), and *The Elements of Geology* (1838). In these books he combated the necessity of stupendous convulsions, and maintained that the greatest geologic changes might be produced by remote causes still in operation. He also *pub.*, among other works, *Geological Evidence of the Antiquity of Man* (1863). He was Prof. of Geology in King's Coll., London, 1831-33, Pres. of the British Association 1864, knighted in 1848, and *cr.* a Baronet in 1864. He was buried in Westminster Abbey. In his later years he was generally recognised as the greatest of living geologists.

LYLY, JOHN (1554?-1606).—Dramatist and miscellaneous writer, was *b.* in the Weald of Kent, and *ed.* at both Oxf. and Camb. He wrote several dramas, most of which are on classical and mythological subjects, including *Campaspe* and *Sapho and Phao* (1584), *Endymion* (1591), and *Midas* (1592). His chief fame, however, rests on his two didactic romances, *Euphues, the Anatomy of Wit* (1579), and *Euphues and his England* (1580). These works, which were largely inspired by Ascham's *Toxophilus*, and had the same objects in view, viz., the reform of education and manners, exercised a powerful, though temporary, influence on the language, both written and spoken, commemorated in our words "euphuism" and "euphuistic." The characteristics of the style have been set forth as "pedantic and far-fetched allusion, elaborate indirectness, a cloying smoothness and drowsy monotony of diction, alliteration, punning, and such-like puerilities, which do not, however, exclude a good deal of wit, fancy, and prettiness." Many contemporary authors, including Shakespeare, made game of it, while others, *e.g.* Greene, admired and practised it. L. also wrote light dramatic pieces for the children of the Chapel Royal, and contributed a pamphlet, *Pappe with an Hatchet* (1589) to the Mar-prelate controversy in which he supported the Bishops. He sat in Parliament for some years.

LYNDESAY, SIR D. (*See* LINDSAY.)

LYTE, HENRY FRANCIS (1793-1847).—Hymn-writer, *b.* at Ednam, near Kelso, of an ancient Somersetshire family, and *ed.* at Trinity Coll., Dublin, took orders, and was incumbent of Lower Brixham, Devonshire. He *pub. Poems: chiefly religious* (1833). He is chiefly remembered for his hymns, one of which, *Abide with Me*, is universally known and loved.

LYTTELTON, GEORGE, 1ST LORD LYTTELTON (1709-1773).—Poet, *s.* of Sir Thomas L., of Hagley, Worcestershire, *ed.* at Eton and Oxf., was the patron of many literary men, including Thomson and Mallet, and was himself a somewhat voluminous author. Among his works are *Letters from a Persian in England to his friend in Ispahan* (1735), a treatise *On the Conversion of St. Paul* (1746), *Dialogues of the Dead* (1760), which had great popularity, and a *History of the Reign of Henry II.*, well-informed, careful, and impartial, but tedious. He is chiefly remembered by his *Monody* on the death of his wife. The stanza in *The Castle of Indolence* in which Thomson is playfully described (canto I, st. lxviii.), is by L., who is himself referred to in lxv. He took some part in public affairs, and was Chancellor of the Exchequer in 1756.

LYTTON, EDWARD GEORGE EARLE LYTTON-BULWER, 1ST LORD (1803-1873).—Novelist and statesman, third son of General Earle Bulwer of Heydon and Dalling, Norfolk, and of Elizabeth Lytton, heiress of Knebworth, Herts, was *b.* in London, and *ed.* privately and at Camb. He began to write when still a boy, and *pub.*, in 1820, *Ismael and other Poems*. His marriage in 1825 to Rosina Wheeler, an Irish beauty, caused a quarrel with his mother, and the loss of his income, and thus incidentally gave the impulse to his marvellous literary activity. The marriage proved an unhappy one, and was terminated by a separation in 1836. During its continuance, however, his life was a busy and productive one, its literary results including *Falkland* (1827), *Pelham* (1828), *Paul Clifford* (1830), *Eugene Aram* (1832), *The Pilgrims of the Rhine*, *Last Days of Pompeii*, *Rienzi* (1835), besides *England and the English*,

Athens, its Rise and Fall, and innumerable tales, essays, and articles in various reviews and magazines, including the *New Monthly*, of which he became ed. in 1831. In the same year he entered Parliament as a Liberal, but gradually gravitated towards Conservatism, and held office in the second government of Lord Derby as Colonial Sec. 1858-59. As a politician he devoted himself largely to questions affecting authors, such as copyright and the removal of taxes upon literature. He continued his literary labours with almost unabated energy until the end of his life, his works later than those already mentioned including the *Last of the Barons* (1843), *Harold* (1848), the famous triad of *The Caxtons* (1850), *My Novel* (1853), and *What will he do with it?* (1859); and his studies in the supernatural, *Zanoni* (1842), and *A Strange Story* (1862). Later still were *The Coming Race* (1870) and *Kenelm Chillingly* (1873). To the drama he contributed three plays which still enjoy popularity, *The Lady of Lyons*, *Richelieu*, both (1838), and *Money* (1840). In poetry he was less successful. *The New Timon*, a satire, is the best remembered, largely, however, owing to the reply by Tennyson which it brought down upon the author, who had attacked him. In his works, numbering over 60, L. showed an amazing versatility, both in subject and treatment, but they have not, with perhaps the exception of the Caxton series, kept their original popularity. Their faults are artificiality, and forced brilliancy, and as a rule they rather dazzle by their cleverness than touch by their truth to nature. L. was raised to the peerage in 1866.

Life, Letters, etc., of Lord Lytton by his son, 2 vols., comes down to 1832 only. Political Memoir prefaced to *Speeches* (2 vols., 1874).

LYTTON, EDWARD ROBERT BULWER, 1ST EARL OF LYTTON (1831-1891).—Poet and statesman, *s.* of the above, was *ed.* at Harrow and Bonn, and thereafter was private sec. to his uncle, Sir H. Bulwer, afterwards Lord Dalling and Bulwer (*q.v.*), at Washington and Florence. Subsequently he held various diplomatic appointments at other European capitals. In 1873 he succeeded his *f.* in the title, and in 1876 became Viceroy of India. He was *cr.* an Earl on his retirement in 1880, and was in 1887 appointed Ambassador at Paris, where he *d.* in 1891. He valued himself much more as a poet than as a man of affairs; but, though he had in a considerable degree some of the qualities of a poet, he never quite succeeded in commanding the recognition of either the public or the critics. His writings, usually appearing under the pseudonym of "Owen Meredith," include *Clytemnestra* (1855), *The Wanderer* (1857), *Lucile* (1860), *Chronicles and Characters* (1868), *Orval, or the Fool of Time* (1869), *Fables in Song* (1874), and *King Poppy* (1892). As Viceroy of India he introduced important reforms, and his dispatches were remarkable for their fine literary form.

MACAULAY, MRS. CATHERINE (SAWBRIDGE) (1731-1791).—*Dau.* of a landed proprietor of Kent, was an advocate of republicanism, and a sympathiser with the French Revolution. She wrote a *History of England from the Accession of James I. to the Elevation of the House of Hanover* (8 vols., 1763-83), which had great popularity in its day, some critics, *e.g.* Horace Walpole, placing it above Hume.

Though a work of no real research or authority, it is in the main well written.

MACAULAY, THOMAS BABINGTON, LORD (1800-1859).—Historian, essayist, and statesman, *s.* of Zachary M., a wealthy merchant, and one of the leaders of the anti-slavery party, was *b.* at Rothley Temple, Leicestershire, and *ed.* at a private school and at Trinity Coll., Camb., of which he became a Fellow in 1824, and where, though he gained distinction as a classical scholar and debater, he did not take a high degree, owing to his weakness in mathematics. About the time of his leaving the Univ. his prospects were entirely changed by the failure of his father's firm. He accordingly read law, and in 1826 was called to the Bar, which led to his appointment two years later as a Commissioner in Bankruptcy. He had by this time made his first appearance in print, in *Knight's Quarterly Magazine,* and in 1825 he formed the connection with the *Edinburgh Review* which redounded so greatly to the fame of both. His first contribution was the famous essay on Milton, which, although he afterwards said of it that "it contained scarcely a paragraph which his matured judgment approved," took the reading public by storm, and at once gave him access to the first society in London, in which his extraordinary conversational powers enabled him to take a leading place. He now began to turn his mind towards public life, and by favour of Lord Lansdowne sat in the House of Commons for his family borough of Calne. Entering the House in 1830 in the thick of the Reform struggle, M. at once leaped into a foremost place as a debater, and after the passage of the Reform Bill sat as one of the two members for the new borough of Leeds, and held office as Sec. to the Board of Control. The acquaintance with Indian affairs which he thus gained led to his appointment as a member of the Supreme Council of India, whither he went in 1834. Here his chief work was the codification of the criminal law, which he carried out with great ability, and by which he wrote his name on the history of the empire. By the regard for the rights of the natives which he showed, he incurred much ill-will in interested quarters. For this he consoled himself with the pleasures of literature, which gradually assumed the preponderance in his mind over political ambitions. In 1838 he returned to England. The next year he began *The History of England,* but for some time to come his energies were still divided between this task, the demands of the *Edinburgh Review,* and politics. He was elected for Edin., for which he sat until 1847, when he was thrown out on the Maynooth question, and from 1839-41 was Sec. for War. The *Lays of Ancient Rome* were *pub.* in 1842, and a collection of his essays in *The Edinburgh* the following year. In 1846 he joined the government of Lord John Russell as Paymaster-General, an office with light duties, his retirement from which, however, followed the loss of his seat in the next year. He was now finally set free for his great work, which became thenceforth the leading interest of his life. The first and second vols. appeared in 1848, and were received with extraordinary applause. In 1852 he was offered, but declined, a seat in the coalition government of Lord Aberdeen, accepting, however, the seat in Parliament which Edin., now repentant, gave him unsolicited. His health began about this time to show symptoms of failure, and he spoke in the House only once or twice. In 1855 the third and fourth vols. of the *History* came out, and meeting with a success both at home and in America unprecedented in the case of an historical work, were translated into various foreign languages. In 1857 M. was raised to the Peerage, a distinction which he appreciated and enjoyed. His last years were spent at Holly Lodge, Kensington, in comparative retirement, and there he *d.* on December 28, 1859. Though never *m.*, M. was a man of the warmest family affections. Outside of his family he was a steady friend and a generous opponent, disinterested and honourable in his public life Possessed of an astonishing memory, knowledge of vast extent, and an unfailing flow of ready and effective speech, he shone alike as a parliamentary orator and a conversationalist. In his writings he spared no pains in the collection and arrangement of his materials, and he was incapable of deliberate unfairness. Nevertheless, his mind was strongly cast in the mould of the orator and the pleader: and the vivid contrasts, antitheses, and even paradoxes which were his natural forms of expression do not always tend to secure a judicial view of the matter in hand. Consequently he has been accused by some critics of party-spirit, inaccuracy, and prejudice. He has not often, however, been found mistaken on any important matter of fact, and in what he avowedly set himself to do, namely, to give a living picture of the period which he dealt with, he has been triumphantly successful. Unfortunately, strength and life failed before his great design was completed. He is probably most widely known by his *Essays*, which retain an extraordinary popularity.

Life by his nephew, Sir G. O. Trevelyan. *See* also J. C. Monson's *Life* (English Men of Letters).

MACCARTHY, DENIS FLORENCE (1817-1882).—Poet, *b.* at Dublin, and *ed.* at Maynooth with a view to the priesthood, devoted himself, however, to literature, and contributed verses to *The Nation*. Among his other writings are *Ballads, Poems, and Lyrics* (1850), *The Bell Founder* (1857), and *Under-Glimpses*. He also ed. a collection of Irish lyrics, translated Calderon, and wrote *Shelley's Early Life* (1872).

M'COSH, JAMES (1811-1894).—Philosophical writer, *s.* of an Ayrshire farmer, was a minister first of the Church of Scotland, and afterwards of the Free Church. From 1851-68 he was Prof. of Logic at Queen's Coll., Belfast, and thereafter Pres. of Princeton Coll., New Jersey. He wrote several works on philosophy, including *Method of the Divine Government* (1850), *Intuitions of the Mind inductively investigated* (1860), *Laws of Discursive Thought* (1870), *Scottish Philosophy* (1874), and *Psychology* (1886).

M'CRIE, THOMAS (1772-1835).—Biographer and ecclesiastical historian, *b.* at Duns, and *ed.* at the Univ. of Edin., became the leading minister of one of the Dissenting churches of Scotland. His *Life of Knox* (1813) ranks high among biographies for the ability and learning which it displays, and was the means of vindicating the great Reformer from a cloud of prejudice and misunderstanding in which he had been enveloped. It was followed by a *Life of Andrew*

Melville (1819), Knox's successor as the leader of the Reformers in Scotland, also a work of great merit. M'C. also *pub.* histories of the Reformation in Italy and Spain. He received the degree of D.D. in 1813.

MACDONALD, GEORGE (1824-1905).—Poet and novelist, *s.* of a farmer, was *b.* at Huntly, Aberdeenshire, and *ed.* at the Univ. of Aberdeen, and at the Independent Coll., Highbury. He became minister of a congregation at Arundel, but after a few years retired, on account partly of theological considerations, partly of a threatened breakdown of health. He then took to literature, and *pub.* his first book, *Within and Without* (1856), a dramatic poem, *Poems* followed in 1857, and *Phantastes, a Faerie Romance*, in 1858. He then turned to fiction, and produced numerous novels, of which *David Elginbrod* (1862), *Alec Forbes* (1865), *Robert Falconer* (1868), *The Marquis of Lossie* (1877), and *Sir Gibbie* (1879), are perhaps the best. He also wrote stories for children of great charm and originality, including *The Princess and the Goblin, At the Back of the North Wind*, and *Ranald Bannerman's Boyhood*. As a novelist he had considerable narrative and dramatic power, humour, tenderness, a genial view of life and character, tinged with mysticism, and within his limits was a true poet. On retiring from the ministry he attached himself to the Church of England, but frequently preached as a layman, never accepting any remuneration for his sermons.

MACKAY, CHARLES (1814-1889).—Poet and journalist, *s.* of a naval officer, was *b.* at Perth, and *ed.* at the Royal Caledonian Asylum, London, and at Brussels, but much of his early life was spent in France. Coming to London in 1834, he engaged in journalism, *pub. Songs and Poems* (1834), wrote a *History of London, Popular Delusions*, and a romance, *Longbeard*. His fame, however, chiefly rests upon his songs, some of which, including *Cheer, Boys, Cheer*, were in 1846 set to music by Henry Russell, and had an astonishing popularity. In 1852 he became ed. of the *Illustrated London News*, in the musical supplement to which other songs by him were set to old English music by Sir H. R. Bishop. M. acted as *Times* correspondent during the American Civil War, and in that capacity discovered and disclosed the Fenian conspiracy. He had the degree of LL.D. from Glasgow in 1846.

MACKENZIE, SIR GEORGE (1636-1691).—Lawyer and miscellaneous writer, *s.* of Sir Simon M., of Lochslin, a brother of the Earl of Seaforth, was *ed.* at St. Andrews, Aberdeen, and Bourges, called to the Bar in 1659, in 1677 became Lord Advocate, in which capacity he was the subservient minister of the persecuting policy of Charles II. in Scotland, and the inhumanity and relentlessness of his persecution of the Covenanters gained for him the name of "Bloody Mackenzie." In private life, however, he was a cultivated and learned gentleman with literary tendencies, and is remembered as the author of various graceful essays, of which the best known is *A Moral Essay preferring Solitude to Public Employment* (1665). He also wrote legal, political, and antiquarian works of value, including *Institutions of the Law of Scotland* (1684), *Antiquity of the Royal Line of Scotland* (1686), *Heraldry*, and *Memoirs of the Affairs of Scotland from the Restoration of Charles II*, a valuable work which was not *pub.* until 1821. M. was the founder of the Advocates' Library in Edin. He retired at the Revolution to Oxf., where he *d.*

MACKENZIE, HENRY (1745-1831).—Novelist and miscellaneous writer, *s.* of a physician in Edin., where he was *b.* and *ed.* He studied for the law, and became Controller of Taxes for Scotland. He was the author of three novels, *The Man of Feeling* (1771), *The Man of the World* (1773), and *Julia de Roubigné* (1777), all written in a strain of rather high-wrought sentimentalism, in which the influence of Sterne is to be seen. He was also a leading contributor to *The Mirror* and *The Lounger*, two periodicals somewhat in the style of the *Spectator*. In his later days he was one of the leading members of the literary society of Edinburgh.

MACKINTOSH, SIR JAMES (1765-1832).—Philosopher and historian, was *b.* at Aldowrie, Inverness-shire, *s.* of an officer in the army and landowner, *ed.* at Aberdeen, whence he proceeded to Edinburgh to study medicine, in which he *grad.* in 1787. In the following year he went to London, where he wrote for the press and studied law, and in 1791 he *pub. Vindiciæ Gallicæ* in answer to Burke's *Reflections on the French Revolution*, which was well received by those who, in its earlier stages, sympathised with the Revolution, and procured for him the friendship of Fox, Sheridan, and other Whigs. Called to the Bar at Lincoln's Inn in 1795, he delivered before that society in 1799 a brilliant course of lectures on *The Law of Nature and Nations*, which greatly increased his reputation. In 1804 he went out to India as Recorder of Bombay, and two years later was appointed a Judge of the Admiralty Court. He remained in India until 1811, discharging his official duties with great efficiency. After his return he entered Parliament in 1813 as member for Nairnshire, and attained a considerable reputation as a forcible and informing speaker on questions of criminal law and general politics. On the accession of the Whigs in 1830 he was made a member of the Board of Control for India. He also held from 1818-24 the Professorship of Law and General Politics at Haileybury. His true vocation, however, was to literature, and it is to be regretted that so much of his time and strength was withdrawn from it, his writings being confined to a *Dissertation on the Progress of Ethical Philosophy* in the *Encyclopædia Britannica*, a sketch of the History of England for Lardner's *Cabinet Cyclopædia*, a Life of Sir Thomas More for the same, a fragment of a projected *History of the Revolution of* 1688, and some articles in the *Edinburgh Review*.

MACKLIN, CHARLES (1697?-1797).—Actor and dramatist, *b.* in the north of Ireland, was one of the most distinguished actors of his day, shining equally in tragedy and comedy. Having killed another actor in a quarrel he was tried for murder but acquitted, and *d.* a centenarian. He wrote, among other comedies, *Love à la Mode* (1759) and *The Man of the World* (1781), which were the only ones printed. He was the creator of Sir Pertinax Macsycophant, a famous burlesque character.

M'LENNAN, JOHN FERGUSON (1827-1881).—Sociologist, *b.* at Inverness, and *ed.* at Aberdeen and Camb., was in 1857 called to the Scottish Bar, and was subsequently Parliamentary Draftsman for Scotland. His main contribution to literature is his original and learned book, *Primitive Marriage* (1865). Another work, *The Patriarchal Theory*, left unfinished, was completed by his brother (1884). These works and other papers by M. gave a great impulse to the study of the problems with which they deal, and cognate questions. M. received the degree of LL.D. from Aberdeen in 1874.

"MACLEOD, FIONA" (*see* SHARP, WILLIAM).

MACLEOD, NORMAN (1812-1872).—Scottish divine and miscellaneous writer, *s.* of the Rev. Norman M., D.D., a distinguished minister of the Scottish Church, studied at Edin., and was ordained in 1838. He became one of the most distinguished ministers, and most popular preachers of his Church, was made one of the Royal Chaplains in Scotland in 1857, and became a trusted friend of Queen Victoria. He was the first ed. of *Good Words*, to which he contributed many articles and stories, including *Wee Davie*, *The Starling*, and *The Old Lieutenant and his Son*.

MACNEILL, HECTOR (1746-1818).—Poet, was in the West Indies 1780-86, and clerk on a flagship. He wrote various political pamphlets, two novels, and several poems, *The Harp* (1789), *The Carse of Forth*, and *Scotland's Skaith*, the last against drunkenness, but is best known for his songs, such as *My Boy Tammy*, *I lo'ed ne'er a Laddie but ane*, and *Come under my Plaidie*.

MACPHERSON, JAMES (1736?-1796).—Alleged translator of the Ossianic poems, *s.* of a small farmer at Ruthven, Inverness-shire, studied for the Church at Aberdeen and Edin., became teacher of the school in his native parish, and afterwards tutor in a gentleman's family. In 1758 he *pub.* *The Highlander*, an ambitious poem in 6 cantos, which, however, attracted no attention. But in the following year he submitted to John Home (*q.v.*), the author of *Douglas*, certain writings which he represented to be translations from ancient Gaelic poems. By the help of Home and some of his friends M. was enabled to *pub.* a considerable number of his *Fragments of Poetry translated from the Gaelic and Erse Languages*. These were received with profound and widely-spread interest, and gave rise to a controversy which can hardly yet be said to be settled. While some authorities received them with enthusiastic admiration, others immediately called their genuineness in question. In the first instance, however, a subscription was raised to enable M. to make a journey in search of further poetic remains, the result of which was the production in 1761 of *Fingal*, an epic in 6 books, and in 1763 of *Temora*, also an epic, in 8 books. The fame which these brought to their discoverer was great, and the sales enormous. In 1764 M. went as sec. to the Governor of Pensacola in Florida. Returning in 1766 he settled in London, became an energetic pamphleteer in support of the Government, and in 1780 entered Parliament, and was next year appointed to the lucrative post of Agent for the Nabob of Arcot. He retired in 1789, and bought an estate in his native parish, where he *d.* in 1796. Great doubt still rests upon the subject of the Ossianic poems: it is, however, generally admitted that M. took great liberties with the originals, even if they ever really existed in anything at all resembling the form given in the alleged translations. No manuscripts in the original have ever been forthcoming. Few, however, will deny that M. either discovered, or composed, a body of poetry unlike anything that has preceded it, of unequal merit, indeed, but containing many striking and beautiful passages, and which unquestionably contributed to break up the tyranny of the classical school and thus prepare the way for the romantic revival.

MAGINN, WILLIAM (1793-1842).—Journalist and miscellaneous writer, *b.* at Cork, became a contributor to *Blackwood's Magazine*, and afterwards foreign correspondent to *The Representative*, a paper started by J. Murray, the publisher, and when its short career was run, one of the leading supporters of *Fraser's Magazine*. One of the most brilliant periodical writers of his time, he has left no permanent work behind him. In his later years he fell into intemperate habits, and *d.* in poverty.

MAHONY, FRANCIS SYLVESTER (FATHER PROUT) (1804-1866).—Humorist, *b.* at Cork, and *ed.* at the Jesuit Coll. at Clongoweswood, Co. Kildare, at Amiens, and at Rome, becoming a member of the society, was Prof. of Rhetoric at Clongoweswood, but was soon after expelled from the order. He then came to London, and became a leading contributor to *Fraser's Magazine*, under the signature of "Father Prout." He was witty and learned in many languages. One form which his humour took was the professed discovery of the originals in Latin, Greek, or mediæval French of popular modern poems and songs. Many of these *jeux d'esprit* were *coll.* as *Reliques of Father Prout*. He wittily described himself as "an Irish potato seasoned with Attic salt." Latterly he acted as foreign correspondent to various newspapers, and *d.* at Paris reconciled to the Church.

MAINE, SIR HENRY JAMES SUMNER (1822-1888).—Jurist, *ed.* at Christ's Hospital and at Camb., where he became Regius Prof. of Civil Law 1847-54. Called to the Bar in 1850, he went in 1862 to India as legal member of the Government. On his return he was in 1870 appointed Prof. of Comparative Jurisprudence at Oxf., which office he held until his election in 1878 as Master of Trinity Hall. He became Whewell Prof. of International Law at Camb. in 1887, and was the author of many valuable works on law and the history of political institutions, and profoundly influenced the study of jurisprudence. Among his writings are *Ancient Law* (1861), *Village Communities* (1871), *Early History of Institutions* (1875), and *Dissertations on Early Law and Customs* (1883).

MAIR, OR MAJOR, JOHN (1469?-1550).—Historian, studied at Camb. and Paris, was the teacher of John Knox and George Buchanan. In 1506 he was a Doctor of the Sorbonne, and in 1519 became Prof. of Divinity at St. Andrews. He wrote, in Latin, treatises on divinity and morals, and a *History of Greater Britain*, in which the separate histories of England and Scotland were brought together, *pub.* at Paris (1521). In his writings, while upholding the doctrinal teaching of Rome, he was outspoken in condemning the corruptions of the clergy.

MAITLAND, SIR RICHARD (1496-1586).—Poet, *f.* of M. of Lethington, Sec. of State to Mary Queen of Scots. In his later years he was blind, and occupied himself in composing a *History of the House of Seaton*, and by writing poems, *e.g. On the New Year, On the Queene's Maryage*, etc. He held various offices, chiefly legal, but appears to have kept as far as possible out of the fierce political struggles of his time, and to have been a genially satirical humorist.

MALCOLM, SIR JOHN (1769-1833).—Indian soldier, statesman, and historian, *b.* at Burnfoot, Dumfriesshire, went to India in 1782, studied Persian, was employed in many important negotiations and held various distinguished posts, being Ambassador to Persia and Governor of Bombay 1826-30. He was the author of several valuable works regarded as authorities, viz., *A History of Persia* (1815), *Memoir of Central India* (1823), *Political History of India from* 1784 *to* 1823 (1826), and *Life of Lord Clive* (1836).

MALLET, ORIGINALLY MALLOCH, DAVID (1705-1765).—Poet and miscellaneous writer, *ed.* at Crieff parish school and the Univ. of Edin., where he became acquainted with James Thomson, and in 1723 went to London as tutor in the family of the Duke of Montrose. In the following year appeared his ballad of *William and Margaret*, by which he is chiefly remembered, and which made him known to Pope, Young, and others. In 1726 he changed his name to Mallet to make it more pronounceable by Southern tongues. His *Excursion*, an imitation of Thomson, was *pub.* in 1728. At the request of the Prince of Wales, whose sec. he had become, he wrote with Thomson a masque, *Alfred* (1740), in which *Rule Britannia* first appeared, which, although he claimed the authorship, is now generally attributed to Thomson. He also wrote a *Life of Bacon*; and on Bolingbroke bequeathing to him his manuscripts and library, he *pub.* an ed. of his works (1754). On the accession of George III., M. became a zealous supporter of Lord Bute, and was rewarded with a sinecure. In addition to the works above named M. wrote some indifferent dramas, including *Eurydice*, *Mustapha*, and *Elvira*. Dr. Johnson said of him that he was "the only Scotsman whom Scotsmen did not commend."

MALONE, EDMUND (1741-1812).—Critic, *s.* of an Irish judge, *b.* in Dublin, and *ed.* at Trinity Coll. there, studied for the law, but coming into a fortune, decided to follow a literary career. Acute, careful, and sensible, he was a useful contributor to the study of Shakespeare, of whose works he *pub.* a valuable ed. in 1790. He also aided in the detection of the Rowley forgeries of Chatterton, and the much less respectable Shakespeare ones of Ireland. At his death he was engaged upon another ed. of Shakespeare, which was brought out under the editorship of James Boswell (*q.v.*). M. also wrote Lives of Dryden and others, and was the friend of Johnson, Goldsmith, Reynolds, and Burke.

MALORY, SIR THOMAS (*fl.* 1470).—Translator of *Morte d'Arthur*. Very little is known of him. An endeavour has been made to identify him with a Sir Thomas Malory of Warwickshire, who fought successively on both sides in the Wars of the Roses, sat in Parliament 1444-45, and *d.* 1471. In his book he strove to make a continuous story of the Arthurian legends, and showed judgment alike in what he included and omitted.

MALTHUS, THOMAS ROBERT (1766-1834).—Economist, *s.* of a landed proprietor, was *b.* near Dorking, and *ed.* at Jesus Coll., Camb., of which he became a Fellow. Taking orders he became incumbent of Albury, Essex. He travelled much on the continent, collecting information as to the means of livelihood and mode of life of various peoples. In 1798 the first ed. of his famous *Essay on Population* appeared, and in 1803 a second greatly enlarged. Its leading proposition, supported by much learning, is that while population increases approximately in a geometrical ratio, the means of subsistence do so in an arithmetical ratio only, which, of course, opened up an apalling prospect for the race. It necessarily failed to take into account the then undreamed-of developments whereby the produce of the whole world has been made available for all nations. The work gave rise to a great deal of controversy, much of it based on misunderstanding. M. was Prof. of Political Economy at Haileybury.

MANDEVILLE, BERNARD DE (1670-1733).—Satirist, a native of Dort in Holland, who having studied medicine at Leyden, came over to England to practise his profession. In 1705 he *pub.* a short poem, *The Grumbling Hive*, which in 1714 reappeared with a prose commentary, and various dissertations on the origin of moral virtue, etc., as *The Fable of the Bees, or Private Vices Public Benefits*, and in 1729 was made the subject of a persecution for its immoral tendency. It was also vigorously combated by, among others, Bishop Berkeley and William Law, author of *The Serious Call*. While the author probably had no intention of subverting morality, his views of human nature were assuredly cynical and degrading in a high degree. Another of his works, *A Search into the Nature of Society* (1723), appended to the later versions of the *Fable*, also startled the public mind, which his last works, *Free Thoughts on Religion* and *An Enquiry into the Origin of Honour and the Usefulness of Christianity* did little to reassure.

MANDEVILLE, SIR JOHN.—Was the ostensible author only of a book of travels bearing his name, written about the middle of the 14th century, giving an account of journeys in the East, including India and the Holy Land. It appears to have been compiled from the writings of William of Boldensele, Oderic of Pordenone, and Vincent de Beauvais. The name of Mandeville was probably fictitious.

MANGAN, JAMES CLARENCE (1803-1849).—Poet, *b.* at Dublin, *s.* of a small grocer, was brought up in poverty, and received most of his education from a priest who instructed him in several modern languages. He then became a lawyer's clerk, and was later an assistant in the library of Trinity College, Dublin. He contributed verses of very various merit to a number of Irish newspapers, and translations from the German to *The Dublin University Magazine*. By some critics his poetical powers were considered to be such as to have gained for him the first place among Irish poets; but his irregular and intemperate habits prevented him from attaining any sure excellence. His best work, generally inspired by the miseries of his country, often rises to a high level of tragic power, and had his strength of character been equal to his poetic gift it is difficult to say to what heights he might have attained. He *d.* of cholera.

MANLEY, MRS. MARY DE LA RIVIERE (1663 or 1672-1724). —Novelist, dramatist, and political writer, *dau.* of Sir Roger Manley, was decoyed into a bigamous connection with her cousin, John M. Her subsequent career was one of highly dubious morality, but considerable literary success. Her principal works are *The New Atalantis* (*sic*) (1709), a satire in which great liberties were taken with Whig notabilities, *Memoirs of Europe* (1710), and *Court Intrigues* (1711). She also wrote three plays, *The Royal Mischief*, *The Lost Lover*, and *Lucius*, and conducted the *Examiner*. In her writings she makes great havoc with classical names and even with spelling. She was a vivacious and effective political writer.

MANNING, ANNE (1807-1879).—Miscellaneous writer. Her best known works are *Mistress Mary Powell*, which first appeared in *Sharpe's Magazine* in 1849, and *The Household of Sir Thomas More*, a delightful picture of More's home life told in the form of a diary written by his daughter Margaret. Her writings have much literary charm, and show a delicate historical imagination.

MANNING, HENRY EDWARD (1808-1892).—Cardinal and theologian. *B.* at Totteridge, Herts, and *ed.* at Harrow and Oxf., where he became notable as an eloquent preacher, and as one of the ablest of the Tractarian party. He was rector of Woollavington-cum-Graffham 1833, and Archdeacon of Chichester 1840. In 1851 he entered the Church of Rome, in which he attached himself to the Ultramontane party. More even than Newman he was the leading spirit of the Roman Church in England. His writings consist of sermons, of which he *pub.* several vols. before his secession from the Church of England, and controversial works, including *Petri Privilegium* (1871), *The Vatican Decrees* (1875), in answer to Gladstone's *Vaticanism*, and *The Eternal Priesthood* (1883). He became Roman Catholic Archbishop of Westminster 1865, and Cardinal 1875.

MANNYNG, ROBERT, OR ROBERT DE BRUNNE (*fl.* 1288-1338).—Was a Canon of the Gilbertine Order. His work, *Handlynge Sinne* (*c.* 1300), translated with original additions from the *Manuel des Péchés*, a book written in French verse by William of Waddington, is practically a collection of tales and short stories on the Commandments, Seven Deadly Sins, Sacraments, etc., and is of value as giving a contemporary picture of the time. He also made (*c.* 1335) a translation in verse of the French *Chronicle* of Peter Langtoft, the second and more interesting part of which covers the period from the death of Cadwallader to the end of the reign of Edward I.

MANSEL, HENRY LONGUEVILLE (1820-1871).—Metaphysician, *s.* of a clergyman, was *b.* at Cosgrave, Northamptonshire, and *ed.* at Merchant Taylors' School and Oxf. He took orders, was Reader in Theology at Magdalen Coll. 1855, Bampton Lecturer 1858, Prof. of Ecclesiastical History 1867, and Dean of St. Paul's 1869. Among his writings are *Prolegomena Logica* (1851), *The Limits of Demonstrative Science* (1853), *Man's Conception of Eternity* (1854), *Limits of Religious Thought* (1858), *Philosophy of the Conditioned* (1866). He was also joint ed. of Sir. W. Hamilton's *Lectures*.

MAP, OR MAPES, WALTER DE (*fl.* 1200).—Ecclesiastical statesman and romancist. Most of the facts about him are gleaned from his *De Nugis Curialium* (Of the Trifles of the Courtiers), a miscellany of contemporary notes and anecdotes, throwing much light on the manners and opinions of the Court of Henry II. He was *b.* probably in Herefordshire, and had Celtic blood in his veins, his *f.* had rendered service to the King, and he had studied at Paris, and on his return attended the Court, where he found favour, and obtained preferment both in Church and State, and in 1173 was a travelling justice. Thereafter he attended the King, probably as chaplain, on his foreign wars, represented him at the French Court, and went to Rome to the Lateran Council of 1179. After the death of Henry II. he seems to have continued in favour under Richard I. and John, and was Archdeacon of Oxf. in 1196. M. is the reputed author of some at least of the *Golias* poems, rough satires on the vices of the clergy, but his great work, which has influenced the future of English literature, was his systematising and spiritualising the Arthurian legends with additions of his own, including the legends of *Launcelot*, of the *Quest of the Holy Grail*, and of the *Morte d'Arthur*.

MARKHAM, GERVASE (1568?-1637).—Translator and miscellaneous writer, served as a soldier in the Low Countries and Ireland. Retiring into civil life about 1593 he displayed extraordinary industry as a translator, compiler, and original writer. Among his original writings are a poem on the *Revenge* (1595) (Sir R. Grenville's ship), a continuation of Sidney's *Arcadia*, *The Discourse of Horsemanshippe* (1593), *The Young Sportsman's Instructor*, *Country Contentments* (1611), and various books on agriculture; also plays and poems, some of the latter of which are religious.

MARLOWE, CHRISTOPHER (1564-1593).—Dramatist, *s.* of a shoemaker at Canterbury, where he was *b.*, was *ed.* at the King's School there, and in 1581 went to Benet's (now Corpus Christi) Coll., Camb., where he graduated B.A. 1583, and M.A. in 1587. Of his life after he left the Univ. almost nothing is known. It has, however, been conjectured, partly on account of his familiarity with military matters, that he saw service, probably in the Low Countries. His first play, *Tamburlaine*, was acted in 1587 or 1588. The story is drawn from the Spanish Life of Timur by Pedro Mexia. Its resounding splendour, not seldom passing into bombast, won for it immediate popularity, and it long held the stage. It was followed in 1604 by *Faustus*, a great advance upon *Tamburlaine* in a dramatic sense. The absence of "material horror" in the treatment, so different in this respect from the original legend, has often been remarked upon. M.'s handling of the subject was greatly admired by Goethe, who, however, in his own version, makes the motive knowledge, while M. has power, and the mediæval legend pleasure.

In his next play, *The Jew of Malta*, M. continues to show an advance in technical skill, but the work is unequal, and the Jew Barabas is to Shylock as a monster to a man. In *Edward II.*, M. rises to his highest display of power. The rhodomontade of *Tamburlaine* and the piled-up horror of *The Jew* are replaced by a mature self-restraint, and in the whole workmanship he approaches more nearly to Shakespeare than any one else has ever done. Speaking of it Lamb says, "The death scene of Marlowe's King moves pity and terror beyond any scene, ancient or modern, with which I am acquainted." M. is now almost certainly believed to have had a large share in the three parts of *Henry VI.*, and perhaps also he may have collaborated in *Titus Andronicus*. His next plays, *The Massacre of Paris* and *The Tragedy of Dido* (written with Nash, *q.v.*), both show a marked falling off; and it seems likely that in his last years, perhaps, breaking down under the effects of a wild life, he became careless of fame as of all else. Greene, in his *Groat's Worth of Wit*, written on his deathbed, reproaches him with his evil life and atheistic opinions, and a few days before his hapless death an information was laid against him for blasphemy. The informer was next year hanged for an outrageous offence, and his witness alone might not be conclusive, but M.'s life and opinions, which he made no secret of, were notorious. On the other hand, his friends, Shakespeare, Nash, Drayton, and Chapman, all make kindly reference to him. To escape the plague which was raging in London in 1593, he was living at Deptford, then a country village, and there in a tavern brawl he received a wound in the head, his own knife being turned against him by a serving man, upon whom he had drawn it. The quarrel was about a girl of the town. The parish record bears the entry, "Christopher Marlowe, slain by ffrancis Archer, the 1 of June 1593." M. is the father of the modern English drama, and the introducer of the modern form of blank verse. In imagination, richness of expression, originality, and general poetic and dramatic power he is inferior to Shakespeare alone among the Elizabethans. In addition to his plays he wrote some short poems (of which the best known is *Come live with me and be my love*), translations from Ovid's *Amores* and Lucan's *Pharsalia*, and a glowing paraphrase of Musaeus' *Hero and Leander*, a poem completed by Chapman.

Ed. of *Works* by Dyce, Cunningham, and Bullen; Ingram's *C. Marlowe and his Associates*, etc.

MARMION, SHACKERLEY (1603-1639).—Dramatist, *s.* of a country gentleman of Northamptonshire, was *ed.* at Oxford. After a youth of extravagance, he fought in the Low Countries. His writings consist of an epic, *Cupid and Psyche*, and three comedies, *Holland's Leaguer*, *A Fair Companion*, and *The Antiquary*. His plays show some power of satire, and were popular, but he had little of the dramatist.

MARRYAT, FREDERICK (1792-1848).—Novelist, *s.* of a West India merchant, was *b.* in London. In 1806 he entered the navy as a midshipman under Lord Cochrane (afterwards Earl of Dundonald), and saw much service in the Mediterranean, at Walcheren, and in the Burmese War of 1824. He returned in 1830 as a

Captain and C.B. The scenes and experiences through which he had passed were the preparation for and the foundation of his numerous novels, of which the first, *Frank Mildmay*, was *pub.* in 1829. It was followed by over 30 others, of which perhaps the best are *Peter Simple*, *Jacob Faithful* (1834), *Mr. Midshipman Easy* (1836), *The Dog Fiend* (1837), and *The Phantom Ship* (1839). M. is the prince of sea story-tellers; his knowledge of the sea, vigorous definition of character, and hearty and honest, if somewhat broad, humour never failing to please.

MARSH, HERBERT (1757-1839).—Theologian and controversialist, *s.* of a clergyman, *ed.* at Canterbury, Cambridge, and Leipsic, was the first to introduce the German methods of Biblical criticism into England, and gave lectures on the subject at Camb., which excited great interest and controversy. In 1816 he was made Bishop of Llandaff, and was translated to Peterborough in 1819. His critical views and his opposition to the evangelical party in the Church, to the Bible Society, to hymns in Divine service, and to Catholic emancipation, involved him in controversy with high, low, and broad churchmen alike. He was the author of a *History of the Politics of Great Bitain and France* (1799), *Comparative View of the Churches of England and Rome*, and *Horæ Pelasgicæ*.

MARSTON, JOHN (1575?-1634).—Dramatist and satirist, *b.* at Coventry, was *ed.* at Oxf. In later life he gave up writing for the stage, took orders, and was incumbent of Christchurch, Hants, 1616-31. He began his literary career in 1598 with satire, *The Scourge of Villanie* and *The Metamorphosis of Pygmalion's Image* (1598), the latter of which was burned by order of Archbishop Whitgift. In 1602 appeared *The History of Antonio and Mellida*, and its sequel, *Antonio's Revenge*, ridiculed by Ben Jonson. In repayment of this M. co-operated with Dekker in attacking Jonson in *Satiromastix* (a Whip for the Satirist). A reconciliation, however, took place, and his comedy, *The Malcontent* (1604), was dedicated to J., another, *Eastward Ho* (1605), was written in collaboration with him and Chapman. Other plays of his are *Sophonisba*, *What You Will* (1607), and possibly *The Insatiate Countess* (1613). Amid much bombast and verbiage there are many fine passages in M.'s dramas, especially where scorn and indignation are the motives. Sombre and caustic, he has been called "a screech-owl among the singing birds."

MARSTON, PHILIP BOURKE (1850-1887).—Poet, was *b.* in London, and lost his sight at the age of 3. His poems, *Song-tide*, *All in All*, and *Wind Voices* bear, in their sadness, the impress of this affliction, and of a long series of bereavements. He was the friend of Rossetti and of Swinburne, the latter of whom has written a sonnet to his memory.

MARTIN, SIR THEODORE (1816-1909).—Poet, biographer, and translator, *s.* of James M., solicitor in Edin., where he was *b.* and *ed.* at the High School and Univ. He practised as a solicitor in Edin. 1840-45, after which he went to London and became head of the firm of Martin and Leslie, parliamentary agents. His first contribution to literature was *The Bon Gaultier Ballads*, written along with W. E. Aytoun (*q.v.*), full of wit and humour, which still retain their popularity; originally contributed to a magazine, they appeared in book form in 1855. His translations include *Dante's Vita Nuova*, Œhlenschläger's *Correggio* and *Aladdin*, Heine's *Poems and Ballads*, Schiller's *Song of the Bell*, and Hertz's *King René's Daughter*. He also *pub.* a complete translation of Horace with a Life, and one of Catullus. He is, however, perhaps best known for his *Life of the Prince Consort* (1874-80), the writing of which was committed to him by Queen Victoria, a work which he executed with such ability and tact as to win for him her lifelong friendship. He also wrote Lives of Prof. Aytoun and Lord Lyndhurst. He *m.* in 1851 Miss Helen Faucit (*d.* 1898), the well-known actress, and authoress of studies on *Shakespeare's Female Characters*, whose Life he *pub.* in 1901. M. kept up his intellectual activity into old age, *pub.* in 1905 a translation of Leopardi's poems, and *Monographs* (1906). He was Lord Rector of St. Andrews 1881, LL.D. of Edin. 1875, and K.C.B. 1880.

MARTINEAU, HARRIET (1802-1876).—Novelist and economist. *b.* at Norwich, where her *f.*, descended from a French family, was a manufacturer. From her earliest years she was delicate and very deaf, and took to literary pursuits as an amusement. Afterwards, when her *f.* had fallen into difficulties, they became her means of support. Her first publication was *Devotional Exercises for Young Persons* (1823). Becoming interested in political economy, she endeavoured to illustrate the subject by tales, of which two were *The Rioters* and *The Turn-out*. Later she *pub.* a more serious treatment of it in *Illustrations of Political Economy* (1832-4), *Poor Law and Paupers* (1833), and *Illustrations of Taxation* (1834). About this time she went to London, and was regarded as an authority on economic questions, being occasionally consulted by Cabinet Ministers. Among her books of travel are *Society in America* (1837), and *Eastern Life, Present and Past* (1848), which she considered her best book: in it she declared herself no longer a believer in revelation. She also wrote two novels, *Deerbrook* (1839), and *The Hour and the Man* (1840), also a number of books for children. Perhaps her most important work is her *History of England during the Thirty Years' Peace*, 1816-46, which appeared in 1849. She translated Comte's *Philosophy* (1853), and *pub.* a collection of letters between herself and Mr. H. G. Atkinson *On the Laws of Man's Nature and Development*, which encountered severe criticism. In addition to her separate publications she wrote innumerable articles for newspapers, specially the *Daily News*, and for periodicals. In 1845 she settled in the Lake District, where she died.

MARTINEAU, JAMES (1805-1900).—Unitarian theologian, younger brother of the above, was *b.* at Norwich. Possessed of considerable inventive and mathematical talents, he was originally intended for engineering, but studied for the Unitarian ministry, to which he was ordained in 1828. After serving as pastor in various places he became in 1840 Prof. of Mental and Moral Philosophy in the Manchester New Coll. (subsequently removed to London), and Principal 1869-85. Among his writings, which were very influential, are *Rationale of Religious Inquiry* (1836), *Ideal Substitutes for God* (1879), *Study of Spinoza* (1882), *Types of Ethical Theory* (1885), *Study of Religion* (1888), *Seat of Authority in Religion* (1890), and religious poems and hymns. M. was a man of very elevated character and powerful intellect; of great acuteness, candour, and openness to new ideas. He was D.D. of Edin. 1884. and D.C.L. of Oxf. 1888.

MARVELL, ANDREW (1621-1678).—Poet and satirist, *s.* of the Rector of Winestead, Yorkshire, where he was *b.*, *ed.* Camb., and thereafter travelled in various Continental countries. He sat in Parliament for Hull, proving himself an assiduous and incorruptible member, with strong republican leanings. In spite of this he was a favourite of Charles II., who took pleasure in his society, and offered him a place at Court, and a present of £1000, which were both declined. In his own day he was best known as a powerful and fearless political writer, and for some time from 1657 was assistant to Milton as Latin Sec. After the Restoration he wrote against the Government, his chief work in this kind being on the *Growth of Popery and Arbitrary Government in England* (1677). He was also the author of an *Historical Essay regarding General Councils.* His controversial style was lively and vigorous, but sometimes coarse and vituperative. His fame now rests on his poems which, though few, have many of the highest poetical qualities. Among the best known are *The Emigrants in the Bermudas, The Nymph complaining for the Death of her Fawn,* and *Thoughts in a Garden.* Of the last Palgrave says that "it may be regarded as a test of any reader's insight into the most poetical aspects of poetry," and his *Horatian Ode on Cromwell's Return from Ireland.* The town of Hull voted him a monument, which was, however, forbidden by the Court. His appearance is thus described, "He was of middling stature, pretty strong-set, roundish-faced, cherry-cheeked, hazel-eyed, brown-haired."

Life and Works by Cooke, 1726, reprinted 1772; Thomson, 1726; Dove, 1832; and specially Grosart (4 vols., 1872-74).

MASON, WILLIAM (1724-1797).—Poet, *s.* of a clergyman, was *b.* at Hull, and *ed.* at Camb. He took orders and rose to be a Canon of York. His first poem was *Musæus,* a monody on the death of Pope, and his other works include *Elfrida* (1752), and *Caractacus* (1759), dramas—an *Heroic Epistle* to Sir William Chambers, the architect, in which he satirised some modern fashions in gardening, *The English Garden,* his largest work, and some odes. He was a close friend of Gray, whose Life he wrote. His language was too magnificent for his powers of thought, but he has passages where the rich diction has a pleasing effect.

MASSEY, GERALD (1828-1907).—Poet, *b.* near Tring, Herts. As a boy he worked in a silk-factory, and as a straw-plaiter and errand boy. When he was 15 he came to London, where he was taken up by Maurice and Kingsley. His first book was *pub.* in 1851, but he first attracted attention by *Babe Christabel* (1854). This was followed by *War Waits, Craigcrook Castle,* and *Havelock's March.* A selection from these was *pub.* 1889, under the title of *My Lyrical Life.* Later he wrote and lectured on spiritualism, and produced prose works on the origin of myths and mysteries in *The Book of Beginnings* (1881), *The Natural Genesis* (1883), and *Ancient Egypt: the Light of the World* (1907). He also wrote a book on the sonnets of Shakespeare. M. had a true lyrical vein, but though often musical, he was at times harsh and rugged, and did not give sufficient attention to form and finish.

MASSINGER, PHILIP (1583-1640).—Dramatist, was probably *b.* at Salisbury. His *f.* appears to have been a retainer of the Earl of Pembroke, by whom and by Queen Elizabeth he was employed in a confidential capacity. M. was at Oxf., but quitted the Univ. suddenly without graduating. He is next found in London writing for the stage, frequently in collaboration with others. Few details of his life have come down, but it seems that he was on the whole unfortunate. He was found dead in bed on March 16, 1640, and was buried in St. Saviour's, Southwark, by some of the actors. The burial register has the entry, "buried Philip Massinger, a stranger." Of the many plays which he wrote or had a hand in, 15 believed to be entirely his are extant, other 8 were burned by a servant in the 18th century. He, however, collaborated so much with others—Fletcher, Dekker, etc., that much fine work probably his can only be identified by internal evidence. Among his plays may be mentioned *The Unnatural Combat* (*pr.* 1639), *The Virgin Martyr* (1622) (partly by Dekker), which contains perhaps his finest writing. His best plays on the whole, however, are *The City Madam* (1632), and *A New Way to pay Old Debts* (*pr.* 1633), which latter kept the stage until the 19th century. He is believed to have joined with Fletcher and Shakespeare in *Henry VIII.* and *The Two Noble Kinsmen.* Other plays which he wrote or had a hand in are *The Duke of Milan, The Bondman, The Renegado, The Roman Actor, The Great Duke of Florence, The Maid of Honour, The Picture,* and *The Fatal Dowry.* His verse is fluent and sweet, and in his grave and reflective passages he rises to a rich and stately music. He often repeats himself, has little humour, and is not seldom coarse. He has, however, much skill in the construction and working out of a story.

MASSON, DAVID (1822-1907).—Biographer and historian, *b.* at Aberdeen, and *ed.* at Marischal Coll. there and at Edin., where he studied theology under Chalmers. He did not, however, enter the Church, but began a literary career by ed. a newspaper in Aberdeen. He then returned to Edin., where he worked for the brothers Chambers, the eminent publishers, and where he became acquainted with Wilson, Sir William Hamilton, and Chalmers, for the last of whom he cherished an extraordinary veneration. Going to London in 1847 he wrote extensively in reviews, magazines, and encyclopædias. In 1852 he became Prof. of English Literature in Univ. Coll., and in 1858 ed. of *Macmillan's Magazine.* He was appointed in 1865 Prof. of English Literature in Edin., where he exercised a profound influence on his students, many of whom have risen to high positions in literature. Though a most laborious student and man of letters, M. took a warm interest in various public questions, including Italian emancipation, and the higher education of women. He was the author of many important works, including *Essays Biographical and Critical* (1856), *British Novelists* (1859), and *Recent British Philosophy* (1865). His *magnum opus* is his monumental *Life of John Milton* (6 vols., 1859-80) the most complete biography of any Englishman, dealing as it does not only with the personal life of the poet, but with the history, political, social, and religious of his time. Other books are *Drummond of Hawthornden* (1873), *De Quincey* (in English Men of Letters Series) (1878), *Edinburgh Sketches and Memories* (1892), and *Carlyle Personally and in his Writings.* He also ed. the standard ed. of De Quincey's works, and the Register of the Privy Council of Scotland, his introductions in connection with which are of great historical value. He was appointed Historiographer for Scotland in 1893. M. was full of learning guided by sagacity, genial, broad-minded, and sane in his judgments of men and things, and thoroughly honest and sincere.

MATHER, COTTON (1663-1728).—Divine, *s.* of Increase M., a leading American divine, was *ed.* at Harvard, became a minister, and was colleague to his *f.* He was laborious, able, and learned, but extremely bigoted and self-sufficient. He carried on a persecution of so-called "witches," which led to the shedding of much innocent blood; on the other hand he was so much of a reformer as to advocate inoculation for small-pox. He was a copious author, his chief work being *Magnalia Christi Americana* (1702), an ecclesiastical history of New England. Others were *Late Memorable Providences relating to Witchcraft and Possession* (1689), and *The Wonders of the Invisible World* (1693). In his later years he admitted that "he had gone too far" in his crusade against witches.

MATHIAS, THOMAS JAMES (1754?-1835).—Satirist, *ed.* at Camb., and held some minor appointments in the Royal household. He was an accomplished Italian scholar, and made various translations from the English into Italian, and *vice versâ.* He also produced a fine ed. of Gray, on which he lost heavily. His chief work, however, was *The Pursuits of Literature* (1794), an undiscriminating satire on his literary contemporaries which went through 16 ed., but is now almost forgotten.

MATURIN, CHARLES ROBERT (1782-1824).—Novelist, *b.* in Dublin of Huguenot ancestry, was *ed.* at Trinity Coll. there, and taking orders held various benefices. He was the author of a few dramas, one of which, *Bertram*, had some success. He is, perhaps, better known for his romances in the style of Mrs. Radcliffe and "Monk" Lewis. The first of these, *The Fatal Revenge* appeared in 1807, and was followed by, among others, *The Milesian Chief* (1812), *Women*, which was the most successful, and lastly by *Melmoth*, in which he outdoes his models in the mysterious, the horrible, and indeed the revolting, without, except very occasionally, reaching their power. His last work, *The Albigenses*, in a somewhat different style, was *pub.* in the year of his death.

MAURICE, FREDERICK DENISON (1805-1872).—Divine, *s.* of a Unitarian minister, was *b.* at Normanston, near Lowestoft, and studied at Camb., but being then a Dissenter, could not graduate. He went to London, and engaged in literary work, writing for the *Westminster Review* and other periodicals, and for a short time ed. the *Athenæum*. His theological views having changed, he joined the Church of England, went to Oxf., graduated, and was ordained 1834. He became Chaplain to Guy's Hospital, and held other clerical positions in London. In 1840 he was appointed Prof. of

English Literature and History at King's Coll., and subsequently Prof. of Theology. He became a leader among the Christian socialists, and for a short time ed. their paper. On the publication of his *Theological Essays* in 1853 he was asked to resign his professorship at King's Coll. In 1854 he was one of the founders of the Working Men's Coll., of which he became Principal, and in 1866 he was made Prof. of Moral Philosophy at Camb. Among his writings are *The Religions of the World and their Relation to Christianity, Moral and Metaphysical Philosophy, The Prophets and Kings of the Old Testament* (1853), *The Doctrine of Sacrifice*, and *Theological Essays*. M.'s style was copious, and was often blamed as obscure; nevertheless, he exercised an extraordinary influence over some of the best minds of his time by the originality of his views, and the purity and elevation of his character.

MAXWELL, WILLIAM HAMILTON (1792-1850).—Novelist, a Scoto-Irishman, *b.* at Newry, and *ed.* at Trinity Coll., Dublin, entered the army, and saw service in the Peninsula, and at Waterloo. Afterwards he took orders, but was deprived of his living for non-residence. His novels, *O'Hara*, and *Stories from Waterloo*, started the school of rollicking military fiction, which culminated in the novels of Lever. M. also wrote a Life of the Duke of Wellington, and a *History of the Irish Rebellion*.

MAX-MÜLLER, FRIEDRICH (1823-1900).—Philologist, *s.* of the German poet, Wilhelm M., was *b.* at Dessau, and *ed.* at Leipzig, Berlin, and Paris. In 1846 he was requested by the East India Company to ed. the *Rig Veda*. He settled at Oxf. in 1848, and in 1850 was appointed deputy Taylorian Prof. of Modern European languages, becoming Prof. 4 years later, and Curator of the Bodleian Library in 1856. In 1868 he was elected first Prof. of Comparative Philology. He ed. *Sacred Books of the East*, and wrote in English *Chips from a German Workshop* (1867-75). He did much to stimulate the study of comparative religion and philology. He was made a Privy Councillor in 1896.

MAY, THOMAS (1595-1650).—Poet and historian, *b.* in Sussex, *s.* of Sir Thomas M., of Mayfield, went to Camb., and thence to Gray's Inn, but discarded law for literature. In 1622 he produced his first comedy, *The Heir*, and also a translation of Virgil's *Georgics*. Six years later, 1627, appeared his translation of *Lucan*, which gained him the favour of Charles I., at whose command he wrote two poems, *The Reigne of King Henry II.*, and *The Victorious Reigne of King Edward III.*, each in 7 books. When the Civil War broke out M., to the disappointment of his friends, took the side of the Parliament, and was made Sec. to the Long Parliament, the historian of which he became, *pub.* 1647, *The History of the Parliament of England, which began Nov.* 3, 1640. This work he prefaced with a short review of the preceding reigns from that of Elizabeth. The narrative closes with the Battle of Newbury, 1643, and is characterised by fulness of information and candour. M. was also the author of several tragedies, including *Antigone*, of no great merit.

MAY, SIR THOMAS ERSKINE, 1ST BARON FARNBOROUGH (1815-1886).—Jurist and historian, *ed.* at Bedford School, and after holding various minor offices became in 1871 clerk to the House of Commons, retiring in 1886, when he was raised to the peerage. He had previously, 1866, been made K.C.B. He was the author of a treatise on the laws, privileges, etc., of Parliament, which, first *pub.* in 1844, reached in 1901 its tenth ed., and was translated into various languages. His *Constitutional History of England*, 1760-1860 is practically a continuation of Hallam's great work. He also wrote *Democracy in Europe*. As an historical writer M. was learned, painstaking, and impartial.

MAYNE, JASPER (1604-1672).—Dramatist, was at Oxf., entered the Church, and became Archdeacon of Chichester. He wrote two dramas, *The City Match* (1639), and *The Amorous War* (1648), in neither of which did he sustain the clerical character. He had, however, some humour.

MAYNE, JOHN (1759-1836).—Poet, was *b.* in Dumfries. In 1780 he *pub.* the *Siller Gun* in its original form in *Ruddiman's Magazine*. It is a humorous poem descriptive of an ancient custom in Dumfries of shooting for the "Siller Gun." He was continually adding to it, until it grew to 5 cantos. He also wrote a poem on *Hallowe'en*, and a version of the ballad, *Helen of Kirkconnel*. His verses were admired by Scott.

MELVILLE, HERMAN (1819-1891).—Novelist, *b.* in New York, and took to the sea, which led to strange adventures, including an imprisonment of some months in the hands of cannibals in the Marquesas Islands. His first novel, *Typee* (1846), is based upon this experience. *Omoo* followed in 1847, *Moby Dick, or the White Whale*, a powerful sea story, in 1852, and *Israel Potter* in 1855. He was a very unequal writer, but occasionally showed considerable power and originality.

MELVILLE, JAMES (1556-1614).—Scottish divine and reformer, *s.* of the laird of Baldovie, in Forfarshire, and nephew of the great reformer and scholar, Andrew M., by whom, when Principal of the Univ. of Glasgow, he was chosen to assist him as a regent or professor. When, in 1580, Andrew became Principal of St. Mary's Coll., St. Andrews, James accompanied him, and acted as Prof. of Hebrew and Oriental Languages. He wrote many poems, but his chief work was his *Diary*, an original authority for the period, written with much naïveté, and revealing a singularly attractive personality. M., who for his part in Church matters, had been banished to England, *d.* at Berwick on his way back to Scotland.

MELVILLE, SIR JAMES (1535-1617).—Historian, *s.* of Sir John M., of Hallhill, was a page to Mary Queen of Scots at the French Court, and afterwards one of her Privy Council. He also acted as her envoy to Queen Elizabeth and the Elector Palatine. He was the author of an autobiography which is one of the original authorities for the period. The MS., which lay for long hidden in Edin. Castle, was discovered in 1660, and *pub.* 1683. A later ed. was brought out in 1827 by the Bannatyne Club. The work is written in a lively style, but is not always to be implicitly relied upon in regard either to facts or the characters attributed to individuals.

MEREDITH, GEORGE (1828-1909).—Novelist and poet, *b.* at Portsmouth, *s.* of Augustus M., a naval outfitter, who afterwards went to Cape Town, and *ed.* at Portsmouth and Neuwied in Germany. Owing to the neglect of a trustee, what means he had inherited were lost, and he was in his early days very poor. Articled to a lawyer in London, he had no taste for law, which he soon exchanged for journalism, and at 21 he was writing poetry for magazines, his first printed work, a poem on the Battle of Chillianwallah, appearing in *Chambers's Journal.* Two years later he *pub.* *Poems* (1851), containing *Love in the Valley.* Meantime he had been ed. a small provincial newspaper, and in 1866 he was war correspondent in Italy for the *Morning Post,* and he also acted for many years as literary adviser to Chapman and Hall. By this time, however, he had produced several of his novels. *The Shaving of Shagpat* had appeared in 1856, *Farina* in 1857, *The Ordeal of Richard Feverel* in 1859, *Evan Harrington* in 1861, *Emilia in England* (also known as *Sandra Belloni*) in 1864, its sequel, *Vittoria,* in 1866, and *Rhoda Fleming* in 1865. In poetry he had produced *Modern Love and Poems of the English Roadside* (1862), generally regarded as his best poetical work. These were followed by *The Adventures of Harry Richmond* (1871), *Beauchamp's Career* (1875), said to be the author's favourite, *The Egoist* (1879), which marks the beginning of a change in style characterised by an even greater fastidiousness in the choice of words, phrases, and condensation of thought than its predecessors, *The Tragic Comedians* (1880), and *Diana of the Crossways,* the first of the author's novels to attain anything approaching general popularity. The same period yielded in poetry, *Poems and Lyrics of the Joy of Earth* (1883), *Ballads and Poems of Tragic Life* (1887), and *A Reading of Earth* (1888). His later novels, *One of our Conquerors* (1891), *Lord Ormont and his Aminta* (1894), and *The Amazing Marriage* (1895), exhibit a tendency to accentuate those qualities of style which denied general popularity to all of M.'s works, and they did little to add to his reputation. The contemporary poems include *The Empty Purse* and *Jump to Glory Jane* (1892). In 1905 he received the Order of Merit, and he *d.* on May 19, 1909. He was twice *m.*, his first wife, who *d.* 1860, being a *dau.* of Thomas Love Peacock (*q.v.*). This union did not prove in all respects happy. His second wife was Miss Vulliamy, who *d.* 1885. In his earlier life he was vigorous and athletic, and a great walker; latterly he lost all power of locomotion.

Though the writings of M. never were and probably never will be generally popular, his genius was, from the very first, recognised by the best judges. All through he wrote for the reader who brought something of mind, thought, and attention, not for him who read merely to be amused without trouble; and it is therefore futile to attribute failure to him because he did not achieve what he did not aim at. Nevertheless, the long delay in receiving even the kind of recognition which he sought was a disappointment to him. Few writers have striven to charge sentences and even words so heavily with meaning, or to attain so great a degree of condensation, with the result that links in the chain of thought are not seldom omitted and left for the careful reader to supply. There is also a tendency to adopt unusual words and forms of expression where plainness and simplicity would have served as well, and these features taken together give reason for the charges of obscurity and affectation so often made. Moreover, the discussion of motive and feeling is often out of proportion to the narrative of the events and circumstances to which they stand related. But to compensate us for these defects he offers humour, often, indeed, whimsical, but keen and sparkling, close observation of and exquisite feeling for nature, a marvellous power of word-painting, the most delicate and penetrating analysis of character, and an invincible optimism which, while not blind to the darker aspects of life, triumphs over the depression which they might induce in a weaker nature. In matters of faith and dogma his standpoint was distinctly negative.

MERES, FRANCIS (1565-1647).—Miscellaneous author, was of a Lincolnshire family, studied at Camb. and Oxf., and became Rector of Wing in Rutland. He *pub.* in 1598 *Palladis Tamia : Wit's Treasury*, containing a comparison of English poets with Greek, Latin, and Italian.

MERIVALE, CHARLES (1808-1893).—Historian, *s.* of John Herman M., a translator and minor poet, *b.* in London, *ed.* at Harrow, Haileybury, and Camb., he took orders, and among other preferments held those of chaplain to the Speaker of the House of Commons, 1863-69, and Dean of Ely. From his college days he was a keen student of Roman history, and between 1850 and 1864 he *pub.* his *History of the Romans under the Empire*, an able and scholarly work, though considered by some critics to be too favourable to the Emperors, and the imperial idea. An earlier work was *The Fall of the Roman Republic* (1853).

MERRIMAN, H. SETON (*See* SCOTT, H. S.).

MESTON, WILLIAM (1688?-1745).—*S.* of a blacksmith, was *ed.* at Marischal Coll., Aberdeen, took part in the '15, and had to go into hiding. His *Knight of the Kirk* (1723) is an imitation of *Hudibras*. It has little merit.

MICKLE, WILLIAM JULIUS (1735-1788).—Poet, *s.* of the minister of Langholm, Dumfriesshire, was for some time a brewer in Edin., but failed. He went to Oxf., where he was corrector for the Clarendon Press. After various literary failures and minor successes he produced his translation of the *Lusiad*, from the Portuguese of Camoens, which brought him both fame and money. In 1777 he went to Portugal, where he was received with distinction. In 1784 he *pub.* the ballad of *Cumnor Hall*, which suggested to Scott the writing of *Kenilworth*. He is perhaps best remembered, however, by the beautiful lyric, *There's nae luck aboot the Hoose*, which, although claimed by others, is almost certainly his.

MIDDLETON, CONYERS (1683-1750).—Divine and scholar, *b.* at Richmond, Yorkshire, and *ed.* at Camb. He was the author of several latitudinarian treatises on miracles, etc., which brought him into controversy with Waterland (*q.v.*) and others, and of a *Life of*

Cicero (1741), largely plagiarised from William Bellenden, a Scottish writer of the 17th century. Another of his controversies was with Bentley on college administration. He was master of a very fine literary style.

MIDDLETON, THOMAS (1570-1627).—Dramatist, was a Londoner and city chronologer, in which capacity he composed a chronicle of the city, now lost. He wrote over 20 plays, chiefly comedies, besides masques and pageants, and collaborated with Dekker, Webster, and other playwrights. His best plays are *The Changeling, The Spanish Gipsy* (both with Rowley), and *Women beware Women.* Another, *The Game of Chess* (1624), got the author and the players alike into trouble on account of its having brought the King of Spain and other public characters upon the stage. They, however, got off with a severe reprimand. M. was a keen observer of London life, and shone most in scenes of strong passion. He is, however, unequal and repeats himself. Other plays are: *The Phœnix, Michaelmas Term* (1607), *A Trick to Catch the old One* (1608), *The Familie of Love* (1608), *A Mad World, My Masters* (1608), *The Roaring Girl* (1611) (with Dekker), *The Old Law* (1656) (with Massinger and Rowley), *A Faire Quarrel* (1617); and among his pageants and masques are *The Triumphs of Truth* (1613), *The Triumphs of Honour and Industry* (1617), *The Inner Temple Masque* (1619), etc.

MILL, JAMES (1773-1836).—Philosopher and historian, *s* of a shoemaker, was *b.* at Montrose, and showing signs of superior ability, was sent to the Univ. of Edin. with a view to the ministry. He was licensed as a preacher in 1798, but gave up the idea of the Church, and going to London in 1802 engaged in literary work, ed. the *St. James's Chronicle*, and wrote for the *Edinburgh Review.* In 1806 he began his *History of British India* (1817-18), and in 1819 received the appointment of Assistant Examiner to the India Office, and in 1834 became head of the department. M. had meanwhile become the intimate friend of Jeremy Bentham, was perhaps the chief exponent of the utilitarian philosophy, and was also one of the founders of the London Univ. His philosophical writings include *Elements of Political Economy* (1821), and *Analysis of the Human Mind* (1824). M.'s intellect was powerful, though rigid and somewhat narrow; his style was clear and precise, and his conversational powers very remarkable, and influential in moulding the opinions of those who came into contact with him, especially his distinguished son, John Stuart (*q.v.*).

MILL, JOHN STUART (1806-1873).—Philosopher, *s.* of the above, *b.* in London, was *ed.* by his *f.* with the view of making him the successor of Bentham and himself, as the exponent of the Utilitarian philosophy. In all respects he proved an apt pupil, and by his 15th year had studied classical literature, logic, political economy, and mathematics. In that year he went to France, where he was under the charge of Sir S. Bentham, a brother of Jeremy. His studies had led him to the adoption of the utilitarian philosophy, and after his return he became acquainted with Grote, the Austins, and other Benthamites. In 1823 he entered the India House as a clerk, and, like his *f.*, rose to be examiner of Indian correspondence; and, on the dissolution of the Company, retired on a liberal pension. In 1825 he ed. Bentham's *Rationale of Judicial Evidence.* During the following years he was a frequent contributor to Radical journals, and ed. the *London Review.* His *Logic* appeared in 1843, and produced a profound impression; and in 1848 he *pub. Principles of Political Economy.* The years between 1858 and 1865 were very productive, his treatises on *Liberty, Utilitarianism, Representative Government,* and his *Examination of Sir W. Hamilton's Philosophy* being *pub.* during this period. In 1865 he entered the House of Commons as one of the members for Westminster, where, though highly respected, he made no great mark. After this political parenthesis he returned to his literary pursuits, and wrote *The Subjection of Women* (1869), *The Irish Land Question* (1870), and an *Autobiography.* M. had *m.* in 1851 Mrs. Taylor, for whom he showed an extraordinary devotion, and whom he survived for 15 years. He *d.* at Avignon. His *Autobiography* gives a singular, and in some respects painful account of the methods and views of his *f.* in his education. Though remaining all his life an adherent of the ulitarian philosophy, M. did not transmit it to his disciples altogether unmodified, but, finding it too narrow and rigid for his own intellectual and moral requirements, devoted himself to widening it, and infusing into it a certain element of idealism.

Bain's *Criticism with Personal Recollections* (1882), L. Courtney's *John Stuart Mill* (1889), *Autobiography,* Stephens's *Utilitarians,* J. Grote's *Examination of the Utilitarian Philosophy of Mill,* etc.

MILLER, HUGH (1802-1856).—Geologist, and man of letters, *b.* at Cromarty, had the ordinary parish school education, and early showed a remarkable love of reading and power of story-telling. At 17 he was apprenticed to a stonemason, and his work in quarries, together with rambles among the rocks of his native shore, led him to the study of geology. In 1829 he *pub.* a vol. of poems, and soon afterwards threw himself as an ardent and effective combatant into the controversies, first of the Reform Bill, and thereafter of the Scottish Church question. In 1834 he became accountant in one of the local banks, and in the next year brought out his *Scenes and Legends in the North of Scotland.* In 1840 the popular party in the Church, with which he had been associated, started a newspaper, *The Witness,* and M. was called to be ed., a position which he retained till the end of his life, and in which he showed conspicuous ability. Among his geological works are *The Old Red Sandstone* (1841), *Footprints of the Creator* (1850), *The Testimony of the Rocks* (1856), and *Sketch-book of Popular Geology.* Other books are: *My Schools and Schoolmasters,* an autobiography of remarkable interest, *First Impressions of England and its People* (1847), and *The Cruise of the Betsy.* Of the geological books, perhaps that on the old red sandstone, a department in which M. was a discoverer, is the best: but all his writings are distinguished by great literary excellence, and especially by a marvellous power of vivid description. The end of his life was most tragic. He had for long been overworking his brain, which at last gave way, and in a temporary loss of reason, he shot himself during the night.

Life and Letters, P. Bayne (1871), etc.

MILLER, THOMAS (1807-1874).—Poet and novelist, of humble parentage, worked in early life as a basket-maker. He *pub.* *Songs of the Sea Nymphs* (1832). Going to London he was befriended by Lady Blessington (*q.v.*) and S. Rogers (*q.v.*), and for a time engaged in business as a bookseller, but was unsuccessful and devoted himself exclusively to literature, producing over 40 vols., including several novels, *e.g.*, *Royston Gower* (1838), *Gideon Giles the Roper*, and *Rural Sketches*. In his stories he successfully delineated rural characters and scenes.

MILMAN, HENRY HART (1791-1868).—Poet and historian, *s.* of Sir Francis M., a distinguished physician, *ed.* at Eton and Oxf. Taking orders he became in 1835 Rector of St. Margaret's, Westminster, and in 1849 Dean of St. Paul's. He also held the professorship of Poetry at Oxf. 1821-31. Among his poetical works may be mentioned *Fazio* (drama) (1815), *Samor* (epic) (1818), *The Fall of Jerusalem* (1820), *The Martyr of Antioch* (1822), and *Anne Boleyn* (1826). It is, however, on his work as an historian that his literary fame chiefly rests, his chief works in this department being his *History of the Jews* (1830), *History of Christianity* (1840), and especially *The History of Latin Christianity* (6 vols. 1854-56), which is one of the most important historical works of the century, characterised alike by literary distinction and by learning and research. M. also brought out a valuable ed. of Gibbon's *Decline and Fall*, and wrote a *History of St. Paul's Cathedral*.

MILNES, R. MONCKTON- (*See* HOUGHTON).

MILTON, JOHN (1608-1674).—Poet, was *b.* 9th December 1608 in Bread Street, London. His *f.*, also John, was the *s.* of a yeoman of Oxfordshire, who cast him off on his becoming a Protestant. He had then become a scrivener in London, and grew to be a man of good estate. From him his illustrious *s.* inherited his lofty integrity, and his love of, and proficiency in, music. M. received his first education from a Scotch friend of his father's, Thomas Young, a Puritan of some note, one of the writers of *Smectymnuus*. Thereafter he was at St. Paul's School, and in 1625 went to Christ's Coll., Camb., where for his beauty and his delicacy of mind he was nicknamed "the lady." His sister Anne had *m.* Edward Phillips, and the death of her first child in infancy gave to him the subject of his earliest poem, *On the death of a Fair Infant* (1626). It was followed during his 7 years' life at the Univ., along with others, by the poems, *On the Morning of Christ's Nativity* (1629), *On the Circumcision*, *The Passion*, *Time*, *At a Solemn Music*, *On May Morning*, and *On Shakespeare*, all in 1630; and two sonnets, *To the Nightingale* and *On arriving at the Age of Twenty-three*, in 1631. In 1632, having given up the idea of entering the Church, for which his *f.* had intended him, he lived for 6 years at Horton, near Windsor, to which the latter had retired, devoted to further study. Here he wrote *L'Allegro* and *Il Penseroso* in 1632, *Arcades* (1633), *Comus* in 1634, and *Lycidas* in 1637. The first celebrates the pleasures of a life of cheerful innocence, and the second of contemplative, though not gloomy, retirement, and the last is a lament for a lost friend, Edward

King, who perished at sea. *Arcades* and *Comus* are masques set to music by Henry Lawes, having for their motives respectively family affection and maiden purity. Had he written nothing else these would have given him a place among the immortals. In 1638 he completed his education by a period of travel in France and Italy, where he visited Grotius at Paris, and Galileo at Florence. The news of impending troubles in Church and State brought him home the following year, and with his return may be said to close the first of three well-marked divisions into which his life falls. These may be called (1) the period of preparation and of the early poems; (2) the period of controversy, and of the prose writings; and (3) the period of retirement and of the later poems. Soon after his return M. settled in London, and employed himself in teaching his nephews, Edward and John Phillips, turning over in his mind at the same time various subjects as the possible theme for the great poem which, as the chief object of his life, he looked forward to writing. But he was soon to be called away to far other matters, and to be plunged into the controversies and practical business which were to absorb his energies for the next 20 years. The works of this period fall into three classes—(1) those directed against Episcopacy, including *Reformation of Church Discipline in England* (1641), and his answers to the writings of Bishop Hall (*q.v.*), and in defence of *Smectymnuus* (*see* under Calamy); (2) those relating to divorce, including *The Doctrine and Discipline of Divorce* (1643), and *The Four Chief Places of Scripture which treat of Marriage* (1645); and (3) those on political and miscellaneous questions, including the *Tractate on Education*, *Areopagitica, A Speech for the Liberty of Unlicensed Printing* (1644) (his greatest prose work), *Eikonoklastes*, an answer to the *Eikon Basilike* of Dr. Gauden (*q.v.*), *The Tenure of Kings and Magistrates* (1649), in defence of the execution of Charles I., which led to the furious controversy with Salmasius, the writing of *Pro Populo Anglicano Defensio* (1650), the second *Defensio* (1654), which carried his name over Europe, and *The Ready and Easy Way to establish a Free Commonwealth*, written on the eve of the Restoration. In 1643 M. had *m.* Mary Powell, the *dau.* of an Oxfordshire cavalier, a girl of 17, who soon found her new life as the companion of an austere poet, absorbed in severe study, too abrupt a change from the gay society to which she had been accustomed, and in a month returned to her father's house on a visit. When the time fixed for rejoining her husband arrived, she showed no disposition to do so, upon which he began to aim at a divorce, and to advocate in the works above mentioned "unfitness and contrariety of mind" as a valid ground for it, views which incurred for him much notoriety and unpopularity. A reconciliation, however, followed in 1645, and three *dau.* were born of the marriage. In 1649 the reputation of M. as a Latinist led to his appointment as Latin or Foreign Sec. to the Council of State, in the duties of which he was, after his sight began to fail, assisted by A. Marvell (*q.v.*) and others, and which he retained until the Restoration. In 1652 his wife *d.*, and four years later he entered into a second marriage with Katharine Woodcock, who *d.* in child-birth in the following year. To her memory he dedicated one of the most touching of his sonnets. At the Restoration he was, of course, deprived of his office, and had to go into hiding; but on the intercession of Marvell (*q.v.*), and perhaps Davenant (*q.v.*), his name was included in the amnesty. In 1663, being now totally blind and somewhat helpless, he asked his friend Dr. Paget to recommend a wife for him. The lady chosen was Elizabeth Minshull, aged 25, who appears to have given him domestic happiness in his last years. She survived him for 53 years. The Restoration closed his second, and introduced his third, and for his fame, most productive period. He was now free to devote his whole powers to the great work which he had so long contemplated. For some time he had been in doubt as to the subject, had considered the Arthurian legends, but had decided upon the Fall of Man. The result was *Paradise Lost*, which was begun in 1658, finished in 1664, and *pub.* in 1667. A remark of his friend, Thomas Ellwood (*q.v.*), suggested to him the writing of *Paradise Regained*, which, along with *Samson Agonistes*, was *pub.* in 1671. Two years before he had printed a *History of Britain*, written long before, which, however, is of little value. The work of M. was now done. In addition to his blindness he suffered from gout, to which it was partly attributable, and, his strength gradually failing, but with mind unimpaired and serene, he *d.* peacefully on November 8, 1674. In M. the influences of the Renaissance and of Puritanism met. To the former he owed his wide culture and his profound love of everything noble and beautiful, to the latter his lofty and austere character, and both these elements meet in his writings. Leaving Shakespeare out of account, he holds an indisputable place at the head of English poets. For strength of imagination, delicate accuracy and suggestiveness of language, and harmony of versification, he is unrivalled, and almost unapproached; and when the difficulties inherent in the subject of his great masterpiece are considered, the power he shows in dealing with them appears almost miraculous, and we feel that in those parts where he has failed, success was impossible for a mortal. In his use of blank verse he has, for majesty, variety, and music, never been approached by any of his successors. He had no dramatic power and no humour. In everything he wrote, a proud and commanding genius manifests itself, and he is one of those writers who inspire reverence rather than affection. His personal appearance in early life has been thus described, " He was a little under middle height, slender, but erect, vigorous, and agile, with light brown hair clustering about his fair and oval face, with dark grey eyes."

SUMMARY.—*B.* 1608, *ed.* at St. Paul's School and Camb., and while at the latter wrote earlier poems including *The Nativity* and Sonnets, lived for 6 years at Horton and wrote *L'Allegro*, *Il Penseroso*, *Arcades*, *Comus*, and *Lycidas*, travelled in France and Italy 1638, settled in London, entered on his political and controversial labours, and wrote *inter alia* on *Reform of Discipline* 1641, *Divorce* 1643-45, *Education* 1644, *Areopagitica* 1644, and the two *Defences* 1650 and 1654, appointed Latin Sec. 1649, this period closed by Restoration 1660, *Paradise Lost* written 1658-64, *pub.* 1667, *Paradise Regained* and *Samson Agonistes* 1671, *d.* 1674, *m.* first 1643 Mary Powell, second 1652 Katharine Woodcock, third 1663 Eliz. Minshull, who survived till 1727.

Life by Prof. Masson (6 vols. 1859-80), also short Lives by M.

Patteson (1880), Garnett (1889). Ed. of *Works* by Boydell, Sir E. Brydges, and Prof. Masson.

MINOT, LAURENCE (1300?-1352?).—Poet. Nothing is certainly known of him. He may have been a soldier. He celebrates in northern English and with a somewhat ferocious patriotism the victories of Edward III. over the Scots and the French.

MINTO, WILLIAM (1845-1893).—Critic and biographer, *b.* at Alford, Aberdeenshire, and *ed.* at Aberdeen and Oxf., went to London, and became ed. of the *Examiner*, and also wrote for the *Daily News* and the *Pall Mall Gazette*. In 1880 he was appointed Prof. of Logic and Literature at Aberdeen. He wrote a *Manual of English Prose Literature* (1873), *Characteristics of the English Poets* (1874), and a *Life of Defoe* for the Men of Letters Series.

MITCHELL, JOHN (1815-1875).—Journalist and political writer, *s.* of a Presbyterian minister, was *b.* in Ulster. For some time he practised as a solicitor, but becoming acquainted with Thomas Davis (*q.v.*), he associated himself with the Young Ireland party, and was a leading contributor to the *Nation* newspaper. His political sympathies and acts were carried so far as to bring about in 1848 his trial for treason-felony, and his transportation for 14 years. After his release he resided chiefly at New York, and ed. various papers, and opposed the abolition of slavery; but in 1874 he was elected M.P. for Tipperary, for which, however, he was declared incapable of sitting. On a new election he was again returned, but *d.* before the resulting petition could be heard. He wrote a *Jail Journal*, a work of great power, *The Last Conquest of Ireland* (*perhaps*) (1860), and a *History of Ireland* of little value.

MITFORD, MARY RUSSELL (1787-1855).—Poetess and novelist, *b.* at Alresford, Hants, *dau.* of a physician, without practice, selfish and extravagant, who ran through three fortunes, his own, his wife's, and his daughter's, and then lived on the industry of the last. After a vol. of poems which attracted little notice, she produced her powerful tragedy, *Julian*. In 1812, what ultimately became the first vol. of *Our Village* appeared in the *Lady's Magazine*. To this four additional vols. were added, the last in 1832. In this work Miss M. may be said to have created a new branch of literature. Her novel, *Belford Regis* (1835), is somewhat on the same lines. She added two dramas, *Rienzi* (1828), and *Foscari, Atherton and other Tales* (1852), and *Recollections of a Literary Life*, and *d.* at her cottage at Swallowfield, much beloved for her benevolent and simple character, as well as valued for her intellectual powers.

MITFORD, WILLIAM (1744-1827).—Historian, *e.s.* of John M. of Exbury, Hants, descended from an old Northumbrian family, was *b.* in London, and *ed.* at Cheam School and Oxf. He studied law, but on succeeding to the family estates devoted himself to study and literature, and to his duties as an officer of the militia. His first *pub.* was an *Essay on the Harmony of Language* (1774). His great work, *The History of Greece*, is said to have been undertaken at the suggestion of Gibbon, who was a fellow-officer in the South Hants Militia. This work, the successive vols. of which appeared at considerable intervals between 1784 and 1810, was long a standard one, though it is now largely superseded by the histories of Thirwall and Grote. M. wrote with strong prejudices against democracy, and in defence of tyrants, but his style is forcible and agreeable, and he brought learning and research to bear on his subject. He sat for many years in Parliament.

MOIR, DAVID MACBETH (1798-1851).—Poet and miscellaneous writer, was a doctor at Musselburgh, near Edin., and a frequent contributor, under the signature of Δ, to *Blackwood's Magazine* in which appeared *Mansie Waugh*, a humorous Scottish tale. He also wrote *The Legend of Genevieve* (1824), *Domestic Verses* (1843), and sketches of the poetry of the earlier half of the 19th century. His poetry was generally grave and tender, but occasionally humorous.

MONBODDO, JAMES BURNETT, LORD (1714-1799).—Philosopher and philologist, *b.* at the family seat in Kincardineshire, was *ed.* at the Univ. of Aberdeen, Edin., and Groningen, and called to the Scottish Bar in 1737. Thirty years later he became a judge with the title of Lord Monboddo. He was a man of great learning and acuteness, but eccentric and fond of paradox. He was the author of two large works alike learned and whimsical, *An Essay on the Origin and Progress of Language* (6 vols. 1773-92), and *Ancient Metaphysics* (6 vols. 1779-99). He mooted and supported the theory that men were originally monkeys, and gradually attained to reason, language, and civilisation by the pressure of necessity. His doctrines do not sound so absurd now as they did in his own day. He was visited by Dr. Johnson at Monboddo.

MONTAGU, ELIZABETH (ROBINSON) (1720-1800).—Critic, *dau.* of a gentleman of Yorkshire, *m.* a grandson of Lord Sandwich. She was one of the original "blue-stockings," and her house was a literary centre. She wrote an *Essay on the Writings and Genius of Shakespeare* (1769), in which she compared him with the classical and French dramatists, and defended him against the strictures of Voltaire. It had great fame in its day, but has long been superseded.

MONTAGU, LADY MARY WORTLEY (PIERREPONT) (1690-1762).—Letter-writer, was the eldest *dau.* of the 1st Duke of Kingston. In her youth she combined the attractions of a reigning beauty and a wit. Her early studies were encouraged and assisted by Bishop Burnet, and she was the friend of Pope, Addison, and Swift. In 1712 she *m.*, against the wishes of her family, Edward Wortley-Montagu, a cousin of the celebrated Charles Montagu, afterwards Earl of Halifax. Her husband having been appointed Ambassador to the Porte, she accompanied him, and wrote the sparkling *Letters from the East* which have given her a place high among the great letter-writers of the world. While in Turkey she became acquainted with the practice of inoculation against smallpox, which she did much to introduce into western countries. After her return to England she settled at Twickenham, and renewed her friendship with Pope, which, however, ended in a violent quarrel, arising out of her publication of *Town Eclogues*. She was furiously attacked by both Pope and Swift, and was not slow to defend herself. In 1737, for reasons which have never been explained, she left her husband and country, and settled in Italy. Mr. M. having *d.*, 1761, she returned at the request of her *dau.*, the Countess of Bute, but *d.* the following year.

MONTGOMERIE, ALEXANDER (1545?-1610?).—Poet, probably *b.* in Ayrshire, was in the service of the Regent Morton and James VI., by whom he was pensioned. He is sometimes styled "Captain," and was laureate of the Court. He appears to have fallen on evil days, was imprisoned on the Continent, and lost his pension. His chief work is *The Cherrie and the Slae* (1597), a somewhat poor allegory of Virtue and Vice, but with some vivid description in it, and with a comparatively modern air. He also wrote *Flyting* (scolding) *betwixt Montgomerie and Polwart, pub.* 1621, and other pieces.

MONTGOMERY, JAMES (1771-1854).—Poet, *s.* of a pastor and missionary of the Moravian Brethren, was *b.* at Irvine, Ayrshire, and *ed.* at the Moravian School at Fulneck, near Leeds. After various changes of occupation and abode, he settled in Sheffield in 1792 as clerk to a newspaper. In 1796 he had become ed. of the *Sheffield Iris*, and was twice imprisoned for political articles for which he was held responsible. In 1797 he *pub. Prison Amusements;* but his first work to attract notice was *The Wanderer of Switzerland* (1806). It was followed by *The West Indies* (1809), *The World before the Flood* (1812), *Greenland* (1819), and *The Pelican Island* (1828), all of which contain passages of considerable imaginative and descriptive power, but are lacking in strength and fire. He himself expected that his name would live, if at all, in his hymns, and in this his judgment has proved true. Some of these, such as *For ever with the Lord*, *Hail to the Lord's Anointed*, and *Prayer is the Soul's sincere Desire*, are sung wherever the English language is spoken. M. was a good and philanthropic man, the opponent of every form of injustice and oppression, and the friend of every movement for the welfare of the race. His virtues attained wide recognition.

MONTGOMERY, ROBERT (1807-1855).—Poet, a minister of the Scottish Episcopal Church, wrote some ambitious religious poems, including *The Omnipresence of the Deity* and *Satan*, which were at first outrageously puffed, and had a wide circulation. Macaulay devoted an essay to the demolition of the author's reputation, in which he completely succeeded.

MOORE, EDWARD (1712-1757).—Fabulist and dramatist, *s.* of a dissenting minister, was *b.* at Abingdon. After being in business as a linen-draper, in which he was unsuccessful, he took to literature, and wrote a few plays, of which *The Gamester* (1753) had a great vogue, and was translated into various languages. He is best known by his *Fables for the Female Sex* (1744), which rank next to those of Gay (*q.v.*).

MOORE, JOHN (1729 or 1730-1802).—Physician and miscellaneous writer, *s.* of an Episcopal minister, was *b.* in Stirling. After studying medicine at Glasgow, he acted as a surgeon in the navy and the army, and ultimately settled in Glasgow as a physician. In 1779 he *pub. View of Manners and Society in France, Switzerland,*

and Germany, which was well received. A similar work, relating to Italy, followed in 1781. He is, however, chiefly remembered by his romance *Zeluco* (1786?). One or two other novels followed, and his last works are a *Journal during a Residence in France* (1792), and *Causes and Progress of the French Revolution* (1795), the latter of which was used both by Scott and Carlyle. M. was one of the friends of Burns, and was the *f.* of Sir John M., the hero of Corunna.

MOORE, THOMAS (1779-1852).—Poet, *b.* in Dublin, *s.* of a grocer and wine-merchant in a small way, was *ed.* at Trinity Coll., after which he went to London, and studied law at the Middle Temple, 1799. He took with him a translation of *Anacreon*, which appeared, dedicated to the Prince Regent, in 1800, was well received, and made a position for him. In the following year appeared *Poems by Thomas Little*. In 1803 he received the appointment of Admiralty Registrar at Bermuda, and after visiting the island and travelling in America, he committed his official duties to a deputy (an unfortunate step as it proved), and returned to England. The literary fruit of this journey was *Epistles, Odes, and other Poems* (1806). In 1807 M. found his true poetic vocation in his *Irish Melodies*—the music being furnished by Sir John Stevenson, who adapted the national airs. The reception they met with was enthusiastic, and M. was carried at once to the height of his reputation. They continued to appear over a period of 25 years, and for each of the 130 songs he received 100 guineas. His charming singing of these airs, and his fascinating conversational and social powers made him sought after in the highest circles. In 1815 there appeared *National Airs* which, however, cannot be considered equal to the *Melodies*. After making various unsuccessful attempts at serious satire, he hit upon a vein for which his light and brilliant wit eminently qualified him—the satirical and pungent verses on men and topics of the day, afterwards *coll.* in *The Twopenny Post Bag*, in which the Prince Regent especially was mercilessly ridiculed, and about the same time appeared *Fables for the Holy Alliance*. In 1818 he produced the *Fudge Family in Paris*, written in that city, which then swarmed with "groups of ridiculous English." *Lalla Rookh*, with its gorgeous descriptions of Eastern scenes and manners, had appeared in the previous year with great applause. In 1818 the great misfortune of his life occurred through the dishonesty of his deputy in Bermuda, which involved him in a loss of £6000, and necessitated his going abroad. He travelled in Italy with Lord John Russell, and visited Byron. Thereafter he settled for a year or two in Paris, where he wrote *The Loves of the Angels* (1823). On the death of Byron his memoirs came into the hands of Moore, who, in the exercise of a discretion committed to him, destroyed them. He afterwards wrote a *Life of Byron* (1830), which gave rise to much criticism and controversy, and he also ed. his works. His last imaginative work was *The Epicurean* (1827). Thereafter he confined himself almost entirely to prose, and *pub.* Lives of Sheridan (1827), and Lord Edward Fitzgerald (1831). His last work, written in failing health, was a *History of Ireland* for Lardner's *Cabinet Cyclopædia*, which had little merit. Few poets have ever enjoyed greater popularity with the public, or the friendship of more men distinguished in all departments of life. This latter was largely owing to his brilliant social qualities, but his genuine and independent character had also a large share in it. He left behind him a mass of correspondence and autobiographical matter which he committed to his friend Lord John (afterwards Earl) Russell for publication. They appeared in 8 vols. (1852-56).

Memoir, Journal, and Correspondence, by Lord John Russell (1856).

MORE, HANNAH (1745-1833).—Miscellaneous and religious writer, was one of the five daughters of a schoolmaster at Stapleton, Gloucestershire. The family removed to Bristol, where Hannah began her literary efforts. Some early dramas, including *The Search after Happiness* and the *Inflexible Captive* brought her before the public, and she went to London in 1774, where, through her friend, Garrick, she was introduced to Johnson, Burke, and the rest of that circle, by whom she was highly esteemed. After publishing some poems, now forgotten, and some dramas, she resolved to devote herself to efforts on behalf of social and religious amelioration, in which she was eminently successful, and exercised a wide and salutary influence. Her works written in pursuance of these objects are too numerous to mention. They included *Hints towards forming the Character of a young Princess* (1805), written at the request of the Queen for the benefit of the Princess Charlotte, *Cœlebs in search of a Wife* (1809), and a series of short tales, the *Cheap Repository*, among which was the well-known *Shepherd of Salisbury Plain*. This enterprise, which had great success, led to the formation of the Religious Tract Society. The success of Miss M.'s literary labours enabled her to pass her later years in ease, and her sisters having also retired on a competency made by conducting a boarding-school in Bristol, the whole family resided on a property called Barley Grove, which they had purchased, where they carried on with much success philanthropic and educational work among the people of the neighbouring district of Cheddar. Few persons have devoted their talents more assiduously to the well-being of their fellow-creatures, or with a greater measure of success.

MORE, HENRY (1614-1687).—Philosopher, *b.* at Grantham, and *ed.* at Camb., took orders, but declined all preferment, including two deaneries and a bishopric; and also various appointments in his Univ., choosing rather a quiet life devoted to scholarship and philosophy, especially the study of writings of Plato and his followers. He led a life of singular purity and religious devotion, tinged with mysticism, and his writings had much popularity and influence in their day. Among them may be mentioned *Psychozoia Platonica* (1642), *repub.* (1647) as *Philosophicall Poems*, *Divine Dialogues* (prose) (1668), *The Mystery of Godliness*, and *The Mystery of Iniquity*. His life was written by his friend Richard Ward.

MORE, SIR THOMAS (1478-1535).—Historical and political writer, *s.* of Sir John M., a Justice of the King's Bench, was *b.* in London. In his 16th year he was placed in the household of Morton, Archbishop of Canterbury, who was wont to say, " This child here waiting at the table . . . will prove a marvellous man." In 1497 he went to Oxf., where he became the friend of Erasmus and others, and came in contact with the new learning. He studied law at New Inn and Lincoln's Inn, and for some time thought of entering the Church. He was, however, in 1504 sent up to Parliament, where his powerful speaking gained for him a high place. Meanwhile, he had brilliant success in the Law Courts, and was introduced by Wolsey to Henry VIII., with whom he soon rose into high favour. He became Chancellor of the Duchy of Lancaster, Speaker of the House of Commons, 1523, and was sent on missions to Charles V. and Francis I. At length, on the fall of Wolsey, M. was, much against his will, appointed Lord Chancellor, an office which he filled with singular purity and success, though he was harsh in his dealings with persons accused of heresy. But differences with the King soon arose. M. disapproved of Henry's ecclesiastical policy, as well as of his proceedings in regard to the Queen, and in 1532 he resigned his office. In 1534 he refused the oath which pledged him to approval of the King's marriage to Anne Boleyn, and for this he was imprisoned in the Tower, and on July 7, 1535, beheaded. His body was buried in St. Peter's in the Tower, and his head exhibited on London Bridge, whence it was taken down and preserved by his *dau.*, the noble Margaret Roper. All Catholic Europe was shocked at the news of what was truly a judicial murder. Among his works are a Life of *Picus, Earl of Mirandula* (1510), and a *History of Richard III.*, written about 1513. His great work, *Utopia*, was written in Latin in two books—the second 1515, and the first 1516. It had immediate popularity, and was translated into French 1530, English 1551, German 1524, Italian 1548, and Spanish 1790. It gives an account of an imaginary island and people, under cover of which it describes the social and political condition of England, with suggested remedies for abuses. The opinions on religion and politics expressed in it are not, however, always those by which he was himself guided. M. wrote many works of controversy, among which are *Dyaloge concerning Heresies*, also epigrams and dialogues in Latin. His pure and religious character, his sweet temper, his wit, his constancy and fortitude under misfortune combine to render him one of the most attractive and admirable figures in English history.

Life by W. Roper (son-in-law), Lord Campbell, *Lives of Chancellors*, *Utopia* was translated by Robinson (1551, etc.), Bishop Burnet (1684, etc.), and ed. by Lupton (1895), and Michelis (1896).

MORGAN, LADY (SYDNEY OWENSON) (1780?-1859).—Novelist, *dau.* of Robert Owenson, an actor, was the author of several vivacious Irish tales, including *The Wild Irish Girl* (1806), *O'Donnel* (1814), and *The O'Briens and the O'Flaherties* (1827); also two books on society in France and in Italy characterised by "more vivacity and point than delicacy," and a Life of Salvator Rosa.

MORIER, JAMES JUSTINIAN (1780?-1849).—Traveller and novelist, *s.* of Isaac M., descended from a Huguenot family resident at Smyrna, where he was *b.*, was *ed.* at Harrow. Returning to the East he became in 1809 Sec. of Legation in Persia. He wrote accounts of travels in Persia, Armenia, and Asia Minor; also novels, in which he exhibits a marvellous familiarity with Oriental manners and modes of thought. The chief of these are *The Adventures of Hajji Baba* (1824), and *Hajji Baba in England* (1828), *Zohrab the Hostage* (1832), *Ayesha* (1834), and *The Mirza* (1841). All these works are full of brilliant description, character-painting, and delicate satire.

MORISON, JAMES COTTER (1832-1888).—Was *ed.* at Oxf. He wrote Lives of *Gibbon* (1878), and *Macaulay* (1882); but his best work was his *Life of St. Bernard* (1863). *The Service of Man* (1887) is written from a Positivist point of view.

MORLEY, HENRY (1822-1894).—Writer on English literature, *s.* of an apothecary, was *b.* in London, *ed.* at a Moravian school in Germany, and at King's Coll., London, and after practising medicine and keeping schools at various places, went in 1850 to London, and adopted literature as his profession. He wrote in periodicals, and from 1859-64 ed. the *Examiner.* From 1865-89 he was Prof. of English Literature at Univ. Coll. He was the author of various biographies, including Lives of *Palissy, Cornelius Agrippa,* and *Clement Marot.* His principal work, however, was *English Writers* (10 vols. 1864-94), coming down to Shakespeare. His *First Sketch of English Literature*—the study for the larger work—had reached at his death a circulation of 34,000 copies.

MORRIS, SIR LEWIS (1833-1907).—Poet, *b.* at Penrhyn, Carmarthenshire, and *ed.* at Sherborne and Oxf., was called to the Bar, and practised as a conveyancer until 1880, after which he devoted himself to the promotion of higher education in Wales, and became honorary sec. and treasurer of the New Welsh Univ. In 1871 he *pub. Songs of Two Worlds,* which showed the influence of Tennyson, and was well received, though rather by the wider public than by more critical circles. It was followed in 1876-77 by *The Epic of Hades,* which had extraordinary popularity, and which, though exhibiting undeniable talent both in versification and narrative power, lacked the qualities of the higher kinds of poetry. It deals in a modern spirit with the Greek myths and legends. Other works are *A Vision of Saints, Gwen, The Ode of Life,* and *Gycia,* a tragedy.

MORRIS, WILLIAM (1834-1896).—Poet, artist, and socialist, *b.* at Walthamstow, and *ed.* at Marlborough School and Oxf. After being articled as an architect he was for some years a painter, and then joined in founding the manufacturing and decorating firm of Morris, Marshall, Faulkner and Co., in which Rossetti, Burne-Jones, and other artists were partners. By this and other means he did much to influence the public taste in furnishing and decoration. He was one of the originators of the *Oxford and Cambridge Magazine,* to which he contributed poems, tales, and essays, and in 1858 he *pub. Defence of Guenevere and other Poems. The Life and Death of Jason* followed in 1867, *The Earthly Paradise* in 1868-70, and *Love is Enough* in 1875. In the last mentioned year he made a translation in verse of Virgil's *Æneid.* Travels in Iceland led to the writing of *Three Northern Love Stories,* and the epic of *Sigurd the Volsung* (1876). His translation of the *Odyssey* in verse appeared 1887. A series of prose romances began with *The House of the Wolfings* (1889).

and included *The Roots of the Mountains, Story of the Glittering Plain. The Wood beyond the World, The Well at the World's End* (1896), and posthumously *The Water of the Wondrous Isles*, and *Story of the Sundering Flood.* In addition to poems and tales M. produced various illuminated manuscripts, including two of Fitzgerald's *Omar Khayyam*, and many controversial writings, among which are tales and tracts in advocacy of Socialism. To this class belong the *Dream of John Ball* (1888), and *News from Nowhere* (1891). In 1890 M. started the Kelmscott Press, for which he designed type and decorations. For his subjects as a writer he drew upon classic and Gothic models alike. He may perhaps be regarded as the chief of the modern romantic school, inspired by the love of beauty for its own sake; his poetry is rich and musical, and he has a power of description which makes his pictures live and glow, but his narratives sometimes suffer from length and slowness of movement.

Life by J. W. Mackail (2 vols., 1899), *The Books of W. Morris*, Forman, etc.

MORTON, THOMAS (1764-1838).—Dramatist, *b.* in Durham, came to London to study law, which he discarded in favour of playwriting. He wrote about 25 plays, of which several had great popularity. In one of them, *Speed the Plough*, he introduced Mrs. Grundy to the British public.

MOTHERWELL, WILLIAM (1797-1835).—Poet, *b.* and *ed.* in Glasgow, he held the office of depute sheriff-clerk at Paisley, at the same time contributing poetry to various periodicals. He had also antiquarian tastes, and a deep knowledge of the early history of Scottish ballad literature, which he turned to account in *Minstrelsy, Ancient and Modern* (1827), a collection of Scottish ballads with an historical introduction. In 1830 he became ed. of the *Glasgow Courier*, and in 1832 he *coll.* and *pub.* his poems. He also joined Hogg in ed. the Works of Burns.

MOTLEY, JOHN LOTHROP (1814-1877).—Historian, *b.* at Dorchester, a suburb of Boston, Massachusetts, was *ed.* at Harvard, where O. W. Holmes (*q.v.*), afterwards his biographer, was a fellow-student. After graduating he went to Europe, studied at Göttingen and Berlin, and visited Italy. On his return he studied law, and was admitted to the Bar in 1837. He did not, however, practise, and was in 1840 sent to St. Petersburg as Sec. of Legation. Meanwhile, having *pub.* two novels, *Morton's Hope* and *Merry Mount*, which had little success, he turned to history, and attracted attention by some essays in various reviews. Having decided to write an historical work on Holland, he proceeded in 1851 to Europe to collect materials, and in 1856 *pub. The Rise of the Dutch Republic.* It was received with the highest approval by such critics as Froude and Prescott, and at once took its place as a standard work. It was followed in 1860 by the first two vols. of *The United Netherlands.* The following year M. was appointed Minister at Vienna, and in 1869 at London. His latest works were a *Life of Barneveldt*, the Dutch statesman, and *A View of . . . the Thirty Years' War.* M. holds a high place among historical writers both on account of his research and accuracy, and his vivid and dramatic style, which shows the influence of Carlyle.

MOULTRIE, JOHN (1799-1874).—Poet, *ed.* at Eton and Camb., took orders and was Rector of Rugby. He wrote several books of poetry, his best known pieces are *My Brother's Grave*, and *Godiva*.

MULOCK, DINAH MARIA (MRS. CRAIK) (1826-1887).—Novelist, *dau.* of a Nonconformist minister of Irish descent. Beginning with stories for children, she developed into a prolific and popular novelist. Her best and most widely known book is *John Halifax, Gentleman* (1857), which had a wide popularity, and was translated into several languages. Others are *The Head of the Family*, *Agatha's Husband*, *A Life for a Life*, and *Mistress and Maid*. She also wrote one or two vols. of essays.

MUNDAY, ANTHONY (1553-1633).—Dramatist, poet, and pamphleteer, *s.* of a draper in London, appears to have had a somewhat chequered career. He went to Rome in 1578, and *pub.* *The Englyshe Romayne Life*, in which he gives descriptions of rites and other matters fitted to excite Protestant feeling; and he appears to have acted practically as a spy upon Roman Catholics. He had a hand in 18 plays, of which four only are extant, including two on *Robert, Earl of Huntingdon* (*Robin Hood*) (1598), and one on the *Life of Sir John Oldcastle*. He was ridiculed by Ben Jonson in *The Case is Altered*. He was also a ballad-writer, but nothing of his in this kind survives, unless *Beauty sat bathing in a Spring* be correctly attributed to him. He also wrote city pageants, and translated popular romances, including *Palladino of England*, and *Amadis of Gaule*. He was made by Stow the antiquary (*q.v.*) his literary executor, and *pub.* his *Survey of London* (1618).

MURE, WILLIAM (1799-1860).—Scholar, laird of Caldwell, Ayrshire, *ed.* at Westminster, Edin., and Bonn, sat in Parliament for Renfrewshire 1846-55. He was a sound classical scholar, and *pub.* *A Critical History of the Language and Literature of Ancient Greece* (5 vols., 1850-57). He held the view that the *Iliad* and *Odyssey* are now substantially as they were originally composed. M. was Lord Rector of Glasgow Univ. 1847-48.

MURPHY, ARTHUR (1727-1805).—Actor and dramatist, *b.* in Ireland, and *ed.* at St. Omer, went on the stage, then studied for the Bar, to which he was ultimately admitted after some demur on account of his connection with the stage. His plays were nearly all adaptations. They include *The Apprentice* (1756), *The Spouter*, and *The Upholsterer*. He also wrote an essay on Dr. Johnson, and a Life of Garrick.

MURRAY, LINDLEY (1745-1826).—Grammarian, was *b.* in Pennsylvania, and practised as a lawyer. From 1785 he lived in England, near York, and was for his last 16 years confined to the house. His *English Grammar* (1795) was long a standard work, and his main claim to a place in literature. His other writings were chiefly religious.

MYERS, FREDERIC WILLIAM HENRY (1843-1901).—Poet and essayist, *s.* of a clergyman, was *b.* at Keswick, and *ed.* at Cheltenham and Camb. He became an inspector of schools, and was the author of several vols. of poetry, including *St. Paul* (1867). He also wrote *Essays Classical and Modern*, and Lives of Wordsworth and Shelley. Becoming interested in mesmerism and spiritualism he aided in founding the Society for Psychical Research, and was joint author of *Phantasms of the Living*. His last work was *Human Personality and its Survival of Bodily Death* (1903).

NABBES, THOMAS (*fl.* 1638).—Dramatist, was at Oxf. in 1621. He lived in London, and wrote comedies, satirising bourgeois society. He was most successful in writing masques, among which are *Spring's Glory* and *Microcosmus*. He also wrote a continuation of Richard Knolles' *History of the Turks*.

NAIRNE, CAROLINA (OLIPHANT), BARONESS (1766-1845). —*B*. at the House of Gask (" the auld house "), *m*. in 1806 her second cousin, Major Nairne, who on reversal of attainder became 5th Lord Nairne. On his death, after residing in various places in England, Ireland, and on the Continent, she settled at the new house of Gask (the old one having been pulled down in 1801). Of her songs—87 in number—many first appeared anonymously in *The Scottish Minstrel* (1821-24); a collected ed. with her name, under the title of *Lays from Strathearn*, was *pub*. after her death. Although the songs, some of which were founded on older compositions, had from the first an extraordinary popularity, the authoress maintained a strict anonymity during her life. For direct simplicity and poetic feeling Lady N. perhaps comes nearer than any other Scottish song-writer to Burns, and many of her lyrics are enshrined in the hearts of her fellow-countrymen. Among the best of them are *The Land of the Leal* (1798), *Caller Herrin'*, *The Laird o' Cockpen*, *The Auld House*, *The Rowan Tree*, *The Hundred Pipers*, and *Will ye no come back Again?* The Jacobitism of some of these and many others was, of course, purely sentimental and poetical, like that of Scott. She was a truly religious and benevolent character, and the same modesty which concealed her authorship withdrew from public knowledge her many deeds of charity.

NAPIER, MARK (1798-1879).—Historian, *s*. of a lawyer in Edinburgh, was called to the Bar, practised as an advocate, and was made Sheriff of Dumfries and Galloway. He *pub*. Memoirs of the Napiers, of Montrose, and of Graham of Claverhouse, the last of which gave rise to much controversy. N. wrote from a strongly Cavalier and Jacobite standpoint, and had remarkably little of the judicial spirit in his methods. His writings, however, have some historical value.

NAPIER, SIR WILLIAM FRANCIS PATRICK (1785-1860).—was one of the sons of Col. the Hon. George N. and Lady Sarah Lennox, *dau*. of the 2nd Duke of Richmond, and the object of a romantic attachment on the part of George III. One of his brothers was Sir Charles N., the conqueror of Scinde. Entering the army at 15, he served with great distinction in the Peninsula under Moore and Wellington. His experiences as a witness and participator in the stupendous events of the war combined with the possession of remarkable acumen and a brilliant style to qualify him for the great work of his life as its historian. *The History of the War in the Penin-*

sula and in the South of France from 1807-14 (1828-40) at once took rank as a classic, and superseded all existing works on the subject. Though not free from prejudice and consequent bias, it remains a masterpiece of historical writing, especially in the description of military operations. It was translated into French, German, Spanish, Italian, and Persian. N. also *pub. The Conquest of Scinde* (1844-46), mainly a defence of his brother Charles, whose life he subsequently wrote. He became K.C.B. in 1848, and General 1859.

NASH, THOMAS (1567-1601).—Satirist, etc., *b.* at Lowestoft, *ed.* at Camb. A reckless life kept him in perpetual poverty, and a bitter and sarcastic tongue lost him friends and patrons. He cherished an undying hatred for the Puritans, and specially for Gabriel Hervey, with whom he maintained a lifelong controversy, and against whose attacks he defended Robert Greene (*q.v.*). Among his writings are *Anatomy of Absurdities* (1589), *Have with you to Saffron Walden*, and *Pierce Pennilesse, his Supplication to the Divell* (1592), all against the Puritans. In *Summer's* (a jester of Henry VIII.) *Last Will and Testament* occurs the well-known song, " Spring, the sweet Spring, is the year's pleasant King." *Christ's Tears over Jerusalem* (1593) may have indicated some movement towards repentance. Another work in a totally different style, *The Unfortunate Traveller, or the Life of Jack Wilton* (1594), a wild tale, may be regarded as the pioneer of the novel of adventure. It had, however, so little success that the author never returned to this kind of fiction. A comedy, *The Isle of Dogs* (now lost), adverted so pointedly to abuses in the state that it led to his imprisonment. His last work was *Lenten Stuffe* (1599), a burlesque panegyric on Yarmouth and its red herrings. N.'s verse is usually hard and monotonous, but he was a man of varied culture and great ability.

NAYLER, JAMES (1617?-1660).—Quaker theologian, *s.* of a Yorkshire yeoman, who, after serving in the Parliamentary army, joined the Quakers in 1651, became one of Foxe's most trusted helpers, and exercised a powerful influence. By some of the more enthusiastic devotees of the sect he was honoured with such blasphemous titles as " the Lamb of God," which, however, he did not arrogate to himself, but asserted that they were ascribed to " Christ in him." He was found guilty of blasphemy, pilloried, whipped, and branded, and cast into prison, from which he was not released until after the death of Cromwell, when he made public confession and resumed preaching. He was the author of a number of short works both devotional and controversial. He ranks high among the Quakers for eloquence, insight, and depth of thought.

NÉAL, JOHN (1793-1876).—Novelist and poet, *b.* at Portland, Maine, was self-educated, kept a dry goods store, and was afterwards a lawyer. He wrote several novels, which show considerable native power, but little art, and are now almost forgotten. Among those which show the influence of Byron and Godwin are *Keep Cool* (1818), *Logan* (1822), and *Seventy-six* (1823). His poems have the same features of vigour and want of finish. In 1823 he visited England, and became known to Jeremy Bentham. He contributed some articles on American subjects to *Blackwood's Magazine*.

NEAVES, CHARLES, LORD (1800-1876). — Miscellaneous author, *b.* and *ed.* in Edinburgh, was called to the Bar, and became a judge. He was a frequent contributor to *Blackwood's Magazine.* His verses, witty and satirical, were *coll.* as *Songs and Verses, Social and Scientific.* He wrote also on philology, and *pub.* a book on the Greek Anthology.

NECKHAM, ALEXANDER (1157-1217).—Scholar, *b.* at St. Albans, was foster-brother to Richard Cœur de Lion. He went to Paris in 1180, where he became a distinguished teacher. Returning to England in 1186 he became an Augustinian Canon, and in 1213 Abbot of Cirencester. He is one of our earliest men of learning, and wrote a scientific work in Latin verse, *De Naturis Rerum* (*c.* 1180-94) in 10 books. Other works are *De Laudibus Divinæ Sapientiæ* (in Praise of the Divine Wisdom), and *De Contemptu Mundi* (on Despising the World), and some grammatical treatises.

NEWCASTLE, MARGARET, DUCHESS OF (1624?-1674).—*Dau.* of Sir Thomas Lucas, and a maid of honour to Queen Henrietta Maria, *m.* in 1645 the 1st Duke of Newcastle (then Marquis), whom she regarded in adversity and prosperity with a singular and almost fantastic devotion, which was fully reciprocated. The noble pair collaborated (the Duchess contributing by far the larger share) in their literary ventures, which filled 12 vols., and consisted chiefly of dramas (now almost unreadable), and philosophical exercitations which, amid prevailing rubbish, contain some weighty sayings. One of her poems, *The Pastimes and Recreations of the Queen of Fairies in Fairyland* has some good lines. Her Life of her husband, in which she rates him above Julius Cæsar, was said by Lamb to be " a jewel for which no casket was good enough."

NEWMAN, FRANCIS WILLIAM (1805-1897).—Scholar and theological writer, brother of Cardinal N., *b.* in London, and *ed.* at Oxf. After spending three years in the East, he became successively classical tutor in Bristol Coll., Professor of Classical Literature in Manchester New Coll. (1840), and of Latin in Univ. Coll., London, 1846-63. Both brought up under evangelical influences, the two brothers moved from that standpoint in diametrically opposite directions, Francis through eclecticism towards scepticism. His writings include a *History of the Hebrew Monarchy* (1847), *The Soul* (1849), and his most famous book, *Phases of Faith* (1850), a theological autobiography corresponding to his brother's *Apologia,* the publication of which led to much controversy, and to the appearance of Henry Rogers' *Eclipse of Faith.* He also *pub. Miscellanea* in 4 vols., a Dictionary of modern Arabic, and some mathematical treatises. He was a vegetarian, a total abstainer, and enemy of tobacco, vaccination, and vivisection. Memoir by I. G. Sieveking, 1909.

NEWMAN, JOHN HENRY (1801-1890).—Theologian, *s.* of a London banker, and brother of the above, was *ed.* at Ealing and Trinity Coll., Oxf., where he was the intimate friend of Pusey and Hurrell Froude. Taking orders he was successively curate of St. Clement's 1824, and Vicar of St. Mary's, Oxford, 1828. He was also Vice-principal of Alban Hall, where he assisted Whately, the Principal, in his *Logic*. In 1830 he definitely broke with the evangelicalism in which he had been brought up; and in 1832, accompanied by H. Froude, went to the South of Europe, and visited Rome. During this lengthened tour he wrote most of his short poems, including "Lead Kindly Light," which were *pub.* 1834 as *Lyra Apostolica*. On his return he joined with Pusey, Keble, and others in initiating the Tractarian movement, and contributed some of the more important tracts, including the fateful No. xc., the publication of which brought about a crisis in the movement which, after two years of hesitation and mental and spiritual conflict, led to the resignation by N. of his benefice. In 1842 he retired to Littlemore, and after a period of prayer, fasting, and seclusion, was in 1845 received into the Roman Catholic Church. In the following year he went to Rome, where he was ordained priest and made D.D., and returning to England he established the oratory in Birmingham in 1847, and that in London in 1850. A controversy with C. Kingsley, who had written that N. "did not consider truth a necessary virtue," led to the publication of his *Apologia pro Vita Sua* (1864), one of the most remarkable books of religious autobiography ever written. N.'s later years were passed at the oratory at Birmingham. In 1879 he was summoned to Rome and *cr.* Cardinal of St. George in Velabro. Besides the works above mentioned he wrote, among others, *The Arians of the Fourth Century* (1833), *Twelve Lectures* (1850), *Lectures on the Present Position of Catholics* (1851), *Idea of a University*, *Romanism and Popular Protestantism*, *Disquisition on the Canon of Scripture*, and his poem, *The Dream of Gerontius*. Possessed of one of the most keen and subtle intellects of his age, N. was also master of a style of marvellous beauty and power. To many minds, however, his subtlety not seldom appeared to pass into sophistry; and his attitude to schools of thought widely differing from his own was sometimes harsh and unsympathetic. On the other hand he was able to exercise a remarkable influence over men ecclesiastically, and in some respects religiously, most strongly opposed to him. His sermons place him in the first rank of English preachers.

Lives or books about him by R. H. Hutton, E. A. Abbott. *Works* (36 vols., 1868-81), *Apologia pro Vita Sua* (1864), etc.

NEWTON, SIR ISAAC (1642-1727).—Natural philosopher, *b.* at Woolsthorpe, Lincolnshire, the *s.* of a small landed proprietor, and *ed.* at the Grammar School of Grantham and at Trinity Coll., Camb. By propounding the binomial theorem, the differential calculus, and the integral calculus, he began in 1665 the wonderful series of discoveries in pure mathematics, optics, and physics, which place him in the first rank of the philosophers of all time. He was elected Lucasian Prof. of Mathematics at Camb. in 1669, and a Fellow of the Royal Society in 1672, over which body he presided for 25 years from 1703. In the same year his new theory of light was *pub.* in a paper before the society. His epoch-making discovery of the law of universal gravitation was not promulgated until 1687, though the first glimpse of it had come to him so early as 1665. The discovery of fluxions, which he claimed, was contested by Leibnitz, and led to a long and bitter controversy between the two philosophers. He twice sat in Parliament for his

Univ., and was Master of the Mint from 1699, in which capacity he presented reports on the coinage. He was knighted in 1705, and *d.* at Kensington in 1727. For a short time, after an unfortunate accident by which a number of invaluable manuscripts were burned, he suffered from some mental aberration. His writings fall into two classes, scientific and theological. In the first are included his famous treatises, *Light and Colours* (1672), *Optics* (1704), the *Principia* (1687), in Latin, its full title being *Philosophiæ Naturalis Principia Mathematica.* In the second are his *Observations upon the Prophecies of Holy Writ* and *An Historical Account of Two Notable Corruptions of Scripture.* In character N. was remarkable for simplicity, humility, and gentleness, with a great distaste for controversy, in which, nevertheless, he was repeatedly involved.

Life by Sir D. Brewster, second ed., 1855, etc.

NEWTON, JOHN (1725-1807).—Divine and hymn-writer, *s.* of a shipmaster, was *b.* in London, and for many years led a varied and adventurous life at sea, part of the time on board a man-of-war and part as captain of a slaver. In 1748 he came under strong religious convictions, and after acting as a tide-waiter at Liverpool for a few years, he applied for orders in 1758, and was ordained curate of Olney in 1764. Here he became the intimate and sympathetic friend of Cowper, in conjunction with whom he produced the *Olney Hymns.* In 1779 he was translated to the Rectory of St. Mary, Woolnoth, London, where he had great popularity and influence, and wrote many religious works, including *Cardiphonia,* and *Remarkable Passages in his Own Life.* He lives, however, in his hymns, among which are some of the best and most widely known in the language, such as *In evil long I took delight, Glorious things of Thee are Spoken, How Sweet the Name of Jesus sounds,* and many others. In his latter years N. was blind.

NICHOL, JOHN (1833-1894).—Poet and biographer, *s.* of John P. N., Prof. of Astronomy in Glasgow, *ed.* at Glasgow and Oxf., and held the chair of English Literature in Glasgow, 1862-1889. Among his writings are *Hannibal* (1873), a drama, *Death of Themistocles and other Poems* (1881), *Fragments of Criticism,* and *American Literature ;* also Lives of Bacon, Burns, Carlyle, and Byron.

NOEL, HON. RODEN BERKELEY WRIOTHESLEY (1834-1894).—Poet, *s.* of the 1st Earl of Gainsborough, was *ed.* at Camb. He wrote *Behind the Veil* (1863), *The Red Flag* (1872), *Songs of the Heights and Deeps* (1885), and *Essays* on various poets, also a Life of Byron.

NORRIS, JOHN (1657-1711).—Philosopher and poet, *ed.* at Oxf., took orders, and lived a quiet and placid life as a country parson and thinker. In philosophy he was a Platonist and mystic, and was an early opponent of Locke. His poetry, with occasional fine thoughts, is full of far-fetched metaphors and conceits, and is not seldom dull and prosaic. From 1692 he held G. Herbert's benefice of Bemerton. Among his 23 works are *An Idea of Happiness* (1683), *Miscellanies* (1687), *Theory and Regulation of Love* (1688), *Theory of the Ideal and Intelligible World* (1701-4), and a *Discourse concerning the Immortality of the Soul* (1708).

NORTH, SIR THOMAS (1535?-1601?).—Translator, 2nd *s.* of the 1st Lord N., may have studied at Camb. He entered Lincoln's Inn 1557, but gave more attention to literature than to law. He is best known by his translation of *Plutarch*, from the French of Amyot, in fine, forcible, idiomatic English, which was the repertory from which Shakespeare drew his knowledge of ancient history: in *Antony and Cleopatra* and *Coriolanus* North's language is often closely followed. Another translation was from an Italian version of an Arabic book of fables, and bore the title of *The Morale Philosophie of Doni.*

NORTON, CAROLINE ELIZABETH SARAH (SHERIDAN) (1808-1877).—Grand-daughter of Richard Brinsley S. (*q.v.*), *m.* in 1827 the Hon. G. C. Norton, a union which turned out most unhappy, and ended in a separation. Her first book, *The Sorrows of Rosalie* (1829), was well received. *The Undying One* (1830), a romance founded upon the legend of the Wandering Jew, followed, and other novels were *Stuart of Dunleath* (1851), *Lost and Saved* (1863), and *Old Sir Douglas* (1867). The unhappiness of her married life led her to interest herself in the amelioration of the laws regarding the social condition and the separate property of women and the wrongs of children, and her poems, *A Voice from the Factories* (1836), and *The Child of the Islands* (1845), had as an object the furtherance of her views on these subjects. Her efforts were largely successful in bringing about the needed legislation. In 1877 Mrs. N. *m.* Sir W. Stirling Maxwell (*q.v.*).

NORTON, CHARLES ELIOT, LL.D., D.C.L., ETC. (1827-1909).—American biographer and critic. *Church Building in the Middle Ages* (1876), translation of the *New Life* (1867), and *The Divine Comedy* of Dante (1891); has ed. *Correspondence of Carlyle and Emerson* (1883), *Carlyle's Letters and Reminiscences* (1887), etc.

OCCAM OR OCKHAM, WILLIAM (1270?-1349?).—Schoolman, *b.* at Ockham, Surrey, studied at Oxf. and Paris, and became a Franciscan. As a schoolman he was a Nominalist and received the title of the Invincible Doctor. He attacked the abuses of the Church, and was imprisoned at Avignon, but escaped and spent the latter part of his life at Munich, maintaining to the last his controversies with the Church, and with the Realists. He was a man of solid understanding and sense, and a masterly logician. His writings, which are of course all in Latin, deal with the Aristotelean philosophy, theology, and specially under the latter with the errors of Pope John XXII., who was his *bête-noir.*

OCCLEVE (*See* HOCCLEVE).

OCKLEY, SIMON (1678-1720).—Orientalist, *b.* at Exeter, and *ed.* at Camb., became the greatest Orientalist of his day, and was made in 1711 Prof. of Arabic in his Univ. His chief work is the *Conquest of Syria, Persia, and Egypt by the Saracens* (3 vols., 1708-57), which was largely used by Gibbon. The original documents upon which it is founded are now regarded as of doubtful authority. O. was a clergyman of the Church of England.

O'KEEFFE, JOHN (1747-1833).—Dramatist, wrote a number of farces and amusing dramatic pieces, many of which had great success. Among these are *Tony Lumpkin in Town* (1778), *Wild Oats*, and *Love in a Camp*. Some of his songs set to music by Arnold and Shield, such as *I am a Friar of Orders Grey*, and *The Thorn*, are still popular. He was blind in his later years.

OLDHAM, JOHN (1653-1683).—Satirist and translator, *s.* of a Nonconformist minister, was at Oxf., and was the friend of most of the literary men of his time, by whom his early death from small-pox was bewailed. He made clever adaptations of the classical satirists, wrote an ironical *Satire against Virtue*, and four severe satires against the Jesuits. He is cynical to the verge of misanthropy, but independent and manly.

OLDMIXON, JOHN (1673-1742).—Historical and miscellaneous writer, belonged to an old Somersetshire family, wrote some, now forgotten, dramas and poems which, along with an essay on criticism, in which he attacked Addison, Swift, and Pope, earned for him a place in *The Dunciad*. He was also the author of *The British Empire in America* (1708), *Secret History of Europe* (against the Stuarts), and in his *Critical History* (1724-26) attacked Clarendon's *History of the Rebellion*. All these works are partisan in their tone. O. was one of the most prolific pamphleteers of his day.

OLDYS, WILLIAM (1696-1761).—Antiquary, wrote a Life of Sir W. Raleigh prefixed to an ed. of his works (1736), a *Dissertation on Pamphlets* (1731), and was joint ed. with Dr. Johnson of the *Harleian Miscellany*. He amassed many interesting facts in literary history, the fruits of diligent, though obscure, industry. The only poem of his that still lives is the beautiful little anacreontic beginning "Busy, curious, thirsty Fly." O. held the office of Norroy-King-at-Arms. He produced in 1737 *The British Librarian*, a valuable work left unfinished.

OLIPHANT, LAURENCE (1829-1888).—Novelist and miscellaneous writer, *s.* of Sir Anthony O., Chief Justice of Ceylon. The first 38 years of his life were spent in desultory study, travel, and adventure, varied by occasional diplomatic employment. His travels included, besides Continental countries, the shores of the Black Sea, Circassia, where he was *Times* correspondent, America, China, and Japan. He was in the Crimean War, Indian Mutiny, Chinese War, the military operations of Garibaldi, and the Polish insurrection, and served as private sec. to Lord Elgin in Washington, Canada, and China, and as Sec. of Legation in Japan. In 1865 he entered Parliament, and gave promise of political eminence, when in 1867 he came under the influence of Thomas L. Harris, an American mystic of questionable character, went with him to America, and joined the Brotherhood of the New Life. In 1870-71 he was correspondent for the *Times* in the Franco-German War. Ultimately he broke away from the influence of Harris and went to Palestine, where he founded a community of Jewish immigrants at Haifa. After revisiting America he returned to England, but immediately fell ill and *d.* at Twickenham. O. was a voluminous and versatile author, publishing books of travel, novels, and works on mysticism. The most important are as follows: *The Russian Shores of the Black Sea* (1853), *Minnesota and the Far West* (1855), *The Transcaucasian Campaign* (1856), *Patriots and Fillibusters* (adventures in Southern States) (1860), *Narrative of a Mission to China and Japan* (1857-59), *The Land of Gilead* (1880), *Piccadilly* (1870), and *Altiora Peto* (1883) (novels), and *Scientific Religion.*

OLIPHANT, MRS. MARGARET OLIPHANT (WILSON) (1828-1897).—Novelist and miscellaneous writer, was *b.* near Musselburgh. Her literary output began when she was little more than a girl, and was continued almost up to the end of her life. Her first novel, *Mrs. Margaret Maitland*, appeared in 1849, and its humour, pathos, and insight into character gave the author an immediate position in literature. It was followed by an endless succession, of which the best were the series of *The Chronicles of Carlingford* (1861-65), including *Salem Chapel*, *The Perpetual Curate*, and *Miss Marjoribanks*, all of which, as well as much of her other work, appeared in *Blackwood's Magazine*, with which she had a lifelong connection. Others of some note were *The Primrose Path*, *Madonna Mary* (1866), *The Wizard's Son*, and *A Beleaguered City*. She did not, however, confine herself to fiction, but wrote many books of history and biography, including *Sketches of the Reign of George II.* (1869), *The Makers of Florence* (1876), *Literary History of England* 1790-1825, *Royal Edinburgh* (1890), and Lives of *St. Francis of Assisi*, *Edward Irving*, and *Principal Tulloch*. Her generosity in supporting and educating the family of a brother as well as her own two sons rendered necessary a rate of production which was fatal to the permanence of her work. She was negligent as to style, and often wrote on subjects to which her intellectual equipment and knowledge did not enable her to do proper justice. She had, however, considerable power of painting character, and a vein of humour, and showed untiring industry in getting up her subjects.

OPIE, MRS. AMELIA (ALDERSON) (1769-1853).—Novelist, *dau.* of a medical man, was *b.* at Norwich. In 1798 she *m.* John Opie, the painter. Her first acknowledged work was *Father and Daughter* (1801), which had a favourable reception, and was followed by *Adeline Mowbray* (1804), *Temper* (1812), *Tales from Real Life* (1813), and others, all having the same aim of developing the virtuous affections, the same merit of natural and vivid painting of character and passions, and the same fault of a too great preponderance of the pathetic. They were soon superseded by the more powerful genius of Scott and Miss Edgeworth. In 1825 she became a Quaker. After this she wrote *Illustrations of Lying* (1825), and *Detraction Displayed* (1828). Her later years, which were singularly cheerful, were largely devoted to philanthropic interests.

ORDERICUS VITALIS (1075-1143?).—Chronicler, *b.* near Shrewsbury, was in childhood put into the monastery of St. Evroult in Normandy, where the rest of his life was passed. He is the author of a chronicle, *Ecclesiastical History of England and Normandy* (*c.* 1142) in 13 books. Those from the seventh to the thirteenth are invaluable as giving a trustworthy, though not very clear, record of contemporary events in England and Normandy. It was translated into English in 1853-55.

ORM, OR ORMIN (*fl.* 1200).—Was an Augustinian canon of Mercia, who wrote the *Ormulum* in transition English. It is a kind of mediæval *Christian Year*, containing a metrical portion of the Gospel for each day, followed by a metrical homily, largely borrowed from Ælfric and Bede. Its title is thus accounted for, " This boc iss nemmed the *Ormulum*, forthi that Orm it wrohhte."

ORME, ROBERT (1728-1801).—Historian, *s.* of an Indian army doctor, *b.* at Travancore, and after being at Harrow, entered the service of the East India Company. Owing to failure of health he had to return home in 1760, and then wrote his *History of the Military Transactions of the British Nation in Indostan from* 1745 (1763-78), a well-written and accurate work, showing great research. He also *pub. Historical Fragments of the Mogul Empire, the Morattoes and English Concerns in Indostan from* 1659 (1782). His collections relating to India are preserved at the India Office.

ORRERY, ROGER BOYLE, 1ST EARL OF (1621-1679).—Statesman and dramatist, third *s.* of the Earl of Cork, was *ed.* at Trinity Coll., Dublin. After having fought on the Royalist side he was, on the death of the King, induced by Cromwell to support him in his Irish wars and otherwise. After the death of the Protector he secured Ireland for Charles II., and at the Restoration was raised to the peerage. He wrote a romance in 6 vols., entitled *Parthenissa*, some plays, and a treatise on the *Art of War*. He has the distinction of being the first to introduce rhymed tragedies.

O'SHAUGHNESSY, ARTHUR WILLIAM EDGAR (1844-1881). Poet, *b.* in London, entered the library of the British Museum, afterwards being transferred to the natural history department, where he became an authority on fishes and reptiles. He *pub.* various books of poetry, including *Epic of Women* (1870), *Lays of France* (1872), and *Music and Moonlight* (1874). Jointly with his wife he wrote *Toyland*, a book for children. He was associated with D. G. Rossetti and the other pre-Raphaelites. There is a certain remoteness in his poetry which will probably always prevent its being widely popular. He has a wonderful mastery of metre, and a " haunting music " all his own.

OTWAY, CÆSAR (1780-1842).—Writer of Irish tales. His writings, which display humour and sympathy with the poorer classes in Ireland, include *Sketches in Ireland* (1827), and *A Tour in Connaught* (1839). He was concerned in the establishment of various journals.

OTWAY, THOMAS (1651 or 1652-1685).—Dramatist, *s.* of a clergyman, was *b.* near Midhurst, Sussex, and *ed.* at Oxf., which he left without graduating. His short life, like those of many of his fellows, was marked by poverty and misery, and he appears to have *d.* practically of starvation. Having failed as an actor, he took to writing for the stage, and produced various plays, among which *Don Carlos, Prince of Spain* (1676), was a great success, and brought him some money. Those by which he is best remembered, however, are *The Orphan* (1680), and *Venice Preserved* (1682), both of which have been frequently revived. O. made many adaptations from the French, and in his tragedy of *Caius Marius* incorporated large parts of *Romeo and Juliet*. He has been called "the most pathetic and tear-drawing of all our dramatists," and he excelled in delineating the stronger passions. The grossness of his comedies has banished them from the stage. Other plays are *The Cheats of Scapin, Friendship in Fashion, Soldier's Fortune* (1681), and *The Atheist*.

OUIDA (*See* RAMÉE).

OUTRAM, GEORGE (1805-1856).—Humorous poet, was a Scottish advocate, a friend of Prof. Wilson, and for some time ed. of the *Glasgow Herald*. He printed privately in 1851 *Lyrics, Legal and Miscellaneous*, which were *pub.* with a memoir in 1874. Many of his pieces are highly amusing, the *Annuity* being the best.

OVERBURY, SIR THOMAS (1581-1613).—Poet and miscellaneous writer, *ed.* at Oxf., became the friend of Carr, afterwards Earl of Rochester and Somerset, and fell a victim to a Court intrigue connected with the proposed marriage of Rochester and Lady Essex, being poisoned in the Tower with the connivance of the latter. He wrote a poem, *A Wife, now a Widowe*, and *Characters* (1614), short, witty descriptions of types of men. Some of those *pub.* along with his are by other hands.

OWEN, JOHN (1560-1622).—Epigrammatist, *b.* at Plas Dhu, Carnarvonshire, *ed.* at Winchester and Oxf., and became head master of King Henry VIII. School at Warwick. His Latin epigrams, which have both sense and wit in a high degree, gained him much applause, and were translated into English, French, German, and Spanish.

OWEN, JOHN (1616-1683).—Puritan divine, *b.* at Stadhampton, Oxfordshire, and *ed.* at Oxf., from which he was driven by Laud's statutes. Originally a Presbyterian, he passed over to Independency. In 1649 he accompanied Cromwell to Ireland, and in 1650 to Edinburgh. He was Dean of Christ Church, Oxf. (1651-60), and one of the "triers" of ministers appointed by Cromwell. After the Restoration he was ejected from his deanery, but was favoured by Clarendon, who endeavoured to induce him to conform to the Anglican Church by offers of high preferment. Strange to say Charles II. also held him in regard, and gave him money for the Nonconformists; and he was allowed to preach to a congregation of Independents in London. His great learning and ability rendered him a formidable controversialist, specially against Arminianism and Romanism. His works fill 28 vols; among the best known being *The Divine Original, etc., of the Scriptures, Indwelling Sin, Christologia, or . . . The Person of Christ*, and a commentary on Hebrews.

OWEN, ROBERT (1771-1858).—Socialist and philanthropist, *b.* at Newton, Montgomeryshire, had for his object the regeneration of the world on the principles of socialism. His sincerity was shown by the fact that he spent most of the fortune, which his great capacity for business enabled him to make, in endeavours to put his theories into practice at various places both in Britain and America. He was sincerely philanthropic, and incidentally did good on a considerable scale in the course of his more or less impracticable schemes. He propounded his ideas in *New Views of Society, or Essays on the Formation of the Human Character* (1816).

OXFORD, EDWARD DE VERE, EARL OF (1550-1604).—Was a courtier of Queen Elizabeth, who lost his friends by his insolence and pride, and his fortune by his extravagance. He *m.* a *dau.* of Lord Burghley, who had to support his family after his death. He had some reputation as a writer of short pieces, many of which are in the *Paradise of Dainty Devices.*

PAINE, THOMAS (1737-1809).—Political and anti-Christian writer, *s.* of a stay-maker and small farmer of Quaker principles at Thetford, became with large classes perhaps the most unpopular man in England. After trying various occupations, including those of schoolmaster and exciseman, and having separated from his wife, he went in 1774 to America where, in 1776, he *pub.* his famous pamphlet, *Common Sense,* in favour of American independence. He served in the American army, and also held some political posts, including that of sec. to a mission to France in 1781. Returning to England in 1787 he *pub.* his *Rights of Man* (1790-92), in reply to Burke's *Reflections on the French Revolution.* It had an enormous circulation, 1,500,000 copies having been sold in England alone; but it made it necessary for him to escape to France to avoid prosecution. Arrived in that country he was elected to the National Convention. He opposed the execution of Louis XVI., and was, in 1794, imprisoned by Robespierre, whose fall saved his life. He had then just completed the first part of his *Age of Reason,* of which the other two appeared respectively in 1795 and 1807. It is directed alike against Christianity and Atheism, and supports Deism. Becoming disgusted with the course of French politics, he returned to America in 1802, but found himself largely ostracised by society there, became embroiled in various controversies, and is said to have become intemperate. He *d.* at New York in 1809. Though apparently sincere in his views, and courageous in the expression of them, P. was vain and prejudiced. The extraordinary lucidity and force of his style did much to gain currency for his writings.

PAINTER, WILLIAM (1540?-1594).—Translator, etc., *ed.* at Camb., was then successively schoolmaster at Sevenoaks, and Clerk of the Ordnance, in which position his intromissions appear to have been of more advantage to himself than to the public service. He was the author of *The Palace of Pleasure* (1566), largely consisting of translations from Boccaccio, Bandello, and other Italian writers, and also from the classics. It formed a quarry in which many dramatists, including Shakespeare, found the plots for their plays.

PALEY, WILLIAM (1743-1805).—Theologian, *s.* of a minor canon of Peterborough, where he was *b.*, went at 15 as a sizar to Christ's Coll., Camb., where he was Senior Wrangler, and became a Fellow and Tutor of his coll. Taking orders in 1767 he held many benefices, and rose to be Archdeacon of Carlisle, and Sub-Dean of Lincoln. P., who holds one of the highest places among English theologians, was the author of four important works—*Principles of Moral and Political Philosophy* (1785), *Horæ Paulinæ*, his most original, but least popular, book (1790), *View of the Evidences of Christianity* (1794), and *Natural Theology* (1802). Though now to a large extent superseded, these works had an immense popularity and influence in their day, and are characterised by singular clearness of expression and power of apt illustration. The system of morals inculcated by P. is Utilitarian, modified by theological ideas. His view of the "divine right of Kings" as on a level with "the divine right of constables" was unpleasing to George III.. notwithstanding which his ecclesiastical career was eminently successful. His manners were plain and kindly.

PALGRAVE, SIR FRANCIS (1788-1861).—Historian, *s.* of Meyer Cohen, a Jewish stockbroker, but at his marriage in 1823, having previously become a Christian, assumed his mother-in-law's name of Palgrave. He studied law, and was called to the Bar in 1827. From 1838 until his death in 1861 he was Deputy Keeper of the Records, and in that capacity arranged a vast mass of hitherto inaccessible documents, and ed. many of them for the Record Commission. His historical works include a *History of England in Anglo-Saxon Times* (1831), *Rise and Progress of the English Commonwealth* (1832), and *History of Normandy and England* (4 vols., 1851-64), *pub.* posthumously. He was knighted in 1832. His works are of great value in throwing light upon the history and condition of mediæval England.

PALGRAVE, FRANCIS TURNER (1824-1897).—Poet and critic, *s.* of the above, *ed.* at Oxf., was for many years connected with the Education Department, of which he rose to be Assistant-Sec.; and from 1886-95 he was Prof. of Poetry at Oxf. He wrote several vols. of poetry, including *Visions of England* (1881), and *Amenophis* (1892), which, though graceful and exhibiting much poetic feeling, were the work rather of a man of culture than of a poet. His great contribution to literature was his anthology, *The Golden Treasury of Songs and Lyrics* (1864), selected with marvellous insight and judgment. A second series showed these qualities in a less degree. He also *pub.* an anthology of sacred poetry.

PALTOCK, ROBERT (1697-1767).—Novelist, was an attorney, and wrote *The Life and Adventures of Peter Wilkins, a Cornish Man* (1751), admired by Scott, Coleridge, and Lamb. It is somewhat on the same plan as *Robinson Crusoe*, the special feature being the *gawry*, or flying woman, whom the hero discovered on his island, and married. The description of Nosmnbdsgrutt, the country of the flying people, is a dull imitation of Swift, and much else in the book is tedious.

PARDOE, JULIA (1806-1862).—Novelist and miscellaneous writer, *b.* at Beverley, showed an early bias towards literature, and became a voluminous and versatile writer, producing in addition to her lively and well-written novels many books of travel, and others dealing with historical subjects. She was a keen observer, and her Oriental travels had given her an accurate and deep knowledge of the peoples and manners of the East. Among her books are *The City of the Sultan* (1836), *Romance of the Harem, Thousand and One Days, Louis XIV. and the Court of France, Court of Francis I.*, etc.

PARIS, MATTHEW (*c.* 1195-1259).—Chronicler, entered in 1217 the Benedictine Monastery of St. Albans, and continued the work of Roger de Wendover (*q.v.*) as chronicler of the monastery. In 1248 he went on the invitation of Hacon King of Norway to reform the Abbey of St. Benet Holm. In this he was successful, and on his return to England enjoyed the favour of Henry III., who conversed familiarly with him, and imparted information as to matters of state, which constitutes a valuable element in his histories. He had a high reputation for piety and learning, was a patriotic Englishman, and resisted the encroachments of Rome. His chief work is *Historia Major*, from the Conquest until 1259. In it he embodied the *Flores Historiarum* of his predecessor Roger, and the original part is a bold and vigorous narrative of the period (1235-59). He also wrote *Historia Minor* and *Historia Anglorum*, a summary of the events (1200-1250).

PARK, MUNGO (1771-1806).—Traveller, *b.* near Selkirk, studied medicine at Edin. As a surgeon in the mercantile marine he visited Sumatra, and on his return attracted the attention of various scientific men by his botanical and zoological investigations. In 1795 he entered the service of the African Association, and made a voyage of discovery on the Niger. His adventures were *pub.* in *Travels in the Interior of Africa* (1799), which had great success. He *m.* and set up in practice in Peebles; but in 1805 accepted an invitation by Government to undertake another journey in Africa. From this he never returned, having perished in a conflict with natives. His narratives, written in a straightforward and pleasing style, are among the classics of travel.

PARKER, THEODORE (1810-1860).—Theologian, *b.* at Lexington, Massachusetts, *ed.* at Harvard, was an indefatigable student, and made himself master of many languages. In 1837 he was settled at West Roxbury as a Unitarian minister, but the development of his views in a rationalistic direction gradually separated him from the more conservative portion of his co-religionists. He lectured on theological subjects in Boston in 1841, travelled in Europe, and in 1845 settled in Boston, where he lectured to large audiences, and exercised a wide influence. He took a leading part in the anti-slavery crusade, and specially in resisting the Fugitive Slave Act. In 1859 his health, which had never been robust, gave way; he went to Italy in search of restoration, but *d.* at Florence. Although he was a powerful theological and social influence, his writings are not of corresponding importance: it was rather as a speaker that he influenced his countrymen, and he left no contribution to literature of much permanent account, though his *coll.* works fill 14 vols. Among the most outstanding of his writings are *A Discourse of Matters Pertaining to Religion*, and *Sermons for the Times.*

PARKMAN, FRANCIS (1823-1893).—Historian, *s.* of a Unitarian minister in Boston, Massachusetts, graduated at Harvard, and qualified as a lawyer, but never practised, and though hampered by a state of health which forbade continuous application, and by partial blindness, devoted himself to the writing of the history of the conflict between France and England in North America. This he did in a succession of works—*The Conspiracy of Pontiac* (1851), *The Pioneers of France in the New World* (1865), *The Jesuits in North America* (1867), *La Salle and the Discovery of the Great West* (1869), *The Old Regime in Canada* (1874), *Count Frontenac and New France* (1877), *Montcalm and Wolfe* (1884), and *A Half Century of Conflict* (1892). In these the style, at first somewhat turgid, gradually improved, and became clear and forcible, while retaining its original vividness. P. spared no labour in collecting and sifting his material, much of which was gathered in the course of visits to the places which were the scenes of his narrative, and his books are the most valuable contribution in existence to the history of the struggle for Canada and the other French settlements in North America. He also wrote two novels, which had little success, and a book upon rose-culture.

PARNELL, THOMAS (1679-1718).—Poet, *b.* and *ed.* in Dublin, took orders in 1700, and was Vicar of Finglas and Archdeacon of Clogher. The death of his young wife in 1706 drove him into intemperate habits. He was a friend of Swift and Pope, a contributor to the *Spectator*, and aided Pope in his translation of the *Iliad*. He wrote various isolated poems showing a fine descriptive touch, of which the most important are *The Hermit, The Night Piece*, and *The Hymn to Contentment*. P. was a scholar, and had considerable social gifts. His Life was written by Goldsmith.

PARR, DR. SAMUEL (1747-1825).—Scholar, *s.* of an apothecary at Harrow, where and at Camb. he was *ed.* He was successively an assistant-master at Harrow and head-master of schools at Colchester and Norwich, and having taken orders, finally settled down at Hatton, Warwickshire, where he took private pupils. He was undoubtedly a great Latinist, but he has left no work to account for the immense reputation for ability which he enjoyed during his life. His chief power appears to have been in conversation, in which he was bold, arrogant, and epigrammatic. He was nicknamed "the Whig Johnson," but fell very far short of his model. His writings, including correspondence, were *pub.* in 8 vols.

PATER, WALTER HORATIO (1839-1894).—Essayist and critic, *s.* of Richard G. P., of American birth and Dutch extraction, a benevolent physician, *b.* at Shadwell, and *ed.* at the King's School, Canterbury, and at Queen's Coll., Oxf., after leaving which he made various tours in Germany and Italy where, especially in the latter, his nature, keenly sensitive to every form of beauty, received indelible impressions. In 1864 he was elected a Fellow of Brasenose, and in its ancient and austere precincts found his principal home. As a tutor, though conscientious, he was not eminently successful; nevertheless his lectures, on which he bestowed much pains, had a fit audience, and powerfully influenced a few select souls. He resigned his tutorship in 1880, partly because he found himself not entirely in his element, and partly because literature was becoming the predominant interest in his life. In 1885 he went to London, where he remained for 8 years, continuing, however, to reside at Brasenose during term. The reputation as a writer which he had gained made him welcome in whatever intellectual circles he found himself. Leaving London in 1893 he settled in a house in St. Giles, Oxf. In the spring of 1894 he went to Glasgow to receive the honorary degree of LL.D., a distinction which he valued. In the summer he had an attack of rheumatic fever, followed by pleurisy. From these he had apparently recovered, but he succumbed to an attack of heart-failure which immediately supervened. Thus ended prematurely in its 55th year a life as bare of outward events as it was rich in literary fruit and influence.

P. is one of the greatest modern masters of style, and one of the subtlest and most penetrating of critics. Though not a philosopher in the technical sense, he deeply pondered the subjects with which philosophy sets itself to deal; but art was the dominating influence in his intellectual life, and it was said of him that "he was a philosopher who had gone to Italy by mistake instead of to Germany." He may also be called the prophet of the modern æsthetic school. His attitude to Christianity, though deeply sceptical, was not unsympathetic. As a boy he came under the influence of Keble, and at one time thought of taking orders, but his gradual change of view led him to relinquish the idea. Among his works may be mentioned an article on Coleridge, and others on Winckelmann, Leonardo da Vinci, Michelangelo, Botticelli, etc., which were *coll.* and *pub.* as *Studies in the History of the Renaissance* (1873); *Appreciations* (1889) contained his great essays on *Æsthetic Poetry* and *Style*, various Shakespearian studies and papers on Lamb and Sir T. Browne; *Imaginary Portraits*, and *Greek Studies* (1894); *Plato and Platonism* (1893). His masterpiece, however, is *Marius the Epicurean* (1885), a philosophical romance of the time of Marcus Aurelius. The style of P. is characterised by a subdued richness, and complicated, but perfect structure of sentences. In character he was gentle, refined, and retiring, with a remarkable suavity of manner and dislike of controversy.

PATMORE, COVENTRY KERSEY DIGHTON (1823-1896).—Poet, *s.* of Peter George P., also an author, *b.* at Woodford, Essex, was in the printed book department of the British Museum. He *pub. Tamerton Church Tower* (1853), and between 1854 and 1862 the four poems which, combined, form his masterpiece, *The Angel in the House*, a poetic celebration of married love. In 1864 he entered the Church of Rome. Thereafter he *pub. The Unknown Eros* (1877), *Amelia* (1878), and *Rod, Root, and Flower* (1895), meditations chiefly on religious subjects. His works are full of graceful and suggestive thought, but occasionally suffer from length and discursiveness. He was successful in business matters, and in character was energetic, masterful, and combative. He numbered Tennyson and Ruskin among his friends, was associated with the pre-Raphaelites, and was a contributor to their organ, the *Germ.*

PATTISON, MARK (1813-1884).—Scholar and biographer, *b.* at Hornby, Yorkshire, *s.* of a clergyman, *ed.* privately and at Oxf., where in 1839 he became Fellow of Lincoln Coll., and acquired a high reputation as a tutor and examiner. At first strongly influenced by Newman and the Tractarian movement, he ultimately abandoned that school. In 1851, failing to be elected head of his coll., he threw up his tutorship, and devoted himself to severe study, occasionally writing on educational subjects in various reviews. In 1861, however, he attained the object of his ambition, being elected Rector of Lincoln Coll. In 1883 he dictated a remarkable autobiography, coming down to 1860. In 1875 he had *pub.* a *Life of Isaac Casaubon*, and he left materials for a Life of Scaliger, which he had intended to be his *magnum opus*. He also wrote *Milton* for the English Men of Letters Series, and produced an ed. of his sonnets.

PAULDING, JAMES KIRKE (1779-1860).—Novelist, etc., *b.* in the state of New York, was chiefly self-educated. He became a friend of W. Irving, and was part author with him of *Salmagundi*—a continuation of which by himself proved a failure. Among his other writings are *John Bull and Brother Jonathan* (1812), a satire, *The Dutchman's Fireside* (1831), a romance which attained popularity, a *Life of Washington* (1835), and some poems.

PAYN, JAMES (1830-1898).—Novelist, *s.* of an official in the Thames Commission, *ed.* at Eton, Woolwich, and Camb. He was a regular contributor to *Household Words* and to *Chambers's Journal*, of which he was ed. 1859-74, and in which several of his works first appeared; he also ed. the *Cornhill Magazine* 1883-96. Among his novels—upwards of 60 in number—may be mentioned *Lost Sir Massingberd*, *The Best of Husbands*, *Walter's Word*, *By Proxy* (1878), *A Woman's Vengeance*, *Carlyon's Year*, *Thicker than Water*, *A Trying Patient*, etc. He also wrote a book of poems and a volume of literary reminiscences.

PEACOCK, THOMAS LOVE (1785-1866).—Novelist, *b.* at Weymouth, the only child of a London merchant, was in boyhood at various schools, but from the age of 13 self-educated. Nevertheless, he became a really learned scholar. He was for long in the India Office, where he rose to be Chief Examiner, coming between James Mill and John Stuart Mill. He was the author of several somewhat whimsical, but quite unique novels, full of paradox, prejudice, and curious learning, with witty dialogue and occasional poems interspersed. Among them are *Headlong Hall* (1816), *Nightmare Abbey* (1818), *Maid Marian* (1822), *Misfortunes of Elphin* (1829), *Crotchet Castle* (1831), and *Gryll Grange* (1860). He was the intimate friend of Shelley, memoirs of whom he contributed to *Fraser's Magazine*.

PEARSON, CHARLES HENRY (1830-1894).—*B.* at Islington, *ed.* at Rugby and King's Coll., London, at the latter he became Prof. of Modern History. Owing to a threatened failure of sight he went to Australia, where he remained for 20 years, and was for a time Minister of Education of Victoria. Returning to England in 1892 he wrote his *National Life and Character: a Forecast*, in which he gave utterance to very pessimistic views as to the future of the race. He also wrote a *History of England during the Early and Middle Ages* (1867).

PEARSON, JOHN (1613-1686).—Theologian, *s.* of an archdeacon of Suffolk, *b.* at Great Snoring, Norfolk, *ed.* at Eton and Camb., took orders, and after holding various preferments, including the archdeaconry of Surrey, the mastership of Jesus Coll., and of Trinity Coll., Camb., was made, in 1673, Bishop of Chester. His *Exposition of the Creed* (1659) has always been regarded as one of the most finished productions of English theology, remarkable alike for logical argument and arrangement, and lucid style. He was also the author of other learned works, including a defence of the authenticity of the epistles of Ignatius. In his youth P. was a Royalist, and acted in 1645 as a chaplain in the Royal army. He was one of the commissioners in the Savoy Conference.

PECOCK, REGINALD (1395?-1460?).—Theologian, *b.* in Wales, entered the Church, and rose to be successively Bishop of St. Asaph 1444, and of Chichester 1450. He was a strenuous controversialist, chiefly against the Lollards; but his free style of argument, and especially his denial of the infallibility of the Church, led him into trouble, and on being offered the choice of abjuration or death at the stake, he chose the former, but nevertheless was deprived of his bishopric, had his books burned, and spent his latter days in the Abbey of Thorney, Cambridgeshire. His chief work is *The Repressor of overmuch blaming of the Clergy* (1455), which, from its clear, pointed style, remains a monument of 15th century English. *The Book of Faith* (1456) is another of his writings.

PEELE, GEORGE (1558?-1597?).—Dramatist and poet, *s.* of a salter in London, *ed.* at Christ's Hospital and Oxf., where he had a reputation as a poet. Coming back to London about 1581 he led a dissipated life. He appears to have been a player as well as a playwright, and to have come into possession of some land through his wife. His works are numerous and consist of plays, pageants, and miscellaneous verse. His best plays are *The Arraignment of Paris* (1584), and *The Battle of Alcazar* (1594), and among his poems *Polyhymnia* (1590), and *The Honour of the Garter* (1593). Other works are *Old Wives' Tale* (1595), and *David and Fair Bethsabe* (1599). P. wrote in melodious and flowing blank verse, with abundance of fancy and brilliant imagery, but his dramas are weak in construction, and he is often bombastic and extravagant.

PENN, WILLIAM (1644-1718).—Quaker apologist, *s.* of Sir William P., a celebrated Admiral, was *b.* in London, and *ed.* at Oxf., where he became a Quaker, and was in consequence expelled from the Univ. His change of views and his practice of the extremest social peculiarities imposed by his principles led to a quarrel with his *f.*, who is said to have turned him out of doors. Thereafter he began to write, and one of his books, *The Sandy Foundation Shaken* (*c.* 1668), in which he attacked the doctrines of the Trinity, the atonement, and justification by faith, led to his being, in 1668, imprisoned in the Tower, where he wrote his most popular work, *No Cross, No Crown* (1668), and a defence of his own conduct, *Innocency with her Open Face* (1668), which resulted in his liberation. Shortly after this, in 1670, on the death of his *f.*, who had been reconciled to him, P. succeeded to a fortune, including a claim against the Government amounting to £15,000, which was ultimately in 1681 settled by a grant of the territory now forming the state of Pennsylvania. Meanwhile, however, he had again suffered imprisonment for preaching, and employed his enforced leisure in writing four treatises, of which one, *The Great Cause of Liberty of Conscience* (*c.* 1671), is an able defence of religious toleration. In 1682, having obtained the grant above referred to, he set sail for America, with the view of founding a community based upon the principles of toleration. Having established a Constitution and set matters in working order there, P. returned to England in 1684 and busied himself in efforts for the relief of those Quakers who had remained at home. The peculiar position of affairs when James II. was endeavouring to use the Dissenters as a means of gaining concessions to the Roman Catholics favoured his views, and he was to some extent successful in his efforts. His connection with the Court at that time has, however, led to his conduct being severely animadverted upon by Macaulay and others. In 1690 and for some time thereafter he was charged with conspiring against the Revolution Government, but after full investigation was completely acquitted. His later years were embittered by troubles in Pennsylvania, and by the dishonesty and ingratitude of an agent by whose defalcations he was nearly ruined, as a consequence of which he was imprisoned for debt. He *d.* soon after his release in 1718.

PENNANT, THOMAS (1726-1798).—Naturalist and traveller, *b.* in Flintshire, and *ed.* at Oxf., was one of the most distinguished naturalists of the 18th century, and *pub.*, among other works on natural history, *British Zoology* (1768), and *History of Quadrupeds* (1781). In literature he is, however, best remembered by his *Tours in Scotland* (1771-75), which did much to make known the beauties of the country to England. He also travelled in Ireland and Wales, and on the Continent, and *pub.* accounts of his journeys. Dr. Johnson said of him, "he observes more things than any one else does."

PEPYS, SAMUEL (1633-1703).—Diarist, *s.* of John P., a London tailor, but of good family and connected with Sir E. Montague, afterwards Earl of Sandwich, was *ed.* at St. Paul's School and at Camb. After leaving the Univ. he entered the household of Montagu, who became his life-long patron. He held various Government posts, including that of Surveyor-General of the Victualling Office, in which he displayed great administrative ability and reforming zeal, and in 1672 he became Sec. of the Admiralty. After being imprisoned in the Tower on a charge in connection with the Popish plot, and deprived of his office, he was in 1686 again appointed Sec. of the Admiralty, from which, however, he was dismissed at the Revolution. Thereafter he lived in retirement chiefly at Clapham. P. was a man of many interests, combining the characters of the man of business, man of pleasure, and *virtuoso*, being skilled in music and a collector of books, manuscripts, and pictures, and he was Pres. of the Royal Society for two years. He wrote *Memoirs of the Royal Navy* (1690), but his great legacy to literature is his unique and inimitable *Diary*, begun January 1, 1660, and coming down to May 31, 1669, when the failure of his sight prevented its further continuance. As an account by an eye-witness of the manners of the Court and of society it is invaluable, but it is still more interesting as, perhaps, the most singular example extant of unreserved self-revelation—all the foibles, peccadilloes, and more serious offences against decorum of the author being set forth with the most relentless *naïveté* and minuteness. It was written in a cypher or shorthand, which was translated into long-hand by John Smith in 1825, and ed. by Lord Braybrooke, with considerable excisions. Later and fuller ed. have followed. P. left his books, MSS., and collections to Magdalene Coll., Camb., where they are preserved in a separate library.

PERCIVAL, JAMES GATES (1795-1854).—Poet, *b.* at Berlin, Conn., was a precocious child, and a morbid and impractical, though versatile man, with a fatal facility in writing verse on all manner of subjects and in nearly every known metre. His sentimentalism appealed to a wide circle, but his was one of the tapers which were extinguished by Lowell. He had also a reputation as a geologist. His poetic works include *Prometheus* and *The Dream of a Day* (1843).

PERCY, THOMAS (1729-1811).—Antiquary and poet, *s.* of a grocer at Bridgnorth, where he was *b.*, *ed.* at Oxf., entered the Church, and became in 1778 Dean of Carlisle, and in 1782 Bishop of Dromore. He *pub.* various antiquarian works, chiefly with reference to the North of England; but is best remembered for his great service to literature in collecting and ed. many ancient ballads, *pub.* in 1765 as *Reliques of Ancient Poetry*, which did much to bring back interest in the ancient native literature, and to usher in the revival of romanticism.

PHILIPS, AMBROSE (1675?-1749).—Poet, *b.* in Shropshire and *ed.* at Camb., wrote pastorals and dramas, was one of the Addison circle, and started a paper, the *Freethinker*, in imitation of the *Spectator*. He also made translations from Pindar and Anacreon, and a series of short complimentary verses, which gained for him the nickname of "Namby Pamby." His *Pastorals*, though poor enough, excited the jealousy of Pope, who pursued the unfortunate author with life-long enmity. P. held various Government appointments in Ireland.

PHILIPS, JOHN (1676-1709).—Poet, *s.* of an archdeacon of Salop, and *ed.* at Oxf. His *Splendid Shilling*, a burlesque in Miltonic blank verse, still lives, and *Cyder*, his chief work, an imitation of Virgil's *Georgics*, has some fine descriptive passages. P. was also employed by Harley to write verses on Blenheim as a counterblast to Addison's *Campaign*. He *d.* at 33 of consumption.

PHILLIPS, SAMUEL (1814-1854).—Novelist, of Jewish descent, studied for the Church at Göttingen and Camb., but his *f.* dying, he was obliged to give up his intention and take to business, in which, however, he was unsuccessful, and fell into great straits. He then tried writing, and produced some novels, of which the best known was *Caleb Stukely*, which appeared in *Blackwood* in 1842. He was latterly a leader-writer for the *Times*.

PICKEN, ANDREW (1788-1833).—Miscellaneous writer, *b.* in Paisley, was in business in the West Indies, and in Glasgow and Liverpool, but not being successful, went to London to try his fortunes in literature. His earlier writings, *Tales and Sketches of the West of Scotland* and *The Sectarian* (1829), gave offence in dissenting circles: his next, *The Dominie's Legacy* (1830), had considerable success, and a book on *Travels and Researches of Eminent Missionaries* (1830) did something to rehabilitate him with those whom he had offended. His last work, *The Black Watch* (1833), had just appeared when he *d.* of an apoplectic seizure. His best work is somewhat like that of Galt (*q.v.*).

PIERPONT, JOHN (1785-1860).—Poet, *b.* at Litchfield, Conn., was first a lawyer, then a merchant, and lastly a Unitarian minister. His chief poem is *The Airs of Palestine*.

PIKE, ALBERT (1809-1891).—Poet, *b.* at Boston, Mass., was in his early days a teacher, and afterwards a successful lawyer. His now little-remembered poems were chiefly written under the inspiration of Coleridge and Keats. His chief work, *Hymns to the Gods*, which appeared in *Blackwood's Magazine*, closely imitates the latter. He also wrote prose sketches.

PINDAR, PETER (*See* WOLCOT, J.).

PINKERTON, JOHN (1758-1826).—Historian and Antiquary, *b.* in Edin., was apprenticed to a lawyer, but took to literature, and produced a number of works distinguished by painstaking research, but disfigured by a controversial and prejudiced spirit. His first publication was *Select Scottish Ballads* (1783), some of which, however, were composed by himself. A valuable *Essay on Medals* (1784) introduced him to Gibbon and Horace Walpole. Among his other works are *Ancient Scottish Poems* (1786), *Dissertation on the Goths* (1787), *Medallic History of England* (1790), *History of Scotland* (1797), and his best work, *Treatise on Rocks* (1811). One of his most inveterate prejudices was against Celts of all tribes and times. He *d.* in obscurity in Paris.

PINKNEY, EDWARD COATE (1802-1828).—*B.* in London, where his *f.* was U. S. ambassador. He wrote a number of light, graceful short poems, but fell a victim to ill-health and a morbid melancholy at 25. His longest poem is *Rudolph* (1825).

PIOZZI, HESTER LYNCH (SALUSBURY) (1741-1821).—Miscellaneous writer, *m.* Henry Thrale, a wealthy brewer, and, after his death, Gabriel Piozzi, an Italian musician. Her chief distinction is her friendship with Dr. Johnson, who was for a time almost domesticated with the Thrales. Her second marriage in the year of Johnson's death, 1784, broke up the friendship. She wrote *Anecdotes of Dr. Johnson*, a work which had a favourable reception, and gives a lifelike picture of its subject, and left an *Autobiography*. Her poem,

The Three Warnings, is supposed to have been touched up by Johnson. Many details of her friendship with J. are given in the *Diary* of Madame D'Arblay (*q.v.*).

PLANCHÉ, JAMES ROBINSON (1796-1880).—Dramatist and miscellaneous writer, *b.* in London of Huguenot descent, was in the Herald Office, and rose to be Somerset Herald, in which capacity he was repeatedly sent on missions to invest foreign princes with the Order of the Garter. He produced upwards of 90 adaptations, and about 70 original pieces for the stage. He also wrote a *History of British Costumes*, *The Pursuivant of Arms* (1852), and *The Conqueror and his Companions* (1874), besides autobiographical *Recollections* (1872).

POE, EDGAR ALLAN (1809-1849).—Poet and writer of tales, was *b.* at Boston, where his parents, who were both actors, were temporarily living. He was left an orphan in early childhood in destitute circumstances, but was adopted by a Mr. Allan of Richmond, Virginia. By him and his wife he was treated with great indulgence, and in 1815 accompanied them to England, where they remained for five years, and where he received a good education, which was continued on their return to America, at the Univ. of Virginia. He distinguished himself as a student, but got deeply into debt with gaming, which led to his being removed. In 1829 he *pub.* a small vol. of poems containing *Al Araaf* and *Tamerlane*. About the same time he proposed to enter the army, and was placed at the Military Academy at West Point. Here, however, he grossly neglected his duties, and fell into the habits of intemperance which proved the ruin of his life, and was in 1831 dismissed. He then returned to the house of his benefactor, but his conduct was so objectionable as to lead to a rupture. In the same year P. *pub.* an enlarged ed. of his poems, and in 1833 was successful in a competition for a prize tale and a prize poem, the tale being the *MS. found in a Bottle*, and the poem *The Coliseum*. In the following year Mr. Allan *d.* without making any provision for P., and the latter, being now thrown on his own resources, took to literature as a profession, and became a contributor to various periodicals. In 1836 he entered into a marriage with his cousin Virginia Clemm, a very young girl, who continued devotedly attached to him notwithstanding his many aberrations, until her death in 1847. *The Narrative of Arthur Gordon Pym* appeared in 1838, and in 1839 P. became ed. of the *Gentleman's Magazine*, in which appeared as *Tales of the Arabesque and Grotesque* many of his best stories. In 1845 his famous poem, *The Raven*, came out, and in 1848 *Eureka, a Prose Poem*, a pseudo-scientific lucubration. The death of his wife gave a severe shock to his constitution, and a violent drinking bout on a visit to Baltimore led to his death from brain fever in the hospital there. The literary output of P., though not great in volume, limited in range, and very unequal in merit, bears the stamp of an original genius. In his poetry he sometimes aims at a musical effect to which the sense is sacrificed., but at times he has a charm and a magic melody all his own. His better tales are remarkable for their originality and ingenuity of construction, and in the best of them he rises to a high level of imagination, as in *The House of Usher*, while *The Gold Beetle* or *Golden Bug* is one of the first examples of the cryptogram story; and in *The Purloined Letters, The Mystery of Marie Roget*, and *The Murders in the Rue Morgue* he is the pioneer of the modern detective story.

Life, Woodberry (American Men of Letters). *Works* ed. by Woodberry and Stedman (10 vols.), etc.

POLLOK, ROBERT (1789-1827).—Poet, *b.* in Refrewshire, studied for the ministry of one of the Scottish Dissenting communions. After leaving the Univ. of Glasgow he *pub.* anonymously *Tales of the Covenanters*, and in 1827, the year of his untimely death from consumption, appeared his poem, *The Course of Time*, which contains some fine passages, and occasionally faintly recalls Milton and Young. The poem went through many ed. in Britain and America. He *d.* at Shirley, near Southampton, whither he had gone in search of health.

POMFRET, JOHN (1667-1702).—Poet, *s.* of a clergyman, entered the Church. He wrote several rather dull poems, of which the only one remembered, though now never read, is *The Choice*, which celebrates a country life free from care, and was highly popular in its day.

POPE, ALEXANDER (1688-1744).—Poet, was *b.* in London, of Roman Catholic parentage. His *f.* was a linen-merchant, who *m.* as his second wife Edith Turner, a lady of respectable Yorkshire family, and of some fortune, made a competence, and retired to a small property at Binfield, near Windsor. P. received a somewhat desultory education at various Roman Catholic schools, but after the age of 12, when he had a severe illness brought on by over-application, he was practically self-educated. Though never a profound or accurate scholar, he had a good knowledge of Latin, and a working acquaintance with Greek. By 1704 he had written a good deal of verse, which attracted the attention of Wycherley (*q.v.*), who introduced him to town life and to other men of letters. In 1709 his *Pastorals* were *pub.* in Tonson's *Miscellany*, and two years later *The Essay on Criticism* appeared, and was praised by Addison. The *Rape of the Lock*, which came out in 1714, placed his reputation on a sure foundation, and thereafter his life was an uninterrupted and brilliant success. His industry was untiring, and his literary output almost continuous until his death. In 1713 *Windsor Forest* (which won him the friendship of Swift) and *The Temple of Fame* appeared, and in 1715 the translation of the *Iliad* was begun, and the work *pub.* at intervals between that year and 1720. It had enormous popularity, and brought the poet £5000. It was followed by the *Odyssey* (1725-26), in which he had the assistance of Broome and Fenton (*q.v.*), who, especially the former, caught his style so exactly as almost to defy identification. It also was highly popular, and increased his gains to about £8000, which placed him in a position of independence. While engaged upon these he removed to Chiswick, where he lived 1716-18, and where he issued in 1717 a *coll.* ed. of his works, including the *Elegy on an Unfortunate Lady* and the *Epistle of Eloisa to Abelard*. In 1718, his *f.* having *d.*, he again removed with his mother to his famous villa at Twickenham, the adornment of the grounds of which became one of his chief interests, and where, now the acknowledged chief of his art, he received the visits of his friends, who included the most distinguished men of letters, wits, statesmen, and beauties of the day. His next task was his ed. of Shakespeare (1725), a work for which he was not well qualified, though the preface is a fine piece of prose. The *Miscellanies*, the joint work of Pope and Swift, were *pub.* in 1727-28, and drew down upon the authors a storm of angry comment, which in turn led to the production of *The Dunciad*, first *pub.* in 1728, and again with new matter in 1729, an additional book—the fourth—being added in 1742. In it he satirised with a wit, always keen and biting, often savage and unfair, the small wits and poetasters, and some of a quite different quality, who had, or whom he supposed to have, injured him. Between 1731 and 1735 he produced his *Epistles*, the last of which, addressed to Arbuthnot, is also known as the *Prologue to the Satires*, and contains his ungrateful character of Addison under the name of "Atticus;" and also, 1733, the *Essay on Man*, written under the influence of Bolingbroke. His last, and in some respects best, works were his *Imitations of Horace*, *pub.* between 1733 and 1739, and the fourth book of *The Dunciad* (1742), already mentioned. A naturally delicate constitution, a deformed body, extreme sensitiveness, over-excitement, and over-work did not promise a long life, and P. *d.* on May 30, 1744, aged 56.

His position as a poet has been the subject of much contention among critics, and on the whole is lower than that assigned him by his contemporaries and immediate successors. Of the higher poetic qualities, imagination, sympathy, insight, and pathos, he had no great share; but for the work which in his original writings, as distinguished from translations, he set himself to do, his equipment was supreme, and the medium which he used—the heroic couplet—he brought to the highest technical perfection of which it is capable. He wrote for his own age, and in temper and intellectual and spiritual outlook, such as it was, he exactly reflected and interpreted it. In the forging of condensed, pointed, and sparkling maxims of life and criticism he has no equal, and in painting a portrait Dryden alone is his rival; while in the *Rape of the Lock* he has produced the best mock-heroic poem in existence. Almost no author except Shakespeare is so often quoted. His extreme vanity and sensitiveness to criticism made him often vindictive, unjust, and venomous. They led him also into frequent quarrels, and lost him many friends, including Lady M. Wortley Montagu, and along with a strong tendency to finesse and stratagem, of which the circumstances attending the publication of his literary correspondence is the chief instance, make his character on the whole an unamiable one. On the other hand, he was often generous; he retained the friendship of such men as Swift and Arbuthnot, and he was a most dutiful and affectionate son.

SUMMARY.—*B.* 1688, *ed.* at various Romanist schools, introduced to Wycherley 1704, *pub. Pastorals* 1709, *Essay on Criticism* 1711, *Rape of the Lock* 1714, *Windsor Forest* and *Temple of Fame* 1713, translation of *Iliad* 1715-20, *Odyssey* 1725-26, *coll. Works* 1717, buys villa at Twickenham 1718, *pub.* ed. of *Shakespeare* 1725, *Miscellanies* 1727-28, *Dunciad* 1728 (fourth book 1742), *Epistles* 1731-35, *Essay on Man* 1733, *Imitations of Horace* 1733-39, *d.* 1744.

The best ed. of the *Works* is that of Elwin and Courthope, with *Life* by Courthope (10 vols., 1871-89).

PORDAGE, SAMUEL (1633-1691?).—Poet, *s.* of a clergyman in Berks, *ed.* at Merchant Taylor's School, studied law at Lincoln's Inn, and made various translations, wrote some poems, two tragedies, *Herod and Mariamne* (1673), and *The Siege of Babylon* (1678), and a romance, *Eliana.* He is best known by his *Azaria and Hushai* (1682), in reply to Dryden's *Absalom and Achitophel*, distinguished from the other replies by its moderation and freedom from scurrility.

PORSON, RICHARD (1759-1808).—Scholar, *s.* of the parish clerk of E. Ruston, Norfolk, was distinguished from childhood by a marvellous tenacity of memory which attracted the attention of the curate of the parish, who *ed.* him, after which he was sent by a gentleman to Eton. Subsequently a fund was collected for the purpose of maintaining him at Camb., where he had a brilliant career, and became a Fellow of Trinity Coll. This position he lost by refusing to take orders. In 1792 he was appointed Prof. of Greek in the Univ., but resided for the most part in London, where he was much courted by literary men, but unfortunately fell into extremely intemperate habits. P. was one of the very greatest of Greek scholars and critics; but he has left little permanent work of his own. He ed. four plays of Euripides, viz., *Hecuba, Orestes, Phœnissæ,* and *Medea.* His most widely read work was his *Letters* to Archdeacon Travis on the disputed passage, 1 John v. 7, which is considered a masterpiece of acute reasoning. He is buried in the chapel of Trinity Coll.

PORTER, ANNA MARIA (1780-1832), PORTER, JANE (1776-1850).—Novelists, were the *dau.* of an Irish army surgeon, and sisters of Sir Robert Ker P., the painter and traveller. After the death of the *f.* the family settled in Edin., where they enjoyed the friendship of Scott. ANNA at the age of 12 *pub. Artless Tales*, the precursor of a series of tales and novels numbering about 50, the best being *Don Sebastian* (1809). JANE, though the elder by four years, did not *pub.* until 1803, when her first novel, *Thaddeus of Warsaw*, appeared. *The Scottish Chiefs* followed in 1810. Both of these works, especially the latter, had remarkable popularity, the *Chiefs* being translated into German and Russian. She had greater talent than her sister, but like her, while possessed of considerable animation and imagination, failed in grasping character, and imparting local verisimilitude. Both were amiable and excellent women. A romance, *Sir Edward Seaward's Diary* (1831), purporting to be a record of actual circumstances, and ed. by Jane, is generally believed to have been written by a brother, Dr. William Ogilvie P.

POWELL, FREDERICK YORK (1850-1904).—Historian, *ed.* at Rugby and Oxf., called to the Bar at the Middle Temple 1874, became an ardent student of history, and succeeded Froude as Prof. of Modern History at Oxf. in 1894. Absorbed in study, he wrote less than his wide and deep learning qualified him for. Among his works are *A History of England to* 1509, and he also wrote on Early England up to the Conquest, and on Alfred and William the Conqueror.

PRAED, WINTHROP MACKWORTH (1802-1839).—Poet, *s.* of a sergeant-at-law, was *b.* in London, *ed.* at Eton and Camb., and called to the Bar 1829. He sat in Parliament for various places, and was Sec. to the Board of Control 1834-35. He appeared to have a brilliant career before him, when his health gave way, and he *d.* of consumption in 1839. His poems, chiefly bright and witty skits and satirical pieces, were *pub.* first in America 1844, and appeared in England with a memoir by Derwent Coleridge in 1864. His essays appeared in 1887.

PRESCOTT, WILLIAM HICKLING (1796-1859).—Historian, *b.* at Salem, Massachusetts, the *s.* of an eminent lawyer, was *ed.* at Harvard, where he graduated in 1814. While there he met with an accident to one of his eyes which seriously affected his sight for the remainder of his life. He made an extended tour in Europe, and on his return to America he *m.*, and abandoning the idea of a legal career, resolved to devote himself to literature. After ten years of study, he *pub.* in 1837 his *History of Ferdinand and Isabella,* which at once gained for him a high place among historians. It was followed in 1843 by the *History of the Conquest of Mexico*, and in 1847 by the *Conquest of Peru.* His last work was the *History of Philip II.*, of which the third vol. appeared in 1858, and which was left unfinished. In that year he had an apoplectic shock, and another in 1859 was the cause of his death, which took place on January 28 in the last-named year. In all his works he displayed great research, impartiality, and an admirable narrative power. The great disadvantage at which, owing to his very imperfect vision, he worked, makes the first of these qualities specially remarkable, for his authorities in a foreign tongue were read to him, while he had to write on a frame for the blind. P. was a man of amiable and benevolent character, and enjoyed the friendship of many of the most distinguished men in Europe as well as in America.

PRICE, RICHARD (1723-1791).—Writer on morals, politics, and economics, *s.* of a dissenting minister, was *b.* at Tynton in Wales, *ed.* at a dissenting coll. in London, and was then for some years chaplain to a Mr. Streatfield, who left him some property. Thereafter he officiated as minister to various congregations near London. In 1758 his *Review of the Principal Questions and Difficulties in Morals,* a work of considerable metaphysical power, appeared; and it was followed in 1766 by a treatise on *The Importance of Christianity.* In 1769 his work on *Reversionary Payments* was *pub.*, and his Northampton Mortality Table was about the same time constructed. These, though long superseded, were in their day most valuable contributions to economical science. His most popular work, *Observations on Civil Liberty and the Justice and Policy of the War with America,* appeared in 1776, had an enormous sale, and led to his being invited to go to America and assist in establishing the financial system of the new Government. This he declined chiefly on the score of age. Simplicity, uprightness, and toleration of opinions opposed to his own appear to have been marked traits in his character.

PRIDEAUX, HUMPHREY (1648-1724).—Divine and scholar, belonged to an ancient Cornish family, was *b.* at Padstow, and *ed.* at

Westminster School and at Oxf. He first attracted notice by his description of the Arundel Marbles (1676), which gained for him powerful patrons, and he rose to be Dean of Norwich. Among his other works are a *Life of Mahomet* (1697), and *The Old and New Testament connected in the History of the Jews and Neighbouring Nations* (1715-17), long an important work, of which many ed. were brought out.

PRIESTLEY, JOSEPH (1733-1804).—Chemist, theologian, and political writer, *s.* of a draper at Fieldhead, Yorkshire, where he was *b.* Brought up as a Calvinist, he gradually became a modified Unitarian, and after attending a dissenting academy at Daventry, he became minister to various congregations. About 1756 he *pub.* *The Scripture Doctrine of Remission,* denying the doctrine of atonement, and in 1761 succeeded Dr. Aiken as teacher of languages and *belles-lettres* in the dissenting academy at Warrington. About the same time he became acquainted with Franklin and Dr. Price (*q.v.*), and began to devote himself to science, the fruits of which were his *History and Present State of Electricity* (1767), and *Vision, Light, and Colours.* He also became a distinguished chemist, and made important discoveries, including that of oxygen. In 1773 he travelled on the Continent as companion to Lord Shelburne, where he was introduced to many men of scientific and literary eminence, by some of whom he was rallied upon his belief in Christianity. In reply to this he wrote *Letters to a Philosophical Unbeliever* (1774), and in answer to the accusations of Atheism brought against him at home, he *pub.* (1777) *Disquisition relating to Matter and Spirit.* In 1780 he settled in Birmingham, in 1782 *pub.* his *Corruptions of Christianity,* and in 1786 his *History of Early Opinions concerning Jesus Christ.* He was one of those who wrote replies to Burke's *Reflections on the French Revolution,* one consequence of which was his election as a French citizen, and another the destruction of his chapel, house, papers, and instruments by a mob. Some years later he went to America, where he *d.* P. has been called the father of modern chemistry. He received many scientific and academic honours, being a member of the Royal Society, of the Academies of France, and of St. Petersburg, and an LL.D. of Edin. He was a man of powerful and original mind, of high character, and of undaunted courage in maintaining his opinions, which were usually unpopular.

PRINGLE, THOMAS (1789-1834).—Poet, *b.* in Roxburghshire, studied at Edin., and became known to Scott, by whose influence he obtained a grant of land in South Africa, to which he, with his *f.* and brothers, emigrated. He took to literary work in Cape Town, and conducted two papers, which were suppressed for their free criticisms of the Colonial Government. Thereupon he returned and settled in London, where he *pub.* *African Sketches.* He also produced a book of poems, *Ephemerides.*

PRIOR, MATTHEW (1664-1721).—Poet, *b.* near Wimborne Minster, Dorset, *s.* of a joiner who, having *d.*, he was *ed.* by an uncle, and sent to Westminster School. Befriended by the Earl of Dorset he proceeded to Camb., and while there wrote, jointly with Charles Montague, *The Town and Country Mouse,* a burlesque of Dryden's

Hind and Panther. After holding various diplomatic posts, in which he showed ability and discretion, he entered Parliament in 1700, and, deserting the Whigs, joined the Tories, by whom he was employed in various capacities, including that of Ambassador at Paris. On the death of Queen Anne he was recalled, and in 1715 imprisoned, but after two years released. In 1719 a folio ed. of his works was brought out, by which he realised £4000, and Lord Harley having presented him with an equal sum, he looked forward to the peace and comfort which were his chief ambition. He did not, however, long enjoy his prosperity, dying two years later. Among his poems may be mentioned *Solomon*, which he considered his best work, *Alma, or the Progress of the Mind, The Female Phaeton, To a Child of Quality*, and some prose tales. His chief characteristic is a certain elegance and easy grace, in which he is perhaps unrivalled. His character appears to have been by no means unimpeachable, but he was amiable and free from any trace of vindictiveness.

PROCTER, ADELAIDE ANN (1825-1864).—Poetess, eldest *dau.* of Bryan W. P. (*q.v.*). Many of her poems were first *pub.* in *Household Words* and *All the Year Round*, and afterwards *coll.* under the title of *Legends and Lyrics* (1858), of which many ed. appeared. In 1851 Miss P. became a Roman Catholic. She took much interest in social questions affecting women. She wrote the well-known songs, *Cleansing Fires* and *The Lost Chord*, and among her many hymns are, *I do not ask, O Lord, that Life may be*, and *My God, I thank Thee who hast made*.

PROCTER, BRYAN WALLER (" BARRY CORNWALL ") (1787-1874).—Poet, *b.* at Leeds, and *ed.* at Harrow, went to London and practised successfully as a solicitor. Thereafter he became a barrister, and was, 1832-61, a Commissioner of Lunacy. By 1823 he had produced four vols. of poetry and a tragedy, *Mirandola* (1821). His works include *Dramatic Scenes* (1819), *A Sicilian Story, Marcian Colonna* (1820), *The Flood of Thessaly* (1823), and *English Songs* (1832), which last will perhaps survive his other writings. P. was the friend of most of his literary contemporaries, and was universally beloved.

PROUT, FATHER (*See* MAHONY, F. S.).

PRYNNE, WILLIAM (1600-1669).—Controversial writer, *b.* near Bath, *ed.* at Oxf., studied law at Lincoln's Inn, of which he became a bencher, but soon became immersed in the writing of controversial pamphlets. After the *Unloveliness of Lovelocks* and *Health's Sicknesse* (1627-30) appeared his best known controversial work, *Histrio-Mastix*, or a *Scourge for Stage Players* (1633), a bitter attack on most of the popular amusements of the day. It was punished with inhuman severity. P. was brought before the Star Chamber, fined £5000, pilloried, and had both his ears cut off. Undeterred by this he issued from his prison a fierce attack upon Laud and the hierarchy, for which he was again fined, pilloried, and branded on both cheeks with the letters S. L. (seditious libeller). Removed to Carnarvon Castle he remained there until liberated in 1641 by the Long Parliament. He soon after became a member of the House, and joined with extreme, but not inexcusable, rancour in the prosecution of Laud. After this he turned his attention to the Independents, whom he hated scarcely less than the Prelatists, and was among those expelled from the House of Commons by Cromwell, whom he had opposed in regard to the execution of the King with such asperity that he again suffered imprisonment, from which he was released in 1652. He supported the Restoration, and was by Charles II. appointed Keeper of the Records in the Tower. Here he did good service by compiling the *Calendar of Parliamentary Writs* and *Records*. He *pub.* in all about 200 books and pamphlets.

PSALMANAZAR, GEORGE (1679? - 1763). — Literary impostor. His real name is unknown. He is believed to have been a native of France or Switzerland, but represented himself as a native of the island of Formosa, and palmed off a Formosan language of his own construction, to which he afterwards added a description of the island. For a time he was in the military service of the Duke of Mecklenburg, and formed a connection with William Innes, chaplain of a Scottish regiment, who collaborated with him in his frauds, and introduced various refinements into his methods. Innes, however, was appointed chaplain to the forces in Portugal, and P. was unable to maintain his impositions, and was exposed. After a serious illness in 1728 he turned over a new leaf and became a respectable and efficient literary hack; his works in his latter days included a *General History of Printing*, contributions to the *Universal History*, and an *Autiobiography* containing an account of his impostures.

PURCHAS, SAMUEL (1575?-1626).—Compiler of travels, *b.* at Thaxton, and *ed.* at Camb., took orders, and held various benefices, including the rectory of St. Martin's, Ludgate Hill. The papers of R. Hakluyt (*q.v.*) came into his hands, and he made several compilations relating to man, his nature, doings, and surroundings. His three works are (1) *Purchas his Pilgrimage, or Relations of the World and the Religions observed in all Ages and Places, etc.*; (2) *Purchas his Pilgrim, Microcosmus, or the History of Man, etc.*; and (3) *Hakluytus Posthumus, or Purchas his Pilgrimes, containing a History of the World in Sea Voyages and Land Travels, etc.* Although credulous, diffuse, and confused, these works have preserved many interesting and curious matters which would otherwise have been lost.

PUSEY, EDWARD BOUVERIE (1800-1882).—Scholar and theologian, *b.* at Pusey, Berks, *ed.* at Eton and Oxf., belonged to the family of Lord Folkstone, whose name was Bouverie, his *f.* assuming that of P. on inheriting certain estates. After studying in Germany, he became in 1828 Regius Prof. of Hebrew at Oxf. His first important work was an *Essay on the Causes of Rationalism in German Theology*, and the arrest of similar tendencies in England became one of the leading objects of his life. He was one of the chief leaders of the Tractarian movement, and contributed tracts on *Baptism* and on *Fasting*. In consequence of a sermon on the Eucharist, he was in 1843 suspended from the office of Univ. Preacher which he then held. Later writings related to *Confession* and *The Doctrine of the Real Presence*, and in 1865 he issued an *Eirenicon* in support of union with the Church of Rome. He was prominent in all movements and controversies affecting the Univ., and was foremost among the prosecutors of Jowett (*q.v.*). Among his other literary labours are commentaries on Daniel and the minor Prophets, a treatise on Everlasting Punishment, and a Catalogue of the Arabic MS. in the Bodleian Library.

PUTTENHAM, GEORGE (1530?-1590).—Was one of the *s.* of Robert P., a country gentleman. There has been attributed to him the authorship of *The Arte of Poesie*, a treatise of some length divided into three parts, (1) of poets and poesy, (2) of proportion, (3) of ornament. It is now thought rather more likely that it was written by his brother RICHARD (1520?-1601). George was the author of an *Apologie* for Queen Elizabeth's treatment of Mary Queen of Scots.

PYE, HENRY JAMES (1745-1813).—A country gentleman of Berkshire, who *pub.* *Poems on Various Subjects* and *Alfred, an Epic*, translated the *Poetics* of Aristotle, and was Poet Laureate from 1790. In the last capacity he wrote official poems of ludicrous dulness, and was generally a jest and a byword in literary circles.

QUARLES, FRANCIS (1592-1644).—Poet, *b.* at the manor-house of Stewards near Romford, was at Camb., and studied law at Lincoln's Inn. Thereafter he went to the Continent, and at Heidelberg acted as cup-bearer to Elizabeth of Bohemia, *dau.* of James I. He next appears as sec. to Archbishop Ussher in Ireland, and was in 1639 Chronologer to the City of London. On the outbreak of the Civil War he sided with the Royalists, and was plundered by the Parliamentarians of his books and rare manuscripts, which is said to have so grieved him as to bring about his death. His first book of poems was *A Feast for Worms* (1620); others were *Hadassa* (Esther) (1621), *Sion's Elegies* (1625), and *Divine Emblems* (1635), by far his most popular book. His style was that fashionable in his day, affected, artificial, and full of "conceits," but he had both real poetical fire and genuine wit, mixed with much that was false in taste, and though quaint and crabbed, is seldom feeble or dull. He was twice *m.*, and had by his first wife 18 children.

RADCLIFFE, MRS. ANN (WARD) (1764-1823).—Novelist, only *dau.* of parents in a respectable position, in 1787 *m.* Mr. William Radcliffe, ed. and proprietor of a weekly newspaper, the *English Chronicle.* In 1789 she *pub.* her first novel, *The Castles of Athlin and Dunbayne*, of which the scene is laid in Scotland. It, however, gave little promise of the future power of the author. In the following year appeared *The Sicilian Romance*, which attracted attention by its vivid descriptions and startling incidents. Next came *The Romance of the Forest* (1791), followed by *The Mysteries of Udolpho* (1794), and *The Italian* (1797), a story of the Inquisition, the last of her works *pub.* during her life-time. *Gaston de Blondeville*, ed. by Sergeant Talfourd, was brought out posthumously. Mrs. R. has been called the Salvator Rosa of British novelists. She excels in the description of scenes of mystery and terror whether of natural scenery or incident: in the former displaying a high degree of imaginative power, and in the latter great ingenuity and fertility of invention. She had, however, little power of delineating character. Though her works belong to a type now out of fashion, they will always possess an historical interest as marking a stage in the development of English fiction.

"RAINE, ALLEN" (MRS. BEYNON PUDDICOMBE).—Novelist. *A Welsh Singer* (1897), *Torn Sails* (1898), *A Welsh Witch* (1901), *Queen of the Rushes* (1906), etc.

RALEIGH, SIR WALTER (1552?-1618).—Explorer, statesman, admiral, historian, and poet, *s.* of Walter R., of Fardel, Devonshire, was *b.* at Hayes Barton in that county. In 1568 he was sent to Oxf., where he greatly distinguished himself. In the next year he began his career of adventure by going to France as a volunteer in aid of the Huguenots, serving thereafter in the Low Countries. The year 1579 saw him engaged in his first voyage of adventure in conjunction with his half-brother, Sir Humphrey Gilbert. Their object was to discover and settle lands in North America; but the expedition failed, chiefly owing to opposition by the Spaniards. The next year he was fighting against the rebels in Ireland; and shortly thereafter attracted the notice of Queen Elizabeth, in whose favour he rapidly rose. In 1584 he fitted out a new colonising expedition to North America, and succeeded in discovering and occupying Virginia, named after the Queen. On his return he was knighted. In the dark and anxious days of the Armada, 1587-88, R. was employed in organising resistance, and rendered distinguished service in action. His favour with the Queen, and his haughty bearing, had, however, been raising up enemies and rivals, and his intrigue and private marriage with Elizabeth Throckmorton, one of the maids of honour, in 1593, lost him for a time the favour of the Queen. Driven from the Court he returned to the schemes of adventure which had so great a charm for him, and fired by the Spanish accounts of the fabulous wealth of Guiana, he and some of his friends fitted out an expedition which, however, though attended with various brilliant episodes, proved unsuccessful. Restored to the favour of the Queen, he was appointed an Admiral in the expeditions to Cadiz, 1596, and in the following year was engaged in an attack on the Azores, in both of which he added greatly to his reputation. The death of Elizabeth in 1603 was the turning point in R.'s fortunes. Thenceforward disaster clouded his days. The new sovereign and his old enemies combined to compass his ruin. Accused of conspiring against the former he was, against all evidence, sentenced to death, and though this was not at the time carried out, he was imprisoned in the Tower and his estates confiscated. During this confinement he composed his *History of the World*, which he brought down to 130 B.C. It is one of the finest specimens of Elizabethan prose, reflective in matter and dignified and grave in style. Released in 1615 he set out on his last voyage, again to Guiana, which, like the former, proved a failure, and in which he lost his eldest *s.* He returned a broken and dying man, but met with no pity from his ungenerous King who, urged, it is believed, by the King of Spain, had him beheaded on Tower Hill, October 29, 1618. R. is one of the most striking and brilliant figures in an age crowded with great men. Of a noble presence, he was possessed of a commanding intellect and a versatility which enabled him to shine in every enterprise to which he set himself. In addition to his great fragment the

History of the World, he wrote *A Report of the Truth of the Fight about the Azores*, and *The Discoverie of the Empire of Guiana*, besides various poems chiefly of a philosophic cast, of which perhaps the best known are *The Pilgrimage*, and that beginning " Go, Soul, the Body's Guest."

The most recent *Lives* are by Stebbing (1892), and Hume (1898). *Works* (1829), with *Lives* by Oldys and Birch.

RAMÉE, LOUISE DE LA (" OUIDA ") (1840?-1908).—Novelist, *b.* at Bury St. Edmunds, *dau.* of an English *f.* and a French mother. For many years she lived in London, but about 1874 she went to Italy, where she *d.* She wrote over 40 novels, which had considerable popularity. Among the best known of them are *Under Two Flags*, *Puck*, *Two Little Wooden Shoes*, *In a Winter City*, *In Maremma.* She also wrote a book of stories for children, *Bimbi.* Occasionally she shows considerable power, but on the whole her writings have an unhealthy tone, want reality, and are not likely to have any permanent place in literature.

RAMSAY, ALLAN (1686-1758).—Poet, *s.* of a mine-manager at Leadhills, Dumfriesshire, who claimed kin with the Ramsays of Dalhousie. In his infancy he lost his *f.*, and his mother *m.* a small " laird," who gave him the ordinary parish school education. In 1701 he came to Edinburgh as apprentice to a wig-maker, took to writing poetry, became a member of the " Easy Club," of which Pitcairn and Ruddiman, the grammarian, were members, and of which he was made " laureate." The club *pub.* his poems as they were thrown off, and their appearance soon began to be awaited with interest. In 1716 he *pub.* an additional canto to *Christ's Kirk on the Green*, a humorous poem sometimes attributed to James I., and in 1719 he became a bookseller, his shop being a meeting-place of the *literati* of the city. A *coll.* ed. of his poems appeared in 1720, among the subscribers to which were Pope, Steele, Arbuthnot, and Gay. It was followed by *Fables and Tales*, and other poems. In 1724 he began the *Tea Table Miscellany*, a collection of new Scots songs set to old melodies, and the *Evergreen*, a collection of old Scots poems with which R. as ed. took great liberties. This was a kind of work for which he was not qualified, and in which he was far from successful. *The Gentle Shepherd*, by far his best known and most meritorious work, appeared in 1725, and had an immediate popularity which, to a certain extent, it retains. It is a pastoral drama, and abounds in character, unaffected sentiment, and vivid description. After this success R., satisfied with his reputation, produced nothing more of importance. He was the first to introduce the circulating library into Scotland, and among his other enterprises was an unsuccessful attempt to establish a theatre in Edin. On the whole his life was a happy and successful one, and he had the advantage of a cheerful, sanguine, and contented spirit. His foible was an innocent and good-natured vanity.

RAMSAY, EDWARD BANNERMAN (1793-1872).—A clergyman of the Scottish Episcopal Church, and Dean of Edinburgh in that communion from 1841, has a place in literature by his *Reminiscences of Scottish Life and Character*, which had gone through 22 ed.

at his death. It is a book full of the engaging personality of the author, and preserves many interesting and entertaining traits and anecdotes which must otherwise, in all probability, have perished. The Dean was deservedly one of the most popular men in Scotland.

RANDOLPH, THOMAS (1605-1635).—Poet and dramatist, *ed.* at Westminster School and Camb., was a friend of Ben Jonson, and led a wild life in London. He wrote six plays, including *The Jealous Lovers*, *Amyntas*, and *The Muses' Looking-glass*, and some poems. He was a scholar as well as a wit, and his plays are full of learning and condensed thought in a style somewhat cold and hard.

RAPIN DE THOYRAS, PAUL (1661-1725).—Historian, *b.* at Castres, Languedoc, belonged to a Protestant Savoyard family, and came to England on the revocation of the Edict of Nantes in 1686. He afterwards served with William III. in Holland, and accompanied him to England in 1688. His *History of England*, written in French, was translated into English, and continued by various writers, and was the standard history until the appearance of Hume's.

RASPE, RUDOLF ERIC- (1737-1794).—*B.* in Hanover, was a prof. in Cassel, and keeper of the Landgrave of Hesse's antique gems and medals, in the purloining of some of which he was detected, and fled to England. Here he won for himself a certain place in English literature by the publication in 1785 of *Baron Munchausen's Narrative.* Only a small portion of the work in its present form is by R., the rest having been added later by another hand. He appears to have maintained more or less during life his character of a rogue, and is the prototype of Douster-swivel in Scott's *Antiquary.*

RAWLINSON, GEORGE (1812-1902).—Historian, *b.* at Chadlington, Oxfordshire, and *ed.* at Oxf., took orders, and was Canon of Canterbury from 1872. He held the Camden Professorship of Ancient History at Oxf. from 1861. Among his works are a translation of Herodotus (1858-62) (with his brother, Sir Henry R., *q.v.*), *Historical Evidences of the Truth of the Scripture Records*, *The Five Great Monarchies of the Ancient Eastern World* (1862-67), *Manual of Ancient History* (1869), *The Sixth and Seventh Great Oriental Monarchies* (1873-77), *History of Ancient Egypt* (1881), Histories of the Phœnicians and Parthians, Memoirs of Sir H. C. Rawlinson (1898).

RAWLINSON, SIR HENRY CRESSWICKE (1810-1895).—Brother of the above, entered the service of the East India Company, and held many important diplomatic posts. He studied the cuneiform inscriptions, and *pub.* *The Cuneiform Inscriptions of Western Asia* (1861-80), *Outlines of the History of Assyria* (1852). He deciphered most of the inscriptions discovered by Sir A. H. Layard (*q.v.*).

RAY, JOHN (1627-1705).—Naturalist, *s.* of a blacksmith at Black Notley, Essex, was at Camb., where he became a Fellow of Trinity, and successively lecturer on Greek and mathematics. His first publication was a Latin catalogue of plants growing near Cambridge, which appeared in 1660. Thereafter he made a tour of Great Britain, and *pub.* in 1670 his *Catalogue of the Plants of England and the adjacent Isles.* In 1663 he had travelled on the Continent for three years with his pupil-friend, F. Willughby, and in 1673 appeared *Observations* on his journeys, which extended over the Low Countries, Germany, Italy, and France, with a catalogue of plants not native to England. On the death of Willughby, R. *ed.* his sons, and in 1679 retired to his native village, where he continued his scientific labours until his death. These included the ed. of W.'s *History of Birds and Fishes*, a collection of English proverbs, *Historia Plantarum Generalis* (1686-1704), and *Synopsis Methodica Animalium.* He was for long popularly known by his treatise, *The Wisdom of God manifested in the works of the Creation* (1691), a precursor of Paley's *Natural Theology.* R. is the father of English botany, and appears to have grasped the idea of the natural classification of plants, afterwards developed by Jussieu and other later naturalists. His greatest successors, including Cuvier, highly commended his methods and acquirements.

READ, THOMAS BUCHANAN (1822-1872).—American poet, was a portrait-painter, and lived much abroad. He wrote a prose romance, *The Pilgrims of the Great St. Bernard*, and several books of poetry, including *The New Pastoral*, *The House by the Sea*, *Sylvia*, and *A Summer Story.* Some of the shorter pieces included in these, *e.g.*, "Sheridan's Ride," "Drifting," and "The Closing Scene," have great merit.

READE, CHARLES (1814-1884).—Novelist, *s.* of a country gentleman of Oxfordshire, *ed.* at Oxf., and called to the Bar at Lincoln's Inn 1843. He did not, however, practise, but began his literary career with some dramas, of which the most remarkable were *Masks and Faces*, *Gold*, and *Drink.* He afterwards rewrote the first of these as a novel, *Peg Woffington* (1852), which attained great popularity. *It is never too late to Mend* appeared in 1856, his historical novel, *The Cloister and the Hearth*, generally regarded as his masterpiece (1861), *Hard Cash* (1863), *Griffith Gaunt* (1867), *Foul Play* (1869), *Put Yourself in his Place* (1870), and *A Terrible Temptation* (1871). Critics have differed very widely as to the merits of R. as a novelist, and have attributed to, and denied him the same qualities; but it will be generally admitted that, while very unequal, he was at his best a writer of unusual power and vividness. Nearly all are agreed as to the great excellence of *The Cloister and the Hearth*, Mr. Swinburne placing it "among the very greatest masterpieces of narrative." Many of his novels were written with a view to the reformation of some abuse. Thus *Hard Cash* exposes certain private asylums, and *Foul Play*, written in collaboration with Dion Boucicault, is levelled against ship-knackers.

REED, HENRY (1808-1854).—Critic, was Prof. of English Literature in the Univ. of Pennsylvania. He *d.* in a shipwreck. He was a sympathetic and delicate critic, and was among the first of American men of letters to appreciate the genius of Wordsworth, of whose works he brought out an ed. in 1837. His lectures on English Literature, English History, and English Poets were *pub.*

REEVE, CLARA (1729-1807).—Novelist, was the author of several novels, of which only one is remembered—*The Old English Baron* (1777), written in imitation of, or rivalry with, H. Walpole's *Castle of Otranto*, with which it has often been printed.

REEVE, HENRY (1813-1895).—Editor, etc., *s.* of a physician, was on the staff of the *Times*, the foreign policy of which he influenced for many years. He was ed. of the *Edinburgh Review* 1855-95, and of the Greville Memoirs 1865. He held a leading place in society, and had an unusually wide acquaintance with men of letters all over the continent.

REID, MAYNE (1818-1883).—Novelist, *b.* in the north of Ireland, he set off at the age of 20 for Mexico to push his fortunes, and went through many adventures, including service in the Mexican War. He also was for a short time settled in Philadelphia engaged in literary work. Returning to this country he began a long series of novels of adventure with *The Rifle Rangers* (1849). The others include *The Scalp Hunters*, *Boy Hunters*, and *Young Voyagers*, and had great popularity, especially with boys.

REID, THOMAS (1710-1796).—Philosopher, was the *s.* of the minister of Strachan, Kincardineshire, where he was *b.* His mother was one of the gifted family of the Gregorys. At the age of 12 he was sent to Marischal Coll., Aberdeen, where he graduated, and thereafter resided for some time as librarian, devoting himself to study, especially of mathematics and the Newtonian philosophy. He was in 1737 ordained minister of New Machar, Aberdeen, and in 1748 he communicated to the Royal Society an *Essay on Quantity*. Four years later he became one of the Prof. of Philosophy (including mathematics and natural philosophy) in King's Coll., Aberdeen, and in 1763 he was chosen to succeed Adam Smith as Prof. of Moral Philosophy in Glasgow. In the following year he *pub.* his great work, *Inquiry into the Human Mind on the Principles of Common Sense*, directed against Hume's *Essay on Human Nature*. Up to the appearance of the latter work in 1739 R. had been a follower of Berkeley, but the conclusions drawn therein from the idealistic philosophy led him to revise his theories, and to propound what is usually known as the "common sense" philosophy, by which term is meant the beliefs common to rational beings as such. In 1785 he *pub.* his *Essay on the Intellectual Powers*, which was followed in 1788 by that *On the Active Powers*. R., who, though below the middle size, was strong and fond of exercise, maintained his bodily and mental vigour until his death at 86. His writings, distinguished by logical rigour of method and clearness of style, exercised a profound influence in France as well as at home; but his attempted refutation of Berkeley is now generally considered to have failed.

Works ed. by Sir W. Hamilton and H. L. Mansel. Sketch by Prof. A. C. Fraser (1898).

REID, SIR THOMAS WEMYSS (1842-1905).—Novelist and biographer, *b.* at Newcastle, and after being connected with various provincial newspapers came to London in 1887 as manager for Cassell and Co. Thereafter he was, 1890-99, ed. of *The Speaker*. Among his more permanent writings are *The Land of the Bey* (1882), *Gladys Fane* (1883), and Lives of W. E. Forster (1888), and Lords Houghton (1891), and Playfair (1899), and William Black (1902). He was knighted in 1894.

REYNOLDS, SIR JOSHUA (1723-1792).—Painter and writer on art, *s.* of a clergyman and schoolmaster at Plympton, Devonshire. After studying art in Italy, he settled in London, where he attained extraordinary fame as a portrait-painter. He is regarded as the greatest English representative of that art, and was first Pres. of the Royal Academy. He was the intimate friend of Johnson, Burke, Goldsmith, and indeed of most of the celebrated men of his time. He has also a place in literature for his *Fifteen Discourses* on painting, delivered to the Academy. He also contributed to the *Idler*, and translated Du Fresney's *Art of Painting*. He suffered from deafness, and in his latter years from failure of sight. He was a man of great worth and amiability. He was knighted in 1769.

RHODES, WILLIAM BARNES (1772-1826).—Dramatist, was in the Bank of England, of which he became Chief Teller. He wrote a burlesque, *Bombastes Furioso*, which achieved great popularity.

RHYMER, THOMAS THE (*See* ERCILDOUN).

RICARDO, DAVID (1772-1823).—Political economist, *s.* of a Jewish stockbroker, himself followed the same business, in which he acquired a large fortune. On his marriage he conformed to Christianity. He was an original and powerful writer on economic subjects, his chief work being *The Principles of Political Economy and Taxation* (1817). After retiring from business he entered the House of Commons, where, owing to his remarkable power of lucid exposition, combined with his reputation as a highly successful man of business, he acquired great influence. The writings of R. are among the classics of his subject.

RICE, JAMES (1844-1882).—Novelist, was *ed.* at Camb., and studied law, from which he drifted into literature. He wrote a number of successful novels in collaboration with W. Besant (*q.v.*).

RICH, BARNABE (1540?-1620?).—Writer of romances, *b.* in Essex, saw military service in the Low Countries. He began to write in 1574, and took Lyly's *Euphues* as his model. Among his numerous romances is *The Strange and Wonderful Adventures of Simonides, a Gentleman Spaniard* and *Riche, his Farewell to the Military Profession* (1581), which furnished Shakespeare with the plot for *Twelfth Night*.

RICHARDSON, SAMUEL (1689-1761).—Novelist, *s.* of a joiner, was *b.* at Derby. His *f.* had intended him for the Church, but means failed, and at the age of 17 he went to London, and was apprenticed to a printer. Careful and diligent, he prospered in business, became printer of the Journals of the House of Commons, and in the year before his death purchased the moiety of the patent of King's Printer. He was twice *m.*, and each of his wives brought him six children, of whom, however, only four daughters were living at his death. R., who was the originator of the modern novel, did not take seriously to literature until he was past 50 when, in 1740, *Pamela* appeared. It originated in a proposal by two printers that R. should write a collection of model letters for the use of persons unaccustomed to correspondence, but it soon developed in his hands into a novel in which the story is carried on in the form of a correspondence. With faults and absurdities, it struck a true note of sentiment, and exploded the prevalent idea that dukes and princesses were the only suitable heroes and heroines (Pamela was a maid-servant), and it won immediate and phenomenal popularity. In 1748 *Clarissa Harlow*, his masterpiece, was *pub.*, and in 1753 *Sir Charles Grandison*, in which the author embodies his ideal of a Christian gentleman. All these suffer from an elaboration of detail which often becomes tedious; but in deep acquaintance with the motives of conduct, and especially of the workings of the female heart, they are almost unrivalled; their pathos also is genuine and deep. R. had an unusual faculty as the platonic friend and counsellor of women, and was the centre of an admiring circle of the sex, who ministered to a vanity which became somewhat excessive. R. has also the distinction of evoking the genius of Fielding, whose first novel, *Joseph Andrews*, was begun as a skit or parody upon *Pamela*. R. is described as "a stout, rosy, vain, prosy little man."

Life by Sir W. Scott in Ballantyne's *Novelists Library*. *Works* with preface by L. Stephen (12 vols., 1883), etc.

RITCHIE, LEITCH (1800?-1865).—Novelist, *b.* at Greenock and in business as a clerk in Glasgow, but about 1820 adopted literature as his profession. He wrote several novels of which the best known is *Wearyfoot Common*; others were *The Robber of the Rhine* and *The Magician*. In his later years he ed. *Chambers's Journal*.

RITSON, JOSEPH (1752-1803).—Antiquary and critic, *b.* at Stockton-on-Tees, settled in London as a conveyancer, at the same time devoting himself to the study of ancient English poetry. By his diligence as a collector and acuteness as a critic he rendered essential service to the preservation and appreciation of our ancient poetry. His chief works are *A Collection of English Songs* (1783), *Ancient Songs from Henry III. to the Revolution* (1790), *A Collection of Scottish Songs* (1794), and *A Collection of all the Ancient Poems, etc., relating to Robin Hood* (1795). Of a jealous and quarrelsome temper, R. was continually in controversy with his fellow-collectors and critics, including Johnson, Warton, and Percy. His acuteness enabled him to detect the Ireland forgeries. He *d.* insane.

ROBERTSON, FREDERICK WILLIAM (1816-1853).—Divine, *s.* of Captain Frederick R., of the Royal Artillery, was *b.* in London, and *ed.* at Edin. and Oxf. After holding various curacies he became in 1847 incumbent of Trinity Chapel, Brighton, where his preaching, though it brought him under the suspicion both of the High and Evangelical parties in the Church, had an extraordinary influence. Always of delicate and highly-strung constitution, his health gave way after his ministry in Brighton had extended to six years, and he *d.* in 1853. The beauty of his life and character had almost conquered the suspicion and dislike with which his views had inspired many. His sermons, of which five series were *pub.* posthumously, have had a very wide popularity.

ROBERTSON, THOMAS WILLIAM (1829-1871).—Dramatist, belonged to a family famous for producing actors. Never a successful actor himself, he produced a number of plays, which had unusual popularity. Among these are *David Garrick, Society, Caste,* and *School.*

ROBERTSON, WILLIAM (1721-1793).—Historian, *s.* of the parish minister of Borthwick, Midlothian, where he was *b.*, received his earlier *ed.* at Dalkeith, which then had a school of some repute; but his *f.* being translated to Edin., he attended school, and afterwards the Univ. there, studying for the Church. In 1743 he became minister of Gladsmuir, near Prestonpans. In the '45 he showed his loyalty by offering himself to Sir J. Cope as a volunteer, a service which was, however, declined. He soon began to take a prominent part in the debates of the General Assembly, of which he rose to be the undisputed leader. In 1758 he became one of the city ministers of Edin., and in the following year *pub.* his *History of Scotland,* which had an extraordinary success, and at once raised him to a foremost place among British historians. Preferment immediately followed: he was made Chaplain of Stirling Castle 1759, King's Chaplain for Scotland 1760, Principal of the Univ. of Edin. 1761, and Historiographer for Scotland 1763. In 1769 appeared the *History of the Reign of the Emperor Charles V.*, in 1777 *The History of America,* and in 1791 *Historical Disquisition on Ancient India.* In 1780 R. retired from the management of Church affairs, in which he had shown conspicuous ability, and gave himself to study, and the society of his friends, among whom were most of his distinguished contemporaries. As a writer he possessed a finished style, clear, measured, and stately, which carried his well-arranged narrative as on a full and steady stream; he was also cool and sagacious, but, like Hume, he was apt to take his facts at second hand, and the vast additional material which has been in course of accumulation since his day has rendered the value of his work more and more literary, and less and less historical.

Lives by Dugald Stewart (1801), Bishop Gleig (1812), and Lord Brougham in *Men of Letters.*

ROBINSON, HENRY CRABB (1775-1867).—Diarist, *b.* at Bury St. Edmunds, was articled to an attorney in Colchester. Between 1800 and 1805 he studied at various places in Germany, and became acquainted with nearly all the great men of letters there, including Goethe, Schiller, Herder, Wieland, etc. Thereafter he became war correspondent to the *Times* in the Peninsula. On his return to London he studied for the Bar, to which he was called in 1813, and became leader of the Eastern Circuit. Fifteen years later he retired, and by virtue of his great conversational powers and other qualities, became a leader in society, going everywhere and knowing everybody worth knowing. He *d.* unmarried, aged 91, and his *Diary, Reminiscences and Correspondence,* which stands in the forefront of its class, was *pub.* in 1869.

ROCHESTER, JOHN WILMOT (2ND EARL OF) (1647-1680).—Poet, *s.* of the 1st Earl, *b.* at Ditchley in Oxfordshire, and *ed.* at Oxf., saw some naval service when he showed conspicuous bravery. He became one of the most dissolute of the courtiers of Charles II., and wore himself out at 33 by his wild life. He was handsome, and witty, and possessed a singular charm of manner. He wrote a number of light, graceful poems, many of them extremely gross. Bishop Burnet, who attended him on his death-bed, believed him to have been sincerely repentant. In addition to his short pieces he wrote a *Satyr against Mankind*, and a tragedy, *Valentinian*, adapted from Beaumont and Fletcher.

ROGERS, HENRY (1806-1877).—Critic and theologian, was a minister of the Congregationalist Church, and ultimately Prof. of English Literature in Univ. Coll., London. He was a contributor to the *Edinburgh Review*, and is best known by his *Eclipse of Faith* (1852), a reply to F. W. Newman's *Phases of Faith.* This work, which displays remarkable acuteness and logical power, had great popularity.

ROGERS, SAMUEL (1763-1855).—Poet, *s.* of a banker in London, received a careful private education, and entered the bank, of which, on his father's death, he became the principal partner. From his early youth he showed a marked taste for literature and the fine arts, which his wealth enabled him to gratify; and in his later years he was a well-known leader in society and a munificent patron of artists and men of letters, his breakfasts, at which he delighted to assemble celebrities in all departments, being famous. He was the author of the following poems: *The Pleasures of Memory* (1792), *Columbus* (1810), *Jacqueline* (1814), *Human Life* (1819), and *Italy* (1822). R. was emphatically the poet of taste, and his writings, while full of allusion and finished description, rarely show passion or intensity of feeling; but are rather the reflections and memory-pictures of a man of high culture and refinement expressed in polished verse. He had considerable powers of conversation and sarcasm. He was offered, but declined, the laureateship.

ROLLE, RICHARD (1290?-1349).—Hermit and poet, *b.* at Thornton, Yorkshire, was at Oxf. Impressed by the uncertainty and the snares of life he decided to become a hermit, a resolution which he carried out with somewhat romantic circumstances. He wrote various religious treatises in Latin and English, turned the Psalms into English verse, and composed a poem—*The Pricke of Conscience*—in 7 books, in which is shown the attitude of protest which was rising against certain Papal pretensions and doctrines.

ROLLOCK, ROBERT (1555?-1599).—Theologian and scholar, *b.* in Stirlingshire, was first a Prof. in St. Andrews, and then the first Principal of the Univ. of Edin. He also held office as Prof. of Theology, and was one of the ministers of the High Church. He was one of the earliest of Protestant commentators. He wrote chiefly in Latin, but some of his sermons and commentaries are in vernacular Scotch.

ROPER, WILLIAM (1496-1578).—Biographer, *s.* of a Kentish gentleman, *m.* Margaret, *dau.* of Sir Thomas More. He has a place in literature for his excellent and appreciative biography of his father-in-law. He was a member of various Parliaments between 1529 and 1558. Although he remained a Roman Catholic, he was permitted to retain his office of prothonotary of the Court of King's Bench after the accession of Elizabeth.

ROSCOE, WILLIAM (1753-1831).—Historian, *s.* of a market-gardener near Liverpool, for a time assisted his *f.*, devoting all his spare time to mental improvement. Subsequently he entered the office of an attorney, and in due time went into business on his own account, continuing, however, his literary studies. In 1799 he joined a local bank as partner and manager, which proved an unfortunate step, as the bank was obliged, in 1816, to suspend payment. In 1795 he rose into fame at a bound by his *Life of Lorenzo de' Medici.* It was followed in 1805 by the *Life and Pontificate of Leo the Tenth*, which, though also a work of great ability, had not the same success—his treatment of the Reformation offending Protestants and Roman Catholics alike. Both works were translated into various languages. He also wrote some poems, including *The Butterfly's Ball and the Grasshopper's Feast*, and several pamphlets on political questions, including the slave-trade, of which he was a determined opponent. He also took a leading part in the public life of Liverpool, which he represented in Parliament for a few years. He was an accomplished botanist.

ROSCOMMON, WENTWORTH DILLON, 4TH EARL OF (1633?-1685).—Poet, nephew of the famous Earl of Strafford, was *b.* in Ireland. He studied and travelled on the Continent, and enjoyed a considerable literary reputation in his own day on the strength of a poetical *Essay on Translated Verse*, and translations from Horace's *Art of Poetry*.

ROSE, WILLIAM STEWART (1775-1843).—Poet and translator, *s.* of George R., who held various Government offices, including that of Treasurer of the Navy. After being *ed.* at Eton and Camb., he was appointed Reading Clerk to the House of Lords. He translated the romance of *Amadis de Gaul* (1803), *Partenopex de Blois* (1807), etc., and from 1823-31 was occupied with the principal work of his life, his translations from the Italian, including the *Orlando Furioso* of Ariosto, in which he was encouraged by Sir W. Scott, whose friend he was. He also produced a vol. of poems, *The Crusade of St. Louis* (1810).

ROSSETTI, CHRISTINA GEORGINA (1830-1894).—Poetess, sister of Dante Gabriel R. (*q.v.*), was *b.* in London, where she lived all her life. She began to write poetry in early girlhood, some of her earliest verse appearing in 1850 in the *Germ*, the magazine of the pre-Raphaelites, of which her brother was one of the founders. Her subsequent publications were *Goblin Market and other Poems* (1862), *The Prince's Progress* (1866), *A Pageant and other Poems* (1881), and *Verses* (1893). *New Poems* (1896) appeared after her death. *Sing-Song* was a book of verses for children. Her life was a very retired one, passed largely in attending on her mother, who lived until 1886, and in religious duties. She twice rejected proposals of marriage. Her poetry is characterised by imaginative power, exquisite expression, and simplicity and depth of thought. She rarely imitated any forerunner, and drew her inspiration from her own experiences of thought and feeling. Many of her poems are definitely religious in form; more are deeply imbued with religious feeling and motive. In addition to her poems she wrote *Commonplace and other Stories*, and *The Face of the Deep*, a striking and suggestive commentary on the Apocalypse.

ROSSETTI, DANTE GABRIEL (1828-1882).—Poet and painter, was *b.* in London. His *f.* was Gabriele Rossetti, an Italian scholar, who came to England in 1824, and was Prof. of Italian in King's Coll., London. His mother was Frances Polidori, English on her mother's side, so that the poet was three-fourths Italian, and one-fourth English. He was *ed.* at King's Coll. School, and began the systematic study of painting in 1842, and in 1848, with Holman Hunt, Millais, and others, founded the pre-Raphaelite school of painting. In 1849 he exhibited the "Girlhood of Mary Virgin," and among his other pictures are "Beata Beatrix," "Monna Vanna," and "Dante's Dream." Simultaneously with art he worked hard at poetry, and by 1847 he had written *The Blessed Damozel* and *Hand and Soul* (both of which appeared in the *Germ*, the magazine of the pre-Raphaelites), *Retro me Sathanas*, *The Portrait*, and *The Choice*, and in 1861 he brought out a vol. of translations from the early Italian poets under the title of *Dante and his Circle*. The death of his wife in 1862, after a married life of less than two years, told heavily upon him, as did various attacks upon his poetry, including that of Robert Buchanan (*q.v.*)—*The Fleshly School of Poetry*—to which he replied with *The Stealthy School of Criticism*. His *Poems* which, in the vehemence of his grief, he had buried in the coffin of his wife, and which were afterwards exhumed, appeared in 1870; and his last literary effort, *Ballads and Sonnets*, containing the sonnets forming *The House of Life*, in 1881. In his later years he suffered acutely from neuralgia, which led to the habit of taking chloral. Rossetti was fastidious in composition; his poems are as remarkable for condensation, finish, and exact expression of the poet's thought as for their sumptuous colouring and rich concrete imagery. In later years he was subject to depression, and became somewhat embittered, and much of a recluse.

Life by A. C. Benson (English Men of Letters). *Family Letters and Memoir* by W. M. Rossetti. Poetical Works with preface by the same, etc.

ROUS, FRANCIS (1579-1659).—Versifier of the Psalms, a Cornishman, and a prominent Puritan, took a leading part in Parliament, was Provost of Eton, and wrote several theological and devotional works. His memory has, however, been chiefly kept green by his translation of the Psalms into verse, which with some modifications was adopted by the Church and Parliament of Scotland for use in public worship, a position which it held almost exclusively until the middle of the 19th century. It is still in universal use in the Presbyterian churches of that country, though now accompanied by hymns. Though rough, and sometimes, through the endeavour to maintain literalness, grotesque, it is strong and simple, and not seldom rises to a certain severe beauty; and association has endeared it to many generations of Scottish Christians.

ROW, JOHN (1568-1646).—Scottish ecclesiastical historian, *b.* at Perth, *s.* of John R., one of the Scottish Reformers, was minister of Carnock in Fife, and a leading opponent of Episcopacy. His *Historie of the Kirk of Scotland*, 1558-1637, left by him in manuscript, was printed in 1842 for the Wodrow Society. It is an original authority for the period.

ROWE, NICHOLAS (1674-1718).—Dramatist and poet, *b.* of a good family at Little Barford, Bedfordshire, was bred to the law, but inheriting an income of £300 a year, he devoted himself to literature, and produced several dramas, including *The Ambitious Stepmother*, *The Fair Penitent*, and *Jane Shore*. The last, which is his best, contains some scenes of true pathos, and holds its place. He also wrote some poems, and translated Lucan. R., who was a man of very engaging manners, was the friend of Pope, Swift, and Addison, and received many lucrative appointments, including that of Under-Sec. of State. He has the distinction of being the first ed. and biographer of Shakespeare (1709). He was appointed Poet Laureate in 1715, and was buried in Westminster Abbey, with an epitaph by Pope.

ROWLEY, WILLIAM (1585?-1642?).—Dramatist, was an actor in the Queen's Company 1610. He collaborated with Middleton in *A Fair Quarrel* and *The Changeling*, and in others with Dekker, Webster, etc., and wrote unassisted *A New Wonder*, *A Match at Midnight*, *A Shoemaker, a Gentleman*, and several others; also a picture of life in London called *A Search for Money*. R. was vigorous and humorous, but his verse lacked sweetness and smoothness.

RUDDIMAN, THOMAS (1674-1757).—Grammarian, *b.* in Banffshire, and *ed.* at King's Coll., Aberdeen, obtained a position in the Advocates' Library in Edin., of which in 1730 he became Librarian. In 1714 he *pub.* his *Rudiments of the Latin Tongue*, which was for long the recognised Latin grammar in the schools of Scotland. He was made printer to the Univ. in 1728. R., who was one of the greatest of Scottish Latinists, produced an ed. of the works of George Buchanan, and an ed. of *Livy* said to be "immaculate." He also reprinted, with notes, Gavin Douglas's version of the *Æneid*.

RUSKIN, JOHN (1819-1900).—Writer on art, economics, and sociology, was *b.* in London, the *s.* of a wealthy wine merchant, a Scotsman. Brought up under intellectually and morally bracing Puritan influences, his education was mainly private until he went to Oxf. in 1836; he remained until 1840, when a serious illness interrupted his studies, and led to a six months' visit to Italy. On his return in 1842 he took his degree. In 1840 he had made the acquaintance of Turner, and this, together with a visit to Venice, constituted a turning point in his life. In 1843 appeared the first vol. of *Modern Painters*, the object of which was to insist upon the superiority in landscape of the moderns, and especially of Turner, to all the ancient masters. The earnestness and originality of the author and the splendour of the style at once called attention to the work which, however, awakened a chorus of protest from the adherents of the ancients. A second vol. appeared in 1846, the third and fourth in 1856, and the fifth in 1860. Meanwhile he had *pub.* *The Seven Lamps of Architecture* (1849), *The Stones of Venice* (1851-53), perhaps his greatest work, *Lectures on Architecture and Painting* (1854), *Elements of Drawing* (1856), and *Elements of Perspective* (1859). During the 17 years between the publication of the first and the last vols. of *Modern Painters* his views alike on religion and art had become profoundly modified, and the necessity of a radical change in the moral and intellectual attitude of the age towards religion, art, and economics in their bearing upon life and social conditions had become his ruling idea. He now assumed the *rôle* of the prophet as Carlyle, by whose teaching he was profoundly influenced, had done, and the rest of his life was spent in the endeavour to turn the mind of the nation in the direction he desired. *The Political Economy of Art* (1857) showed the line in which his mind was moving; but it was in *Unto this Last, pub.* in the *Cornhill Magazine* in 1860, that he began fully to develop his views. It brought down upon him a storm of opposition and obloquy which continued for years, and which, while it acted injuriously upon his highly sensitive nervous system, had no effect in silencing him or modifying his views. There followed *Munera Pulveris* (Gifts of the Dust), *The Crown of Wild Olive, Sesame and Lilies* (1865), *Time and Tide by Wear and Tyne*, and innumerable fugitive articles. In 1869 R. was appointed first Slade Prof. of the Fine Arts at Oxf., and endowed a school of drawing in the Univ. His successive courses of lectures were *pub.* as *Aratra Pentelici* (Ploughs of Pentelicus) (1870), *The Eagle's Nest* (1872), *Ariadne Florentina* (1872), and *Love's Meinie* (1873). Contemporaneously with these he issued, with more or less regularity, as health permitted, *Fors Clavigera* (Chance the Clubbearer), a series of miscellaneous notes and essays, sold by the author himself direct to the purchasers, the first of a series of experiments—of which the Guild of St. George, a tea room, and a roadmaking enterprise were other examples—in practical economics. After the death of his mother in 1871 he purchased a small property, Brantwood, in the Lake district, where he lived for the remainder of his life, and here he brought out in monthly parts his last work, *Præterita*, an autobiography, 24 parts of which appeared, bringing down the story to 1864. Here he *d.* on January 20, 1900. R. was a man of noble character and generous impulses, but highly strung, irritable, and somewhat intolerant. He is one of our greatest stylists, copious, eloquent, picturesque, and highly coloured. His influence on his time was very great, at first in the department of art, in which he was for a time regarded as the supreme authority, later and increasingly in the realms of economics and morals, in which he was at first looked upon as an unpractical dreamer. He *m.* in 1848, but the union proved unhappy, and was dissolved in 1855.

For his Life *see* his own works, especially *Præterita. Life and Works* by Collingwood (2 vols., 1893). *Bibliography*, T. J. Wise (1889-93). Shorter works by Mrs. Meynell, J. A. Hobson, F. Harrison, etc.

RUSSELL, LORD JOHN, 1ST EARL RUSSELL (1792-1878).—Statesman, biographer, and historical writer, third *s.* of the 6th Duke of Bedford, was *ed.* at Westminster School and the Univ. of Edin. He entered Parliament in 1813, and became one of the most eminent English statesmen of the 19th century. He uniformly acted with the Whig and afterwards with the Liberal party, advocated all measures of progress, especially the removal of tests, the extension of education, and Parliamentary reform. He was the leader of his party in the House of Commons from 1834-55, represented the City of London from 1841 until his elevation to the peerage in 1861, and held the offices of Paymaster of the Forces, Home Sec., Colonial Sec., Foreign Sec., and Prime Minister, which last he held twice, 1846-52, and 1865-66. His contributions to literature were considerable, both in number and importance, and include *Essay on the English Constitution* (1821), *Memoirs of the Affairs of Europe from the Peace of Utrecht* (1824), *Correspondence of the 4th Duke of Bedford, Life, Diary, and Letters of Thomas Moore, Correspondence of Charles James Fox*, and a *Life* of the same statesman, *Essays on the Rise and Progress of the Christian Religion in the West of Europe* (1873), and *Recollections and Suggestions* (1875).

RUSSELL, WILLIAM (1741-1793).—Historian, *b.* in Selkirkshire, and apprenticed to a bookseller in Edin., he was patronised by Lord Elibank, and went to London, where he followed literature as a profession. He wrote poems and fables, a *History of America* (1779), and a *History of Modern Europe*, which he left unfinished.

RUSSELL, SIR WILLIAM HOWARD (1821-1907).—War correspondent, *b.* in Co. Dublin, was called to the Bar in 1850. Having joined the staff of the *Times*, he was sent as war correspondent to the Crimea, his letters from which caused a profound sensation, and led to an improved condition of things in regard to the army. He was also correspondent in India during the Mutiny, in America during the Civil War, and during the Austro-Prussian War of 1866, and the Franco-German War of 1870-71, in South Africa in 1879, and in Egypt in 1883. Among his books are *The Adventures of Dr. Brady* (1868), *Hesperothen* (1882), *A Visit to Chili* (1890), and *The Great War with Russia* (1895). He was knighted in 1895, and also received various foreign decorations.

RUTHERFORD, SAMUEL (1600?-1661).—Theologian and controversialist, *b.* at Nisbet, Roxburghshire, *ed.* at Edin. Univ., where he became in 1623 Regent of Humanity (Prof. of Latin). In 1627 he was settled as minister of Anwoth in Galloway, whence he was banished to Aberdeen for nonconformity. On the re-establishment of Presbytery in 1638 he was made Prof. of Divinity at St. Andrews, and in 1651 Principal of St. Mary's Coll. there, and he was one of the Scottish Commissioners to the Westminster Assembly. At the Restoration he was deprived of all his offices. He was a formidable controversialist, and a strenuous upholder of the divine right of Presbytery. Among his polemical works are *Due Right of Presbyteries* (1644), *Lex Rex* (1644), and *Free Disputation against Pretended Liberty of Conscience*. *Lex Rex* was, after the Restoration, burned by the common hangman, and led to the citation of the author for high treason, which his death prevented from taking effect. His chief fame, however, rests upon his spiritual and devotional works, such as *Christ Dying and drawing Sinners to Himself*, but especially upon his *Letters*, which display a fervour of feeling and a rich imagery which, while highly relished by some, repel others.

RYCAUT, OR RICAUT, SIR PAUL (1628-1700).—Historian, was at Camb., and held various diplomatic positions. He wrote *Present State of the Ottoman Empire* (1668), and a continuation of *Knolles's General Historie of the Turks*, and translated Platina's *Latin History of the Popes*.

RYMER, THOMAS (1641-1713).—Archæologist and critic, *ed.* at Camb., became a barrister at Gray's Inn. He *pub.* in 1678 *Tragedies of the last Age Considered*, in which he passed judgments, very unfavourable, upon their authors, including Shakespeare. He was of much more use as the collector of English treaties, which he *pub.* under the title of *Fœdera*, in 20 vols., the last 5 of which were ed. after his death by R. Sanderson (*q.v.*). R. also *pub.* poems and a play, *Edgar*. He held the office of historiographer to William III. His learning and industry have received the recognition of many subsequent historians.

ST. JOHN, H. (*See* BOLINGBROKE).

SALA, GEORGE AUGUSTUS HENRY (1828-1895).—Journalist and novelist, *b.* in London of Italian ancestry, began life as an illustrator of books and scene-painter, afterwards taking to literature. He contributed to many periodicals, including *Household Words*, and the *Illustrated London News*, and was the founder and first ed. of *Temple Bar*. Among his novels were *The Buddington Peerage* and *Quite Alone*. He also wrote books of travel, and an autobiographical work, his *Life and Adventures* (1895).

SALE, GEORGE (1697?-1736).—Orientalist, a Kentish man and practising solicitor. In 1734 he *pub.* a translation of the *Koran*, He also assisted in the *Universal History*, and was one of the correctors of the Arabic New Testament issued by the S.P.C.K.

SANDERSON, ROBERT (1587-1663).—Theologian and casuist, *b.* of good family at Rotherham in Yorkshire, was at Oxf. Entering the Church he rose to be Bishop of Lincoln. His work on logic, *Logicæ Artis Compendium* (1615), was long a standard treatise on the subject. His sermons also were admired; but he is perhaps best remembered by his *Nine Cases of Conscience Resolved* (1678), in consideration of which he has been placed at the head of English casuists. He left large collections of historical and heraldic matter in MS.

SANDS, ROBERT CHARLES (1799-1832).—Miscellaneous writer, *b.* at New York, was a scholarly and versatile writer, but without much originality. His best work is in his short stories. His chief poem was *Yamoyden*, an Indian story written in collaboration with a friend.

SANDYS, GEORGE (1578-1644).—Traveller and translator, *s.* of an Archbishop of York, *b.* at Bishopsthorpe, and *ed.* at Oxf., is one of the best of the earlier travellers, learned, observant, and truth-loving. He *pub.* in 1615 an account of his journeys in the East which was highly popular. He also translated when in America the *Metamorphoses* of Ovid, produced a metrical *Paraphrase on the Psalms*, with music by Henry Lawes, and another on the Canticles, and wrote *Christ's Passion*, a tragedy. He held various public offices, chiefly in connection with the colony of Virginia.

SAVAGE, RICHARD (1697?-1743).—Poet, was probably of humble birth, but claimed to be the illegitimate *s.* of the Countess of Macclesfield. He was the friend of Johnson in the early and miserable days of the latter in London; and in *The Lives of the Poets* J. has given his story as set forth by himself, which is, if true, a singular record of maternal cruelty. There are strong reasons, however, for doubting whether it was anything but a tissue of falsehoods mingled with gross exaggerations of fact. He led a wildly irregular life, killed a gentleman in a tavern brawl, for which he was sentenced to death, but pardoned; and by his waywardness alienated nearly all who wished to befriend him. For a time he had a pension of £50 from Queen Caroline on condition of his writing an ode yearly on her birthday. He wrote *Love in a Veil* (1718) (comedy) and *Sir Thomas Overbury* (1723) (tragedy), and two poems, *The Bastard* (1728) and *The Wanderer* (1729). He *d.* in prison at Bristol.

SAVILE, SIR HENRY (1549-1622).—Scholar, *ed.* at Oxf., where he lectured on mathematics. He was afterwards Warden of Merton Coll. and Provost of Eton, and made a translation from Tacitus entitled, *The Ende of Nero and Beginning of Galba, etc.* (1581), and in the same year *pub. Rerum Anglicarum Scriptores post Bedam Præcipui*, a collection of some of the chronicles subsequent to Bede, William of Malmesbury, Roger of Hoveden, etc. He founded the Savilian Professorship of Astronomy and Geometry at Oxf.

SAXBY, EDWARD (*d.* 1658).—*B.* in Suffolk, and was in Cromwell's Horse. His extreme republican views, however, led him into the bitterest antagonism when C. assumed the Protectorship. This received expression in his extraordinary pamphlet, *Killing no Murder*, in which the assassination of C. is advocated, and which displays in a remarkable degree perverted ingenuity of argument combined with considerable literary power. S. *d.* demented in the Tower in 1658.

SCOTT, ALEXANDER (1525?-1584?).—Scottish poet, Almost nothing is known of his life, but he is believed to have spent most of his time in or near Edin. Thirty-six short poems are attributed to him, including *Ane New Yeir Gift to Quene Mary*, *The Rondel of Love*, and a satire, *Justing at the Drum*. He has great variety of metre, and is graceful and musical, but his satirical pieces are often extremely coarse.

SCOTT, HUGH STOWELL (1863?-1903).—Novelist (under the name of Henry Seton Merriman). He was an underwriter in Lloyd's, but having a strong literary bent, latterly devoted himself to writing novels, many of which had great popularity. They include *The Slave of the Lamp* (1892), *The Sowers* (generally considered his best) (1896), *In Kedar's Tents* (1897), *Roden's Corner* (1898), *Isle of Unrest* (1900), *The Velvet Glove* (1901), *The Vultures* (1902), and *Barlasch of the Guard* (1903). He worked with great care, and his best books hold a high place in modern fiction. He was unusually modest and retiring in character.

SCOTT, JOHN (1730-1783).—Poet, *s.* of a Quaker draper who in his later years lived at Amwell, a village in Herts, which the poet celebrates in his descriptive poem, *Amwell.* He wrote much other verse now forgotten.

SCOTT, LADY JOHN (ALICIA ANN SPOTTISWOODE) (1801-1900).—*M.* Lord John Scott. She was the writer of a number of Scottish songs characterised by true poetic feeling. Among them may be mentioned *Annie Laurie, Douglas,* and *Durrisdeer.* She also composed the music for them.

SCOTT, MICHAEL (1789-1835).—Novelist, *b.* near and *ed.* at Glasgow, and settled in business at Kingston, Jamaica, which led to his making frequent sea voyages, and thus yielded him experiences which he turned to account in two vivacious novels, *Tom Cringle's Log* and *The Cruise of the Midge,* both of which first appeared in *Blackwood's Magazine,* where they attained deserved popularity. They have frequently been reprinted. The author, however, maintained a strict *incognito* during his life.

SCOTT, SIR WALTER (1771-1832).—Poet, novelist, and biographer, *s.* of Walter S., a Writer to the Signet in Edinburgh, and Margaret Rutherford, *dau.* of one of the Prof. of Medicine in the Univ. there. Through both parents he was connected with several old Border families; his *f.* was a scion of the Scotts of Harden, well known in Border history. In early childhood he suffered from a severe fever, one of the effects of which was a permanent lameness, and for some time he was delicate. The native vigour of his constitution, however, soon asserted itself, and he became a man of exceptional strength. Much of his childhood was spent at his grandfather's farm at Sandyknowe, Roxburghshire, and almost from the dawn of intelligence he began to show an interest in the traditionary lore which was to have so powerful an influence on his future life, an interest which was nourished and stimulated by several of the older members of his family, especially one of his aunts. At this stage he was a quick-witted, excitable child, who required rather to be restrained than pressed forward. At the age of 7 he was strong enough to be sent to the High School of Edinburgh, where he was more remarkable for miscellaneous and out-of-the-way knowledge and his powers of story-telling than for proficiency in the ordinary course of study; and notwithstanding his lameness, he was found in the forefront wherever adventure or fighting was to be had. Thereafter he was for three sessions at the Univ., where he bore much the same character as at school. He was, however, far from idle, and was all the time following the irresistible bent, which ultimately led to such brilliant results, in a course of insatiable reading of ballads and romances, to enlarge which he had by the time he was 15 acquired a working knowledge of French and Italian, and had made the acquaintance of Dante and Ariosto in the original. Percy's *Reliques of Ancient Poetry, pub.* in 1765, came into his hands in 1784, and proved one of the most formative influences of this period. At 15 he was apprenticed to his *f.*, but preferring the higher branch of the profession, he studied for the Bar, to which he was called in 1792. He did not, however, forego his favourite studies, but ransacked the Advocates' Library for old manuscripts, in the deciphering of which he became so expert that his assistance soon came to be invoked by antiquarians of much longer standing. Although he worked hard at law his ideal was not the attainment of an extensive practice, but rather of a fairly paid post which should leave him leisure for his favourite pursuits, and this he succeeded in reaching, being appointed first in 1799 Sheriff of Selkirk, and next in 1812 one of the Principal Clerks to the Court of Session, which together brought him an income of £1600. Meanwhile in 1795 he had translated Bürger's ballad of *Lenore*, and in the following year he made his first appearance in print by publishing it along with a translation of *The Wild Huntsman* by the same author. About the same time he made the acquaintance of "Monk" Lewis, to whose collection of *Tales of Wonder* he contributed the ballads of *Glenfinlas*, *The Eve of St. John*, and *The Grey Brother*; and he *pub.* in 1799 a translation of Goethe's *Goetz von Berlichingen*. In 1797 he was *m.* to Miss Charlotte Margaret Charpentier, the *dau.* of a French gentleman of good position. The year 1802 saw the publication of Scott's first work of real importance, *The Minstrelsy of the Scottish Border*, of which 2 vols. appeared, the third following in the next year. In 1804 he went to reside at Ashestiel on the Tweed, where he ed. the old romance, *Sir Tristrem*, and in 1805 he produced his first great original work, *The Lay of the Last Minstrel*, which was received with great favour, and decided that literature was thenceforth to be the main work of his life. In the same year the first few chapters of *Waverley* were written; but the unfavourable opinion of a friend led to the MS. being laid aside for nearly 10 years. In 1806 S. began, by a secret partnership, that association with the Ballantynes which resulted so unfortunately for him 20 years later. *Marmion* was *pub.* in 1808: it was even more popular than the *Lay*, and raised his reputation proportionately. The same year saw the publication of his elaborate ed. of Dryden with a Life, and was also marked by a rupture with Jeffrey, with whom he had been associated as a contributor to the *Edinburgh Review*, and by the establishment of the new firm of J. Ballantyne and Co., of which the first important publication was *The Lady of the Lake*, which appeared in 1810, *The Vision of Don Roderick* following in 1811. In 1812 S. purchased land on the Tweed near Melrose, and built his famous house, Abbotsford, the adornment of which became one of the chief pleasures of his life, and which he made the scene of a noble and kindly hospitality. In the same year he *pub. Rokeby*, and in 1813 *The Bridal of Triermain*, while 1814 saw *The Life and Works of Swift* in 19 vols., and was made illustrious by the appearance of *Waverley*, the two coming out in the same week, the latter, of course, like its successors, anonymously. The next year, *The Lord of the Isles*, *Guy Mannering*, and *The Field of Waterloo* appeared, and the next again, 1816, *Paul's Letters to his Kinsfolk*, *The Antiquary*, *The Black Dwarf*, and

Old Mortality, while 1817 saw *Harold the Dauntless* and *Rob Roy*. The enormous strain which S. had been undergoing as official, man of letters, and man of business, began at length to tell upon him, and in this same year, 1817, he had the first of a series of severe seizures of cramp in the stomach, to which, however, his indomitable spirit refused to yield, and several of his next works, *The Heart of Midlothian* (1818), by many considered his masterpiece, *The Bride of Lammermoor*, *The Legend of Montrose*, and *Ivanhoe*, all of 1819, were dictated to amanuenses, while he was too ill to hold a pen. In 1820 *The Monastery*, in which the public began to detect a falling off in the powers of the still generally unknown author, appeared. The immediately following *Abbot*, however, showed a recovery. *Kenilworth* and *The Pirate* followed in 1821, *The Fortunes of Nigel* in 1822; *Peveril of the Peak*, *Quentin Durward*, and *St. Ronan's Well* in 1823; *Redgauntlet* in 1824, and *Tales of the Crusaders* (*The Betrothed* and *The Talisman*) in 1825. By this time S. had long reached a pinnacle of fame such as perhaps no British man of letters has ever attained during his lifetime. He had for a time been the most admired poet of his day, and though latterly somewhat eclipsed by Byron, he still retained great fame as a poet. He also possessed a great reputation as an antiquary, one of the chief revivers of interest in our ancient literature, and as the biographer and ed. of several of our great writers; while the incognito which he maintained in regard to his novels was to many a very partial veil. The unprecedented profits of his writings had made him, as he believed, a man of wealth; his social prestige was immense; he had in 1820 been made a baronet, when that was still a real distinction, and he had been the acknowledged representative of his country when the King visited it in 1822, All this was now to change, and the fabric of prosperity which he had raised by his genius and labour, and which had never spoiled the simplicity and generosity of his character, was suddenly to crumble into ruin with, however, the result of revealing him as the possessor of qualities even greater and nobler than any he had shown in his happier days. The publishing and printing firms with which he had been connected fell in the commercial crisis of 1826, and S. found himself at 55, and with failing health, involved in liabilities amounting to £130,000. Never was adversity more manfully and gallantly met. Notwithstanding the crushing magnitude of the disaster and the concurrent sorrow of his wife's illness, which soon issued in her death, he deliberately set himself to the herculean task of working off his debts, asking only that time might be given him. The secret of his authorship was now, of course, revealed, and his efforts were crowned with a marvellous measure of success. *Woodstock*, his first publication after the crash, appeared in the same year and brought £8000; by 1828 he had earned £40,000. In 1827 *The Two Drovers*, *The Highland Widow*, and *The Surgeon's Daughter*, forming the first series of *Chronicles of the Canongate*, appeared together with *The Life of Napoleon* in 9 vols., and the first series of *Tales of a Grandfather*; in 1828 *The Fair Maid of Perth* and the second series of *Tales of a Grandfather*, *Anne of Geierstein*, a third series of the *Tales*, and the commencement of a complete ed. of the novels in 1829; a fourth and last series of *Tales*, *History of Scotland*, and other work in 1830. Then at last the overworked brain gave way, and during this year he had more than one paralytic seizure. He was sent abroad for change and rest, and a Government frigate was placed at his disposal. But all was in vain; he never recovered, and though in temporary rallies he produced two more novels, *Count Robert of Paris* and *Castle Dangerous*, both in 1831, which only showed that the spell was broken, he gradually sank, and *d.* at Abbotsford on September 21, 1832.

The work which S. accomplished, whether looked at as regards its mass or its quality, is alike marvellous. In mere amount his output in each of the four departments of poetry, prose fiction, history and biography, and miscellaneous literature is sufficient to fill an ordinary literary life. Indeed the quantity of his acknowledged work in other departments was held to be the strongest argument against the possibility of his being the author of the novels. The achievement of such a result demanded a power of steady, methodical, and rapid work almost unparalleled in the history of literature. When we turn to its quality we are struck by the range of subject and the variableness of the treatment. In general there is the same fulness of mind directed by strong practical sense and judgment, but the style is often heavy, loose, and even slipshod, and in most of his works there are "patches" in which he falls far below his best. His poetry, though as a whole belonging to the second class, is full of broad and bold effects, picturesqueness, and an irresistible rush and freshness. As a lyrist, however, he stands much higher, and in such gems as "Proud Maisie" and "A weary lot is thine, Fair Maid," he takes his place among our greatest singers. His chief fame rests, of course, upon the novels. Here also, however, there is the same inequality and irregularity, but there is a singular command over his genius in virtue of which the fusing, creating imagination responds to his call, and is at its greatest just where it is most needed. For the variety, truth, and aliveness of his characters he has probably no equal since Shakespeare, and though, of course, coming far behind, he resembles him alike in his range and in his insight. The most remarkable feature in his character is the union of an imagination of the first order with practical sagacity and manly sanity, in this also resembling his great predecessor.

SUMMARY.—*B.* 1771, *ed.* Edin., called to Bar 1792, Sheriff of Selkirk 1799, Principal Clerk of Session 1812, first *pub.* translation of *Lenore*, etc., wrote ballads and made translation from German, *pub.* *Minstrelsy of Scottish Border* 1802-3, *Lay of Last Minstrel* 1805, began *Waverley* 1805, partner with Ballantynes 1806, *pub. Marmion* 1808, *Lady of Lake* 1810, began to build Abbotsford 1812, Waverley novels began and continued 1814-31, health began to fail 1817, made Baronet 1820, ruined by failure of Ballantynes 1826, devotes rest of his life to clearing off debt by novels and historical works, *Tales of a Grandfather*, *Life of Napoleon*, etc., health finally gave way 1830, *d.* 1832.

The great authority is the *Life* by Lockhart, but it has been supplemented by the *Journal* (1890) and *Letters* (1893). Short *Lives* by G. Gilfillan, R. H. Hutton, etc., etc.

SCOTT, WILLIAM BELL (1811-1890).—Poet and painter, *s.* of Robert S., an engraver, and brother of David S., painter, *b.* in

Edin., settled in London, and painted chiefly historical subjects. He *pub.* five vols. of poetry, including *Hades* and *The Year of the World,* and many fine sonnets, a form of poetry in which he excelled, and in prose *Half-hour Lectures on Art* and *The Little Masters* in the Great Artists Series. He also ed. a series of " English Poets," and wrote a Life of his brother and one of Albrecht Dürer, etc.

SEDLEY, SIR CHARLES (1639?-1701).—Poet, *s.* and heir of a Kentish baronet, was at Oxf. and, coming to the Court of Charles II., became one of the most popular and brilliant members of its dissipated circles. He was the author of two tragedies and three comedies, now forgotten, though extravagantly lauded in their day, and of some poems and songs, of which the best known are *Phyllis* and *Chloris.* His only child was the witty and profligate Catherine S., mistress of James II., who created her Countess of Dorset. *Bellamira* and *The Mulberry Garden,* founded respectively on Terence and Molière, are his best plays. His prose in pamphlets and essays is better than his verse.

SEELEY, SIR JOHN ROBERT (1834-1895).—Historian and essayist, *s.* of a publisher in London, *ed.* at City of London School and Camb. In 1863 he became Prof. of Latin at Univ. Coll., London, and was Prof. of Modern History at Camb. from 1869 until his death. In 1865 appeared anonymously *Ecce Homo,* a work which created intense excitement and keen controversy in the theological and religious world. Other works were *The Life and Times of Stein,* the Prussian statesman (1879), *Natural Religion* (1882), *The Expansion of England* (1883), *Life of Napoleon* (1885), and a work on Goethe. *The Growth of British Policy* (1895) was left finished but unrevised at his death. In recognition of his services to the empire in his political writings he was, in 1894, made K.C.M.G.

SELDEN, JOHN (1584-1654).—Jurist and scholar, *b.* near Worthing, Sussex, the *s.* of a farmer who was also a musician, *ed.* at Chichester and Oxf., and studied law at Clifford's Inn and the Inner Temple. His learning soon attracted attention and, though practising little, he was consulted on points involving legal erudition. His first work, *Analecton Anglo-Britannicon,* a chronological collection of English records down to the Norman invasion, was written in 1606, though not *pub.* till 1615. In 1610 appeared a treatise on the *Duello, or Single Combat*; and in 1614 his largest English work on *Titles of Honour,* full of profound learning, and still a high authority. Three years later, 1617, he wrote in Latin his treatise, *De Deis Syris* (on the Gods of Syria), an inquiry into polytheism, specially with reference to the false deities mentioned in Scripture. His reputation as a scholar had now become European. In 1618 he incurred the indignation of the King and the clergy by his *History of Tithes,* in which he denied their claim to be a divine institution. Called before the High Commission he made a statement regretting the publication of the book though not withdrawing any of its statements. In 1621 he suffered a brief imprisonment for withstanding some of James's doctrines as to the privileges of Parliament. Two years later he was elected member for Lancaster. As a politician his views were moderate, and all along he endeavoured to repress the zeal of the extremists on both sides. He was imprisoned in the Tower for four years, 1630-34. During the final struggle of King and Parliament he was much employed; but like most men of moderate views, was frequently under suspicion, and after the execution of the King, to which he was strongly opposed, he took little to do with public matters. He was a lay member of the Westminster Assembly, 1643, where his profound knowledge of the original tongues made him somewhat of a terror to certain extremists among the divines. He had at an early age been appointed steward to the Earl of Kent, and at the house of his widow, with whom he had long lived in such close friendship as to give rise to the belief that they were *m.*, he *d.* Among other works may be mentioned a description of the Arundel Marbles (1629), a treatise concerning the Jewish calendar (1646), and, specially, his *Table Talk, pub.* 1689, of which Coleridge said " there is more weighty bullion sense in this book than I can find in the same number of pages of any uninspired writer." He was likewise the author of various treatises on constitutional matters and the law of nations, including *Mare Clausum* (a Closed Sea), in defence of the property of England in its circumfluent seas. Most of these were written in Latin.

Coll. Works with *Life*, Dr. Wilkins (3 vols., folio, 1726), Aikin's *Lives* of Selden and Ussher.

SELLAR, WILLIAM YOUNG (1825-1890).—Scholar, *b.* in Sutherlandshire, his *f.* being factor to the Duke of Sutherland, *ed.* at Glasgow Univ. and Oxf., became in 1859 Prof. of Greek at St. Andrews and, in 1863, of Latin at Edin. He *pub.* a work on the *Roman Poets of the Republic* (1863), followed by *The Roman Poets of the Augustan Age.* Both of these hold a high place among modern works of scholarship.

SEMPILL, ROBERT (1530?-1595), SEMPILL, ROBERT (1595?-1659?), SEMPILL, FRANCIS (1616?-1682). — Scottish poets, all belonging to the same family, the last two being *f.* and *s.* The first was mainly a satirist, was in Paris at the massacre of St. Bartholomew, and belonged to the extremist division of the Reforming party, *The Regente's Tragedy* laments the death of Murray, *Ane Complaint upon Fortoun*, the fall of Morton. The second Robert wrote *The Life and Death of Habbie Simson, the Piper*, a humorous description of old Scottish life. Francis wrote occasional pieces. The song *She Rose and let me in*, formerly attributed to him, is now known to be by Tom D'Urfey (*q.v.*).

SENIOR, NASSAU WILLIAM (1790-1864).—Economist and essayist, *s.* of a clergyman, was *b.* at Compton Beauchamp, Berks, *ed.* at Eton and Oxf., studied law, and was called to the Bar in 1819. He twice held the Professorship of Political Economy at Oxf., 1825-30 and 1847-52, rendered important service as a member of the Poor Law Commission of 1833, and wrote its Report. S. holds a high position among English economists, and made many contributions to the literature of the science, including *Outline of the Science of Political Economy* (1836). He was, moreover, a writer of considerable versatility, his works in general literature including *Essays on Fiction* (1864), *Historical and Philosophical Essays* (1865), and specially his notes of conversations with many eminent persons, chiefly political, *e.g.*, De Tocqueville, Thiers, and Guizot, which combine fulness of information with discretion; he also *pub.* journals of his travels in Turkey, Greece, Egypt, etc.

SETTLE, ELKANAH (1648-1724).—Poet and dramatist, *ed.* at Oxf., was the author of a number of turgid dramas, now unreadable and unread, but which in their day were held to rival Dryden, who pilloried S. as Doeg in the second part of *Absalom and Achitophel.* S. essayed a reply in *Absalom Senior.* He wrote against the Papists, but recanted, and made amends by a *Narrative of the Popish Plot,* in which he exposed the perjuries of Titus Oates. He was appointed City Poet. Latterly he had a booth in Bartholomew Fair. He *d.* in the Charterhouse. His plays include *Cambyses* (1666), *Empress of Morocco* (1671), *Love and Revenge* (1675), *The Female Prelate, Distressed Innocence* (1691), and the *Ladies' Triumph* (1718).

SHADWELL, THOMAS (1640 or 1642-1692).—Dramatist and poet, belonged to a good Staffordshire family, was *b.* in Norfolk, *ed.* at Camb., and after studying law travelled, and on his return became a popular dramatist. Among his comedies, in which he displayed considerable comic power and truth to nature, may be mentioned *The Sullen Lovers* (1668), *Royal Shepherdess* (1668), *The Humourists* (1671), and *The Miser* (1672). He attached himself to the Whigs, and when Dryden attacked them in *Absalom and Achitophel* and *The Medal,* had the temerity to assail him scurrilously in *The Medal of John Bayes* (1682). The castigation which this evoked in *MacFlecknoe* and in the second part of *Absalom and Achitophel,* in which S. figures as "Og," has conferred upon him an unenviable immortality. He may have found some consolation in his succession to Dryden as Poet Laureate when, at the Revolution, the latter was deprived of the office.

Other plays are *Epsom Wells* (1673), *The Virtuoso* (1676), *Lancashire Witches* (1681), *The Volunteers* (1693), etc.

SHAFTESBURY, ANTHONY ASHLEY COOPER, 3RD EARL OF (1671-1713).—Philosopher, *b.* in London, grandson of the 1st Earl, the eminent statesman, the "Achitophel" of Dryden. After a private education under the supervision of Locke, and a short experience of Winchester School, he travelled much on the Continent. On succeeding to the earldom in 1699 he took a prominent part in the debates of the House of Lords, but devoted himself mainly to philosophical and literary pursuits. His *coll.* writings were *pub.* in 1711 under the title of *Characteristics of Men, Manners, Opinions, and Times.* In his philosophy he maintains, as against Hobbes, the existence of a moral sense, a view subsequently developed by the Scottish school of philosophy. The style of S. is stately and sonorous but laboured. He *d.* at Naples, whither he had gone in search of health, at the early age of 42. Though his writings are directed strongly against Atheism, they have been held to be hostile to a belief in revelation.

SHAIRP, JOHN CAMPBELL (1819-1885).—Poet and critic, *ed.* at Glasgow and Oxf., became Prof. of Latin at St. Andrews 1861, Principal of the United Coll. there 1868, and Prof. of Poetry at Oxf.

1877-87. Among his writings are *Kilmahoe and other Poems* (1864), *Studies in Poetry and Philosophy* (1868), *Culture and Religion* (1870), and a Life of Burns in the English Men of Letters Series. He also collaborated with Prof. Tait in writing the Life of Principal Forbes (*q.v.*), and ed. the Journal of Dorothy Wordsworth.

SHAKESPEARE, WILLIAM (1564-1616).—Dramatist and poet, *b.* at Stratford-on-Avon, Warwickshire, on 22nd or 23rd, and baptised on 26th April, 1564. On his father's side he belonged to a good yeoman stock, though his descent cannot be certainly traced beyond his grandfather, a Richard S., settled at Snitterfield, near Stratford. His *f.*, John S., appears to have been a man of intelligence and energy, who set up in Stratford as a dealer in all kinds of agricultural produce, to which he added the trade of a glover. He became prosperous, and gained the respect of his neighbours, as is evidenced by his election in succession to all the municipal honours of his community, including those of chief alderman and high bailiff. He *m.* Mary, youngest *dau.* of Robert Arden, a wealthy farmer at Wilmcote, and a younger branch of a family of considerable distinction, and whose tenant Richard S. had been. On her father's death Mary inherited Asbies, a house with 50 acres of land attached to it. The first children of the marriage were two *dau.*, who *d.* in infancy. William was the third, and others followed, of whom three sons, Gilbert, Richard, and Edmund, and a *dau.* Joan, reached maturity. He was *ed.* with his brother Gilbert at Stratford Grammar School, where he learned Latin from Lilly's Grammar, English, writing, and arithmetic. He probably read some of the Latin classics and may have got a little Greek, and though his learned friend Ben Jonson credits him with "little Latin and less Greek," Aubrey says he "knew Latin pretty well." This happy state of matters continued until he was about 13, when his *f.* fell into misfortune, which appears to have gone on deepening until the success and prosperity of the poet in later years enabled him to reinstate the family in its former position. Meanwhile, however, he was taken from school, and appears to have been made to assist his *f.* in his business. The next certain fact in his history is his marriage in November, 1582, when he was 18, to Ann Hathaway, *dau.* of a yeoman at the neighbouring hamlet of Shottery, and 8 years his senior. Various circumstances point to the marriage having been against the wishes of his own family, and pressed on by that of his wife, and that it was so urged in defence of the reputation of the lady, and as perhaps might be expected, they indicate, though not conclusively, that it did not prove altogether happy. The birth, in May, 1583, of his eldest child Susannah (who is said to have inherited something of his wit and practical ability, and who *m.* a Dr. John Hall), followed in the next year by that of twins, Hamnet and Judith, and the necessity of increased means, led to his departure from Stratford, whence he travelled on foot to London, where the next 23 years of his life were mainly spent. The tradition that his departure was also caused by trouble into which he had got by killing the deer of Sir Thomas Lucy, of Charlcote, is credible. Leaving Stratford in 1585 or the beginning of 1586, he seems at once to have turned to the theatres, where he soon found work, although, as Rowe, his first biographer, says, "in a very mean rank." It was not long, however, before he had opportunities of showing his capacities as an actor, with the result that he shortly became a member of one of the chief acting companies of the day, which was then under the patronage of the Earl of Leicester, and after being associated with the names of various other noblemen, at last on the accession of James I. became known as the King's Company. It played originally in "The Theatre" in Shoreditch, the first playhouse to be erected in England, and afterwards in the "Rose" on the Bankside, Southwark, the scene of the earliest successes of S. as an actor and playwright. Subsequently to 1594, he acted occasionally in a playhouse in Newington Butts, and between 1595 and 1599 in the "Curtain." In the latter year the "Globe" was built on the Bankside, and 10 years later the "Blackfriars:" and with these two, but especially with the former, the remainder of his professional life was associated. It is not unlikely that he visited various provincial towns; but that he was ever in Scotland or on the Continent is improbable. Among the plays in which he appeared were Jonson's *Every Man in his Humour* and *Sejanus*, and in *Hamlet* he played "The Ghost;" and it is said that his brother Gilbert as an old man remembered his appearing as "Adam" in *As You Like It.* By 1595 S. was famous and prosperous; his earlier plays had been written and acted, and his poems *Venus and Adonis*, and *Lucrece*, and probably most of the sonnets, had been *pub.* and received with extraordinary favour. He had also powerful friends and patrons, including the Earl of Southampton, and was known at Court. By the end of the century he is mentioned by Francis Meres (*q.v.*) as the greatest man of letters of the day, and his name had become so valuable that it was affixed by unscrupulous publishers to works, *e.g. Locrine*, *Oldcastle*, and *The Yorkshire Tragedy*, by other and often very inferior hands. He had also resumed a close connection with Stratford, and was making the restoration of the family position there the object of his ambition. In accordance with this he induced his *f.* to apply for a grant of arms, which was given, and he purchased New Place, the largest house in the village. With the income derived from his profession as an actor and dramatist, and his share of the profits of the Globe and Blackfriars theatres, and in view of the business capacity with which he managed his affairs, he may be regarded as almost a wealthy man, and he went on adding to his influence in Stratford by buying land. He had enjoyed the favour of Elizabeth, and her death in 1603 did nothing to disturb his fortunes, as he stood quite as well with her successor. His company received the title of the "King's Servants," and his plays were frequently performed before the Court. But notwithstanding this, the clouds had gathered over his life. The conspiracy of Essex in 1601 had involved several of his friends and patrons in disaster; he had himself been entangled in the unhappy love affair which is supposed to be referred to in some of his sonnets, and he had suffered unkindness at the hands of a friend. For a few years his dramas breathe the darkness and bitterness of a heart which has been sounding the depths of sad experience. He soon, however, emerged from this and, passing through the period of the great tragedies, reached the serene triumph and peace of his later dramas. In 1611 S. severed his long connection with the stage, and retired to Stratford, where the remaining five years of his life were spent in honour and prosperity. Early in 1616 his health began to give way, and he made his will. In the spring he received a visit from his friends, Jonson and Drayton, and the festivity with which it was celebrated seems to have brought on a fever, of which he *d.* on April 23. He was survived by his wife and his two *dau.*, both of whom were married. His descendants *d.* out with his granddaughter, Elizabeth Hall.

Immense research has been spent upon the writings of S., with the result of substantial agreement as to the order of their production and the sources from which their subjects were drawn; for S. rarely troubled himself with the construction of a story, but adopting one already existing reared upon it as a foundation one of those marvellous superstructures which make him the greatest painter and interpreter of human character the world has ever seen. His period of literary production extends from about 1588 to 1613, and falls naturally into four divisions, which Prof. Dowden has named, "In the Workshop" ending in 1596; "In the World" 1596-1601; "Out of the Depths" 1601-1608; and "On the Heights" 1608-1613. Of the 37 plays usually attributed to him, 16 only were *pub.* during his lifetime, so that the exact order in which they were produced cannot always be determined with certainty. Recent authorities are agreed to the extent that while they do not invariably place the individual plays in the same order, they are almost entirely at one as to which belong to the four periods respectively. The following list shows in a condensed form the order according to Mr. Sidney Lee (*Dictionary of National Biography*) with the most probable dates and the original sources on which the plays are founded.

CHRONOLOGICAL TABLE OF SHAKESPEARE'S PLAYS

FIRST PERIOD—1588?-1596

LOVE'S LABOUR LOST (1591)—Plot probably original.
TWO GENTLEMEN OF VERONA (1591)—*The Shepherdess Felismena* in George of Montmayor's *Diana*.
COMEDY OF ERRORS (1591)—*Menæchmi* of Plautus and earlier play.
ROMEO AND JULIET (1591)—Italian romance in Painter's *Palace of Pleasure* and Broke's *Romeus and Juliet*.
HENRY VI. 1, 2, and 3 (1592)—Retouched old plays, probably with Marlowe.
RICHARD III. (1592-3)—Holinshed's *Chronicle*.
RICHARD II. (1593-4?)— do.
TITUS ANDRONICUS (1594)—Probably chiefly by Kyd, retouched.
KING JOHN (1594)—Old play retouched.

SECOND PERIOD—1596-1601-2

MERCHANT OF VENICE (1594)—Italian novels, *Gesta Romanorum*, and earlier plays.
MIDSUMMER NIGHT'S DREAM (1595)—North's *Plutarch*, Chaucer, Ovid.
ALL'S WELL THAT ENDS WELL (1595)—Painter's *Palace of Pleasure*.
TAMING OF THE SHREW (1596?)—Old play retouched, and *Supposes* of G. Gascoigne, Shakespeare's in part only.
HENRY IV. 1 and 2 (1597?)—Holinshed and earlier play.
MERRY WIVES OF WINDSOR (1597-8)—Italian novels (?).
HENRY V. (1599).

MUCH ADO ABOUT NOTHING (1599).—Partly from Italian.
AS YOU LIKE IT (1599)—Lodge's *Rosalynde, Euphues' Golden Legacie.*
TWELFTH NIGHT (1599)—B. Riche's *Apolonius and Silla.*

THIRD PERIOD—1602–1608

JULIUS CÆSAR (1601)—North's *Plutarch.*
HAMLET (1601-2)—Belleforest's *Histoires Tragiques.*
TROILUS AND CRESSIDA (1603?)—Probably Chaucer's *Troilus and Cresseide* and Chapman's *Homer.*
OTHELLO (1604)—Cinthio's *Hecatommithi.*
MEASURE FOR MEASURE (1604?)—Cinthio's *Epithia.*
MACBETH (1605-6?)—Holinshed.
LEAR (1606)— do.
TIMON OF ATHENS (1607?)—*Palace of Pleasure* and Plutarch written with G. Wilkins (?) and W. Rowley (?).
PERICLES (1607-8)—Gower's *Confessio Amantis,* with G. Wilkins (?).
ANTONY AND CLEOPATRA (1608)—North's *Plutarch.*
CORIOLANUS (1608)— do.

FOURTH PERIOD—1608–1613

CYMBELINE (1610-11?) — Holinshed and *Ginevra* in Boccaccio's *Decamerone.*
WINTER'S TALE (1610-11)—Green's *Dorastus and Fawnia.*
TEMPEST (1611?)—S. Jourdain's *Discovery of the Bermudas.*
HENRY VIII. (1612-13)—Draft by S. completed by Fletcher and perhaps Massinger.

POEMS

VENUS AND ADONIS (1593).
RAPE OF LUCRECE (1594).
SONNETS (1591-94?).

The evidence as to chronology is three-fold—(1) External, such as entries in registers of Stationers' Company, contemporary references, or details as to the companies of actors; (2) External and internal combined, such as references in the plays to events or books, etc.; (3) Internal, content and treatment, progressive changes in versification, presence of frequency of rhyme, etc. The genius of S. was so intensely dramatic that it is impossible to say confidently when he speaks in his own character. The sonnets, written probably 1591-94 have, however, been thought to be of a more personal nature, and to contain indications as to his character and history, and much labour and ingenuity have been expended to make them yield their secrets. It is generally agreed that they fall into two sections, the first consisting of sonnets 1 to 126 addressed to a young man, probably Henry Wriothesley, Earl of Southampton, the friend and patron of S., and 9 years his junior; and the second from 127 to 154 addressed or referring to a woman in whose snares the writer had become entangled, and by whom he was betrayed. Some, however, have held that they are allegorical, or partly written on behalf of others, or that the emotion they express is dramatic and not personal.

There are contemporary references to S. which show him to have been generally held in high regard. Thus Ben Jonson says, "I loved the man, and do honour to his memory, on this side idolatry, as much as any," and Chettle refers to "His demeanour no lesse civil than exelent in the qualities he professes." The only exception is a reference to him in Greene's *Groat's-worth of Wit*, as "an upstart crow beautified with our feathers, that with his tyger's heart wrapt in a player's hide supposes he is as well able to bumbast out a blanke verse as the best of you . . . and is in his own conceit the only Shake-scene in a countrie." He is said to have written rapidly and with facility, rarely requiring to alter what he had set down. In addition to his generally received works, others have been attributed to him, some of which have been already mentioned: the only two which appear to have serious claims to consideration are *The Two Noble Kinsmen*, partly by Fletcher, and *Edward III.*, of which part of Act I. and the whole of Act II. have been thought to be Shakespeare's. On the other hand a theory has been propounded that none of the plays bearing his name were really his, but that they were written by Bacon (*q.v.*). This extraordinary view has been widely supported, chiefly in America, and has been sometimes maintained with considerable ability and misplaced ingenuity.

SUMMARY.—*B.* 1564, *ed.* at Stratford School, *f.* falls into difficulties *c.* 1577, *m.* Ann Hathaway 1582, goes to London end of 1585, finds employment in theatres and acts in chief companies of the time, first in "The Theatre" afterwards the "Rose," the "Curtain," the "Globe" and "Blackfriars," appearing in Jonson's *Every Man in his Humour* and *Sejanus*. *Venus and Adonis*, *Lucrece*, earlier plays, and perhaps most of sonnets *pub.* by 1595, when he was friend of Southampton and known at Court, purchases New Place at Stratford, falls into trouble *c.* 1600, having lost friends in Essex's conspiracy, and has unfortunate love affair; emerges from this into honour and peace, retires to Stratford and *d.* 1616. Productive period *c.* 1588-1613, 4 divisions, first (1588-96), second (1596-1601), third (1601-1608), fourth (1608-1613). Of 37 plays usually attributed, only 16 *pub.* in his life.

As might have been expected, there is a copious literature devoted to Shakespeare and his works. Among those dealing with biography may be mentioned Halliwell Phillipps's *Outline of the Life of Shakespeare* (7th ed., 1887), Fleay's *Shakespeare Manual* (1876), and *Life of Shakespeare* (1886). *Life* by S. Lee (1898), Dowden's *Shakespeare, his Mind and Art* (1875), Drake's *Shakespeare and his Times* (1817), Thornberry's *Shakespeare's England* (1856), Knight's *Shakespeare* (1843). *See* also Works by Guizot, De Quincey, Fullom, Elze, and others. Criticisms by Coleridge, Hazlitt, Swinburne, T. S. Baynes, and others. Concordance by Mrs. Cowden Clarke. Ed., Rowe (1709), Pope (1725), Theobald (1733), Johnson (1765), Capell (1768), Steevens's improved re-issue of Johnson (1773), Malone (1790), Reed's *1st Variorum* (1803), *2nd Variorum* (1813), *3rd Variorum* by Jas. Boswell the younger (1821), Dyce (1857), Staunton (1868-70), Camb. by W. G. Clark and Dr. Aldis Wright (1863-66), Temple (ed. I. Gollancz, 1894-96), *Eversley Shakespeare* (ed. Herford, 1899).

SHARP, WILLIAM ("FIONA MACLEOD") (1856-1905).—Wrote under this pseudonym a remarkable series of Celtic tales, novels, and poems, including *Pharais, a Romance of the Isles*, *The Mountain Lovers*, *The Sin-Eater* (1895), *The Washer of the Ford*, and

Green Fire (1896), *The Laughter of Peterkin* (1897), *The Dominion of Dreams* (1899), *The Divine Adventure* (1900), *Drostan and Iseult* (1902). He was one of the earliest and most gifted promoters of the Celtic revival. In verse are *From the Hills of Dream, Through the Ivory Gate*, and *The Immortal Hour* (drama). Under his own name he wrote *Earth's Voices, Sospiri di Roma, Sospiri d'Italia*, poems, and books on Rossetti, Shelley, Browning, and Heine; also a few novels.

SHAW, HENRY WHEELER ("JOSH BILLINGS") (1818-1885).—Humorist, *b.* in Massachusetts. After working on steamboats and farming, he became an auctioneer, and settled at Poughkeepsie. Stripped of the fantastic spelling by which he first succeeded in catching the public attention, the shrewd and droll maxims of his *Farmers' Allminax* have something in common with Franklin's *Poor Richard*. Other books with the same features are *Josh Billings' Sayings, Everybody's Friend, Josh Billings' Trump Kards*, etc.

SHELLEY, MRS. MARY WOLLSTONECRAFT (GODWIN) (1797-1851).—Novelist, *b.* in London, the only child of William Godwin (*q.v.*) and Mary Wollstonecraft, his wife (*q.v.*). In 1814 she went to the Continent with P. B. Shelley (*q.v.*), and *m.* him two years later. When abroad she saw much of Byron, and it was at his villa on the Lake of Geneva that she conceived the idea of her famous novel of *Frankenstein* (1818), a ghastly but powerful work. None of her other novels, including *The Last Man* and *Lodore*, had the same success. She contributed biographies of foreign artists and authors to Lardner's *Cabinet Cyclopædia*, and ed. her husband's poems.

SHELLEY, PERCY BYSSHE (1792-1822).—Poet, *s.* of Sir Timothy S., was *b.* at Field Place, near Horsham, Sussex, and *ed.* at Brentford, Eton, and Univ. Coll., Oxf., whence for writing and circulating a pamphlet, *The Necessity of Atheism*, he was expelled. One immediate result of this was a difference with his *f.*, which was deepened into a permanent breach by his marriage in the following year to Harriet Westbrook, the pretty and lively *dau.* of a retired innkeeper. The next three years were passed in wandering about from place to place in Ireland, Wales, the Lake District, and other parts of the kingdom, and in the composition of *Queen Mab* (1813), the poet's first serious work. Before the end of that period he had separated from his wife, for which various reasons have been assigned, one being her previous desertion of him, and the discovery on his part of imperfect sympathy between them; the principal one, however, being that he had conceived a violent passion for Mary Wollstonecraft Godwin (*see* Shelley, Mrs. M. W.), *dau.* of William Godwin (*q.v.*), with whom he eloped to Italy in 1814, and whom he *m.* in 1816, his first wife having drowned herself. The custody of his two children, whom he had left with their mother, was refused him by the Court of Chancery. In Switzerland he had made the acquaintance of Byron, with whom he afterwards lived in intimacy in Italy. Returning to England in 1815 he wrote his first really great poem, *Alastor* (1816), followed by the *Hymn to Intellectual Beauty, Prince Athanase, Rosalind and Helen*, and *Laon and Cythna*, afterwards called the *Revolt of Islam* (1817). In 1818 he left England never to return, and went to Italy, and in the next two years—while at

Rome—produced his two greatest works, the tragedy of *The Cenci* (1819) and *Prometheus Unbound* (1820). He removed to Venice in 1820 in the company of Byron, and there wrote *Julian and Maddalo*, a poetic record of discussions between them. *Epipsychidion*, *Hellas*, and *Adonais*, a lament for Keats, were all produced in 1821. After a short residence at Pisa he went to Lerici on the Gulf of Spezzia, where he indulged in his favourite recreation of boating, and here on July 8, 1822, he went, in company with a friend, Mr. Williams, on that fatal expedition which cost him his life. His body was cast ashore about a fortnight later, and burnt, in accordance with the quarantine law of the country, on a pyre in the presence of Byron, Leigh Hunt, and Trelawny. His ashes were carefully preserved and buried in the Protestant cemetery at Rome near those of Keats. The character of S. is a singularly compounded one. By the unanimous testimony of his friends, it was remarkable for gentleness, purity, generosity, and strong affection: on the other hand he appears to have had very inadequate conceptions of duty and responsibility, and from his childhood seems to have been in revolt against authority of every kind. The charge of Atheism rests chiefly on *Mab*, the work of a boy, printed by him for private circulation, and to some extent repudiated as personal opinion. As a poet he stands in the front rank: in lyrical gift, shown in *Prometheus*, *Hellas*, and some of his shorter poems, such as "The Skylark," he is probably unsurpassed, and in his *Cenci* he exhibits dramatic power of a high order. Among his shorter poems are some which reach perfection, such as the sonnet on "Ozymandias," "Music when soft voices die," "I arise from dreams of thee," "When the lamp is shattered," the "Ode to the West Wind," and "O world! O life! O time!" During his short life of 30 years he was, not unnaturally, the object of much severe judgment, and his poetic power even was recognised by only a few. Posterity has taken a more lenient view of his serious errors of conduct, while according to his genius a shining place among the immortals.

The best ed. of the *Works* is that of Buxton Forman (4 vols.). There are ed. of the Poems by W. M. Rossetti (1894), Dowden (1891), etc. *Lives* by Medwin (1847), J. A. Symonds (1887), W. M. Rossetti, Prof. Dowden, T. Jefferson Hogg, and others.

SHENSTONE, WILLIAM (1714-1763).—Poet, *s.* of Thomas S., owner of a small estate at Hales Owen, Shropshire. At this place, called the Leasowes, the poet was *b.* In 1732 he went to Oxf. On his father's death he retired to the Leasowes where he passed his time, and ran through his means in transforming it into a marvel of landscape gardening, visited by strangers from all parts of the kingdom. The works of S. consist of poems and prose essays. Of the former two, *The Schoolmistress*, a humorous imitation of Spenser, with many quaint and tender touches, and the *Pastoral Ballad* in four parts, perhaps the best of its kind in the language, survive. The essays also display good sense and a pointed and graceful style. The last years of S. were clouded by financial embarrassments and perhaps also by disappointed affections. After his death his works were *coll.* and *pub.* by Dodsley.

SHERIDAN, RICHARD BRINSLEY (1751-1816).—Dramatist and orator, *b.* in Dublin, the *s.* of an actor, was *ed.* at Harrow. In 1772 he eloped with Miss Linley, a famous singer, went with her to France, fought two duels, and *m.* her in 1773. S. has a reputation of the highest in two distinct walks, those of the dramatist and the Parliamentary orator. By his three great comedies, *The Rivals* (1775), *The School for Scandal* (1777), and *The Critic* (1779), he raised himself to the first place among the writers of the comedy of manners; and by his speeches, specially those in support of the impeachment of Warren Hastings, he has a position among the greatest of Parliamentary orators. Unfortunately he had little turn for business, and too great a love of pleasure and conviviality, which led to lifelong pecuniary embarrassment, completed by the destruction by fire of Drury Lane Theatre, of which he had become proprietor. As a politician S. supported the Whig party, and held the offices of Under-Sec. for Foreign Affairs, Sec. to the Treasury, and Treasurer of the Navy. He was also confidential adviser to George IV. when Prince of Wales, but like everybody else who had to do with him suffered from the ingratitude of "the first gentleman in Europe." The accounts long prevalent of the poverty and misery of his last years have been shown to be greatly exaggerated, though he was in reduced circumstances. As a dramatist S. shines in the construction of amusing situations, and in a sparkling flow of witty dialogue which never flags. His only other play was *Pizarro* (1799), a patriotic melodrama.

Lives by Walkins (1817), T. Moore (1825), and Mrs. Oliphant (1883).

SHERLOCK, WILLIAM (1641?-1707).—Divine and controversialist, *b.* at Southwark, *ed.* at Eton and Camb., took orders, and became in 1684 Master of the Temple, and in 1691 Dean of St. Paul's. He exercised a powerful influence in the Church. His most popular work was his *Discourse concerning Death*, and his principal controversial effort was his *Vindication of the Doctrine of the Trinity*. Other works were on *Future Judgment* and on *The Divine Providence*. His son, THOMAS SHERLOCK (1678-1761), who was also Master of the Temple, became Bishop successively of Bangor, Salisbury, and London, and was, like his *f.*, a noted controversialist. His best known work is his *Tryal of the Witnesses of the Resurrection of Jesus* (1729).

SHERWOOD, MRS. MARY MARTHA (BUTT) (1775-1851).—Writer of children's books, *m.* in 1803 Captain H. Sherwood, and went to India, where she took much interest in soldiers' children. Among her books, many of which attained great popularity, are *Susan Gray*, *Little Henry and his Bearer*, and *The Fairchild Family*.

SHIRLEY, JAMES (1596-1666).—Dramatist, *b.* in London, *ed.* at Merchant Taylor's School, London, and at Oxf. and Camb., became a master of St. Alban's Grammar School, and afterwards joined the Roman Catholic Church, and going to London wrote for the stage, producing 39 plays. His talents and his religion recommended him to Queen Henrietta Maria, and he appears to have led a fairly prosperous life until the interdict of plays by Parliament in 1642. In the Civil War he bore arms on the Royalist side, and during the Commonwealth he returned to his occupation of schoolmaster. The Restoration does not appear to have improved his fortunes much; he was burnt out in the great fire of 1666, and very soon afterwards he and his wife *d.* on the same day. The plays of S. include *Loves Tricks* (1625), *The Cardinal* (1641), *The Gamester* (1633), *Hyde Park* (1632), and *The Lady of Pleasure* (1635). He also wrote poems, including the well-known lines beginning "The Glories of our blood and State." S. has fancy, liveliness, and the style of a gentleman, but he lacks depth and interest. He is less gross than most of his contemporaries.

Other plays are *The Ball* (1632), *The Maid's Revenge* (1626), *The Grateful Servant* (1629), *Bird in a Cage* (1633), *The Example* (1634), *The Constant Maid* (*c.* 1640), *Doubtful Heir, or Rosania* (1640), *Court Secret* (1653), *Contention of Ajax and Ulysses* (1659), etc.

SHORTHOUSE, JOSEPH HENRY (1834-1903).—Novelist, *b.* at Birmingham, where he was a chemical manufacturer. Originally a Quaker, he joined the Church of England. His first, and by far his best book, *John Inglesant*, appeared in 1881, and at once made him famous. Though deficient in its structure as a story, and not appealing to the populace, it fascinates by the charm of its style and the "dim religious light" by which it is suffused, as well as by the striking scenes occasionally depicted. His other novels, *The Little Schoolmaster Mark*, *Sir Percival*, *The Countess Eve*, and *A Teacher of the Violin*, though with some of the same characteristics, had no success comparable to his first. S. also wrote an essay, *The Platonism of Wordsworth*.

SIBBES, RICHARD (1577-1635).—Divine, was at Camb., where he held various academic posts, of which he was deprived by the High Commission on account of his Puritanism. He was the author of several devotional works expressing intense religious feeling—*The Saint's Cordial* (1629), *The Bruised Reed and Smoking Flax*, etc. He was a man of great learning.

SIDNEY, OR SYDNEY, ALGERNON (1622-1683).—Political writer, *s.* of the 2nd Earl of Leicester, and grand-nephew of Sir Philip S., in his youth travelled on the Continent, served against the Irish Rebels, and on the outbreak of the Civil War, on the side of the Parliament. He was one of the judges on the trial of Charles I., and though he did not attend, he thoroughly approved of the sentence. He opposed the assumption of the supreme power by Cromwell. After the Restoration he lived on the Continent, but receiving a pardon, returned in 1677 to England. He, however, retained the republican principles which he had all his life advocated, fell under the suspicion of the Court, and was in 1683, on the discovery of the Rye House Plot, condemned to death on entirely insufficient evidence, and beheaded on Tower Hill, December 7, 1683. Though no charge of personal venality has been substantiated, yet it appears to be certain that he received money from the French King for using his influence against war between the two countries, his object being to prevent Charles II. from obtaining command of the war supplies. S. was deeply versed in political theory, and wrote *Discourses concerning Government*, *pub.* in 1698.

SIDNEY, SIR PHILIP (1554-1586).—Poet and romancist, *s.* of Sir Henry S., Deputy of Ireland, and Pres. of Wales, *b.* at the family seat of Penshurst, and *ed.* at Shrewsbury School and Oxf. He was at the French Court on the fateful August 24, 1572—the massacre of St. Bartholomew—but left Paris soon thereafter and went to Germany and Italy. In 1576 he was with his *f.* in Ireland, and the next year went on missions to the Elector Palatine and the Emperor Rudolf II. When his father's Irish policy was called in question, he wrote an able defence of it. He became the friend of Spenser, who dedicated to him his *Shepherd's Calendar.* In 1580 he lost the favour of the Queen by remonstrating against her proposed marriage with the Duke of Anjou. His own marriage with a *dau.* of Sir Francis Walsingham took place in 1583. In 1585 he was engaged in the war in the Low Countries, and met his death at Zutphen from a wound in the thigh. His death was commemorated by Spenser in his *Astrophel.* S. has always been considered as the type of English chivalry; and his extraordinary contemporary reputation rested on his personal qualities of nobility and generosity. His writings consist of his famous pastoral romance of *Arcadia,* his sonnets *Astrophel and Stella,* and his *Apologie for Poetrie,* afterwards called *Defence of Poesie.* The *Arcadia* was originally written for the amusement of his sister, afterwards Countess of Pembroke, the "Sidney's sister, Pembroke's mother," of William Browne. Though its interest now is chiefly historical, it enjoyed an extraordinary popularity for a century after its appearance, and had a marked influence on the immediately succeeding literature. It was written in 1580-81 but not *pub.* until 1590, and is a medley of poetical prose, full of conceits, with occasional verse interspersed. His *Defence of Poesie,* written in reply to Gosson (*q.v.*), is in simple and vigorous English. S. also made a translation of the Psalms.

Poems ed. by Grosart, *Apologie* by Arber and others, *Astrophel* by Gray, Arber, and others. *Life* by Fulke Greville (1652), ed. by Sir E. Brydges (1816). *Arcadia* (*facsimile*), by Somner. Lives by J. A. Symonds, Fox Bourne, and others.

SIGOURNEY, MRS. LYDIA (HUNTLEY) (1791-1865).—American verse writer, was an extraordinarily copious writer of smooth, sentimental verse, which had great popularity in its day. Her most ambitious effort was a blank verse poem, *Traits of the Aborigines of America* (1822). Other books were *Connecticut Forty Years Since, Pocahontas,* etc.

SIMMS, WILLIAM GILMORE (1806-1870).—Novelist, etc., *b.* at Charleston, South Carolina, began his literary life with journalism. He then for some time tried poetry, but without any distinct success except occasionally in *Southern Passages and Pictures* (1839). But in fiction, which he began in 1833 with *Martin Faber,* he was more successful, though rather an imitator of Cooper. *The Yemassee* (1835) is generally considered his best novel. He was less happy in his attempts at historical romance, such as *Count Julian* and *The Damsel of Darien.* During the war, in which he was naturally a strong partisan of the South, he was ruined, and his library was burned; and from these disasters he never recovered. He had a high repute as a journalist, orator, and lecturer. He was the first Southerner to achieve any name in literature.

SKELTON, JOHN (1460?-1529).—Poet, *b.* in Norfolk, and *ed.* at Oxf. and Camb., of both of which he was *cr.* Poet Laureate, and perhaps held the same office under the King. He was appointed tutor to Henry VIII., and notwithstanding his sharp tongue, enjoyed some favour at Court. In 1498 he entered the Church, and became Rector of Diss in his native county. Hitherto he seems to have produced some translations only, but about this time he appears to have struck upon the vein which he was to work with such vigour and popularity. He turned his attention to abuses in Church and State, which he lashed with caustic satire, conveyed in short doggerel rhyming lines peculiar to himself, in which jokes, slang, invectives, and Latin quotations rush out pell-mell. His best works in this line are *Why come ye not to Court?* and *Colin Clout*, both directed against the clergy, and the former against Wolsey in particular. Piqued at his inconstancy (for S. had previously courted him) the Cardinal would have imprisoned him, had he not taken sanctuary in Westminster, where he remained until his death. Other works of his are *The Tunning* (brewing) *of Elynor Rummynge*, a coarsely humorous picture of low life, and the tender and fanciful *Death of Philip Sparrow*, the lament of a young lady over her pet bird killed by a cat.

SKELTON, SIR JOHN (1831-1897).—Miscellaneous writer. *B.* in Edinburgh, *ed.* at the Univ. there, and called to the Scottish Bar 1854, he was Sec. and ultimately Chairman of the Local Government Board for Scotland. He wrote *Maitland of Lethington and the Scotland of Mary Stuart* (1887), *The Crookit Meg* (1880), and *The Table Talk of Shirley*. He contributed to *Fraser's* and *Blackwood's Magazines*. He received the degree of LL.D. from Edin. 1878, and was made K.C.B. 1897.

SKENE, WILLIAM FORBES (1807-1892).—Historian, 2nd *s.* of James S. of Rubislaw, friend of Sir Walter Scott, was a Writer to the Signet in Edinburgh, and Clerk of the Bills in the Court of Session. He wrote and ed. historical works of considerable authority, *The Highlanders of Scotland* (1837), and his most important work, *Celtic Scotland* (1876-80), and ed. of *The Four Ancient Books of Wales* (1868), and other Celtic writings.

SKINNER, JOHN (1721-1807).—Historian and song-writer, *s.* of a schoolmaster at Birse, Aberdeenshire, was *ed.* at Marischal Coll. Brought up as a Presbyterian, he became an Episcopalian and ministered to a congregation at Longside, near Peterhead, for 65 years. He wrote *The Ecclesiastical History of Scotland* from the Episcopalian point of view, and several songs of which *The Reel of Tullochgorum* and *The Ewie wi' the Crookit Horn* are the best known, and he also rendered some of the Psalms into Latin. He kept up a rhyming correspondence with Burns.

SKIPSEY, JOSEPH (1832-1903).—Poet, *b.* near North Shields, and from childhood worked in the mines. He *pub.* a few pieces of poetry in 1859, and soon after left working underground and became caretaker of Shakespeare's house at Stratford-on-Avon. During the last 30 years of his life he *pub.* several vols. of poetry, including *The Collier Lad* and *Carols from the Coal Fields;* and he ed. some vols. for the "Canterbury Poets." *Memoir* by R. S. Watson (1908).

SMART, CHRISTOPHER (1722-1771).—Poet, *s.* of the steward to Lord Vane, was *b.* at Shipbourne, Kent, and by the bounty of the Duchess of Cleveland sent to Camb. Here his ill-balanced mind showed itself in wild folly. Leaving the Univ. he came to London and maintained himself by conducting and writing for periodicals. His *Poems on Several Occasions*, which contained "The Hop Garden," was issued in 1752, and *The Hilliad* in 1753 against "Sir" John Hill, a notoriety of the day who had attacked him. His mind ultimately gave way, and it was in confinement that he produced by far his most remarkable work, the *Song to David*, a most original and powerful poem. Unfortunate to the last, he *d.* in the King's Bench prison, to which he had been committed for debt. He also translated Horace.

SMEDLEY, FRANK (1818-1864).—Novelist, was the author of several novels which had considerable popularity, including *Frank Fairleigh* (1850), *Lewis Arundel* (1852), and *Harry Coverdale's Courtship* (1855). S. was a life-long cripple.

SMILES, SAMUEL (1812-1904).—Biographer and miscellaneous writer, *b.* at Haddington, *ed.* at the Grammar School there, studied medicine at Edin., and settled in practice in his native town. Subsequently he betook himself to journalism, and ed. a paper in Leeds. Afterwards he was sec. to various railways. His leisure was devoted to reading and writing, and his first publication was *The Life of George Stephenson* (1857). *Self-Help*, his most popular work, followed in 1859; it had an immense circulation, and was translated into 17 languages. It was followed up by *Character* (1871), *Thrift* (1875), and *Duty* (1880). *The Lives of the Engineers* and *Industrial Biography* appeared in 1863, *The Huguenots, their Settlements, Churches, and Industries in England and Ireland* (1867), and *The Huguenots in France* a little later. He also wrote biographies of Telford and James Watt, and of the Scottish naturalists, Edwards the shoemaker and Dick the baker. He received the degree of LL.D. from Edin. in 1878.

SMITH, ADAM (1723-1790).—Philosopher and economist, *b.* at Kirkcaldy, Fife, the *s.* of the Controller of Customs there. His *f. d.* shortly before his birth. The first and only adventure in his tranquil life was his being kidnapped by gipsies. After being at the Grammar School of Kirkcaldy, he went to the Univ. of Glasgow, whence he proceeded to Oxf. On the conclusion of his Univ. course he returned to Kirkcaldy, going subsequently to Edinburgh, where he was soon recognised as a man of unusual intellect. In 1751 he was appointed to the Chair of Logic at Glasgow, which he next year exchanged for that of Moral Philosophy, and in 1759 he *pub.* his *Theory of the Moral Sentiments.* He received in 1762 the degree of LL.D. from his Univ., and two years later resigned his chair and became travelling tutor to the young Duke of Buccleuch, accompanying him to the Continent. He remained for nearly a year in Paris, and made the acquaintance of the brilliant circle of *savans* in that city. Returning to Kirkcaldy in 1766 he lived there with his mother for nearly ten years in retirement and close study, the results of which were given to the world in 1776 in the publication of his epoch-making work, *Inquiry into the Nature and Causes of the Wealth of Nations* (1776). This book may be said to have founded the science of political economy, and to have created a new department of literature; and very few works have, to the same extent, influenced the practical history of the world. In 1778 S. was made a Commissioner of Customs, and settled in Edinburgh; and in 1787 he was elected Lord Rector of the Univ. of Glasgow. In addition to the works above mentioned, he wrote various essays on philosophical subjects, and an account of the last days of David Hume. The style of his works was plain and lucid, and he had a remarkable faculty of apt illustration.

SMITH, ALBERT (1816-1860).—Humorous writer, studied medicine, and for a short time assisted his *f.* in practice. He was one of the original contributors to *Punch*, and among his books are *The Adventures of Mr. Ledbury* and *The Scattergood Family.* He also lectured and gave entertainments, including *The Ascent of Mont Blanc*, which were highly popular.

SMITH, ALEXANDER (1830-1867).—Poet and essayist, *s.* of a Paisley pattern-designer, at first followed the same occupation in Glasgow, but having become known as a poet of promise was, in 1854, appointed Sec. of Edin. Univ. After contributing to the *Glasgow Citizen* he *pub. A Life Drama* (1853), which received much admiration. Thereafter appeared *War Sonnets* (in conjunction with S. Dobell, *q.v.*), *City Poems* (1857), and *Edwin of Deira* (1861). In prose he wrote *Dreamthorpe* (essays), *A Summer in Skye,* and two novels, *Alfred Hagart's Household* and *Miss Dona M'Quarrie.* His poems were in a rich and glowing style, but by some good judges were held to show fancy rather than imagination. He belonged to what was called the "spasmodic" school of poetry.

SMITH, MRS. CHARLOTTE (TURNER) (1749-1806).—Was *m.* at 15 to a West Indian merchant, who by a series of misfortunes and imprudences was reduced from affluence to poverty. She had in her youth shown considerable promise as a poetess, and in her misfortunes she was able to maintain herself and her family by her pen. In addition to a poem, *Beachy Head,* and sonnets, she wrote several novels of more than usual merit, including *Emmeline* (1788), and, her best work, *The Old English Manor House.*

SMITH, HORACE (1779-1849), SMITH, JAMES (1775-1839). —Humorists, *s.* of a London lawyer who was solicitor to the Board of Ordnance. James succeeded his *f.*; Horace became a successful stockbroker. Both brothers were distinguished for brilliant wit and humour. Their first great hit was *Rejected Addresses* (1812), extremely clever parodies on leading contemporary poets. To this *jeu d'ésprit* James contributed among others imitations of Wordsworth, Coleridge, and Crabbe, while Horace's share included Scott and Moore. James *pub.* little more, but anonymously gave Charles Matthews assistance in his entertainments. Horace *pub.* several novels which, with perhaps the exception of *Brambletye House*, are now forgotten. He also wrote *The Address to a Mummy*, a remarkable poem in which wit and true sentiment are admirably combined. Both brothers were highly esteemed not only for their social qualities, but for their benevolence and goodness of heart.

SMITH, SYDNEY (1771-1845).—Miscellaneous writer, *b.* at Woodford, Essex, the *s.* of a gentleman of independent means, and *ed.* at Winchester and Oxf., took orders 1794, becoming curate of Amesbury. He came to Edinburgh as tutor to a gentleman's *s.*, was introduced to the circle of brilliant young Whigs there, and assisted in founding the *Edinburgh Review.* He then went to London, where he was for a time preacher at the Foundling Hospital, and lectured on moral philosophy at the Royal Institution. His brilliant wit and general ability made him a favourite in society, while by his power of clear and cogent argument he exercised a strong influence on the course of politics. His *Plymley Letters* did much to advance the cause of Catholic emancipation. He received various preferments, and became a canon of St. Paul's. In politics he was a Whig, in his Church views an Erastian; and in the defence of his principles he was honest and courageous. Though not remarkable for religious devotion he was a hard-working and, according to his lights, useful country parson. By the death of a younger brother he in his later years came into a considerable fortune.

SMITH, WALTER CHALMERS (1824-1908).—*B.* in Aberdeen and *ed.* there and at Edin., was a minister of the Free Church of Scotland at Orwell, Glasgow, and Edinburgh successively, a distinguished preacher and a man of kindly nature and catholic sympathies. He attained considerable reputation as a poet. Among his works are *The Bishop's Walk* (1861), *Olrig Grange* (1872), *Hilda among the Broken Gods* (1878), *Raban* (1880), *Kildrostan* (1884), and *A Heretic* (1890). Some of these were written under the names of "Orwell" and Hermann Kunst. He received the degrees of D.D. and LL.D.

SMITH, SIR WILLIAM (1813-1893).—Lexicographer, *ed.* at Univ. Coll., London, was a contributor to the *Penny Magazine* and compiled or ed. many useful works of reference, including *Dictionary of Greek and Roman Antiquities* (1842), and dictionaries of the Bible, of Christian Antiquities, and Christian Biography, etc., also various school series and educational handbooks, including *The Classical Dictionary.* He held various academical degrees, including Ph.D. of Leipsic, and was knighted in 1892.

SMITH, WILLIAM ROBERTSON (1846-1894).—Theologian and Semitic scholar, *s.* of the Free Church minister of Keig, Aberdeenshire, studied for the ministry of that Church. In 1870 he was appointed Prof. of Hebrew, etc., in its coll. at Aberdeen, a position which he had to resign on account of his advanced critical views. He became joint ed. of *The Encyclopædia Britannica*, and in 1883 Prof. of Arabic at Camb. S. was a man of brilliant and versatile talents, a mathematician as well as a scholar, somewhat uncompromising and aggressive in the exposition and defence of his views.

His works include *The Old Testament in the Jewish Church* (1881), and *The Religion of the Semites* (1889).

SMOLLETT, TOBIAS GEORGE (1721-1771).—Novelist, 2nd *s.* of Archibald S., of Dalquhurn, Dumbartonshire, and *ed.* at Glasgow, proceeded to London in 1739 with the view of having a tragedy, *The Regicide*, put on the stage, in which, however, he failed. In this disappointment he took service as surgeon's mate on one of the vessels of the Carthagena expedition, 1741, an experience which he turned to account in his novels. On his return he settled in London, and endeavoured to acquire practice as a physician, but was not very successful, and having discovered where his talent lay, he thenceforth devoted himself to literature. *Roderick Random* appeared in 1748, *The History of an Atom* (1749), *Peregrine Pickle* in 1751, *Ferdinand, Count Fathom* in 1753, *Sir Lancelot Greaves* in 1766, and *Humphrey Clinker*, generally considered his best novel, in 1770. Besides these works, however, he translated Voltaire, wrote a *History of England* in continuation of Hume's, an *Ode to Independence*, travels and satires, and contributed to various periodicals. He was repeatedly involved in acrimonious controversy, and on one occasion fined and imprisoned for a libel, which, with various private misfortunes, embittered his life, and he *d.* disappointed and worn out near Leghorn. Had he lived four years longer he would have succeeded to his grandfather's estate of Bonhill. The novels of S. display great narrative power, and he has a remarkable comic vein of a broad type, which enables him to present ludicrous scenes and circumstances with great effect. There is, however, a strong infusion of coarseness in his treatment of his subjects.

SOMERVILLE, MRS. MARY (FAIRFAX) (1780-1872).—Mathematician and writer on science, *dau.* of Admiral Sir William G. Fairfax, *b.* at Jedburgh, was twice *m.*, first to Mr. Greig, an officer in the Russian Navy, and second to her cousin Dr. William S. Although she had early manifested a taste for study, and specially for science, she had, until after the death of her first husband, little opportunity of following out her favourite subjects. With Dr. S., who was in full sympathy with her scientific tastes, she went to reside in London, and there her talents made her known in scientific circles. In 1823 she was requested by Lord Brougham to popularise the *Mechanique Celeste* of La Place. This she did with great success, publishing her work as *The Celestial Mechanism of the Heavens* (1830). She also *pub. The Connection of the Physical Sciences* (1834), and other works. She received a pension from Government, and *d.* aged 92 at Naples, where she had resided for the last ten or twelve years of her life.

SOMERVILLE, WILLIAM (1675-1742).—Poet, a Warwickshire squire of literary tastes, wrote among others a poem, *The Chase*, in 4 books, which has some passages of considerable descriptive power.

SOTHEBY, WILLIAM (1757-1833).—Poet and translator, belonged to a good family, and was *ed.* at Harrow. In early life he was in the army. He *pub.* a few dramas and books of poems, which had no great popularity, and are now forgotten; his reputation rests upon his admirable translations of the *Oberon* of Wieland, the *Georgics* of Virgil, and the *Iliad* and *Odyssey*. The last two were begun when he was upwards of 70, but he lived to complete them. His *Georgics* is considered one of the best translations from the classics in the language.

SOUTH, ROBERT (1634-1716).—Divine, *s.* of a London merchant, was *b.* at Hackney, and *ed.* at Westminster School and Oxf., where in 1660 he was appointed Univ. Orator. He became domestic chaplain to the Lord Chancellor Clarendon, and in 1663 the degree of D.D. was conferred upon him. After accompanying an embassy to Poland he became Rector of Islip, and a chaplain to Charles II. Thereafter he steadily declined higher preferment, including the bishopric of Rochester. He was opposed to the Romanising measures of James II., but owing to his views as to the duty of passive obedience he declined to associate himself in any way with the Revolution, to which nevertheless he submitted. He was an expert controversialist, but it is chiefly by his sermons, which are among the classics of English divinity, that he is remembered. He has the reputation of being the wittiest of English preachers, and this characteristic is sometimes present to a degree not quite suitable to the subjects treated.

SOUTHERNE, THOMAS (1660-1746).—Dramatist, *b.* in Dublin, and *ed.* at Trinity Coll. there, came to London and studied law at the Middle Temple. Afterwards he entered the army and saw service. He wrote ten plays, of which two were long acted and are still remembered, *The Fatal Marriage* (1694) and *Oroonoko* (1696), in the latter of which he appeals passionately against the slave-trade. Unlike most preceding dramatists he was a practical man, succeeded in his theatrical management, and retired on a fortune. Other plays are *The Loyal Brother* (1682), *The Disappointment* (1684), *The Wives' Excuse* (1692), *The Spartan Dame* (1719), etc.

SOUTHEY, MRS. CAROLINE ANNE (BOWLES) (1786-1854).—Poetess, *dau.* of a captain in the navy, submitted a poem, *Ellen Fitzarthur* to Southey (*q.v.*), which led to a friendship, and to a proposed joint poem on Robin Hood, not, however, carried out, and eventually to her becoming the poet's second wife. She wrote various other works, including *Chapters on Churchyards* and *Tales of the Factories*.

SOUTHEY, ROBERT (1774-1843).—Poet, biographer, etc., *s.* of an unsuccessful linen-draper in Bristol, where he was *b.*, was sent to Westminster School, and in 1792 went to Oxf. His friendship with Coleridge began in 1794, and with him he joined in the scheme of a "pantisocracy" (*see* Coleridge). In 1795 he *m.* his first wife, Edith Fricker, and thus became the brother-in-law of Coleridge. Shortly afterwards he visited Spain, and in 1800 Portugal, and laid the foundations of his thorough knowledge of the history and literature of the Peninsula. Between these two periods of foreign travel he had attempted the study of law, which proved entirely uncongenial; and in 1803 he settled at Greta Hall, Keswick, to which neighbourhood the Coleridges had also come. Here he set himself to a course of indefatigable literary toil which only ended with his life. *Thalaba* had appeared in 1801, and there followed *Madoc* (1805), *The Curse of Kehama* (1810), *Roderic, the Last of the Goths* (1814), and *A Vision of Judgment* (1821); and in prose a *History of Brazil*, Lives of Nelson (1813), Wesley (1820), and Bunyan (1830), *The Book of the Church* (1824), *History of the Peninsular War* (1823-32), *Naval History*, and *The Doctor* (1834-37). In addition to this vast amount of work he had been from 1808 a constant contributor to the *Quarterly Review*. In 1839 when he was failing both in body and mind he *m.*, as his second wife, Miss Caroline Ann Bowles, who had for 20 years been his intimate friend, and by whom his few remaining years were soothed. Though the name of S. still bulks somewhat largely in the history of our literature, his works, with a few exceptions, are now little read, and those of them (his longer poems, *Thalaba* and *Kehama*) on which he himself based his hopes of lasting fame, least of all. To this result their length, remoteness from living interests, and the impression that their often splendid diction is rather eloquence than true poetry, have contributed. Some of his shorter poems, *e.g.*, " The Holly Tree," and " The Battle of Blenheim " still live, but his fame now rests on his vigorous prose and especially on his classic *Life of Nelson*. Like Wordsworth and Coleridge, S. began life as a democratic visionary, and was strongly influenced by the French Revolution, but gradually cooled down into a pronounced Tory. He was himself greater and better than any of his works, his life being a noble record of devotion to duty and unselfish benevolence. He held the office of Poet Laureate from 1813, and had a pension from Government. He declined a baronetcy.

Life and Correspondence (6 vols., 1849-50) by his younger son, Rev. C. Southey. *Life* by Dowden in Men of Letters (1880).

SOUTHWELL, ROBERT (1561?-1595).—Poet, *b.* at Horsham St. Faith's, Norfolk, of good Roman Catholic family, and *ed.* at Douay, Paris, and Rome, he became a Jesuit, and showed such learning and ability as to be appointed Prefect of the English Coll. In 1586 he came to England with Garnett, the superior of the English province, and became chaplain to the Countess of Arundel. His being in England for more than 40 days then rendered him liable to the punishment of death and disembowelment, and in 1592 he was apprehended and imprisoned in the Tower for three years, during which he was tortured 13 times. He was then put on trial and executed, February 22, 1595. He was the author of *St. Peter's Complaint* and *The Burning Babe*, a short poem of great imaginative power, and of several prose religious works, including *St. Mary Magdalene's Teares, A Short Rule of Good Life, The Triumphs over Death*, etc.

SPEDDING, JAMES (1808-1881).—Editor of Bacon's works, *s.* of a Cumberland squire, and *ed.* at Bury St. Edmunds and Camb., was for some years in the Colonial Office. He devoted himself to the ed. of Bacon's works, and the endeavour to clear his character against the aspersions of Macaulay and others. The former was done in conjunction with Ellis and Heath, his own being much the largest share in their great ed. (1861-74); and the latter, so far as possible, in *The Life and Letters*, entirely his own. In 1878 he brought out an abridged *Life and Times of Francis Bacon.* He strongly combated the theory that B. was the author of Shakespeare's plays. His death was caused by his being run over by a cab. He enjoyed the friendship of many of his greatest contemporaries, including Carlyle, Tennyson, and Fitzgerald.

SPEED, JOHN (1552?-1629).—Historian, *b.* at Farington, Cheshire, and brought up to the trade of a tailor, had a strong taste for history and antiquities, and wrote a *History of Great Britain* (1611), which was long the best in existence, in collecting material for which he had assistance from Cotton, Spelman, and other investigators. He also *pub.* useful maps of Great Britain and Ireland, and of various counties, etc. In 1616 appeared his *Cloud of Witnesses confirming . . . the truth of God's most holie Word.* His maps were *coll.* and with descriptions *pub.* in 1611 as *Theatre of the Empire of Great Britain.*

SPEKE, J. H. (*See under* GRANT, J. A.)

SPELMAN, SIR HENRY (1564?-1641).—Historian and antiquary, *b.* at Congham, Norfolk, studied at Camb., and entered Lincoln's Inn. He wrote valuable works on legal and ecclesiastical antiquities, including *History of Sacrilege* (*pub.* 1698), *Glossarium Archæologicum* (1626 and 1664), a glossary of obsolete law-terms, *A History of the English Councils* (1639), and *Tenures by Knight-service* (1641). His writings have furnished valuable material for subsequent historians. He sat in Parliament and on various commissions, and in recompense of his labours was voted a grant of £300.

SPENCE, JOSEPH (1699-1768).—Anecdotist, *b.* at Kingsclere, Hants, and *ed.* at Winchester and Oxf., he entered the Church, and held various preferments, including a prebend at Durham, and was Prof. of Poetry at Oxf. He wrote an *Essay on Pope's Odyssey,* which gained for him the friendship of the poet, of whose conversation he made notes, collecting likewise anecdotes of him and of other celebrities which were *pub.* in 1820, and are of great value, inasmuch as they preserve much matter illustrative of the literary history of the 18th century which would otherwise have been lost.

SPENCER, HERBERT (1820-1903).—Philosopher, *b.* at Derby, the *s.* of a teacher, from whom, and from his uncle, mentioned below, he received most of his education. His immediate family circle was strongly Dissenting in its theological atmosphere, his *f.*, originally a Methodist, having become a Quaker, while his mother remained a Wesleyan. At 13 he was sent to the care of his uncle, Thomas S., a clergyman, near Bath, but a Radical and anti-corn-law agitator. Declining a Univ. career he became a school assistant, but shortly after accepted a situation under the engineer of the London and Birmingham railway, in which he remained until the great railway crisis of 1846 threw him out of employment. Previous to this he had begun to write political articles in the *Nonconformist;* he now resolved to devote himself to journalism, and in 1848 was appointed sub-ed. of the *Economist.* Thereafter he became more and more absorbed in the consideration of the problems of sociology and the development of the doctrine of evolution as applied thereto, gradually leading up to the completion of a system of philosophy which was the work of his life. His fundamental proposition is that society, like the individual, is an organism subject to evolution, and the scope of this idea is gradually expanded so as to embrace in its sweep the whole range of cognisible phenomena. Among the books which he *pub.* in exposition of his views may be mentioned *Social Statics* (1850), *Principles of Psychology* (1855), *First Principles* (1862), *Principles of Biology* (1867), *Data of Ethics* (1879), *Principles of Sociology* (1877), *Political Institutions* (1882), and *Man versus the State* (1884). His works have been translated into most European languages—some of them into Chinese and Japanese. The most characteristic qualities of S. as a thinker are his powers of generalisation and analysis. He left an autobiography, in which he subjects his own personality to analysis with singular detachment of mind.

Life by David Duncan, LL.D., *Life* by J. A. Thompson. *See* also *Outlines of Cosmic Philosophy*, Fishe (1874), and books on S. and his philosophy by Hudson (1894), White (1897), and Macpherson (1890).

SPENCER, WILLIAM ROBERT (1769-1834).—Poet, *ed.* at Harrow and Oxf., belonged to the Whig set of Fox and Sheridan. He wrote graceful *vers de societé*, made translations from Bürger, and is best remembered by his well-known ballad of *Gelert*. After a life of extravagance he *d.* in poverty in Paris.

SPENSER, EDMUND (1552?-1599).—Poet, was *b.* in East Smithfield, London, the *s.* of John S., described as gentleman and journeyman in the art of cloth-making, who had come to London from Lancashire. In 1561 the poet was sent to Merchant Taylor's School, then newly opened, and in 1569 he proceeded to Pembroke Hall, Camb., as a sizar, taking his degree in 1576. Among his friends there were Edward Kirke, who ed. the *Shepheard's Calendar*, and Gabriel Harvey, the critic. While still at school he had contributed 14 sonnet-visions to Van der Noot's *Theatre for Worldlings* (1569). On leaving the Univ. S. went to the north, probably to visit his relations in Lancashire, and in 1578, through his friend Harvey, he became known to Leicester and his brother-in-law, Philip Sidney. The next year, 1579, saw the publication of *The Shepheard's Calendar* in 12 eclogues. It was dedicated to Sidney, who had become his friend and patron, and was received with acclamation, all who had ears for poetry perceiving that a new and great singer had arisen. The following year S. was appointed sec. to Lord Grey of Wilton, Deputy for Ireland, a strict Puritan, and accompanied him to Ireland. At the same time he appears to have begun the *Faerie Queen*. In 1581 he was appointed Registrar of Chancery, and received a grant of the Abbey and Castle of Enniscorthy, which was followed in 1586 by a grant of the Castle of Kilcolman in County Cork, a former possession of the Earls of Desmond, with 3000 acres attached. Simultaneously, however, a heavy blow fell upon him in the death of Sidney at the Battle of Zutphen. The loss of this dear friend he commemorated in his lament of *Astrophel* In 1590 he was visited by Sir Walter Raleigh, who persuaded him to come to England, and presented him to the Queen, from whom he received a pension of £50, which does not, however, appear to have been regularly paid, and on the whole his experiences of the Court did not yield him much satisfaction. In the same year his reputation as a poet was vastly augmented by the publication of the first three books of the *Faerie Queen*, dedicated to Elizabeth. The enthusiasm with which they were received led the publisher to bring out a collection of other writings of S. under the general title of *Complaints*, and including *Mother Hubbard's Tale* (a satire on the Court and on the conflict then being waged between the old faith and the new), *Teares of the Muses*, and *The Ruins of Time*. Having seen these ventures launched, S. returned to Kilcolman and wrote *Colin Clout's come Home Again*, one of the brightest and most vigorous of his poems, not, however, *pub.* until 1595. In the following year appeared his *Four Hymns*, two on *Love and Beauty* and two on *Heavenly Love and Beauty*, and the *Prothalamion* on the marriage of two daughters of the Earl of Worcester. He also *pub.* in prose his *View of Ireland*, a work full of shrewd observation and practical statesmanship. In 1594 he was *m.* to Elizabeth Boyle, whom he had courted in *Amoretti*, and his union with whom he now celebrated in the magnificent *Epithalamion*, by many regarded as his most perfect poem. In 1595 he returned to England, taking with him the second part of the *Faerie Queen*, *pub.* in 1596. In 1598 he was made Sheriff of Cork, and in the same year his fortunes suffered a final eclipse. The rebellion of Tyrone broke out, his castle was burned, and in the conflagration his youngest child, an infant, perished, he himself with his wife and remaining children escaping with difficulty. He joined the President, Sir T. Norris, who sent him with despatches to London, where he suddenly *d.* on January 16, 1599, as was long believed in extreme destitution. This, however, happily appears to be at least doubtful. He was buried in Westminster Abbey near Chaucer, and a monument was erected to his memory in 1620 by the Countess of Dorset.

The position of S. in English poetry is below Chaucer, Shakespeare, and Milton only. The first far excels him in narrative and constructive power and in humour, and the last in austere grandeur of conception; but for richness and beauty of imagination and exquisite sweetness of music he is unsurpassed except by Shakespeare. He has been called the poets' poet, a title which he well merits, not only by virtue of the homage which all the more imaginative poets have yielded him, but because of the almost unequalled influence he has exercised upon the whole subsequent course and expression of English poetry, which he enriched with the stanza which bears his name, and which none since him have used with more perfect mastery. His faults are prolixity, indirectness, and want of constructive power, and consequently the sustained sweetness and sumptuousness of his verse are apt to cloy. His great work, the *Faerie Queen*, is but a gorgeous fragment, six books out of a projected twelve; but probably few or none of its readers have regretted its incompleteness. In it Protestantism and Puritanism receive their most poetic and imaginative presentation and vindication.

SUMMARY.—*B.* 1552, *ed.* Merchant Taylor's School and Camb., became known to Leicester and Sir P. Sidney 1578, *pub. Shepheard's Calendar* 1579, appointed sec. to Lord Deputy of Ireland 1580, and began *Faerie Queen*, receives various appointments and grants

1581-6, *pub. Astrophel* in memory of Sidney 1586, visited by Raleigh and by him presented to Queen Elizabeth, who pensioned him 1590, and in same year *pub.* first three books of *Faerie Queen, Teares of Muses,* etc., writes *Colin Clout, pub.* 1595, and in 1596 *pub. Four Hymns* and *Prothalamion, m.* E. Boyle 1594, whom he had courted in *Amoretti,* and now celebrated in the *Epithalamion,* returned to England 1595, Sheriff of Cork 1598, in which year the rebellion broke out and ruined his fortunes, returned to London and *d.* 1599.

There have been very numerous ed. of the works, among which may be mentioned the Globe (1899), and Dr. Grosart's (10 vols., 1882-84). There is an excellent biography by Dean Church (1879).

SPOTTISWOOD, JOHN (1565-1639).—Historian, *s.* of John S., minister of Midcalder and Superintendent of Lothian. Entering the Church he gained the favour of James VI., and was his chief instrument in his endeavours to restore Episcopal church-government in Scotland. He became Archbishop successively of Glasgow and St. Andrews, and in 1635 Lord Chancellor of Scotland. On the rising caused by the introduction of the service-book, he had to flee from Scotland, and was excommunicated by the General Assembly (1638). He wrote a *History of the Church and State of Scotland, pub.* 1655. It is, of course, written from the Episcopalian standpoint, as Calderwood's is from the Presbyterian.

SPRAGUE, CHARLES (1791-1875).—Poet, *b.* at Boston, Mass., had some reputation as a writer of prize poems, odes, and domestic poems. To the first class belong *Curiosity* and *Shakespeare Ode,* and to the latter, *The Family Meeting* and *I see Thee Still,* an elegy on his sister.

SPRAT, THOMAS (1635-1713).—Divine and writer of memoirs, *b.* at Beaminster, Dorset, *ed.* at Oxf., was a mathematician, and one of the group of scientific men among whom the Royal Society, of which he was one of the first members and the historian, had its origin. He wrote a Life of his friend Cowley the poet, and an account of Young's plot for the restoration of James II. His *History of the Royal Society* is his principal work, but he also wrote poems, and had a high reputation as a preacher. His literary style gives him a distinguished place among English writers. He held various high preferments, and *d.* Bishop of Rochester.

SPURGEON, CHARLES HADDON (1834-1892).—*B.* at Kelvedon, Essex, left the Independents and joined the Baptist communion and became, at the age of 20, pastor of New Park Street Chapel, London, where he attained an unprecedented popularity. In 1859 the Metropolitan Tabernacle was erected for him. He was a decided Calvinist in his theological views, and was strongly opposed to modern critical movements. He possessed in an eminent degree two of the great requisites of effective oratory, a magnificent voice and a command of pure idiomatic Saxon English. His sermons, composed and *pub.* weekly, had an enormous circulation, and were regularly translated into several languages. In addition to his pastoral labours he superintended an almshouse, a pastor's coll., and an orphanage; and he was likewise a voluminous author, publishing, in addition to his sermons, numerous works, including *The Treasury of David* (a commentary on the Psalms).

STANHOPE, PHILIP HENRY, 5TH EARL STANHOPE (1805-1875).—Historian, was *b.* at Walmer, and *ed.* at Oxf. He sat in the House of Commons for Wootton Bassett and Hertford, held some minor official appointments under Peel, and identified himself with many useful measures, specially in regard to literature and art. His writings, which are all remarkable for industrious collection of facts, careful and impartial sifting and weighing of evidence, and a clear, sober, and agreeable style, include *History of England from the Peace of Utrecht to the Peace of Versailles* (1836-63), and histories of the *War of the Spanish Succession* (1832), and of the *Reign of Queen Anne* (1870), besides Lives of the younger Pitt (1861) and of Lord Chesterfield. As an author he is best known as Viscount Mahon.

STANLEY, ARTHUR PENRHYN (1815-1881).—Historian, biographer, and theologian, *s.* of Edward S., Bishop of Norwich, *b.* at Alderley, Cheshire, of which his *f.* was then rector, *ed.* at Rugby and Oxf., became a Fellow of Univ. Coll. Taking orders in 1839 he became Canon of Canterbury 1851, and of Christ Church 1858, and Dean of Westminster 1864. He was also Prof. of Ecclesiastical History at Oxf. 1856. His ecclesiastical position was Erastian and latitudinarian, and his practical aim in Church politics comprehension. He gave great offence to the High Church party by his championing of Colenso, W. G. Ward, Jowett, and others, by his preaching in the pulpits of the Church of Scotland and in other ways, and his latitudinarianism made him equally obnoxious to many others. On the other hand, his singular personal charm and the fascination of his literary style secured for him a very wide popularity. He was a prolific author, his works including *Life of Dr. Arnold* (of Rugby) (1844), whose favourite pupil he was, and *Memorials of Canterbury* (1854), *Sinai and Palestine* (1855), *Lectures on the Eastern Church* (1861), *History of the Jewish Church* (1863, etc.), *Historical Memorials of Westminster Abbey* (1867), *Lectures on the History of the Church of Scotland* (1872), besides various commentaries. In his historical writings he aimed rather at conveying a vivid and picturesque general effect than at minute accuracy of detail or philosophical views. His masterpiece is his *Life of Dr. Arnold*, which is one of the great biographies in the language. His wife was Lady Augusta Bruce, to whom he was *m.* in 1868.

STANLEY, SIR HENRY MORTON (1841-1904).—Traveller in Africa, *b.* in America, went to find, and found, Livingstone, and wrote an account of his adventures in the quest, *How I found Livingstone.* Other works were *In Darkest Africa* and *Through the Dark Continent.*

STANLEY, THOMAS (1625-1678).—Philosopher and scholar, connected with the Derby family, *ed.* at Camb., was the author of some poems and of a biographical *History of Philosophy* (4 vols., 1655-62). He was learned in the classics, and translated from the Latin and late Greek as well as from the Italian and Portuguese, and ed. Æschylus. His poetry is thoughtful and gracefully expressed.

STANYHURST, RICHARD (1547-1618).—Translator, was at Oxf., and studied law at Furnivall's Inn and Lincoln's Inn. He collaborated with Holinshed (*q.v.*). His principal literary achievement was a grotesquely stiff, clumsy, and prosaic translation of the first four books of the *Æneid* into English hexameters. He also translated some of the Psalms.

STEDMAN, EDMUND CLARENCE, L.H.D., LL.D., (1833-1908).—American poet and critic. *Poems Lyric and Idyllic* (1860), *Alice of Monmouth* (1864), *The Blameless Prince* (1869), *Victorian Poets* (1875-87), *Lyrics and Idylls* (1879), *Poets of America* (1885), *Victorian Anthology* (1896), *American Anthology* (1896), etc.

STEELE, SIR RICHARD (1672-1729).—Essayist and dramatist, *s.* of a Dublin attorney, who *d.* when his *s.* was 5 years old, was, on the nomination of the Duke of Ormond, sent to the Charterhouse School, where his friendship with Addison began, and thence went to Oxf., but left without taking a degree, and enlisted in the Horse Guards, for which he was disinherited by a rich relation. He, however, gained the favour of his colonel, Lord Cutts, himself a poet, and rose to the rank of captain. With the view of setting before himself a high ideal of conduct (to which unhappily he was never able to attain), he at this time wrote a treatise on morals entitled *The Christian Hero* (1701). Abandoning this vein, he next produced three comedies, *The Funeral, or Grief à la Mode* (1702), *The Tender Husband* (1703), and *The Lying Lover* (1704). Two years later he was appointed Gentleman Waiter to Prince George of Denmark, and in 1707 he was made Gazetteer; and in the same year he *m.* as his second wife Mary Scurlock, his "dear Prue," who seems, however, to have been something of a termagant. She had considerable means, but the incorrigible extravagance of S. soon brought on embarrassment. In 1709 he laid the foundations of his fame by starting the *Tatler*, the first of those periodicals which are so characteristic a literary feature of that age. In this he had the invaluable assistance of Addison, who contributed 42 papers out of a total of 271, and helped with others. The *Tatler* was followed by the *Spectator*, in which Addison co-operated to a still greater extent. It was even a greater success, and ran to 555 numbers, exclusive of a brief revival by Addison in which S. had no part, and in its turn was followed by the *Guardian*. It is on his essays in these that the literary fame of S. rests. With less refinement and delicacy of wit than Addison, he had perhaps more knowledge of life, and a wider sympathy, and like him he had a sincere desire for the reformation of morals and manners. In the keen political strife of the times he fought stoutly and honestly on the Whig side, one result of which was that he lost his office of Gazetteer, and was in 1714 expelled from the House of Commons to which he had just been elected. The next year gave a favourable turn to his fortunes. The accession of George I. brought back the Whigs, and S. was appointed to various offices, including a commissionership on forfeited estates in Scotland, which took him to Edinburgh, where he was welcomed by all the *literati* there. Nothing, however, could keep him out of financial embarrassments, and other troubles followed: his wife *d.*; differences arose with Addison, who *d.* before a reconciliation could be effected.

The remaining years were clouded by financial troubles and ill-health. His last work was a play, *The Conscious Lovers* (1722). He left London and lived at Hereford and at Carmarthen, where he *d.* after a partial loss of his faculties from paralysis.

Lives by Austin Dobson (1886) and G. A. Aitken (1889). Ed., *Plays* by Aitken (1893), Essays (selected) Clarendon Press (1885), *Tatler*, Aitken (1898), *Spectator*, H. Morley (1868), Gregory Smith (1897-8), Aitken (1898).

STEEVENS, GEORGE (1736-1800).—Shakespearian commentator, *ed.* at Eton and Camb. He issued various reprints of quarto ed. of Shakespeare, and assisted Dr. Johnson in his ed., and also in his *Lives of the Poets*. In 1793 he himself brought out a new ed. of Shakespeare, in which he dealt somewhat freely with the text. He was in constant controversy with Ritson and other literary antiquaries, and was also an acute detector of literary forgeries, including those of Chatterton and Ireland.

STEEVENS, GEORGE WARRINGTON (1869-1900).—Journalist and miscellaneous writer, *b.* at Sydenham, and *ed.* at City of London School and Oxf., took to journalism, in which he distinguished himself by his clearness of vision and vivid style. Connected successively with the *National Observer*, the *Pall Mall Gazette*, and the *Daily Mail*, he utilised the articles which appeared in these and other publications in various books, such as *The Land of the Dollar* (America) (1897), *With Kitchener to Kartoum*, and *The Tragedy of Dreyfus*. His most striking work, however, was *Monologues of the Dead* (1895). He went as war correspondent to South Africa in 1900, and *d.* of enteric fever at Ladysmith.

STEPHEN, SIR JAMES (1789-1859).—Statesman and historical writer, *s.* of James S., Master in Chancery, *ed.* at Camb., and called to the Bar at Lincoln's Inn 1811. After practising with success, accepted appointment of permanent counsel to Colonial Office and Board of Trade 1825, and was subsequently, 1826-47, permanent Under-Sec. for the Colonies, in which capacity he exercised an immense influence on the colonial policy of the empire, and did much to bring about the abolition of the slave trade. Impaired health led to his resignation, when he was made K.C.B. and a Privy Councillor. He was afterwards Prof. of Modern History at Camb. 1849-59, and of the same subject at the East India Coll. at Haileybury 1855-57. He wrote *Essays in Ecclesiastical Biography* (1849) and *Lectures on the History of France* (1852).

STEPHEN, SIR LESLIE (1832-1904).—Biographer and critic, *s.* of the above, was *b.* in London, and *ed.* at Eton, King's Coll., London, and Camb., where he obtained a tutorial Fellowship, and took orders. He came under the influence of Mill, Darwin, and H. Spencer, and devoted himself largely to the study of economics. His religious views having undergone a change, he gave up the clerical character and his Fellowship, and became a pronounced Agnostic. In 1865 he definitely adopted a literary career, and contributed to the *Saturday Review*, *Fraser's Magazine*, and other periodicals. In 1873 he *pub.* a collection of his essays as *Free Thinking and Plain Speaking*, which he followed up with *An*

Agnostic's Apology (1893). He became ed. in 1871 of the *Cornhill Magazine*, in which appeared the essays afterwards *coll.* as *Hours in a Library* (3 series, 1874-79). His chief work was *The History of English Thought in the Eighteenth Century* (1876-81). He also wrote *Science of Ethics* (1882), and biographies of *Dr. Johnson* (1878), *Pope* (1880), *Swift* (1882), and *George Eliot* (English Men of Letters Series). In 1882 he became ed. of the *Dictionary of National Biography*, to which he devoted much labour, besides contributing many of the principal articles. *The English Utilitarians* appeared in 1900. As a biographical and critical writer he holds a very high place. His first wife was a *dau.* of Thackeray. In recognition of his literary eminence he was made a K.C.B.

Life and Letters by F. W. Maitland (1906).

STEPHENS, THOMAS (1821-1875).—Welsh historian and critic, *b.* at Pont Nedd Fechan, Glamorganshire, *s.* of a shoemaker. His works include *The Literature of the Kymry* (1849), *The History of Trial by Jury in Wales*, and an essay in which he demolished the claim of the Welsh under Madoc to the discovery of America. He also wrote on the life and works of the bard Aneurin. The critical methods which he adopted in his works often made him unpopular with the less discriminating enthusiasts for the glory of Wales, but he earned the respect of serious scholars.

STERLING, JOHN (1806-1844).—Essayist and miscellaneous writer, *s.* of Edward S., a well-known writer in the *Times*, was *b.* in Bute, and *ed.* at Glasgow and Camb. At the latter he became acquainted with a group of brilliant men, including F. D. Maurice, Trench, and Monckton Milnes. He took orders and became curate to Julius Hare (*q.v.*); but intellectual difficulties and indifferent health led to his resignation within a year, and the rest of his life was passed in alternating between England and warmer climes. He wrote for *Blackwood's Magazine*, the *London and Westminster*, and *Quarterly Reviews*, and *pub. Essays and Tales*, *The Election*, a humorous poem, *Strafford*, a tragedy, and *Richard Cœur de Lion*, a serio-comic poem of which three books out of eight were *pub.* His memory, perpetuated in a remarkable memoir by Carlyle, lives rather by what he was than by anything he did. His character and intellect appear to have exercised a singular influence on the eminent men he numbered among his friends.

STERNE, LAURENCE (1713-1768).—Novelist, *s.* of an officer in the army, and the great-grandson of an Archbishop of York, was *b.* at Clonmel, where his father's regiment happened to be stationed, and passed part of his boyhood in Ireland. At the age of 10 he was handed over to a relation, Mr. Sterne of Elvington in Yorkshire, who put him to school at Halifax, and thereafter sent him to Camb. He entered the Church, a profession for which he was very indifferently fitted, and through family influence procured the living of Sutton, Yorkshire. In 1741 he *m.* a lady—Miss Lumley—whose influence obtained for him in addition an adjacent benefice, and he also became a prebendary of York. It was not until 1760 that the first two vols. of his famous novel, *Tristram Shandy*, appeared. Its peculiar and original style of humour, its whimsicality, and perhaps also its defiance of conventionality, and even its frequent lapses into indecorum, achieved for it an immediate and immense popularity. S. went up to London and became the lion of the day. The third and fourth vols. appeared in 1761, the fifth and sixth in 1762, the seventh and eighth in 1765, and the last in 1767. Meanwhile he had *pub.* the *Sermons of Mr. Yorick* (1760), and his remaining work, *The Sentimental Journey* appeared in 1768. From the time of his finding himself a celebrity his parishioners saw but little of him, his time being passed either in the gaieties of London or in travelling on the Continent. Latterly he was practically separated from his wife and only *dau.*, to the former of whom his behaviour had been anything but exemplary. His health, which had begun to give way soon after his literary career had commenced, finally broke down, and he fell into a consumption, of which he *d.* in London on March 18, 1768, utterly alone and unattended. His body was followed to the grave by one coach containing his publisher and another gentleman; and it was exhumed and appeared in a few days upon the table of the anatomical professor at Camb. He *d.* in debt, but a subscription was raised for his wife and *dau.*, the latter of whom *m.* a Frenchman, and is said to have perished under the guillotine. Worthless as a man, S. possessed undoubted genius. He had wit, originality, and pathos, though the last not seldom runs into mawkishness, and an exquisitely delicate and glancing style. He has contributed some immortal characters to English fiction, including Uncle Toby and Corporal Trim. His great faults as a writer are affectation and a peculiarly deliberate kind of indecency, which his profession renders all the more offensive; and he was by no means scrupulous in adopting, without acknowledgment, the good things of previous writers.

Works ed. by Prof. Saintsbury (6 vols., 1894). *See* also Macmillan's Library of English classics. *Lives* by P. Fitzgerald (1896) and H. D. Traill in English Men of Letters Series.

STERNHOLD, THOMAS (1500-1549), HOPKINS, JOHN (*d.* 1570).—Were associated in making the metrical version of the Psalms, which was attached to the Prayer-book, and was for 200 years the chief hymn-book of the Church of England. It is a commonplace and tame rendering. The collection was not completed until 1562. It was gradually superseded by the version of Tate and Brady.

STEVENSON, ROBERT LOUIS (1850-1894).—Novelist and essayist, was *b.* at Edin., the *s.* of Thomas S., a distinguished civil engineer. His health was extremely delicate. He was destined for the engineering profession, in which his family had for two generations been eminent, but having neither inclination nor physical strength for it, he in 1871 exchanged it for law, and was called to the Bar in 1875, but never practised. From childhood his interests had been literary, and in 1871 he began to contribute to the *Edinburgh University Magazine* and the *Portfolio.* A tour in a canoe in 1876 led to the publication in 1878 of his first book, *An Inland Voyage.* In the same year, *The New Arabian Nights*, afterwards separately *pub.*, appeared in magazines, and in 1879 he brought out *Travels with a Donkey in the Cevennes.* In that year he went to California and *m.* Mrs. Osbourne. Returning to Europe in 1880 he entered upon a period of productiveness which, in view of his wretched health, was, both as regards quantity and worth, highly remarkable. The year 1881 was marked by his unsuccessful candidature for the Chair of Constitutional Law and History at Edin., and by the publication of *Virginibus Puerisque*. Other works followed in rapid succession. *Treasure Island* (1882), *Prince Otto* and *The Child's Garden of Verse* (1885), *Dr. Jekyll and Mr. Hyde* and *Kidnapped* (1886), *Underwoods* (poetry), *Memories and Portraits* (essays), and *The Merry Men*, a collection of short stories (1887), and in 1888 *The Black Arrow*. In 1887 he went to America, and in the following year visited the South Sea Islands where, in Samoa, he settled in 1890, and where he *d.* and is buried. In 1889 *The Master of Ballantrae* appeared, in 1892 *Across the Plains* and *The Wrecker*, in 1893 *Island Nights Entertainments* and *Catriona*, and in 1894 *The Ebb Tide* in collaboration with his step-son, Mr. Lloyd Osbourne. By this time his health was completely broken, but to the last he continued the struggle, and left the fragments *St. Ives* and *Weir of Hermiston*, the latter containing some of his best work. They were *pub.* in 1897. Though the originality and power of S.'s writings was recognised from the first by a select few, it was only slowly that he caught the ear of the general public. The tide may be said to have turned with the publication of *Treasure Island* in 1882, which at once gave him an assured place among the foremost imaginative writers of the day. His greatest power is, however, shown in those works which deal with Scotland in the 18th century, such as *Kidnapped*, *Catriona*, and *Weir of Hermiston*, and in those, *e.g.*, *The Child's Garden of Verse*, which exhibit his extraordinary insight into the psychology of child-life; *Dr. Jekyll and Mr. Hyde* is a marvellously powerful and subtle psychological story, and some of his short tales also are masterpieces. Of these *Thrawn Janet* and *Will of the Mill* may be mentioned as examples in widely different kinds. His excursions into the drama in collaboration with W. E. Henley—*Deacon Brodie*, *Macaire*, *Admiral Guinea*, *Beau Austin*,—added nothing to his reputation. His style is singularly fascinating, graceful, various, subtle, and with a charm all its own.

Works, Edinburgh ed. (28 vols., 1894-98). *Life* by Grahame Balfour (1901), *Letters*, S. Colvin (1899).

STEWART, DUGALD (1753-1828).—Philosopher, *s.* of Matthew S., Prof. of Mathematics at Edin., was *b.* in the Coll. buildings, and at the age of 19 began to assist his *f.* in his classes, receiving the appointment of regular assistant two years later. In 1785 he became Prof. of Moral Philosophy, and rendered the chair illustrious by his learning and eloquence, his pupils including Lords Palmerston, Russell, and Lansdowne. S. was, however, rather a brilliant expositor than an original thinker, and in the main followed Reid (*q.v.*). His works include *Philosophy of the Human Mind*, in three vols., *pub.* respectively in 1792, 1813, and 1827, *Outlines of Moral Philosophy* (1793), *Philosophical Essays* (1810), *Dissertation on the Progress of Metaphysical and Ethical Philosophy* (1815, part II. 1821), and *View of the Active and Moral Powers of Man*. He also wrote memoirs of Robertson the historian, Adam Smith, and Reid. The Whig party, which he had always supported, on their accession to power, created for him the office of Gazette-writer for Scotland, in recognition of his services to philosophy. His later years were passed in retirement at Kinneil House on the Forth. His works were ed. by Sir William Hamilton.

STILLINGFLEET, EDWARD (1635-1699). — Theologian, *b.* at Cranbourne, Dorsetshire, *ed.* at Camb., entered the Church, and held many preferments, including a Royal Chaplaincy, the Deanery of St. Paul's (1678), and the Bishopric of Worcester (1689). He was a frequent speaker in the House of Lords, and had considerable influence as a Churchman. A keen controversialist, he wrote many treatises, including *The Irenicum* (advocating compromise with the Presbyterians), *Antiquities of the British Churches*, and *The Unreasonableness of Separation.* S. was a good and honest man and had the respect of his strongest opponents.

STIRLING, JAMES HUTCHISON (1820-1909).—Philosopher, *b.* in Glasgow, and *ed.* there and at Edin., where he studied medicine, which he practised until the death of his *f.* in 1851, after which he devoted himself to philosophy. His *Secret of Hegel* (1865) gave a great impulse to the study and understanding of the Hegelian philosophy both at home and in America, and was also accepted as a work of authority in Germany and Italy. Other works, all characterised by keen philosophical insight and masterly power of exposition are *Complete Text-book to Kant* (1881), *Philosophy and Theology* (1890), *What is Thought? or the Problem of Philosophy* (1900), and *The Categories* (1903). Less abstruse are *Jerrold, Tennyson, and Macaulay* (1868), *Burns in Drama* (1878), and *Philosophy in the Poets* (1885).

STIRLING, WILLIAM ALEXANDER, EARL OF (1567-1640).—Poet, *s.* of A. of Menstrie, and *cr.* Earl of S. by Charles I., 1633, was a courtier, and held many offices of state. He studied at Glasgow and Leyden, and wrote among other poems, partly in Latin, sonnets and four *Monarchicke Tragedies, Darius, Crœsus, The Alexandræan Tragedy*, and *Julius Cæsar* (1603-7), the motive of which is the fall of ambition, and which, though dignified, have little inspiration. He also assisted James I. in his metrical version of the Psalms. He *d.* insolvent in London. The grant of Nova Scotia which he had received became valueless owing to the French conquests in that region.

STIRLING-MAXWELL, SIR WILLIAM (1818-1878).—Historian and writer on art, *s.* of Archibald Stirling of Keir, succeeded to the estates and title of his uncle, Sir John Maxwell of Pollok, as well as to Keir, *ed.* at Camb., afterwards travelled much. He sat in the House of Commons for Perthshire, which he twice represented, 1852-68 and 1874-80, served on various commissions and public bodies, and was Lord Rector successively of the Univ. of St. Andrews and Edin. and Chancellor of that of Glasgow. His works include *Annals of the Artists of Spain* (1848), *The Cloister Life of the Emperor Charles V.* (1852), and *Don John of Austria*, *pub.* posthumously in 1885. They were all distinguished by research and full information, and the last two are standard authorities He *m.* as his second wife the Hon. Mrs. Norton (*q.v.*).

STOCKTON, FRANCIS RICHARD (1834-1902).—*B.* at Philadelphia, was an engraver and journalist. He became well known as a writer of stories for children, and of amusing books of which *Rudder Grange* (1879) is the best known. *The Lady and the Tiger* was also highly popular. Others are *Adventures of Captain Horne, Mrs. Null, Casting Away of Mrs. Lecks and Mrs. Aleshine, The Hundredth Man, Great Stone of Sardis, Captain's Toll-gate,* etc. His work was very unequal in interest.

STODDARD, RICHARD HENRY (1825-1903).—Poet, *b.* at Hingham, Mass., worked in a foundry, and afterwards in New York Custom House, wrote a Life of Washington, but is chiefly known as a poet, his poetical works including *Songs in Summer* (1857), *The King's Bell, The Lion's Cub,* etc.

STORER, THOMAS (1571-1604).—Poet, *b.* in London, and *ed.* at Oxf., wrote a long poem, *The Life and Death of Thomas Wolsey, Cardinal.*

STORY, WILLIAM WETMORE (1819-1895).—Sculptor, poet, etc., *b.* at Salem, Mass., was intended for the law, but became a sculptor and an eminent man of letters. His writings include *Roba di Roma* (1862), *The Tragedy of Nero* (1875), *The Castle of St. Angelo* (1877), *He and She* (1883), *Conversations in a Studio, A Poet's Portfolio* (1894), etc.

STOW, JOHN (1525-1605).—Historian and antiquary, *b.* in London, *s.* of a tailor, and brought up to the same trade. He had, however, an irresistible taste for transcribing and collecting ancient documents, and pursuing antiquarian and historical researches, to which he ultimately entirely devoted himself. This he was enabled to do partly through the munificence of Archbishop Parker. He made large collections of old books and manuscripts, and wrote and ed. several works of importance and authority, including *The Woorkes of Geoffrey Chaucer, Summarie of Englyshe Chronicles* (1561), afterwards called *Annales of England,* ed. of the chronicles of Matthew Paris and others, of Holinshed's *Chronicle,* and *A Survey of London* (1598). It is sad to think that the only reward of his sacrifices and labours in the public interest was a patent from James I. to collect "among our loving subjects their voluntary contributions and kind gratuities."

STOWE, MRS. HARRIET BEECHER (1811?-1896).—Novelist and miscellaneous writer, *dau.* of Dr. Lyman Beecher, a well-known American clergyman, and sister of Henry Ward B., one of the most popular preachers whom America has produced, was *b.* at Litchfield, Connecticut, in 1811 or 1812. After spending some years as a teacher, she *m.* the Rev. Calvin E. Stowe. Up till 1852 all she had written was a little vol. of stories which failed to attract attention. In that year, at the suggestion of a sister-in-law, she decided to write something against slavery, and produced *Uncle Tom's Cabin,* which originally appeared in serial form in a magazine, *The National Era.* It did not at the time receive much attention, but on its appearance in a separate form it took the world by storm. Its sale soon reached 400,000 copies, and the reprints have probably reached a far greater number. It was translated into numerous foreign languages, and had a powerful effect in hurrying on the events which ultimately resulted in emancipation. Her later works include *Dred, The Minister's Wooing, Agnes of Sorrento, The Pearl of Orr's Island,* and *Old Town Folks.* Some of these, especially the last, are in a literary sense much superior to *Uncle Tom's Cabin,* but none of them had more than an ordinary success. In 1869 an article on Lord Byron involved her in a somewhat unfortunate controversy.

STRICKLAND, AGNES (1796 or 1806-1874).—Historical writer, *dau.* of Thomas S., of Royden Hall, Suffolk, was *ed.* by her *f.*, and began her literary career with a poem, *Worcester Field,* followed by *The Seven Ages of Woman* and *Demetrius.* Abandoning poetry she next produced among others *Historical Tales of Illustrious British Children* (1833), *The Pilgrims of Walsingham* (1835), *Tales and Stories from History* (1836). Her chief works, however, are *Lives of the Queens of England from the Norman Conquest,* and *Lives of the Queens of Scotland, and English Princesses, etc.* (8 vols., 1850-59), *Lives of the Bachelor Kings of England* (1861), and *Letters of Mary Queen of Scots,* in some of which she was assisted by her sister Elizabeth. Though laborious and conscientious she lacked the judicial faculty, and her style does not rise above mediocrity.

STRODE, WILLIAM (1600-1645).—Poet, only *s.* of Philip S., who belonged to an old Devonshire family, he was *b.* at Plympton, Devonshire, and showing studious tendencies, was sent to Westminster School and Oxf. While at the Univ. he began to manifest his poetic talents, and generally distinguished himself, being elected in 1629 Public Orator. He took orders and, on Richard Corbet (*q.v.*) becoming Bishop of Oxf., became his chaplain. Later he was Rector of E. Bredenham, Norfolk, and of Badley, Northants, and Canon of Christ Church. On the outbreak of the Civil War he attached himself warmly to the cause of the King. He was a High Churchman, and had a reputation as "a witty and sententious preacher, an exquisite orator, and an eminent poet." It is therefore singular that, until the recovery of his poems by Mr. B. Dobell, he had fallen into absolute oblivion. As a poet he shines most in lyrics and elegies. With much of the artificiality of his age he shows gracefulness, a feeling for the country, and occasional gleams of tenderness. His play, *The Floating Island,* a political allegory, was produced in 1633 and played before the Court then on a visit to Oxf., where it was a subject of complaint that it had more moralising than amusement. Mr. Dobell, who ed. his poems in 1907, claims for S. the poem on "Melancholy" ("Hence all you vain delights"), hitherto attributed to Fletcher.

STRYPE, JOHN (1643-1737).—Ecclesiastical historian, *b.* at Hackney, and *ed.* at St. Paul's School and Camb., took orders and, among other livings, held the Rectory of Low Leyton, Essex, for upwards of 60 years. He made a large collection of original documents, chiefly relating to the Tudor period, and was a voluminous author. Among his works are *Memorials of Archbishop Cranmer* (1694), *Life of Sir Thomas Smith, Secretary of State to*

Edward VI. and Elizabeth (1698), *Annals of the Reformation* (1709-31), and *Ecclesiastical Memorials* (1721); besides Lives of Bishop Aylmer and Archbishops Grindal, Parker, and Whitgift. S., who was a painstaking and honest, but dull and unmethodical, writer, remains an authority.

STUART, GILBERT (1742-1786).—Historical writer, *s.* of George S., Prof. of Humanity (Latin) at Edin. Among his publications were *An Historical Dissertation on the English Constitution* (1768), *Discourse on the Government and Laws of England* (1772), *A View of Society in Europe* (1778), and a *History of Scotland* (1782). He was a man of extremely jealous and implacable temper, and made venomous attacks on the historical works of Robertson and Henry. His own writings, though well-written, are inaccurate.

STUBBS, WILLIAM (1825-1901).—Historian, *s.* of a solicitor, *b.* at Knaresborough, Yorkshire, and *ed.* there and at the Grammar School of Ripon, and Oxf. In 1848 he became a Fellow of Trinity Coll., and in the same year took orders and was appointed to the coll. living of Navestock in Essex, where he remained for 16 years, during which he began his historical researches, and *pub.* his earlier works. His first publication was *Hymnale Secundum Usum Sarum.* In 1858 appeared *Registrum Sacrum Anglicanum,* a calendar of English bishops from Augustine; and then followed ed. of several Chronicles in the Rolls Series. The learning and critical insight displayed in these works commanded the attention and admiration of historical scholars both at home and on the Continent. In 1862 he was appointed librarian of Lambeth Palace, and in 1866 Prof. of Modern History at Oxf. There he *pub.* in 1870 his *Select Charters,* and his chief work, *The Constitutional History of England* (3 vols., 1874-78), which at once became the standard authority on its subject. It deals with the period preceding that with which the great work of Hallam begins. In 1879 he was appointed a Canon of St. Paul's, and in 1884 Bishop of Chester, whence he was translated five years later to Oxf. As an active prelate he was necessarily largely withdrawn from his historical researches; but at Chester he ed. two vols. of William of Malmesbury. S. was greater as a historian than as a writer, but he brought to his work sound judgment, insight, accuracy, and impartiality. He was a member of the French and Prussian Academies, and had the Prussian Order "Pour le Mérite" conferred upon him. Since his death his prefaces to the Rolls Series have been *pub.* separately.

STUKELEY, WILLIAM (1687-1765).—Antiquary, *ed.* at Camb., and after practising as a physician took orders in 1729 and held benefices at Stamford and in London. He made antiquarian tours through England, and was one of the founders of the Society of Antiquaries, to which he acted as sec. He *pub. Itinerarium Curiosum* (1724) and *Stonehenge* (1740). He made a special study of Druidism, and was called "the Arch-Druid."

SUCKLING, SIR JOHN (1609-1642).—Poet, *s.* of a knight who had held office as Sec. of State and Comptroller of the Household to James I., was *b.* at Whitton, Middlesex, *ed.* at Camb., and thereafter went to Gray's Inn. On the death of his *f.* in 1627, he inherited large estates. After travelling in France and Italy, he is said to have served for a short time under Gustavus Adolphus. On his return he was knighted, and went to Court, where his wealth, generosity, and wit made him a general favourite. When Charles I. was moving against the Scots S. fitted out a gorgeously appointed troop for his service which, however, were said to have fled at first sight of the Scots army at Duns, an exploit which is ridiculed in the ballad of *Sir John Suckling's Campaign.* He got into trouble in connection with a plot to rescue Strafford from the Tower, and fled to the Continent. He *d.* at Paris, it is now believed by his own hand. He was a noted gambler, and has the distinction of being the inventor of the game of cribbage. He wrote four plays, *Aglaura* (1637), *Brennoralt* (1646), *The Goblins,* and *The Sad One* (unfinished), now forgotten; his fame rests on his songs and ballads, including *The Wedding,* distinguished by a gay and sparkling wit, and a singular grace of expression.

SURREY, HENRY HOWARD, EARL OF (1517?-1547).—Poet, *s.* of Thomas H., 3rd Duke of Norfolk, was *ed.* by John Clerke, a learned and travelled scholar, and sec. to his *f.* He became attached to the Court, was cup-bearer to the King (Henry VIII.), ewerer at the Coronation, and Earl Marshall at the trial of Anne Boleyn. In 1542 he was made a Knight of the Garter a few weeks after the execution of his cousin, Queen Catherine Howard. He suffered imprisonment more than once for being implicated in quarrels and brawls, did a good deal of fighting in Scotland and France, and was the last victim of Henry's insensate jealousy, being beheaded on a frivolous charge of conspiring against the succession of Edward VI. The death of Henry saved Norfolk from the same fate. S. shares with Sir Thomas Wyatt (*q.v.*) the honour of being the true successor of Chaucer in English poetry, and he has the distinction of being, in his translation of the *Æneid,* the first to introduce blank verse, and, with Wyatt, the sonnet. The poems of S., though well known in courtly circles, were not *pub.* during his life; 40 of them appeared in *Tottel's Miscellany* in 1557. He also paraphrased part of Ecclesiastes and a few of the Psalms. The Geraldine of his sonnets was Elizabeth Fitzgerald, *dau.* of the Earl of Kildare, then a lonely child at Court, her *f.* being imprisoned in the Tower.

SURTEES, ROBERT SMITH (1802-1864).—Sporting novelist, a country gentleman of Durham, who was in business as a solicitor, but not succeeding, started in 1831 the *Sporting Magazine.* Subsequently he took to writing sporting novels, which were illustrated by John Leech. Among them are *Mr. Sponge's Sporting Tour, Ask Mamma, Plain or Ringlets,* and *Mr. Facey Romford's Hounds.*

SWIFT, JONATHAN (1667-1745).—Satirist, was *b.* at Dublin of English parents. Dryden was his cousin, and he also claimed kin with Herrick. He was a posthumous child, and was brought up in circumstances of extreme poverty. He was sent to school at Kilkenny, and afterwards went to Trinity Coll., Dublin, where he gave no evidence of ability, but displayed a turbulent and unruly temper, and only obtained a degree by "special grace." After the Revolution he joined his mother, then resident at Leicester, by whose influence he was admitted to the household of Sir William Temple (*q.v.*) at Moor Park, Lady T. being her distant kinswoman. Here he acted as sec., and having access to a well-stocked library, made good use of his opportunities, and became a close student. At Moor Park he met many distinguished men, including William III., who offered him a troop of horse; he also met Esther Johnson (Stella), a natural *dau.* of Sir William, who was afterwards to enter so largely into his life. Dissatisfied, apparently, that Temple did not do more for his advancement, he left his service in 1694 and returned to Ireland, where he took orders, and obtained the small living of Kilroot, near Belfast. While there he wrote his *Tale of a Tub*, one of the most consummate pieces of satire in any language, and *The Battle of the Books*, with reference to the "Phalaris" controversy (*see* Bentley), which were *pub.* together in 1704. In 1698 he threw up his living at the request of Temple, who felt the want of his society and assistance, and returned to Moor Park. On the death of his patron in 1699 he undertook by request the publication of his works, and thereafter returned to Ireland as chaplain to the Lord Deputy, the Earl of Berkeley, from whom he obtained some small preferments, including the vicarage of Laracor, and a prebend in St. Patrick's Cathedral. At this time he made frequent visits to London and became the friend of Addison, Steele, Congreve, and other Whig writers, and wrote various pamphlets, chiefly on ecclesiastical subjects. In 1710, disgusted with the neglect of the Whigs, alike of himself and of the claims of his Church, he abandoned them and attached himself to Harley and Bolingbroke. The next few years were filled with political controversy. He attacked the Whigs in papers in the *Examiner* in 1710, and in his celebrated pamphlets, *The Conduct of the Allies* (1712), *The Barrier Treaty* (1713), and *The Public Spirit of the Whigs* (1714). In 1713 he was made Dean of St. Patrick's, the last piece of patronage which he received. The steady dislike of Queen Anne had proved an insurmountable obstacle to his further advancement, and her death proved the ruin of the Tories. On the destruction of his hopes S. retired to Ireland, where he remained for the rest of his life a thoroughly embittered man. In 1713 he had begun his *Journal to Stella*, which sheds so strange a light upon his character, and on his return to Ireland his marriage to her is now generally believed to have taken place, though they never lived together. Now also took place also his final rupture with Miss Van Homrigh (Vanessa), who had been in love with him, with whom he had maintained a lengthened correspondence, and to whom he addressed his poem, *Cadenus and Vanessa* (1726). Though he disliked the Irish and considered residence in Ireland as banishment, he interested himself in Irish affairs, and attained extraordinary popularity by his *Drapier's Letters*, directed against the introduction of " Wood's halfpence." In 1726 he visited England and joined with Pope and Arbuthnot in publishing *Miscellanies* (1727). In the same year, 1726, he *pub. Gulliver's Travels*, his most widely and permanently popular work. His last visit to England was paid in 1727 and in the following year " Stella," the only being, probably, whom he really loved, *d.* Though he had a circle of friends in Dublin, and was, owing to his championing the people in their grievances, a popular idol, the shadows were darkening around him. The fears of insanity by which he had been all his life haunted, and which may account for and perhaps partly excuse some of the least justifiable portions of his conduct, pressed more and more upon him. He became increasingly morose and savage in his misanthropy, and though he had a rally in which he produced some of his most brilliant work—the *Rhapsody on Poetry*, *Verses on the Death of Dr. Swift*, and the *Modest Proposal* (a horrible but masterly piece of irony)—he gradually sank into almost total loss of his faculities, and *d.* on October 19, 1745.

The character of S. is one of the gloomiest and least attractive among English writers. Intensely proud, he suffered bitterly in youth and early manhood from the humiliations of poverty and dependence, which preyed upon a mind in which the seeds of insanity were latent until it became dominated by a ferocious misanthropy. As a writer he is our greatest master of grave irony, and while he presents the most humorous ideas, the severity of his own countenance never relaxes. The *Tale of a Tub* and *Gulliver's Travels* are the greatest satires in the English language, although the concluding part of the latter is a savage and almost insane attack upon the whole human race. His history is a tragedy darkening into catastrophe, and as Thackeray has said, " So great a man he seems that thinking of him is like thinking of an Empire falling."

S. was tall and powerfully made. His eyes, blue and flashing under excitement, were the most remarkable part of his appearance.

SUMMARY.—*B.* 1667, *ed.* at Trinity Coll., Dublin, entered household of Sir W. Temple at Moor Park 1692, and became his sec., became known to William III., and met E. Johnson (Stella), left T. in 1694 and returned to Ireland, took orders and wrote *Tale of a Tub* and *Battle of Books* (*pub.* 1704), returned to Sir W. T. 1698, and on his death in 1699 *pub.* his works, returned to Ireland and obtained some small preferments, visits London and became one of the circle of Addison, etc., deserts the Whigs and joins the Tories 1710, attacking the former in various papers and pamphlets, Dean of St. Patrick's 1713, death of Anne and ruin of Tories destroyed hopes of further preferment, and he returned to Ireland and began his *Journal to Stella*, *Drapier's Letters* appeared 1724, visits England, and joins with Pope and Arbuthnot in *Miscellanies* 1726, *pub. Gulliver's Travels* 1727, " Stella " *d.* 1728, gradually lost his faculties and *d.* 1745.

Lives by Craik (1882), Leslie Stephen (1882), Churton Collins (1893), etc. *Works* ed. by Sir Walter Scott (19 vols., 1814, etc.), Bohn's Standard Library (1897-1908).

SWINBURNE, ALGERNON CHARLES (1837-1909).—Poet, *s.* of Admiral S. and of Lady Jane Ashburnham, *dau.* of the 3rd Earl of A., *b.* in London, received his early education in France, and was at Eton and at Balliol Coll., Oxf., where he attracted the attention of Jowett, and gave himself to the study of Latin, Greek, French, and Italian, with special reference to poetic form. He left Oxf. without graduating in 1860, and in the next year *pub.* two plays, *The Queen Mother* and *Rosamund*, which made no impression on the public, though a few good judges recognised their promise. The same year he visited Italy, and there made the acquaintance of Walter Savage Landor (*q.v.*). On his return he lived for some time in Cheyne Row, Chelsea, with D. G. Rossetti (*q.v.*), and G. Meredith (*q.v.*). The appearance in 1865 of *Atalanta in Calydon* led to his immediate recognition as a poet of the first order, and in the same year he *pub. Chastelard, a Tragedy,* the first part of a trilogy relating to Mary Queen of Scots, the other two being *Bothwell* (1874), and *Mary Stuart* (1881). *Poems and Ballads, pub.* in 1866, created a profound sensation alike among the critics and the general body of readers by its daring departure from recognised standards, alike of politics and morality, and gave rise to a prolonged and bitter controversy, S. defending himself against his assailants in *Notes on Poems and Reviews.* His next works were the *Song of Italy* (1867) and *Songs before Sunrise* (1871). Returning to the Greek models which he had followed with such brilliant success in *Atalanta* he produced *Erechtheus* (1876), the extraordinary metrical power of which won general admiration. *Poems and Ballads,* second series, came out in 1878. *Tristram of Lyonesse in* heroic couplets followed in 1882, *A Midsummer Holiday* (1884), *Marino Faliero* (1885), *Locrine* (1887), *Poems and Ballads,* third series (1889), *The Sisters* (1892), *Astrophel* (1894), *The Tale of Balen* (1896), *Rosamund, Queen of the Lombards* (1899), *A Channel Passage* (1904), and *The Duke of Gandia* (1908). Among his prose works are *Love's Cross Currents* (1905) (fiction), *William Blake, a Critical Essay* (1867), *Under the Microscope* (1872), in answer to R. Buchanan's *Fleshly School of Poetry, George Chapman, a Critical Essay* (1875), *A Study of Shakespeare* (1879), *A Study of Victor Hugo* (1886), and *A Study of Ben Jonson* (1889).

S. belongs to the class of "Poets' poets." He never became widely popular. As a master of metre he is hardly excelled by any of our poets, but it has not seldom been questioned whether his marvellous sense of the beauty of words and their arrangement did not exceed the depth and mass of his thought. *The Hymn to Artemis* in *Atalanta* beginning "When the hounds of Spring are on Winter's traces" is certainly one of the most splendid examples of metrical power in the language. As a prose writer he occupies a much lower place, and here the contrast between the thought and its expression becomes very marked, the latter often becoming turgid and even violent. In his earlier days in London S. was closely associated with the pre-Raphaelites, the Rossettis, Meredith, and Burne-Jones: he was thus subjected successively to the classical and romantic influence, and showed the traces of both in his work. He was never *m.*, and for the last 30 years of his life lived with his friend, Mr. Theodore Watts-Dunton, at the Pines, Putney Hill. For some time before his death he was almost totally deaf.

SYLVESTER, JOSHUA (1563-1618).—Poet and translator, is chiefly remembered by his translation from the French of Du Bartas' *Divine Weeks and Works,* which is said to have influenced Milton and Shakespeare. He seconded the *Counterblast against Tobacco* of James I. with his *Tobacco Battered and the Pipes Shattered . . . by a Volley of Holy Shot thundered from Mount Helicon* (1620), and also wrote *All not Gold that Glitters, Panthea: Divine Wishes and Meditations* (1630), and many religious, complimentary, and other occasional pieces. S., who was originally engaged in commerce, acted later as a sort of factor to the Earl of Essex.

SYMONDS, JOHN ADDINGTON (1840-1893).—Writer on art and literature, *s.* of a physician in Bristol, was *ed.* at Harrow and Oxf. His delicate health obliged him to live abroad. He *pub.* (1875-86) *History of the Italian Renaissance,* and translated the *Autobiography of Benvenuto Cellini.* He also *pub.* some books of poetry, including *Many Moods* (1878) and *Animi Figura* (1882), and among his other publications were *Introduction to the Study of Dante* (1872), *Studies of the Greek Poets* (1873 and 1876), *Shakespeare's Predecessors in the English Drama* (1884), and Lives of various poets, including Ben Jonson, Shelley, and Walt Whitman. He also made remarkable translations of the sonnets of Michelangelo and Campanella, and wrote upon philosophical subjects in various periodicals.

SYNGE, JOHN MILLINGTON (1871-1909).—Miscellaneous writer, *b.* near Dublin, *ed.* privately and at Trinity Coll., Dublin. He wrote *Riders to the Sea, In the Shadow of the Glen* (1905), *The Well of the Saints* (1905), *The Play Boy of the Western World* (1907), and *The Aran Islands* (1907).

TABLEY DE, JOHN BYRON LEICESTER WARREN, 3RD LORD (1835-1895).—Poet, eldest *s.* of the 2nd Lord, *ed.* at Eton and Oxf., was for a time attached to the British Embassy at Constantinople. He wrote poems of a very high order, some of them *pub.* under the *pseudonyms* of "George F. Preston" and "William Lancaster." They include *Ballads and Metrical Sketches, The Threshold of Atrides, Glimpses of Antiquity,* etc. These were followed by two dramas, *Philoctetes* (1866) and *Orestes* (1868). Later works in his own name were *Rehearsals* (1870), *Searching the Net* (1873), *The Soldier's Fortune,* a tragedy. *Poems, Dramatic and Lyrical* (1893) included selections from former works. After his death appeared *Orpheus in Thrace* (1901). He was a man of sensitive temperament, and was latterly much of a recluse. He was an accomplished botanist, and *pub.* a work on the *Flora of Cheshire.*

TALFOURD, SIR THOMAS NOON (1795-1854).—Poet and biographer, *s.* of a brewer at Reading, where he was *b.*, and which he represented in Parliament, 1835-41, was *ed.* at Mill Hill School. He studied law, was called to the Bar in 1821, and became a Judge in 1849. He *d.* suddenly of apoplexy while charging the Grand Jury at Stafford. He wrote much for reviews, and in 1835 produced *Ion,* a tragedy, followed by *The Athenian Captive* (1838), and *The Massacre of Glencoe,* all of which were acted with success. T. was the friend and literary executor of Charles Lamb (*q.v.*), and *pub.* in two sections his *Memoirs and Letters.* In 1837 he introduced the Copyright Bill, which was passed with modifications in 1842.

TANNAHILL, ROBERT (1774-1810).—Poet, *b.* in Paisley where he was a weaver. In 1807 he *pub.* a small vol. of poems and songs, which met with success, and carried his hitherto local fame over his native country. Always delicate and sensitive, a disappointment in regard to the publication of an enlarged ed. of his poems so wrought upon a lowness of spirits, to which he was subject, that he drowned himself in a canal. His longer pieces are now forgotten, but some of his songs have achieved a popularity only second to that of some of Burns's best. Among these are *The Braes of Balquhidder*, *Gloomy Winter's now awa'* and *The Bonnie Wood o' Craigielea*.

TATE, NAHUM (1652-1715).—Poet, *s.* of a clergyman in Dublin, was *ed.* at Trinity Coll. there. He *pub. Poems on Several Occasions* (1677), *Panacea, or a Poem on Tea*, and, in collaboration with Dryden, the second part of *Absalom and Achitophel*. He also adapted Shakespeare's *Richard II.* and *Lear*, making what he considered improvements. Thus in *Lear* Cordelia is made to survive her *f.*, and marry Edgar. This desecration, which was defended by Dr. Johnson, kept the stage till well on in the 19th century. He also wrote various miscellaneous poems, now happily forgotten. He is best remembered as the Tate of Tate and Brady's metrical version of the Psalms, *pub.* in 1696. T., who succeeded Shadwell as Poet Laureate in 1690, figures in *The Dunciad*. NICHOLAS BRADY (1659-1726).—Tate's fellow-versifier of the Psalms, *b.* at Bandon, and *ed.* at Westminster and Oxf., was incumbent of Stratford-on-Avon. He wrote a tragedy, *The Rape*, a blank verse translation of the *Æneid*, an *Ode*, and sermons, now all forgotten.

TATHAM, JOHN (*fl.* 1632-1664).—Dramatist. Little is known of him. He produced pageants for the Lord Mayor's show and some dramas, *Love Crowns the End*, *The Distracted State*, *The Scots Figgaries, or a Knot of Knaves*, *The Rump*, etc. He was a Cavalier, who hated the Puritans and the Scotch, and invented a dialect which he believed to be their vernacular tongue.

TAUTPHŒUS, BARONESS (MONTGOMERY) (1807-1893).—*Dau.* of an Irish gentleman, *m.* the Baron T., Chamberlain at the Court of Bavaria. She wrote several novels dealing with German life of which the first, *The Initials* (1850), is perhaps the best. Others were *Cyrilla* (1883), *Quits* (1857), and *At Odds* (1863).

TAYLOR, BAYARD (1825-1878).—Poet, *b.* in Pennsylvania of Quaker descent, began to write by the time he was 12. Apprenticed to a printer, he found the work uncongenial and, purchasing his indentures, went to Europe on a walking tour, and thereafter he was a constant and enterprising traveller. After his return from Europe he ed. a paper, got on the staff of the *New York Tribune*, and *pub.* several books of travel and poetry, among which are *Views Afoot* (1846), an account of his travels in Europe, and *El Dorado* (1850), which described the Californian gold-fields. After some experience and some disappointments in the diplomatic sphere, he settled down to novel-writing, his first venture in which, *Hannah Thurston* (1863), was very successful, and was followed by *John Godfrey's Fortunes* (1864), partly autobiographical, and *The Story of Kenneth* (1866). His poetic works include *Poems of the Orient* (1854), *Poet's Journal* (1862), *Masque of the Gods* (1872), *Lars* (1873), *The Prophet* (1874), a tragedy, *Prince Deucalion*, and *Home Pastorals* (1875). In 1878 he was appointed to the German Embassy, and *d.* in Berlin in the following year. His translation of Goethe's *Faust* is perhaps his best work. He was a man of untiring energy and great ability and versatility, but tried too many avenues to fame to advance very far in any of them.

TAYLOR, SIR HENRY (1800-1886).—Dramatist, *s.* of a gentleman farmer in the county of Durham. After being at sea for some months and in the Naval Stores Department, he became a clerk in the Colonial Office, and remained there for 48 years, during which he exercised considerable influence on the colonial policy of the Empire. In 1872 he was made K.C.M.G. He wrote four tragedies—*Isaac Comnenus* (1827), *Philip van Artevelde* (1834), *Edwin the Fair* (1842), and *St. Clement's Eve* (1862); also a romantic comedy, *The Virgin Widow*, which he renamed *A Sicilian Summer*, *The Eve of the Conquest and other Poems* (1847). In prose he *pub.* *The Statesman* (1836), *Notes from Life* (1847), *Notes from Books* (1849), and an *Autobiography*. Of all these *Philip van Artevelde* was perhaps the most successful. T. was a man of great ability and distinction, but his dramas, with many of the qualities of good poetry, lack the final touch of genius.

TAYLOR, ISAAC (1787-1865).—Philosophical and historical writer, artist, and inventor, was the most eminent member of a family known as the Taylors of Ongar, which has shown a remarkable persistence of ability in various departments, but especially in art and literature. His grandfather and *f.*, who bore the same name, were both eminent engravers, and the latter was the author of various books for children. T. was brought up to the hereditary art of engraving, in which he displayed pre-eminent skill, his work gaining the admiration of D. G. Rossetti. He decided, however, to devote himself to literature, and for 40 years continued to produce works of originality and value, including *Elements of Thought* (1823), *Natural History of Enthusiasm* (1829), *Spiritual Despotism* (1831), *Ancient Christianity* (1839), *Restoration of Belief* (1855), *The Physical Theory of Another Life*, *History of Transmission of Ancient Books*, and *Home Education*, besides numerous contributions to reviews and other periodicals. Besides his literary and artistic accomplishments T. was an important inventor, two of his inventions having done much to develop the manufacture of calico. Two of his sisters had considerable literary reputation. ANN T., afterwards MRS. GILBERT (1782-1866), and JANE (1783-1824) were, like their brother, taught the art of engraving. In 1804-5 they jointly wrote *Original Poems for Infant Minds*, followed by *Rhymes for the Nursery* and *Hymns for Infant Minds*. Among those are the little poems, "My Mother" and "Twinkle, twinkle, little Star," known to all well-conditioned children. Jane was also the author of *Display*, a tale (1815), and other works, including several hymns, of which the best known is "Lord, I would own Thy tender Care." The hereditary talents of the family were represented in the next generation by CANON ISAAC T. (1829-1901), the *s.* of Isaac last mentioned, who, in addition to *The Liturgy and the Dissenters*, *pub.* works in philology and archæology, including *Words and Places* and *Etruscan Researches;* and by JOSIAH GILBERT, *s.* of Ann T., an accomplished artist, and author of *The Dolomite Mountains*, *Cadore, or Titian's Country*, and ed. of the *Autobiography* of his mother.

TAYLOR, JEREMY (1613-1667).—Divine, was *b.* at Camb. His *f.*, though of gentle descent, followed the trade of a barber, and

Jeremy entered Caius Coll. as a sizar. After his graduation in 1634 he was asked to preach in London, where his eloquence attracted the attention of Laud, who sent him to Oxf., caused him to be elected a Fellow of All Souls Coll., and made him his chaplain. He also became a chaplain to the King, and soon attaining a great reputation as a preacher, was presented to the living of Uppingham. In 1639 he *m.* his first wife, and in 1643 he was made Rector of Overstone. On the outbreak of the Civil War T. sided with the King, and was present, probably as a chaplain, at the battle fought in 1645 near Cardigan Castle, when he was taken prisoner. He was soon released, but the Royalist cause being practically lost, he decided to remain in Wales, and with two friends started a school at Newtonhall, Caermarthenshire, which had some success. T. also found a friend in Lord Carbery, whose chaplain he became. During the period of 13 years from 1647-60, which were passed in seeming obscurity, he laid the foundations and raised the structure of his splendid literary fame. The *Liberty of Prophesying* (that is, of preaching), one of the greatest pleas for toleration in the language, was *pub.* in 1647, *The Life of Christ* in 1649, *Holy Living* in 1650, and *Holy Dying* in 1651. These were followed by various series of sermons, and by *The Golden Grove* (1655), a manual of devotion which received its title from the name of the seat of his friend Lord Carbery. For some remarks against the existing authorities T. suffered a short imprisonment, and some controversial tracts on *Original Sin, Unum Necessarium* (the one thing needful), and *The Doctrine and Practice of Repentance* involved him in a controversy of some warmth in which he was attacked by both High Churchmen and Calvinists. While in Wales T. had entered into a second marriage with a lady of some property which, however, was seriously encroached upon by the exactions of the Parliamentarians. In 1657 he ministered privately to an Episcopalian congregation in London, and in 1658 accompanied Lord Conway to Ireland, and served a cure at Lisburn. Two years later he *pub. Ductor Dubitantium, or the Rule of Conscience in all her General Measures*, a learned and subtle piece of casuistry which he dedicated to Charles II. The Restoration brought recognition of T.'s unswerving devotion to the Royalist cause; he was made Bishop of Down and Connor, and to this was added the administration of the see of Dromore. In his new position, though, as might have been expected, he showed zeal, diligence, and benevolence, he was not happy. He did not, probably could not, entirely practise his own views of absolute toleration, and found himself in conflict with the Presbyterians, some of whose ministers he had extruded from benefices which they had held, and he longed to escape to a more private and peaceful position. He *d.* at Lisburn of a fever caught while ministering to a parishioner. T. is one of the great classical writers of England. Learned, original, and impassioned, he had an enthusiasm for religion and charity, and his writings glow with an almost unequalled wealth of illustration and imagery, subtle argument, and fullness of thought. With a character of stainless purity and benevolence, and gracious and gentle manners, he was universally beloved by all who came under the spell of his presence.

TAYLOR, JOHN (1580-1653).—Known as the "Water Poet," *b*. at Gloucester of humble parentage, was apprenticed to a London waterman, and pressed for the navy. Thereafter he returned to London and resumed his occupation on the Thames, afterwards keeping inns first at Oxf., then in London. He had a talent for writing rollicking verses, enjoyed the acquaintance of Ben Jonson, and other famous men, superintended the water pageant at the marriage of the Princess Elizabeth 1613, and composed the "triumphs" at the Lord Mayor's shows. He made a journey on foot from London as far as to Braemar, of which he wrote an account, *The Pennyless Pilgrimage . . . of John Taylor, the King's Majesty's Water Poet* (1618). He visited the Queen of Bohemia at Prague in 1620, and made other journeys, each of which was commemorated in a book. His writings are of little literary value, but have considerable historical and antiquarian interest.

TAYLOR, PHILIP MEADOWS (1808-1876).—Novelist, *b*. at Liverpool, *s*. of a merchant there. When still a boy went out to a mercantile situation in Calcutta, but in 1826 got a commission in the army of the Nizam of Hyderabad. From this he rose to a high civil position in the service of the Nizam, and entirely reorganised his government. He wrote several striking novels dealing with Indian life, including *Confessions of a Thug* (1639), *Tara*, and *A Noble Queen*. He left an autobiography, *The Story of my Life*, ed. by his *dau*.

TAYLOR, THOMAS (1758-1835).—Translator, *b*. in London and *ed*. at St. Paul's School, devoted himself to the study of the classics and of mathematics. After being a bank clerk he was appointed Assistant Secretary to the Society for the encouragement of Arts, etc., in which capacity he made many influential friends, who furnished the means for publishing his various translations, which include works of Plato, Aristotle, Proclus, Porphyry, Apuleius, etc. His aim indeed was the translation of all the untranslated writings of the ancient Greek philosophers.

TAYLOR, TOM (1817-1880).—Dramatist, *b* at Sunderland, ed. at Glasgow and Camb., and was Prof. of English Literature in London Univ. from 1845-47. In 1846 he was called to the Bar, and from 1854-71 he was Sec. to the Local Government Board. He was the author of about 100 dramatic pieces, original and adapted, including *Still Waters run Deep*, *The Overland Route*, and *Joan of Arc*. He was likewise a large contributor to *Punch*, of which he was ed. 1874-80, and he ed. the autobiographies of Haydon and Leslie, the painters, and wrote *Life and Times of Sir Joshua Reynolds*.

TAYLOR, WILLIAM (1765-1836).—Translator, etc., *s*. of a merchant, travelled on the Continent, learned German, and became an enthusiastic student of German literature, which he was one of the first to introduce to his fellow-countrymen. His articles on the subject were *coll*. and *pub*. as *Historic Survey of German Poetry* (1828-30). He translated Bürger's *Lenore*, Lessing's *Nathan*, and Goethe's *Iphigenia*. He also wrote *Tales of Yore* (1810) and *English Synonyms Described* (1813).

TEMPLE, SIR WILLIAM (1628-1699).—Statesman and essayist, *s.* of Sir John T., Master of the Rolls in Ireland, was *b.* in London, and *ed.* at Camb. He travelled on the Continent, was for some time a member of the Irish Parliament, employed on various diplomatic missions, and negotiated the marriage of the Prince of Orange and the Princess Mary. On his return he was much consulted by Charles II., but disapproving of the courses adopted, retired to his house at Sheen, which he afterwards left and purchased Moor Park, where Swift was for a time his sec. He took no part in the Revolution, but acquiesced in the new *régime*, and was offered, but refused, the Secretaryship of State. His works consist for the most part of short essays *coll.* under the title of *Miscellanea*, but longer pieces are *Observations upon the United Provinces*, and *Essay on the Original and Nature of Government*. T. is best known in literary history as being the recipient of the famous *Letters from Dorothy Osborne*, who became his wife in 1655.

TENNANT, WILLIAM (1784-1848).—Poet and scholar, a cripple from his birth, was *b.* at Anstruther (commonly called Anster) in Fife. As a youth he was clerk to his brother, a corn-merchant, but devoted his leisure to the study of languages, and the literature of various countries. In 1813 he became parish schoolmaster of Lasswade, near Edinburgh, thereafter classical master at Dollar Academy, and in 1835 Prof. of Oriental Languages at St. Andrews. In 1812 he *pub. Anster Fair*, a mock-heroic poem, in *ottava rima*, full of fancy and humour, which at once brought him reputation. In later life he produced two tragedies, *Cardinal Beaton* and *John Baliol*, and two poems, *The Thane of Fife* and *Papistry Stormed*. He also issued a *Syriac and Chaldee Grammar*.

TENNYSON, ALFRED, 1ST LORD (1809-1892).—Poet, was the fourth *s.* of George T., Rector of Somersby, Lincolnshire, where he was *b.* His *f.* was himself a poet of some skill, and his two elder brothers, Frederick T. (*q.v.*) and Charles T. Turner (*q.v.*), were poets of a high order. His early education was received from his *f.*, after which he went to the Grammar School of Louth, whence in 1828 he proceeded to Trinity Coll., Camb. In the previous year had appeared a small vol., *Poems by Two Brothers*, chiefly the work of his brother Charles and himself, with a few contributions from Frederick, but it attracted little attention. At the Univ. he was one of a group of highly gifted men, including Trench (*q.v.*), Monckton Milnes, afterwards Lord Houghton (*q.v.*), Alford (*q.v.*), Lushington, his future brother-in-law, and above all, Arthur Hallam, whose friendship and early death were to be the inspiration of his greatest poem. In 1829 he won the Chancellor's medal by a poem on *Timbuctoo*, and in the following year he brought out his first independent work, *Poems chiefly Lyrical*. It was not in general very favourably received by the critics, though Wilson in *Blackwood's Magazine* admitted much promise and even performance. In America it had greater popularity. Part of 1832 was spent in travel with Hallam, and the same year saw the publication of *Poems*, which had not much greater success than its predecessor. In the next year Hallam *d.*, and T. began *In Memoriam* and wrote *The Two Voices*. He also became engaged to Emily Sellwood, his future wife, but owing to various circumstances their marriage did not take place until 1850. The next few years were passed with his family at various places, and, so far as the public were concerned, he remained silent until 1842, when he *pub.* *Poems* in two volumes, and at last achieved full recognition as a great poet. From this time the life of T. is a record of tranquil triumph in his art and of the conquest of fame; and the publication of his successive works became almost the only events which mark his history. *The Princess* appearing in 1847 added materially to his reputation : in the lyrics with which it is interspersed, such as "The Splendour Falls" and "Tears, idle Tears" he rises to the full mastery of this branch of his art. The year 1850 was perhaps the most eventful in his life, for in it took place his marriage which, as he said, "brought the peace of God into his life," his succession to the Laureateship on the death of Wordsworth, and the publication of his greatest poem, *In Memoriam*. In 1852 appeared his noble *Ode on the Death of the Duke of Wellington ;* and two years later *The Charge of the Light Brigade*. The publication of *Maud* in 1855 gave his rapidly growing popularity a perceptible set-back, though it has since risen in favour. But this was far more than made up for by the enthusiasm with which the first set of *The Idylls of the King* was received on its appearance four years later. *Enoch Arden*, with the *Northern Farmer*, came out in 1864; *The Holy Grail* and *Gareth and Lynette*, both belonging to the *Idyll* series, in 1869 and 1872 respectively. Three years later in 1875 T. broke new ground by beginning a series of dramas with *Queen Mary*, followed by *Harold* (1876), *The Falcon* (1879), *The Cup* (1881), *The Promise of May* (1882), *Becket* (1884), and *Robin Hood* (1891). His later poems were *The Lovers' Tale* (1879) (an early work retouched), *Tiresias* (1885), *Locksley Hall—60 Years after* (1886), *Demeter and other Poems* (1889), including "Crossing the Bar," and *The Death of Œnone* (1892). T., who cared little for general society, though he had many intimate and devoted friends, lived at Farringford, Isle of Wight, from 1853-69, when he built a house at Aldworth, near Haslemere, which was his home until his death. In 1884 he was raised to the peerage. Until he had passed the threescore years and ten he had, with occasional illnesses, enjoyed good health on the whole. But in 1886 the younger of his two sons *d.*, a blow which told heavily upon him; thereafter frequent attacks of illness followed, and he *d.* on October 6, 1892, in his 84th year, and received a public funeral in Westminster Abbey.

The poetry of T. is characterised by a wide outlook, by intense sympathy with the deepest feelings and aspirations of humanity, a profound realisation of the problems of life and thought, a noble patriotism finding utterance in such poems as *The Revenge*, the *Charge of the Light Brigade*, and the *Ode on the Death of the Duke of Wellington*, an exquisite sense of beauty, marvellous power of vivid and minute description often achieved by a single felicitous phrase, and often heightened by the perfect matching of sense and sound, and a general loftiness and purity of tone. No poet has excelled him in precision and delicacy of language and completeness of expression. As a lyrist he has, perhaps, no superiors, and only two or three equals in English poetry, and even of humour he possessed no small share, as is shown in the *Northern Farmer* and in other pieces. When the volume, variety, finish, and duration of his work are considered, as well as the influence which he exercised on his time, a unique place must be assigned him among the poets of his country.

SUMMARY.—*B.* 1809, *ed.* Camb., *Poems by Two Brothers* 1827, *Poems chiefly Lyrical* 1830, his chief works *Poems in two Volumes* 1842, *Princess* 1847, *In Memoriam* 1850, *Maud* 1855, *Idylls of the King* 1869-72, Poet Laureate 1850, *d.* 1892.

Life by his *s.* (2 vols., 1897). There are also numerous books, biographical and critical, by, among others, W. E. Wace (1881), A. C. Benson, A. Lang, F. Harrison, Sir A. Lyell, C. F. G. Masterman (T. as a Religious Teacher), Stopford Brooke, Waugh, etc.

TENNYSON, FREDERICK (1807-1898).—Poet, was the eldest *s.* of the Rector of Somersby, Lincolnshire, and brother of Alfred T. (*q.v.*). *Ed.* at Eton and Camb., he passed most of his life in Italy and Jersey. He contributed to the *Poems by Two Brothers*, and produced *Days and Hours* (lyrics) (1854), *The Isles of Greece* (1890), *Daphne* (1891), and *Poems of the Day and Night* (1895). All his works show passages of genuine poetic power.

TENNYSON TURNER, CHARLES (1808-1879).—Poet, elder brother of Alfred T. (*q.v.*), *ed.* at Camb., entered the Church, and became Vicar of Grasby, Lincolnshire. The name of Turner he assumed in conformity with the will of a relation. He contributed to *Poems by Two Brothers*, and was the author of 340 sonnets, which were greatly admired by such critics as Coleridge, Palgrave, and his brother Alfred.

THACKERAY, WILLIAM MAKEPEACE (1811-1863).—Novelist, *s.* of Richmond T., who held various important appointments in the service of the East India Company, and who belonged to an old and respectable Yorkshire family, was *b.* at Calcutta, and soon after the death of his *f.*, which took place in 1816, sent home to England. After being at a school at Chiswick, he was sent to the Charterhouse School, where he remained from 1822-26, and where he does not appear to have been very happy. Meanwhile in 1818 his mother had *m.* Major H. W. C. Smythe, who is believed to be, in part at any rate, the original of Colonel Newcome. In 1829 he went to Trinity Coll., Camb., where he remained for a year only, and where he did not distinguish himself particularly as a student, but made many life-long friends, including Spedding (*q.v.*), Tennyson, Fitzgerald (*q.v.*), and Monckton Milnes (*see* Houghton), and contributed verses and caricatures to two Univ. papers, "The Snob" and "The Gownsman." The following year, 1831, was spent chiefly in travelling on the Continent, especially Germany, when, at Weimar, he visited Goethe. Returning he entered the Middle Temple, but having no liking for legal studies, he soon abandoned them, and turning his attention to journalism, became proprietor, wholly or in part, of two papers successively, both of which failed. These enterprises, together with some unfortunate investments and also, it would seem, play, stripped him of the comfortable fortune which he had inherited; and he now found himself dependent on his own exertions for a living. He thought at first of art as a profession, and studied for a time at Paris and Rome. In 1836, while acting as Paris correspondent for the second of his journals, he *m.* Isabella, *dau.* of Colonel Shawe, an Irish officer, and the next year he returned to England and became a contributor to *Fraser's Magazine,* in which appeared *The Yellowplush Papers, The Great Hoggarty Diamond, Catherine,* and *Barry Lyndon,* the history of an Irish sharper, which contains some of his best work. Other works of this period were *The Paris Sketch-book* (1840) and *The Irish Sketch-book* (1843). His work in *Fraser,* while it was appreciated at its true worth by a select circle, had not brought him any very wide recognition: it was his contributions to *Punch*—the *Book of Snobs* and *Jeames's Diary*—which first caught the ear of the wider public. The turning point in his career, however, was the publication in monthly numbers of *Vanity Fair* (1847-48). This extraordinary work gave him at once a place beside Fielding at the head of English novelists, and left him no living competitor except Dickens. *Pendennis,* largely autobiographical, followed in 1848-50, and fully maintained his reputation. In 1851 he broke new ground, and appeared, with great success, as a lecturer, taking for his subject *The English Humourists of the Eighteenth Century,* following this up in 1855 with the *Four Georges,* first delivered in America. Meanwhile *Esmond,* perhaps his masterpiece, and probably the greatest novel of its kind in existence, had appeared in 1852, and *The Newcomes* (1853), *The Virginians,* a sequel to *Esmond,* which, though containing much fine work, is generally considered to show a falling off as compared with its two immediate predecessors, came out in 1857-59. In 1860 the *Cornhill Magazine* was started with T. for its ed., and to it he contributed *Lovell the Widower* (1860), *The Adventures of Philip* (1861-62), *The Roundabout Papers,* a series of charming essays, and *Denis Duval,* left a mere fragment by his sudden death, but which gave promise of a return to his highest level of performance. In addition to the works mentioned, T. for some years produced Christmas books and burlesques, of which the best were *The Rose and the Ring* and *The Kickleburys on the Rhine.* He also wrote graceful verses, some of which, like *Bouillabaisse,* are in a strain of humour shot through with pathos, while others are the purest rollicking fun. For some years T. suffered from spasms of the heart, and he *d.* suddenly during the night of December 23, 1863, in his 53rd year. He was a man of the tenderest heart, and had an intense enjoyment of domestic happiness; and the interruption of this, caused by the permanent breakdown of his wife's health, was a heavy calamity. This, along with his own latterly broken health, and a sensitiveness which made him keenly alive to criticism, doubtless fostered the tendency to what was often superficially called his cynical view of life. He possessed an inimitable irony and a power of sarcasm which could scorch like lightning, but the latter is almost invariably directed against what is base and hateful. To human weakness he is lenient and often tender, and even when weakness passes into wickedness, he is just and compassionate. He saw human nature "steadily and saw it whole," and paints it with a light but sure hand. He was master of a style of great distinction and individuality, and ranks as one of the very greatest of English novelists.

Lives by Merivale and Marzials (Great Writers), A. Trollope (English Men of Letters), Whibley ((Modern English Writers). Article in *Dictionary of National Biography* by Leslie Stephen.

THEOBALD, LEWIS (1688-1744).—Editor of Shakespeare, and translator, originally an attorney, betook himself to literature, translated from Plato, the Greek dramatists, and Homer, and wrote also essays, biographies, and poems. In 1715 he *pub. Shakespeare Restored, etc.*, in which he severely criticised Pope's ed., and was in consequence rewarded with the first place in *The Dunciad*, and the adoption of most of his corrections in Pope's next ed.

THIRWALL, CONNOP (1797-1875).—Historian, was *b.* at Stepney, the *s.* of a clergyman, and *ed.* at the Charterhouse and Camb. He studied law, was called to the Bar in 1825, and in the same year *pub.* a translation of Schleiermacher's *Critical Essay on the Gospel of St. Luke*. After this, having changed his mind, he took orders in 1827, and the next year translated, with Julius Hare (*q.v.*), the first vol. of Niebuhr's *History of Rome*, and *pub.*, also with him, *The Philological Museum* (1831-33). He was an advocate for the admission of Dissenters to degrees, and in consequence of his action in the matter had to resign his Univ. tutorship. Thereupon Lord Brougham, then Lord Chancellor, presented him to the living of Kirkby Underdale. Between 1835 and 1847 he wrote his great *History of Greece*, which has a place among historical classics. In 1840 he was made Bishop of St. David's, in which capacity he showed unusual energy in administering his see. As a Broad Churchman T. was regarded with suspicion by both High and Low Churchmen. He was the only Bishop who was in favour of the disestablishment of the Irish Church.

THOMPSON, FRANCIS (1860–1907).—Poet, *b.* at Preston, the *s.* of a doctor. He was *ed.* at Ushaw Coll., Durham, and afterwards studied medicine at Owen's College, Manchester. Failing to obtain a degree he came to London in 1885 in an attempt to earn a living. For some years he lived a life of extreme poverty, and in ill-health took to opium. Fortunately for him he submitted some poetry to Wilfrid Meynell, who, together with his wife, Alice Meynell, sought T. out and rescued him from failure and starvation. Under the care of these fellow Roman Catholics he published his first volume of *Poems* in 1893 (including *The Hound of Heaven*). There followed two more volumes, *Sister Songs* (1895) and *New Poems* (1897). He died from consumption in London and was buried at Kensal Green. Besides his poetry he showed no little power as a prose writer (*Health and Holiness* (1905), *Essay on Shelley* (1909), *Life of Ignatius Loyola* (1909). Mr. Wilfrid Meynell edited the complete edition of Thompson's work (1913).

THOMS, WILLIAM JOHN (1803-1885).—Antiquary and miscellaneous writer, for many years a clerk in the secretary's office of Chelsea Hospital, was in 1845 appointed Clerk, and subsequently Deputy Librarian to the House of Lords. He was the founder in 1849 of *Notes and Queries*, which for some years he also ed. Among his publications are: *Early Prose Romances* (1827–8), *Lays and Legends* (1834), *The Book of the Court* (1838), *Gammer Gurton's Famous Histories* (1846), *Gammer Gurton's Pleasant Stories* (1848).

THOMSON, JAMES (1700-1748).—Poet, *s.* of the minister of Ednam, Roxburghshire, spent most of his youth, however, at Southdean, a neighbouring parish, to which his *f.* was translated. He was *ed.* at the parish school there, at Jedburgh, and at Edin., whither he went with the view of studying for the ministry. The style of one of his earliest sermons having been objected to by the Prof. of Divinity as being too flowery and imaginative, he gave up his clerical views and went to London in 1725, taking with him a part of what ultimately became his poem of *Winter*. By the influence of his friend Mallet he became tutor to Lord Binning, *s.* of the Earl of Haddington, and was introduced to Pope, Arbuthnot, Gay, and others. *Winter* was *pub.* in 1726, and was followed by *Summer* (1727), *Spring* (1728), and *Autumn* (1730), when the whole were brought together as *The Seasons*. Previous to 1730 he had produced one or two minor poems and the tragedy of *Sophonisba*, which, after promising some success, was killed by the unfortunate line, "Oh! Sophonisba, Sophonisba, oh!" being parodied as "Oh! Jemmy Thomson, Jemmy Thomson, oh!" In 1731 T., accompanied Charles Talbot, *s.* of the Lord Chancellor, to the Continent as tutor, and on his return received the sinecure Secretaryship of Briefs which, however, he lost in 1737, through omitting to apply for its continuance to Talbot's successor. He then returned to the drama and produced *Agamemnon* in 1738, and *Edward and Eleanora* in 1739. The same year he received from the Prince of Wales a pension of £100, and was made Surveyor-General of the Leeward Islands which, after providing for a deputy to discharge the duties, left him £300 a year. He was now in comfortable circumstances, and settled in a villa near Richmond, where he amused himself with gardening and seeing his friends. In conjunction with Mallet he wrote, in 1740, the masque of *Alfred*, in which appeared *Rule Britannia*, which M. afterwards claimed, or allowed to be claimed, for him, but which there is every reason to believe was contributed by T. In 1745 appeared *Tancred and Sigismunda*, the most successful of his dramas, and in 1748 *Coriolanus*. In May of the latter year he *pub.* *The Castle of Indolence*, an allegorical poem in the Spenserian stanza, generally considered to be his masterpiece. In August following he caught a chill which developed into a fever, and carried him off in his 48th year. Though T. was undoubtedly a poet by nature, his art was developed by constant and fastidious polishing. To *The Seasons*, originally containing about 4000 lines, he added about 1400 in his various revisions. He was the first to give the description of nature the leading place, and in his treatment of his theme he showed much judgment in the selection of the details to be dwelt upon. His blank verse, though not equal to that of a few other English poets, is musical and wielded in a manner suitable to his subject. In all his poems he displays the genial temper and kindly sympathies by which he was characterised as a man. He was never *m.*, and lived an easy, indolent life, beloved by his many friends. (*See also* Lyttelton, Lord)

THOMSON, JAMES (1834-1882).—Poet, *b.* at Port Glasgow and brought up in the Royal Caledonian Asylum, was for some years an army teacher, but was dismissed for a breach of discipline. He became associated with Charles Bradlaugh, the free-thought protagonist, who introduced him to the conductors of various secularist publications. His best known poem is *The City of Dreadful Night*, deeply pessimistic. Others are *Vane's Story* and *Weddah and Om-el-Bonain.* His views resulted in depression, which led to dipsomania, and he *d.* in poverty and misery. His work has a certain gloomy power which renders it distinctly noteworthy.

THOREAU, HENRY DAVID (1817-1862).—Essayist, poet, and naturalist, was *b.* at Concord, Massachusetts. His *f.*, of French extraction, from Jersey, was a manufacturer of lead-pencils. He was *ed.* at Harvard, where he became a good classical scholar. Subsequently he was a competent Orientalist, and was deeply versed in the history and manners of the Red Indians. No form of regular remunerative employment commending itself to him, he spent the 10 years after leaving coll. in the study of books and nature, for the latter of which he had exceptional qualifications in the acuteness of his senses and his powers of observation. Though not a misanthropist, he appears in general to have preferred solitary communion with nature to human society. "The man I meet," he said, "is seldom so instructive as the silence which he breaks;" and he described himself as "a mystic, a transcendentalist, and a natural philosopher." He made such money as his extremely simple mode of life called for, by building boats or fences, agricultural or garden work, and surveying, anything almost of an outdoor character which did not involve lengthened engagement. In 1837 he began his diaries, records of observation with which in ten years he filled 30 vols. In 1839 he made the excursion the record of which he in 1845 *pub.* as *A Week on the Concord and Merrimac Rivers.* Two years later, in 1841, he began a residence in the household of Emerson, which lasted for two years, when he assisted in conducting the *Dial*, and in 1845, after some teaching in New York, he retired to a hut near the solitary Walden Pond to write his *Week on the Concord*, etc. Later works were *Walden* (1854), and *The Maine Woods* (1864), and *Cape Cod* (1865), accounts of excursions and observations, both *pub.* after his death. T. was an enthusiast in the anti-slavery cause, the triumph of which, however, he did not live to see, as he *d.* on May 6, 1862, when the war was still in its earlier stages. The deliberate aim of T. was to live a life as nearly approaching naturalness as possible; and to this end he passed his time largely in solitude and in the open air. As he says, "I went to the woods because I wished to live deliberately, to front only the essential facts of life, and see if I could not learn what it had to teach." To his great powers of observation he added great powers of reflection, and two of the most characteristic features of his writings are immediateness and individuality in his descriptions of nature, and a remarkable power of giving permanent and clear form to the most subtle and evanescent mental impressions.

TICKELL, THOMAS (1686-1740).—Poet, *b.* at Bridekirk Vicarage, Cumberland, and *ed.* at Oxf. became the friend of Joseph

Addison (*q.v.*), contributed to the *Spectator* and *Guardian*, and accompanied him when he went to Ireland as sec. to the Lord Lieutenant. His translation of the first book of the *Iliad* came out at the same time as Pope's, and led to a quarrel between the latter and Addison, Pope imagining that the publication was a plot to interfere with the success of his work. On Addison becoming Sec. of State in 1717 he appointed T. Under-Sec. Among the writings of T. are the well-known ballad, *Colin and Lucy, Kensington Gardens*, a poem, and an *Elegy* on the death of Addison, of which Macaulay says that it "would do honour to the greatest name in our literature." In 1725 he became sec. to the Lords Justices of Ireland, and retained the post until his death.

TICKNOR, GEORGE (1791-1871).—Historian and biographer, *s.* of a rich man, was *b.* at Boston, Mass., and *ed.* for the law. He, however, gave himself to study and writing, and also travelled much. After being a Prof. at Harvard, 1819-35, he went in the latter year to Europe, where he spent some years collecting materials for his *magnum opus*, *The History of Spanish Literature* (1849). He also wrote Lives of Lafayette and Prescott, the historian. His *Letters and Journals* were *pub.* in 1876, and are the most interesting of his writings.

TIGHE, MARY (BLACKFORD) (1772-1810).—Poet, *dau.* of a clergyman, made an unhappy marriage, though she had beauty and amiable manners, and was highly popular in society. She wrote a good deal of verse; but her chief poem was a translation in Spenserian stanza of the tale of *Cupid and Psyche*, which won the admiration of such men as Sir J. Mackintosh, Moore, and Keats.

TILLOTSON, JOHN (1630-1694).—Divine, *s.* of a Presbyterian clothier, was *b.* near Halifax, and *ed.* at Camb., where his originally Puritan views became somewhat modified. At the Savoy Conference in 1661 he was still a Presbyterian, but submitted to the Act of Uniformity, and became next year Rector of Keddington, and in 1664 preacher at Lincoln's Inn, where he became very popular. In 1672 he was made Dean of Canterbury. He vainly endeavoured to secure the comprehension of the Nonconformists in the Church. After the Revolution he gained the favour of William III., who made him Clerk of the Closet, and Dean of St. Paul's, and in 1691 he succeeded Sancroft as Archbishop of Canterbury. His sermons, which had extraordinary popularity, give him a place in literature, and he was one of those writers who, by greater simplicity and greater attention to clearness of construction, helped to introduce the modern style of composition.

TIMROD, HENRY (1829-1867).—Poet, *b.* at Charleston, S. Carolina, of German descent, was ruined by the Civil War, and *d.* in poverty. He wrote one vol. of poems, *pub.* 1860, which attained wide popularity in the South. He had notable descriptive power.

TOBIN, JOHN (1770-1804).—Dramatist, was for long unsuccessful, but in the year of his death made a hit with *The Honey Moon*, which had great success, and maintained its place for many years. Other plays were *The Curfew* and *The School for Authors*.

TOLAND, JOHN (1670?-1722).—Deistical writer, *b.* in Ireland of Roman Catholic parentage, completed his education at Glasgow, Edin., and Leyden. Very early in life he had become a Protestant, and at Leyden he studied theology with the view of becoming a Nonconformist minister, but imbibed Rationalistic views. He then resided for some time at Oxf., and in 1696 *pub.* his first work, *Christianity not Mysterious*, which was censured by Convocation and gave rise to much controversy. Next year he returned to Ireland, where, however, he was not more popular than in England, and where his book was burned by the common hangman. Returning to England he took to writing political pamphlets, including one, *Anglia Libera*, in support of the Brunswick succession, which gained him some favour at Hanover, and he was sent on some political business to the German Courts. He then served Harley in Holland and Germany practically as a political spy. His later years were passed in literary drudgery and poverty. Among his numerous writings may be mentioned *Account of Prussia and Hanover, Origines Judaicæ, History of the Druids*, and a Life of Milton prefixed to an ed. of his prose works.

TOOKE, JOHN HORNE (1736-1812).—Philologist, *s.* of a poulterer called Horne, added the name of Tooke in 1782 in anticipation of inheriting from his friend W. Tooke, of Purley. He was at Camb. and took orders, but disliking the clerical profession, travelled abroad. Returning he became prominent as a radical politician, and espoused the cause of Wilkes, with whom, however, he afterwards quarrelled. He also supported the revolted American colonists, and was fined and imprisoned for endeavouring to raise a subscription for them. An effort to be admitted to the Bar was unsuccessful; and in 1786 he published his *Diversions of Purley*, a work on philology which brought him great reputation, and which, containing much that has been proved to be erroneous, showed great learning and acuteness. T. twice endeavoured unsuccessfully to enter Parliament for Westminster, but ultimately sat for the rotten burgh of Old Sarum, making, however, no mark in the House. He was the author of numerous effective political pamphlets.

TOPLADY, AUGUSTUS MONTAGUE (1740-1778).—Hymn-writer, *s.* of an officer in the army, was *b.* at Farnham, *ed.* at Westminster and Trinity Coll., Dublin, after which he took orders and became incumbent of Broad Hembury. He was a strong Calvinist and entered into a bitter controversy with Wesley. His controversial works are forgotten; but he will always be remembered as the author of "Rock of Ages," perhaps the most widely known of English hymns.

TOURNEUR, OR TURNER, CYRIL (1575?-1626).—Dramatist, perhaps *s.* of Richard T., Lieutenant of the Brill, served in the Low Countries, and was sec. to Sir Edward Cecil in his unsuccessful expedition to Cadiz, returning from which he was disembarked with the sick at Kinsale, where he *d.* He wrote two dramas, *The Revenger's Tragedy* (*pr.* 1607), and *The Atheist's Tragedy* (*pr.* 1611), in both of which, especially the former, every kind of guilt and horror is piled up, the author displaying, however, great intensity of tragic power. Of *The Revenger* Lamb said that it made his ears tingle. Another play of his, *Transformed Metamorphosis*, was discovered in 1872.

TRAHERNE, THOMAS (1636?-1674).—Poet and theological writer, *s.* of a shoemaker at Hereford where, or at Ledbury, he was probably *b.* Very few facts concerning him have been preserved, and indeed his very existence had been forgotten until some of his MS. were discovered on a bookstall in 1896, without, however, anything to identify the author. Their discoverer, Mr. W. T. Brooke, was inclined to attribute them to Henry Vaughan (*q.v.*), in which he was supported by Dr. Grosart (*q.v.*), and the latter was about to bring out a new ed. of Vaughan's poems in which they were to be included. This was, however, prevented by his death. The credit of identification is due to Mr. Bertram Dobell, who had become the possessor of another vol. of MS., and who rejecting, after due consideration, the claims of Vaughan, followed up the very slender clues available until he had established the authorship of Traherne. All the facts that his diligent investigations were successful in collecting were that T. was " entered as a commoner at Brasenose Coll., Oxf., in 1652, took one degree in arts, left the house for a time, entered into the sacred function, and in 1661 was actually created M.A. About that time he became Rector of Crednell, near Hereford . . . and in 1669 Bachelor of Divinity; " and that after remaining there for over 9 years he was appointed private chaplain to the Lord Keeper, Sir Orlando Bridgeman, who on his retirement from office retained him as a member of his household at Teddington until his death in 1674, T. himself dying three months later. T. also appears to have been incumbent of Teddington, or perhaps more probably, curate to a pluralist incumbent. The complete oblivion into which T. had fallen is the more remarkable when the quality of his poetry, which places him on a level with Herbert, Vaughan, and Crashaw, is considered; and that he appears in his own day to have had some reputation as a scholar and controversialist. His *Roman Forgeries* (1673) achieved some note. His next work, *Christian Ethics*, which was not *pub.* until after his death, appears to have fallen dead, and is extremely rare: it is described by Mr. Dobell as " full of eloquence, persuasiveness, sagacity, and piety." *Centuries of Meditations* consists of short reflections on religious and moral subjects, etc. The *Poems* constitute his main claim to remembrance and, as already stated, are of a high order. With occasional roughness of metre they display powerful imagination, a deep and rich vein of original thought, and true poetic force and fire. It has been pointed out that in some of them the author anticipates the essential doctrines of the Berkeleian philosophy, and in them is also revealed a personality of rare purity and fascination.

TRELAWNY, EDWARD JOHN (1792-1881).—Biographer, entered the navy, from which, however, he deserted, after which he wandered about in the East and on the Continent. In Switzerland he met Byron and Shelley, and was living in close friendship with the latter when he was drowned, and was one of the witnesses at the cremation of his remains. He took part in the Greek war of independence, and *m.* the sister of one of the insurgent chiefs. After various adventures in America he settled in London, where he was a distinguished figure in society, and enjoyed the reputation of a picturesque, but somewhat imaginative, conversationalist. He wrote *The Adventures of a Younger Son* (1831), a work of striking distinction, and the intensely interesting *Records of Shelley, Byron, and the Author* (1858). The last survivor of that brilliant group, he was buried by the side of Shelley.

TRENCH, RICHARD CHENEVIX (1807-1886).—Poet and theologian, *b.* in Dublin, and *ed.* at Harrow and Camb., took orders, and after serving various country parishes, became in 1847 Prof. of Theology in King's Coll., London, in 1856 Dean of Westminster, and in 1864 Archbishop of Dublin. As Primate of the Irish Church at its disestablishment, he rendered valuable service at that time of trial. In theology his best known works are his *Hulsean Lectures, Notes on the Parables*, and *Notes on the Miracles*. His philological writings, *English Past and Present* and *Select Glossary of English Words* are extremely interesting and suggestive, though now to some extent superseded. His *Sacred Latin Poetry* is a valuable collection of mediæval Church hymns. He also wrote sonnets, elegies, and lyrics, in the first of which he was specially successful, besides longer poems, *Justin Martyr* and *Sabbation*.

TREVISA, JOHN OF (1326-1412).—Translator, a Cornishman, *ed.* at Oxf., was Vicar of Berkeley, Gloucestershire, and chaplain to the 4th Lord Berkeley, and Canon of Westbury. He translated for his patron the *Polychronicon* of Ranulf Higden, adding remarks of his own, and prefacing it with a *Dialogue on Translation between a Lord and a Clerk*. He likewise made various other translations.

TROLLOPE, ANTHONY (1815-1882).—Novelist, *s.* of Thomas Anthony T., a barrister who ruined himself by speculation, and of Frances T. (*q.v.*), a well-known writer, was *b.* in London, and *ed.* at Harrow and Winchester. His childhood was an unhappy one, owing to his father's misfortunes. After a short time in Belgium he obtained an appointment in the Post Office, in which he rose to a responsible position. His first three novels had little success; but in 1855 he found his line, and in *The Warden* produced the first of his Barsetshire series. It was followed by *Barchester Towers* (1857), *Doctor Thorne* (1858), *Framley Parsonage* (1861), *The Small House at Allington* (1864), and *The Last Chronicle of Barset* (1867), which deal with the society of a small cathedral city. Other novels are *Orley Farm, Can you forgive Her? Ralph the Heir, The Claverings, Phineas Finn, He knew he was Right*, and *The Golden Lion of Grandpré*. In all he wrote about 50 novels, besides books about the West Indies, North America, Australia, and South Africa, a translation of *Cæsar*, and monographs on Cicero and Thackeray. His novels are light of touch, pleasant, amusing, and thoroughly healthy. They make no attempt to sound the depths of character or either to propound or solve problems. Outside of fiction his work was generally superficial and unsatisfactory. But he had the merit of providing a whole generation with wholesome amusement, and enjoyed a great deal of popularity. He is said to have received £70,000 for his writings.

TROLLOPE, MRS. FRANCES (MILTON) (1780-1863).—Novelist and miscellaneous writer, *b.* at Stapleton near Bristol, *m.* in 1809 Thomas A. T., a barrister, who fell into financial misfortune. She then in 1827 went with her family to Cincinnati, where the efforts which she made to support herself were unsuccessful. On her return to England, however, she brought herself into notice by publishing *Domestic Manners of the Americans* (1832), in which she gave a very unfavourable and grossly exaggerated account of the subject; and a novel, *The Refugee in America*, pursued it on similar lines. Next came *The Abbess* and *Belgium and Western Germany*, and other works of the same kind on *Paris and the Parisians*, and *Vienna and the Austrians* followed. Thereafter she continued to pour forth novels and books on miscellaneous subjects, writing in all over 100 vols. Though possessed of considerable powers of observation and a sharp and caustic wit, such an output was fatal to permanent literary success, and none of her books are now read. She spent the last 20 years of her life at Florence, where she *d.* in 1863. Her third *s.* was Anthony T., the well-known novelist (*q.v.*). Her eldest *s.*, Thomas Adolphus, wrote *The Girlhood of Catherine de Medici*, a *History of Florence*, and *Life of Pius IX.*, and some novels.

TRUMBULL, JOHN (1750-1831).—Poet, *b.* at Waterbury, Conn., was a lawyer, and became a judge. He wrote much verse, his principal productions being *The Progress of Dulness* (1772) and *McFingal* (1782), written in support of the Revolution in imitation of *Hudibras*.

TUCKER, ABRAHAM (1705-1774).—Philosophic writer, *b.* in London, and *ed.* at Oxf., was a country gentleman, who devoted himself to the study of philosophy, and wrote under the name of Edward Search, a work in 7 vols., *The Light of Nature Followed* (1768-78). It is rather a miscellany than a systematic treatise, but contains much original and acute thinking.

TUCKER, GEORGE (1775-1861).—Economist, etc., *b.* in Bermuda, became Prof. of Moral Philosophy, etc., in the Univ. of Virginia. He wrote a *Life of Jefferson*, *Political History of the United States*, *Essays Moral and Philosophical*, *The Valley of the Shenandoah*, a novel. *A Voyage to the Moon* (satire), and various works on economics.

TUCKER, NATHANIEL BEVERLY (1784-1851).—*B.* in Virginia, became a Prof. of Law in William and Mary Coll. He wrote a novel, *The Partisan Leader* (1836), a prophecy of the future disunion which led to the Civil War. It was *re-pub.* in 1861 as *A Key to the Southern Conspiracy*. Another novel was *George Balcombe*.

TUCKERMAN, HENRY THEODORE (1813-1871).—Essayist, etc., *b.* in Boston, Mass. He was a sympathetic and delicate critic, with a graceful style. He lived much in Italy, which influenced his choice of subjects in his earlier writings. These include *The Italian Sketch-book*, *Isabel, or Sicily*, *Thoughts on the Poets*, *The Book of the Artists*, *Leaves from the Diary of a Dreamer*, etc.

TULLOCH, JOHN (1823-1886).—Theologian and historical writer, *b.* at Bridge of Earn, Perthshire, studied at St. Andrews and

Edin. He was ordained to the ministry of the Church of Scotland at Dundee, whence he was translated to Kettins, Forfarshire, and became in 1854 Principal and Prof. of Theology in St. Mary's Coll., St. Andrews. He was a leader of the liberal party in the Church of Scotland, and wrote *Literary and Intellectual Revival of Scotland in the Eighteenth Century* (1883), *Movements of Religious Thought in the Nineteenth Century* (1884-85), *Rational Theology and Christian Philosophy in England in the Seventeenth Century*, and a book on Pascal, etc.

TUPPER, MARTIN FARQUHAR (1810-1889).—Versifier, *s.* of a surgeon, was *b.* in London, *ed.* at Charterhouse School and Oxf., and called to the Bar in 1835. He, however, believed that literature was his vocation, and wrote many works in prose and verse, only one of which, *Proverbial Philosophy*, had much success. But the vogue which it had was enormous, especially in America. It is a singular collection of commonplace observations set forth in a form which bears the appearance of verse, but has neither rhyme nor metre, and has long since found its deserved level. He also wrote *War Ballads, Rifle Ballads*, and *Protestant Ballads*, various novels, and an autobiography.

TURBERVILLE, OR TURBERVILE, GEORGE (1540?-1610).—Poet, belonging to an ancient Dorsetshire family, was *b.* at Whitchurch, and *ed.* at Winchester and Oxf. He became sec. to Thomas Randolph, Ambassador to Russia, and made translations from the Latin and Italian, and in 1570 *pub. Epitaphes, Epigrams, Songs, and Sonets*. He also wrote books on *Falconrie* and *Hunting*, and was one of the first to use blank verse.

TURNER, SHARON (1768-1847).—Historian, *b.* in London, was a solicitor, and becoming interested in the study of Icelandic and Anglo-Saxon literature, *pub.* the results of his researches in his *History of the Anglo-Saxons* (1799-1805). Thereafter he continued the narrative in *History of England* (1814-29), carrying it on to the end of the reign of Elizabeth. These histories, especially the former, though somewhat marred by an attempt to emulate the grandiose style of Gibbon, were works of real research, and opened up, and to a considerable extent developed, a new field of inquiry. T. also wrote a *Sacred History of the World*, and a poem on Richard III.

TUSSER, THOMAS (1524?-1580).—Versifier on agriculture, was an Essex man. Having a good voice he was trained in music, and was a chorister in St. Paul's, and afterwards in Norwich Cathedral, and held the post of musician to Lord Paget. He tried farming at different places, but unsuccessfully, which did not, however, prevent his undertaking to instruct others. This he does with much shrewdness and point in his *Hundreth Goode Pointes of Husbandrie* (1557), expressed in rude but lively verse; thereafter he added *Hundreth Goode Pointes of Husserie* (Housewifery). The two joined, and with many additions, were repeatedly reprinted as *Five Hundredth Pointes of Goode Husbandrie united to as many of Goode Huswifery*. Many proverbs may be traced back to the writings of T., who, in spite of all his shrewdness and talent, *d.* in prison as a debtor.

TWAIN, MARK (*see* CLEMENS).

TYNDALE, WILLIAM (1484?-1536).—Translator of the Bible, belonged to a northern family which, migrating to Gloucestershire during the Wars of the Roses, adopted the alternative name of Huchyns or Hychins, which T. himself bore when at Oxf. in 1510. After graduating there, he went to Camb., where the influence of Erasmus, who had been Prof. of Theology, still operated. He took orders, and in 1522 was a tutor in the household of Sir John Walsh of Old Sodbury, and was preaching and disputing in the country round, for which he was called to account by the Chancellor of the diocese. At the same time he translated a treatise by Erasmus, the *Enchiridion Militis Christiani* (Manual of the Christian Soldier), and in controversy with a local disputant prophesied that he would cause that "a boye that driveth the plough" should know the Scriptures better than his opponent. Having formed the purpose of translating the New Testament T. went in 1523 to London, and used means towards his admission to the household of Tunstal, Bishop of London, but without success; he then lived in the house of a wealthy draper, Humphrey Monmouth, where he probably began his translation. Finding, however, that his work was likely to be interfered with, he proceeded in 1524 to Hamburg, whence he went to visit Luther at Wittenberg. He began printing his translation at Cologne the following year, but had to fly to Worms, where the work was completed. The translation itself is entirely T.'s work, and is that of a thorough scholar, and shows likewise an ear for the harmony of words. The notes and introduction are partly his own, partly literal translations, and partly the gist of the work of Luther. From Germany the translation was introduced into England, and largely circulated until forcible means of prevention were brought to bear in 1528. In this year T. removed to Marburg, where he *pub.* *The Parable of the Wicked Mammon*, a treatise on Justification by Faith, and *The Obedience of a Christian Man*, setting forth that Scripture is the ultimate authority in matters of faith, and the King in matters of civil government. Thereafter, having been at Hamburg and Antwerp, T. returned to Marburg, and in 1530 *pub.* his translation of the *Pentateuch* and *The Practice of Prelates*, in which he attacked Wolsey and the proposed divorce proceedings of Henry VIII., the latter of whom endeavoured to have him apprehended. Thereafter he was involved in a controversy with Sir Thomas More. In 1533 he returned to Antwerp, Henry's hostility having somewhat cooled, and was occupied in revising his translations, when he was in 1535 betrayed into the hands of the Imperial officers and carried off to the Castle of Vilvorde, where the next year he was strangled and burned. T. was one of the most able and devoted of the reforming leaders, and his, the foundation of all future translations of the Bible, is his enduring monument. He was a small, thin man of abstemious habits and untiring industry.

TYNDALL, JOHN (1820-1893).—Scientific writer, *b.* at Leighlin Bridge, County Carlow, was in early life employed in the ordnance survey and as a railway engineer. He was next teacher of mathematics and surveying at Queenwood Coll., Hampshire, after which he went to Marburg to study science, and while there became joint author of a memoir *On the Magneto-optic Properties of*

Crystals (1850). After being at Berlin he returned in 1851 to Queenwood, and in 1853 was appointed Prof. of Natural Philosophy in the Royal Institution, which in 1867 he succeeded Faraday as Superintendent. With Huxley (*q.v.*) he made investigations into the Alpine glaciers. Thereafter he did much original work on heat, sound, and light. In addition to his discoveries T. was one of the greatest popularisers of science. His style, remarkable for lucidity and elegance, enabled him to expound such subjects with the minimum of technical terminology. Among his works are *The Glaciers of the Alps* (1860), *Mountaineering* (1861), *Fragments of Science*, two vols. (1871), including his address to the British Association at Belfast, which raised a storm of controversy and protest in various quarters, *Hours of Exercise on the Alps*, etc. T. *d.* from an overdose of chloral accidentally administered by his wife.

TYTLER, ALEXANDER FRASER (1747-1813).—Historian, *s.* of William T. (*q.v.*), studied at Edin., was called to the Bar in 1770 and raised to the Bench as Lord Woodhouselee in 1802. He was Prof. of History in Edin., and wrote *Elements of General History* (1801), *An Essay on the Principles of Translation* (1791), besides various legal treatises.

TYTLER, PATRICK FRASER (1791-1849).—Historian, *s.* of the above, studied at Edin., and was called to the Bar in 1813. Among his many writings are an *Essay on the History of the Moors in Spain, The Life of the Admirable Crichton* (1819), *History of Scotland* (1828-43), and *England under the Reigns of Edward VI. and Mary* (1839). His *History of Scotland*, which was the result of 20 years of study and research, is still authoritative.

TYTLER, WILLIAM (1711-1792).—Historical writer, was a lawyer in Edin., and wrote *An Inquiry into the Evidence against Mary Queen of Scots*, in which he combated the views of Robertson. He discovered the *King's Quhair* of James I., and *pub.* in 1783 *The Poetical Remains of James I., King of Scotland*, with a Life.

UDALL, NICOLAS (1505-1556).—Dramatist and scholar, *b.* in Hampshire, and *ed.* at Oxf. In 1534 he became headmaster of Eton, from which he was dismissed for misconduct, 1541. In 1537 he became Vicar of Braintree, in 1551 of Calborne, Isle of Wight, and in 1554 headmaster of Westminster School. He translated part of the *Apophthegms* of Erasmus, and assisted in making the English version of his *Paraphrase of the New Testament*. Other translations were Peter Martyr's *Discourse on the Eucharist* and Thomas Gemini's *Anatomia*, but he is best remembered by *Ralph Roister Doister* (1553?), the first English comedy, a rude but lively piece.

UNDERDOWN, THOMAS (*fl.* 1566-1587).—Translator. He translated the *Æthiopian History* of Heliodorus 1566; also from Ovid.

UNDERWOOD, FRANCIS HENRY (1825-1894).—Critic and biographer, *b.* in Massachusetts, was American Consul at Glasgow and Leith. He wrote *Hand-books of English Literature, Builders of American Literature*, etc., some novels, *Lord of Himself, Man Proposes*, and *Dr. Gray's Quest*, and biographies of Lowell, Longfellow, and Whittier.

URQUHART, SIR THOMAS (1611-1660).—Eccentric writer and translator, was *ed.* at King's Coll., Aberdeen, after leaving which he travelled in France, Spain, and Italy. He was bitterly opposed to the Covenanters, and fought against them at Turriff in 1639. His later life was passed between Scotland, England (where he was for some time a prisoner in the Tower), and the Continent, where he lived, 1642-45. A man of considerable ability and learning, his vanity and eccentricity verged upon insanity, and he is said to have *d.* from the effects of an uncontrollable fit of joyful laughter on hearing news of the Restoration. Among his extravagances was a genealogy of his family traced through his *f.* to Adam, and through his mother to Eve, he himself being the 153rd in descent. He *pub.* *Trissotetras*, a work on trigonometry (1645), an invective against the Presbyterians (1652), a scheme for a universal language, *Logopandecteision* (1653), and a partial translation of Rabelais (1653), a further portion being *pub.* in 1693. In the last he was assisted by Peter Anthony Motteux, a Frenchman who had established himself in England, who continued the work.

USK, THOMAS (*d.* 1388).—Poet, *b.* in London, was sec. to John of Northampton, the Wyclifite Lord Mayor of London, whom he betrayed to save himself, in which, however, he failed, being executed in 1388. During his imprisonment, which lasted from 1384 until his death, he composed *The Testament of Love*, a didactic poem long attributed to Chaucer.

USSHER, JAMES (1581-1656).—Divine and scholar, *b.* in Dublin, the *s.* of a lawyer there, and *ed.* at Trinity Coll., took orders, and became Chancellor of St. Patrick's, Dublin, 1605, and Prof. of Divinity, 1607-21. On the Irish clergy, in 1715, deciding to assert themselves as an independent church, U. had the main hand in drawing up the constitution, certain features of which led to the suspicion of his being in favour of Puritanism. To defend himself he went in 1619 to England, and had a conference with the King (James I.), in which he so completely succeeded that he was in 1621 made Bishop of Meath, and four years later Archbishop of Armagh. He constantly used his influence in favour of reform, and endeavoured to introduce such modifications of Episcopacy as would conciliate and comprehend the Presbyterians. During the troubles which led to the Civil War U. maintained the unlawfulness of taking up arms against the King. The Rebellion in Ireland in 1641 drove him away, and he settled first at Oxf., but ultimately at the house of Lady Peterborough at Reigate, where he *d.* in 1656. His works dealt chiefly with ecclesiastical antiquities and chronology, his *magnum opus* being *Annales*, a chronology of the world from the creation to the dispersion of the Jews in the reign of Vespasian, a work which gained him great reputation on the Continent as well as at home. The date of the creation was fixed as 4004 B.C., which was long universally received. It has, of course, been altogether superseded, alike by the discovery of ancient records, and by geology.

VANBRUGH, SIR JOHN (1664-1726).—Dramatist and architect, *b.* in London of Flemish descent, was in France from 1683 to 1685, studying architecture, for which he had early shown a taste.

The next year he got a commission in the army, and in 1690 he was a prisoner first at Vincennes and then in the Bastille. In 1696 he began his dramatic career with *The Relapse*, which had great success. *Æsop* followed in 1697, and *The Provoked Wife* in the same year. The latter was severely handled by Jeremy Collier (*q.v.*) in his *Short View*, etc., which produced a vindication by the author. In addition to these he wrote or collaborated in various other plays. His leading features as a dramatist are the naturalness of his dialogue and his lively humour. Like all his contemporaries he is frequently extremely gross. He obtained great fame as an architect, as well as a dramatist. Among his most famous designs are Castle Howard, Blenheim Palace, and Dalkeith Palace. He was knighted by George I., was controller of the Royal works, and succeeded Wren as architect to Greenwich Hospital. In addition to the plays above mentioned V. wrote *The Confederacy* and *The Country House*. He was a handsome and jovial person, and highly popular in society.

VAUGHAN, HENRY (1622-1695).—Poet, *b.* in the parish of Llansaintffraed, Brecknock, and as a native of the land of the ancient Silures, called himself "Silurist." He was at Jesus Coll., Oxf., studied law in London, but finally settled as a physician at Brecon and Newton-by-Usk. In his youth he was a decided Royalist and, along with his twin brother Thomas, was imprisoned. His first book was *Poems, with the Tenth Satire of Juvenal Englished.* It appeared in 1646. *Olor Iscanus* (the Swan of Usk), a collection of poems and translations, was surreptitiously *pub.* in 1651. About this time he had a serious illness which led to deep spiritual impressions, and thereafter his writings were almost entirely religious. *Silex Scintillans* (Sparks from the Flint), his best known work, consists of short poems full of deep religious feeling, fine fancy, and exquisite felicities of expression, mixed with a good deal that is quaint and artificial. It contains "The Retreat," a poem of about 30 lines which manifestly suggested to Wordsworth his *Ode on the Intimations of Immortality*, and "Beyond the Veil," one of the finest meditative poems in the language. *Flores Solitudinis* (Flowers of Solitude) and *The Mount of Olives* are devout meditations in prose. The two brothers were joint authors of *Thalia Rediviva : the Pastimes and Diversions of a Country Muse* (1678), a collection of translations and original poems.

VAUGHAN, ROBERT (1795-1868).—A minister of the Congregationalist communion, Prof. of History in London Univ., 1830-43, and Pres. of the Independent Coll., Manchester, 1843-57. He founded, and for a time ed. the *British Quarterly*. He wrote, among various other works, *A History of England under the Stuarts*, *Revolutions of History*, and a Life of Wycliffe.

VEITCH, JOHN (1829-1894).—Philosophic and miscellaneous writer, *b.* at Peebles, *ed.* at Univ. and New Coll., Edin., was assistant to Sir Wm. Hamilton (*q.v.*), 1856-60, Prof. of Logic at St. Andrews, 1860-64, and Glasgow, 1864-94. He was a voluminous and accomplished writer, his works including Lives of *Dugald Stewart* (1857) and *Sir W. Hamilton* (1869), *Tweed and other Poems* (1875), *History and Poetry of the Scottish Border* (1877), *Feeling for Nature in Scottish*

Poetry (1887), *Merlin and other Poems* (1889), *Border Essays* (1896), and *Dualism and Monism* (1895).

VERY, JONES (1813-1880).—Essayist and poet, *b.* at Salem, Mass., where he became a clergyman and something of a mystic. He *pub.* one small volume, *Essays and Poems*, the latter chiefly in the form of the Shakespearian sonnet. Though never widely popular, he appealed by his refined, still thoughtfulness to a certain small circle of minds.

WACE (*fl.* 1170).—Chronicler, *b.* in Jersey, and *ed.* at Caen, was influenced by the Chronicle of Geoffrey of Monmouth (*q.v.*), and based upon it a French metrical romance, *Brut.* Later, at the command of Henry II., he rewrote with additions a chronicle of the life of William the Conqueror and entitled it *Roman de Rou.*

WADE, THOMAS (1805-1875). — Poet, *b.* at Woodbridge, *pub.* poems, dramas, sonnets, and a translation of Dante's *Inferno.* Among his writings are *Tasso and the Sisters* (1825), *Mundi et Cordis Carmina* (1835); *Duke Andrea* (1828), and *The Jew of Arragon* (1830), both tragedies, and the *Phrenologists* (1830), a farce.

WAKEFIELD, GILBERT (1756-1801).—Scholar and controversialist, *b.* at Nottingham, *ed.* at Camb., took orders, but becoming a Unitarian renounced them and acted as classical tutor in various Unitarian academies. He was a strong defender of the French Revolution, and was imprisoned for two years for writing a seditious pamphlet. He *pub.* ed. of various classical writers, and among his theological writings are *Early Christian Writers on the Person of Christ* (1784), *An Examination of Paine's Age of Reason* (1794), and *Silva Critica* (1789-95), illustrations of the Scriptures.

WALLACE, LEWIS (1827-1905).—Novelist, *b.* at Brookville, Indiana, served with distinction in the Mexican and Civil Wars, and rose to the rank of General. He was also a politician of some note, and was Governor of Utah and Minister to Turkey. His novel, *Ben Hur* (1880), dealing with the times of Christ, had great popularity, and was followed by *The Fair God*, *The Prince of India*, and other novels, and by a work on the *Boyhood of Christ.*

WALLER, EDMUND (1606-1687).—Poet, *b.* at Coleshill, Herts, and *ed.* at Eton and Camb., belonged to an old and wealthy family, and in early childhood inherited the estate of Beaconsfield, Bucks, worth £3500 a year. He was related to John Hampden, and was distantly connected with Oliver Cromwell, his own family, however, being staunch Royalists. He studied law at Lincoln's Inn, and at the age of 16 became a member of Parliament, in which he sat for various constituencies for the greater part of his life, and in which his wit and vivacity, as well as his powers of adapting his principles to the times, enabled him to take a prominent part. In 1631 he added to his fortune by marrying Anne Banks, a London heiress, who *d.* in 1634, and he then paid assiduous but unsuccessful court to Lady Dorothea Sidney, to whom, under the name of Sacharissa, he addressed much of his best poetry. Though probably really a Royalist in his sympathies, W. supported the popular cause in Parliament, and in 1641 conducted the case against Sir Francis Crawley for his opinion in favour of the legality of ship-money. His speech, which was printed, had an enormous circulation and brought him great fame. Two years later, however, he was detected in a plot for seizing London for the King, was expelled from the House, fined £10,000, and banished. On this occasion he showed cowardice and treachery, humiliating himself in the most abject manner, and betraying all his associates. He went to the Continent, living chiefly in France and Switzerland, and showing hospitality to Royalist exiles. Returning by permission in 1652 he addressed some laudatory verses, among the best he wrote, to Cromwell, on whose death nevertheless he wrote a new poem entitled, *On the Death of the late Usurper, O. C.* On the Restoration the accommodating poet was ready with a congratulatory address to Charles II., who, pointing out its inferiority as a poem to that addressed to Cromwell, elicited the famous reply, " Poets, Sire, succeed better in fiction than in truth." The poem, however, whatever its demerits, succeeded in its prime object, and the poet became a favourite at Court, and sat in Parliament until his death. In addition to his lighter pieces, on which his fame chiefly rests, W. wrote an epic, *The Summer Islands* (Bermudas), and a sacred poem, *Divine Love.* His short poems, such as " On a Girdle," often show fancy and grace of expression, but are frequently frigid and artificial, and exhibit absolute indifference to the charms of Nature. As a man, though agreeable and witty, he was time-serving, selfish, and cowardly. Clarendon has left a very unflattering " character " of him. He *m.* a second time and had five sons and eight daughters.

WALLER, JOHN FRANCIS (1810-1894).—Poet, *b.* at Limerick, and *ed.* at Trinity Coll., Dublin, became a contributor to and ultimately ed. of the *Dublin University Magazine*, usually writing under the pseudonym of " Jonathan Freke Slingsby." His works include *Ravenscroft Hall* (1852), *The Dead Bridal* (1856), and *Peter Brown* (1872).

WALPOLE, HORATIO OR HORACE (1717 - 1797). — Miscellaneous writer, third *s.* of Sir Robert W., the great minister of George II., was *b.* in London, and *ed.* at Eton and Camb., after which he travelled on the Continent with Gray, the poet (*q.v.*). His *f.* bestowed several lucrative appointments upon him, and he sat in Parliament for various places, but never took any prominent part in public business. By the death of his nephew, the 3rd Earl, he became in 1791 4th Earl of Orford. In 1747 he purchased the villa of Strawberry Hill, Twickenham, the conversion of which into a small Gothic Castle and the collection of the works of art and curios with which it was decorated was the main interest of his subsequent life. His position in society gave him access to the best information on all contemporary subjects of interest, and he was as successful in collecting gossip as curios. He also erected a private press, from which various important works, including Gray's *Bard*, as well as his own writings, were issued. Among the latter are *Letter from Xo Ho to his Friend Lien Chi at Pekin* (1757), *The Castle of Otranto*, the forerunner of the romances of terror of Mrs. Radcliffe and " Monk " Lewis, *The Mysterious Mother* (1768), a tragedy of considerable power, *Cata-*

logue of Royal and Noble Authors, Anecdotes of Painting, Catalogue of Engravers (1763), *Essay on Modern Gardening, Memoirs of the Last Ten Years of George II., Memoirs of the Reign of George III.*, and above all his *Letters*, 2700 in number, vivacious, interesting, and often brilliant. W. never *m.*

WALPOLE, SIR SPENCER (1839-1907).—Historian, *s.* of the Right Hon. Spencer W., Home Sec. in the three Derby Cabinets, belonged to the same family as Sir Robert W. *Ed.* at Eton he became a clerk in the War Office, and was thereafter successively Inspector of Fisheries 1867, Lieutenant-Governor of the Isle of Man 1882, and Sec. to the Post Office, where he made a reputation as an efficient administrator, and was made K.C.B. in 1898. He *pub. History of England from* 1815 in 6 vols., bringing the story down to 1858, and followed it up with *The History of Twenty-five Years.* He also wrote Lives of Spencer Percival, Prime Minister 1809-12, who was assassinated in the lobby of the House of Commons in the latter year, and who was his maternal grandfather, and of Earl Russell. His latest book was *Studies in Biography.* He wrote with much knowledge, and in a clear and sober style.

WALTON, IZAAK (1593-1683).—Biographer, and author of *The Compleat Angler*, *s.* of a yeoman, was *b.* at Stafford. Of his earlier years little is known. He carried on business as a hosier in London, in which he made a modest competence, which enabled him to retire at 50, the rest of his long life of 90 years being spent in the simple country pleasures, especially angling, which he so charmingly describes. He was twice *m.*, first to Rachel Floud, a descendant of Archbishop Cranmer, and second to Ann Ken, half-sister of the author of the Evening Hymn. His first book was a *Life of Dr. Donne* (1640), followed by Lives of Sir Henry Wotton (1651), Richard Hooker (1662), George Herbert (1670), and Bishop Sanderson (1678). All of these, classics in their kind, short, but simple and striking, were *coll.* into one vol. His masterpiece, however, was *The Compleat Angler*, the first ed. of which was *pub.* in 1653. Subsequent ed. were greatly enlarged; a second part was added by Charles Cotton (*q.v.*). With its dialogues between Piscator (angler), Venator (hunter), and Auceps (falconer), full of wisdom, kindly humour, and charity, its charming pictures of country scenes and pleasures, and its snatches of verse, it is one of the most delightful and care-dispelling books in the language. His long, happy, and innocent life ended in the house of his son-in-law, Dr. Hawkins, Prebendary of Winchester, where in the Cathedral he lies buried.

WARBURTON, BARTHOLOMEW ELIOT GEORGE (1810-1852).—Miscellaneous writer, *b.* in County Galway, travelled in the East, and *pub.* an account of his experiences, *The Crescent and the Cross*, which had remarkable success, brought out an historical work, *Memoirs of Prince Rupert and the Cavaliers* (1849), and ed. *Memoirs of Horace Walpole and his Contemporaries.* He perished in the burning of the steamer *Amazon.*

WARBURTON, WILLIAM (1698-1779).—Theologian, *b.* at Newark, where his *f.* was an attorney. Intended for the law, he was for a few years engaged in its practice, but his intense love of, and capacity for, study led him to enter the Church, and in 1728 he was presented to the Rectory of Brand-Broughton, where he remained for many years. His first important work was *The Alliance between Church and State* (1736), which brought him into notice. But it was entirely eclipsed by his *Divine Legation of Moses*, of which the first part appeared in 1737, and the second in 1741. The work, though learned and able, is somewhat paradoxical, and it plunged him into controversies with his numerous critics, and led to his publishing a *Vindication*. It, however, obtained for him the appointment of chaplain to Frederick, Prince of Wales. In 1739 W. gained the friendship of Pope by publishing a defence of *The Essay on Man*. Through Pope he became acquainted with most of the men of letters of the time, and he was made by the poet his literary executor, and had the legacy of half his library, and the profits of his posthumous works. On the strength of this he brought out an ed. of Pope's works. He also *pub.* an ed. of Shakespeare with notes, which was somewhat severely criticised, and his *Doctrine of Grace*, a polemic against Wesley. He became Dean of Bristol in 1757 and Bishop of Gloucester in 1759. W. was a man of powerful intellect, but his temper was overbearing and arrogant.

"WARD, ARTEMUS" (*see* BROWN, C. F.).

WARD, ROBERT PLUMER (1765-1846).—Novelist and politician, *b.* in London, *ed.* at Oxf., and called to the Bar 1790, held various political offices, and wrote some books on the law of nations; also three novels, *Tremaine, or the Man of Refinement*, full of prolix discussions; *De Vere, or the Man of Independence*, in which Canning is depicted under the character of Wentworth; and *De Clifford, or the Constant Man*.

WARD, WILLIAM GEORGE (1812-1882).—Theologian, *ed.* at Winchester and Oxf., and came under the influence of J. H. Newman, whose famous Tract No. XC. he defended, and whom he followed into the Church of Rome. In 1844 he *pub. The Ideal of a Christian Church* from the Romanist point of view, whence his soubriquet of "Ideal Ward." He was lecturer on Moral Philosophy at St. Edward's Coll., Ware, and wrote various treatises on controversial theology.

WARDLAW, ELIZABETH, LADY (1677-1727).—Poetess, *dau.* of Sir Charles Halkett of Pitfirrane, and wife of Sir Henry Wardlaw of Pitreavie, is believed to have written the pseudo-ancient ballad of "Hardyknute." The ballad of "Sir Patrick Spens" and others have also, but doubtfully, been attributed to her.

WARNER, SUSAN (1819-1885).—Writer of tales, *b.* at New York, and wrote, under the name of "Elizabeth Wetherell," a number of stories, of which *The Wide, Wide World* (1851) had an extraordinary popularity. Others were *Queechy* (1852), *The Old Helmet* (1863), and *Melbourne House* (1864). They have no particular literary merit or truth to nature, and are rather sentimental and "gushy."

WARNER, WILLIAM (1558-1609).—Poet, *b.* in London or Yorkshire, studied at Oxf., and was an attorney in London. In

1585 he *pub.* a collection of seven tales in prose entitled *Pan his Syrinx*, and in 1595 a translation of the *Menæchmi* of Plautus. His chief work was *Albion's England*, *pub.* in 1586 in 13 books of fourteen-syllabled verse, and republished with 3 additional books in 1606. The title is thus explained in the dedication, "This our whole island anciently called Britain, but more anciently Albion, presently containing two kingdoms, England and Scotland, is cause . . . that to distinguish the former, whose only occurrants I abridge from our history, I entitle this my book *Albion's England*." For about 20 years it was one of the most popular poems of its size—it contains about 10,000 lines—ever written, and he and Spenser were called the Homer and Virgil of their age. They must, however, have appealed to quite different classes. The plain-spoken, jolly humour, homely, lively, direct tales, vigorous patriotic feeling, and rough-and-tumble metre of Warner's muse, and its heterogeneous accumulation of material—history, tales, theology, antiquities—must have appealed to a lower and wider audience than Spenser's charmed verse. The style is clear, spirited, and pointed, but, as has been said, "with all its force and vivacity . . . fancy at times, and graphic descriptive power, it is poetry with as little of high imagination in it as any that was ever written." In his narratives W. allowed himself great latitude of expression, which may partly account for the rapidity with which his book fell into oblivion.

WARREN, SAMUEL (1807-1877).—Novelist, *b.* in Denbighshire, *s.* of a Nonconformist minister. After studying medicine at Edin. he took up law, and became a barrister, wrote several legal text-books, and in 1852 was made Recorder of Hull. He sat in the House of Commons for Midhurst 1856-59, and was a Master in Lunacy 1859-77. He was the author of *Passages from the Diary of a late Physician*, which appeared (1832-37) first in *Blackwood's Magazine*, as did also *Ten Thousand a Year* (1839). Both attracted considerable attention, and were often reprinted and translated. His last novel, *Now and Then*, had little success. W. entertained exaggerated ideas as to the importance of his place in literature.

WARTON, JOSEPH (1722-1800).—Critic, elder *s.* of the Rev. Thomas W., Prof. of Poetry at Oxf., was *ed.* at Basingstoke School, (of which his *f.* was headmaster), Winchester, and Oxf. He took orders, held various benefices, and became headmaster of Winchester Coll., and Prebendary of Winchester and of St. Paul's. He *pub.* miscellaneous verses, 2 vols. of *Odes* (1744 and 1746), in which he displayed a then unusual feeling for nature, and revolted against the critical rules of Pope and his followers. He was a good classical scholar, and made an approved translation of the *Eclogues* and *Georgics* of Virgil. He and his brother Thomas (*q.v.*) were friends of Johnson, and members of the Literary Club. His last work of importance was an *Essay on the Writings and Genius of Pope*, of which the first vol. appeared in 1757, and the second in 1782, and which gave an impulse to the romantic movement in English literature. He also ed. Pope's works, and had begun an ed. of Dryden when he *d.*

WARTON, THOMAS (1728-1790).—Literary historian and critic, younger *s.* of Thomas W., Prof. of Poetry at Oxf., and brother of the above, was *ed.* under his *f.* at Basingstoke and at Oxf. At the age of 19 he *pub.* a poem of considerable promise, *The Pleasures of Melancholy*, and two years later attracted attention by *The Triumph of Isis* (1749), in praise of Oxf., and in answer to Mason's *Isis.* After various other poetical excursions he *pub. Observations on Spenser's Faery Queen* (1754), which greatly increased his reputation, and in 1757 he was made Prof. of Poetry at Oxf., which position he held for 10 years. After bringing out one or two ed. of classics and biographies of college benefactors, he issued, from 1774-81, his great *History of English Poetry*, which comes down to the end of the Elizabethan age. The research and judgment, and the stores of learning often curious and recondite, which were brought to bear upon its production render this work, though now in various respects superseded, a vast magazine of information, and it did much to restore our older poetry to the place of which it had been unjustly deprived by the classical school. His ed. of Milton's minor poems has been pronounced by competent critics to be the best ever produced. W. was a clergyman, but if the tradition is to be believed that he had only two sermons, one written by his *f.* and the other printed, and if the love of ease and of ale which he celebrates in some of his verses was other than poetical, he was more in his place as a critic than as a cleric. As a poet he hardly came up to his own standards. He was made Poet Laureate in 1785, and in the same year Camden Prof. of History, and was one of the first to detect the Chatterton forgeries, a task in which his antiquarian lore stood him in good stead.

WATERLAND, DANIEL (1683-1740).—Theologian, *b.* at Waseley Rectory, Lincolnshire, and *ed.* at Camb., took orders, and obtained various preferments, becoming Master of Magdalene Coll., Camb. 1713, Chancellor of York 1722, and Archdeacon of Middlesex 1730. He was an acute and able controversialist on behalf of the orthodox doctrine of the Trinity, on which he wrote several treatises. He was also the author of a *History of the Athanasian Creed* (1723).

WATERTON, CHARLES (1782-1865).—Naturalist, belonged to an old Roman Catholic family in Yorkshire, and was *ed.* at Stonyhurst Coll. Sent out in 1804 to look after some family estates in Demerara, he wandered through the wildest parts of Guiana and Brazil, in search of plants and animals for his collections. His adventures were related in his highly-spiced and entertaining *Wanderings in South America, etc.* (1825), in which he details certain surprising episodes in connection with the capture of serpents, and specially of a cayman, on the back of which he rode. He also wrote an interesting account of his family.

WATSON, JOHN (1850-1907) "IAN MACLAREN."—Novelist and theological writer, *b.* at Manningtree, where his *f.* was an Inland Revenue official, *ed.* at Stirling and Edin., and the New Coll. there. He came, after serving in a country charge, to Sefton Park Presbyterian Church, Liverpool, where he was a popular preacher, and took a prominent part in the social and religious life of the city. He wrote, under the name of "Ian Maclaren," several novels belonging to the "Kailyard" school, including *Beside the Bonnie Briar Bush* and *The*

Days of Auld Lang Syne, which had great popularity both at home and in America. He also wrote religious works, of which *The Mind of the Master* is the best known.

WATSON, ROBERT (1730-1781).—Historian, *s.* of an apothecary in St. Andrews, where and at Edin. and Glasgow, he was *ed.* He became Prof. of Logic, and afterwards Principal of St. Salvador's Coll., at St. Andrews, and wrote a History of Philip II. of Spain, and part of a continuation on Philip III., which were long standard works.

WATSON, THOMAS (1557?-1592).—Poet, *b.* in London, was at Oxf., and studied law. He was a scholar, and made translations, one of which was a Latin version of the *Antigone* of Sophocles. In 1582 he *pub. Hecatompathia, or The Passionate Centurie of Love*, consisting of 100 eighteen-line poems, which he called sonnets. It was followed by *Amyntas* (1585) and *Teares of Fansie* (1593).

WATTS, ALARIC ALEXANDER (1797-1864).—Poet, *b.* in London, had an active career as a journalist. He founded the *United Service Gazette*, and ed. various newspapers and an annual, the *Literary Souvenir*. His poems were *coll.* as *Lyrics of the Heart*. His numerous journalistic ventures finally resulted in bankruptcy.

WATTS, ISAAC (1674-1748).—Poet and theologian, *b.* at Southampton, where his *f.* kept a school, and *ed.* at a Nonconformist academy at Stoke Newington, became minister of an Independent congregation in Mark Lane; but his health proving insufficient for his pastoral duties, he resigned, and gave himself chiefly to literary work, continuing to preach occasionally. For the last 36 years of his life he resided at Theobald's, the house of his friend, Sir Thomas Abney. Among his writings were various educational treatises, including those on *Logic* and *The Improvement of the Mind*, and some works on theological subjects. But his fame rests on his sacred poems and his hymns, which number over 500, and with much that is prosaic comprised "There is a Land of Pure Delight," "O God our Help in Ages Past," and "When I survey the Wondrous Cross," which has been called "the most majestic hymn in English speech." His *Horæ Lyricæ* was *pub.* in 1706, *Hymns* (1707), *Divine Songs* (for children) (1715), *Metrical Psalms* (1719). Some of his poems, such as his exquisite cradle song, "Hush, my dear, lie still and slumber" have a perfect beauty and tenderness.

WAUGH, EDWIN (1817-1890).—Poet, *s.* of a shoemaker, was *b.* at Rochdale and, after a little schooling, apprenticed to a printer. He read eagerly, and became assistant sec. to the Lancashire Public School Association. He first attracted attention by his sketches of Lancashire life and character in the *Manchester Examiner*. He wrote also in prose *Factory Folk, Besom Ben Stories*, and *The Chimney Corner*. His best work was, perhaps, his dialect songs, *coll.* as *Poems and Songs* (1859), which brought him great local fame. He was possessed of considerable literary gift, and has been called "the Lancashire Burns."

WEBBE, WILLIAM (*b.* 1550).—Critic and translator. Almost nothing is known of him except that he was at Camb. and acted as tutor in certain distinguished families, and was a friend of Spenser. He wrote a *Discourse of English Poetrie* (1586), in which he discusses metre, rhyme (the use of which he reprehends), and reviews English poetry up to his own day. He also translated the first two of the *Eclogues* of Virgil in singularly unmelodious hexameters.

WEBSTER, MRS. AUGUSTA (DAVIES) (1837-1894).—Poet and translator, *dau.* of Admiral Davies, *m.* Mr. Thomas Webster, a solicitor. She wrote a novel, *Lesley's Guardians*, and several books of poetry of distinguished excellence, including *Blanche Lisle*, *Dramatic Studies* (1866), *Portraits* (1870), *A Book of Rhyme* (1881), and some dramas, including *The Auspicious Day* (1874), *Disguises*, and *The Sentence* (1887). She also made translations of *Prometheus Bound* and *Medea*.

WEBSTER, DANIEL (1782-1852).—Orator, *s.* of a farmer in New Hampshire, was a distinguished advocate in Boston, and afterwards a member of the United States Senate and Sec. of State 1841-43 and 1850-52. He was the greatest orator whom America has produced, and has a place in literature by virtue of his *pub.* speeches.

WEBSTER, JOHN (1580?-1625?).—Dramatist. Though in some respects he came nearest to Shakespeare of any of his contemporaries, almost nothing has come down to us of the life of W. Even the dates of his birth and death are uncertain. He appears to have been the *s.* of a London tailor, to have been a freeman of the Merchant Taylor's Company, and clerk of the parish of St. Andrews, Holborn. Four plays are known to be his, *The White Devil, or the Life and Death of Vittoria Corombona* (1612), *Appius and Virginia* (1654), *The Devil's Law Case* (1623), and *The Duchess of Malfi* (1623), and he collaborated with Drayton, Middleton, Heywood, Dekker, etc., in the production of others. He does not appear to have been much regarded in his own day, and it was only in the 19th century that his great powers began to be appreciated and expounded by such critics as Lamb and Hazlitt, and in later days Swinburne. The first says, " To move a horror skilfully, to touch a soul to the quick, to lay upon fear as much as it can bear, to wean and weary a life till it is ready to drop, and then step in with mortal instruments to take its last forfeit, this only a Webster can do." W. revels in the horrible, but the touch of genius saves his work from mere brutality, and evokes pity and sorrow where, without it, there would be only horror and disgust. His work is extremely unequal, and he had no power of construction, but his extraordinary insight into motives and feelings redeem all his failings and give him a place second only to Marlowe and Ben Jonson among the contemporaries of Shakespeare.

WEBSTER, NOAH (1758-1843).—Lexicographer, etc., *b.* at Hartford, Conn., and *ed.* at Yale. His long life was spent in unremitting diligence as teacher, lawyer, and man of letters. His great work is his American *Dictionary of the English Language* (1828), for which he prepared himself by 10 years' study of philology.

Many abridgments of it have appeared, and in 1866 a new and enlarged ed. was *pub.* His *Elementary Spelling Book* is believed to have attained a circulation of 70,000,000 copies. He also *pub.* *A Philosophical and Practical Grammar of the English Language* (1807), and many other works.

WELLS, CHARLES JEREMIAH (1800?-1879).—Poet, *b.* in London, where he practised as a solicitor, *pub.* in 1822 *Stories after Nature*, written in poetic prose, which attracted no attention, and a biblical drama, *Joseph and his Brethren* (1824), which had an almost similar fate until D. G. Rossetti called attention to it in 1863, giving it a high meed of praise. In 1874, stung by want of appreciation, he had burned his manuscripts of plays and poems; but on the new interest excited in his *Joseph* he added some new scenes. In his later years he lived in France. *Joseph and his Brethren* ed. in the World's Classics, 1909.

WENDOVER, ROGER DE (*d.* 1236).—Chronicler, a monk of St. Albans, became Prior of Belvoir, from which he was deposed for extravagance, but was recalled to St. Albans, where he *d.* He wrote *Flores Historiarum* (Flowers of History), a history of the world in 2 books, the first from the creation to the incarnation, the second to the reign of Henry III., his own time. The latter is of value as a contemporary authority, and is an impartial and manly account of his own period.

WESLEY, CHARLES (1707-1788).—Hymn-writer, younger brother of John W. (*q.v.*), was *b.* at Epworth, and *ed.* at Westminster School and Oxf. He was all his life closely associated with his elder and greater brother, one of whose most loyal helpers he was, though not agreeing with him in all points. His chief fame is founded upon his hymns, of which he is said to have written the almost incredible number of 6500, many of them among the finest in the language. They include "Jesus, Lover of my Soul," "Love Divine all Loves excelling," "Come, oh Thou Traveller Unknown," "Hark the Herald Angels Sing," and "Come, let us join our Friends above."

WESLEY, JOHN (1703-1791).—Theological writer, diarist, and founder of Methodism, was the second surviving *s.* of the Rev. Samuel W., Rector of Epworth, Lincolnshire. The name was also written Westley and Wellesley, and the family appears to be the same as that to which the Duke of Wellington and his brother the Marquis Wellesley belonged. W. was *ed.* at the Charterhouse and at Oxf., and was ordained deacon in 1725, and priest in 1728. After assisting his *f.* for a short time as curate, he returned to Oxf., where he found that his brother Charles, along with G. Whitefield (*q.v.*) and others, had begun that association for religious improvement from which sprang the great religious movement known as Methodism. About the same time the two brothers came under the influence of William Law (*q.v.*), author of the *Serious Call*, and in 1735 John went on a mission to Georgia to preach to the Indians and colonists, and became closely associated with the Moravian Brethren. Difficulties of a personal character, however, led to his return in 1738 to London, where he continued to associate with the Moravians.

It was at this time that, hearing Luther's preface to the Epistle to the Romans read at a meeting, he found his religious and ecclesiastical views revolutionised. Hitherto holding strong High Church views in some directions, he now assumed a position which ultimately led to his abandoning the doctrine of Apostolical succession, and ordaining pastors and bishops, and finally creating a separate ecclesiastical organisation. Consequences soon followed; the pulpits of the Church were closed against him, and he began his marvellous career of itinerant and out-of-door preaching, which was continued to the close of his long life. He soon became a mighty power in the land; vast crowds waited on his ministrations, which were instrumental in producing a great revival of religious interest, and improved morality among the people. At the same time violent opposition was aroused, and W. was often in danger of his life from mobs. In the end, however, he lived down this state of things to a large extent, and in his old age was the object of extraordinary general veneration, while in his own communion he exercised a kind of pontifical sway. During the 50 years of his apostolic journeyings he is said to have travelled 250,000 miles in Britain, Ireland, and the Continent; but notwithstanding this phenomenal activity he was able, by extreme economy of time, to write copiously, his works including educational treatises, translations from the classics, histories of Rome and England, a history of the Church, biblical commentaries, manifold controversial treatises and ed. of religious classics. Most of them had an enormous circulation and brought him in £30,000, all of which he expended on philanthropic and religious objects. The work, however, on which his literary fame chiefly rests is his *Journal*, extending from 1735-90, which is one of the most graphic and interesting records of its kind in existence. He also wrote many hymns, largely translations from the German, and he had a considerable hand in giving their final form to the almost innumerable hymns of his brother Charles. W. was a man of practical and organising ability of the first order, of intense religious earnestness and sincerity, benevolent feelings, and agreeable manners. At the same time he was of an autocratic temper, and often showed keenness and even intolerance in his controversies, which were largely against the extreme Calvinism of his old friend and fellow-labourer, Whitefield, and Toplady, the author of the hymn "Rock of Ages," himself a bitter polemic. In 1740 he had formally withdrawn from association with the Moravians. W. was *m.* in 1751 to a widow, Mrs. Vazeille, with whom, however, he did not live happily, and who separated from him in 1776.

WESTALL, WILLIAM (1834-1903).—Novelist, was originally in business, but later betook himself to journalism, and also wrote a large number of novels, including *The Old Factory*, *Strange Crimes*, *Her Ladyship's Secret*, etc., which, while healthy in tone and interesting, have no literary distinction.

WHARTON, THOMAS WHARTON, 1ST MARQUIS OF (1648-1715).—Statesman and writer of "Lillibullero," *s.* of the 4th Baron W., was one of the most profligate men of his age. He was a supporter of the Exclusion Bill, and consequently obnoxious to James II. His only contribution to literature was the doggerel ballad,

"Lillibullero" (1688), which had so powerful a political effect that its author claimed to have sung a King out of three kingdoms. He was generally disliked and distrusted, but held for a short time, from 1708, the Lord Lieutenancy of Ireland, when he had Addison as his chief sec.

WHATELEY, RICHARD (1787-1863).—Theologian and economist, *s.* of the Rev. Dr. Joseph W., *b.* in London, and *ed.* at a school in Bristol, and at Oxf., where he became a coll. tutor. Taking orders he became Rector of Halesworth, Suffolk. In 1822 he delivered his Bampton lectures on *The Use and Abuse of Party Feeling in Religion.* Three years later he was made Principal of St. Alban's Hall, in 1829 Prof. of Political Economy, and in 1831 Archbishop of Dublin. As head of a coll. and as a prelate W. showed great energy and administrative ability. He was a vigorous, clear-headed personality, somewhat largely endowed with contempt for views with which he was not in sympathy, and with a vein of caustic humour, in the use of which he was not sparing. These qualities made him far from universally popular; but his honesty, fairness, and devotion to duty gained for him general respect. He had no sympathy with the Oxf. movement, was strongly anti-Calvinistic, and somewhat Latitudinarian, so that he was exposed to a good deal of theological odium from opposite quarters. He was a voluminous writer, and among his best known works are his treatises on *Logic* (1826) and *Rhetoric* (1828), his *Historic Doubts relative to Napoleon Buonaparte* (1819), intended as a *reductio ad absurdum* of Hume's contention that no evidence is sufficient to prove a miracle, *Essays on some Peculiarities of the Christian Religion* (1825), *Christian Evidences* (1837), and ed. of Bacon's *Essays* with valuable notes, and of Paley's *Evidences.*

WHETSTONE, GEORGE (1544?-1587?).—Dramatist, one of the early, roistering playwrights who frequented the Court of Elizabeth, later served as a soldier in the Low Countries, accompanied Sir Humphrey Gilbert's expedition to Newfoundland in 1578, and was at the Battle of Zutphen in 1586. He was a trenchant critic of the contemporary drama, contending for greater reality and rationality. His play, *Promos and Cassandra,* translated from Cinthio's *Hecatomithi,* was used by Shakespeare in *Measure for Measure.*

WHEWELL, WILLIAM (1794-1866).—Philosopher, theologian and mathematician, *s.* of a joiner at Lancaster, where he was *b.*, *ed.* at Camb., where he had a brilliant career. He became Prof. of Mineralogy at Camb. 1828, of Moral Theology 1838, was Master of Trinity from 1841 until his death, and he held the office of Vice-Chancellor of the Univ. in 1843 and 1856. W. was remarkable as the possessor of an encyclopædic fund of knowledge, perhaps unprecedented, and he was the author of a number of works of great importance on a variety of subjects. Among the chief of these may be mentioned his Bridgewater Treatise on *Astronomy and General Physics considered with Reference to Natural Theology* (1833), *History of the Inductive Sciences* (1837), *The Philosophy of the Inductive Sciences* (1840), *Essay on Plurality of Worlds* (anonymously), *Elements of Morality* (1845), *History of Moral Philosophy in England*

(1852), and *Platonic Dialogues.* In addition to these he wrote innumerable articles, reviews, and scientific papers. It was as a co-ordinator of knowledge and the researches of others that W. excelled; he was little of an original observer or discoverer. He is described as a large, strong, erect man with a red face and a loud voice, and he was an overwhelming and somewhat arrogant talker.

WHICHCOTE, BENJAMIN (1609-1683).—Divine, belonged to a good Shropshire family, and was at Camb., where he became Provost of King's Coll., of which office he was deprived at the Restoration. He was of liberal views, and is reckoned among the Camb. Platonists, over whom he exercised great influence. His works consist of *Discourses* and *Moral and Religious Aphorisms.* In 1668 he was presented to the living of St. Lawrence, Jewry, London, which he held until his death.

WHIPPLE, EDWIN PERCY (1819-1886).—Essayist and critic, *b.* in Massachusetts, was a brilliant and discriminating critic. His works include *Character and Characteristic Men, Literature and Life, Success and its Conditions, Literature of the Age of Elizabeth, Literature and Politics,* etc.

WHISTON, WILLIAM (1667-1752).—Theologian, and man of science, *b.* at Norton, Leicestershire, and *ed.* at Camb., where he succeeded Newton as Lucasian Prof. of Mathematics, was a prominent advocate of the Newtonian system, and wrote a *Theory of the Earth* against the views of Thomas Burnet (*q.v.*). He also wrote several theological works, *Primitive Christianity Revived* and the *Primitive New Testament.* The Arian views promulgated in the former led to his expulsion from the Univ. His best known work was his translation of *Josephus.* He was a kindly and honest, but eccentric and impracticable man, and an insatiable controversialist.

WHITE, GILBERT (1720-1793).—Naturalist, *b.* at Selborne, Hants, and *ed.* along with the Wartons (*q.v.*) at their father's school at Basingstoke, and thereafter at Oxf., entered the Church, and after holding various curacies settled, in 1755, at Selborne. He became the friend and correspondent of Pennant the naturalist (*q.v.*), and other men of science, and *pub.* in the form of letters the work which has made him immortal, *The Natural History and Antiquities of Selborne* (1789). He was never *m.*, but was in love with the well-known bluestocking Hester Mulso, afterwards Mrs. Chapone, who rejected him. He had four brothers, all more or less addicted to the study of natural history.

WHITE, HENRY KIRKE (1785-1806).—Poet, *s.* of a butcher at Nottingham. At first assisting his *f.*, next a stocking weaver, he was afterwards placed in the office of an attorney. Some contributions to a newspaper introduced him to the notice of Capel Lofft, a patron of promising youths, by whose help he brought out a vol. of poems, which fell into the hands of Southey, who wrote to him. Thereafter friends raised a fund to send him to Camb., where he gave brilliant promise. Overwork, however, undermined a constitution originally delicate, and he *d.* at 21. Southey wrote a short memoir of him with some additional poems. His chief poem was the *Christiad*, a fragment. His best known production is the hymn, "Much in sorrow, oft in Woe."

WHITE, JOSEPH BLANCO (1775-1841).—Poet, *s.* of a merchant, an Irish Roman Catholic resident at Seville, where he was *b.*, became a priest, but lost his religious faith and came to England, where he conducted a Spanish newspaper having for its main object the fanning of the flame of Spanish patriotism against the French invasion, which was subsidised by the English Government. He again embraced Christianity, and entered the Church of England, but latterly became a Unitarian. He wrote, among other works, *Internal Evidences against Catholicism* (1825), and *Second Travels of an Irish Gentleman in search of a Religion*, in answer to T. Moore's work, *Travels, etc.* His most permanent contribution to literature, however, is his single sonnet on "Night," which Coleridge considered "the finest and most grandly conceived" in our language.

WHITE, RICHARD GRANT (1822-1885).—Shakespearian scholar, *b.* in New York State, was long Chief of the Revenue Marine Bureau, and was one of the most acute students and critics of Shakespeare, of whose works he *pub.* two ed., the first in 1865, and the second (the Riverside) in 1883. He also wrote *Words and their Uses*, *Memoirs of Shakespeare*, *Studies in Shakespeare*, *The New Gospel of Peace* (a satire), *The Fate of Mansfield Humphreys* (novel), etc.

WHITEHEAD, CHARLES (1804-1862).—Poet, novelist, and dramatist; is specially remembered for three works, all of which met with popular favour: *The Solitary* (1831), a poem, *The Autobiography of Jack Ketch* (1834), a novel, and *The Cavalier* (1836), a play in blank verse. He recommended Dickens for the writing of the letterpress for R. Seymour's drawings, which ultimately developed into *The Pickwick Papers*.

WHITEHEAD, WILLIAM (1715-1785).—Poet, *s.* of a baker at Camb., and *ed.* at Winchester School and Camb., became tutor in the family of the Earl of Jersey, and retained the favour of the family through life. In 1757 he succeeded Colley Cibber as Poet Laureate. He wrote plays of only moderate quality, including *The Roman Father* and *Creusa*, tragedies, and *The School for Lovers*, a comedy; also poems, *The Enthusiast* and *Variety*. His official productions as Laureate were severely attacked, which drew from him in reply *A Charge to the Poets*.

WHITMAN, WALTER OR WALT (1819-1892).—Poet, was *b.* at Huntingdon, Long Island, New York. His mother was of Dutch descent, and the farm on which he was *b.* had been in the possession of his father's family since the early settlement. His first education was received at Brooklyn, to which his *f.* had removed while W. was a young child. At 13 he was in a printing office, at 17 he was teaching and writing for the newspapers, and at 21 was editing one. The next dozen years were passed in desultory work as a printer with occasional literary excursions, but apparently mainly in "loafing" and observing his fellow-creatures. It was not till 1855 that his first really characteristic work, *Leaves of Grass*, appeared. This first ed. contained only 12 poems. Notwithstanding its startling departures from conventionality both in form and substance it was well received by the leading literary reviews and, with certain reserves to be expected, it was welcomed by Emerson. It did not, however, achieve general acceptance, and was received with strong and not unnatural protest in many quarters. When a later ed. was called for Emerson unsuccessfully endeavoured to persuade the author to suppress the more objectionable parts. On the outbreak of the Civil War W. volunteered as a nurse for the wounded, and rendered much useful service. The results of his experiences and observations were given in verse in *Drum Taps* and *The Wound Dresser*, and in prose in *Specimen Days*. From these scenes he was removed by his appointment to a Government clerkship, from which, however, he was soon dismissed on the ground of having written books of an immoral tendency. This action of the authorities led to a somewhat warm controversy, and after a short interval W. received another Government appointment, which he held until 1873, when he had a paralytic seizure, which rendered his retirement necessary. Other works besides those mentioned are *Two Rivulets* and *Democratic Vistas*. In his later years he retired to Camden, New Jersey, where he *d*. W. is the most unconventional of writers. Revolt against all convention was in fact his self-proclaimed mission. In his versification he discards rhyme almost entirely, and metre as generally understood; and in his treatment of certain passions and appetites, and of unadulterated human nature, he is at war with what he considered the conventions of an effeminate society; but after all reservations, there is real poetic insight and an intense and singularly fresh sense of nature in the best of his writings.

Works, 12 vols. with *Life*. *See* Stedman's *Poets of America*. Monographs by Symonds, Clarke, and Salter.

WHITNEY, WILLIAM DWIGHT (1827-1894).—Philologist, *b*. at Northampton, Mass., was Prof. of Sanskrit, etc., at Yale, and chief ed. of a remarkable work, *The Century Dictionary*. Among his books are *Darwinism and Language* and *The Life and Growth of Language*.

WHITTIER, JOHN GREENLEAF (1807-1892).—Poet, was *b*. at Haverhill, Massachusetts, of a Quaker family. In early life he worked on a farm. His later years were occupied partly in journalism, partly in farming, and he seems also to have done a good deal of local political work. He began to write verse at a very early age, and continued to do so until almost his latest days. He was always a champion of the anti-slavery cause, and by his writings both as journalist and poet, did much to stimulate national feeling in the direction of freedom. Among his poetical works are *Voices of Freedom* (1836), *Songs of Labour* (1851), *Home Ballads* (1859), *In War Time* (1863), *Snow Bound* (1866), *The Tent on the Beach* (1867),

Ballads of New England (1870), *The Pennsylvania Pilgrim* (1874). W. had true feeling and was animated by high ideals. Influenced in early life by the poems of Burns, he became a poet of nature, with which his early upbringing brought him into close and sympathetic contact; he was also a poet of faith and the ideal life and of liberty. He, however, lacked concentration and intensity, and his want of early education made him often loose in expression and faulty in form; and probably a comparatively small portion of what he wrote will live.

WHYTE-MELVILLE, GEORGE JOHN (1821-1878).—Novelist, *s.* of a country gentleman of Fife, *ed.* at Eton, entered the army, and saw service in the Crimea, retiring in 1859 as Major. Thereafter he devoted himself to field sports, in which he was an acknowledged authority, and to literature. He wrote a number of novels, mainly founded on sporting subjects, though a few were historical. They include *Kate Coventry*, *The Queen's Maries*, *The Gladiators*, and *Satanella*. He also wrote *Songs and Verses* and *The True Cross*, a religious poem. He *d.* from an accident in the hunting-field.

WICLIF, OR WYCLIF, JOHN (1320?-1384).—Theologian and translator of the Bible, *b.* near Richmond, Yorkshire, studied at Balliol Coll., Oxf., of which he became in 1361 master, and taking orders, became Vicar of Fillingham, Lincolnshire, when he resigned his mastership, and in 1361 Prebendary of Westbury. By this time he had written a treatise on logic, and had won some position as a man of learning. In 1372 he took the degree of Doctor of Theology, and became Canon of Lincoln, and in 1374 was sent to Bruges as one of a commission to treat with Papal delegates as to certain ecclesiastical matters in dispute, and in the same year he became Rector of Lutterworth, where he remained until his death. His liberal and patriotic views on the questions in dispute between England and the Pope gained for him the favour of John of Gaunt and Lord Percy, who accompanied him when, in 1377, he was summoned before the ecclesiastical authorities at St. Paul's. The Court was broken up by an inroad of the London mob, and no sentence was passed upon him. Another trial at Lambeth in the next year was equally inconclusive. By this time W. had taken up a position definitely antagonistic to the Papal system. He organised his institution of poor preachers, and initiated his great enterprise of translating the Scriptures into English. His own share of the work was the Gospels, probably the whole of the New Testament and possibly part of the Old. The whole work was ed. by John Purvey, an Oxf. friend, who had joined him at Lutterworth, the work being completed by 1400. In 1380 W. openly rejected the doctrine of transubstantiation, and was forbidden to teach at Oxf., where he had obtained great influence. In 1382 a Court was convened by the Archbishop of Canterbury, which passed sentence of condemnation upon his views. It says much for the position which he had attained, and for the power of his supporters, that he was permitted to depart from Oxf. and retire to Lutterworth, where, worn out by his labours and anxieties, he *d.* of a paralytic seizure on the last day of 1384. His enemies, baffled in their designs against him while living, consoled themselves by disinterring his bones in 1428 and throwing them into the river Swift, of which Thomas Fuller (*q.v.*) has said, "Thus this brook has conveyed his ashes into Avon, Avon into Severn, Severn into the Narrow Seas, they into the main ocean, and thus the ashes of Wicliffe are the emblem of his doctrine, which now is dispersed all the world over." The works of W. were chiefly controversial or theological and, as literature, have no great importance, but his translation of the Bible had indirectly a great influence not only by tending to fix the language, but in a far greater degree by furthering the moral and intellectual emancipation on which true literature is essentially founded.

WILBERFORCE, WILLIAM (1759-1833).—Philanthropist and religious writer, *s.* of a merchant, was *b.* at Hull, *ed.* at Camb., entered Parliament as member for his native town, became the intimate friend of Pitt, and was the leader of the crusade against the slave-trade and slavery His chief literary work was his *Practical View of Christianity*, which had remarkable popularity and influence, but he wrote continually and with effect on the religious and philanthropic objects to which he had devoted his life.

WILCOX, CARLES (1794-1827).—Poet, *b.* at Newport, N. H., was a Congregationalist minister. He wrote a poem, *The Age of Benevolence*, which was left unfinished, and which bears manifest traces of the influence of Cowper.

WILDE, OSCAR FINGAL O'FLAHERTY WILLS (1856-1900). —Poet and dramatist, *s.* of Sir William W., the eminent surgeon, was *b.* at Dublin, and *ed.* there at Trinity Coll. and at Oxf. He was one of the founders of the modern cult of the æsthetic. Among his writings are *Poems* (1881), *The Picture of Dorian Gray*, a novel, and several plays, including *Lady Windermere's Fan*, *A Woman of no Importance*, and *The Importance of being Earnest*. He was convicted of a serious offence, and after his release from prison went abroad and *d.* at Paris. *Coll.* ed. of his works, 12 vols., 1909.

WILKES, JOHN (1727-1797).—Politician, *s.* of a distiller in London, was *ed.* at Leyden. Witty, resourceful, but unprincipled and profligate, he became from circumstances the representative and champion of important political principles, including that of free representation in Parliament. His writings have nothing of the brilliance and point of his social exhibitions, but his paper, *The North Briton*, and especially the famous "No. 45," in which he charged George III. with uttering a falsehood in his speech from the throne, caused so much excitement, and led to such important results that they give him a place in literature. He also wrote a highly offensive *Essay on Woman*. W. was expelled the House of Commons and outlawed, but such was the strength of the cause which he championed that, notwithstanding the worthlessness of his character, his right to sit in the House was ultimately admitted in 1774, and he continued to sit until 1790. He was also Lord Mayor of London.

WILKIE, WILLIAM (1721-1772).—Poet, *b.* in Linlithgowshire, *s.* of a farmer, and *ed.* at Edin., he entered the Church, and became minister of Ratho, Midlothian, in 1756, and Prof. of Natural

Philosophy at St. Andrews in 1759. In 1757 he *pub.* the *Epigoniad*, dealing with the Epigoni, sons of the seven heroes who fought against Thebes. He also wrote *Moral Fables in Verse.*

WILKINS, JOHN (1614-1672).—Mathematician and divine, *s.* of a goldsmith in Oxf., but *b.* at Daventry and *ed.* at Oxf., entered the Church, held many preferments, and became Bishop of Chester. He *m.* a sister of Oliver Cromwell, and being of an easy temper and somewhat accommodating principles, he passed through troublous times and many changes with a minimum of hardship. He was one of the band of learned men whom Charles II. incorporated as the Royal Society. Among his writings are *The Discovery of a World in the Moon*, *Mathematical Magic*, and *An Essay towards . . . a Philosophical Language.*

WILKINSON, SIR JOHN GARDNER (1797-1875).—Egyptologist, *s.* of a Westmoreland clergyman, studied at Oxf. In 1821 he went to Egypt, and remained there and in Nubia exploring, surveying, and studying the hieroglyphical inscriptions, on which he made himself one of the great authorities. He *pub.* two important works, of great literary as well as scholarly merit, *Materia Hieroglyphica* (1828) and *Manners and Customs of the Ancient Egyptians* (6 vols., 1837-41). He wrote various books of travel, and was knighted in 1839.

WILLIAM OF MALMESBURY (*fl.* 12th cent.).—Historian, was an inmate of the great monastery at Malmesbury. His name is said to have been Somerset, and he was Norman by one parent and English by the other. The date of his birth is unknown, that of his death has sometimes been fixed as 1142 on the ground that his latest work stops abruptly in that year. His history, written in Latin, falls into two parts, *Gesta Regum Anglorum* (Acts of the Kings of the English), in five books, bringing the narrative down from the arrival of the Saxons to 1120, and *Historia Novella* (Modern History), carrying it on to 1142. The work is characterised by a love of truth, much more critical faculty in sifting evidence than was then common, and considerable attention to literary form. It is dedicated to Robert, Earl of Gloucester, the champion of Queen Matilda. Other works by W. are *De Gestis Pontificum Anglorum*, Lives of the English Bishops, and a history of the Monastery of Glastonbury.

WILLIAM OF NEWBURGH, OR NEWBURY (1136-1198?).—Historian, belonged to the monastery of Newburgh in Yorkshire. His own name is said to have been Little. His work, *Historia Rerum Anglicarum* (History of English affairs), is written in good Latin, and has some of the same qualities as that of William of Malmesbury (*q.v.*). He rejects the legend of the Trojan descent of the early Britons, and animadverts severely on what he calls " the impudent and impertinent lies " of Geoffrey of Monmouth (*q.v.*). His record of contemporary events is careful.

WILLIAMS, SIR CHARLES HANBURY (1708-1759).—Diplomatist and satirist, *s.* of John Hanbury, a Welsh ironmaster, assumed the name of Williams on succeeding to an estate, entered

Parliament as a supporter of Walpole, held many diplomatic posts, and was a brilliant wit with a great contemporary reputation for lively and biting satires and lampoons.

WILLIS, BROWNE (1682-1760).—Antiquary, *ed.* at Westminster and Oxf., entered the Inner Temple 1700, sat in the House of Commons 1705-8. He wrote *History of the Counties, Cities, and Boroughs of England and Wales* (1715), *Notitia Parliamentaria*, etc.

WILLIS, NATHANIEL PARKER (1806-1867).—Poet, *b.* at Portland, and *ed.* at Yale, was mainly a journalist, and conducted various magazines, including the *American Monthly*; but he also wrote short poems, many of which were popular, of which perhaps the best is "Unseen Spirits," stories, and works of a more or less fugitive character, with such titles as *Pencillings by the Way* (1835), *Inklings of Adventure, Letters from under a Bridge* (1839), *People I have Met, The Rag-Tag, The Slingsby Papers*, etc., some of which were originally contributed to his magazines. He travelled a good deal in Europe, and was attached for a time to the American Embassy in Paris. He was a favourite in society, and enjoyed a wide popularity in uncritical circles, but is now distinctly a spent force.

WILLS, JAMES (1790-1868).—Poet and miscellaneous writer, younger *s.* of a Roscommon squire, was *ed.* at Trinity Coll., Dublin, and studied law in the Middle Temple. Deprived, however, of the fortune destined for him and the means of pursuing a legal career by the extravagance of his elder brother, he entered the Church, and also wrote largely in *Blackwood's Magazine* and other periodicals. In 1831 he *pub. The Disembodied and other Poems; The Philosophy of Unbelief* (1835) attracted much attention. His largest work was Lives of *Illustrious and Distinguished Irishmen*, and his latest publication *The Idolatress* (1868). In all his writings W. gave evidence of a powerful personality. His poems are spirited, and in some cases show considerable dramatic qualities.

WILLS, WILLIAM GORMAN (1828-1891).—Dramatist, *s.* of above, *b.* in Dublin. After writing a novel, *Old Times*, in an Irish magazine, he went to London, and for some time wrote for periodicals without any very marked success. He found his true vein in the drama, and produced over 30 plays, many of which, including *Medea in Corinth, Eugene Aram, Jane Shore, Buckingham*, and *Olivia*, had great success. Besides these he wrote a poem, *Melchior*, in blank verse, and many songs. He was also an accomplished artist.

WILSON, ALEXANDER (1766-1813).—Poet and ornithologist, *b.* at Paisley, where he worked as a weaver, afterwards becoming a pedlar. He *pub.* some poems, of which the best is *Watty and Maggie*, and in 1794 went to America, where he worked as a pedlar and teacher. His skill in depicting birds led to his becoming an enthusiastic ornithologist, and he induced the publisher of *Rees's Cyclopædia*, on which he had been employed, to undertake an American ornithology to be written and illustrated by him. Some vols. of the work were completed when, worn out by the labour and exposure entailed by his journeys in search of specimens, he succumbed to a fever. Two additional vols. appeared posthumously. The work, both from a literary and artistic point of view, is of high merit. He also *pub.* in America another poem, *The Foresters.*

WILSON, SIR DANIEL (1816-1892).—Archæologist and miscellaneous writer, *b.* and *ed.* in Edin., and after acting as sec. of the Society of Antiquaries there, went to Toronto as Prof. of History and English Literature. He was the author of *Memorials of Edinburgh in the Olden Time, The Archæology and Pre-historic Annals of Scotland* (1851), *Civilisation in the Old and the New World,* a study on "Chatterton," and *Caliban, the Missing Link,* etc.

WILSON, JOHN ("CHRISTOPHER NORTH") (1785-1854).—Poet, essayist, and miscellaneous writer, *s.* of a wealthy manufacturer in Paisley, where he was *b.*, was *ed.* at Glas. and Oxf. At the latter he not only displayed great intellectual endowments, but distinguished himself as an athlete. Having succeeded to a fortune of £50,000 he purchased the small estate of Elleray in the Lake District, where he enjoyed the friendship of Wordsworth, Southey, Coleridge, and De Quincey. In 1812 he *pub. The Isle of Palms,* followed four years later by *The City of the Plague,* which gained for him a recognised place in literature, though they did not show his most characteristic gifts, and are now almost unread. About this time he lost a large portion of his fortune, had to give up continuous residence at Elleray, came to Edinburgh, and was called to the Scottish Bar, but never practised. The starting of *Blackwood's Magazine* brought him his opportunity, and to the end of his life his connection with it gave him his main employment and chief fame. In 1820 he became Prof. of Moral Philosophy in the Univ. of Edin. where, though not much of a philosopher in the technical sense, he exercised a highly stimulating influence upon his students by his eloquence and the general vigour of his intellect. The peculiar powers of W., his wealth of ideas, felicity of expression, humour, and animal spirits, found their full development in the famous *Noctes Ambrosianæ,* a medley of criticism on literature, politics, philosophy, topics of the day and what not. *Lights and Shadows of Scottish Life* and *The Trials of Margaret Lyndsay* are contributions to fiction in which there is an occasional tendency to run pathos into rather mawkish sentimentality. In 1851 W. received a Government pension of £300. The following year a paralytic seizure led to his resignation of his professorial chair, and he *d.* in 1854. He was a man of magnificent physique, of shining rather than profound intellectual powers, and of generous character, though as a critic his strong feelings and prejudices occasionally made him unfair and even savage.

WILSON, JOHN (1804-1875).—Missionary and orientalist, *b.* at Lauder, Berwickshire, and *ed.* at Edin. for the ministry of the Church of Scotland, went in 1828 to India as a missionary, where, besides his immediate duties, he became a leader in all social reform, such as the abolition of the slave-trade and *suttee,* and also one of the greatest authorities on the subject of caste, and a trusted adviser of successive Governors-General in regard to all questions affecting the natives. He was in addition a profound Oriental scholar as to languages, history, and religion. He was D.D., F.R.S., and Vice-

Chancellor of Bombay Univ. Among his works are *The Parsi Religion* (1812), *The Lands of the Bible* (1847), *India Three Thousand Years Ago*, and *Memoirs of the Cave Temples of India*.

WILSON, THOMAS (1525?-1581).—Scholar and statesman, *b*. in Lincolnshire, was at Camb., and held various high positions under Queen Elizabeth. He was the author of *The Rule of Reason containing the Arte of Logique* (1551), and *The Arte of Rhetorique* (1553), and made translations from Demosthenes. He endeavoured to maintain the purity of the language against the importation of foreign words.

WINGATE, DAVID, (1828-1892).—Poet, was employed in the coal-pits near Hamilton from the time he was 9. He *pub*. *Poems and Songs* (1862), which was favourably received, and followed by *Annie Weir* (1866). After this he studied at the Glasgow School of Mines, became a colliery manager, and devoted his increased leisure to study and further literary work. *Lily Neil* appeared in 1879, followed by *Poems and Songs* (1883), and *Selected Poems* (1890). W. was a man of independent character. He was twice *m*., his second wife being a descendant of Burns.

WINTHROP, THEODORE (1828-1861).—Novelist, *b*. at New Haven, Conn., descended through his *f*. from Governor W., and through his mother from Jonathan Edwards, *ed*. at Yale, travelled in Great Britain and on the Continent, and far and wide in his own country. After contributing to periodicals short sketches and stories, which attracted little attention, he enlisted in the Federal Army, in 1861, and was killed in the Battle of Great Bethel. His novels, for which he had failed to find a publisher, appeared posthumously—*John Brent*, founded on his experiences in the far West, *Edwin Brothertoft*, a story of the Revolution War, and *Cecil Dreeme*. Other works were *The Canoe and Saddle*, and *Life in the Open Air*. Though somewhat spasmodic and crude, his novels had freshness, originality, and power, and with longer life and greater concentration he might have risen high.

WITHER, GEORGE (1588-1667).—Poet, *b*. near Alton, Hampshire, was at Oxf. for a short time, and then studied law at Lincoln's Inn. In 1613 he *pub*. a bold and pungent satire, *Abuses Stript and Whipt*, with the result that he was imprisoned for some months in the Marshalsea. While there he wrote *The Shepheard's Hunting*, a pastoral. *Wither's Motto, Nec Habeo, nec Careo, nec Curo* (I have not, want not, care not) was written in 1618, and in 1622 he *coll*. his poems as *Juvenilia*. The same year he *pub*. a long poem, *Faire Virtue, the Mistress of Philarete*, in which appears the famous lyric, "Shall I wasting in despair." Though generally acting with the Puritans he took arms with Charles I. against the Scotch in 1639; but on the outbreak of the Civil War he was on the popular side, and raised a troop of horse. He was taken prisoner by the Royalists, and is said to have owed his life to the intercession of a fellow-poet, Sir John Denham. After the establishment of the Commonwealth he was considerably enriched out of sequestrated estates and other spoils of the defeated party; but on the Restoration was obliged to surrender his gains, was impeached, and committed to the Tower. In his later years he wrote many religious poems and hymns, *coll.* as *Hallelujah.* Before his death his poems were already forgotten, and he was referred to by Pope in *The Dunciad* as "the wretched Withers." He was, however, disinterred by Southey, Lamb, and others, who drew attention to his poetical merits, and he has now an established place among English poets, to which his freshness, fancy, and delicacy of taste well entitle him.

WODROW, ROBERT (1679-1734).—Church historian, *s.* of James W., Prof. of Divinity in Glasgow. Having completed his literary and theological education there, he entered the ministry of the Church of Scotland, and was ordained to the parish of Eastwood, Renfrewshire. Here he carried on the great work of his life, his *History of the Sufferings of the Church of Scotland* 1660 *to* 1688. W. wrote when the memory of the persecutions was still fresh, and his work is naturally not free from partisan feeling and credulity. It is, however, thoroughly honest in intention, and is a work of genuine research, and of high value for the period with which it deals. It was *pub.* in two folio vols. in 1721 and 1722. W. made large collections for other works which, however, were not *pub.* in his lifetime. *The Lives of the Scottish Reformers and Most Eminent Ministers* and *Analecta, or a History of Remarkable Providences,* were printed for the Maitland Club, and 3 vols. of his correspondence in 1841 for the Wodrow Society. The *Analecta* is a most curious miscellany showing a strong appetite for the marvellous combined with a hesitating doubt in regard to some of the more exacting narratives.

WOLCOT, JOHN (1738-1819).—Satirist, *b.* near Kingsbridge, Devonshire, was *ed.* by an uncle, and studied medicine. In 1767 he went as physician to Sir William Trelawny, Governor of Jamaica, and whom he induced to present him to a Church in the island then vacant, and was ordained in 1769. Sir William dying in 1772, W. came home and, abandoning the Church, resumed his medical character, and settled in practice at Truro, where he discovered the talents of Opie the painter, and assisted him. In 1780 he went to London, and commenced writing satires. The first objects of his attentions were the members of the Royal Academy, and these attempts being well received, he soon began to fly at higher game, the King and Queen being the most frequent marks for his satirical shafts. In 1786 appeared *The Lousiad, a Heroi-Comic Poem,* taking its name from a legend that on the King's dinner plate there had appeared a certain insect not usually found in such exalted quarters. Other objects of his attack were Boswell, the biographer of Johnson, and Bruce, the Abyssinian traveller. W., who wrote under the *nom-de-guerre* of "Peter Pindar," had a remarkable vein of humour and wit, which, while intensely comic to persons not involved, stung its subjects to the quick. He had likewise strong intelligence, and a power of coining effective phrases. In other kinds of composition, as in some ballads which he wrote, an unexpected touch of gentleness and even tenderness appears. Among these are *The Beggar Man* and *Lord Gregory.* Much that he wrote has now lost all interest owing to the circumstances referred to being forgotten, but enough still retains its peculiar relish to account for his contemporary reputation.

WOLFE, CHARLES (1791-1823).—Poet, *s.* of a landed gentleman in Kildare, was *b.* in Dublin, where he completed his *ed.* at Trinity Coll., having previously been at Winchester. He took orders, and was Rector of Donoughmere, but his health failed, and he *d.* of consumption at 32. He is remembered for one short, but universally known and admired poem, *The Burial of Sir John Moore*, which first appeared anonymously in the *Newry Telegraph* in 1817.

WOOD, OR À WOOD, ANTHONY (1632-1695).—Antiquary, was *b.* at Oxf., where he was *ed.* and spent most of his life. His antiquarian enthusiasm was awakened by the collections of Leland, and he early began to visit and study the antiquities of his native county. This with history, heraldry, genealogies, and music occupied his whole time. By 1669 he had written his *History and Antiquities of the University of Oxford*, which was translated into Latin not to his satisfaction by the Univ. authorities, and he wrote a fresh English copy which was printed in 1786. His great work was *Athenæ Oxonienses; an exact History of all the Writers and Bishops who have had their Education in the University of Oxford, to which are added the Fasti or Annals of the said University* (1691-92). For an alleged libel on the Earl of Clarendon in that work the author was expelled in 1694. He also wrote *The Ancient and Present State of the City of Oxford*, and *Modius Salium, a Collection of Pieces of Humour*, generally of an ill-natured cast.

WOOD, MRS. ELLEN (PRICE) (1814-1887).—Novelist, writing as "Mrs. Henry Wood," was *b.* at Worcester. She wrote over 30 novels, many of which, especially *East Lynne*, had remarkable popularity. Though the stories are generally interesting, they have no distinction of style. Among the best known are *Danesbury House, Oswald Cray, Mrs. Halliburton's Troubles, The Channings, Lord Oakburn's Daughters*, and *The Shadow of Ashlydyat*. Mrs. W. was for some years proprietor and ed. of the *Argosy*.

WOOD, JOHN GEORGE (1827-1889).—Writer on natural history, *s.* of a surgeon, *b.* in London, and *ed.* at home and at Oxf., where he worked for some time in the anatomical museum. He took orders, and among other benefices which he held was for a time chaplain to St. Bartholomew's Hospital. He was a very prolific writer on natural history, though rather as a populariser than as a scientific investigator, and was in this way very successful. Among his numerous works may be mentioned *Illustrated Natural History* (1853), *Animal Traits and Characteristics* (1860), *Common Objects of the Sea Shore* (1857), *Out of Doors* (1874), *Field Naturalist's Handbook* (with T. Wood) (1879-80), books on gymnastics, sport, etc., and an ed. of White's *Selborne*.

WOOLMAN, JOHN (1720-1772).—Quaker diarist, *b.* at Burlington, New Jersey, began life as a farm labourer, and then became a clerk in a store. He underwent deep religious impressions, and the latter part of his life was devoted to itinerant preaching and doing whatever good came to his hand. To support himself he worked as a tailor. He was one of the first to witness against the evils of slavery, on which he wrote a tract, *Some Considerations on the Keeping of Negroes* (1753). His *Journal* "reveals his life and character with rare fidelity" and, though little known compared with some similar works, gained the admiration of, among other writers, Charles Lamb, who says, "Get the writings of John Woolman by heart." In 1772 he went to England, where he *d.* of smallpox in the same year.

WOOLNER, THOMAS (1826-1892).—Sculptor and poet, *b.* at Hadleigh, attained a high reputation as a sculptor. He belonged to the pre-Raphaelite Brotherhood, and contributed poems to their magazine, the *Germ.* He wrote several vols. of poetry, including *My Beautiful Lady* (1863), *Pygmalion*, *Silenus*, *Tiresias*, and *Nelly Dale.* He had a true poetic gift, though better known by his portrait busts.

WORDSWORTH, CHRISTOPHER (1774-1846).—Biographer, etc., was a younger brother of the poet, *ed.* at Camb., took orders, and became Chaplain to the House of Commons, and Master of Trinity Coll., Camb. 1820-41. He was also Vice-Chancellor of the Univ. 1820-21 and 1826-27. He *pub. Ecclesiastical Biography* (1810), and *Who wrote Eikon Basilikè?* in which he argued for the authorship of Charles I.

WORDSWORTH, CHRISTOPHER (1807-1885).—*S.* of above, *ed.* at Camb., took orders and became a Canon of Westminster 1844, and Bishop of Lincoln 1868. He travelled in Greece, and discovered the site of Dodona. His writings include in theology a commentary on the Bible (1856-70), *Church History to* A.D. 451 (1881-83), and in other fields, *Athens and Attica* (1836), and *Theocritus* (1844).

WORDSWORTH, DOROTHY (1771-1855).—Diarist, etc., was the only sister of the poet, and his lifelong and sympathetic companion, and endowed in no small degree with the same love of and insight into nature as is evidenced by her *Journals.* Many of her brother's poems were suggested by scenes and incidents recorded by her, of which that on Daffodils beginning "I wandered lonely as a cloud" is a notable example.

WORDSWORTH, WILLIAM (1770-1850).—Poet, *s.* of John W., attorney and agent to the 1st Lord Lonsdale, was *b.* at Cockermouth. His boyhood was full of adventure among the hills, and he says of himself that he showed "a stiff, moody, and violent temper." He lost his mother when he was 8, and his *f.* in 1783 when he was 13. The latter, prematurely cut off, left little for the support of his family of four sons and a *dau.*, Dorothy (afterwards the worthy companion of her illustrious brother), except a claim for £5000 against Lord Lonsdale, which his lordship contested, and which was not settled until his death. With the help, however, of uncles, the family were well *ed.* and started in life. William received his earlier education at Penrith and Hawkshead in Lancashire; and in 1787 went to St. John's Coll., Camb., where he graduated B.A. in 1791. In the preceding year, 1790, he had taken a walking tour on the

Continent, visiting France in the first flush of the Revolution with which, at that stage, he was, like many of the best younger minds of the time, in enthusiastic sympathy. So much was this the case that he nearly involved himself with the Girondists to an extent which might have cost him his life. His funds, however, gave out, and he returned to England shortly before his friends fell under the guillotine. His uncles were desirous that he should enter the Church, but to this he was unconquerably averse; and indeed his marked indisposition to adopt any regular employment led to their taking not unnatural offence. In 1793 his first publications—*The Evening Walk* and *Descriptive Sketches of a Pedestrian Tour in the Alps*—appeared, but attracted little attention. The beginning of his friendship with Coleridge in 1795 tended to confirm him in his resolution to devote himself to poetry; and a legacy of £900 from a friend put it in his power to do so by making him for a time independent of other employment. He settled with his sister at Racedown, Dorsetshire, and shortly afterwards removed to Alfoxden, in the Quantock Hills, to be near Coleridge, who was then living at Nether Stowey in the same neighbourhood. One result of the intimacy thus established was the planning of a joint work, *Lyrical Ballads*, to which Coleridge contributed *The Ancient Mariner*, and W., among other pieces, *Tintern Abbey*. The first ed. of the work appeared in 1798. With the profits of this he went, accompanied by his sister and Coleridge, to Germany, where he lived chiefly at Goslar, and where he began the *Prelude*, a poem descriptive of the development of his own mind. After over a year's absence W. returned and settled with Dorothy at Grasmere. In 1800 the second ed. of *Lyrical Ballads*, containing the same contributions, with several additions, appeared. In the same year Lord Lonsdale *d.*, and his successor settled the claims already referred to with interest, and the share of the brother and sister enabled them to live in the frugal and simple manner which suited them. Two years later W.'s circumstances enabled him to marry his cousin, Mary Hutchinson, to whom he had been long attached. In 1803 he made a tour in Scotland, and began his friendship with Scott. The year 1807 saw the publication of *Poems in two Volumes*, which contains much of his best work, including the "Ode to Duty," "Intimations of Immortality," "Yarrow Unvisited," and the "Solitary Reaper." In 1813 he migrated to Rydal Mount, his home for the rest of his life; and in the same year he received, through the influence of Lord Lonsdale, the appointment of Distributor of Stamps for Westmoreland, with a salary of £400. The next year he made another Scottish tour, when he wrote *Yarrow Visited*, and he also *pub.* *The Excursion*, "being a portion of *The Recluse*, a Poem." W. had now come to his own, and was regarded by the great majority of the lovers of poetry as, notwithstanding certain limitations and flaws, a truly great and original poet. The rest of his life has few events beyond the publication of his remaining works (which, however, did not materially advance his fame), and tokens of the growing honour in which he was held. *The White Doe of Rylstone* appeared in 1815, in which year also he made a collection of his poems; *Peter Bell* and *The Waggoner* in 1819; *The River Duddon*, 1820; *Memorials of a Tour on the Continent* in 1822; *Ecclesiastical Sonnets*, 1822; and *Yarrow Revisited* in 1835. In 1831 he paid his last visit to Scott; in 1838 he received the degree of D.C.L. from Durham, and in 1839 the same from Oxf. Three years later he resigned his office of Distributor of Stamps in favour of his *s.*, and received a civil list pension of £300. The following year, 1843, he succeeded Southey as Poet Laureate. His long, tranquil, and fruitful life ended in 1850. He lies buried in the churchyard of Grasmere. After his death the *Prelude*, finished in 1805, was *pub.* It had been kept back because the great projected poem of which it was to have been the preface, and of which *The Excursion* is a part, was never completed.

The work of W. is singularly unequal. When at his best, as in the "Intimations of Immortality," "Laodamia," some passages in *The Excursion*, and some of his short pieces, and especially his sonnets, he rises to heights of noble inspiration and splendour of language rarely equalled by any of our poets. But it required his poetic fire to be at fusing point to enable him to burst through his natural tendency to prolixity and even dulness. His extraordinary lack of humour and the, perhaps consequent, imperfect power of self-criticism by which it was accompanied, together with the theory of poetic theme and diction with which he hampered himself, led him into a frequent choice of trivial subjects and childish language which excited not unjust ridicule, and long delayed the general recognition of his genius. He has a marvellous felicity of phrase, an unrivalled power of describing natural appearances and effects, and the most ennobling views of life and duty. But his great distinguishing characteristic is his sense of the mystic relations between man and nature. His influence on contemporary and succeeding thought and literature has been profound and lasting. It should be added that W., like Milton, with whom he had many points in common, was the master of a noble and expressive prose style.

SUMMARY.—*B.* 1770, *ed.* at Camb., sympathiser with French Revolution in earlier stages, first publication *Tour in the Alps* and *Evening Walk* 1793, became acquainted with Coleridge 1795, *pub.* with him *Lyrical Ballads* 1798, visits Germany and begins *Prelude*, returns to England and settles at Grasmere, *pub.* second ed. of *Lyrical Ballads*, with some additions, 1800, *m.* Mary Hutchinson 1802, visits Scotland 1804 and becomes acquainted with Scott, *pub. Poems in Two Volumes* 1807, goes to Rydal Mount 1813, appointed Distributor of Stamps, revisits Scotland, writes *Yarrow Visited* and *pub. The Excursion* 1814, *White Doe* and *coll.* works 1815, *Waggoner*, *Ecclesiastical Sonnets*, etc., 1819-35, pensioned 1842, Poet Laureate 1843, *d.* 1850.

There are numerous good ed. of the poems, including his own by Moxon (1836, 1845, and 1850), and those by Knight (1882-86), Morley (1888), Dowden (1893), Smith (1908). Another by Knight in 16 vols. includes the prose writings and the *Journal* by Dorothy (1896-97). *Lives* by Christopher Wordsworth (1857), Myers (1880), and others. See also criticism by W. Raleigh (1903).

WOTTON, SIR HENRY (1568-1639).—Diplomatist and poet, *s.* of a Kentish gentleman, was *b.* at Boughton Park, near Maidstone, and *ed.* at Winchester and Oxf. After spending 7 years on the Continent, he entered the Middle Temple. In 1595 he became sec. to the Earl of Essex, who employed him abroad, and while at Venice he wrote *The State of Christendom or a Most Exact and Curious Discovery of many Secret Passages and Hidden Mysteries of the Times*, which was not, however, printed until 1657. Afterwards he held various diplomatic appointments, but Court favour latterly failed him and he was recalled from Venice and made Provost of Eton in 1624, to qualify himself for which he took deacon's orders. Among his other works were *Elements of Architecture* (1624) and *A Survey of Education*. His writings in prose and verse were *pub.* in 1651 as *Reliquiæ Wottonianæ*. His poems include two which are familiar to all readers of Elizabethan verse, *The Character of a Happy Life*, "How happy is he born and taught," and *On his Mistress, the Queen of Bohemia*, beginning "Ye meaner Beauties of the Night." He was the originator of many witty sayings, which have come down.

WRAXALL, SIR NATHANIEL WILLIAM (1751-1831).—Historical writer, *b.* at Bristol, was for a few years in the service of the East India Company, and thereafter employed on diplomatic missions, and sat for some years in the House of Commons. In addition to a book of travels and some historical works relating to the French and other foreign Courts, he wrote *Historical Memories of my own Time* 1772-84, *pub.* in 1815. The work was severely criticised by both political parties, and in particular by Macaulay; but W. made a reply which was considered to be on the whole successful. A continuation bringing the narrative down to 1790 was *pub.* in 1836. The *Memoirs* are valuable for the light they throw on the period, and especially for the portraits of public men which they give.

WRIGHT, THOMAS (1810-1877).—Antiquary, *b.* near Ludlow, of Quaker parentage, was *ed.* at Camb. His first work was a *History of Essex* (1831-36). In 1836 he went to London, and adopted literature as a profession, devoting himself specially to archæology, history, and biography. He held office in various societies such as the "Camden," "Percy," and "Shakespeare," and ed. many works for them. In all he was the author of over 80 publications, of which some of the chief are *The Celt, the Roman, and the Saxon, Biographia Britannica Literaria, Queen Elizabeth and her Times*, and *History of Domestic Manners and Sentiments in England during the Middle Ages*. He was superintendent of the excavation of the Roman city at Wroxeter in 1859.

WYATT, SIR THOMAS (1503-1542).—Poet, *s.* of Sir Henry W., a servant of Henry VII., and *ed.* at St. John's Coll., Camb., came to Court and was frequently employed by Henry VIII. on diplomatic missions. He is said to have been an admirer of Anne Boleyn before her marriage, and on her disgrace was thrown into the Tower for a short time. In 1537 he was knighted, and two years later was against his will sent on a mission to the Emperor Charles V. On the death in 1540 of Thomas Cromwell, to whose party he belonged, W. was accused of misdemeanours during his embassy and again imprisoned in the Tower, where he wrote a defence which resulted in his release. In 1542 he was sent to meet the Spanish Ambassador at Falmouth, and conduct him to London, but on the way caught a chill, of which he *d.* W. shares with the Earl of Surrey (*q.v.*) the honour of being the first real successor of Chaucer, and also of introducing the sonnet into England. In addition to his sonnets, which are in a more correct form than those of Surrey, W. wrote many beautiful lyrics; in fact he may be regarded as the reviver of the lyrical spirit in English poetry which, making its appearance in the 13th century, had fallen into abeyance. In the anthology known as *Tottel's Miscellany*, first *pub.* in 1557, 96 pieces by W. appear along with 40 by Surrey, and others by different hands. W. has less smoothness and sweetness than Surrey, but his form of the sonnet was much more difficult as well as more correct than that invented by the latter, and afterwards adopted by Shakespeare, and his lyrical gift is more marked.

WYCHERLEY, WILLIAM (1640?-1716).—Dramatist, was *b.* at Clive, near Shrewsbury, where his *f.* had an estate. He was at the Inner Temple in 1659, and at Oxf. in 1660. Part of his youth had been spent in France, where he became a Roman Catholic, but at the Restoration he returned to Protestantism. He wrote four comedies, *Love in a Wood, The Gentleman Dancing Master, The Country Wife*, and *The Plain Dealer*, all produced in the reign of Charles II., and nothing of consequence afterwards, a vol. of poems doing little to add to his reputation. About 1679 he *m.* the widowed Countess of Drogheda, who *d.* in 1681, and he entered into a second marriage eleven days before his death. In his later years he formed a friendship with Pope, then a boy of 16. W. was one of the founders of the Comedy of Manners. The merit of his plays lies in smart and witty dialogue rather than in construction. *The Plain Dealer*, his best, is founded upon Molière's *Misanthrope*. His plays are notoriously coarse.

WYNTOUN, ANDREW OF (1350?-1420?).—Chronicler, was a canon of St. Andrews, who became Prior of St. Serf's island in Loch Leven. His work, entitled *The Orygynale Cronykil*, begins with the creation of angels and men and comes down to 1406. It is poetic in form though rarely so in substance, and is of considerable historical value in its later parts and as regards the see of St. Andrews.

YALDEN, THOMAS (1670-1736).—Poet, *s.* of an exciseman at Oxf., and *ed.* at Magdalen Coll., entered the Church, in which he obtained various preferments. He was the author of a considerable number of poems, including a *Hymn to Darkness*, Pindaric Odes, and translations from the classics.

YATES, EDMUND (1831-1894).—Novelist and dramatist, *b.* at Edin., held for some years an appointment in the General Post Office. He did much journalistic work, mainly as a dramatic writer, and wrote many dramatic pieces and some novels, including *Running the Gauntlet* and *The Black Sheep*. He was perhaps best known as ed. of *The World* society journal.

YONGE, CHARLOTTE MARY (1823-1901).—Novelist, only *dau.* of a landed gentleman of Hampshire, was *b.* near Winchester, and in her girlhood came under the influence of Keble, who was a near neighbour. She began writing in 1848, and *pub.* during her long life about 100 works, chiefly novels, interesting and well-written, with a High Church tendency. Among the best known are *The Heir of Redclyffe*, *Heartsease*, and *The Daisy Chain*. She also wrote *Cameos from English History*, and Lives of Bishop Patteson and Hannah More. The profits of her works were devoted to religious objects.

YOUNG, ARTHUR (1741-1820).—Writer on agriculture, was *b.* in London, the *s.* of a Suffolk clergyman. In his early years he farmed, making many experiments, which though they did not bring him financial success, gave him knowledge and experience, afterwards turned to useful account. Various publications had made his name known, and in 1777 he became agent to Lord Kingsborough on his Irish estates. In 1780 he *pub.* his *Tour in Ireland*, and four years later started the *Annals of Agriculture*, 47 vols. of which appeared. His famous tours in France were made 1787-90, the results of his observations being *pub.* in *Travels in France* (1792). He was in 1793 appointed sec. to the newly founded Board of Agriculture, and *pub.* many additional works on the subject. He is justly regarded as the father of modern agriculture, in which, as in all subjects affecting the public welfare, he maintained an active interest until his death. In his later years he was blind.

YOUNG, EDWARD (1683-1765).—Poet, *s.* of the Rector of Upham, Hampshire, where he was *b.* After being at Winchester School and Oxf. he accompanied the Duke of Wharton to Ireland. Y., who had always a keen eye towards preferment, and the cult of those who had the dispensing of it, began his poetical career in 1713 with *An Epistle to Lord Lansdowne*. Equally characteristic was the publication in the same year of two poems, *The Last Day* and *The Force of Religion*. The following year he produced an elegy *On the Death of Queen Anne*, which brought him into notice. Turning next to the drama he produced *Busiris* in 1719, and *The Revenge* in 1721. His next work was a collection of 7 satires, *The Love of Fame, the Universal Passion*. In 1727 he entered the Church, and was appointed one of the Royal Chaplains, and Rector of Welwyn, Herts, in 1730. Next year he *m.* Lady Elizabeth Lee, the widowed *dau.* of the Earl of Lichfield, to whom, as well as to her *dau.* by her former marriage, he was warmly attached. Both *d.*, and sad and lonely the poet began his masterpiece, *The Complaint, or Night Thoughts* (1742-44), which had immediate and great popularity, and which still maintains its place as a classic. In 1753 he brought out his last drama, *The Brothers*, and in 1761 he received his last piece of preferment, that of Clerk to the Closet to the Princess Dowager of Wales. Four years later, in 1765, he *d.* The poems of Y., though in style artificial and sometimes forced, abound in passages of passion and power which sometimes reach the sublime. But the feelings and sentiments which he expresses with so much force as a poet form an unpleasantly harsh contrast with the worldliness and tuft-hunting of his life.

written with a High Church tendency. Among the best known are *The Heir of Redclyffe*, *Heartsease*, and *The Daisy Chain*. She also wrote *Cameos from English History*, and Lives of Bishop Patteson and Hannah More. The profits of her works were devoted to religious objects.

YOUNG, ARTHUR (1741-1820).—Writer on agriculture, was b. in London, the s. of a Suffolk clergyman. In his early years he turned to farming, making many experiments, which though they did not bring him financial success, gave him knowledge and experience afterwards turned to good account. Various publications had made his name known, and in 1777 he became agent to Lord Kingsborough on his Irish estates. In 1780 he pub. his *Tour in Ireland*, and four years later started the *Annals of Agriculture*, 47 vols. of which appeared. His famous tours in France were made 1787-89, the results of his observations being pub. as *Travels in France* (1792). He was in 1793 appointed sec. to the newly founded Board of Agriculture, and pub. many additional works on the subject. He is justly regarded as the father of modern agriculture, in which, as in all subjects affecting the public welfare, he maintained an active interest up to his death. In his later years he was blind.

YOUNG, EDWARD (1683-1765).—Poet, s. of the Rector of Upham, Hampshire, where he was b. After being at Winchester School and Oxf. he accompanied the Duke of Wharton to Ireland. Y., who had always a keen eye towards preferment, and the rest of those who had the disposing of it, began his poetical career in 1713 with his *Epistle to Lord Lansdowne*. Equally characteristic was the publication in the same year of two poems, *The Last Day* and *The Force of Religion*. The following year he produced an *Essay on the Death of Queen Anne*, which brought him into notice. Turning next to the drama he produced *Busiris* in 1719, and *The Revenge* in 1721. His next work was a collection of satires, *The Love of Fame, the Universal Passion*. In 1727 he entered the Church, and was appointed one of the Royal Chaplains, and Rector of Welwyn, Herts, in 1730. Next year he m. Lady Elizabeth Lee, the d. of the Earl of Lichfield, to whom, as well as to her d. by her former marriage, he was warmly attached. Their d., and subsequently the [illegible] were among his masterpiece, *The Complaint, or Night Thoughts* (1742-45), which had immediate and great popularity, and which still maintains its place as a classic. In 1753 he brought out his last drama, *The Brothers*, and in 1761 he received the last piece of preferment, that of Clerk of the Closet to the Princess Dowager of Wales. [illegible] The poetry of Y., though marked by artifice, and sometimes forced, abounds in passages of vigour and power which sometimes reach the sublime. But the feelings and sentiments which he expresses with so much force as a poet were apparently little exemplified in the conduct of his life.

APPENDIX OF CONTEMPORARY WRITERS

NOTE

THE two hundred writers noticed in this Appendix are either living or have died since 1909. All are to be taken as British, unless the contrary is definitely stated. In order to give as much space as possible to the biographical side, criticism has been kept to a minimum and only the most representative works of each author mentioned, though it is natural that the more important the figure is the fuller the list of works.

ABERCROMBIE, LASCELLES (1881).—*Ed.* at Malvern and Victoria Univ., Manchester. Lectured on literature and poetry at the universities of Liverpool, London, Belfast, and Leeds. First volume of poems was *Interludes and Poems* (1908). *Collected Poems* (1930). Also a writer on æsthetics and a critic of high standing.

ALDINGTON, RICHARD (1892).—Made his literary reputation as a leader of the Imagists in poetry, *m.* Hilda Doolittle (*q.v.*) in 1913. *Collected Poems*, published 1929. His novels *Death of a Hero* (1929), *The Colonel's Daughter* (1931), and *All Men are Enemies* (1933), also established his fame as a prose writer. Is a classical scholar of some standing and has made a number of important translations from Latin, Greek, French, and Italian.

ANDERSON, SHERWOOD (1876). — American novelist. Took up a commercial career in Chicago; *pub.* his first novel, *Windy McPherson's Son*, in 1916. Other novels are *Marching Men* (1917), *Dark Laughter* (1925). Has achieved a great reputation as a short-story writer with *Winesburg, Ohio* (1919), *The Triumph of the Egg* (1921), and *Horses and Men* (1923).

ARCHER, WILLIAM (1856–1924).—*B.* at Perth, *ed.* at Edin. Univ., went to Australia and returned in 1877 to take up a distinguished position in the literary world as dramatic critic. Best known for his work as a translator and editor of Ibsen.

AUSTIN, ALFRED (1835–1913).—*B.* at Headingley, *ed.* at London Univ., became a barrister in 1857, but quickly abandoned the law for literature. Aroused attention by his satirical poem *The Season* (1861). He published about twenty volumes of verse, and although it is of very little value on the whole, it gave him a position which, when coupled to his position of ed. of the *National Review* (from 1883) and some audacious criticism of contemporary poets, led to his being appointed Poet Laureate in 1896.

BALFOUR, ARTHUR JAMES, 1ST EARL (1848–1930).—*B.* in London, *ed.* at Eton. and Camb., entered parliament in 1874, became Chief Secretary for Ireland in 1887 and later, First Lord of the Treasury. Premier in 1902 for a few months, resigned leadership of Conservative party in 1911. Enhanced his reputation as statesman in the Great War and at the post-war conferences. Raised to peerage in 1922. Made a literary reputation with his philosophic works, *A Defence of Philosophic Doubt* (1879), *The Foundations of Belief* (1895), etc.

BARING, MAURICE (1874).—*Ed.* at Eton and Cambridge. Entered the diplomatic service in 1898; acted as special correspondent in Manchuria, Russia, Turkey, and the Balkans, 1904–12; served in the Great War. His collected poems were *pub.* in 1925, and besides several novels he has written a large number of miscellaneous works, which include records of his experiences abroad, books on Russian literature, essays, stories, *Diminutive Dramas* (1910–19), and a study of Mary Stuart—*In the End is My Beginning* (1931).

BARING-GOULD, SABINE (1834–1924).—*B.* at Exeter, *ed.* at Camb. and took orders in the Anglican Church. From 1854 produced works in folk-lore, including his valuable *Songs and Ballads of the West* (1890), theology, *Lives of the Saints* (1872-7), fiction, *Mehalah* (1880), history, and mythology. A prolific, versatile, though unequal writer.

BARRIE, SIR JAMES MATTHEW (1860).—*B.* at Kirriemuir, Angus, *ed.* at Dumfries and Edin. Univ. Early life spent as a journalist in Nottingham and London. First book was *Better Dead* (1887), and there followed a number of novels, often in the "Kailyard" manner. The fame of Barrie rests chiefly on his plays, the children's play *Peter Pan* (1904) being perhaps the most popular. Other plays are: *What Every Woman Knows* (1908), *The Admirable Crichton* (1902), *Dear Brutus* (1907), *Mary Rose* (1920). Rector of St. Andrews Univ. 1919–22, and Chancellor of Edin. Univ. 1930.

BEERBOHM, MAX (1872).—*B.* in London, *ed.* at Charterhouse and Oxf. First became known as a writer in the *Yellow Book* (1894–7). Dramatic critic for *Saturday Review* (1898–1910). The first of his famous caricatures appeared in 1896 (*Caricatures of Twenty-five Gentlemen*). Has lived at Rapallo since 1910.

BEITH, JOHN HAY ("IAN HAY") (1876).—*Ed.* at Fettes and Camb., served with a Highland regiment during the Great War. Author of many whimsical and romantic light novels: *Pip* (1907), *The First Hundred Thousand* (1915), and some successful plays: *Tilly of Bloomsbury* (1919), *The Sport of Kings* (1924).

BELLOC, HILAIRE (1870).—*B.* in France, *ed.* at the Oratory School, Edgbaston and at Oxf. Served in a Fr. artillery regiment, became a naturalised Br. subject in 1902. Entered parliament in 1906, but withdrew in disagreement with the practices of politicians and established a paper in 1911, *The Eye Witness.* A versatile writer, he has produced notable work in history, *History of England* (1925–), poetry, *Verses and Sonnets* (1895, 1924), essays, *On Nothing* (1908), fiction, *Belinda* (1928), travel, *The Path to Rome* (1902), juvenile literature, *The Bad Child's Book of Beasts* (1896).

BENNETT, ENOCH ARNOLD (1867–1931).—*B.* May 27, nr. Hanley, Staffs, *ed.* locally and at London Univ. Leaving a solicitor's office, turned to journalism in his early twenties. Ed. of *Woman* (1896-1900). After this he devoted himself to more serious work, and within a few years had established his position as an accomplished novelist with *The Old Wives' Tale* (1908). Other novels include: *A Man from the North* (1898), *The Grand Babylon Hotel* (1902), *Clayhanger* (1910) and its sequels, *Hilda Lessways* and *These Twain* (1911 and 1916), *Riceyman Steps* (1923). He wrote a vast quantity of miscellaneous literature, *Journalism for Woman* (1898), *How to Live on Twenty-four Hours a Day* (1912), *Things That Have Interested Me* (1921-5), and his *Journals* (1930-3). He also wrote a few plays, of which the most successful were *Milestones* (with E. Knoblock, 1912) and *The Great Adventure* (1913).

BENSON, ARTHUR CHRISTOPHER (1862–1925).—Eldest *s.* of Archbishop Benson. Master of Magdalen Coll. 1915, a novelist and writer of critical studies and sketches. Of his brothers, Edward Frederic (1867) made a reputation as a novelist with *Dodo* (1893), and Robert Hugh (1871–1914) became a priest in the Roman Catholic Church, his romances being vehicles for his religious philosophy.

BERESFORD, JOHN DAVYS (1873).—*S.* of a clergyman, *ed.* at Oundle and Peterborough, studied architecture but turned to literature definitely about 1907. Has written innumerable short stories and novels from a realist's point of view, *History of Jacob Stahl* (1911), *The Invisible Event* (1915), *These Lynnekers* (1916), etc.

BIERCE, AMBROSE (1838–1914?).—American short-story writer, *b.* in Ohio, the *s.* of a farmer. Served in the Civil War. Came to London in 1872 but soon returned to America, living a journalist's life. Ed. his own *Collected Works* in 1912, and in 1913 went to Mexico to take part in civil war. Last note was received from him in Dec. 1913. His end is unknown.

BINYON, LAWRENCE (1869).—*B.* at Lancaster and *ed.* at St. Paul's School and Oxf. Won the Newdigate Prize in 1890. Joined the staff of the British Museum in 1893; until recently Keeper of Oriental Prints. An authority on Oriental art. First volume of poems: *Lyric Poems* (1894). *Collected Poems* (1930). Has also written a few plays.

BIRRELL, AUGUSTINE (1850).—*B.* near Liverpool, studied at Camb., became a barrister in 1875. Entered parliament in 1889, Chief Sec. for Ireland, 1907 to 1916, retired from public life in 1918. An accomplished essayist, as revealed by his *Obiter Dicta* (1884, 1887, and 1924), and *Et Cetera* (1930), he has also written important works on Hazlitt and Marvell.

BLACKWOOD, ALGERNON (1869).—*Ed.* at Wellington Coll. and Edin. Univ. and abroad. Went to America and after some varied experiences became a journalist. Began writing books in 1906, and has specialised in novels and stories of terror and the supernatural: *The Centaur* (1911), *Incredible Adventures* (1914), etc.

BLUNDEN, EDMUND CHARLES (1896).—*Ed.* at Christ's Hospital and Oxf. Served in France during the Great War and produced a notable piece of prose in *Undertones of War* (1928). Besides his poetry (*Coll.* ed., 1930), he has written a standard life of Leigh Hunt (1930), and as an ed. has won fame with his ed. of Clare's poems (1920) and early autobiography (1931). Prof. of English Literature at Tokio Univ. (1924–7).

BLUNT, WILFRID SCAWEN (1840–1922).—*B.* in Sussex; in the Diplomatic Service, 1858–69. Travelled Egypt, Arabia, and Persia with his wife; strong supporter of Home Rule for Ireland, and in 1887 was imprisoned for two months in Ireland in connection with agitations. Best remembered for his poems, *Love Sonnets of Proteus* (1880), but *pub.* his views on Islam, Egypt, India, and Ireland, generally analysing British Imperialism.

BRADDON, MARY ELIZABETH (1837–1915).—*B.* in London. Showed literary talent at an early age, but achieved no success as poet or novelist until the enormous popularity of *Lady Audley's Secret* (1862). Continued thereafter to produce numerous novels, full of sensation and facility of invention, but of little serious literary merit. Published successful novels up to the last few years of her life. *M.* the publisher, J. Maxwell, in 1874.

BRADLEY, ANDREW CECIL (1851).—Brother of F. H. Bradley, *ed.* at Cheltenham and Oxf. Prof. of Literature at Liverpool, Glas., and Oxf. Univ., held successively. Best known for his *Shakesperean Tragedy* (1904) and *Oxford Lectures on Poetry* (1909).

BRADLEY, FRANCIS HERBERT (1846–1924).—*B.* at Glasbury, Brecon, *ed.* at Oxf. An important figure in British philosophy of the nineteenth century. *Ethical Studies* (1876 and 1927), *Principles of Logic* (1883 and 1922), *Appearance and Reality*, his most important work (1893); *Essays on Truth* (1914).

BRIDGES, ROBERT (1844–1930).—*Ed.* at Eton and Oxf. and later became a physician. Forsook medicine for literature in 1882. His period of greatest activity as a poet was from 1885 to 1916. Was created Poet Laureate in 1913. Besides a considerable output of shorter poems he wrote eight plays, and at the age of eighty-five (1929) he produced his long philosophical poem *The Testament of Beauty*.

BROOKE, RUPERT (1887–1915).—*B.* Aug. 3 at Rugby, *ed.* at Rugby and Camb., visited Germany and Italy in 1911, and in the same year *pub.* his first volume of poems and suffered a nervous breakdown. In 1913 visited America and New Zealand. At the defence of Antwerp, 1914; was being transferred to the Dardanelles when he had an attack of sunstroke and developed blood poisoning, *d.* on the island of Skyros on April 23. *Collected Poems* (1918). His prose work includes a study of John Webster and *Letters from America* (1916).

BROOKE, STOPFORD AUGUSTUS (1832–1916).—*B.* in Donegal, Ireland, *ed.* at Dublin, ordained in 1857. After gaining a good position in London seceded from the Anglican Church in 1880 and became a Unitarian minister. Was a prominent man of letters in his day. *Theology in the English Poets* (1874), *History of English Literature* (1894), and works on the nineteenth-century poets.

BROWNING, OSCAR (1837–1923).—*B.* in London, *ed.* at Eton and Camb. Master at Eton, 1860, dismissed from post in 1873, and became lecturer in history at Camb. Historical works include *History of England* (1890), *History of Europe* (1901). Also wrote works on Dante, Napoleon, and Italian History.

BRYCE, VISCOUNT (1838–1922).—*B.* at Belfast, studied at Glas. and Oxf., became a barrister (1867), entered parliament (1880), Liberal cabinet minister (1892), ambassador to the U.S.A. (1907–12). Achieved a position of note as historian with *The Holy Roman Empire* (1862), and *The American Commonwealth* (1888–1910). Created viscount in 1914.

BUCHAN, JOHN (1875).—*B.* at Perth, studied at Glas. and Oxf. Univs.; a barrister, 1901; on the Headquarters Staff in the Great War; entered parliament in 1927. A director of the publishing house of Nelson for some years. His literary work chiefly consists of novels: *Prester John* (1910), *Greenmantle* (1916), etc; but he produced a *History of the Great War* in 1921–2.

BURNAND, SIR FRANCIS COWLEY (1836–1917).—*B.* in London, *ed.* at Eton and Camb., studied for Anglican orders but became a Roman Catholic in 1858. Obtained a success with the burlesque *Black-Eyed Susan*, and produced a number of humorous dramatic works, including the libretto of *Cox and Box*. After being a contributor for years became editor of *Punch* in 1880.

BURNETT, MRS. FRANCES ELIZA HODGSON (1849–1924).—Anglo-American novelist, *b.* at Manchester. Divorced Dr. Burnett in 1898 and re-married in 1900. Chiefly remembered for *Little Lord Fauntleroy* (1886), and other works for children. *d.* in New York.

BURROUGHS, JOHN (1837–1921).—American essayist and naturalist, *b.* at Roxbury, New York. Became teacher, journalist, farmer, and civil servant, finally settling on a farm in 1874 in New York. Produced nature books from 1871 almost to the year of his death, two books on Whitman and miscellaneous sketches.

CABELL, JAMES BRANCH (1879).—American novelist, *b.* at Richmond, Va., was a teacher and journalist. Novels include *Gallantry* (1907), *Jurgen* (1919) (usually held to be his best work), *Something about Eve* (1927). Is a leading figure among American fiction writers, but is especially prominent in Virginian literary life.

CAINE, SIR THOMAS HENRY HALL (1853–1931).—*B.* in Cheshire, *ed.* in the Isle of Man and at Liverpool. After journalistic work began his long career as a popular novelist with *The Shadow of a Crime* (1885). Other novels are *The Bondman* (1890), *The Eternal City* (1901), *The Master of Man* (1921).

CAMPBELL, WILLIAM WILFRID (1861–1918).—Canadian poet, *b.* in Ont, *ed.* at Toronto and Camb., Mass. Entered the Episcopal Church, but resigned. Volumes of poems: *Lake Lyrics* (1889), *War Poems* (1915), etc.

CARMAN, WILLIAM BLISS (1861–1929).—Canadian poet, *b.* at Fredericton, N. B., related to R. W. Emerson on his mother's side, *ed.* at the univs. of New Brunswick, Edin. and Harvard. Took up journalism for a career. His earliest and perhaps his best poetical publication was *Low Tide on Grand Pré* (1893). Crowned Canadian poet laureate after the Great War. *d.* at New Canaan, Conn. Other works: *Ballads of Lost Haven* (1897), *Later Poems* (1921), and a prose work developing his philosophy of nature worship, *The Kinship of Nature* (1904).

CARPENTER, EDWARD (1844–1929).—*B.* at Brighton, studied at Camb., renounced a Church career, taught science, adopted socialism, and became an agriculturist doing his own work in the fields. Wrote poetry: *Narcissus* (1873) and *Towards Democracy* (1883–1902); treatises in social and moral psychology, and an autobiography, *My Days and Dreams* (1916).

CATHER, WILLA SIBERT (1876).—American novelist, *b.* in Virginia, studied at a number of American Univs. A journalist of experience; her most famous novel is *Death Comes for the Archbishop* (1927). Other titles, *My Antonia* (1918), *One of Ours* (1922), *Shadows on the Rock* (1931).

CHESTERTON, GILBERT KEITH (1874).—*B.* in London and *ed.* at St. Paul's School, entered the Slade School to study art. Took up literature as a career in 1900 and has since contributed to a number of periodicals on very varied subjects. He has written novels, *The Napoleon of Notting Hill* (1904), short stories (*The Father Brown Stories*), poetry, *Collected Poems* (1927), criticism, *Browning* (1904), *Shaw* (1909), essays and dramas. His great force comes from his religious philosophy (he entered the Roman Church in 1922) which dominates all his work; see especially *Orthodoxy* (1909), *The Catholic Church and Conversion* (1926), and *The Thing* (1929).

CHURCHILL, WINSTON (1871).—American novelist, *b.* at St. Louis, Mo., graduated from U.S. Naval Academy, and obtained good experience as a journalist. Novels: *Richard Carvel* (1899), *The Inside of the Cup* (1913).

COLE, GEORGE DOUGLAS HOWARD (1889).—*Ed.* at St. Paul's School and Oxf. Early interested in social science and economics, associating himself with the Socialist movement. See *The World of Labour* (1913), *The Payment of Wages* (1918), *Short History of the British Working-class Movement* (1925–27), *Intelligent Man's Guide Through the World Chaos* (1932). Has also written a number of detective stories in collaboration with his wife, and is an authority on William Cobbett.

COLUM, PADRAIC (1881).—Irish poet, *b.* at Longford, Ireland. Part founder and ed. of the *Irish Review*, took prominent part in the Irish Theatre movement. Visited America in 1914 and Hawaii in 1923. Now lives in America. Known chiefly for his poems (*Wild Earth*, etc.), but has done good work in drama and fiction.

CONRAD, JOSEPH (FEODOR JÓZEF KONRAD KORZENIOWSKI) (1857–1924).—*B.* Dec. 3 at Bordiczew in the Ukraine, of

Polish parents. Became a sailor and made a number of transatlantic voyages, landed in England in 1878, and after seven more years of seafaring life, chiefly in Indian and Australian waters, became a naturalised British subject. It was not for another ten years that he finally abandoned his seafaring life. His literary career began with a short story in *Tit-Bits* (1886). His long-prepared first novel appeared in 1895 (*Almayer's Folly*). This was quickly followed by other sea novels, *An Outcast of the Islands* (1896), *The Nigger of the Narcissus* (1897), *Lord Jim* (1900), etc., and it is as a writer of the sea that C. is best known, but *Nostromo* (1904), *Under Western Eyes* (1911), and the Napoleonic unfinished novel *Suspense* (1927) show his versatility. He was also a master of the short story: *Youth* (1902), *Typhoon* (1903), *Within the Tides* (1915).

COPPARD, ALFRED EDGAR (1878).—*B.* at Folkestone. Best known as a short story writer: *Adam and Eve and Pinch Me* (1921), *Black Dog* (1923), but has written some poetry: *Collected Poems* (1928).

CORELLI, MARIE (1864–1924).—English novelist, with an Italian father and Scots mother, *ed.* in a French convent, and trained for musical career, but at the age of 22 published a highly successful romantic story, *A Romance of Two Worlds.* Continued to produce novels in this vein with great success, though her serious literary value is small. Lived at Stratford-on-Avon.

CROCKETT, SAMUEL RUTHERFORD (1860–1914).—*B.* in Galloway, became a minister in the Free Church of Scotland, but gave this career up for a literary one. Achieved success with *The Stickit Minister* (1893), and many other novels of the "Kailyard" class, but was also successful with a different type as represented by *The Raider* (1894).

CUNNINGHAME GRAHAM, ROBERT BONTINE (1852).—*B.* in Scotland, *ed.* at Harrow, member of parliament, 1886-92, associated with socialism and Scottish nationalism. Has written a mass of miscellaneous literature: fiction, travel, and historical studies.

DAVIES, WILLIAM HENRY (1871).—*B.* in Wales. Lived an extremely varied and mostly vagrant life, first in England, then in America, and then in England again (see his *Autobiography of a Super-Tramp*, 1908). Began to write poetry when over thirty and published his first volume in 1907 (*The Soul's Destroyer*). *Collected Poems* (1928).

DE LA MARE, WALTER (1873).—*B.* in Kent, *ed.* at St. Paul's Cathedral Choir School. Entered on a business career, but wrote poetry in spare time. Published *Songs of Childhood* in 1902 under the name of "Walter Ramal". Two years later *pub.* his first novel, *Henry Brocken.* Has since written other volumes of verse and fiction, a play, and compiled a famous poetry anthology for children, *Come Hither* (1923); also miscellaneous prose works such as *Desert Islands* (1930), and *Stories from the Bible* (1929).

DE MORGAN, WILLIAM FREND (1839–1917).—*B.* in London, studied to be an artist at the Royal Academy. Experimented in lustre and pottery work and was a friend of the Pre-Raphaelites. Produced his first novel with success when over sixty years of age, *Joseph Vance* (1906). Other novels: *Alice for Short* (1907), *When Ghost Meets Ghost* (1914).

DOBSON, HENRY AUSTIN (1840–1921).—*B.* at Plymouth, Board of Trade official 1856–1901. First volume of poems issued 1873, *Vignettes in Rhyme*, which was followed by *Proverbs in Porcelain* (1877), showing his strong preference for the French poetic forms. Later concentrated on critical and biographical studies in the Georgian era: *Fielding* (1883), *Steele* (1886), *Richardson* (1902), etc. *Collected Poems* (1897 and 1923).

DOOLITTLE, HILDA (1886). — American poetess, *m.* Richard Aldington in 1913, both being important members of the Imagist group of poets. Uses 'H. D.' as her literary pseudonym.

DOUGHTY, CHARLES MONTAGU (1843–1926).—*Ed.* at Camb. His fame rests on his *Travels in Arabia Deserta* (1888), a record of travels carried out some ten years earlier. Has also written some long poetical works with an archaic flavour.

DOUGLAS, NORMAN (*c.* 1867).—Created a reputation by an unusual novel, *South Wind* (1917). Followed this up by another, *They Went* (1920), and some equally original travel books, *Old Calabria* (1920), *Alone* (1921), etc.

DOWDEN, EDWARD (1843–1913).—*B.* in Cork, became Prof. of Oratory and Literature at Dublin Univ. Was an authority on Shakespeare (*Shakespeare: his mind and art*, 1875) and on Shelley (*Life of Shelley*, 1886). Wrote many other sound works on the nineteenth-century poets, Shakespeare, and French literature.

DOYLE, SIR ARTHUR CONAN (1859–1930).—English author, chiefly known as the creator of Sherlock Holmes, *A Study in Scarlet* (1887), etc., but wrote successful historical romances and devoted the latter part of his career to psychic research.

DREISER, THEODORE (1871).—American novelist, *b.* in Indiana. Began a journalistic career in 1892, ed. various periodicals up to 1910. First novel was *Sister Carrie* (1900), and his next *Jennie Gerhardt* (1911). Others: *An American Tragedy* (1925), *Dawn* (1931). Has written a few plays, a number of short stories, autobiographical works, essays, and some poetry.

DRINKWATER, JOHN (1882).—*Ed.* at Oxf. High School and Birmingham Univ. Twelve years as an insurance clerk, became connected with the stage and wrote poetry. His success as a playwright came with *Abraham Lincoln* (1918). *Collected Plays* (1925), *Collected Poems* (1923).

ELIOT, THOMAS STEARNS (1888).—Anglo-American poet and critic, *b.* in U.S.A., *ed.* at Harvard, Oxf., and the Sorbonne. Made his poetical reputation with *The Waste Land* (1922). His prose works include *Homage to John Dryden* (1924), *Dante* (1929), and *Selected Essays* (1932). Associates himself with Anglo-Catholic thought in the Anglican Church (*For Lancelot Andrewes*, 1928, *Thoughts after Lambeth*, 1931). Ed. of *The Criterion*. A director of the publishing house of Faber and Faber.

ELLIS, HENRY HAVELOCK (1859).—*B.* at Croydon, Surrey, studied at St. Thomas's Hospital, qualified as a doctor, but turned to literary work in the 'eighties. An authority on psychology: *The Criminal* (1890), *Man and Woman* (1894 and 1929), and a series of volumes of *Studies in the Psychology of Sex*.

FARNOL, JOHN JEFFERY (1878).—*B.* Feb. 10, went to America in 1902 for eight years, returning as a writer of some experience, and *pub.* his great success, *The Broad Highway* (1910). Other novels: *Beltane the Smith* (1915), *The Loring Mystery* (1905), etc.

FLECKER, JAMES ELROY (1884–1915).—*B.* at Lewisham, *ed.* at Oxf., after studying oriental tongues for the Consular Service was sent to Constantinople in 1910. Vice-Consul at Beirut 1911–13. *d.* of consumption at Davos Platz. *Pub.* poems and a novel in his lifetime, and the plays *Hassan* and *Don Juan* were issued posthumously.

FORD, FORD MADOX (FORD MADOX HUEFFER) (1873).—Founder of *The English Review*; a poet, *Collected Poems* (1914); novelist, *The Spirit of the People* (1907), *A Man Could Stand Up* (1926), collaborated with Joseph Conrad in *The Inheritors* (1901) and *Romance* (1903); critic, *Rossetti*, *Henry James* (1914), *The English Novel* (1930).

FORSTER, EDWARD MORGAN (1879).—Fellow of King's Coll., Camb., where he had graduated. Established a high literary reputation with *A Passage to India* (1924), though he had *pub.* his first work in 1905. He is a critic with much influence on the young serious writers: *Aspects of the Novel* (1927).

FRAZER, SIR JAMES GEORGE (1854).—*B.* at Glasgow. A fellow of Trinity Coll., Camb., was prof. of social anthropology at Liverpool, 1907–22. His works almost entirely deal with mythology and comparative religion, and his most famous publication is *The Golden Bough* (1890–1915, 12 volumes).

GALSWORTHY, JOHN (1867–1933).—*B.* in Surrey, *ed.* at Harrow and Oxf. Called to the Bar in 1890, but turned to literature after travelling round the world. After issuing a few novels under the name of John Sinjohn, *pub. The Island Pharisees* in 1904 under his own name. In 1906 came *The Man of Property*, the first of the famous trilogy known as *The Forsyte Saga*, (*In Chancery*, 1920, *To Let*, 1921). In 1906 also he became known as a dramatist with

The Silver Box. Other plays: *Strife* (1909), *Justice* (1910), *Loyalties* (1922), etc. Other novels: *The Country House* (1907), *Fraternity* (1909), and *The Modern Comedy* trilogy (1924–28). Poetry: *Verses New and Old* (1921). Short stories: *Caravan* (1905). Essays: *Castles in Spain* (1927), etc. Awarded the Nobel Prize for Literature in 1932.

GALTON, SIR FRANCIS (1822–1911).—*B.* in Warwickshire, cousin of Charles Darwin, studied at Camb. Explored unknown parts of S. Africa in 1850 and *pub.* two books on his experiences. Best known for his connection with the science of eugenics. His book *Human Faculty and its Development* (1883) can be reckoned to be the starting point in favour of National Eugenics. Endowed a fellowship for the study of eugenics at London Univ. in 1904. Knighted in 1909.

GARNETT, DAVID (1892).—Grandson of Richard Garnett (*q.v.*), *ed.* at Royal Coll. of Science, studied botany, and turned from bookselling to publishing. Is now literary editor of the *New Statesman and Nation*. Has produced some decidedly original fiction: *Lady into Fox* (1922), *Man in the Zoo* (1924), *Go She Must* (1927), *No Love* (1929), and a biography: *Pocahontas* (1933).

GASQUET, FRANCIS AIDAN (1846–1929).—*B.* in London, *ed.* at Downside Coll., Bath. Rose to be abbot pres. of the English Benedictines, and was finally raised by Pope Pius XI to the dignity of cardinal priest. An authority on Pre-Reformation monasticism in England. Works include *Henry VIII and the English Monasteries* (1888–9), *Parish Life in Medieval England* (1906), *Monastic Life in the Middle Ages* (1922). *d.* at Rome.

GIBSON, WILFRID WILSON (1878).—Was for a time a social worker in the East End of London, and during the Great War served in the ranks, and these experiences form the background of much of his poetry, *Daily Bread* (1910), *Liveliness* (1917), *Battle* (1915), *Collected Poems*, 1905–25 (1926), *Hazards* (1930).

GILBERT, SIR WILLIAM SCHWENCK (1836–1911).—*B.* in London, graduated at London Univ. After a few years in the Privy-Council office, went in for law, became a barrister (1864) and a magistrate (1891). Contributed to magazines from 1861; *Bab Ballads*, a collection of his work, appeared in 1869. Turned his attention to the stage and entered into partnership with Sullivan in 1871, producing with him the famous series of comic operas. Knighted in 1907.

GOLLANCZ, SIR ISRAEL (1864–1930).—*Ed.* at London and Camb. Became univ. lecturer in English at Camb. and London, director of the Early English Text Society, and secretary of the British Academy from its foundation. An authority on old English texts and Elizabethan literature; his chief function was that of an editor.

GORE, CHARLES (1853–1932).—*Ed.* at Harrow and Oxf., Bishop of Worcester, 1902, of Birmingham, 1905, of Oxf., 1911. Resigned in 1919 and ceased to have a see. A high-churchman and worked for the re-union of Christendom. *The Church and the Ministry* (1889), *Roman Catholic Claims* (1889), *Belief in God* (1921), *The Philosophy of the Good Life* (1930). He was also ed. of the famous *Commentary on Holy Scripture* (1928).

GOSSE, SIR EDWARD WILLIAM (1849–1928).—*B.* in London. After work at the British Museum was made translator to the Board of Trade. Later became lecturer on English literature at Camb. and librarian to the House of Lords. *Collected Poems* (1911), *History of Eighteenth-Century Literature* (1889), *Collected Essays* (1913), *Father and Son*, a study of his early family life (1907). Exercised considerable influence as a critic.

GRAND, SARAH (FRANCES ELIZABETH MCFALL) (1862).—*B.* in Ireland of English parents. Travelled in the Far East, *m.* at sixteen. Became famous by her first novel *Ideala* (1888) and by *The Heavenly Twins* (1893). Has six times been Mayoress of Bath.

GRAVES, ROBERT RANKE (1895).—*B.* in London, *ed.* at Charterhouse and Oxf., served in France in the Great War, Prof. of English Literature, Egyptian Univ., 1926. Became known as a war poet. *Collected Poems, 1914–27* (1927). His prose autobiography, *Goodbye to All That* (1929), was a popular success.

GREGORY, ISABELLA AUGUSTA, LADY (1852–1932).—*B.* in Ireland. In the last few years of the nineteenth century was foremost in founding a national drama in Ireland, and in 1904 obtained a patent for the Abbey Theatre, Dublin, now the home of that drama. Wrote a number of successful plays: *The Golden Apple* (1916), *Three Lost Plays* (1928), etc.

HAGGARD, SIR HENRY RIDER (1856–1925).—*B.* in Norfolk. At nineteen he went to S. Africa and filled various important public positions. To this period belong his best-known romances, *King Solomon's Mines* (1886), *She* (1887). Also an authority on agriculture, for his services to which he was knighted in 1912.

HARDY, THOMAS (1840–1928).—*B.* June 2 nr. Dorchester. Originally an architect, but after a short and successful career took to literature, with a preference for poetry, although it was in fiction that he first made his mark. After *Desperate Remedies* (1871), *Under the Greenwood Tree* (1872), and *A Pair of Blue Eyes* (1873) he achieved a popular success with *Far from the Madding Crowd* in 1874. Then followed his one comedy *The Hand of Ethelberta* (1876) and several other novels in his more usual sombre style: *The Return of the Native* (1878), *Two on a Tower* (1882), *Tess of the D'Urbervilles* (1891), *Jude the Obscure* (1895), etc. The rather hostile reception of the last book sent Hardy back to poetry. The result of several years' work was his great epic, *The Dynasts* (1904–8). After this he turned to lyrical poetry: *Satires of Circumstance* (1915),

Late Lyrics and Earlier (1922), *Human Shows: Far Phantasies* (1925), etc. Hardy also wrote a number of short stories with no little success: *Wessex Tales* (1888), *A Group of Noble Dames* (1891), *Life's Little Ironies* (1894). His *Memoirs* appeared 1928–30. *d.* Jan. 11.

HARRIS, FRANK (1856–1931).—*Ed.* at continental and American univs. One time ed. of the *Fortnightly Review, the Saturday Review,* and *Vanity Fair,* founder and ed. of the *Candid Friend.* Works include: *The Man Shakespeare* (1909), five series of *Contemporary Portraits* (1915–30), short stories, plays, an autobiography, and sensational lives of Oscar Wilde and Bernard Shaw (1920 and 1931).

HARRISON, FREDERIC (1831–1923).—*B.* in London, *ed.* at King's Coll. School, London, and Oxf. Called to the Bar, 1858, pres. of the English Positivist Committee, 1880–1905, an authority on civil and international law, history, and Comte. *The Meaning of History* (1862), *Introduction to Comte's Positive Philosophy* (1896), *Among My Books* (1912).

HASSALL, ARTHUR (1853–1931).—*B.* at Bebington, Cheshire, *ed.* at Uppingham and Oxf., lecturer in history at Keble Coll., 1880, and at Christ Church, 1883. Works include: *Life of Bolingbroke* (1889), *The Balance of Power* (1896 and 1898), *Modern Europe* (1910), *A British History* (1919).

HAWKINS, SIR ANTHONY HOPE ("ANTHONY HOPE") (1863).—*Ed.* at Marlborough and Oxf., called to the Bar 1887. Achieved a sudden and wide popular success in 1894 with *The Dolly Dialogues* (reprinted from the *Westminster Gazette*) and *The Prisoner of Zenda.* Has written a number of novels since. Knighted 1918.

HERGESHEIMER, JOSEPH (1880).—American writer, *b.* at Philadelphia, Pa., *ed.* at a Quaker School and the Pennsylvania School of Fine Arts. Early established a reputation for careful and stylish fiction, and rose to his greatest height, possibly, in *Java Head* (1919). Other titles: *The Lay Anthony* (1914), *The Three Black Pennys* (1917), *Balisand* (1924), *The Limestone Tree* (1931).

HEWLETT, MAURICE (1861–1923).—*B.* in Kent and became a barrister and magistrate. Produced imaginative and historical novels, frequently in an Italian setting, some short stories and plays. In his last fifteen years he concentrated more on poetry, producing a narrative poem of real merit, *The Song of the Plow* (1916). Novels: *The Forest Lovers* (1898), *Life and Death of Richard Yea-and-Nay* (1900), etc.

HOCKING, JOSEPH (1855).—*B.* in Cornwall, younger brother of S. K. Hocking (*q.v.*), studied at Victoria Univ., Manchester, Nonconformist minister 1884–1910. Travelled the Near East in the 'eighties. Novels include: *Jabez Easterbrook* (1891), *The Jesuit* (1911), *The Man Who Was Sure* (1931).

HOCKING, SILAS KITTO (1850).—*B.* in Cornwall, Nonconformist minister from 1870 to 1896, unsuccessfully contested parliamentary seats 1906 and 1910. Novels include: *Alec Green* (1878), *The Flaming Sword* (1906), *The Greater Good* (1922).

HODGSON, RALPH (1871).—Awarded Polignac Prize for his poems *The Bull* and *Song of Honour* by the Royal Society of Literature. Nearly all his poetry issued in loose broadsheets, each containing one poem, or in small chapbooks. Works include *The Last Blackbird* (1907) and *Poems* (1917).

HOPE, ANTHONY (*see* HAWKINS).

HOUSMAN, ALFRED EDWARD (1859).—Studied at Oxf. Professor of Latin at Univ. Coll., London, 1892–1911, and at Camb. since then. One of the foremost classical scholars in the country (ed. of Manilius, Juvenal, and Lucan), but is best known to the general public for his lyrics, *The Shropshire Lad* (1896) and *Last Poems* (1922).

HOUSMAN, LAURENCE (1865).—Brother of A. E. Housman (*q.v.*), studied art at S. Kensington and has illustrated a number of books. He has written novels and shorter tales, but is best known for his poetry, *Spikenard* (1906), *Selected Poems* (1909), and his plays, *Prunella*, with Granville Barker (1906), *Little Plays of St. Francis* (1922). He is also the author of the well-known *An Englishwoman's Love Letters* (1900).

HOWELLS, WILLIAM DEAN (1837–1920). — American novelist, critic, and poet, *b.* in Ohio. Began life as a journalist and printer; United States consul at Venice, 1861–5; editor of the *Atlantic Monthly* (1872). The recognised leader of the realistic school in the U.S.A. in his time. His enormous output included *Poems* (1873, 1886, and 1895), *A Modern Instance* (novel, 1882), *Years of My Youth* (1916), *Literature and Life* (1902).

HUDSON, WILLIAM HENRY (1841–1922).—*B.* in Rio de la Plata, Argentina, came to England in 1869. Best known for his nature-books, *Naturalist in La Plata* (1892), *Idle Days in Patagonia* (1893), *Birds and Man* (1901), *A Hind in Richmond Park* (1922), but produced a striking romance, *Green Mansions* (1904). Other works: *Far Away and Long Ago* (reminiscences, 1918), *A Traveller in Little Things* (sketches, 1921).

HUXLEY, ALDOUS LEONARD (1894).—*S.* of Leonard Huxley (ed. of the *Cornhill Magazine*), grandson of T. H. Huxley, and brother of Julian S. Huxley, the scientist. *Ed.* at Eton and Oxf., on the staff of the *Athenæum* and *Westminster Gazette*, 1919–21. Attracted attention as a poet of the Imagist school (*Leda*, 1920), and as a short story writer (*Limbo*, 1920), but reached a wider public through his novels *Antic Hay* (1923), *Point Counter Point* (1928), etc. In 1932 came his futuristic fantasy, *Brave New World*. Has written essays on philosophical subjects, *Do What You Will* (1929) and a travel book, *Jesting Pilate* (1926).

HYDE, DOUGLAS (1850).—*B.* in Roscommon, Ireland, *ed.* at Trinity Coll., Dublin. One of the leading figures in Irish literature. Pres. of Gaelic League 1893–1915, and of many other Irish national and literary societies. Has also been a senator in the I.F.S. government (1925). His literary reputation is based chiefly on his poetry and plays, but he has written an important history of Gaelic literature and collected Irish folk-tales.

JACOBS, WILLIAM WYMARK (1863). — Employed in Savings Bank Dept. of the Civil Service 1883–99, since when he has confined himself to literary work, mostly consisting of humorous stories, *Many Cargoes* (1896), *Sea Whispers* (1926) etc. Has also done a little work in drama, sensational or humorous.

JAMES, HENRY (1843–1916).—American author, *b.* April 15 in New York, *ed.* in Europe and Harvard; intended for the law but turned to literature. First story appeared in 1865 in the *Atlantic Monthly*; achieved success as a novelist with *Roderick Hudson* (1875) and *Daisy Miller* (1878). Came to Europe in 1869 and settled in Rye, England; became naturalised as a British subject in 1915. A master in the art of the short story, he was also a distinguished critic. *d.* Feb. 28.

JAMES, WILLIAM (1842–1910).—Elder brother of Henry James, *b.* in New York, *ed.* at Harvard, became lecturer there in anatomy and physiology in 1872, later becoming a Prof. of Philosophy and Psychology. Visited Europe on various occasions. Outstanding works: *Principles of Psychology* (1890), *The Will to Believe* (1897), *Pragmatism* (1907).

JEROME, JEROME KLAPKA (1859–1927).—*B.* at Walsall. Was schoolmaster, clerk, and actor before taking up journalism. Made his reputation as a humorist with *Idle Thoughts of an Idle Fellow* and *Three Men in a Boat* (1889). Wrote various plays, of which *The Passing of the Third Floor Back* (1907) had the greatest success. Served in France during the Great War.

JONES, HENRY ARTHUR (1851–1929).—*B.* in Bucks, obliged to become a shop assistant at thirteen. In 1879 he gained a hearing with *A Clerical Error* (a one-act comedy) and *Only Round the Corner.* Wrote a number of other—generally popular and successful—plays ranging from melodrama, *Saints and Sinners* (1884), to comedy and satire, *The Liars* (1897), *The Knife* (1909). He also wrote a rather vindictive soliloquy, *My Dear Wells* (1921).

JOYCE, JAMES (1882).—*B.* in Dublin, *ed.* at Royal Univ., Dublin. Has lived chiefly on the Continent. First appeared in print as a poet (*Chamber Music*, 1907). Has written short stories (*Dubliners*, 1914), an autobiographical novel, *Portrait of the Artist as a Young Man* (1916), and a play, *Exiles* (1918), but is best known for his novel *Ulysses* (1925), which is often held to be the most significant novel—in style and thought—of modern times. Has also published fragments from an unfinished work referred to as *Work in Progress*.

KIPLING, RUDYARD (1865).—*B.* in Bombay, *ed.* in England, returned to India at the age of seventeen and took up journalism. In 1886 appeared *Departmental Ditties* and in the following year the first of a number of volumes of short stories, *Plain Tales from the Hills,* which made him famous. His first novel appeared in 1891, *The Light That Failed.* In 1894 came the first of his children's books, *The Jungle Book.* He has since written other volumes in each of these classes, besides a *History of England,* volumes of essays and speeches and other miscellaneous works, but his most successful medium is undoubtedly the short story. *Inclusive Verse* (1919). Awarded the Nobel Prize for Literature in 1907.

LANG, ANDREW (1844–1912).—*B.* at Selkirk, Scotland, *ed.* at Edin. and Oxf. Elected a fellow of Merton Coll. and embarked on a varied literary career. Began with poetry, *Ballads and Lyrics of Old France* (1872), went on to fairy tales and folk-lore, *Blue Fairy Tale Book* (1889), *Custom and Myth* (1884). *Pub.* works on historical mysteries such as Mary Stuart and the Man in the Iron Mask, and showed his powers as a Greek scholar by his participation in the prose translations of the *Odyssey* and *Iliad* (1879 and 1883), and in other translations and works on Homer.

LAWRENCE, DAVID HERBERT (1885–1930).—*B.* Sept. 11 at Eastwood, Notts, *s.* of a coal miner, gained place in Univ. Coll., Nottingham by scholarships. Was a clerk and school teacher, came to London and wrote history books as "L. H. Davidson". Gained increasing attention with his novels *The White Peacock* (1911), *The Trespasser* (1912), *Sons and Lovers* (1913). *Pub.* poems in 1917, *Collected Poems* (1928). Travelled in Europe and Mexico: *Twilight in Italy* (1916), *Mornings in Mexico* (1927). Wrote volumes of short stories, plays, a philosophical essay, *Fantasia on the Unconscious* (1922). Interest in Aztec civilisations and Mexico shown in novels such as *The Plumed Serpent* (1926). Analysis of sex his main theme in novels: *Sons and Lovers* and *Lady Chatterley's Lover,* (1928). Was also a competent artist. *Letters* published 1932.

LEACOCK, STEPHEN BUTLER (1869).—Canadian economist and humorist, *b.* in Hampshire, England, *ed.* at Toronto Univ., became head of dept. of economics and political science at McGill Univ. Has written on economics and Canadian history, but is best known as a humorous writer: *Literary Lapses* (1910), *Short Circuits* (1928), etc.

LEE, SIR SIDNEY (1859–1926).—*B.* in London of Jewish parents, *ed.* at London and Oxf. Became assistant-ed. of the *Dictionary of National Biography* in 1883 and ed. in 1891. Also produced standard lives of Shakespeare (1898), Queen Victoria (1902), Edward VII (1912). Professor of English Literature and Dean of the Faculty of Arts at London Univ. *d.* at Kensington.

LE GALLIENNE, RICHARD (1866).—*B.* in Liverpool, literary critic for the *Star,* 1891, and joined the *Daily Chronicle* and the *Speaker* (*Retrospective Reviews,* 1896). Visited U.S.A. in 1898 and decided to live in New York. Besides his reviews and essays he has written novels, *The Quest of the Golden Girl* (1896), and poetry, *English Poems* (1892).

LEWIS, SINCLAIR (1885).—American novelist, *b.* in Minnesota, graduated at Yale, worked for some years in journalism. First novel appeared in 1914, *Our Mr. Wrenn*; wrote others, but did not make a hit until 1920 (*Main Street*). Since then he has become the most celebrated living American novelist with *Babbitt* (1922), *Martin Arrowsmith* (1925), *Elmer Gantry* (1927), *Dodsworth* (1929), *Ann Vickers* (1933). Awarded Nobel Prize for Literature in 1930.

LOCKE, WILLIAM JOHN (1863–1930).—*B.* in Barbados, *ed.* at Trinidad and Camb., became sec. to the Royal Institute of British Architects and other architectural societies. His novels attained wide popularity, the most successful being *The Beloved Vagabond* (1906).

LODGE, SIR OLIVER JOSEPH (1851).—*B.* at Penkhull, Staffs, studied at Univ. Coll., London, became Prof. of Physics at Liverpool Univ., 1881–1900, and during that period wrote various scientific works. Principal of Birmingham Univ. 1900–19, knighted in 1902. A leading figure in psychic research and an advocate of a Christianity in a scientific setting. His fame rests on strictly scientific work. Works include *Modern Views of Electricity* (1889), *Life and Matter* (1905), *Atoms and Rays* (1924), *Energy* (1928), *The Reality of a Spiritual World* (1930).

LONDON, JOHN GRIFFITH ("JACK") (1876–1916).—American novelist, *b.* in San Francisco. Became oyster pirate, sailor, prisoner, journalist, and wanderer. Chiefly famous for his sympathetic animal stories such as *The Call of the Wild* (1903), and *White Fang* (1906). Produced a number of wild and sensational short stories.

LOWELL, AMY (1874–1925).—American poetess, *b.* in Mass. Took to writing poetry about 1902, *pub.* her first volume in 1912 (*A Dome of Many Coloured Glass*). Became the leader of the poetic group called the Imagists. Besides other volumes of verse, *Sword Blades and Poppy Seeds* (1914), *Ballads for Sale* (1927), wrote critical works and an important study of Keats (1925).

M'CARTHY, JUSTIN (1830–1911).—Irish historian, novelist, journalist, and politician, *b.* at Cork. Ed. of the *Morning Star*, 1864–8; from 1870 leader writer to the *Daily News*. Elected M.P. in 1879, closely associated with the Home Rule movement. Chief historical work, *A History of Our Own Times* (1882–7 and 1905).

MACAULAY, ROSE.—One of the foremost contemporary women writers. She has written several novels, including *Crewe Train* (1926), *Staying with Relations* (1930), and a novel written round Herrick, *They Were Defeated* (1932); poetry, 1914 and 1919; essays, and a few literary studies.

MACKENZIE, COMPTON (1883).—*B.* at W. Hartlepool, *ed.* at St. Paul's School, London, and at Oxf. After a volume of poems (1907) took to fiction of a delicate romantic type, *The Passionate Elopement* (1911), *Carnival* (1912), *Guy and Pauline* (1915), etc. Saw active service at the Dardanelles and was later in the Secret Service in Greece during the Great War: *Gallipoli Memories* (1929), *First Athenian Memories* (1931), *Greek Memories* (1932, suppressed).

MANSFIELD, KATHERINE (KATHLEEN BEAUCHAMP) (1890-1923).—*B.* in New Zealand, *ed.* in England. *Pub.* a volume of short stories in 1911, *In a German Pension.* *M.* J. M. Murry in 1913 and found a steady outlet for her work while he was ed. of the *Athenæum.* Contracted pleurisy in 1917 and had to struggle for her health to the end of her life, living chiefly on the Continent, Excelled at the short story, but her posthumously published *Journal* (1924) and *Letters* (1928) are perhaps more widely read.

MAUGHAM, WILLIAM SOMERSET (1874).—*Ed.* at King's School, Canterbury, Heidelberg Univ., and St. Thomas's Hospital. Began as a novelist with *Liza of Lambeth* (1897). Other novels, *Merry-go-round* (1904), *Of Human Bondage* (1915), *Cakes and Ale* (1930). Wrote his first play in German in 1902. Other plays, *A Man of Honour* (1904), *Our Betters* (1923), *The Letter* (1927). Has written volumes of short stories, *Ashenden* (1928), and sketches, *The Land of the Blessed Virgin* (1905).

MARTYN, EDWARD (1859–1924).—*B.* in Co. Galway, studied at Oxf., best known for his work on behalf of the Irish national theatre, music and education. He wrote a number of plays, *The Heather Field* (1899), etc.

MASEFIELD, JOHN EDWARD (1875).—*B.* in Liverpool, ran away to sea, worked in various lowly jobs in U.S.A., returned to England and became a journalist. *Pub.* his first volume of poems in 1902 (*Salt-Water Ballads*). Wrote more poems, one or two plays, and essays, but became famous as a writer of long narrative poems, *The Everlasting Mercy* (1911), *Dauber* (1913), *Reynard the Fox* (1919). Also wrote thrilling novels, *Jim Davis* (1914), *Sard Harker* (1924), *Odtaa* (1926), miscellaneous works such as studies of Shakespeare (1911), Synge (1915), and Ruskin (1920), war books—*Gallipoli* (1916), Naval History books, and religious dramas—*Coming of Christ* (1928) and *Easter* (1929). Created poet laureate in 1930.

MENCKEN, HENRY LEWIS (1880).—American author, *b.* at Baltimore, began a journalistic career in 1899 and occupied various important positions on Baltimore papers. Now ed. of the *American Mercury* and one of the eds. of the New York *Nation.* Has written books on Shaw and Nietzsche, and some verse, but is best known as a satirist: *Prejudices* (six series, 1919–27), etc.

MERRICK, LEONARD (1864).—*B.* in London (original surname, Miller), *ed.* at Brighton Coll., the author of several novels in the realist manner, *The Actor-Manager* (1898), *The Quaint*

Companions (1903). A *coll.* ed., *pub.* in 1918, was sponsored by a number of important people in the literary world. Has also written a few plays.

MEYNELL, ALICE CHRISTIANA (MRS. WILFRID MEYNELL) (1849–1922).—English poetess, spent much of her youth in Italy. Her first volume was *Preludes* (1875), but *Poems* (1893) definitely established her reputation. *Collected Poems* (1913), *Last Poems* (1923). Produced prose works in the form of essays, studies in art and religion.

MILNE, ALAN ALEXANDER (1882).—*Ed.* at Westminster and Camb., began serious journalism at 21 and after a few years became assistant ed. of *Punch.* Has since issued many volumes of essays, and some plays, *Michael and Mary* (1930), etc., but his greatest success has been his work for children, *When We Were Very Young* (1924), *Winnie-the-Pooh* (1926), *Now We Are Six* (1927), *The House at Pooh Corner* (1928).

MOLESWORTH, MRS. MARY LOUISA (1839–1921).—Scottish novelist, *b.* in Rotterdam. Wrote novels under the pseudonym of "Ennis Graham" but is best known because of her books for children such as *Carrots, Cuckoo Clock*, and *The House that Grew.*

MONRO, HAROLD EDWARD (1879–1932).—*B.* at Brussels, *ed.* at Camb. Volumes of poems issued from 1906 onward. Became noted as proprietor of a remarkable London literary centre, The Poetry Bookshop.

MONTAGUE, CHARLES EDWARD (1867–1928).—*Ed.* at City of London School and Oxf. On leaving Oxf. he began a distinguished career in journalism, and his early novel, *A Hind Let Loose,* is a novel of journalistic life. Served as an infantry man in the Great War, but became a censor at G.H.Q. After the war he *pub.* several other volumes of fiction: *Disenchantment* (1922), *Fiery Particles* (1925), *Rough Justice* (1926), *Right off the Map* (1927), and *Action* (1928). He also *pub.* volumes of dramatic criticism and a posthumous work, *A Writer's Notes on His Trade* (1929).

MOORE, GEORGE (1853–1933).—*B.* in Co. Mayo, Ireland, *ed.* in Ireland, studied painting in Paris, produced poetry, *Flowers of Passion* (1878), *Pagan Poetry* (1882). Came to England to issue fiction, *A Modern Lover* (1883), *A Mummer's Wife* (1885). Increased his growing importance with *Confessions of a Young Man* (1888). Established his reputation with three novels, *Esther Waters* (1894), *Evelyn Innes* (1898), *Sister Teresa* (1901). Returned to Ireland for about ten years, and in 1911–14 issued a trilogy of autobiographical revelations, *Hail and Farewell.* Has produced volumes of criticism, *Avowals* (1919 and 1926), *Conversations in Ebury Street* (1924), plays, *The Making of an Immortal* (1927), etc., and a volume on *Modern Painting* (1893), but has chiefly enhanced his reputation by his versions of the story of Christ, *The Brook Kerith* (1916 and 1927), and of *Héloïse and Abélard* (1921).

MOORE, THOMAS STURGE (1870).—*B.* at Hastings. Best known for his poetry, *The Vinedresser*, etc. (1899), *Collected Poems* (1931–). Is also a wood engraver and art critic: *Art and Life* (1910), etc.

MORLEY OF BLACKBURN, JOHN MORLEY, 1ST VISCOUNT (1838–1923).—*B.* at Blackburn, ed. of the *Literary Gazette* and *Morning Star* and *Fortnightly Review*. In 1880 became ed. of *Pall Mall Gazette*. Entered Parliament as a Liberal in 1883, Irish Sec. 1886, Sec. of State for India 1906, raised to peerage in 1908. As a pacifist retired from public life in 1914. Wrote valuable studies and lives of Gladstone (1903), Cromwell (1900), Cobden (1881), Voltaire, Rousseau, Burke, and Walpole.

MOTTRAM, RALPH HALE (1883).—*B.* at Norwich, served throughout the Great War and produced three of the best war books in the trilogy, *The Spanish Farm* (1924–6). Has also written works on finance, *History of Financial Speculation* (1929), etc., and a volume of *Poems* (1930).

MURRAY, SIR JAMES AUGUSTUS HENRY (1837–1915).—*B.* at Denholm, Roxburghshire. *Ed.* at London, Oxf., and Edin. Took up teaching for a career, assistant examiner at London Univ. (1875–9). Appointed ed. of the *New Oxford English Dictionary* in 1879, and produced more than half of it under his direct editorship.

MURRY, JOHN MIDDLETON (1889).—*B.* in London, *ed.* at Christ's Hospital and Oxf., on staff of *Westminster Gazette* (1912–13), *m.* Kathleen Mansfield (*q.v.*) in 1913. In War Office in the Great War and became chief censor in 1919. Ed. of the *Athenæum*, 1919–21, and of the *Adelphi*, 1923–30. Has written *Poems* (1919), various critical works on philosophy of religion, *God* (1929), and a study of D. H. Lawrence, *Son of Woman* (1931).

NEWBOLT, SIR HENRY JOHN (1862).—*Ed.* at Clifton and Oxf., called to the Bar 1887. Began his literary career as a novelist in 1892 and issued a play in 1895, but it was his spirited ballads in *Admirals All* (1897), *The Island Race* (1898), *Songs of the Sea* (1904) which brought him success. An authority on naval matters, he wrote a *Naval History of the War* (1920). Has *pub.* other novels, verse, and miscellaneous works.

NICHOLS, ROBERT MALISE BOWYER (1893).—*Ed.* at Winchester and Oxf., served from the beginning of the Great War and became known as a war poet, *Invocation* (1915), *Ardours and Endurances* (1917), etc. Has written plays and other verse. Prof. of English Literature at Tokio Univ., 1921–4.

NOYES, ALFRED (1880).—*B.* in Staffs, *ed.* at Oxf. His first volume of poems appeared in 1902, *The Loom of Years*; other volumes appeared in rapid succession and two volumes of *Collected Poems* were *pub.* in 1910. He went to America in 1913, where he was honoured by American universities. His great achievement is, however, his epic *The Torch-bearers* (1922–30). He has written critical studies, short stories, novels and plays. He was received into the Roman Catholic Church in 1930.

O'CONNOR, THOMAS POWER (1848–1929).—Irish politician and journalist, *b.* at Athlone. Began career as journalist in Dublin, but soon came to London, and gained posts on the *Daily Telegraph* and *New York Herald*. Entered parliament in 1880 and became "Father of the House". Founded and ed. the *Star*, the *Sun*, *The Weekly Sun*, *M.A.P.*, *T.P.'s Weekly*. Wrote works on Beaconsfield, Napoleon, Gladstone, and the Parnell movement.

OMAN, SIR CHARLES WILLIAM CHADWICK (1860).—*Ed.* at Winchester and Oxf. Fellow of All Soul's, Oxf., since 1883 after a distinguished scholastic career, especially in history. Has written numerous historical works, the principal one being *A History of the Peninsular War*, 1902–30.

O'NEILL, EUGENE GLADSTONE (1888).—American dramatist, *b.* in New York, *ed.* at Princeton and Harvard. For several years lived a varied and adventurous life in C. and S. America and as a sailor. Returned to Harvard for further study and produced some one-act plays. His first full-length play appeared in 1919, *Beyond the Horizon*, and this with *The Emperor Jones* (1920) established his reputation. His plays since then include *Anna Christie* (1922), *The Hairy Ape* (1922), *The Great God Brown* (1925), *Lazarus Laughed* (1927). He is generally accepted to be the greatest living American dramatist.

OSBOURNE, LLOYD (1868).—American novelist, *b.* in San Francisco; his mother married R. L. Stevenson. From 1887 to 1897 was United States Vice-Consul-General at Samoa and Friendly Islands. Best known from his collaboration with Stevenson in three tales, *The Wrong Box* (1889), *The Wrecker* (1892), *The Ebb Tide* (1894). He has also written several novels by himself.

PARKER, SIR GILBERT (1862–1932).—Canadian novelist, *b.* in Ontario, lived in England since 1889, after short career in Australia as journalist. First novel *pub.* in 1892, *Pierre and His People*. Sat in parliament from 1900 to 1918, made a knight in 1915, member of Privy Council, 1916. Novels chiefly have a French-Canadian interest.

PHILLIPS, STEPHEN (1868–1915).—*B.* July 28 at Somerton, Oxf., *ed.* at Oundle, acted on the stage for six years in Shakespeare, and finally devoted himself to poetry, including verse-dramas, of which *Paolo and Francesca* (1899) was hailed as a masterpiece. The popularity and sale of his work was extraordinarily large. *d.* Dec. 9.

PHILLPOTTS, EDEN (1862).—*B.* in India, *ed.* at Plymouth; an insurance clerk until 1890, studied for the stage but abandoned the idea for that of a literary career. Made his name by his novels, generally dealing with Devonshire life, *Lying Prophets* (1896), *The Good Red Earth* (1901), *The Forest on the Hill* (1912), etc., but his greatest success was a play, *The Farmer's Wife* (1917). Has written several other plays, poems, and short stories.

PINERO, SIR ARTHUR WING (1855).—*B.* in London, *ed.* privately; on the stage from 1874–81, when he retired to write plays. His early period, 1881–9, was almost completely concerned with farces and comedies, *The Magistrate* (1885), etc., but he turned to serious drama with *The Profligate* (1889) and *The Second Mrs. Tanqueray* (1893), and these and other similar plays gave him his position in drama. Nearly all of his very numerous plays have been successful with the public. He was knighted in 1909.

POUND, EZRA (1885).—American poet. Came to England as a young man; took great interest in medieval literature (ed. Cavalcanti's Sonnets). Has taken a hand in founding many modernist publications and has lived on the Continent for many years. Now lives at Rapallo, and ed. *Il Mare.* Poems, *Exultations* (1909), etc. The founder of the Imagist group of poets.

POWYS, THEODORE FRANCIS (1875).—*Ed.* privately. The most outstanding member of a literary family; from his youth has lived a secluded life in Dorset, which is the scene of all his tales and allegories. *The Left Leg* (1923), *The House of the Echo* (1928), *Fables* (1929), and *The White Paternoster* (1930) are collections of short stories. His chief novels, all of which are largely allegorical, are *Black Bryony* (1933), *Mark Only* (1924), *Mr. Weston's Good Wine* (1927), which is probably his greatest work, and *Unclay* (1931). Has also published *Soliloquies of a Hermit* (1918) and an interpretation of *Genesis* (1929). Most of his work was written some years before publication.

PRIESTLEY, JOHN BOYNTON (1894).—*B.* at Bradford, *ed.* at Camb., served throughout the Great War. Issued a volume of verses in 1918 and some short stories and sketches in 1922 (*Brief Diversions*). There followed volumes of essays and critical works, *Meredith* (1926), *Peacock* (1927). His outstanding success was his novel *Good Campanions* (1929, dramatised, 1931). This was followed by two little less successful novels, *Angel Pavement* (1930), *Faraway* (1932).

QUILLER-COUCH, SIR ARTHUR THOMAS (1863).—*B.* in Cornwall, *ed.* at Clifton Coll. and Oxf. Issued a novel in 1887, when he was a lecturer in Classics at Oxf. (*Dead Man's Rock*), and continued to write fiction, frequently in a Cornish setting, *Troy Town* (1888), until the outbreak of war. It was under his pseudonym of "Q" that most of this early work was done. In 1910 he was knighted and made Prof. of English Literature at Camb. Since then has mainly issued volumes of critical work based on his lectures, *Studies in Literature* (1918), etc., *Shakespeare's Workmanship* (1920). Has also written poetry (*coll.* in 1929) and ed. a number of anthologies, *The Golden Pomp* (1895), and the Oxf. books of *English Verse, Ballads, Victorian Verse,* and *Prose.*

RALEIGH, SIR WALTER ALEXANDER (1861–1922).—*Ed.* at Univ. Coll., London, and at Camb. Prof. of English literature at Liverpool and Glas., and at Oxf. from 1904. Knighted in 1911. His literary works are mainly critical, *The English Novel* (1894), *Milton* (1900), *Wordsworth* (1903), *Shakespeare* (1907). Also did the first volume of the official History of the War in the Air (1922).

READ, HERBERT (1893).—*Ed.* at the Univ. of Leeds, served in the Great War, 1915–18. Assistant keeper, Victoria and Albert Museum, 1922–31, Prof. of Fine Art in Univ. of Edin. since 1931. His first poems were *pub.* in 1919; *Collected Poems* (1926). He is chiefly known for his literary criticism, of which the more important books are *Reason and Romanticism* (1926), *English Prose Style* (1928), *Wordsworth* (1930). Has also written a story of the Great War, *In Retreat* (1925).

RHYS, ERNEST (1859).—*B.* in London. Began his career as a mining engineer but abandoned it for literature. Ed. the *Camelot Series* 1886–91, and in 1905 planned *Everyman's Library* in conjunction with J. M. Dent and has remained editor. He has written critical works, poems, and fiction. His autobiography, *Everyman Remembers*, appeared in 1931. Has been closely associated with a large number of the great contemporary literary figures.

RICHARDS, IVOR ARMSTRONG (1893).—*Ed.* at Clifton and Camb. Fellow of Magdalene Coll., Camb. since 1926. Visiting Lecturer, Tsing Hua Univ., Peking, 1929–30 and Harvard, 1931. His *Principles of Literary Criticism* (1924) and *Practical Criticism* (1929), like the critical writings of T. S. Eliot (*q.v.*), have had a powerful influence upon younger writers.

RICHARDSON, DOROTHY M. (Mrs. Alan Odle).—The originator of the style of technique in fiction known as the "stream of consciousness". Her novels include *Pointed Roofs* (1915), *The Tunnel* (1919), *The Trap* (1925).

ROBERTS, CHARLES GEORGE DOUGLAS (1860).—Canadian poet and author, *b.* in New Brunswick, *ed.* at the Univ. of N. B. Ed. the Toronto *Week* 1883–4 and then became a univ. prof. for ten years in literature and economics, when he resumed journalism. Served in the Great War. His first publications were poetry (*Collected*, 1900; and four later vols.). Has written many novels, but his most characteristic work is his animal stories, *Wisdom of the Wilderness* (1922), etc.

ROBERTS, MORLEY (1857).—*B.* in London, went to Australia in 1876 and worked in the bush, returned to England in 1879. Travelled widely in N. America 1884–6, and later in the South Seas. Works include reminiscences of his travels, *The Western Avernus* (1877), etc., a number of novels, *The Purification of Dolores Silva* (1894), etc., plays, and a few miscellaneous books.

ROBERTSON, JOHN MACKINNON (1856–1933).—*B.* in the Isle of Arran, left school at 13, did journalistic work in Edin., and came to London in 1884 to work on the *National Reformer.* Edited it from 1891 to its suppression in 1893. Entered parliament in 1906 as a liberal. Associated himself with the Free Thought movement, *History of Free Thought* (1900). Wrote books on Shakespearian problems, *The Problem of Hamlet* (1919), and politics, *Introduction to British Politics* (1899).

ROSEBERY, ARCHIBALD PHILIP PRIMROSE, 5TH EARL OF (1847–1929).—*Ed.* at Eton and Oxf. A brilliant orator, he rose to be Prime Minister in 1894. He published *Pitt* in 1891, *Peel* in 1899, and (his most famous book) *Napoleon, The Last Phase* in 1900. Studies of Cromwell, Lord Randolph Churchill, and Chatham, followed in the next ten years.

RUSSELL, BERTRAND ARTHUR WILLIAM RUSSELL, 3RD EARL (1872).—*Ed.* at Camb., became lecturer there in 1910. His pronounced pacificism lost him his lectureship, and in 1918 he was imprisoned for an article. He is a leading Freethinker, *The Conquest of Happiness* (1930), and a socialist in politics, *Practice and Theory of Bolshevism* (1920). He is also a scientist, specialising in mathematics. Other works, *Introduction to Mathematical Philosophy* (1919), *Sceptical Essays* (1928), etc.

RUSSELL, GEORGE WILLIAM ("Æ") (1867).—*B.* in Co. Armagh, studied art, became leader of the circle that *pub.* the *Irish Theosophist* in which appeared his first poems. He signed one poem "Æon" and it was printed as "Æ", which pseudonym he has since adopted. Was ed. of the Irish agricultural paper *The Irish Homestead* 1905–23 and founder and ed. of the *Irish Statesman* 1923–30. His poems were *coll.* in 1913, but further volumes have appeared since. His play *Deirdre* (1907) was an important landmark for the Irish National Theatre movement.

SAINTSBURY, GEORGE EDWARD BATEMAN (1845–1933).—*B.* at Southampton, *ed.* at Oxf. After various scholastic appointments became Prof. of English Literature at Edin. University (1895–1915). A leading authority on English and French literature. Works include histories of French literature (1882) and of English literature (1878), a *History of Criticism* (1900–4), a *History of English Prosody* (1906–10), and *Collected Essays* (1926).

SASSOON, SIEGFRIED (1886).—Became known as a war poet, *War Poems* (1919). Later volumes of poetry include *Satirical Poems* (1926), *The Heart's Journey* (1928). He has recently widened his public by two autobiographical prose works, *Memoirs of a Fox-Hunting Man* (1928; issued anonymously), *Memoirs of an Infantry Officer* (1930).

SCOTT, DUNCAN CAMPBELL (1862).—*B.* and *ed.* in Canada of British parents. Entered the Canadian Civil Service and is now in the Dept. of Indian Affairs. He is one of the foremost Canadian poets (*Collected Poems,* 1926). Has also written some fiction.

SEAMAN, SIR OWEN (1861).—*Ed.* at Shrewsbury and Camb., became a schoolmaster, a professor of literature and a barrister; joined the staff of *Punch* in 1897, and rose to be ed. in 1906. His writings consist chiefly of humorous verse and parodies, *In Cap and Bells* (1899), *Salvage* (1908). Retired from *Punch* in 1932.

SERVICE, ROBERT WILLIAM (1874).—Canadian author, *b.* in Lancashire. Emigrated to Canada in 1895. Farmed, and then joined the staff of a bank, travelling extensively. He *pub.* poems in 1907 (*Songs of a Sourdough*) and 1909, which gained him the reputation of being the "Canadian Kipling". His poetry was collected in 1930. Has also written a few novels. Was a war correspondent in the Balkan War and the Great War.

SHAW, GEORGE BERNARD (1856).—*B.* in Dublin, came to London in 1876. Wrote a number of immature novels 1880–3 (*Cashel Byron's Profession*, etc.). Joined the Fabian Society in 1884, and *pub.* a number of tracts for the society (see also books such as *Fabianism and the Empire*, 1900). Became music critic (*Star*, 1888–90, *World* 1890–4) and dramatic critic (*Saturday Review*, 1895–8). During this period he published *The Quintessence of Ibsenism* (1891), *The Sanity of Art* (1895), *The Perfect Wagnerite* (1898). It was in this last year that he began to publish the plays that have made him famous (*Plays, Pleasant and Unpleasant*, including the banned *Mrs. Warren's Profession*). There followed *Three Plays for Puritans* (1900), *Getting Married* (1908), *Pygmalion* (1922), etc. The War saw some slackening in Shaw's output, but in the year 1921 came the five-play cycle *Back to Methuselah*, and in 1923 came *Saint Joan*. His last two plays have been *The Apple Cart* (1929) and *Too True to be Good* (1931). Of all his miscellaneous books the most important is *The Intelligent Woman's Guide to Socialism and Capitalism* (1928). Awarded the Nobel Prize for Literature in 1925.

SINCLAIR, MAY.—*B.* in Cheshire. Began her career as a poet and critic, *pub.* first novel in 1896, and with *The Divine Fire* (1904) established her position as one of the foremost women novelists. Other novels: *The Creators*, *The Three Sisters* (1914), *Mary Olivier* (1919). Has written volumes of short stories, and a study of the Brontë sisters (1912).

SINCLAIR, UPTON (1878).—American novelist, *b.* at Baltimore, Maryland, *ed.* at Columbia Univ. He is a fervent Socialist and his books are nearly all directed to the examination of capitalism. He achieved wide fame by his exposure of the American meat-packing industry, *The Jungle* (1906). Other novels in the same vein are *King Coal* (1917), *Oil* (1927), *Boston* (1928).

SITWELL, EDITH (1887).—*B.* at Scarborough, sister of O. and S. Sitwell (*qq.v.*), *ed.* privately. Issued first volume of poems in 1915 (*The Mother and Other Poems*). Ed. the modernist annual anthology of poetry, *Wheels* (1916-21); *Collected Poems* (1930). Has written a life of Pope (1930) and ed. an anthology of English poetry, *The Pleasures of Poetry* (1930–2).

SITWELL, OSBERT (1892).—*B.* in London, *ed.* at Eton, served in the Grenadier Guards throughout the Great War. Issued his first poetry during the war; has become known as a satirist in prose and verse, *Argonaut and Juggernaut* (1919), *England Reclaimed* (1927), *Collected Poems and Satires* (1931). He has also written novels, *Before the Bombardment* (1926), *The Man Who Lost Himself* (1929), and several volumes of short stories.

SITWELL, SACHEVERELL (1897).—*B.* at Scarborough, *ed.* at Eton and Oxf. He became known as a poet in company with his brother and sister, and his first volume was *pub.* in 1918 (*The People's Palace*). Has *pub.* other poetry since, but is also an accomplished prose writer: *Southern Baroque Art* (1924), *German Baroque Art* (1927), *The Gothick North* trilogy (1929–30).

SKEAT, WALTER WILLIAM (1835–1912).—*B.* in London, took orders in the Anglican Church in 1860, but abandoned this career because of throat trouble, and was appointed Prof. of Anglo-Saxon at Camb. in 1878. Produced a number of important works on philology, including his *Etymological Dictionary* (1879–82), and standard eds. of Early and Middle English writers such as Chaucer and Langland.

SQUIRE, JOHN COLLINGS (1884).—*B.* at Plymouth, *ed.* at Camb. Literary ed. of the *New Statesman* (1913), acting ed. 1917–18. In 1919 he founded and has since ed. the *London Mercury*. He has written various volumes of poetry (collected edition, 1926), but the bulk of his work consists of criticism, *Books in General* (1918, 1920, 1921), *Books Reviewed* (1922), *Sunday Mornings* (1930). Other works: *Collected Parodies* (1921), *Grub Street Nights* (stories, 1924). He has ed. several poetical anthologies, and is a leading figure in the campaign to preserve England's historic architecture.

STEEL, MRS. FLORA ANNIE (1847–1929).—Anglo-Indian novelist, *b.* at Harrow and *m.* a Bengal civilian, lived in India until 1889 when she returned to England and took a leading part in the feminist movement. Her stories and novels include, *Wideawake Stories* (1884), *On the Face of the Waters* (1896), *The Curse of Eve* (1929).

STEPHENS, JAMES (1882).—*B.* in Dublin. An Irish nationalist in sympathy. *Pub.* a volume of fairy stories in 1912 (*The Crock of Gold*) and in 1923 a *coll.* of *Irish Fairy Tales*. He has also written several volumes of poems (collected edition, 1926).

STRACHEY, GILES LYTTON (1880–1932).—*Ed.* at Camb. Contributed literary articles to a number of periodicals, and achieved some prominence with *Landmarks of French Literature* (1912). It was in biography, however, that he became really famous. His *Eminent Victorians* (1918) and *Queen Victoria* (1921) may be said to have created the vogue for the modern light and well-informed biography. Other works: *Elizabeth and Essex* (1928), *Portraits in Miniature* (1931), and another volume of criticism, *Books and Characters* (1922).

SWINNERTON, FRANK ARTHUR (1884).—*B.* in London. From work in a publisher's office, became a literary adviser, and finally novelist and critic. His novels include *The Merry Heart* (1909), *Nocturne* (1917), and *Georgian House* (1932). Criticism: *A London Bookman* (1928) and studies of Stevenson (1914) and Gissing (1912).

SYMONS, ARTHUR (1865).—*B.* in Wales, made his name as a poet who wrote under the influence of Baudelaire and the Symbolist movement as a whole. Symons wrote a study of Baudelaire (1921) and *The Symbolist Movement in Literature* (1899). His work, *Days and Nights* (1889), *Silhouettes* (1892), *London Nights* (1895), gained him the close friendship of Verlaine. Has also written charming travel books, *Cities of Italy* (1907), *Wanderings* (1931), a book of *Confessions* (1930), and several other literary studies.

TAGORE, SIR RABINDRANATH (1861).—Indian poet, *b.* in Calcutta. Managed his father's estates from 1885, founded a school in 1901 which became an international institute—the Visva Bharata. T. writes mainly in Bengali, but has written in English besides translating some of his poetry into English: *Kabir's Poems* (1915), *Gitanjali* (1913). Has also written fiction, volumes of essays and *My Reminiscences* (1917). Awarded the Nobel Prize for literature in 1919 and knighted in 1915.

THOMAS, PHILIP EDWARD (1878–1917).—*B.* March 3, killed at Arras, April 9. A writer in the tradition of Borrow, Cobbett, and Clare. *The Heart of England* (1906), *The South Country* (1909), *Collected Poems* (1920). Also wrote critical studies of Jefferies, Borrow, Swinburne, and Pater.

TOMLINSON, HENRY MAJOR (1873).—*B.* in London. Spent his early life travelling in Africa, America, and the East Indies. Took up journalism in 1904, and in 1912 published *The Sea and the Jungle* with which he made an immediate reputation. War correspondent during the Great War, after which he became literary ed. of the *Nation and Athenæum*. Has written several novels, of which *Gallions Reach* (1927) is perhaps the best known.

TRENCH, FREDERICK HERBERT (1865–1923).—*B.* in Co. Cork, *ed.* at Haileybury and Oxf. An examiner on the Board of Education, later turned his attention to the stage, producing Maeterlinck's *Blue Bird* in 1908. His literary reputation rests on his poems, *Deirdre Wedded* (1901; a collection of early poems), *New Poems* (1907), *Poems: with Fables in Prose* (1918), *Collected Works* (1924). Also wrote a play, *Napoleon* (1919).

TREVELYAN, GEORGE MACAULAY (1876).—*S.* of Sir G. O. Trevelyan (*q.v.*), *ed.* at Harrow and Camb., became Regius Prof. of Modern History at Camb. in 1927. His chief works are the three volumes on Garibaldi (1907, 1909, 1911), a *History of England* (1926), and *England under Queen Anne* (1930).

TREVELYAN, SIR GEORGE OTTO (1838–1928).—*B.* in Leicestershire, nephew of Lord Macaulay, *ed.* at Harrow and Camb. Entered parliament in 1865 and held important posts until 1897. Made his literary reputation with *Life and Letters of Lord Macaulay* (1876), and his works on American history, *The Early History of Charles James Fox* (1880), *The American Revolution* (1909), *George III and Charles Fox* (1912–14).

TYNAN, KATHARINE (MRS. KATHARINE TYNAN HINKSON) (1861–1931).—*B.* in Dublin and *ed.* at Drogheda. Began writing at the age of seventeen and was a prominent figure in the Celtic movement at the end of last century. *Pub.* a volume of poems in 1885, but her work chiefly consisted of fiction, *The Dear Irish Girl* (1899), *The Lost Angel* (1908), *The Innocence of Peter* (1926). *Collected Poems* (1930).

VACHELL, HORACE ANNESLEY (1861).—*Ed.* at Harrow and Sandhurst. The writer of a number of novels and plays. Novels include *Romance of Judge Ketchum* (1895), *Brothers* (1904), *Quinney's Adventures* (1924). Plays, *Quinney's* (1915), *Searchlights* (1916).

WALLACE, ALFRED RUSSEL (1823–1913).—*B.* at Usk, Mon. When a schoolmaster in a private school at Leicester met H. W. Bates, and in 1848 set out with him for the Amazon. Later travelled to the Malay Archipelago, and while there (in 1858) he hit upon the idea of natural selection and communicated with Darwin who had already been working independently on the idea. He wrote works on his theory and on his travels, and an autobiography (1905).

WALLACE, EDGAR (1875–1932).—*B.* a destitute orphan, worked up to the position of war correspondent for Reuter's agency during Boer War, by way of such positions as milk boy and newspaper seller and soldier. Became a regular journalist and the creator of numerous thrillers in which capacity he outshone every other writer in his lifetime. *The Four Just Men* (1906) etc. Was also a successful playwright in the same vein. *d.* while visiting Hollywood, U.S.A.

WALPOLE, HUGH SEYMOUR (1884).—*B.* in New Zealand. Came to England at age of five and was *ed.* at King's School, Canterbury, and at Camb. Began to write in 1908. With Russian Red Cross in the Great War. Novels include *The Wooden Horse* (1909), *Prelude to Adventure* (1912), *Jeremy* (1919), *The Cathedral* (1922), *Portrait of a Man with Red Hair* (1925), and an historical sequence, *Rogue Herries* (1930), *Judith Paris* (1931), *The Fortress* (1932).

WARD, MARY AUGUSTA (MRS. HUMPHRY WARD) (1851–1920).—Niece of Matthew Arnold, *b.* in Tasmania. Achieved a success with *Robert Elsmere*, a novel of religious crisis (1888). Produced novels at regular intervals until her death.

WATSON, SIR WILLIAM (1858).—*B.* in Yorks. First book *pub.* in 1880, *The Prince's Quest*, but he did not obtain recognition until 1890 (*Wordsworth's Grave*). From then onwards he produced volume after volume which so enhanced his reputation that some surprise was felt when he was not appointed to the position of Poet Laureate in 1913. His avowed disagreement with England's foreign policy possibly accounted for his non-appointment. Other volumes, *The Eloping Angels* (1893), *The Purple East* (1896), *For England* (1903), *Poems Brief and New* (1925). *Coll.* eds. 1898 and 1905.

WATTS-DUNTON, WALTER THEODORE (1832–1914).—*B.* in Hunts. A solicitor, who turned to literary criticism for a career. Was critic on the *Athenæum* 1875–98. He also wrote a very successful novel *Aylwin* (1898) and some poetry, *The Coming of Love* (1897). Was a close friend of Swinburne.

WEBB, MARY, MRS. (1881–1927).—*B.* at Leighton, nr. Cressage, *m.* in 1912. After 1914 she and her husband became market gardeners, and at the same time she turned her attention to writing novels. By 1921 (when she removed to London) she had published *The Golden Arrow, Gone to Earth, The House in Dormer Forest. Seven for a Secret* was *pub.* in 1922, and her most famous book, *Precious Bane,* in 1924. In spite of the fact that this was awarded the *Femina Vie Heureuse* Prize it is possible that she would never have become popular but for a recommendation given by the then Prime Minister, Stanley Baldwin, shortly after her death.

WELLS, HERBERT GEORGE (1866).—*B.* at Bromley, the *s.* of a small tradesman and professional cricketer. Became a draper's assistant (see his novel *The Wheels of Chance*, 1896), a chemist's apprentice (see *Tono-Bungay*, 1909), a teacher in a preparatory school. He then studied intensely and in eight or nine years, after a brilliant career, had taken the London degree of B.Sc. in 1890. A breakdown in health forced him into writing for a living. His studies found an outlet in scientific romances, *The Time Machine* (1895), *The War of the Worlds* (1898), etc. Gradually he turned to more human themes in original social-scientific novels, *Love and Mr. Lewisham* (1900), *Kipps* (1905), *Marriage* (1912), *Mr. Britling Sees it Through* (1916), *The World of William Clissold* (1926). He is also an accomplished short story writer. His non-fiction works include a *Text Book of Biology* (1893), *Outline of History* (1920), *The Open Conspiracy* (1928), *The Science of Life* (1931). He has long been associated with the Fabian Society.

WEYMAN, STANLEY JOHN (1855–1928).—*B.* at Ludlow, Salop, *ed.* at Shrewsbury and Oxf. Called to the Bar 1881, and practised for about eight years, when he devoted himself to literature. His novels are nearly all historical and include *The House of the Wolf* (1890), *Under the Red Robe* (1894), *Shrewsbury* (1897), *The Abbess of Vlaye* (1904), *Chippinge* (1906), *The Lively Peggy* (1928).

WHARTON, MRS. EDITH (1862).—American novelist, *b.* in New York City and *m.* in 1885. She has travelled extensively, living most of her later years in France, and her work bears evidence of the experiences. She *pub.* her first volume of stories in 1899 (*The Greater Inclination*), and other *coll.* of stories followed it, but it was with the novel *House of Mirth* (1905) that she became known to the general public. Other novels, *Ethan Frome* (1911), *Age of Innocence* (1920), *The Children* (1928), *Hudson River Bracketed* (1929).

WHITE, WILLIAM HALE ("MARK RUTHERFORD") (1830–1913).—*B.* at Bedford, prepared to enter the Congregational ministry, but, debarred on account of his free ideas on biblical inspiration, entered the Admiralty. Famous for his psychological novels, *The Autobiography of Mark Rutherford* (1881) and *Mark Rutherford's Deliverance* (1885).

WHYMPER, EDWARD (1840–1911).—Mountaineer, artist, and author. Among other alpine feats he was one of the party to make the tragic ascent of the Matterhorn in 1865. Also visited Greenland (1867, 1872), Ecuador and the Andes (1879–80), and Canada (1901–5). His best-known work is *Scrambles among the Alps* (1871).

WILDER, THORNTON NIVEN (1897).—American writer, graduated at Yale, and took up teaching for a profession. After publishing *The Cabala* in 1926 he had a great success in America and England with *The Bridge of San Luis Rey* (1927).

WILLIAMSON, HENRY (1897).—*B.* in Bedfordshire. Has written a number of stories and studies of nature-life, the best known being *The Old Stag* (1926) and *Tarka the Otter* (1927). His novels are *The Beautiful Years* (1921), *Dandelion Days* (1922), *The Dream of Fair Women* (1924), *The Pathway* (1928), all of which bear witness to his love for nature and are linked together under the general title of *The Flax of Dream*.

WOOLF, VIRGINIA.—Youngest daughter of Sir Leslie Stephen, *m.* in 1912 to Leonard Woolf and founded with him in 1917 the Hogarth Press. Her novels have placed her in the front rank of living novelists by virtue of their finish and successful experimentation. They consist of *The Voyage Out* (1915), *Jacob's Room* (1922), *Mrs. Dalloway* (1925), *The Lighthouse* (1927), *Orlando* (1929), *The Waves* (1931). Her miscellaneous books include *The Common Reader* (1925), *A Room of One's Own* (1929).

YEATS, WILLIAM BUTLER (1865).—*B.* in Dublin of Anglo-Irish parentage, *ed.* in England and Dublin. Studied painting but turned to literature as a profession, and in 1889 *pub.* a first book of poems. He became a leader in the movement for an Irish National Theatre, *pub.* his first play in 1892, *The Countess Cathleen.* He then issued a *coll.* of essays, *The Celtic Twilight* (1893), and other prose works. He has since written many other plays, *The King's Threshold* (1904), *Deirdre* (1907), etc., literary and critical essays, *Ideas of Good and Evil* (1903), *Per Amica Silentia Lunae* (1918), and more miscellaneous work, but his literary reputation rests chiefly on his lyric poems, *The Wind Among the Reeds* (1899), *The Wild Swans at Coole* (1917), *Later Poems* (1923), *The Tower* (1927), etc. A coll. ed. of his work was issued in 1908, but is now being superseded by a new ed. (1923–). He was created a Senator of the Irish Free State in 1922 and was awarded the Nobel Prize for Literature in 1923.

YOUNG, FRANCIS BRETT (1884).—Ed. at Epsom College and University of Birmingham. Became a major in the R.A.M.C., and wrote of his war experiences in *Marching on Tanga* (1918). He had done a little work in fiction previous to the war, but it is since the war that he has really made his reputation with novels, which include *The Black Diamond* (1921), *Portrait of Clare* (1927), *My Brother Jonathan* (1928), *The House under the Water* (1932). He is also an accomplished musician, and has composed a setting to some poems of Robert Bridges.

ZANGWILL, ISRAEL (1864–1926).—Jewish man of letters, *b.* in London, took up teaching and launched on a literary career. Eventually became a central figure in Anglo-Jewish affairs, including the Zionist Movement. He is best known by his novels, *The Children of the Ghetto* (1892), *The King of Schnorrers* (1894), but he also produced some creditable plays, *The Next Religion* (1912), *We Moderns* (1923).

Made At The Temple Press Letchworth in Great Britain

EVERYMAN'S LIBRARY

By ERNEST RHYS

"A good book is the precious life-blood of a master-spirit."
MILTON

VICTOR HUGO said a Library was "an act of faith," and another writer spoke of one so beautiful, so perfect, so harmonious in all its parts, that he who made it was smitten with a passion. In that faith Everyman's Library was planned out originally on a large scale; and the idea was to make it conform as far as possible to a perfect scheme. However, perfection is a thing to be aimed at and not to be achieved in this difficult world; and since the first volumes appeared some years ago, there have been many interruptions, chief among them the Great War of 1914–18, during which even the City of Books felt a world commotion. But the series is now getting back into its old stride and looking forward to complete its scheme of a Thousand Volumes.

One of the practical expedients in the original plan was to divide the volumes into separate sections, as Biography, Fiction, History, Belles-lettres, Poetry, Philosophy, Romance, and so forth; with a shelf for Young People. Last, and not least, there was one of Reference Books, in which, beside the dictionaries and encyclopædias to be expected, there was a special set of literary and historical atlases, which have been revised from time to time, so as to chart the New Europe and the New World at large, which we hope will preserve Kant's "Perpetual Peace" under the auspices of the League of Nations at Geneva.

That is only one small item, however, in a library list which is running on to the final centuries of its Thousand. The largest slice of this huge provision is, as a matter of course, given to the tyrannous demands of fiction. But in carrying out the scheme, publishers and editors contrived to keep in mind that books, like men and women, have their elective affinities. The present volume, for instance, will be found to have its companion books, both in the same section and just as significantly in other sections. With that idea too, novels like Walter Scott's *Ivanhoe* and *Fortunes of Nigel*, Lytton's *Harold*, and Dickens's *Tale of Two Cities*, have been used as pioneers of history and treated as a sort of holiday history books. For in our day history is tending to grow more documentary and less literary; and "the historian who is a stylist," as one of our contributors, the late Thomas Seccombe, said, "will soon be regarded as a kind of Phœnix."

As for history, Everyman's Library has been eclectic enough to choose its historians from every school in turn, including Gibbon, Grote, Finlay, Macaulay, Motley, and Prescott, while among earlier books may be noted the Venerable Bede and the Anglo-Saxon Chronicle. On the classic shelf too, there is a Livy in an admirable new translation by Canon Roberts, and Cæsar, Tacitus, Thucydides, and Herodotus are not forgotten.

"You only, O Books," said Richard de Bury, "are liberal and independent; you give to all who ask." The variety of authors old and new, the wisdom and the wit at the disposal of Everyman in his own Library may well, at times, seem to him a little embarrassing. In the Essays, for instance, he may turn to Dick Steele in the *The Spectator* and learn how Cleomira dances, when the elegance of her motion is unimaginable and "her eyes are chastized with the simplicity and innocence of her thoughts." Or he may take *A Century of Essays*, as a key to the whole roomful of the English Essayists, from Bacon to Addison, Elia to Augustine Birrell. These are the golden gossips of literature, the writers who have learnt the delightful art of talking on paper. Or again, the reader who has the right spirit and looks on all literature as a great adventure may dive back into the classics, and in Plato's *Phædrus* read how every soul is divided into three parts (like Cæsar's Gaul). The poets next, and we may turn to the finest critic of Victorian times, Matthew Arnold, as their showman, and find in his essay on Maurice de Guerin a clue to the "magical power of poetry," as in Shakespeare, with his

> daffodils
> That come before the swallow dares, and take
> The winds of March with beauty.

William Hazlitt's "Table Talk" may help again to show the relationship of one author to another, which is another form of the Friendship of Books. His incomparable essay, "On Going a Journey," forms a capital prelude to Coleridge's "Biographia Literaria;" and so throughout the long labyrinth of the Library shelves, one can follow the magic clue in prose or verse that leads to the hidden treasury. In that way every reader becomes his own critic and Doctor of Letters. In the same way one may turn to the Byron review in Macaulay's *Essays* as a prelude to the three volumes of Byron's own poems, remembering that the poet whom Europe loved more than England did was as Macaulay said: "the beginning, the middle and the end of all his own poetry." This brings us to the provoking reflection that it is the obvious authors and the books most easy to reprint which have been the signal successes out of the many hundreds in the series, for Everyman is distinctly proverbial in his tastes. He likes best of all an old author who has worn well or a comparatively new author who has gained something like newspaper notoriety. In attempting to lead him on from the good books that are known to those that are less known, the publishers may have at times been even too adventurous. But the elect reader is or ought to be a party to this conspiracy of books and bookmen. He can make it possible, by his help and his co-operative zest, to add still some famous old authors like Burton of the *Anatomy of Melancholy*, or longer novels like Richardson's *Clarissa Harlowe*, a cut-and-come-again book for a winter fireside, or more modern foreign writers like Heine whom Havelock Ellis has promised to sponsor. "Infinite riches in a little room," as the saying is, will be the reward of every citizen who helps year by year to build the City of Books. It was with that belief in its possibilities that the old Chief (J. M. Dent) threw himself into the enterprise. With the zeal of a true book-lover, he thought that books might be alive and productive as dragons' teeth, which, being "sown up and down the land, might chance to spring up armed men." That is a great idea, and it means a fighting campaign in which every recruit, every new reader who buys a volume, counts.

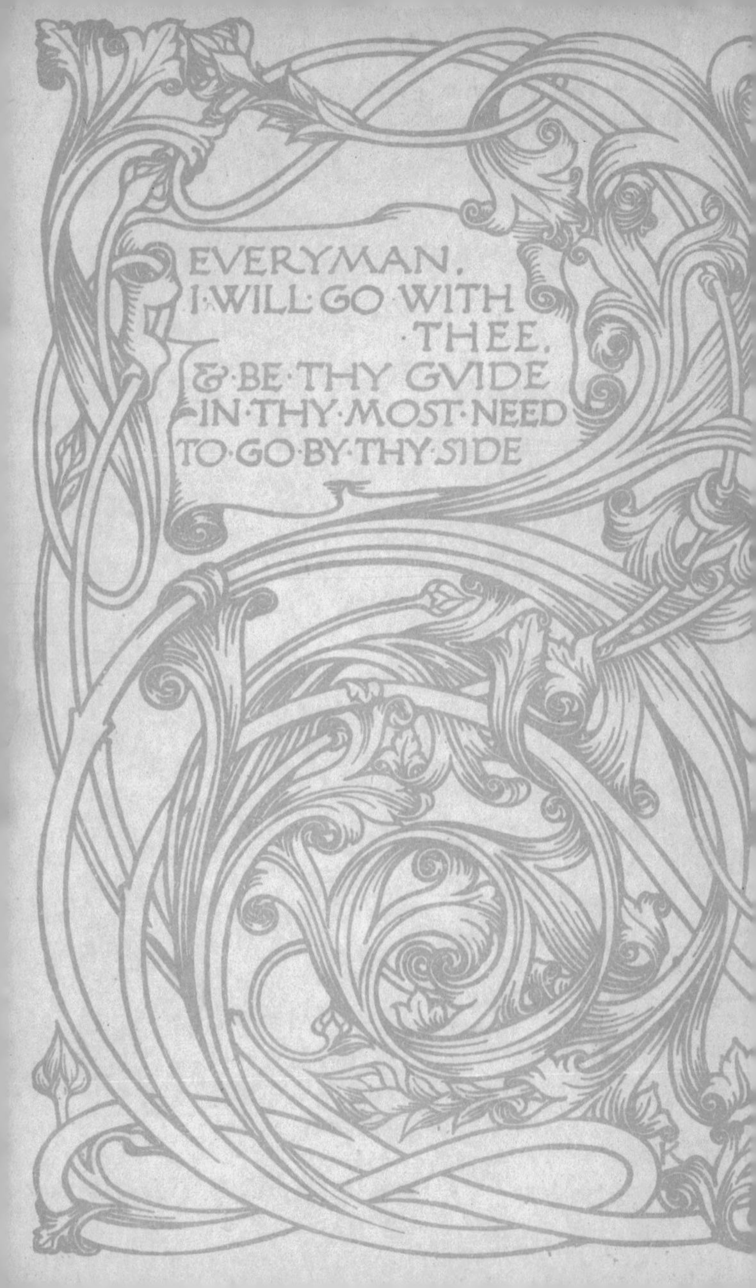
EVERYMAN.
I·WILL·GO·WITH
·THEE.
&·BE·THY·GVIDE
IN·THY·MOST·NEED
TO·GO·BY·THY·SIDE